A Companion to Nō and Kyōgen Theatre

Volume 1

Handbook of Oriental Studies

HANDBUCH DER ORIENTALISTIK

SECTION FIVE
JAPAN

Edited by

R. Kersten

VOLUME 19/1

The titles published in this series are listed at *brill.com/ho5*

A Companion to Nō and Kyōgen Theatre

VOLUME 1

Edited by

Yamanaka Reiko
Monica Bethe
Eike Grossmann
Tom Hare
Diego Pellecchia
Michael Watson

BRILL

LEIDEN | BOSTON

Cover illustration: Performers in Okina: Senzai (right), Okina (center), and Sanbasō (left). From Illustrated Scroll of the Tenpō Kanjin nō (Tenpō kanjin nō zukan). By Unzui Kyūtei (dates unknown). 1831. Handscroll, ink and color on paper. 27.7 × 559.2 cm. Kōzan Bunko, Hōsei University, Tokyo.

The Library of Congress Cataloging-in-Publication Data is available online at https://catalog.loc.gov

Typeface for the Latin, Greek, and Cyrillic scripts: "Brill". See and download: brill.com/brill-typeface.

ISSN 0921-5239
ISBN 978-90-04-72279-8 (hardback, set)
ISBN 978-90-04-53966-2 (hardback, volume 1)
ISBN 978-90-04-72273-6 (hardback, volume 2)
ISBN 978-90-04-70084-0 (e-book, volume 1)
ISBN 978-90-04-72278-1 (e-book, volume 2)
DOI 10.1163/9789004700840

Copyright 2024 by Yamanaka Reiko, Monica Bethe, Eike Grossmann, Tom Hare, Diego Pellecchia, and Michael Watson. Published by Koninklijke Brill BV, Plantijnstraat 2, 2321 JC Leiden, The Netherlands.
Koninklijke Brill BV incorporates the imprints Brill, Brill Nijhoff, Brill Schöningh, Brill Fink, Brill mentis, Brill Wageningen Academic, Vandenhoeck & Ruprecht, Böhlau and V&R unipress.
Koninklijke Brill BV reserves the right to protect this publication against unauthorized use. Requests for re-use and/or translations must be addressed to Koninklijke Brill BV via brill.com or copyright.com.

Brill has made all reasonable efforts to trace all rights holders to any copyrighted material used in this work. In cases where these efforts have not been successful the publisher welcomes communications from copyright holders, so that the appropriate acknowledgements can be made in future editions, and to settle other permission matters.
For more information: info@brill.com.

This book is printed on acid-free paper and produced in a sustainable manner.

Contents

VOLUME 1

Preface XI
Notes to Readers XIV
List of Illustrations XVI
Notes on Contributors XXVII

Introducing Nō and Kyōgen 1
  Tom Hare and Yamanaka Reiko 1

1   **The History of Nō** 14
    Edited by Eike Grossmann and Miyamoto Keizō
    1.1   The Origins of Nō, *Sangaku*, and *Sarugaku* until the Fourteenth Century (*Eike Grossmann and Miyamoto Keizō*) 14
    1.2   The Emergence of "Nō" and the Formation of Performers' Organizations during the Fourteenth and Fifteenth Centuries (*Eike Grossmann and Miyamoto Keizō*) 29
    1.3   Nō in Kyoto and Its Dispersion during the Fifteenth and Sixteenth Centuries (*Eike Grossmann and Miyamoto Keizō*) 46
    1.4   Nō in the Age of Exploration (*Patrick Schwemmer*) 63
    1.5   Nō and Political Leaders from the Late Sixteenth to the Early Eighteenth Century (*Eike Grossmann and Miyamoto Keizō*) 68
    1.6   Nō Practices and Nō Culture during the Seventeenth and Eighteenth Centuries (*Eike Grossmann and Miyamoto Keizō*) 85
    1.7   The Reorganization and Standardization of Nō Practices during the Eighteenth and Nineteenth Centuries (*Eike Grossmann and Miyamoto Keizō*) 97
    1.8   The Crisis of Nō in the Late Nineteenth and Early Twentieth Centuries (*Eike Grossmann and Miyamoto Keizō*) 108
    1.9   Nō from World War I through the 1980s (*Eike Grossmann and Miyamoto Keizō*) 121
          References 133

2   **Nō Performance** 149
    Edited by Monica Bethe and Diego Pellecchia
    2.1   Fundamentals of Nō Performance (*Monica Bethe*) 149
    2.2   The Stage (*Monica Bethe, Yamanaka Reiko, and Diego Pellecchia*) 154

	2.3	Performance Conventions (*Monica Bethe*) 158
	2.4	Movement (*Monica Bethe with Diego Pellecchia*) 180
	2.5	Music (*Takakuwa Izumi with Monica Bethe*) 196
	2.6	The History of Nō Chant (*Takakuwa Izumi with Monica Bethe*) 221
	2.7	*Shōdan*: the Building Blocks of Nō (*Monica Bethe and Takakuwa Izumi*) 226
	2.8	Masks (*Monica Bethe*) 238
	2.9	Costumes (*Monica Bethe*) 252
	2.10	Nō Fans (*Diego Pellecchia*) 274
	2.11	Properties (*Monica Bethe*) 278
	2.12	Interpreting Conventions for Standard and Variant Performances (*Yamanaka Reiko*) 292
	2.13	Underlying Principles of Nō Dramaturgy (*Monica Bethe*) 311
		References 308
3	**Training, Practice, and Production** 316
	Edited by Diego Pellecchia and Yamanaka Reiko
	3.1	Introduction (*Diego Pellecchia and Yamanaka Reiko*) 316
	3.2	Training (*Diego Pellecchia and Yamanaka Reiko*) 324
	3.3	Female Performers in Nō (*Barbara Geilhorn*) 334
	3.4	Practice and Production (*Diego Pellecchia and Yamanaka Reiko*) 341
	3.5	The Role of Amateur Practitioners (*Diego Pellecchia and Yamanaka Reiko*) 368
	3.6	*Kurokawa Nō* (*Eike Grossmann*) 374
	3.7	Recent Developments and Future Perspectives (*Diego Pellecchia and Yamanaka Reiko*) 377
		References 380
4	**Plays: Their Conventions and Backgrounds** 384
	Edited by Tom Hare, Takeuchi Akiko, Michael Watson, and Yamanaka Reiko
	4.1	Introduction (*Takeuchi Akiko*) 384
	4.2	Categories of Nō Plays (*Yamanaka Reiko*) 385
	4.3	Sources of Nō Plays (*Takeuchi Akiko*) 395
	4.4	Nō and Its Belief Systems (*Tom Hare and Takahashi Yūsuke*) 404
	4.5	Reading Nō: *Mugen nō* and *Genzai nō* (*Monogurui nō*) (*Yamanaka Reiko*) 419
	4.6	Aspects of Time and Character Relations (*Paul S. Atkins*) 440
	4.7	Stylistics and Poetics (*Takeuchi Akiko*) 446

CONTENTS   VII

    4.8   Narration and Ambiguous Voice (*Takeuchi Akiko*)   451
    4.9   Religious and Political Allegory in Nō (*Susan Blakeley Klein*)   457
    4.10 Medieval Commentaries and Nō Theatre
           (*Susan Blakeley Klein*)   462
    4.11 *Bangai kyoku* and *Shinsaku nō*: Noncanonical Plays and Modern
           Nō Plays (*Fukazawa Nozomi and Takeuchi Akiko*)   464
    4.12 Conclusion (*Takeuchi Akiko*)   474
    4.13 Excursus: Dramaturgy in Nō and Greek Tragedy
           (*Mae J. Smethurst*)   475
           References   477

5   **Authors**   486
    Edited by Tom Hare and Yamanaka Reiko
    5.1   Introduction (*Tom Hare and Yamanaka Reiko*)   486
    5.2   Kan'ami (*Tom Hare and Yamanaka Reiko*)   488
    5.3   Zeami (*Tom Hare and Yamanaka Reiko*)   490
    5.4   Motomasa (*Tom Hare and Yamanaka Reiko*)   498
    5.5   Zenchiku (*Tom Hare and Takahashi Yūsuke*)   502
    5.6   Nobumitsu (*Ikai Takamitsu and Lim Beng Choo*)   507
    5.7   Nagatoshi (*Ikai Takamitsu and Lim Beng Choo*)   512
    5.8   Zenpō (*Ikai Takamitsu and Lim Beng Choo*)   515
    5.9   Miyamasu (*Ikai Takamitsu and Lim Beng Choo*)   517
    5.10 Amateurs (*Ikai Takamitsu and Lim Beng Choo*)   520
           References   522

VOLUME 2

6   **Treatises and Criticism**   525
    Edited by Tamamura Kyō and Shelley Fenno Quinn
    6.1 Introduction (*Tamamura Kyō*)   525
    6.2 Zeami's Treatises: An Overview (*Shelley Fenno Quinn*)   527
    6.3 Zeami as Philosopher: Who Makes the Flower Bloom?
         (*Tamamura Kyō*)   543
    6.4 Zenchiku's Treatises and Criticism (*Takahashi Yūsuke*)   547
    6.5 Konparu Zenpō's Treatises and Criticism (*Ikai Takamitsu*)   553
    6.6 Nō Treatises from the Late Muromachi to Edo Periods
         (*Miyamoto Keizō*)   557
    6.7 Modern Theories of Nō (*Yokoyama Tarō*)   563
         References   570

7 **Material Culture of Nō and Kyōgen** 575
   Edited by Eike Grossmann
   7.1 Introduction (*Eike Grossmann*) 575
   7.2 The Production of Costumes, Masks, and Fans
        (*Monica Bethe*) 578
   7.3 The Transmission of Masks: Carvers and Their Lineages
        (*Adam Zollinger*) 589
   7.4 Instruments: Artistic Value and Development of Their Forms
        (*Takakuwa Izumi*) 601
   7.5 Performance Spaces: History and Materiality of the Nō Stage
        (*Miyamoto Keizō*) 604
   7.6 *Tsuke*: Notes on Movements, Gestures, Music, and Stage Properties
        (*Fukazawa Nozomi, Nakatsuka Yukiko, and Yamanaka Reiko*) 617
   7.7 *Utaibon* for Amateurs and Connoisseurs (*Ikai Takamitsu*) 622
   7.8 Nō and Kyōgen Illustrations (*Monica Bethe*) 627
   7.9 Nō and Kyōgen Prints and Paintings in Modern Japan
        (*Richard Smethurst*) 642
   7.10 Nō Culture in Everyday Life: *Koutaibon, Sugoroku, Karuta,
        Yubimen, Netsuke,* and *Nō Ningyō* (*Eike Grossmann*) 649
        References 661

8 **Reception** 669
   Edited by Diego Pellecchia and Yokoyama Tarō
   8.1 Introduction (*Yokoyama Tarō*) 669
   8.2 Reception of Nō in the Late Nineteenth and Early
        Twentieth Centuries (*Diego Pellecchia*) 671
   8.3 Nō and Modernism (*Diego Pellecchia and Takeuchi Akiko*) 682
   8.4 Nōgaku and Film (*Kodama Ryūichi*) 690
   8.5 Nō and Contemporary Theatre Abroad and in Japan (*Diego
        Pellecchia and Yokoyama Tarō*) 694
   8.6 Why Not Nō? (*Reginald Jackson and Yokoyama Tarō*) 707
   8.7 Nōgaku and Kabuki (*Kodama Ryūichi*) 723
        References 714

9 **Kyōgen** 726
   Edited by Monica Bethe
   9.1 Introduction (*Monica Bethe*) 726
   9.2 Plays, Plots, and Role Types (*Jonah Salz*) 728
   9.3 Dramaturgy (*Jonah Salz*) 741
   9.4 Costumes and Masks (*Monica Bethe*) 746

9.5 Organization, Training, and Creativity (*Jonah Salz*) 761
9.6 History (*Monica Bethe*) 775
9.7 The Evolution of Texts (*Taguchi Kazuo*) 796
9.8 Discourses (*Taguchi Kazuo*) 815
9.9 Sagi kyōgen (*Alex Rogals*) 829
9.10 Women in Kyōgen (*Barbara Geilhorn*) 831
9.11 Inspiration, Fusion, and Form: Kyōgen outside Japan (*Ondřej Hýbl*) 834
References 839

10 **Research Overview** 845
Edited by Yamanaka Reiko, Tom Hare, and Michael Watson
10.1 Introduction (*Yamanaka Reiko*) 845
10.2 Research into Nō before the Meiji Period (*Yamanaka Reiko*) 846
10.3 Nō Scholarship from the Meiji, Taishō, and Shōwa Periods to World War II (*Tom Hare and Yamanaka Reiko*) 849
10.4 Postwar Studies of Nō (*Yamanaka Reiko*) 852
10.5 The History of Nō Research and Translations in Western Languages: French, Italian, German, and English (*Diego Pellecchia, Eike Grossmann, and Tom Hare*) 858
References 875

11 **Appendices** 877
11.1 Finding List for Nō Texts (*Michael Watson*) 877
11.2 Summaries of Nō Plays (*Nakatsuka Yukiko and Michael Watson, with contributions by Fukazawa Nozomi, Inoue Megumi, Hana Lethen, Pia Schmitt, Patrick Schwemmer, and Tomiyama Takahiro*) 889
11.3 Summaries of Kyōgen Plays (*Monica Bethe*) 994
References (*Michael Watson*) 986

Glossary 1015
Index 1052

Preface

Nō and kyōgen are classical Japanese performing arts with a revered history spanning nearly seven hundred years. At the same time they are major dramatic forms existing very much in the present. The aim of the *Companion to Nō and Kyōgen Theatre* is to provide a broad-ranging examination and elucidation of the dual performing arts of nō and kyōgen that together constitute nōgaku. How did nōgaku come into being, how did it develop, and how was it transmitted from generation to generation? How has it found support and continued to operate in the sociopolitical and economic workings of the modern world? Are the characteristics of nōgaku so different from modern drama in the West? And what of the aesthetic standards and theoretical grounding that underlie nōgaku? Finally, has nō influenced and in turn been influenced by Japanese literature and other performing arts, not to mention dramatic forms from outside Japan? This publication seeks to present the most recent research on these questions, while also providing a "handbook" for those who have never seen nō or kyōgen. A further aim of the book is to demonstrate and to encourage the truly international scope of the study of nōgaku.

To date, the foundations in Japanese nōgaku scholarship have primarily been rooted in meticulous text-based research. The scope of these studies, however, was relatively narrowly defined and principally directed at a select Japanese audience. As a result, they have been rather restricted in acknowledging research from outside Japan. Even though there has been great interest from outside Japan in the artistic synthesis effected in nōgaku—nōgaku is, in its own right, an art of totalizing aspirations, a type of Gesamtkunstwerk—access to the achievements of the most recent Japanese scholarship on nōgaku has been limited for this diverse international body of researchers and performers because of its reliance on outdated pre-World War II Japanese commentaries and folklore about the history of nōgaku. For this reason, we have intended "the project" underlying the publication of this volume to open the study of nōgaku to the widest possible international field.

From its inception, this project has involved both Japanese and non-Japanese scholars, who joined forces to realize this project. The material covered in this publication has been considered from diverse perspectives in an effort to present the latest scholarship to an English-language audience. We have considered the connections between nōgaku and the ever-changing modern philosophical and intellectual disciplines, including gender studies and material culture, perspectives not often encountered in earlier research. These emerging intellectual approaches, alongside those long familiar in the field, such as the conventions governing performance and the achievements of the earliest proponents of nōgaku, form the basis for the *Companion to Nō and Kyōgen Theatre*.

More than a decade has passed since our project was launched. First and foremost, I would like to express my deepest gratitude to the twenty-nine authors whose diligence and commitment will finally bear fruit (see "Notes on Contributors"). Sadly, the earliest contributor to this volume, Mae J. Smethurst (see ch. 4 *Plays*, 4.13), passed away in 2019, and then in 2024, her husband, Richard J. Smethurst (see ch. 7 *Material Culture*, 7.9) passed away, too. It is with real regret that we will not be able to show the finished book to the two people who sowed the very first seeds of this project. We are also indebted to the individuals and institutions who have generously agreed to lend images to augment the rich visual materials presented here.

In my capacity as the general editor, I would like to express my deep appreciation to the four members of the editorial committee: Monica Bethe, Eike Grossmann, Diego Pellecchia, and Michael Watson. Their invaluable contributions in the form of meticulous authorship, translation, and editing encompassed all facets of the book. Throughout the course of this project, they demonstrated steady commitment to addressing the many challenges it presented. Without their dedication, this publication would not have been realized—I am profoundly grateful to all of them.

As relates to the structural, development stage of this book, managing editor Tom Hare offered much advice and assistance regarding the publication's content. This project would never have been conceived without his and Shelley Fenno Quinn's input. Shelley wrote sections of chapter 6, *Treatises and Criticism* and was also that chapter's editor. Although Shelley displayed remarkable modesty in her involvement in the project, her contribution has been unstinting. I have formed a deep respect for both Tom's and Shelley's work and to them I express my heartfelt thanks.

Editors for other chapters also deserve mention. In particular, I would like to acknowledge the exacting and devoted work by Tamamura Kyō in the *Treatises and Criticism* chapter and Takeuchi Akiko in chapter 4, *Plays: Their Conventions and Backgrounds*. Miyamoto Keizō not only wrote extensively on nōgaku history, but as a colleague at the Noh Theatre Research Institute he also aided in securing funding for the publication. He undertook many of the administrative tasks associated with the project and helped us work through the numerous challenges that such an ambitious project entails; I have been immensely encouraged by his support. Invaluable help has also come from others. In particular, my colleague Steven G. Nelson, an expert on Japanese traditional music and literature, offered assistance in reworking and fine-tuning numerous sections. And finally, we are grateful to Fukazawa Nozomi, Inoue Megumi, Hana Lethen, Pia Schmitt, Patrick Schwemmer, and Tomiyama Takahiro for their assistance with the "Summaries of Nō Plays."

This project has been the child of many parents, and the list of those who have assisted along the way would be too long to include here. I am most grateful, however, to Brill Publishers, who saw the importance of this project, with special thanks to Patricia Radder, Brill's Associate Editor. Thanks must also go to our editor Amy Reigle Newland for her tireless efforts in bringing cohesion to the manuscript and working toward its completion. This publication, in its entirety, has served to draw attention to the achievements of scholars and practitioners as well as introduce those interested in drama and other performance arts throughout the world to nogaku—a cultural treasure for all people.

This work is part of an international research project of The Nogami Memorial Noh Theatre Research Institute, Hosei University, and was supported by: a Grant-in-Aid for Scientific Research(B) (16H03369) from the Japan Society for the Promotion of Science (JSPS) and the Science Research Promotion Fund of Promotion and Mutual Aid Corporation for Private Schools of Japan.

>   *Yamanaka Reiko, General Editor*
>   The Nogami Memorial Noh Theatre Research Institute
>   of Hōsei University, Tokyo

Notes to Readers

Japanese Romanization adopts a modified Hepburn system. Japanese names and terms that have entered into English usage, e.g., Tokyo, Hokkaido, do not generally appear in their accented form unless in an original language context. Exceptions include terms such as shōgun, daimyō, and Shintō.

Names

Names of historical figures and contemporary Japanese working and writing in Japan are in traditional order (family name before given name); scholars/artists/performers who have worked primarily outside Japan appear in Western order (given name before family name). The British spelling "theatre" has been adopted in this publication. Sanskrit and Chinese names and terms appear without any diacritical.

A publication of this complexity and with multiple contributors must take into account the differences in the use of names and titles of individuals and places, and authorial preference. Japanese names often change with age, status, or transmission tradition, as seen in the names of historical figures like Zeami or more modern figures like Kanze Shizuo who became Tetsunojō VIII. The inclusion (or not) of titles, e.g., "-dayū," may vary from chapter to chapter and in the glossary. Most temple names appear in their original form, e.g., Kōfukuji, not Kōfuku Temple. Depending on the shrine, some appear in its original language form, e.g., Kasuga Taisha, Wakamiya Jinja, or Hachimangū, others not, e.g., Sumiyoshi Shrine. This in part has to do with the changeability in shrine names and rank over time. Generally, the term "monk" is reserved for Buddhist clerics and "priest" for Shintō.

Translations of Titles

For premodern books, established translations of titles have been used when known (i.e., *The Tale of Genji* for *Genji monogatari*), and otherwise either literal or explanatory translations (i.e., *Diary of Madenokōji Tokifusa* for *Kennaiki*) have been made.

NOTES TO READERS

Captions

Short rather than explanatory captions have been used in most instances. Whenever known, the dates and venues for performances, as well as the materials and sizes of objects have been included. Measurements are height before width in centimetres. All the drawings are by Monica Bethe.

Dates

For dates before the adoption of the Western calendar in 1873, both Western years and Japanese *nengō* (era name, together with month and day) are included, e.g., 1380 (Kōryaku 2.4.13); thereafter, a Western system is used. Birth and death dates of individuals are generally included at first mention in chapter when known; dates of living performers and scholars are not included. The designation "premodern" indicates the period before the twentieth century and "early modern" indicates Edo period. The Japanese period dates used are as follows:

Heian (794–1185)
Kamakura (1185–1333)
Muromachi (1336–1573)
Momoyama (1573–1603)
Edo (1603–1868)
Meiji (1868–1912)
Taishō (1912–1926)
Shōwa (1926–1989)
Heisei (1989–2019)
Reiwa (2019–)

References

Each chapter is followed by a bibliography of sources referenced in that chapter, occasioning the inevitable repetition of certain sources in several chapters. Whenever possible the original date of a publication is listed in ( ); when warranted the reprint date is included. The inclusion of * designates sources for further reading that are not necessarily referenced in the text.

Illustrations

Figures

0.1 The nō play *Ema*   1
1.1 Detail of *sangaku* acrobatics from *Illustrated Scroll of Old Entertainments (Kogaku zu)*. Date unknown   18
1.2 Performers in *Okina* from *Illustrated Scroll of the Tenpō Kanjin nō (Tenpō kanjin nō zukan)*. 1831   24
1.3 *Record of the Tadasugawara Sarugaku nō of Kanshō 5 [1464]* from *Old Records of Nōgaku (Nōgaku kokirokushū)*. 17th–19th centuries   33
1.4 Performance of *gonichi nō* or *gonichi sarugaku* at the *Kasuga Wakamiya onmatsuri*. *Illustrations of the Wakamiya Festival at the Kasuga Taisha (Kasuga Ōmiya Wakamiya gosairei zu)*. 1780   35
1.5 *Zeshi rokujū igo sarugaku dangi (Talks on Sarugaku by Zeami after Sixty)*. 19th century   39
1.6 Chant book (*utaibon*) for *Tenko*. Late 16th century   55
1.7 Entry on Miyamasu Yazaemon Chikakata from *Catalogue of the Performers of the Four Troupes (Yoza yakusha mokuroku)*. 1653   61
1.8 Votive tablet (*ema*) for a safe voyage to Đông Kinh in present-day Vietnam. 1634   65
1.9 *Illustration of Viewing Nō (Kannō zu)*. Early 17th century   66
1.10 Handwritten letter with Oda Nobunaga's official seal sent to Kanze Kojirō Motoyori. 1572   69
1.11 *Nō Program of the Bunroku Performance at the Imperial Palace (Bunroku kinchū nō bangumi)*. 1680   72
1.12 *Illustration of the Theatre for Kanze-dayū's Kanjin nō in 1599 (Keichō yonen Kanze-dayū kanjin nō sajiki zu)*. Early 17th century   74
1.13 *List of Names of Nō Performers and Retainers of the Kii Domain Summoned [to Edo] (Yakusha Kii hanshi yori meshiidashinin seimei-gaki)*. Ca. 1800   79
1.14 List of *nō-dayū* in Kyoto who could be hired as nō teachers from *Illustrated Encyclopedia of Nō (Nō no kinmō zui)*. 1687   86
1.15 The site of a *kanjin nō* held in 1848 from *Illustrated Handscroll of the Kōka Kanjin nō (Kōka kanjin nō emaki)*. Meiji period (1868–1912)   91
1.16 *Regulations for the Participants in Asakura's [Asakura Rokujirō] Utaikō (Asakura shachū utaikō sadame-gaki)*. 1804   93
1.17 *Records of Nō Performances [between 1721 and 1862 at Edo Castle] (Furenagashi o-nōgumi)*. 19th century   98
1.18 *Report of Kyōhō 6 [1721] (Kyōhō rokunen kakiage)*. 1721   100

ILLUSTRATIONS

1.19a–b	*Utaibon Revised in the Meiwa Era* [1764–1772] (*Meiwa kaisei utaibon*). 1765 102	
1.20	*Picture of Townspeople Attending Nō* (*Machiiri nō no zu*) at the Honmaru Goten of Edo Castle. 1889 104	
1.21a–b	*Complete Records of Kanjin nō and Kanjin kyōgen in Osaka* (*Ōsaka kanjin nō narabi ni kyōgen tsukushi roku*). Late 18th century 107	
1.22	*Daily Program of an Officially Authorized Kanjin nō* (*Gomen kanjin nō hiwari bangumi*) held at Umewaka Minoru's residence in 1872. Late 19th century 113	
1.23	*Illustration of a Nō Performance at the Temporary Aoyama Imperial Palace* (*Aoyama kari kōkyo onō no zu*). 1878 115	
1.24a–b	English program for a performance of *Kantan, Utsubozaru,* and *Momijigari* at the Shiba Nōgakudō. 1894 117	
1.25	Performance of *Tsuchigumo*. 1926 122	
1.26a–b	Women's nō (*fujin nō*) on Awaji Island. 1922 125	
1.27	Outdoor nō (*yagai nō*) organized by the *Tōkyō Nichinichi Shinbun*. 1923 128	
1.28	*A Collection of Short Nō Chants on the Greater East Asia War* (*Daitōa sensō koutaishū*). 1943 130	
1.29	*Agreement on the Revision of the Contents of Nō Plays* (*Yōkyoku shishō kaitei mōshiawase*). 1940 131	
2.1	The parts of the nō stage 155	
2.2	Sketch of the placement of the chorus and instrumentalists 156	
2.3	Top-view sketch of a nō stage with the names of areas and pillars as well as placement of performers 157	
2.4a–e	A progression of scenes in nō 160–162	
2.5a–b	Performance of *Tadanori*: a) *mae shite* and b) *nochi shite*. 2021 165	
2.6–2.25	Key to the marking in the stage diagrams 166	
2.6a–b	*Tadanori*: *waki* and *waki tsure* entrance 166	
2.7a–b	*Tadanori*: *shite* entrance 167	
2.8a–b	*Tadanori*: *waki-shite* dialogue 167	
2.9a–b	*Tadanori*: *shite* presentation 168	
2.10a–b	*Tadanori*: *waki* waiting 169	
2.11a–b	*Tadanori*: *shite* entrance in act 2 169	
2.12a–b	*Tadanori*: *shite* dance 170	
2.13a–b	*Tadanori*: *shite* final dance 171	
2.14a–b	Performance of *Miidera*: a) *mae shite* and b) *nochi shite*. 2017 172	
2.15a–b	*Miidera*: *shite* entrance 173	
2.16a–b	*Miidera*: *shite-ado ai* dialogue 174	
2.17a–b	*Miidera*: *waki* entrance 174	

2.18a–b	*Miidera*: *omo ai* presentation	175
2.19a–b	*Miidera*: *nochi shite* entrance	176
2.20a–b	*Miidera*: *shite* monologue	176
2.21a–b	*Miidera*: servant ringing bell	177
2.22a–b	*Miidera*: *shite* bell scene	177
2.23a–b	*Miidera*: *shite* narrative	178
2.24a	*Miidera*: *shite kokata* reunion	178
2.25a–b	*Miidera*: *shite* and *kokata* exit	179
2.26	Basic stance: *kamae*	181
2.27	Sliding step: *hakobi* or *suriashi*	181
2.28a–b	The forward point pattern: a) woman's mode, fan open (left) and b) martial mode, fan closed (right)	184
2.29a–b	The *hiraki* pattern: a) woman's mode (left) and b) martial mode (right)	185
2.30a–c	The series of *kata*: a) *sayū* ("left-right"); b) *uchikomi* ("overhead circling point"); and c) *hiraki* ("open")	188
2.31a–c	Design patterns: a) *hane-ōgi* (feather fan); b) *makura-ōgi* (pillow fan); and c) *shiori* ("weeping")	189
2.32a–c	Martial patterns: a) grappling (*ryōte o kumiawase*); b) setting the shield; and c) striking the enemy (*utsu*)	190
2.33a–c	Fan holds marking sections of a *kuse* dance: a) closed for first circling; b) opened in the middle; and c) extended for closure	191
2.34a–c	Movement around the stage during a *kuse* dance	191
2.35	The fan holds marking the sections of a *mai*	194
2.36	Placement on the stage where each *mai* section begins	195
2.37	*Fue* or *nōkan* with its lacquer case	198
2.38a–b	The process of making a *nōkan*	199
2.39a–b	Hourglass-shaped hand drums: a) the assembled larger *ōtsuzumi* and b) the assembled smaller *kotsuzumi*	201
2.40	The stick drum (*taiko*) set on its stand with the sticks resting underneath	204
2.41	Chant book (*utaibon*) by Kanze Sakon (Motoshige), Kanze school. 1931	216
2.42	Zō onna mask (sub-name: Aioi Zō). 17th century	241
2.43	Ko-omote mask (sub-name: Sawarabi). 17th century	241
2.44	Shakumi mask. 17th century	242
2.45	Uba mask. 17th century	242
2.46	Dōji mask. 17th century	243
2.47	Chūjō mask. 17th century	243
2.48	Heita mask. 17th century	244

ILLUSTRATIONS

2.49	Kojō mask. Late 17th century to early 18th century	244
2.50	Deigan mask. 16th century	245
2.51	Hannya mask. 17th century	245
2.52	Kurohige mask. Late 16th century	246
2.53	Chōrei Beshimi mask. 17th century	246
2.54	Shikami mask. 18th century	247
2.55	Hanakobu Akujō mask. 18th century	247
2.56	Yase otoko mask. 17th century	248
2.57	Mikazuki mask. 17th century	248
2.58	Okina (Hakushikijō) mask. 15th to early 16th centuries	249
2.59	Chichinojō mask	249
2.60a–e	Examples of nō costumes from each category	254
2.61	*Karaori* in straight *kinagashi* draping	255
2.62a–b	a) *karaori* with autumn flowers and grasses and b) detail. 19th century	256
2.63	Headbands (*kazura obi*). Late 18th century	257
2.64a–b	a) *chōken* with fans and maple leaves in gold and silver on a purple gauze weave and b) detail. 18th century	258
2.65	*Uikanmuri* courtier's cap	259
2.66	*Koshimaki* draping	259
2.67a–b	a) *surihaku* with Chinese bellflowers and b) detail. 18th century	260
2.68a–b	a) *nuihaku* with design of chrysanthemum sprigs and flower-filled hexagon lattice and b) detail. 18th century	260
2.69a–c	*Karaori* draping examples: a) *nugisage*; b) *tsuboori* over *koshimaki*; and c) *tsuboori* over *ōkuchi*	261
2.70a–c	*Mizugoromo* draping examples	262
2.71a–b	a) *mizugoromo* with displaced wefts. 19th century	263
2.72	Lined *happi* with *tomoe* design. 19th century	264
2.73	*Hangiri* pleated trousers with leaf design. 19th century	265
2.74a–c	*Happi* draping over *hangiri* examples	265
2.75a–b	Lined *kariginu* with ginkgo leaves, feather fans, and pines over a fence-weave lattice. 19th century	267
2.76a–d	*Kariginu* draping examples	268
2.77a–b	*Ōkuchi*: front and back views	269
2.78a–b	Construction of outer jackets: a) *happi* and b) *chōken*	270
2.79a–b	Warrior-courtier attire	270
2.80	Commoner in *suō* top and trailing trousers (*naga-bakama*) decorated with the same pattern	272
2.81a–b	*Hitatare* draping examples	272
2.82	Townsman in *kamishimo* vest and trailing trousers (*naga-bakama*)	272

2.83a–b	a) *hitatare* (matched suit) of jacket and trousers (*han-bakama*) with cranes and long-tailed tortoises over undulating vertical lines filled with flowers and b) detail. 19th century	273
2.84a–b	*Chūkei* fan: a) closed and b) open	276
2.85	The shrine prop for *Miwa*, covered and unveiled. 1849	280
2.86	Props for *Hashitomi* (left) and *Kurozuka* (right). 17th to 19th centuries	281
2.87	Performance of *Tsuchigumo*. 2016	282
2.88	The well prop for *Izutsu*. 1849	283
2.89	The platform with cherry trees attached used in *Arashiyama*. 1849	284
2.90	The bell tower used in *Miidera* (left) and the cart used in *Yuya* (right). 17th to 19th centuries	285
2.91	Performance of *Adachigahara* (*Kurozuka*). 2014	286
2.92	Handheld tools indicating profession or activity. 17th to 19th centuries	287
2.93	*Miwa* (left) and *Kantan* (right). 1573–1603	288
2.94a–c	a) *Shunkan*: the stage is an island, the bridgeway the sea; b) *Eguchi*: riverboat near the shore; and c) *Funa Benkei*: the boat at sea	290
2.95a–c	a) *Sakuragawa*: netting cherry blossoms; b) *Tōru*: dipping buckets to collect water; and c) *Matsukaze*: collecting brine by the seashore	290
2.96	The unveiled cherry-tree prop in *Saigyōzakura*. 1849	291
2.97	A nō performance program from 1602	296
2.98	Performance of *Kantan*. 2021	303
2.99	*Kantan, Waraya* variant with thatched roof. 1922	304
2.100	Performance of *Hagoromo*. 2017	306
3.1	Kita-school actor Ōshima Teruhisa training his son Iori at a student's private practice space	327
3.2	A student of Kanze Yoshimasa polishing the stage of the Yarai Nōgakudō, Tokyo	329
3.3	Kongō-school actor Sōmyō Tadasuke preparing the *tsukurimono* for the play *Kanawa* in the "mirror room" of the Kongō Nōgakudō, Kyoto	329
3.4	National Noh Theatre call for applications to the 2020 training program in the three arts (*san'yaku kenshū*)	333
3.5	Uzawa Hisa performing *Sagi*. 2021	340
3.6	Kanze Yoshimasa preparing for a performance. 2021	344
3.7	Kyōgen actors Ōkura Noriyoshi, Ōkura Yatarō, and Zenchiku Daijirō preparing for the revived play *Kakuregasa*. 2017	345
3.8	Kongō-school actor Udaka Michishige as *shite* in the *mōshiawase* of the play *Tōru*. 2012	347
3.9	The National Noh Theatre stage and seating area	361

ILLUSTRATIONS   XXI

3.10   National Noh Theatre monthly performance series. 2022   365
3.11   National Noh Theatre summer holiday nō and kyōgen series for parents and children. 2018   366
3.12   Kanze Yoshimasa teaching an amateur student. 2021   370
3.13   Kurokawa resident performing as *shite* in *Dōjōji*. 2006   376
4.1   *Naniwa*. From *An Illustrated Model of Nō* (*Nō on'ekagami*), vol. 1. Late 17th or early 18th century   391
4.2   *Sanemori*. From *An Illustrated Model of Nō* (*Nō on'ekagami*), vol. 1. Late 17th or early 18th century   391
4.3   *Bashō*. From *An Illustrated Model of Nō* (*Nō on'ekagami*), vol. 1. Late 17th or early Late 17th or early 18th century   392
4.4   *Tsuchigumo*. From *An Illustrated Model of Nō* (*Nō on'ekagami*), vol. 2. Late 17th or early 18th century   392
4.5   Map of the route taken by the monk in *Tadanori* as he travels from the capital to Ichinotani in Suma   422
4.6   *Blue Moon Over Memphis*. 2017   473
5.1   *Sotoba Komachi*. From *An Illustrated Model of Nō* (*Nō on'ekagami*), vol. 2. Late 17th or early 18th century   490
5.2   A human-hearted demon (left) and a demon-hearted demon (right). From *Figure Drawings of the Two Arts and the Three Modes* (*Nikyoku santai ningyō zu*). 1421   492
5.3   *Eguchi*. From *An Illustrated Model of Nō* (*Nō on'ekagami*), vol. 1. Late 17th or early 18th century   495
5.4   *Sumidagawa*. From *An Illustrated Model of Nō* (*Nō on'ekagami*), vol. 2. Late 17th or early 18th century   501
5.5   *Teika*. From *An Illustrated Model of Nō* (*Nō on'ekagami*), vol. 1. Late 17th or early 18th century   506
5.6   The inscription text from *The Inscription on Nobumitsu's Portrait* (*Kanze Nobumitsu gazō san*). 1488   509
5.7   *Funa Benkei*. From *An Illustrated Model of Nō* (*Nō on'ekagami*), vol. 1. Late 17th or early 18th century   511
5.8   *Ōyashiro*. From *An Illustrated Model of Nō* (*Nō on'ekagami*), vol. 1. Late 17th or early 18th century   513
5.9   *Arashiyama*. From *An Illustrated Model of Nō* (*Nō on'ekagami*), vol. 1. Late 17th or early 18th century   517
5.10   *Kosode Soga*. From *An Illustrated Model of Nō* (*Nō on'ekagami*), vol. 2. Late 17th or early 18th century   519
5.11   *Zegai*. From *An Illustrated Model of Nō* (*Nō on'ekagami*), vol. 1. Late 17th or early 18th century   521
6.1   *Tōbu* (*The Child Dancing*). From *Figure Drawings of the Two Arts and the Three Modes* (*Nikyoku santai ningyō zu*). 1421   536

6.2	The passage on *omoshiroki*, or "The interesting." From *Pick Up a Jewel and Take the Flower in Hand* (*Shūgyoku tokuka*). 1428	539
6.3	*Zōrin* (*The Sphere of Likening*). From *Notes on the Confidential Account of The Six Spheres and Single Dewdrop*, Bunshō version (*Rokurin ichiro hichū*). 1466	550
6.4	*Kamae* (*Posture*) sketches. From the *Eight-Volume Flower Transmission* (*Hachijō-bon kadensho*), vol. 5, folio 20. Late 16th century	561
7.1	*Karaori* with cherry-blossom designs and fretwork in bands of blue and red. 18th century	582
7.2	*Karaori* woven on a loom at the Sasaki Nō Ishō Studio, Kyoto	583
7.3	Detail of the MET *karaori* (fig. 7.1)	584
7.4	Pattern variations in the MET *karaori* (fig. 7.1)	584
7.5	Detail of the MET *karaori* (fig. 7.1)	585
7.6	Fan parts, "closed-tip" (*shizume ōgi*) style	588
7.7	Diagrammed templates of the Shinsha mask with note "Made by Shakuzuru" (*Shakazuru saku*). From *Nō Mask Template Diagrams* (*Nōmen kirigata zu*). Ca. late 16th century	591
7.8a–b	Sankōjō mask: front (a) and back (b). 15th–16th centuries	596
7.9a–b	Sankōjō mask: front (a) back (b). Seal: *Tenka ichi Kawachi* (*Best under Heaven Kawachi*). 17th century	597
7.10a–b	Sankōjō mask: front (a) back (b). Seal: *Tenka ichi Kawachi* (*Best under Heaven Kawachi*). Early 17th century	597
7.11	Lacquered *kotsuzumi* drum body with design of lightning and clouds (*raiun*), presented to the Chikubushima Shrine in 1430	603
7.12	*Kashiragane "Horomusha"* ("Mounted Warrior"). Decorative metal fitting at the head end of the *nōkan* with the image of a warrior on a galloping horse. 17th century	603
7.13	*Illustrated Handscroll of the Kōka Kanjin nō* (*Kōka kanjin nō emaki*) depicting a Hōshō event in 1848	605
7.14	*Kanjin nō* performance on the banks of the Kamo River in Kyoto. Detail from the *Scenes In and Around the Capital* (*Rakuchū rakugai zu*). 1525	610
7.15	*Abbreviated Sarugaku Illustrations* (*Sarugaku zuryaku*) portraying a Nagoya performance in 1836	611
7.16	*Illustrated Handscroll of the Kōka Kanjin nō* (*Kōka kanjin nō emaki*) depicting a Hōshō event in 1848	614
7.17	A *hayashitsuke* presented by nō performers of the Sendai domain to their daimyo. 17th–18th centuries	621
7.18	Extract from the *Kurumaya utaibon*. Ca. 1600–1601	625
7.19	Page from the nō *Ohara gokō* in a *Kōetsu utaibon*	626

7.20a–b	The Aged Mode and the Old Man's Dance from *Figure Drawings of the Two Arts and the Three Modes* (*Nikyoku santai ningyō zu*). 1421	628
7.21	*Eight-Volume Flower Transmission* (*Hachijō-bon kadensho*), vol. 5, folio 19, verso. Late 16th century	629
7.22	*Illustrated Handscroll of the Kōka Kanjin nō* (*Kōka kanjin nō emaki*) showing benefit performances mounted by Hōshō-dayū in 1848	631
7.23	The depiction of *Dōjōji* at a Nagoya performance in 1836 from *Abbreviated Sarugaku Illustrations* (*Sarugaku zuryaku*). 1836	632
7.24	"Nō the Day After" (*gonichi no nō*) from *Illustrations of the Wakamiya Festival at the Kasuga Taisha* (*Kasuga Ōmiya Wakamiya gosairei zu*). 1780	633
7.25	Scene from *Ataka*. From *An Illustrated Model of Nō* (*Nō on'ekagami*), vol. 2. Late 17th or early 18th century	636
7.26	The kyōgen *Kubihiki*. 18th century	638
7.27	*Kantan*. From *Illustrated Nō Stories* (*Utai no ehon / Yōkyoku gashi*). 1735	639
7.28	Portrait of the *kotsuzumi* player Miyamasu Yazaemon (1482–1556)	641
7.29	*Yorimasa*. From *Illustrations of Nō* (*Nōgaku zue*). 1898	644
7.30	*Short Nō Chants in Temple Schools* (*Terakoya koutai*). Late 18th or early 19th century	649
7.31	*The Joy of Ten Thousand Years: Celebratory Short Nō Chants, Newly Cut* (*Shinkoku shūgi koutai banzei no raku*). 1846	652
7.32	*Short Nō Chants from Takasago, Rotation Sugoroku Game* (*Takasago koutai mawari sugoroku*). Possibly Edo period	654
7.33	Square no. 22 (detail fig. 7.32). From *Short Nō Chants from Takasago, Rotation Sugoroku Game* (*Takasago koutai mawari sugoroku*)	655
7.34	*Cards with Illustrated Nō Texts* (*Yōkyoku karuta*). 1910	657
7.35	Collection of *yubimen* belonging to the Uwajima Date daimyō clan	658
7.36	*Nara ningyō*. *Shite* and *waki* with removable masks, from the play *Aoi no ue*	660
8.1	An excerpt from a page from "Les masques japonais" in *Le monde moderne*, vol. 12 (1900)	678
8.2	A *tsuba* (sword hilt) with nō masks	678
8.3	Performance by Michio Itō (1892–1961) as "The Guardian of the Well" from W. B. Yeats's *At the Hawk's Well*. 1916	686
8.4	Performance of *Der Jasager* (*He Who Said Yes*). 1933	688
8.5	Performance of *Woman and Shadow* (*Onna to kage*). 1993	690
8.6	Film poster for *Noh Mask Murders* (*Tenkawa densetsu satsujin jiken*). 1991	693

8.7	Michio Itō (1892–1961) posing as "Boy" for his adaptation of the nō *Tamura*. 1918 696
8.8	Performance of *Takahime*. 2022 696
8.9	Performance of *Tsuki ni tsukareta Piero* (*Pierrot Lunaire*). 1955 699
8.10	From left to right: Kanze Hisao, Nomura Mansaku, Kanze Shizuo, Watanabe Moriaki, Jean-Louis Barrault. 1977 703
8.11	Performance of *The Diver*. 2008 707
8.12	The "Tochōmae" act from the play *Nō Theater*. 2018 709
9.1	Performance of *Kagyū* (*The Snail*). 2013 737
9.2	Kyōgen *suō* jacket with design of lotuses. Early 19th century 747
9.3a–b	a) *naga-bakama* trailing pleated hemp trousers with design of flowers in a diamond lattice and b) detail. Late 19th century 747
9.4a–c	Examples of matched suit costumes 748
9.5a–b	Examples of *kataginu* costumes 749
9.6	*Kataginu* vest with design of a Japanese lobster and grasses. 18th century 750
9.7	Kyōgen *han-bakama* with design of scattered medallions. 19th century 752
9.8a–c	Nō-style garments for kyōgen roles 753
9.9	Kokushikijō mask worn for the roles of Sanbasō. 17th–18th centuries 754
9.10	Ebisu mask. 18th century 755
9.11	Buaku mask. 18th century 756
9.12	Performance of *Setsubun*. 2019 757
9.13	Saru (monkey) mask. 18th–19th centuries 758
9.14	Kentoku mask. 18th century 759
9.15	Usofuki mask. 17th century 760
9.16	Oto mask. 16th–17th centuries 761
9.17	Ōji mask. 18th century 762
9.18	*Kyōgen Records* (*Kyōgenki*). 1699 792
9.19	Performance of *Busu*. 2017 807

Musical Scores

2.1	Horizontal (left to right) schematic rendition of the eight-beat metrical unit 202
2.2	Sparse hand-drum ground pattern: *koiai* (*ōtsuzumi*) and *mitsuji* (*kotsuzumi*) 202
2.3	Dense hand-drum ground pattern: *tsuzuke* in both *kotsuzumi* and *ōtsuzumi* 203
2.4	The basic *taiko* pattern (*kizami*) 204

2.5   *Sashinori. Yowagin* mode in unmatched rhythm (*hyōshi awazu*)   206
2.6   *Hiranori.* Twelve syllables distributed over sixteen half-beats   208
2.7   *Hiranori* with a short first half-line   208
2.8   *Mitsuji utai*   208
2.9   *Ōnori.* The basic seven-syllable line   210
2.10   *Ōnori.* A seven-syllable line with the first syllable a half-beat delayed for rhythmic variation   210
2.11   *Ōnori.* A seven-syllable line with the first and third syllables extended and the last four syllables packed into three-and-a-half beats   210
2.12   *Chūnori.* Syllables are distributed one on each half beat   211
2.13   *Yowagin* tone names and relationships   213
2.14   *Tsuyogin* pitch names and their relationships   213
2.15   *Tsuyogin* "ascending"   213
2.16   *Tsuyogin* "descending"   213
2.17   *Yowagin* (melodic) mode in matched rhythm (*hyōshi ai*)   215
2.18   *Tsuyogin* (dynamic) mode in matched rhythm (*hyōshi ai*)   215
2.19   *Kotoba* (speech) inflection. Typical *waki* intonation for a standard line   216
2.20   *Kotoba* (speech) inflection. Typical intonation for a female character   216
2.21   Basic flute repeat used for dances to instrumental music (*mai*)   219
2.22   The basic *yowagin* scale set on a Western staff   223
2.23a–b   Modern-day melodic movement   224
2.24a–b   Momoyama-period melodic movement   224
2.25   Muromachi-period style *hiranori*   226

Tables

2.1   The five categories of nō plays   163
2.2   The sounds produced by the two hand drums with their aural and visual representations   201
2.3   The drummer's calls and their functions   201
2.4   Types of language and rhythmic attributes that define *shōdan*   228
2.5   The progression of *shōdan* in the opening scene of *Tadanori*   228
2.6   Types of language found in nō   229
2.7   Types of rhythm found in nō   229
2.8   Types of chant *shōdan* by their name designation with correspondence between language, rhythmic systems, and musical register   230
2.9   The main types of long instrumental dances and their characteristics   233

2.10	The main types of short instrumental dances and their characteristics	236
2.11	The main types of entrance and exit music, their use and characteristics	236
2.12	Mask categories and examples	239
2.13	Types of nō and kyōgen costume garments	253
2.14	Types of fans categorized by character and decorative style	277
3.1	A representation of the current structure of the nōgaku social system	319
3.2	The various schools of nō and kyōgen divided by specialization	322
3.3	The nōgaku professional population registered at the Tokyo branch of the Nohgaku Performers' Association (Nōgaku Kyōkai)	322
3.4	The nōgaku professional population registered at the Kyoto branch of the Nohgaku Performers' Association (Nōgaku Kyōkai)	323
3.5	The nōgaku professional population divided by area	323
3.6	Main performance series produced by the five schools of *shite* actors	352
7.1	The eleven carvers included in the *Sarugaku dangi*, with their locations and associated masks	590
7.2	Key documents that list nō mask carvers	592
7.3	Hereditary lineages of mask carvers with the principal carvers of the Edo period	598
7.4	Notable museum collections of nō masks	600
9.1	Members of the main and branch lines of the Ōkura and Sagi families affiliated with the five nō schools	793
9.2	Ōkura Toraakira's categorization of kyōgen plays	801
9.3	The number of kyōgen plays in early texts and their relation to the current repertory	811

Notes on Contributors

Paul S. ATKINS
is professor of Asian Languages and Literature at the University of Washington, Seattle. His publications include *Revealed Identity: The Noh Plays of Komparu Zenchiku* (2006) and *Teika: The Life and Works of a Medieval Japanese Poet* (2017). He is presently preparing an annotated English translation of poems in classical Chinese by the Japanese Zen monk Zekkai Chūshin (1336–1405).

Monica BETHE
is director of the Medieval Japanese Studies Institute, Kyoto. Her fields of research have grown out of experience with nō practice and textile arts, and from the investigation of historical textiles. Publications include *Nō as Performance: An Analysis of the Kuse Scene of Yamamba* (1978) and *Dance in the Nō Theater* (1982, 1983), both coauthored with Karen Brazell; *Noh Performance Guides* (1992–1997), coauthored with Richard Emmert; and *Miracles and Mischief: Noh and Kyōgen Theater in Japan* (2002), coauthored with Sharon Sadako Takeda.

FUKAZAWA Nozomi
is a member of the research staff at the Nogami Memorial Noh Theatre Research Institute of Hōsei University, Tokyo, and is currently investigating phylogenetic studies of *katatsuke* (notes on movements and gestures) and aspects of the transmission of nō techniques in the Sendai domain. Recent publications include "Date Yoshimura to Ōkura Shōzaemon Tsuneharu," *Nōgaku kenkyū* 47 (2023, 91–113).

Barbara GEILHORN
is a professor of Cultural Resource Studies at the University of Tokyo and an adjunct researcher at the Tsubouchi Memorial Theatre Museum, Waseda University, Tokyo. Her research interests focus on negotiations of gender and power in classical Japanese culture, cultural representations of the Fukushima disaster, and stagings of contemporary society in Japanese performance. Recent coedited books include *Okada Toshiki & Japanese Theatre* (with Peter Eckersall et al., 2021) and *Literature after 3.11* (with Linda Flores, 2023).

Eike GROSSMANN
is professor of Japanese Cultural History and Theatre at University of Hamburg. Her research areas include Japanese traditional theatre and folk performing arts, the history of childhood and material culture, and perceptions of the body. Authored publications include *Kurokawa Nō: Shaping the Image and the Perception of Japan's Folk Traditions, Performing Arts and Rural Tourism* (2013) and the edited volume *Transformationen: Dimensionen des Körpers im vormodern Japan* (2019). She is currently working on a monograph on the nō manuscripts of Shimotsuma Shōshin (1551–1616).

Tom HARE
is professor of Comparative Literature at Princeton University. He has translated the writings of Zeami on training and performance as *Zeami. Performance Notes* (2008) and written on ancient Egyptian semiotics and systems of representation in *ReMembering Osiris* (1999). His current research projects include a biography of *The Great Hymn to Aten* and a translation of Zeami's artistic memoir, *Sarugaku dangi*. His forthcoming volume from Zone Books is entitled *Like It Says: the Writing on Portraits*.

Ondř HÝBL
is a freelance Czech/Japanese/English interpreter, Czech language kyōgen actor, and in 2004 the cofounder of The Kyōgen Theatre (Divadlo kjógen) troupe. He has translated over twenty kyōgen plays into Czech, and is also active in the Czech-Japanese Association (president since 2017) and Eiga-sai festival of Japanese cinema in Prague (coordinator, translator, and subtitle preparation). He also gives occasional lectures at the Masaryk University in Brno and Palacky University in Olomouc. Currently, he is working on the book *25 Kyōgen in Czech Language*.

IKAI *Takamitsu*
is a professor in the Faculty of Letters at Hōsei University, Tokyo. His current research centers on productions of nō plays and nō chant books (*utaibon*). Recent publications include "Kōetsu utaibon saiken: hanshiki, bunrui, kannen, kankōsha no mondai," *Nōgaku kenkyū* 46 (2022, 23–64) and "Naki nō no sakugeki-hō: *Gobō Soga* o chūshin ni," *Nihon bungaku ronkyū* 82 (2023, 11–21).

Reginald JACKSON
is the director of the Center for Japanese Studies and professor of premodern Japanese literature and performance at the University of Michigan in Ann Arbor. His research interests include medieval illustrated handscrolls,

nō dance-drama, Black Studies, and queer theory. He founded and coorganizes the Japanese Antiracist Pedagogy Project and has authored *Textures of Mourning: Calligraphy, Mortality, and the Tale of Genji Scrolls* (2018) and *A Proximate Remove: Queering Intimacy and Loss in The Tale of Genji* (2021).

Susan Blakeley KLEIN
is professor of Japanese Literature, Director of Religious Studies, at the University of California, Irvine. Publications include *Ankoku Butō: The Premodern and Postmodern Influences on the Dance of Utter Darkness* (1989); *Allegories of Desire: The Esoteric Literary Commentaries of Medieval Japan* (2003); and *Dancing the Dharma: Religious and Political Allegory in Japanese Noh Theater* (2021). Her next project is on changing constructions of gender and subjectivity in Japanese literature and theatre, using the historical development of premodern Japanese ghosts as a locus for analysis.

KODAMA Ryūichi
is a professor at Waseda University, Tokyo, and a specialist in kabuki studies. He is president of the academic society, Kabuki, and director of the Tsubouchi Memorial Theatre Museum, Waseda University. Edited works include *Nōgaku, Bunraku, Kabuki* (2002), *Eiga no naka no koten geinō* (2010) and *Saishinban kabuki daijiten* (2012), and the publications "Shintomi-za Yōkai Hikimaku no raireki o megutte," *Engeki kenkyū* 45 (2022, 1–12). He has been writing reviews of kabuki for the newspaper, *Asahi Shinbun*, for around two decades.

LIM Beng Choo
is associate professor in the Department of Japanese Studies, National University of Singapore. Her earliest training was in traditional Japanese theatre and literature, although her research interests include different fields of both traditional and contemporary Japanese culture. Publications include *Another Stage: Kanze Nobumitsu & the Late Muromachi Noh Theater* (2012). She is currently working on two projects: the relationship between traditional Japanese theatre and digital technologies, and the Chineseness in *karamono nō*.

MIYAMOTO Keizō
is a professor at the Nogami Memorial Noh Theatre Research Institute of Hōsei University, Tokyo, and specializes in the history of nō, philological research, and the study of nō masks. His recent publications include *Kindai Nihon to nōgaku* (2017), *Konparu-ke monjo no sekai* (2017), "Shushibashiri to Okina saikō," *Geinō* 28 (2022, 134–51), and "Oheya yakusha kō," *Nōgaku kenkyū* 47 (2023, 55–90).

Nakatsuka Yukiko
is a member of the research staff at the Nogami Memorial Noh Theatre Research Institute of Hōsei University, Tokyo. Her present research interests are on the production of nō plays, especially on their staging. Publications including "Kyōgen *Kakuregasa* to *Takara no Tsuchi* no shukō," *Nōgaku kenkyū* 44 (2020, 167–90).

Diego Pellecchia
is associate professor in the Faculty of Cultural Studies at Kyoto Sangyō University. His research focuses on nō training, performance, and reception. Recent publications include "Noh Creativity? The Role of Amateurs in Japanese Noh Theatre," *Contemporary Theatre Review* 27, no. 1 (2017, 34–45) and the editing of *Mime Journal* 27 "Present-time Nō plays: Ataka and Mochizuki" (2021). As a certified instructor (*shihan*) of the Kongō school, he coordinates the activities of the International Noh Institute in Kyoto.

Shelley Fenno Quinn
is an academy professor and emerita faculty member in the Department of East Asian Languages and Literatures at the Ohio State University in Columbus. Her primary interests are theatre studies and medieval Japanese literature; she has also trained in nō performance in Japan. Her book *Developing Zeami: The Noh Actor's Attunement in Practice* (2005) is a critical study of the drama theory of Zeami Motokiyo. Other interests include translation of nō librettos into English (*Morihisa, Takasago*) and reception of Zeami's critical writings in the twentieth century.

Alex Rogals
is a distinguished lecturer at Hunter College, New York, where he teaches courses in Japanese performance, arts, literature, and culture. His research centers on the intersections between art, artist, and community, and Sagi-ryū kyōgen. His work "Trapping the Heron: The Curious Case of Sagi School Kyōgen" was published in *Asian Theatre Journal* 36, no. 1 (2019, 189–204). His current project focuses on the nonprofessional performer's role in both professional and non-professional contemporary kyōgen.

Jonah Salz
taught traditional Japanese comparative theatre as a founding member of the Faculty of International Studies at Ryukoku University, Kyoto. In 1981, he cofounded the Noho Theatre Group (1981) with kyōgen actor Shigeyama Akira. Publications include translations of kyōgen and Super-kyōgen, Issey Ogata, and

Mishima Yukio; he was the editor of the special kyōgen issue of *Asian Theatre Journal* (2007) and the chief editor of *A History of Japanese Theatre* (2016). His interests include intercultural theatre, Asian performance transmission methods, and Samuel Beckett.

Patrick SCHWEMMER
is associate professor of Humanities at Musashi University, Tokyo, and specializes in the literature of Japan's medieval to early modern transition (16th–17th c.) and its global context. Recent publications on Japanese Christian and anti-Christian literature, their Spanish Golden Age equivalents, as well as the latter's roots in the medieval Islamic Mediterranean, have appeared in journals including *Gunki to katarimono*, *Kirishitan bunka kenkyūkai kaihō*, and *Setsuwa bungaku kenkyū*.

Mae J. SMETHURST (1935–2019)
was a professor of classical Latin, Greek, and Japanese literature at the University of Pittsburgh. She authored and assisted in the translation of four prize-winning books comparing nō and Greek tragedy, including *Dramatic Action in Greek Tragedy and Noh: Reading With and Beyond Aristotle* (2013). She not only compared nō and Greek tragedy, but also turned to a study of woodblock prints and lithographs of the nō theatre by Tsukioka Kōgyo, his daughter Tsukioka Gyokusei, and his student Matsuno Sōfū.

Richard SMETHURST (1933–2024)
was a professor at the University of Pittsburgh and a specialist in modern Japanese history. His important publications, such as *From Foot Soldier to Finance Minister: Takahashi Korekiyo, Japan's Keynes* (2009), investigated the changing technology of war, with a focus on the composition and technology of the Japanese military in World War II. His interest in nō theatre complemented that of his wife, the classicist Mae J. Smethurst. Together they amassed extensive holdings of woodblock prints of nō by Tsukioka Kōgyo, his daughter Tsukioka Gyokusei, and his student Matsuno Sōfū. He puplished on the impact this had in creating interest in nō both in Japan and abroad.

TAGUCHI Kazuo
is professor emeritus at Bunkyo University, Tokyo, and specializes in the history of the performing arts, with a particular interest in narrative literary aspects of nō and kyōgen. Publications include *Kyōgen ronkō: setsuwa karano keisei to sono tenkai* (1977), *Nō kyōgen kenkyū: chūsei bungei ronkō* (1997) and "Nō Hakudaiō to ai kyōgen: Man'yōshū, setsuwa, geinō," *Nō to kyōgen* 12 (2014, 78–89).

TAKAHASHI Yūsuke
is a professor at the Institute of Oriental Classics (Shidō Bunko), Keiō University, Tokyo. He is currently researching the religious background of medieval Japanese literature and performing arts, primarily nō, as well as the written materials handed down in temples. Publications include *Zenchiku nōgakuron no sekai* (2014); he was the editor of *Shūkyōgeinō toshite no nō* (2022).

TAKAKUWA Izumi
is a researcher emeritus of Tokyo National Research Institute for Cultural Properties (Tobunken), Tokyo. The analysis of nō music, especially on its musical structure, stage effects, and the historical evolution of music and musical instruments related to nō are areas of current research. Recent publications include *Nō no hayashi to enshutsu* (2003), *Nō kyōgen utai no hensen* (2015), "Jibyōshi no kotai," *Noh and Kyogen*, no. 14 (2016, 67–77), and "Nagauta Kurui aikata kō," in *Nagauta no denshō* (2023, 110–32).

TAKEUCHI Akiko
is professor of Comparative Theatre at Hōsei University, Tokyo. Her recent interests focus on the analysis of nō plays, in particular, their linguistic ambiguity. Recent publications include "Nō to oratorio shiron: gasshō narēshon shūkyōteki kinō to iu kanten kara," in *Chūsei ni kakeru hashi* (2020, 159–80) and "The Fusion of Narration and Character Voices in Noh Drama: A Narratological Approach to Zeami's God Plays and Warrior Plays," *BmE* 7 (2020, 113–49).

TAMAMURA Kyō
is associate professor of Musicology at Jōetsu University of Education, Niigata, with a current focus on the history of Japanese traditional performing arts, and analyzing the various ways of thinking about players, composers and audiences, regardless of whether they are professionals or amateurs. Recent publications include *Onozukara idekuru nō: Zeami no nōgakuron mata wa jōju no shigaku* (2020) and "Meliorate Meliorism: A Review of *Somaesthetics and the Philosophy of Culture: Projects in Japan*," *The Journal of Somaesthetics* 7, no. 2 (2022, 103–6).

Michael WATSON
is professor emeritus at Meiji Gakuin University, Tokyo. His research has focused on the *Heike monogatari*, nō drama, narratology, translation, and reception history. Publications include *Like Clouds or Mists: Studies and Translations of Nō Plays of the Genpei War* (coedited with Elizabeth Oyler, 2013) and an analysis of noncanonical warrior plays (2023). He is currently involved in a diachronic and cross-genre study of style and narrative in medieval Japanese texts.

YAMANAKA Reiko
is professor at the Nogami Memorial Noh Theatre Research Institute of Hōsei University, Tokyo, and has a research focus on individual nō plays and the ways in which they have been staged throughout nō history. Publications include *Expressions of the Invisible: A Comparative Study of Noh and Other Theatrical Traditions* (coedited with Michael Watson, 2015) and "Fraternizing with the Spirits in Noh Plays *Saigyōzakura* and *Yamamba*," in *Rethinking Nature in Japan: From Tradition to Modernity* (2017, 133–40).

YOKOYAMA Tarō
is professor of Theatre Studies at Rikkyo University, Tokyo. His main research topics are the historical transformation process of the body and performance in nō and the intellectual reception of Zeami in modern times. Recent publications include "Nō to gendai shisō: 1970–80 nendai o chūshin ni," in *Chūsei ni kakeru hashi* (2020, 303–32) and "Hataraki kō," in *ZEAMI: Chūsei no geijutsu to bunka* 5 (2021, 82–112). His current research projects include poetics of Japanese theatre, nō in contemporary drama, and ethnographic analysis of the transmission process between master and apprentice.

Adam ZOLLINGER
is a professor in Japan Studies at Dokkyo University, Saitama. He is the author of *The Manufacture and Procurement of "Daimyo Masks" as Revealed through Original Records and Hereditary Possessions of the Saga-Nabeshima Domain* (2010) and has published extensively on *nō* masks, including "Men-uchi Daikōbō to 'Iseki Meisokusai'," *Nōgaku kenkyū* 43 (2019, 25–39) and "Men-uchi Iseki no Okina-kei men," *Minzoku geijutsu* 35 (2019, 40–48).

Introducing Nō and Kyōgen

Tom Hare and Yamanaka Reiko

Nō and kyōgen together form an exemplary Japanese classical performing art with a unique body of theory and formal conventions regarding playtexts, music, staging, and other aspects of performance. They have been performed for more than six hundred years without interruption, their foundations laid and artistic standards refined in the middle of the fourteenth century and the first part of the fifteenth under the auspices of Kan'ami (1333–1384) and his son Zeami (1363 or 1364–1443?). They count among the oldest continuously performed dramatic forms in the world, and in the twenty-first century, they are referenced and quoted in modern theatre, opera, and dance, occupying an important position among forms of drama throughout the world. In 2001, UNESCO listed them on the registry of the Masterpiece of the Oral and Intangible Heritage of Humanity.

FIGURE 0.1   The nō play *Ema*. *Shite* (goddess dancing), Kagawa Seiji; *tsure* (heavenly maiden, masked at stage left), Uchida Shigenobu; *tsure* (strong deity, stage right), Kaneko Keiichirō (Kita school). Performance January 23, 2019. National Noh Theatre, Tokyo
PHOTO: MAEJIMA PHOTO STUDIO

The many unique features of nō and kyōgen have led to various characterizations. One of the most memorable must be that of the French dramatist and actor Paul Claudel (1868–1955), who described nō as a dramatic form in which "someone arrives," as distinguished from a typical Western drama in which "something happens."[1] Even in acknowledging Claudel's insight, our aims here nonetheless lie in sharp contrast to his witty brevity: the present book has been created with the intention of presenting nō and kyōgen for readers of English as comprehensively as possible.

But we have not approached this project as merely a concatenation of technical terms arranged alphabetically, as if in a dictionary or encyclopedia. We wanted to consider nō and kyōgen from a different direction. Our intent has been to explain them by selecting, classifying, and systematizing the most important elements from which the two dramatic forms are fashioned.

A similar general interpretation and analysis in Japanese was achieved initially between 1942 and 1944 under the direction of Nogami Toyoichirō (1883–1950) as *Nōgaku zensho*, published in six volumes by Sōgensha. This collection was revised and expanded between 1979 and 1981 under the direction of Nishino Haruo and Matsumoto Yasushi, and remains a very useful reference.[2] Shortly thereafter, from 1987 to 1992, Yokomichi Mario (1916–2012), Koyama Hiroshi (1921–2011), and Omote Akira (1927–2010) oversaw the publication of another important collection incorporating state-of-the-art research, in eight volumes, entitled *Iwanami kōza: nō kyōgen* (*Iwanami Lectures on Nō and Kyōgen*).[3] Although the present book is just only two volumes, it aspires to the same kinds of accomplishment achieved with those earlier projects: to classify and contextualize the most salient elements of nō and kyōgen. That said, however, it has not been our intention simply to rehearse and rehash developments in these arts over the past several decades. In addition to a focus on their development during that period, we have also looked further afield to the ways in which they have been supported and sustained. This publication aims to present a new understanding of their systems, taking advantage of research methodologies that were unavailable or unnoticed by previous generations.

This book is organized into ten chapters, each forming an independent unit such that readers may start anywhere depending on their interests and needs. For those who have never seen or are new to nō or kyōgen it might be instructive to first outline some basic information regarding their underlying

---

1   In the original French, a homophone makes the statement even cleverer: "le drame grec, c'est quelque chose qui *arrive*, le Nô, c'est quelqu'un qui *arrive*." Claudel 1965: 1167.
2   Nogami 1942–1944.
3   Yokomichi, Koyama, and Omote, eds. 1987–1992.

concepts and to introduce essential technical terms that appear frequently in this book and are difficult to translate into English, pointing out the characteristics that are relevant to each of the chapters. This is followed by summaries of the book's ten chapters, arranged in order of their appearance in the publication, to offer an outline of the characteristics of nō and kyōgen as well as to demonstrate how they differ from other forms of theatre and performing arts. At the back of the book, the reader will find five appendices and an extensive glossary.

1   Fundamentals

This study sometimes uses the term nōgaku, a relatively new word coined in the nineteenth century to refer to both the gorgeously costumed, masked drama with song and dance, which is nō proper, and to kyōgen, a variety of comic drama with straightforward plots. Nō and kyōgen stem from the same source and are performed on the same "nō stage," but over the past six centuries the two genres have cultivated their own conventions. Kyōgen actors also have an important role in nō plays, and the musical ensemble of flute and drums of nō likewise finds a place in a select group of plays in the kyōgen repertory. As a form of drama with song and dance, nō primarily treats complex human emotions such as sadness, anger, longing, and the anguish of passion, whereas kyōgen takes up the humorous aspects of human behavior, with spoken dialogue in highly refined comic plays.

Nō basically means "capabilities" or "skills." From this sense of "the skills that an actor exhibits" the word has come to designate a performing art in which the skills of the actor are represented in the most exemplary fashion in dramatic form. Kyōgen, for its part, means in its original sense "words and/or actions that depart from common sense," and on this basis, the art of kyōgen has come to connote purposely comical language and amusing actions intended to entertain an audience. It is, thus, a comic counterpart of nō.

The plots of nō and kyōgen plays are straightforward, the characters stereotypical. Ghosts number prominently among the most typical roles. There are the ghosts of warriors who died in famous battles and the spirits of men and women suffering in hell but also noteworthy historical figures and celebrated characters from literary classics, including *The Tale of Genji* or *The Tales of Ise*. There are, besides the spirits of plants and trees such as the pine and cherry, gods, heavenly beings, *tengu* goblins, demons, and many other figures that lie outside the realm of humanity. These figures appear in the human world and entertain various relationships with us. Human beings who existed historically appear in many nō, frequently depicted in the anguished circumstances of searching for a lost lover or exacting vengeance for past enmity. More or less happy human beings who lead routine lives, such as one might find in familial life, belong not to nō, but to kyōgen. In kyōgen plays, one finds clever, resourceful servants and retainers (and their masters), domineering wives, pusillanimous husbands, not-so-reverent priests and ascetics, merchants selling all sorts of goods, swindlers and crooks—in other words, they paint scenes of daily life.

Viewed from the performer's perspective, the types of characters outlined above also fall within certain categories, mirroring the division of labor among the various types of performers on the nō stage.

The *shite* is the central or main role in a nō play. Nō plays focus on the *shite*, literally, "the doer," who wears beautiful costumes and a mask, and performs dances. Nō is said to be an art centered on the *shite*. Although one might say that in any drama, the main character or protagonist is at the heart of the drama, in nō the commitment to the position afforded the *shite* is something altogether different. In drama more generally speaking, in film and indeed in other forms of traditional Japanese drama such as kabuki or the puppet plays of bunraku, the characters represented alongside or in opposition to the central character are depicted with lives of their own, whether they be the lovers, the followers, or the enemies of that character. In most cases in nō, however, and particularly in *mugen nō*, these figures do not even appear onstage.

The figure who encounters the *shite* and draws out the *shite*'s performance is called the *waki* ("beside" or "next to"). This *waki* is not merely the secondary role in a play, as the Japanese term *waki yaku* ("side role") might suggest. Especially in *mugen nō*, the *waki* serves as a kind of reporter or interlocutor. He travels to such and such a destination, meets the *shite* there, and draws forth the *shite*'s story. When the *shite* or the *waki* is accompanied by another figure or figures onstage, they are known respectively by the terms *tsure* or *waki tsure*.

The main role in a kyōgen play is also called a *shite*, but since kyōgen is a drama of dialogue, it is not focused on the *shite* in the same way as nō and develops a plot through interaction between the *shite* and a counter-role known as the *ado*. Some plays include a third person, who plays the *koado* role.

The *waki* in nō and the *ado* in kyōgen differ in function. In kyōgen, the *ado* is the *shite*'s partner, and frequently a person plays the *shite* one day and the *ado* another. In nō, the *shite* and *waki* are totally distinct roles, and a performer of *shite* roles almost never performs *waki* roles, and vice versa. The only exception would be a very unusual carnivalesque performance called a *ran nō* ("riotous nō"), in which actors take on roles they would normally never perform as a kind of joke or amusement. Other similarly attired actors accompanying the *tsure*, *ado*, and *koado* onstage are termed *tachishū*. Children's roles are played by children (*kokata*), and there are a number of nō plays in which a child actor performs the role of an adult, often the emperor or the early medieval hero, Minamoto no Yoshitsune (1159–1189).

All nō include a chorus (*jiutai*), which describes the action, scenery, and emotions of the characters from a third-person perspective. In addition to such objective observation, at times they may also voice in their stead lines understood to represent the speech of the *shite* or *waki*. The chorus members (generally eight) chant together. Unlike a Western chorus, however, they do not match their pitches perfectly, instead use a range of vibratos and tone qualities, effectively evoking a myriad of worlds.

Four instruments comprise the nō ensemble, or *hayashi*. They are the *fue* or *nōkan* (flute), the *kotsuzumi* (shoulder drum), the *ōtsuzumi* (hip drum), and the *taiko* (stick drum). The *kotsuzumi and ōtsuzumi* are hourglass-shaped hand drums of lacquered wood with drumheads of animal skin tightly held together with chords at each end. The *taiko* is a cylindrical drum, again with animal-skin heads tied together to enclose the body of the drum. The two *tsuzumi* are struck directly with the performers' hands, whereas the *taiko* is struck with thick drumsticks and only joins the ensemble in select plays. Some kyōgen also include a chorus and/or an instrumental accompaniment, but it is played in a much simpler, lighter way.

The three or four ensemble performers in nōgaku perform complex interlaced rhythmic patterns without the benefit of a conductor. This frequently provokes questions about how they relate to one another: are they simply ad-libbing or have they memorized a meticulously notated composition so perfectly that they can perform it beginning to end without a conductor?

They are clearly not ad-libbing, but neither are they rendering exactly a score that they have memorized. This not only applies to the instrumentalists but also for the way in which the *shite* interacts with the chorus and the ensemble and for the way the chorus interacts with the ensemble. In other words, the manner in which each part in the performance interacts with all the other parts follows fixed patterns of engagement while constantly keeping track of fellow performers. When the *shite* stomps rhythmically onstage or performs a specific gesture with the fan, the *hayashi* pairs it with a cadential pattern as if to punctuate the performance with a partial stop. When the *ōtsuzumi* begins to play such a pattern, the *kotsuzumi* and flute join in with patterns of their own that bring the passage to conclusion. The musical accompaniment keeps in time with markers and performance conventions like these.

2   What Is Special in Nō?: *mugen nō*

As stated at the beginning of this introduction, nō is a performing art with a unique body of theory and formal conventions. Most prominent among the plays in which these characteristics are apparent are the *mugen nō* ("dream" or "phantom" nō; see ch. 4 *Plays*). There are many other plays in the nō repertory in which a number of characters come onstage, something happens to them, and then a resolution or conclusion is reached through the course of the play. These are called *genzai nō* ("present-time" nō) in contradistinction to *mugen nō*, and they include many popular, highly regarded plays. Nevertheless, when considering the art and its philosophical or psychological basis, these plays do not come up for discussion nearly as often as the plays in the *mugen nō* category. It is generally the *mugen nō* that are cited by directors, dancers, musicians, and other creatives, whether in Japan or abroad. Nō drama would probably not have the lofty, if challenging, reputation that it has garnered as a form of "classical drama" had it not been for the forms and conventions of *mugen nō*.

In a *mugen* nō, the *waki* serves as a representative of the audience and draws out the tale and emotions of the *shite*, and the audience often hears them via such conversations with the *waki*. In this manner, emotions not directly visible onstage, such as longing, suffering, jealousy, and other psychological states become the focus of dramatic attention.

Imagine, for a minute, how it works with our memories. Sometimes a surprising string of associations that has nothing to do with the time or place in which we find ourselves at that particular moment happens to coalesce by virtue of the interaction of our emotions and memories. It is almost like cleaning out a dresser drawer, where blouses and stockings and scarves and handkerchiefs are all jumbled up, and when we pull one out, another comes along, tangled up with it. In a similar fashion, in *mugen nō*, somebody who died ages ago might appear and tell us about their memories. The conventions of realistic time and place disappear, and the *shite* may remember those things they want to remember. All the twists and turns of a long love affair, for instance, can be set aside, and a specific memory that a woman has of her lover, a memory that she has long cherished, can instead become the focus of what she recounts to the audience.

When we said earlier that nō is an art centered on the *shite*, it was the structure of such a *mugen nō* that we had in mind. What a *mugen nō* depicts is not a full picture or an objective account of an event, but rather the truth of that event as it resides in the *shite*'s recollection. The audience, consequently, does not appreciate all the vicissitudes of a given course of events; instead, it follows the *shite*'s lead through the events with empathy, casting their own memories and impressions onto that event. The story the *shite* tells comes to the audience through any events that might remain in the heart and memory of the *shite*. All the *waki* needs to do is sit and listen as the audience simply watches the *shite*. Within the structure of a *mugen nō*, it may be that only a few characters are onstage. There are some plays in which, apart from the chorus and ensemble, only the *shite* and *waki* are present. But this is fully sufficient to allow the *shite* to recollect the distant past in his or her own words.

The techniques of performance and the staging of a *mugen nō* have progressed in such a way as to be as effective as possible. The refined body of movement and gesture, together with the minimalist staging of *mugen* plays, have also come to serve the aims of actors performing in the rough and tumble of *genzai* plays, the techniques and staging of which are discussed in chapter 4. The deliberate, dignified performance techniques and strict formalism in staging did not develop exclusively on their own because of the *mugen nō* plays. These characteristics are closely related to the history of nō as a performing art developed under the military elite, and the interrelation of cultural and military contexts is covered in chapter 1. The forms of nō performance and the trajectory of their evolution could hardly have failed to influence the development of the performance conventions of kyōgen, which has been continually performed on the same stage as nō. In addition to the comprehensive study of kyōgen in chapter 9, further information, where relevant, is to be found in other chapters.

3 An Overview

3.1 *The History of Nō*

Chapter 1 begins with a discussion of sundry Chinese performing arts known in Mandarin as *sanle* (also *sanyue*; J. *sangaku*) as antecedents of nō. It aims to shed light on a number of areas that have previously been unclear: how, for example, was *sanle* gradually domesticated as *sangaku*; what was the process by which the ancient play *Okina* and nō evolved from *sangaku*; what was the significance of the adoption of masks in rituals for quelling demons from the performances in Buddhist institutions where *sarugaku* (the direct ancestor of nōgaku) came into being; and as the fusion of Buddhism and the native religious traditions termed "Shintō," proceeded, how did these performances in Buddhist temples transform into performances for Shintō shrines? This chapter also situates the development of nōgaku in social and cultural terms, from the activities of Kan'ami and Zeami and their successors, whose activities coincided with the expansion and growth of Japanese cities as the military class adopted nō performance as its own. It also discusses how *sarugaku* continued to grow with performances by women and amateurs who were not part of the "orthodox" tradition. This chapter only touches briefly on Zeami, even though his accomplishments include many wonderful plays that continue to be performed today, and his ideals inform performance practices on the modern stage. Zeami's activities and accomplishments are more extensively the subject of chapters 4, 5, and 6.

Chapter 1 also deals extensively with the vicissitudes nō experienced and the influences exerted on it as it has survived into the present through the early modern and modern periods of the Meiji Restoration (1868), the era of Taishō Democracy (1905–1926), and the militarism of the mid-twentieth century.

3.2   *Nō Performance*

Chapter 2 offers an in-depth look at the structure of nō and the conventions its actors observe based on its playscripts, music, and staging. It starts with a description of the stage and its use. A general introduction to the dramaturgical conventions introduces individual plays selected from among the *mugen* and *genzai* categories to clarify how they are assembled in a sequence of episodes. Separate essays then set out the basics of movement and stage business, as well as the vocal and instrumental music. Dissatisfied with clichés that simply characterize nō performance as minimalist or as the expression of the aesthetic concept *yūgen*, we have endeavored instead to explain objectively what actually happens onstage. Also included here is a discussion of *shōdan*, an important structural concept for understanding the performance techniques and staging of nō. *Shōdan* standard units are identified through poetic, melodic, rhythmic, instrumental, and kinetic conventions. They inform not only the performance but also the literary composition of the nō (see chapter 4 for further coverage of this topic).

The individual sections are devoted to masks, costuming, and props. Numerous examples of the different levels and variations in performance that appear in the staging of nō are discussed extensively. Note, however, that information regarding the aesthetic value of masks and costumes and what is known about their creators is included in chapter 7 on material culture. By contrast, in this chapter, we consider the assignment of masks and costumes to different kinds of roles, and the conventions according to which they are worn.

3.3   *Training, Practice, and Production*

The world of nōgaku, like other traditional performing arts and artistic traditions, is organized under the *iemoto* system. According to this system, all professional nō and kyōgen actors belong to one of the various "stylistic schools" (*ryūgi*) of performance, each of which centers on a specific hereditary line held responsible for the transmission of the art. This operates entirely differently from the methods of many theatrical arts of the early modern period from other cultures, whether in its training protocols, its economic structure, or the manner in which it directs occasions of performance. Chapter 3 explains in detail this unique system whereby the world of nōgaku functions in the modern world.

Who is in a position to become a nō or kyōgen actor? What types of groups do they belong to? What kinds of training do they undertake to become mature performers? And once they accomplish this goal, what sorts of lives do they have? How are performances of nō and kyōgen planned and put together, what publicity is used to attract audiences and to mount their productions? Who sells tickets, who pays performance fees, who profits? Who makes up the audience for nōgaku? What is the nature of the relationship between professionals and amateurs? Our account of these matters relies on both written materials and interviews with performers and scholars who hold differing perspectives on these arts.

The systems described above did not, of course, appear overnight. They evolved in tandem with the social conditions of the respective times in which nōgaku developed. That will likewise be the case in the future.

3.4   *Plays: Their Conventions and Backgrounds*

Nōgaku represents an important field for any history of the literary arts of Japan. The texts of nō are, of course, playscripts, but many are also dramatic poetry that can bear the attention of careful reading. Chapter 4 approaches nōgaku as literature and survey the various conventions and set patterns that govern it. Introduced here are the types of plays, the distinction between *mugen nō* and *genzai nō*, the characters and themes in the different types of plays, the structural patterns that occur in the treatment of a diverse range of source materials, the means of understanding that readers of nō have themselves formulated, and the forms taken in works for the stage as in their marriage of a wide variety of literary and religious materials to create plays.

It is clear that these patterns are not absolute, as they have often served as models to be disrupted intentionally for the creation of new works. In other words, this paradoxical feature of nōgaku possesses patterns that in their firmly settled underlying structure are nonetheless capable of a degree of flexibility with the potential for innumerable variations. As a result, this has enabled nō to engender numerous "new" (*shinsaku*) *nōgaku* plays and nō or kyōgen plays in foreign languages.

3.5 *Authors*

The current repertory consists of two hundred and some tens of plays. This represents less than a tenth of the playscripts that were composed but subsequently abandoned. Even among the most highly regarded plays in the repertory, the authorship of a number remains undecided. The authors whose plays are identifiable today were the heads of their troupes and were actors themselves. There were many actors who performed nō, but did not compose plays; most composers of nō, though, were also actors. In chapter 5, we follow the biographies and examine the styles of the authors of nō beginning with the founders, Kan'ami and Zeami, in the fourteenth and fifteenth centuries, proceeding until the seventeenth century when the creation of new plays effectively ceased until the emergence of *shinsaku nō* ("newly created nō") in modern times. A few plays survive in the repertory that were composed by so-called amateurs, who created them once having acquainted themselves with the conventions of nōgaku. Among them were samurai, court nobles, and a physician, and in the plays by such authors that still exist, there are discernible individual styles of composition.

3.6 *Treatises and Criticism*

Chapter 6 examines "treatises," or transmitted texts. These transmitted texts, which contain essential information about the art and its professional secrets, were handed down from generation to generation within acting lines. For modern scholars, they serve as resources on the activities and techniques entailed in historical performance. They demonstrate the worldviews and aesthetic orientations of acting lineages. Individuals in the fifteenth century who were actors, playwrights, and directors of troupes or guilds left their ideas about performance in these transmitted texts. Here, we take up the careers of three of these for examination: Zeami, Konparu Zenchiku (also Ujinobu, 1405–ca. 1470), and Konparu Zenpō (1454–?).

In the sixteenth century, the various forms assumed by nōgaku solidify, and focus is directed more tightly on theory, aesthetic disposition, and features of technique. The groups of individuals writing texts for transmission broaden to include instrumentalists and samurai class amateurs who recorded the teachings and artistic secrets of their professional instructors. In more recent times, furthermore, the range of public engagement with nōgaku has expanded to include the artistic chats and occasional essays by famous nōgaku actors as well as the declarations of intellectuals and artists working in modern and postmodern theatre. All of the above are considered here, expanding the rubric "transmitted texts" to include them in any discourse relating to nōgaku.

3.7 Material Culture of Nō and Kyōgen

The numerous objects necessary for nō performance are the focus of chapter 7. In the traditions of nōgaku, important objects have been handed down from generation to generation within the acting lineages to be employed in performance, among them, costumes, masks, the instruments played by the *hayashi*, and libretti for plays (*utaibon*) and handbooks (*katatsuke*) on how to dance and how to play the instruments. The sixteenth and seventeenth centuries, when the elements of nōgaku performance were in large part codified, were times of significant advancements in several sophisticated crafts such as weaving, dyeing, and lacquerware. As prosperous classes of feudal lords, aristocrats, and wealthy merchants cultivated a passion for nō, they spared no expense in the production of things for use in their own performances: countless costumes, masks, instruments, art objects, and other items of great value were made and have survived to the present day. Moreover, developments in commercial woodblock-printing technology at this time went hand-in-hand with the publication of sets numbering up to one hundred matched volumes of exquisite libretti that testify to the spread of interest in nō beyond stage performance to encompass a culture of nō chanting for its own sake. Given its unique structure, the nō stage too has received attention in the field of architectural history.

This chapter therefore considers the evolution of the many diverse objects utilized in the production of nō during this era. In addition, a range of visual representations of nō and kyōgen in performance, along with portraits of celebrated actors and elements of material culture such as playing cards, board games, dolls, and toys associated with the broader culture of nōgaku, will be introduced.

3.8 Reception

Chapter 8 interprets "reception" to mean the ways in which nōgaku has been taken up by mostly early modern and modern performing arts, and more broadly in cultural and intellectual terms.

Following its discovery by Westerners in the nineteenth century, nōgaku went on influence major figures such as Bertolt Brecht (1898–1956) and W. B. Yeats (1865–1939). In the West, its nonnaturalistic and celebratory nature, its masks and recitations, were seen to be entirely at odds with the dramatic conventions then current in Western Europe, and it became a catalyst for the transformation of drama by artists such as Jean-Louis Barrault (1910–1994) and Benjamin Britten (1913–1976). In combination with the currents of modernism, nōgaku exerted a broad and significant influence. This chapter provides an overview of these features and discusses the impact of nōgaku on film and contemporary theatre. In due course, nōgaku came to be treated as a figure for postmodernism; it is in that context that we consider its circumstances with an eye to philosophy, modern thought, and current affairs.

It was not the case that nōgaku, developing as it did in the Japanese medieval period, only began to exert an influence on culture more generally in the nineteenth century. When new plays ceased, for the most part, to be composed in the seventeenth century, nōgaku became "classical," and from that context it exerted a strong impact on Japanese literary arts. But its influence did not stop there, extending to fine arts and crafts and entering the lives of commoners, which are dealt with in chapter 7. The effect it had on *waka* and *renga* (linked verse) poetry, on narratives, novels, and other literary genres, are too far-reaching to be dealt with in depth here, but we have given thought to how the "high culture" of nōgaku was incorporated and reflected in kabuki, a popular or mass cultural counterfoil to nō from the Edo period (1603–1868) to the present day.

3.9   *Kyōgen*

As noted earlier, nō and kyōgen grew from the same roots and have been performed on the same stage for most of their centuries-long history. In the modern world, nō and kyōgen actors are both called *nōgakushi*, which means something like "masters of nōgaku." In the Edo period, they were both termed "*sarugaku* actors" since both arts belong within the same social sphere and share a common history and institutional structure. That being the case, this volume treats nō and kyōgen in a single text when the subject is their common history (as in ch. 1 *History*, 1.1) or modern institutional structure (as in ch. 3 *Training, Practice, and Production*, 3.1). When, however, the subject concerns the classification of individual plays, as well as the masks and costumes selected for those plays, along with the several centuries-old techniques of portrayal or the processes of training and discipline in the arts, we opted not to combine the separate sections relating to nō and kyōgen. Instead, we have concentrated on the information on kyōgen in this chapter, discussing individual topics in separate chapters. Our intent in doing so has been to treat kyōgen *as* kyōgen within its own world, rather than to explain it as an appendage of nō with certain variations.

The three shorter essays concluding this chapter explore the status and barriers facing female kyōgen players, the regional players who continue the near-extinct art of Sagi kyōgen, and the challenges of producing and performing kyōgen in different Western languages.

3.10   *Research Overview*

Chapter 10 furnishes an overview of research into nōgaku, beginning from the sixteenth century, and attempts to provide the context within which the accumulation of new insights and information that have contributed to our knowledge. This does not extend as far as the assessment of contemporary research on nōgaku since such information is embodied in this volume. The sources and scholarship quoted and referred to in this chapter will serve as a comprehensive guide to the current state of scholarship.

While the encounters by Western societies with nōgaku are discussed in chapter 8, here we sought to examine the history of research into nōgaku not only in Europe and North America but also very briefly touched on trends in Asia.

References

Claudel, Paul. 1965. *Oeuvres en prose*. Edited and annotated by Jacques Petit and Charles Galpérine. Paris: Gallimard.

Nogami Toyoichirō 野上豊一郎. 1944. *Nōmen ronkō* 能面論考. Tokyo: Koyama Shoten. Reprinted in Nogami Toyoichirō, ed. 1979, 1994. *Nō no enshutsu* 能の演出. *Nōgaku zensho* 能楽全書 4. Tokyo: Sogensha.

Yokomichi Mario 横道萬里雄, Koyama Hiroshi 小山弘志, and Omote Akira 表章, eds. 1987–1992. *Iwanami kōza: nō kyōgen* 岩波講座—能・狂言. 8 vols. Tokyo: Iwanami Shoten.

1

The History of Nō

Edited by Eike Grossmann and Miyamoto Keizō

1.1 **The Origins of Nō, *Sangaku*, and *Sarugaku* until the Fourteenth Century**
Eike Grossmann and Miyamoto Keizō

Nō is often presented as a coherent, highly stylized, and sometimes even static preservation of a sophisticated performing art, downplaying change and motion while stressing aspects of tradition and preservation. Nevertheless, nō has been in a constant and unceasing process of transformation and reinvention since its beginnings in the eighth century. Throughout its history, nō was attributed various meanings—not as a mere stage performance but as a multifaceted identifier practiced in different sociocultural settings. While nō was (and still is) constructed as an icon of Japan's high culture, it was firmly located in everyday customs at least until the end of the nineteenth century.

The history of nō is informed by reoccurring patterns that become visible when we follow its historic development within a field of tension between two extremes, which on occasion opposed and contradicted but also complemented and reinforced. At one end of the spectrum was the warrior patronage of nō practitioners, locations, infrastructures, artifacts, and so forth that triggered the standardization and regulation of performance practices. On the other, was the interest in nō by rich urban merchants, townspeople, and farmers that stimulated its popularization and nurtured the freedom to evolve new modes of performance. As a consequence of this tension, performers acquired a special vocabulary, thorough knowledge, and a number of skills in an effort to appeal to all social groups—aristocrats, monks, priests, warriors, and commoners. They displayed a remarkable ability to adapt to social and political changes and to survive, and even flourish, in turbulent times.

In order to throw these reoccurring patterns into sharp relief and to reveal the in-depth structure of nō, this chapter focuses on those parties that engaged in nō, be they performers, learners, spectators, or patrons, and the diverse social, regional, ritual, and ideological contexts in which nō took root. It traces the different meanings attributed to nō in its practice, not only as a performance form but also as a tool for building sociopolitical networks.

In this chapter, both nō and kyōgen actors, actresses, and musicians are subsumed under the term "performer." These are treated separately when a clearer distinction is required. The discussion here introduces and builds on primary sources and data. It will additionally provide the reader with an overview of research materials in Japanese and other languages.

1.1.1 Performances from the Asian Continent

The claim that nō is over six hundred years old usually locates its origins in the fourteenth century when, for the first time, a performing art with theoretical treatises and plays emerged along with performers who considered themselves a part of this cultural production. But in fact, it took nō several centuries to reach that point. Various aspects of nō's prehistory remain elusive and the attempt to grasp the beginnings of performing arts in Japan involves a degree of speculation. Extant materials are scant and often unreliable, thereby creating challenges and contributing to the comparatively little research on the early history of nō and on the history of preceding performing traditions.[1] The following discussion draws on documentation such as accounts of early performances in the *Shoku Nihongi* (*The Chronicles of Japan, Continued*, 797), descriptions of performance arts in the fictional work *Shin sarugakuki* (*A Record of New Sarugaku*, 1061–ca. 1065) by Fujiwara no Akihira (989–1066), and illustration of performers found at the treasure house Shōsōin at Tōdaiji in Nara.

Many elements of Japanese culture originated on the East Asian mainland and through a process of cultural assimilation evolved into distinctly native Japanese arts, including nō. Between the sixth and eighth centuries, sustained and ongoing efforts were made to acquire the administrative structures and cultural achievements of the Chinese Sui (581–618) and Tang (618–907) dynasties. Performing arts were also embraced alongside components of state organization and bureaucracy, as well as sophisticated cultural accomplishments such as writing, literature, the visual arts, and religious worldviews, most notably Buddhism. These elements, after undergoing various stages of implementation and transformation, became the foundation of the new state emerging on the Japanese archipelago, which relied heavily on the legitimizing effects of celebrations, ceremonies, and rituals. It is within this context that the ancestors of nō can be discovered.

---

1 See, for example, Nose 1938; Gotō 1975, 1981; Ishii 2017. For a history of Japanese theatre in English, see Ortolani 1995: esp. 1–53; Terauchi 2016: 4–19; in French, see Tschudin 2011.

Nō has its origins in the miscellaneous performances that came to Japan in the eighth century, which were collectively called *sangaku* (C. *sanyue* or *sanle*) or *tōsangaku* (Tang-dynasty *sangaku*). In addition, there were performances called *tōgaku* from Tang China and *sangokugaku* from the Three Kingdoms (57 BCE–935 CE) on the Korean Peninsula.[2] All performing arts were integrated into court politics. In order to train ceremonial performers, the Gagakuryō (also Utamai no Tsukasa or Utaryō), or the Bureau of Court Music, was created, and it administered all performing arts: *tōgaku, sangokugaku, sangaku*, the masked dance performances of *gigaku* (theatrical performances, presumably pantomime, with masks), and others. It seems safe to assume that the term *sangaku* was employed for performances that took place in between or after religious or state-sponsored ceremonies. These included magic tricks, acrobatics, the embodiment of imaginary and legendary animals, such as unicorns or *kirin* (a mythical one-horned chimerical creature), by performers disguised in animal suits or rod puppetry (C. *kuileixi*; J. *kairaigi* or *kugutsu*). The circus-like *sangaku* performances were considered a counterpart to the official court dances and music that would later be called *gagaku* (refined performing arts).[3]

There is evidence that some *sangaku* performers were systematically grouped into *gakko* (performing arts registers), which included a special category for *sangaku* performers known as *sangakko*. People registered with a *sangakko* were exempt from paying taxes and delivering compulsory labor, a fact that allowed them to concentrate on their art practice. While the precise nature of *sangakko* remains elusive, it is clear that there was at least one *sangakko* for the Yamato area (present-day Nara Prefecture), the geographical center of the Nara state. Most of the performers who were involved in the creation of nō during the fourteenth century came from this area, and it can be conjectured that they were descendants of *sangakko* performers.

In all probability due to the informal character of *sangaku*, its promotion and institutionalization by the Nara state was soon discontinued, and the *sangakko* system was abolished in 782 (Enryaku 1).[4] Subsequently, the performers

---

2 The *san* 散 in *sangaku* can connote the "unsophisticated" and thus implies something "primitive" or "unrefined." During the eighth century, performing arts originating in the Tang empire were subsumed under the Japanese term *tōgaku* (Tang-dynasty music and dance pieces). In contrast, performing arts originating from the Korean Peninsula were called *sangokugaku* (also *sankangaku*)—that is, dances and music from the Three Korean Kingdoms (*shiragigaku* from Silla, *kudaragaku* from Baekje, and *komagaku* from Goguryeo). For a brief overview on the relation of Japanese and Chinese performing arts, see Inoura and Kawatake 1981: 126–30.
3 See Nelson 2008a, 2008b; Ortolani 1995: 39–53.
4 *Shoku Nihongi* 5: 242–43.

affiliated with *sangakko* lost their livelihood, and their already sparse traces vanish almost entirely: there are no records on how *sangaku* performers lived and practiced their art during the ninth century. It stands to reason that in order to avoid paying taxes and being recruited for compulsory labor, some *sangaku* performers gave up their permanent residences officially recorded in their *koseki* (family registers) and either took up unregistered residences or were peripatetic. The *sangaku* performers make their next appearance only in historical materials that date from the end of the tenth century, some two hundred years after the relocation of the capital to Heiankyō (present-day Kyoto) in 794 (Enryaku 13).

1.1.2   *From* Sangaku *to* Sarugaku

The new capital of Heiankyō brought the court aristocracy and the common people into close proximity, and this cultural milieu fostered the further development of *sangaku*. The Heian period (794–1185) experienced repeated and severe epidemics. One countermeasure to deal with such calamities was to entice the spirits (*ekishin*, or "pestilence deities") allegedly responsible for the plague to sit below a splendid baldachin, which was carried outside of the city in a procession. In a concerted effort to attract all the spirits, the people moved through the city with decorated baldachins, playing cymbals and drums. These events, called *goryōe* (ritual for the appeasement of departed spirits), are considered to be among the earliest festivals to include all Kyoto residents, regardless of their social status. During the *goryōe* parade, miscellaneous arts were performed that appear to have derived from those transmitted from the East Asian mainland during the Nara period. One famous illustration of a *goryōe* is the *Gion goryōe*, the predecessor of today's famous *Gion matsuri* (Gion Festival), which was held at Yasaka Jinja for the first time in 972 (Tenroku 3).[5]

In general, reinterpreting and recreating "foreign" elements was in fashion during the Heian period, with the performances during the *goryōe* just one example. Counted among the performing arts that were part of the *goryōe* were: 1) the *ō no mai* ("dance of the sovereign"), a less sophisticated dance emerging from the courtly *gagaku* tradition in which performers used a mask with an extraordinarily long nose; 2) the *shishi mai* ("lion dance"), a dance derived from *gigaku*; and 3) *dengaku* (rice-paddy dances), a new performing art that

---

5 See, for example, Ueki 2010; Wakita 2016, or in English McMullin 1988; Kuroda 1996.

FIGURE 1.1 Detail of *sangaku* acrobatics. From *Illustrated Scroll of Old Entertainments* (*Kogaku zu*). Copy of a 12th-century scroll. Date unknown. Handscroll, ink on paper. 27.0 × 1520 cm. The Tsubouchi Memorial Theatre Museum, Waseda University, Tokyo

combined the rhythmic music accompanying rice-planting festivals with *sangaku* acrobatics such as antics on a pogo stick and sword juggling (fig. 1.1).[6]

Entries in the diaries of court nobles quoted, for instance, in the *Honchō seiki* (*The Chronicle of Imperial Reigns*, late 10th–early 11th c.) or the *Nihon sandai jitsuroku* (*True History of the Three Reigns of Japan*, 901) record *sangaku* performers participating in the parade of the *goryōe* on something resembling a float but do not describe exactly the appearance of their performances.[7] One of the few sources that allows us to at least imagine, if not reconstruct, a *sarugaku* performance is the fictional account *Shin sarugakuki* by Fujiwara no Akihira. Its opening pictures a festival site assumed to be at Kyoto's Inari Taisha. The first half of the show consists mainly of *sangaku* such as rod puppetry, sword and ball juggling, magic tricks, throwing and spinning tops, and so on. The program of the latter half includes comic mimicry, such as "A Nun Called Myōkō Asks for Diapers" or "A Man from the Eastern Provinces Visits the Capital for the First Time." Akihira writes that "[a]musing and foolish words twisted the audience's bellies and invited great laughter; it almost made them dislocate their jaws."[8] He lists names of popular *sangaku* performers, including Hakuta, Jinnan, Jōen, and Keinō, and describes their artistic talent as follows: "Just by looking at the appearance of the performers entering and the attire they wore, the audience started laughing." Furthermore, he notes that "[e]ven before the

---

6 On *dengaku* in relation to the development of nō, see Terauchi 2016: 14–15; Ortolani 1995: 73–74.
7 See, for example, *Honchō seiki*: 213; *Nihon sandai jitsuroku*: 112–13.
8 *Shin sarugakuki*: 3. For an English translation, see Piggott 2007: 491–97.

performers had spoken a word, the audience roared with laughter."[9] Although fictional, Fujiwara no Akihira's account nonetheless gives an idea of what a contemporary audience expected of *sangaku* performances during festivals.

Besides the acrobatic elements of *sangaku*, comic mimicry was extraordinarily popular during the Heian period. The titles of the program in the *Shin sarugakuki* indicate that such mimicry was mostly improvised and relied on the comic appearance of the performer and their humorous verbalizations. This shift in the repertory from acrobatics to theatrical mimicry led to the disappearance of performances that were originally part of *sangaku*. What merits attention is that the *Shin sarugakuki* replaces *sangaku*, the general term for miscellaneous performances, with the term *sarugaku* or *sarugō*, written with the Chinese character for "monkey" and "entertainment/dance." Already some time before the *Shin sarugakuki*, *sarugaku* came to be used synonymously with *sangaku*. A couple of reasons for this change have been suggested: 1) whereas the modern Japanese reading of the character 散 is *san*, the Heian-period pronunciation appears to have been closer to *saru*, which is a homonym of the character 猿 (monkey); or 2) there was a piece in the repertory that either included a performer mimicking a monkey or the participation of a real monkey. There are other hypotheses, but none convincingly provides a definitive explanation. What we can safely say is that the change of *sangaku* from acrobatics to improvised comical skits accompanied the change of terms from *sangaku* to *sarugaku*.

That *sangaku/sarugaku* performances, their actors and repertory, in addition to their audiences, became more diverse is a fact that can be observed not just in *goryōe*. A similar development takes place from the latter half of the tenth to the eleventh century within aristocratic court society in which ritual and ceremonial performances become increasingly elaborate. *Sarugaku* by lower-ranking aristocrats referred to as *beijū* (attendants to the emperor or higher aristocrats), for example, came to be performed after the sacred rituals and dances called *mikagura* (sacred dances for the venerable deities) that were presented exclusively at court and at certain shrines. Again, members of the *konoefu* (inner palace guards) enacted *sarugaku* during the *sumai no sechie* (wrestling ceremonies) held at the imperial court until the late thirteenth century. In all these cases, *sarugaku* is believed to have displayed comical elements in ritualized entertainment contexts and to have closely resembled the *goryōe sarugaku*.

The relation between *sarugaku* at the imperial court and that at festivals among the people of Kyoto remains far from clear, but one basic fact seems

---

9 *Shin sarugakuki*: 22–23.

obvious: the members of the aristocracy must have observed *sarugaku* performances during festivals such as the *Gion goryōe*. It seems equally plausible to conjecture that common *sarugaku* trends were adapted for courtly practices. The fashion of *sarugaku* must have found its way from the city into the imperial court and into aristocratic *mikagura* performances.[10] Extant materials, however, do not allow for a clarification of the precise nature of this process or whether this was a unidirectional influence or a mutual exchange. Nonetheless, it is important to remember that within the history of nō *sangaku*, as a predecessor separated from acrobatic feats, developed a strong tendency toward improvised mimicry during the tenth and eleventh centuries. This led to the evolution of *sarugaku*, a form from which the more elaborate theatrical variations discussed below emerged.

1.1.3 Sarugaku, *Buddhist Seasonal Ceremonies, and the Birth of* Okina

If we assume that the *goryōe* in Kyoto and the court performances during *mikagura* were triggers that accelerated the gradual shift from *sangaku* to *sarugaku*, the Buddhist New Year ceremonies called *shushōe* (also read *shujōe*, or "rectifying the wrongdoings of the past year") and *shunie* (ceremony of the second month of the lunisolar calendar, also *shunigatsue*) were another factor. These *hōe* (Buddhist ritual services) were conducted at large monasteries such as Hōjōji and Hosshōji in Kyoto and Kōfukuji in Nara during the first and the second months of the year in order to establish peace and safety in the realm. They centered around ritual practices, including sutra readings, and were accompanied by theatre-like performances referred to as *tsuina* ("driving away pestilence"), which were supposed to ward off evil and effect good fortune. *Tsuina* practice has predecessors on the East Asian mainland where an exorcism rite called *nuo* in Chinese (J. *na* 儺, as in *tsuina* 追儺) had been performed since the Tang dynasty, in all probability even earlier. It is assumed that these rites reached Japan as early as the eighth century, and the festival-like character of *shushōe* and *shunie* as religious rituals that integrated performances can be ascertained from around the end of the eleventh to the beginning of the twelfth century.[11]

The theatrical performance of *tsuina*, which contained a visual representation of the evil to be exorcised and the staging of its expulsion, generally occurred on the evening of the last day of a *shushōe* or *shunie*. In one scene, for example, a person wearing a *oni* (demon) mask is driven out by the Buddhist superhuman protective deities Bishamonten (Skt. Vaiśravaṇa) or Ryūten

---

10   On *sarugaku* at the imperial court, see Akiyama 2003: esp. 131–49.
11   On *shunie* ceremonies at the Kōfukuji-Kasuga Taisha temple-shrine complex, see Grapard 1992: 167–71. On the possible relation of *nuo* and nō, see Tian 2003.

(Skt. Nagadeva), parts played by actors who seemingly wore masks as well.[12] This raises questions about the identity of the performers. The aristocrat Hirohashi Kanenaka (1244–1308) reports in his diary *Kanchūki* (*Record of Kanenaka of the Kade Area in Kyoto*) that the *sarugaku* performers and *shushi* (incantation masters) who participated in a *shushōe* on Kōan 2 (1279).1.18 received a stipend.[13] In their role as ritual specialists, *shushi* manipulated swords or halberds to fend off evil, an art that might be traced back to the magical performances with swords and knives that were part of the *sangaku* repertory. On the one hand, the *shushi* may have taken the *sangaku* sword displays, elaborated on them, and adapted them to a performance in which religious aspects dominated. On the other, the *sarugaku* performed during Buddhist rituals seems to have consisted primarily of short and improvised comical plays. The records on *shushōe* and *shunie* also show that *shushi* and *sarugaku* performers often appeared side by side in a performance, with the *shushi* performing Bishamonten or Ryūten and the *sarugaku* players embodying the *oni*.[14]

While the early comical *sarugaku* of the tenth and eleventh centuries did not make use of masks, the performance of masked *oni* roles in *tsuina* enabled the *sarugaku* performers to extend their repertory. More precisely, the usage of an *oni* mask in *tsuina*—especially by performers in the Yamato area—triggered the development of *sarugaku* into a masked performing art and permits the first glimpse of what will become the dramatic art called nō some centuries later. It was not just the mask that assisted *sarugaku* performers in refining their art and their performances. *Oni* can also have the meaning of "something/someone hidden from and invisible to human beings." *Oni* on a theatre stage are beings that are imperceptible by normal standards. *Tsuina*, accordingly, led to the realization that a performance could make visible through the use of masks that which was ordinarily invisible. This realization of the masks' power set *sarugaku* on a new path, enabling it to evolve into a theatre form that focused on visualizing and staging the invisible.

---

12   Even today, *tsuina* are incorporated in *shushōe* and *shunie* for example, at Yakushiji and Hōryūji in Nara; the exorcism of demons by Bishamonten is still performed. The roles are played by priests or devotees; *sarugaku* and nō performers are not connected to these performances anymore.

13   *Kanchūki* 1: 83a. Materials related to nō generally read 呪師 as *shushi*. Other readings are *jushi*, *zushi*, or *noronji*, which are predominantly used in Buddhist contexts. Compare Pinnington 2019: 33–40.

14   On the relation of *shushi* and *sarugaku* performers, see Matsuo 2011: 46–100. For images and videos of contemporary *shunie* ceremonies with *shushi-bashiri* (running of the incantation masters) and *oni oi* (demon expulsion) at Yakushiji in Nara, see *Yakushiji shunie hana eshiki* below under References: *Websites of Works Cited*.

This raises the question of how *sarugaku* skits, with their strong emphasis on comical entertainment, became an indispensable part of ritual performances. One reason is that the *shushōe* and *shunie* of that time were not exclusively devoted to solemn rituals but were occasions when both performers and monks staged various amusements, including comical performances. While *shushi* were responsible for driving demons out, *sarugaku* performers were given the task of inviting luck in. This is comparable to the celebration of *setsubun*, which likewise is believed to share its roots with the demon expulsion in *tsuina*.[15] Through this division of labor, the comical character of *sarugaku* was no obstacle to its integration into Buddhist contexts, and it was in fact quite the opposite in that the comical aspects of *sarugaku* played a crucial function since laughter was assumed to bring good fortune. *Sarugaku* was able to fill this role perfectly since it made the audience laugh, and the performance of *sarugaku* during *shushōe* and *shunie* was the comical counterpart to the dignified rituals and ceremonies performed by monks and *shushi*.

During the early years of the Kamakura period (1185–1333), a performance by *shushi* became the forerunner to the ritual performance known as Okina that would be integral to the development of nō. Evidence of Okina appears around the mid-thirteenth century in the form of an Okina mask. The oldest extant Okina mask, which is in the collection of the Ethnographic Museum Berlin, has the year 1278 (Kōan 1) written with black ink on the inside. The traits and gestalt of the Okina mask have remained unchanged.[16]

Until recently, it was generally acknowledged that Okina was performed initially by *shushi* and latter assumed by *sarugaku* performers. This implies either a break in the tradition of *sarugaku* or possibly the coexistence of two different types of *sarugaku*: one of profane, another of sacred content, with only the sacred form surviving and maturing into today's nō.[17] A reevaluation of

---

15 *Setsubun* (seasonal division) are the celebrations on the day before spring, today performed every year on February 3, during which beans are scattered (*mamemaki*), while the participants exclaim: "Demons out! Fortune in!" (*oni wa soto, fuku wa uchi*). See, for example, Nakagawa 2016: 83–100; in English Foster 2015: 124–27.

16 Okina is today also referred to as *Shikisanban* (Three Ceremonial Pieces), a term that emerged at the end of the Muromachi period (1336–1573) and was frequently used thereafter. It is assumed that *Shikisanban* refers to the three persons onstage: Okina, Chichinojō, and Sanbasō. Chichinojō does not feature in contemporary performances, and although Okina belongs to today's nō repertory, it is treated as special in many ways. It is usually only performed on formal occasions and at ceremonial events such as the beginning of the year. See Rath 2000.

17 This line of argumentation can be seen, for instance, in Nose 1938: esp. 94–252; Omote and Amano (1987) 1999: 20–22; Amano 1995. It was subsequently taken up by non-Japanese scholarship. See, for example, Pinnington 1998.

historical sources and the discovery of new materials, however, necessitates an adjustment of this view. Based on the above argument that *shushi* and *sarugaku* performers were two groups of performers with shared roots in *sangaku* and that they subsequently split and then reunited in Buddhist ritual services, a fresh interpretation of the development of *Okina* is outlined here, which argues that this piece was created by *sarugaku* performers.[18]

Kamakura-period records state that there was a *shushi-bashiri* (running of the incantation masters, also read *shushi hashiri*) to be followed by the performance of *Okina*. In this part of the ritual, the *shushi*, holding and swinging bells in their hands, ran around and stamped their feet on the ground (*henbai*), thus preparing and purifying the stage for the performance. The obvious physicality of *shushi-bashiri* was mirrored in the vocality of *Okina* by *sarugaku* performers, auspicious sounds and phrases were supposed to "invite good fortune in," as was the case with the comical expulsion of demons during *tsuina*. In historical records, this performance is often dubbed *shushi-bashiri no okina*, a description that gave rise to the misunderstanding that both were staged by the same group of performers. Records document that both *shushi* and *sarugaku* performers received a salary for their performances. This is irrefutable evidence that they belonged to two different groups of performers.

Shushi-bashiri and *Okina* only parted ways when the site for the performance of *Okina* was transferred from the Nara temple Kōfukuji to the Nara shrine Kasuga Taisha.[19] While the *shushi* remained bound to the services at Kōfukuji, *sarugaku* performers relocated to the new performance site and emancipated *Okina* from *shushi-bashiri*. In an attempt to recreate the ritual and perform the *shushi-bashiri* segments themselves, *sarugaku* performers began to alter the content of *Okina*. An additional role called Senzai ("One Thousand Years") functioned to purify the performance space with an energetic stomping dance, thereby replacing the *shushi*. The following briefly describes the content of *Okina* in its contemporary form as an elaboration of older styles.[20]

Although Senzai is alleged to have lived for more than a thousand years, he symbolizes eternal youth and his age is not evident. Today, the role is performed by a younger actor who delivers a dashing, spirited dance. During Senzai's performance, the actor who plays Okina is already sitting on the stage and prepares for the part by donning an Okina mask, which reveals the vestiges of *Okina*'s

---

18 The findings of this research were published in Japanese in Miyamoto 2011.
19 This was probably an attempt to display an extension of Buddhist rule and Kōfukuji's control over Kasuga Taisha. On the Kōfukuji-Kasuga complex, see Tyler 1990; Grapard 1992: esp. 100–14.
20 For more details on the genesis of the text and on its performance history, see, for example, de Poorter (1986) 2002; Pinnington 1998; Rath 2000.

FIGURE 1.2 Performers in *Okina*: Senzai (right), Okina (center), and Sanbasō (left). From *Illustrated Scroll of the Tenpō Kanjin nō* (*Tenpō kanjin nō zukan*). By Unzui Kyūtei (dates unknown). 1831. Handscroll, ink and color on paper. 27.7 × 559.2 cm. Kōzan Bunko, Hōsei University, Tokyo

comical heritage in its benign and gentle expression with several laughter lines carved into it. As a result, the audience directly participates in the transformation of the human actor into a numinous, otherworldly being. Okina then prays for the realm to be peaceful, its reign fortunate. He is shrouded in mystery, however, and even when asked, he does not disclose his identity. Taking off his mask, the actor staging Okina returns to his human form and exits the stage. Then Sanbasō, today performed by a kyōgen actor, appears and dances the *momi no dan* ("stamping section") and *suzu no dan* ("bell section"). The part of Sanbasō repeats, in an exaggerated and parodic style the dances of Senzai, with the *momi no dan* as a purification dance, and of Okina, with the *suzu no dan* as a dance of fertility and felicitation. The dramatic construction of Okina and Sanbasō as counterparts is likewise evident in their staging—Okina dons a white mask (see fig. 2.58), Sanbasō a black one (see fig. 9.9)—and their characters personify both old and young, shadow and light, solemnity and comedy (fig. 1.2).[21] Sanbasō additionally parodies *shushi-bashiri*, in that he uses handbells during his stamping performance of purification.

The environment in which *Okina* developed and the manner in which it was performed indicate the close relationship of *sarugaku* as a performing art

---

21 In the Kamakura-period version of *Okina*, another pair, Chichinojō and Enmei Kaja, appeared together onstage and verbalized auspicious phrases.

(and also of its performers) with *shushōe* and *shunie* at Buddhist temples. At the same time, the history of *Okina* manifests the ability of *sarugaku* performers to expand new performance contexts and recruit new audiences. From the thirteenth to the fourteenth century onward, when *sarugaku* performers used *Okina* as a stepping stone to the maturation of their repertory and performance styles, this antecedent comes to light even more prominently.

1.1.4 Sarugaku *Performances in Shrines and Temples*

1.1.4.1   *Okina* at Kasuga Taisha and Other Festival Performances

Unquestionably, the development of *Okina* was epoch-making and innovative for Japanese theatre, and its formative influence on nō cannot be underestimated. The play was used by the performers to emphasize their mythical and historical heritage, and their endeavor triggered an artistic consciousness that clearly distinguished *sarugaku* performance from other traditions. The performer Konparu Zenchiku (also Ujinobu, 1405–ca. 1470; see ch. 5 *Authors*, 5.5), for example, referred to *Okina* as a *shukujin*, or "a deity in residence"—in other words, a guardian deity. Even today, the Okina mask is respectfully treated as a divine vessel by nō performers. The fact that it was possible to transfer *Okina* from a Buddhist stage to a Shintō shrine means that the play itself was not defined by a singular religious context. The nondisclosure of Okina's name allows for the play to be performed in various settings, and the interpretation of Okina as an individual belonging to a variable realm of deities in general is most persuasive. The element that enables this variability and transformability is the mask. As was the case with the *oni* mask in *tsuina* rites, the Okina mask is the innovative instrument that reveals the invisible.

The characters appearing in *Okina* are, without exception, otherworldly creatures that manifest onstage in a visible form and may be seen as members of either the Buddhist or Shintō pantheons. Regardless of whether the *Okina* performance takes place in Buddhist temples or Shintō shrines, the audience is part of the transformation process of the actor from a human being into a deity by virtue of the onstage donning of the mask. The progression from human without mask to deity with mask and back to human without mask onstage resembles the way the *kami-gakari* (the mounting of the deity) occurs in *kagura*.[22] In other words, *Okina* is the visualization of a *kami-gakari* on a theatre stage, and the only difference is that here the performer is not a vessel for the deities but rather transforms into one. Thus, the nameless Okina is of

---

22   During a *kagura* (dances for the deities or *kami*) performance the performer enters a trancelike state and becomes the vessel for a divinity uttering the words of the *kami*. Their possessed body experiences *kami-gakari*. See Averbuch 1995.

ubiquitous existence and the performance of *Okina* is in itself neutral, having the ability to take on various meanings that emerge from the performance context with regard to time, space, location, and audience. This flexibility of the repertory enabled *sarugaku* performers to stage their art not only in Buddhist temples but also in Shintō shrines. It explains why it was possible to easily transfer *Okina* from the *shunie* at Kōfukuji to the festivals at Kasuga Taisha.

During the annual *shunie*, an event called *takigi nō*, "torchlight" or "firelight" nō, took place at Kōfukuji's Tōkondō (Eastern Golden Hall) and Saikondō (Western Golden Hall). *Takigi nō* is another illustration highlighting the multifaceted character of *sarugaku*. Although held within Buddhist temple grounds, *takigi nō* crossed religious boundaries by using trees from Mount Kasuga that belonged to the Kasuga Taisha as fuel for the torches that lit the performance. In the fourteenth century, *Okina* was also performed at Kasuga Taisha. Concomitantly, the organizing group of Buddhist monks called *shuto* were incorporated into the festivals of the Kasuga Taisha; their responsibility for monastic administration and the supervision of labor is proof of the power and influence that Buddhism exerted over shrines. The interrelation of these religious worlds also allowed for *sarugaku* performers to venture beyond the limits set for the staging of *Okina* at Buddhist temples and extend their performance contexts and spaces.

Okina soon became an indispensable feature of shrine rituals and festivals, not only at large shrines such as the Kasuga Taisha but also at minor shrines, mostly in the area around Kyoto, Nara and the Kii Peninsula known as Kinki, one of the social and political centers in Japan during the thirteenth and fourteenth centuries. Smaller shrines emerged in self-governed rural communities (*sōson* or *sō*) that frequently asked permission to establish a branch shrine of the Kasuga Taisha.[23] Kasuga Taisha's deities thus became tutelary deities of these shrines, and their newly created communal festivals subsequently contained *sarugaku* performances in order to entertain the deities and parishioners. With this, *Okina* as the representative *sarugaku* play moved to another performance space, to local communities where it was able to develop even faster into a full-fledged form of entertainment.

It appears that in this process the ritual aspects of *sarugaku* connected to shrine festivals intensified, while its affiliation to Buddhist temples and their services (such as *tsuina*) gradually dwindled and finally ceased altogether. Exactly when this change took place has yet to be determined. An *oni* mask called Osoroshidono (Lord Dreadful) that was probably used for *tsuina* performances and which was owned by the Konparu family until the nineteenth

---

23 On the development and organization of *sōson*, see, for example, Ikegami 1997: 129–32.

century might be compelling evidence of the relation between *sarugaku* and *tsuina*, but currently it remains inaccessible to scholars. All we have is information gathered from documentary reports: the seventeenth-century text *Yoza men kagami* (*Mirror of the Masks of the Four Troupes*) states that "this mask is not used for nō plays."[24] It is assumed that the characteristics of the Osoroshidono differ significantly from those of nō masks, making it unsuitable for the nō stage. In his treatise *Fūshi kaden* (*Transmitting the Flower through Effects and Attitudes*, 1400–ca. 1418), Zeami (1363 or 1364–1443?) writes in corroboration that "[*oni* are] a specialty of Yamato [*sarugaku*]. They are of great importance,"[25] and emphasize the pivotal function of demon roles for the *sarugaku* troupes performing in the Yamato area (see chs. 5 *Authors*, 5.3; 6 *Treatises*, 6.2). These sources point to remnants of a continuously performed lineage of the staging of *oni* by *sarugaku* performers in *tsuina* rites, at least through the fifteenth century. The lack of documentation means that the exact relationship between *sarugaku* and *tsuina* remains speculative.

1.1.4.2   *Ennen* Performances and *Sōka*

Without doubt, *Okina* was the main attraction of *sarugaku* performances during the thirteenth century. It was, however, not the only play in the *sarugaku* repertory, and while sources are sparse, they nonetheless indicate that *sarugaku* performers never abandoned the comical dramatic performances they created during the twelfth century (see ch. 9 *Kyōgen*, 9.6). The repertories of the fourteenth and fifteenth centuries still consisted of the miscellaneous performances originating from the Heian period. At Mōtsūji in Hiraizumi in northeastern Honshu, so-called *ennen* (longevity) performances accompanied the *shushōe* at the Jōgyōdō (Hall of Incessant Practice). These reveal one of the few promising leads about the character of the *sarugaku* repertory apart from *Okina*. *Ennen* were entertainment performances hosted by Buddhist monks during banquets after religious ceremonies. They included the latest fashion of performing arts between the twelfth and fourteenth centuries, such as *sarugaku*, *dengaku*, and *bugaku*.[26]

---

24   The text is part of a manuscript collection called *Menronki* (*Record of a Debate on Masks*) and is accessible as a microform at the National Diet Library, Japan, bibliographic ID 000007325330.

25   *Fūshi kaden*: 227. A slightly different translation is "[t]his role is a specialty of Yamato *sarugaku*. It is very difficult." Hare, trans. 2008: 36.

26   Matsuo 1997. For an overview on *ennen*, its repertory, and performance, see Tschudin 2011: 111–16. An Okina mask continues to be used at the *shushōe* at Mōtsūji in Hiraizumi (January 20 every year) and at the *shushōe* at Tōnomine Myōrakuji in Nara for the *ennen*

The *ennen* performances at Mōtsūji contained various dramatic plays that employed masks.[27] One of these masked plays is *Jakujo negi* (*The Young Maiden and the Shrine Priest*), the story of a female spirit medium and a shrine priest who travel to Hiraizumi together in order to offer a performance as an act of devotion to the temple deities. Another play with mask, *Rōjo* (*Old Woman*), has an elderly female spirit medium serving at a shrine performing a maiden dance—that is, the actor imitating an old woman with a bent back shakily performing a young girl's dance. The records of Mōtsūji also list the play *Kyōdono mai* (*Dance of the Lord from the Capital*), which mainly consists of a comical dialogue between a boisterous, foul-mouthed local servant and an imperial envoy to Mutsu Province (present-day Fukushima, Miyagi, Iwate, and Aomori Prefectures) where Mōtsūji is situated.

The paucity of extant sources makes it impossible to undertake a detailed comparison with nō, or to draw any definite conclusions, but the repertory of *ennen* certainly presents elements that seem to have originated with the comical *sarugaku* performances of the twelfth century. These developed dramatic structures with features such as dances, dialogues, and the narration of travel scenes, seeds from which initial theatrical constituents grew, matured, and later bore fruit in nō. Mōtsūji and Chūsonji are removed almost one thousand kilometers to the northeast of Nara and Kyoto, and the examples of their performance traditions support the assumption that masked performances were carried out in many places, both in the political center and in the remote peripheries, in temples and shrines, and in larger cities as well as smaller communities. They were staged at the imperial court and soon in warriors' residences. As the case of Mōtsūji shows, *ennen* even found their way to distant places and served as carriers of knowledge, for instance, of new trends and fashions in theatre performances. Obviously, *ennen* had not yet grown into mature theatre, but they mark a milestone in the emergence of performing arts that contain theatrical characteristics.

Another stimulus to the development of nō were *sōka* or "fast songs" (also pronounced *sōga*; alternatively known as *enkyoku* or "banquet pieces"). These were taken up by the warrior elite around 1270 as a refined form of entertainment that used to be popular with Kyoto's aristocracy and clerical elites in the earlier Heian period. Extant *sōka* date between 1270 and 1319—that is, in the

---

performance. This gives rise to speculation that *ennen* performances at temples imitated the *Okina* performances in Nara or Kyoto.

27 One of the oldest extant masks is preserved at Chūsonji and is inscribed with the dates 1291 (Shōō 4). It was used as an *ennen* mask for young women and suggests the possibility that dramatic performances with masks already existed in the thirteenth century. For an image of the mask, see Tokyo National Research Institute for Cultural Properties below under References: *Websites of Works Cited*.

late Kamakura period—and warriors continued to learn, perform, and enjoy them until the beginning of the sixteenth century. By that time, they had fallen out of fashion but had nonetheless influenced the evolution of nō as a dramatic art, especially the contents of plays, with parts of the songs appearing as *kouta* (short songs) integrated into nō performances.[28]

Sarugaku performers adopted and enhanced the system of musical annotations from *sōka* as well as the general structure of combining dialogue and songs in their plays. The most striking resemblance between *sōka* and nō plays, however, are the *michiyuki* (travel) passages. Kamakura-period *sōka* consisted of long lyrical parts, some of which, such as the *Kaidō kudari* ("traveling from Kyoto along the ocean route to the East"), vividly described scenes experienced by the journeyer. While these narratives were presented as songs and cannot conclusively be labeled theatrical performances, the setting of a traveler describing the scenery they witness is directly related to one of the central constituents of nō plays. These *michiyuki* later resurface in various performing arts, among them the narrative *kusemai* dances, which likewise impacted the development of nō plays. The nō play *Miidera*, for example, quotes a *kusemai* called *Saikoku kudari* ("Traveling from Kyoto to the Western Provinces"), which was influenced by a *sōka* referred to as *Hirefuru koi* ("Scarf-Waving Love").[29] *Sarugaku* performances not only went to remote places where they gained new input, as in *ennen*, but also drew on a wide variety of popular entertainments favored by the court and military aristocracy. In the process, they integrated techniques and fragments of *sōka* and other songs into plays, thereby eliciting associations of interest to their audience.

1.2 The Emergence of "Nō" and the Formation of Performers' Organizations during the Fourteenth and Fifteenth Centuries
Eike Grossmann and Miyamoto Keizō

1.2.1 The "Dengaku of the Collapsing Gallery" and the Record of the Special Festival at Kasuga Wakamiya

It is not until the Muromachi period (1336–1573) that defined features of *sarugaku* with dramatic content were referred to as "nō." It is plausible that the

---

28   Okada 2009: 79–80; Araki 1978: 56–57. On the relation of *sōka* and the warrior elite, see Tonomura 2005. See also Geinōshi Kenkyūkai 1983: 253–81.
29   References to the singing style of *sōka* are found in Zeami's *Shudōsho* (*Learning the Profession*) and *Zeshi rokujū igo sarugaku dangi* (*Talks on Sarugaku by Zeami after Sixty*), both from 1430. Hare, trans. 2008: 420; original in *Shudōsho*: 405; de Poorter (1986) 2002: 97, 103, original passages from *Sarugaku dangi* are in Omote and Katō, eds. (1974) 1995: 275, 281. On *kusemai*, see O'Neill 1958; Ortolani 1995: 75–77; Tschudin 2011: 132–35.

sarugaku repertory contained plays that were considered "nō," and both terms seem to have been used synonymously. And while *sarugaku* performers may have been the first to utilize the term and to perform "nō," their repertory was subsequently integrated by *dengaku* performers. In short, "nō" began to be performed by both *dengaku* and *sarugaku* performers in the fourteenth century. "Nō" in their usage, was a dramatic form that was performed by troupes with either *dengaku* or *sarugaku* backgrounds. The first two sources that present records of dramatic performances suggestive of "nō" date from 1349 (Jōwa 5).

The first documents a *kanjin*, or "benefit" or "subscription," *dengaku* performance at the riverbank in Kyoto's Shijō area.[30] During the fourteenth century, *dengaku*, which began as rice-planting dances and acrobatics derived from *sangaku* performance traditions, integrated elements of *sarugaku* into its repertory. This form then came to be referred to as *dengaku nō*. In 1349, two *dengaku* troupes, the *honza* (original troupe) and the *shinza* (new troupe), performed *dengaku nō* in a *tachiai* ("facing each other") style in which the older actors of both troupes competed against the younger members. There were frequent *tachiai* performances during this time, invariably rivalrous in nature: actors of different troupes performed either simultaneously or alternately, or troupes performed one after the other, vying against each other. The special construction of a stage with two *hashigakari* (bridgeways), one for each troupe, also stressed the dynamic character of this performance (see ch. 7 *Material Culture*, 7.5).[31]

This epoch-making performance was attended by Ashikaga Takauji (1305–1358; r. 1338–1358), the first shōgun of the Muromachi *bakufu*. The event came to be known as the *sajiki kuzure no dengaku*—"Dengaku of the Collapsing Gallery"—so called because during the performance the temporary gallery seats collapsed due to the enthusiasm of the audience and resulted in a number of casualties. The *Taiheiki* (*The Chronicle of the Great Peace*, late 14th c.) gives a short description of the program, explaining that a child donned a monkey mask, impersonating the manifestation of the deity of Hiyoshi Taisha and performing miracles onstage.[32]

Insight into the contents of these emerging *dengaku nō* and *sarugaku nō* can be found in the *Jōwa gonen Kasuga Wakamiya rinjisaiki* (*Record of the Special Festival at Kasuga Wakamiya in Jōwa 5* [1349]). The record recounts that

---

30   Initially, *kanjin* were Buddhist-inspired fundraising campaigns for the construction or repair of monastic and devotional buildings, or for copying scriptures. See Goodwin 1994.
31   *Taiheiki* 3: 322–28. See also Matsuoka 2008: 44–45; Pinnington 2019: 57–60.
32   *Taiheiki* 3: 325.

miko (female spirit mediums) were instructed by a *sarugaku* performer and that *negi* (shrine priests) trained with a *dengaku* performer in preparation of the festival's performances at Wakamiya Jinja, a branch shrine of the Kasuga Taisha in Nara (see ch. 9 *Kyōgen*, 9.6). The *miko* performed *Okina*, and pieces entitled "How Satō Norikiyo [i.e., the monk-poet Saigyō, 1118–1190] Composed Ten Poems at the Palace of [Retired Emperor] Toba" and "How Murasaki Shikibu [ca. 978–1014] Visited an Indisposed Izumi Shikibu [ca. 976–?]." The priests performed *dengaku* dances, including "How [the Indian] Prince Hanzoku Captured King Fumyō" and "How a Retainer Was Sent to the Chinese Mainland by Emperor Murakami, Where he Received the Secret Teachings of Three Musical Pieces by Ren Shōbu and, on his Way Home, Faced a Dragon Deity Who Tried to Snatch One of Them."[33] Although there are no extant scripts of these plays, the long descriptions in the *Jōwa gonen Kasuga Wakamiya rinjisaiki* suggest plays with a dramatic structure.

The *sarugaku nō* and *dengaku nō* repertories were inspired by narratives and tales appreciated by aristocracy and warriors, as well as by common people. The poems of Saigyō refer to the *Saigyō monogatari* (*The Tale of Saigyō*); the tale of Izumi Shikibu fallen ill is adapted from the Muromachi-period short story *Koshikibu* ("Little Shikibu"); the legend of the transmission of secret musical pieces to Japan is found, among others, in the *Heike monogatari* (*The Tale of the Heike*); and the Indian prince Hanzoku is a figure from the *Sangoku denki* (*The Chronicle of the Three Countries*).[34] From these descriptions and the respective casting lists it is apparent that the plays dramatized preexisting legends and tales.

1.2.2   *Expansion of Venues:* Kanjin sarugaku *and* Kanjin dengaku
During the fourteenth and fifteenth centuries, *dengaku* and *sarugaku* performers performed nō in a rather competitive way, and it is safe to assume that *dengaku* and *sarugaku* had a profoundly reciprocal influence. The 1430 *Zeshi rokujū igo sarugaku dangi* (*Talks on Sarugaku by Zeami after Sixty*; hereafter *Sarugaku dangi* or *Talks on Sarugaku*), a record of conversations with the *sarugaku nō* performer Zeami, states that there were numerous differences in the styles of nō as staged by *dengaku* and *sarugaku* troupes.[35]

---

33   For an English translation, see O'Neill 1958/1959. On the festival in general, see Grapard 1992: 157–67; Pinnington 2019: 52–60.

34   For a translation of *The Tale of Saigyō*, see McKinney, trans. 1998; Heldt, trans. 1997. A translation of *Koshikibu* is in Kimbrough 2008: 281–99. See McCullough, trans. 1988 for a translation of the *Heike monogatari*.

35   Omote and Katō, eds. (1974) 1995: 260–61; de Poorter (1986) 2002: 80–81.

A *dengaku* program, for instance, included the following performances: 1) a dance called *chūmon-guchi* ("entrance to the inner gate"); 2) *sōodori* (group dances), or dances in which all performers participated; and 3) *romai* or *ronmai*, a dance variously translated as "dance of the path" or "dance of the dispute" with the performer jumping sideways, forward, or diagonally on one or both legs.[36] These dances were followed by nō performances. In comparison, a *sarugaku* performance was far more focused, starting with a staging of *Okina* and then moving on to nō. In addition, competitive *tachiai* performances between *dengaku* and *sarugaku* troupes flourished until the beginning of the fifteenth century. In these, several actors would sing and dance onstage, all the while exchanging rhetoric, flowery dialogues, and beautiful phrases, which were listed as *koi no tachiai* (love competition) or *To ryo kyo no tachiai* (Miyako no Yoshika [834–879] [poetry] competition) in the repertory. But with the refinement of nō, these *tachiai* gradually disappeared from the main repertories of *dengaku* and *sarugaku*. At present, only one *yumiya no tachiai* (competition of bow and arrow) is preserved as a part of a variant staging of *Okina*, and even this *tachiai* is rarely performed. Among the diverse segments of *sarugaku* and *dengaku* repertories, nō quickly became the most popular performance, with other acts gradually relegated to the fringe until they ceased altogether.

When nō shifted to the center of the *dengaku* and *sarugaku* repertories, the performance contexts likewise expanded. The most substantial change was that *dengaku* and *sarugaku* now began to separate from religious institutions (temples and shrines) and move into more secular environments. *Kanjin* performances were markers of this shift, and numerous types of entertainment used *kanjin* in temples and shrines for their own fundraising. Anybody willing and able to make a donation or to pay the entrance fees could attend. In most cases, the term was used as a prefix, as seen in *kanjin mai* (benefit dances), with *kusemai* or *kōwakamai* narrative dances accompanied by music, or *kanjin Heike* (benefit performance of the [songs of the] Heike) by *biwa hōshi* (blind male singers playing the *biwa* or lute). One of the earliest records of a *kanjin sarugaku* dates to Shōwa 6 (1317).11.6, when a *kanjin sarugaku* took place at Hōryūji in Nara. The earliest mention of *kanjin dengaku* dates to Jōwa 2 (1346).2.23 and was held at Daigoji in Kyoto.[37]

Already during this era, the term *kanjin* was used for fundraising performances that were not necessarily staged on temple or shrine grounds. For example, *kanjin dengaku* and *kanjin sarugaku nō* performances were mostly held on the outskirts of large cities, often on riverbanks (*kawara*). They drew the largest crowds from the fourteenth to the sixteenth century and particularly

---

36   Note that the characters *ro* 路 in *romai* and *ron* 論 in *ronmai* are used for their sound only and the English translations do not convey the dance's actual meaning.
37   *Kagenki*: 38; *Sanbōin Kenshun sōjō nikki*: 141.

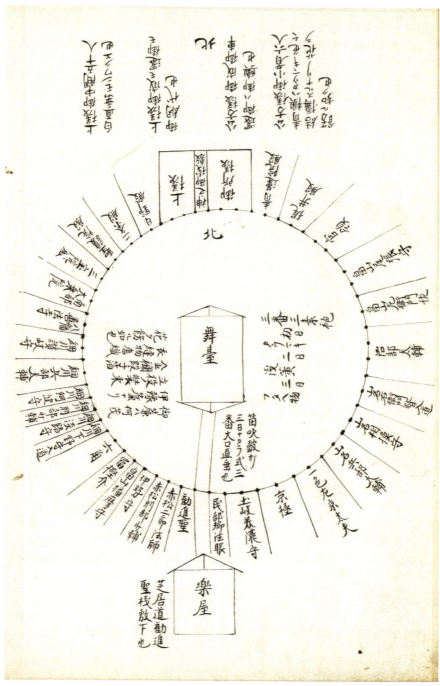

FIGURE 1.3 *Record of the Tadasugawara Kanjin Sarugaku of Kanshō 5 [1464]* (*Kanshō gonen Tadasugawara Sarugaku nō ki*). From *Old Records of Nōgaku* (*Nōgaku kokirokushū*). 17th–19th centuries. Handwritten copy, ink on paper. 28.0 × 20.1 cm. Noh Theatre Research Institute, Hōsei University, Tokyo

flourished in Kyoto. Since extant records on these *kanjin* events are sparse at best, the documentation of a *kanjin sarugaku* by Kanze-dayū[38] Saburō Motoshige (also On'ami; 1398–1467) held on the riverbank of Kyoto's Tadasu area (Tadasugawara) in 1464 (Kanshō 5) is extraordinary. Records indicate how intertwined religious context and entertainment were, including a detailed sketch of the tiered seating showing a *kami osajiki*, or "loge dedicated to the deities" to the north (fig. 1.3). This seat for deities was placed among those for the human audience such that they faced the stage directly, presumably because it offered the best view.[39] Even if *kanjin sarugaku* was held as an entertainment for humans, it was also imagined as a dedication to the deities.

Kanjin performances contributed immensely to the evolution of nō into an independent performing art. The appearance of *dengaku* and *sarugaku* performers at *kanjin* events enabled access to more sophisticated and more profitable contexts. This, in turn, led to the growth and diversification of their audience. Moreover, performers realized that nō was the main attraction of their repertory. As Zeami noted in his *Fūshi kaden*: "… the performing arts generally exist to mollify people's hearts and create excitement in the high and low; they are the foundation of long-term prosperity and increase the means of gaining longevity." He goes on to explain that this is reciprocal: "… this art depends on the affection and respect of the masses for the long-term prosperity of the troupe."[40] Zeami's argument clearly refers to an artistic consciousness and illustrates how *dengaku* and *sarugaku* performers perceived the potential of nō.

1.2.3 *Performers' Organizations:* Dengaku za *and* Sarugaku za

Accompanying the gradual transformation of *dengaku* and *sarugaku* repertories was the formation of performers into troupes. While the activities of performers in the thirteenth and early fourteenth centuries concentrated on their participation in ceremonies and festivals at affiliated religious institutions, at some point in the early fourteenth century they began to organize themselves into *za* (troupes, literally "guilds"), a trend that had accelerated by the middle of the century. It is assumed that the establishment of *sarugaku za* occurred

---

38 大夫 or 太夫, that is, the leader of a nō troupe but initially and not necessarily the senior actor, is usually read *tayū*, only in combination with a name is the consonant voiced and transcribed with a "d," thus treated as a personal name; the same applies for *nō-dayū*. Around the mid-seventeenth century, *tayū* was only used for the four Yamato troupes (Kanze, Konparu, Hōshō, Kongō) and for the Kita troupe. The name fell out of use with the abolishment of the Tokugawa *bakufu* in 1868.

39 *Inryōken nichiroku* 1: 459b–64a.

40 Hare, trans. 2008: 55; *Fūshi kaden*: 258.

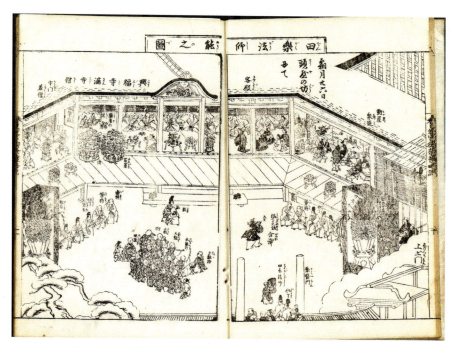

FIGURE 1.4 Performance of *gonichi nō* or *gonichi sarugaku* at the *Kasuga Wakamiya onmatsuri*. Illustrations of the Wakamiya Festival at the Kasuga Taisha (*Kasuga Ōmiya Wakamiya gosairei zu*) showing nō performed in the courtyard without a stage, roof, or bridgeway, vol. 2. By Fujiwara Nakatomo (dates unknown). 1780. Woodblock-printed book. 25.8 × 17.8 cm. Noh Theatre Research Institute, Hōsei University, Tokyo

slightly after *dengaku za*. *Dengaku*'s *honza* was located at Uji Shirakawa south of Kyoto and the *shinza* in Nara. The *honza* performed during the *Uji rikyū matsuri* (Uji Rikyū Festival) at Uji Jinja, whereas both troupes performed at the *Kasuga Wakamiya onmatsuri* (Kasuga Wakamiya Grand Festival; fig. 1.4). Both troupes performed in a competitive *tachiai* during the 1349 *sajiki kuzure no dengaku* described above.

Sarugaku groups were active across the Kinki region and appeared, for instance, at the *Uji rikyū matsuri*, at Kōfukuji's *takigi nō*, and at the *Kasuga Wakamiya onmatsuri*. There were several ways to address these groups: either by an individual company's name or by the area from which they originated. Historical sources mention Uji and Yamato *sarugaku*, as well as groups from the provinces of Ōmi (present-day Shiga Prefecture), Tanba (present-day northern Kyoto Prefecture), and Settsu (present-day eastern Hyōgo Prefecture), and document their nō styles as vastly different. It is unclear, however, when such distinctions came into usage and to what degree they reflect identifiable entities, as the first records noting *sarugaku* in Nara only state that it was performed and do not list any individual troupes.

What is certain is that by the fourteenth century, these groups presented themselves as *za*. In the case of Yamato *sarugaku*, for example, four troupes (*yoza*) have been identified as *Yamato sarugaku yoza*: Enman'i, Yūzaki, Sakado, and Tobi. During the Muromachi period, they would respectively form the Konparu, Kanze, Kongō, and Hōshō *za*, the precursors of the present-day nō schools. Their identification is supported since they were troupes affiliated with Nara's religious institutions and therefore were obliged to perform at the *Kasuga Wakamiya onmatsuri* as well as the Kōfukuji *takigi nō*. They also staged the *Hakkō sarugaku* (*Sarugaku after Eight Lectures*) during the *Yuima hakkōe* (Ceremony of the Eight Lectures on the *Vimalakirti Sutra*) at Tōnominedera (present-day Tanzan Jinja) on the southeastern edge of the Nara basin.[41]

The Yata *za* was active in the Tanba region, and the Enami *za* in Settsu or Kawachi. It is assumed that a troupe referred to as Hōjō *za* might have also been active in Settsu, but due to sparse evidence this remains speculative. During the Kamakura period, the Yata *za* was recognized as the *honza*, while the Enami *za* was the *shinza*, not to be confused with the *honza* and *shinza* of *dengaku*. Both troupes performed during *shushōe* and shrine festivals, but the Yata *za* was affiliated most closely with the Hosshōji in Kyoto and participated in the *Mitoshiro matsuri* (Mitoshiro Festival) of the Kamigamo Jinja. The troupe also appeared with the Enami *za* during the rice-planting rituals of the Sumiyoshi Taisha in Osaka. Six troupes referred to as Ōmi *sarugaku* surface in the early Muromachi period: Yamashina, Shimosaka, Hie, Mimaji, Ōmori, and Sakaudo. Judging from extant records, the Hie *za* was most popular until the end of the Muromachi period, competing with the Yamato troupes over performance styles, patrons, and audiences.

Numerous other *za* were active in each area and there are troupes recorded in Echizen Province (present-day northern Fukui Prefecture) and Ise Province (present-day Mie Prefecture). But records on these other *za* are largely missing. Nevertheless, following the introduction of the *haitōmai* system of allotting a rice stipend by the regent Toyotomi Hideyoshi (1537–1598) to the four Yamato troupes at the end of the sixteenth century, the troupes of Ōmi, Tanba and other areas either disappeared or merged with one of the *Yamato sarugaku*

---

41 On *sarugaku* at Tōnomine, see Omote 1974. See also the six contributions in *Nō to kyōgen*. "Tēma kenkyū: Tōnomine to sarugaku" 2007: 87–107.

yoza. Members of the Hie and Yamashina troupes, for example, became part of the Kanze *za*.[42]

The *sarugaku* and *dengaku za* operated under a strict principle of seniority. Based on the year a performer joined a troupe, he was counted as the *ichirō* ("the eldest," also referred to as *osa*, or "leader"), *nirō* ("the second eldest"), *sanrō* ("the third eldest"), and so forth. This hierarchy fulfilled an important purpose during actual performances. In *dengaku* dances, the musicians were chosen according to age grade.[43] In *sarugaku* troupes, convention dictated that in a staging of *Okina* the most prominent role of Okina could only be performed by the eldest member of the troupe. In contrast, other parts were assigned independent of seniority. For the lead roles in nō it was by no means an exception for the youngest member of a *sarugaku* or *dengaku* troupe to take the stage. With the increasing significance of nō in the repertoire of *dengaku* and *sarugaku*, the actors who performed the main roles gradually became the representatives of their troupes. This caused power shifts within the groups, especially from the latter half of the fourteenth century onward.

An episode in the *Sarugaku dangi* presents evidence of this development. The performance in question probably took place in either 1374 or 1375 (Ōei 7 or 8), when the *sarugaku za* of Kanze-dayū Kan'ami (1333–1384) (see ch. 5 *Authors*, 5.2) staged *sarugaku* at Kyoto's Imagumano Jinja (also read Imakumano) in the presence of the shōgun Ashikaga Yoshimitsu (1358–1408; r. 1368–1394). Before the performance took place, Yoshimitsu's retainer Ebina Naamidabutsu (d. 1381) stated that Okina should not be performed by the senior actor of the troupe but instead by its leader Kan'ami, who by this time was referred to as Kanze-dayū and in the following quote as Kiyotsugu:

> *Okina* in ancient times was danced by the eldest actor [of the troupe], but during the *Sarugaku* [performance] at Imagumano, on the advice of Naamidabutsu who said: "As the shōgun (Rokuon'in) is coming for the first time, he will probably ask about the actor who will appear in the first play. Therefore, this should be the leader," Kiyotsugu participated and performed [Okina], and from then it all started. So Yamato *Sarugaku* made a rule of it.[44]

---

42   On *sarugaku* troupes in English, see de Poorter (1986) 2002: 20–22; Rath 2004: 37–40, 93–97.

43   For an overview on *dengaku* performances, performers, and instruments, see Groemer 2011.

44   de Poorter (1986) 2002: 115; Japanese in Omote and Katō, eds. 1974: 293.

Kan'ami's performance of Okina set a precedent that completely undermined the seniority principle of the troupe, and subsequently, the troupe stipulated that its *tayū* should be the principal actor in *Okina*. Although the descriptive title *osa* continued to exist, the status of the *tayū* changed from the managing director to the prestigious representative of the *za*.

1.2.4 The Rise of Celebrity Performers: Kan'ami, Zeami, Inuō, and Zōami

As nō became a performance art in its own right, the environment and organization of the *dengaku* and *sarugaku* troupes changed rapidly. The appearance of star performers is one distinguishing feature between the first half of the fourteenth and the early fifteenth centuries. Particularly renowned were the *dengaku* performers Itchū (fl. early 14th c.) and Ako (dates unknown) from the *honza* who performed in the *kanjin dengaku* of 1349 on the Shijō riverbank. Itchū must have left a deep impression on Zeami, who praised him in his *Fūshi kaden* as "Itchū of the Honza, who in recent times was considered a veritable saint in this vocation."[45] The *Sarugaku dangi* (fig. 1.5, first two sentences on the left page) even claims that *sarugaku* performers learned nō from *dengaku* performers: "Itchū (Dengaku), Kiyotsugu (Buddhist name Kan'a [Kan'ami]), Inuō (Buddhist name Dōa [Dōami]) and Kia [Kiami] must be called the ancestors of our art. Kan'a said that Itchū was the teacher of his own style. Dōa too is a pupil of Itchū."[46]

During the second half of the fourteenth century, *dengaku nō* may indeed have been more popular than *sarugaku nō*. The majority of *kanjin nō* performances in Kyoto between the mid-fourteenth and early fifteenth centuries were *kanjin dengaku*.[47] One reason why *dengaku nō* was more successful than *sarugaku nō* lay in their respective performance styles. Zeami's *Fūshi kaden* and the *Sarugaku dangi* note that the styles of nō performed by *dengaku*, on the one hand, and by Yamato and Ōmi *sarugaku*, on the other, were strikingly different. *Dengaku nō* consisted of fierce, furious movements that were connected to and in sync with the songs and the music. Ōmi *sarugaku nō* excelled in the elegant, graceful performance of the *tennyo mai*, or the "dance of the heavenly maiden." The performance style of Yamato *sarugaku*, again, may have been rather mimetic, as Zeami's usage of the term *monomane* (imitation) indicates, and unsophisticated, with the performance of *oni* its strong point.

Nevertheless, toward the end of the fourteenth century performers of *dengaku*, Ōmi *sarugaku*, and Yamato *sarugaku* frequently visited Kyoto for

---

45 Hare, trans. 2008: 53–54; *Fūshi kaden*: 254–55.
46 de Poorter (1986) 2002: 81; Omote and Katō, eds. 1974: 261.
47 For a detailed list of (*dengaku* and *sarugaku*) *kanjin nō* performances between 1317 and 1904, see Miyamoto 2020: 11–23.

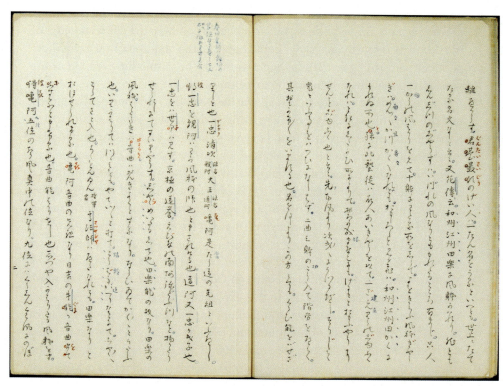

FIGURE 1.5 Pages from *Zeshi rokujū igo sarugaku dangi* (*Talks on Sarugaku by Zeami after Sixty*). Copy by Kurokawa Harumura (1799–1866). 19th century. Handwritten book. 26.5 × 19.1 cm. Noh Theatre Research Institute, Hōsei University, Tokyo

performances where they were favored by the shōguns of the Muromachi *bakufu*. This patronage offered occasions for players from different troupes to perform together for the shōgun, and this presented an unmissable chance for Yamato *sarugaku* performers, such as Kan'ami and Zeami, to learn and imitate the more popular performance styles of *dengaku* and Ōmi *sarugaku*. That Kan'ami claimed Itchū to be the "teacher of his performance style," and that Zeami was able to implement the trademark dance *tennyo mai* of Inuō (later known as Dōami; d. 1413), shows how perceptively Yamato *sarugaku* representatives observed and absorbed the stylistic strengths of *dengaku* and Ōmi *sarugaku*. Zeami goes so far as to proclaim that a master of the art "is skilled in the full diversity of roles whether in Yamato or Ōmi, even in the expressive manner of *dengaku*—all in accord with the preferences and expectations of the audience."[48] By integrating other performance styles, Yamato *sarugaku*

---

48   Hare, trans. 2008: 55; *Fūshi kaden*: 257.

performers were able to increase their popularity, which led to the first boom of *sarugaku nō*. Zeami's efforts, in particular, to combine the characteristics of the different performance styles contributed to the creation of nō as an independent performing art. This is one reason why he is so often credited as the person responsible for bringing nō to its maturity.

That *sarugaku* outperformed *dengaku* between the mid-fourteenth century and the early fifteenth centuries was likewise due to the rising prominence of Kan'ami, his son Zeami, and Inuō (see ch. 5 *Authors*, 5.2, 5.3). Kan'ami (1333–1384) was the third son of an adopted son of Mino-dayū (dates unknown) from the Yamada *sarugaku*, a group that was active in the Yamato basin. His older brothers Hōshō (later *tayū* of the Hōshō *za*) and Shōichi were also active *sarugaku* performers. Until recently, it was generally assumed that Kan'ami founded the Yūzaki *za* and traveled to Obata in Iga Province (present-day Mie Prefecture) for the sole purpose of acquiring an Okina mask. This theory was based on the *Sarugaku dangi*: "The *okina* [mask] of our troupe is made by Miroku. When he founded the troupe in Obata in Iga, he selected the mask in Iga."[49] Omote Akira objected to this explanation, arguing that because the Yūzaki *za* was founded during the Kamakura period and that Kan'ami was born in 1333 (i.e., the last year of the Kamakura period) he cannot have established the troupe.[50] Indeed, since the *Sarugaku dangi* does not state the name of the troupe in question, the assumption that the quoted section refers to Yūzaki *za* could be mistaken. The development of nō troupes and their structure evinces that Kan'ami founded the Kanze *za* and that the Kanze troupe was part of a larger umbrella organization called Yūzaki *za*.[51]

The Yūzaki *za* and the three other Yamato *sarugaku* troupes Enman'i, Sakado, and Tobi were umbrella groups for a number of troupes each centering around one *tayū*. To be precise, most *tayū* active in the Yamato region led their own independent troupes in different areas in the Yamato region and belonged to one of the *Yamato sarugaku yoza*. *Tayū* usually toured the villages in the vicinity of their individual troupe where they performed in shrines and temples. On special occasions, such as the *takigi nō*, the *Kasuga Wakamiya onmatsuri*, or the *Hakkō sarugaku* at Tōnominedera, *tayū* gathered and participated under the name of their umbrella troupe. Kan'ami, as a member of the older Yūzaki *za*, might have chosen to lead his own troupe, which was then referred to as Kanze *za*, citing his stage name "Kanze." That this troupe was associated with the Iga area might have been because his original family shared its lineage

---

49 de Poorter (1986) 2002: 123.
50 Omote 1983; see also de Poorter (1986) 2002: 145, 223n5; Omote and Katō, eds. 1974: 501a–b.
51 The following paragraphs are based on this newer hypothesis. See Miyamoto 2017c.

with the Hattori family of Iga but also because Iga had no other local *sarugaku* group. Seen from this perspective, the Iga area provided fertile soil for Kan'ami to develop his own *sarugaku nō* style. At the same time, it allowed him, as Kanze-dayū of the Kanze *za*, to take part in the *takigi nō* performances and the *Kasuga Wakamiya onmatsuri* in Nara as a member of the Yūzaki *za*.

Kan'ami's almost overnight fame can be traced to his *sarugaku* performance at Kyoto's Imagumano Jinja in 1374 or 1375. It seems that years after forming his troupe in Iga, the Kanze *za* was successful enough to branch out to Kyoto where the main competition between the *sarugaku* and *dengaku* troupes took place—the Imagumano performance was thus a turning point in the Kanze *za*'s fortunes. According to the *Sarugaku dangi*, this was the first performance that was honored by the presence of a shōgun, in this case Ashikaga Yoshimitsu,[52] who subsequently became a patron of *sarugaku*, not only for Kan'ami and his young son Fujiwaka (Zeami) but also for *sarugaku* performers generally. During the next three decades or more, *sarugaku* performers became the official artists for Yoshimitsu and his family, resulting in individual prestige as well as the thriving of their respective troupe. From this point onward, numerous troupes sought to secure the patronage of either the shogunal family or daimyō households.

Zeami succeeded Kan'ami upon his death in 1384 as the second Kanze-dayū. Fifteen years later, in 1399, Zeami performed in a three-day *kanjin sarugaku* at Ichijō Takegahana in Kyoto. This *kanjin sarugaku* was sponsored by Yoshimitsu, and this public recognition facilitated the smooth progress of Zeami's career as a performer.[53] Zeami's achievements for and contributions to the development of nō were manifold: he was not only a keen observer of performance practices but also actively integrated more popular styles of his contemporaneous rivals into his nō style. In doing so he created an aesthetic world of nō revolving around poetic songs and dances, and his sophisticated nō plays came to be considered superior and as the fundaments of the nō repertory. While the extant manuscripts of Zeami's treatises on nō represent the first writings that outline a theoretical framework for this stage art, recent research has completely refuted the assumption that he was the greatest performer in Kyoto during the second half of the thirteenth and the first half of the fourteenth century.[54] Rather, the records in *Sarugaku dangi* note that Inuō from the Ōmi *sarugaku* Hie troupe became the eminent official performer for the Ashikaga

---

52 de Poorter (1986) 2002: 115.
53 On Zeami's *kanjin sarugaku* at Ichijō Takegahana, see Matsuoka 2021.
54 See, for example, Ochiai 1994; Shigeta 2006.

shogunal family and dominated the world of nō performances.⁵⁵ Inuō's popularity apparently reached its zenith in 1408 (Ōei 15) when he took the lead in several performances at Yoshimitsu's residence, attended by the retired emperor Gokomatsu (1377–1433; r. 1382–1392).

Yoshimitsu's death in 1408 impacted all *sarugaku* performers. The new shōgun Ashikaga Yoshimochi (1389–1428; r. 1394–1423) favored *dengaku* performances, while *sarugaku nō* disappeared from large events. Yoshimochi's favorite performer, Zōami (dates unknown) from the *dengaku shinza*, was licensed to organize a yearly *kanjin dengaku* performance in Kyoto between 1412 and 1422 and became the star performer of the early fifteenth century. The *Sarugaku dangi* has Zeami being moved to "tears of admiration" by merely remembering a performance of Zōami, which was "chillingly beautiful."⁵⁶

The loss of the support of the Ashikaga family was just one reason for the lack of activities by *sarugaku* performers during Yoshimochi's tenure as shōgun. Another crucial factor was the generational change that the *sarugaku* troupes were experiencing. Inuō's death in 1413 (Ōei 20) left a void in the Hie troupe as his successor Iwatō never enjoyed Inuō's fame. Zeami, at the same time, was still active as a performer but no longer able to generate enthusiasm, and he instead concentrated on training the next representative for his troupe. But the fate of *sarugaku* changed yet again during the second half of the 1420s when documents on Zōami's activities inexplicably cease. Ashikaga Yoshimochi's death in 1428 marks the rapid and final decline of the popularity of *dengaku*, and *sarugaku* performers reemerged as the avant-garde of the nō community. Not all troupes were a part of this new popularity: while the Kanze troupe of the Yamato *sarugaku* succeeded in restoring its previous glory, Ōmi *sarugaku* failed.

1.2.5 *The Position of Kanze-dayū: Zeami and His Successors*

When Zeami retired from the stage in around 1420 he was referred to by the honorific title of Kanze nyūdō (Lay Monk Kanze).⁵⁷ With Saburō Motoshige (1398–1467, i.e., On'ami), his adopted son and nephew, and his own son Jūrō Motomasa (?–1432), the Kanze troupe had two talented and acclaimed performers (see ch. 5 *Authors*, 5.4). Until recently, it was generally acknowledged that in around 1422 (Ōei 29), Zeami's son Jūrō Motomasa succeeded Zeami as the

---

55 On Yoshimitsu's patronage of Inuō, see Pinnington 2019: 93–95.
56 Omote and Katō, eds. 1974: 262; de Poorter (1986) 2002: 82–83. On Yoshimochi's patronage of Zōami, see Pinnington 2019: 95–97.
57 See *Daigoji shin yōroku* 1: 428.

tayū of the Kanze troupe, thereby inheriting the title of Kanze-dayū.[58] Judging from extant materials from the first half of the fifteenth century, however, the generational change did not go smoothly. In fact, there was a dispute within the Kanze *za* concerning who should be the next Kanze-dayū. Of paramount importance in reevaluating the Kanze troupe's development are the diaries of two monks, Mansai (1378–1435) and Ryūgen (1342–1426) of Daigoji, one of the main monasteries in Kyoto where *sarugaku* was regularly performed. An investigation of the *Mansai jugō nikki* (*Diary of Eminent Monk Mansai*), together with the entries from the *Ryūgen sōjō nikki* (*Diary of Senior Prelate Ryūgen*) quoted in *Daigoji shin yōroku* (*New Record of the Essentials of Daigoji*), sheds fresh light on the putative rivalry within the Kanze troupe. These sources indicate how easily performers could fall victim to political intrigues even when favored by the shōgun.

The rivalry we may suppose existed between Jūrō Motomasa and Saburō Motoshige is at least in part due to the fact that before Jūrō Motomasa was born, Zeami adopted Saburō Motoshige with the aim of raising him as successor. Zeami's intention is evident from his decision to bestow his own childhood name of "Saburō" on Motoshige. On Ōei 29 (1422).4.18, he also assisted Saburō Motoshige, who by then was referred to as Kanze-dayū, when performing at Seiryūgū, a shrine affiliated with Daigoji.[59] This implies that in 1422, Saburō Motoshige was the head of the Kanze troupe. Until 1424, the Seiryūgū's annual *jinji sarugaku*, or "sacred" *sarugaku*, was organized by Enami-dayū of the Enami troupe, who held the prestigious position of *gakutō* (master of performances). For some reason, Enami and his brother fell out of favor with Daigoji; Enami died not long after. The beneficiary of this incident was the Kanze-dayū, who succeeded to the position of *gakutō*. According to the senior prelate Ryūgen (1342–1426), this Kanze-dayū was "Kanze Saburō," which means that Saburō Motoshige held the position of Kanze-dayū at least between 1422 and 1424.[60]

This situation seems to have changed in 1427, when a Kanze-dayū performed at Daigoji's Seiryūgū on the seventeenth day of the fourth month. Only six days later, a "Kanze Saburō" performed at a *kanjin sarugaku* in the vicinity of Kyoto's Fushimi Inari Taisha, supported by Gien, a monk of Shōren'in who would later become the sixth Ashikaga shōgun Yoshinori (1394–1441; r. 1429–1441).[61] There is a high probability that these two entries refer to two distinct performers:

---

58   See, for example, Takemoto 2009: 396; Imaizumi 2009: 71–72.
59   *Mansai jugō nikki* 1: 200b–1a.
60   *Mansai jugō nikki* 1: 264b–65a. *Daigoji shin yōroku* 1: 426–28. On *sarugaku* at Daigoji, the demise of the Enami brothers, and Yoshinori's patronage of Saburō Motoshige, see Pinnington 2019: 98–103.
61   *Mansai jugō nikki* 1: 429a–30b.

"Kanze Saburō" most likely indicates Saburō Motoshige while "Kanze-dayū" designates Zeami's son Jūrō Motomasa. Another entry in the *Mansai jugō nikki* from 1429 (Shōchō 2) adds to the confusion with the mention of "Kanze-dayū ryōza," the two troupes of the Kanze-dayū.[62]

These entries allow us to speculate that Saburō Motoshige, after succeeding Zeami as Kanze-dayū and becoming *gakutō* at Seiryūgū, split from the Kanze *za* and founded his own troupe. One result was that both Saburō Motoshige and Jūrō Motoshige held the title of Kanze-dayū. What might have provoked this situation was Gien's favoritism of Saburō Motoshige, which continued— even increased—after Gien was appointed shōgun in 1428. In 1429, Gien, now Yoshinori, removed Zeami and Jūrō Motomasa from the program of a performance at the residence of the retired emperor Gokomatsu. It was to Yoshinori's patronage that Saburō Motoshige owed the renewal of his position as *gakutō* of the Seiryūgū performance venue in 1430 (Eikyō 2).[63] Jūrō Motomasa, on the other hand, disappeared from Kyoto and Nara, dying shortly after in 1432 (Eikyō 4) in Anotsu in Ise Province (present-day Tsu in Mie Prefecture). Saburō Motoshige was left the sole Kanze-dayū and undisputed leader of the Kanze troupe.[64]

To announce and celebrate his succession as the head of the Kanze troupe, Saburō Motoshige organized a *kanjin sarugaku* on Kyoto's Tadasugawara in 1433 (Eikyō 5). The performance was attended once more by the shōgun Yoshinori, demonstrating the full support of the *bakufu* and the strengthening of Saburō Motoshige's position as the foremost nō performer of his time.[65] Indeed, many records corroborate Saburō Motoshige's exceptional skill. The monk and *renga* poet Shinkei (1406–1475), for example, notes in his *Hitorigoto* (*Solitary Ramblings*, 1468) that Saburō Motoshige "is the most talented" performer and "peerless in this realm."[66] With Zeami's exile to Sado Island just one year later in 1434 (Eikyō 6) and the loss of momentum of *dengaku* and of Ōmi's Hie *za*, there was no one left to contest the position of Kanze-dayū. This enabled Saburō Motoshige to pave the way for his troupe's future success.

Performance records confirm the supremacy of Saburō Motoshige and the Kanze *za*. On Eikyō 12 (1440).1.28, a staging at the shōgun's residence consisted of five *dengaku nō*, five nō by Hie *za*'s Iwatō, and nine by Saburō Motoshige.[67] While this also establishes that actors of the *dengaku*, Ōmi, and Yamato

---

62 *Mansai jugō nikki* 2: 51a.
63 *Mansai jugō nikki* 2: 52b, 141a.
64 On Motomasa and his fate, see de Poorter (1986) 2002: 37–38; Rath 2004: 128–32.
65 *Daijōin nikki mokuroku*: 648a–b.
66 *Hitorigoto*: 474.
67 *Kennaiki* 3: 13.

sarugaku traditions still performed on the same occasion, Saburō Motoshige clearly dominated the stage. Records further state that performances attended by Yoshinori almost always had Saburō Motoshige as main actor. The shōgun Yoshinori, however, appears to not have been the most reliable of patrons. He was feared for being erratic in his arbitrations and prone to violence. In his diary *Kanmon nikki* (*Diary of Things Seen and Heard*) Prince Fushimi no Miya Sadafusa (1372–1456) uses the words *bannin kyōfu*, or "the horror of all people," to describe the atmosphere of the period.[68] Yoshinori's despotic behavior did not spare his favorite performer. In his 1439 (Eikyō 9.2.8) entry, Sadafusa voices his astonishment that even Saburō Motoshige, who was held in such high esteem, was reprimanded by Yoshinori, and laments that the incident is "a typical happening in this uncertain world." Sadafusa does not give the reason for Saburō Motoshige's falling out of favor, but Yoshinori obviously did not forgive easily. More than a week later, however, on the evening of the sixteenth day, the warrior governor Akamatsu Mitsusuke (1381–1441) intervened on Motoshige's behalf and secured his pardon.[69]

In 1441, only two years after this incident, Yoshinori was assassinated in Akamatsu Mitsusuke's residence during an evening nō performance, presumably including Saburō Motoshige as a performer.[70] For the Kanze-dayū and his *za* this meant the loss of their economic base, and for some years the troupe struggled to survive. In addition, financial circumstances for the Kanze troupe were strained because the patronage of *sarugaku* was temporarily reduced under the two young child shōguns Ashikaga Yoshikatsu (1434–1443; r. 1441–1443) and Ashikaga Yoshimasa (1436–1490; r. 1449–1473). Before long, though, the eighth shōgun Yoshimasa became a fervent patron of nō.[71] Ise Sadayori (d. 1529), a steward at the Muromachi shogunate house office in charge of protocol and ceremonies, remembers that when Yoshimasa became aware of the Kanze troupe's impoverishment, he commanded the daimyō to provide financial support to the troupe.[72] Saburō Motoshige regained his prominence and continued performing well into his sixties, even after his son Matasaburō

---

68   *Kanmon gyoki* 2: 259a (Eikyō 7 [1437].2.8). Japanese scholars assume that *gyoki* is not the original title of the diary, but rather added at a later time. Subsequently *gyoki* was replaced with *nikki*, a custom followed here. Quotes are from the edition entitled *Kanmon gyoki*.
69   *Kanmon gyoki* 2: 448b–50b.
70   On the assassination of Yoshinori, see Varley 1967: 65–75.
71   Yoshimasa, who had the Silver Pavilion at Jishōji (Ginkakuji) built, was a central figure of the so-called *Higashiyama bunka* ("Eastern Mountain" culture), when nō, the tea and flower ceremonies, and other cultural activities championed by aristocrats, monks, and warriors flourished. On Konparu Zenchiku and Higashiyama culture, see Thornhill 1993: 186–89. On cultural life in Muromachi Japan, see Varley 1990.
72   *Sōgo ōzōshi*: 560a–b. Compare Pinnington 2019: 149–51.

(1429–1470) became Kanze-dayū, and he himself had taken Buddhist vows and changed his name to On'ami. In 1464 (Kanshō 5), for example, he performed as *shite* in twelve nō during the famous *kanjin sarugaku* in Tadasugawara organized by his son Kanze-dayū Matasaburō (fig. 1.3).[73]

Unlike Zeami, Saburō Motoshige left no treatises. And although Kan'ami and Zeami are often referred to as the founders of nō, it was Saburō Motoshige who monopolized the world of nō for more than three decades and has to be credited with the establishment of the dominant position of the Kanze za during the Muromachi period and for centuries to come. Until the latter half of the sixteenth century, every Kanze-dayū became an official performer directly under the command of the Muromachi *bakufu*, and the Kanze za held sole responsibility for the performances at the shogunal residence. Even though sixteenth-century sources note that *dengaku* performers and members of the Hie za were also present on such occasions, their participation was merely perfunctory. In most instances, they were *homemōsu yakunin*, or "those tasked with praising,"[74] and were planted in the audience, expected to compliment and applaud the performance of the Kanze-dayū.

1.3 Nō in Kyoto and Its Dispersion during the Fifteenth and Sixteenth Centuries
Eike Grossmann and Miyamoto Keizō

1.3.1 *Fierce Competition:* Shōmoji, Onna sarugaku, *and Disappearing Performers*

During the fourteenth and fifteenth centuries, *dengaku nō* and *sarugaku nō* performers vied for larger audiences outside Buddhist temples and Shintō shrines. In the process, they gradually cultivated new spaces and contexts for their art, among them *kanjin nō* and performances sponsored by warriors. The main competition of the era took place in and around Kyoto, and nō performers from all over the country swarmed to Kyoto in the hope of finding stardom. Inuō's rapid rise to fame, for example, came with a *kanjin sarugaku* on the riverbank at Kyoto's Ayanokōji on Kōryaku 2 (1380).4.13.[75] Even if they were not equipped with enough to counter the rising influence of performers form Yamato *sarugaku*—in particular, the Kanze and Konparu troupes—nō performers from other troupes were busily jockeying for a niche

---

73   See *Tadasugawara kanjin sarugaku nikki*: 717b–21b.
74   Such was the case in 1561 (Eiroku 4); *Miyoshi tei o-nari ki*: 241b.
75   *Kōyōki* 1: 52; Ogawa 2008: 43.

in the emerging performance market. Among those whose appearances in Kyoto are documented were Konparu Gonnokami (Zenchiku's grandfather), Kongō Gonnokami, Ōkura-dayū from Yamato *sarugaku*, and Umewaka-dayū, Yata-dayū from Tanba, and Enami-dayū from Settsu or Kawachi, to name just a few. *Sarugaku* performers from Echizen led by one Fukurai-dayū paid their respects at the shogunal residence on Eikyō 7 (1435).2.21, when they came to the capital for the first time and performed in a *tachiai* with the Kanze troupe.[76]

Dengaku and *sarugaku* performers were not the only actors whose nō attracted the attention of broader audiences. The cultivation of urban spaces for performances provided opportunities for many performers formerly affiliated with shrines and temples, and it offered new sources of income for those who were quick to pick up the latest performance fashions. Almost in tandem with the movement of *sarugaku* and *dengaku* performers to the cities was the emergence of other groups of performers. This era of nō thus represents a liberalization of performance spaces and is dominated by the popularity of nō among Kyoto residents. In addition, it reveals processes of specialization and professionalization.

Shōmoji ("those who hear the voice," also *shōmonji*, or "chanters at the gate") seem to have been the most serious competitors in the eyes of *sarugaku nō* performers. They may have belonged to a mendicant group initially specialized in purification and later on blessing households during the New Year celebrations with auspicious phrases in a performance called *senzu manzai* ("one thousand autumns and ten thousand years"). Some *shōmoji* performed celebratory chants called *matsu-bayashi* ("pine music"), another variation of magical blessing, while yet others picked up *sarugaku nō* and *kusemai* dances as a side performance, managing to perform these with considerable success.[77] For example, a *shōmoji* called Koinu ("Little Dog" or "Puppy," d. ca. 1470s) from the village of Yanagihara near Kyoto regularly delivered *matsu-bayashi* and *sarugaku nō* at the imperial palace and at the gates of aristocratic residences during the New Year festivities. In 1432, the *Kanmon nikki* declares Koinu "a master of *sarugaku*" who "performs frequently," for instance, in eleven nō at the imperial palace on Kyōtoku 4 (1455).1.28.[78]

This does not mean that *shōmoji* were held in high esteem. In fact, on several occasions *shōmoji* appearing at the gates for the New Year celebrations were

---

76   *Kanmon gyoki* 2: 263a. On Umewaka-dayū and Yata-dayū, see Miyamoto 2005b: 343–47; Nose 1938: 956–87. On Ōkura-dayū, see Nose 1938: 541–58. The *Sarugaku dangi* contains a critique of Konparu Gonnokami and Kongō Gonnokami. Omote and Katō, eds. 1974: 298–99; de Poorter (1986) 2002: 120–21. See also Pinnington 2019: 74–76.
77   On *shōmoji*, see Groemer 2016: 50, 152–57; Rath 2002: 175–92; Rath 2004: 37–47, 58–67.
78   *Kanmon gyoki* 2: 7a; *Yasutomiki* 4: 132a.

turned away. Even Koinu repeatedly experienced rejection. Although he was hugely popular and is reported to have been favored by Ashikaga Yoshinori, in 1437 (Eikyō 9) he was violently beaten by the guards at the shogunal residence when he showed up uninvited to perform *matsu-bayashi*.[79] Still, Yoshinori, in all probability, was the reason why Koinu was given license to organize *kanjin nō* at the Kyoto monastery Rokudō Chinnōji on Hōtoku 2 (1450).2.23 and in Ōmi Province in 1466 (Bunshō 1).[80]

Sarugaku troupes must have perceived *shōmoji* as a greater threat to their authority than other troupes. They attempted to prevent appearances by *shōmoji* and to establish rules in an effort to stop "outsiders" from performing nō. Members of the Kanze and Konparu troupes, as well as of other *sarugaku* troupes, used their position and political leverage to discourage *shōmoji* like Koinu, whose fate exemplifies what Eric Rath calls "Kanze's triumph over the *shōmonji*."[81] Koinu's *kanjin nō* at Rokudō Chinnōji in 1450, for example, was canceled by the Muromachi *bakufu* after the Kanze and Konparu troupes lodged a formal complaint to Kyoto authorities.[82] In addition to complaining regularly to the authorities about non-*sarugaku kanjin nō*, *sarugaku* performers arranged for a rule to be implemented that afforded them the exclusive right to don masks during performances. The event that led to Koinu's ultimate demise occurred in 1466, when he was arrested in Kyoto for donning a nō mask during the *kanjin nō* performance in Ōmi Province. After this time, he cannot be traced.[83]

Female performers, on the other hand, were not regarded as a serious threat to *sarugaku* performers. One reason may have been the fact that performances by female troupes, which were referred to as *onna sarugaku* or *nyōbō sarugaku* (women's or lady's *sarugaku*), were popular for only a short interlude during the fifteenth century. During this period, *onna sarugaku* was looked upon favorably, and some troupes managed to perform for the shōgun and at the imperial palace. From Eikyō 4 (1432).10.10, for instance, a troupe of female *sarugaku* performers organized a four-day *kanjin nō* at Toba on the southern outskirts of Kyoto. According to the *Kanmon nikki*, this troupe came to the capital from one of the western provinces and established a reputation for their exceptional skills: "The women's chanting, like that of court ladies, is praiseworthy and not inferior to Kanze[-dayū]. Their style of *sarugaku* is marvelous." Since a female

---

79 *Kanmon gyoki* 1: 580a; *Kanmon gyoki* 2: 439a.
80 *Yasutomiki* 3: 152b; *Inryōken nichiroku* 2: 638b–39a.
81 Rath 2004: 64.
82 *Yasutomiki* 3: 152b.
83 *Inryōken nichiroku* 2: 638b–39a.

performance was a rare occasion, an immense group of spectators gathered in the large audience "gallery of 63 *ken*" (ca. 115 m) to watch the beautiful women dance and chant.[84] The troupe stayed in Kyoto for some time, and only thirteen days after its first performance (Eikyō 4.10.23) the group was invited to perform three *sarugaku nō* at the shōgun's residence. The day's performance closed with a competitive *tachiai* performance with Kanze-dayū Saburō Motoshige, and all performers were lavishly rewarded with *kosode* ("small-sleeved" kimono) and coins.[85] The *Kanmon nikki* suggests that the troupe consisted of both female and male performers, with the latter being responsible for the musical accompaniment (*hayashi*) and the kyōgen performances (*okashi*).[86]

The diary *Gohōkōinki* of the aristocrat Konoe Masaie (1444–1505) makes note of a female troupe from Echizen that performed on Kyoto's Hachijō Horikawa on Kanshō 7 (1466).2.23, and mentions that "... the *fue*, *ōtsuzumi*, and *kotsuzumi* players are all men. The kyōgen is also performed by men." After the performance this troupe was invited to perform five *sarugaku nō* at the imperial palace, again followed by a performance of the "old but still fit" Kanze Saburō Motoshige.[87] There are other records of performances by female troupes in Kyoto—one, for instance, speaks of a *sarugaku* at the Katsura riverbank in 1436 (Eikyō 8) that was discontinued after several male and female spectators died following a public disturbance.[88] In the main, however, the background of most female *sarugaku* troupes is unknown. No documentation of the origins of the female performers, the organization of their troupes, or the specifics of their training has yet come to light.

Not surprisingly, competition in Kyoto resulted in some performers being unable to attract enough audience attention to make a living from their art. They left the bustling capital and found new performance contexts in the provinces. Around the mid-fourteenth century, the festivals and rituals of rural communities offered a stable source of income. By participating in performances connected to ceremonies at country shrines, it could be argued that these performers were reconnecting with their roots. Among those whose activities were concentrated on rural communities were the Kongō-dayū and the Ōkura-dayū (both Yamato *sarugaku*), and troupes belonging to Uji *sarugaku*. Various opportunities for performers notwithstanding, some would-be

---

84 *Kanmon gyoki* 2: 63b–64a.
85 *Kanmon gyoki* 2: 66b.
86 *Kanmon gyoki* 2: 63b.
87 *Gohōkōinki* 1: 10; *Inryōken nichiroku* 2: 602a–3b.
88 *Kanmon gyoki* 2: 391a.

nō performers succeeded neither in urban centers nor in rural areas. They probably just disappeared from the scene by changing their profession.

The most prominent examples of this shift are *dengaku* performers. Once favored by the Ashikaga shogunate and popular with audiences, their fame had rapidly declined by the mid-fifteenth century, and toward the end of the fifteenth century *dengaku* could no longer draw in urban audiences. The last record of a full-scale *dengaku* performance in Kyoto dates to 1446 (Bun'an 3), when, on two consecutive days, the *honza* performed eighteen nō at the temple Jūshin'in.[89] Thereafter, they vanished from Kyoto records, although they continued to be involved in the *Kasuga Wakamiya onmatsuri*. Their activities seem to have ceased altogether by the sixteenth century, at which time most *dengaku* performers were no longer able to live solely from their art because they also had no roots in other local community festivals except for Nara's Kasuga Taisha. Some of those who are known to us today became farmers in the Nara area and continued to perform *dengaku* dances during the *Kasuga Wakamiya onmatsuri*. Some of the *dengaku* nō repertory survived into the Edo period (1603–1868), if only through a handful of plays, such as *Kappo* (*Hépǔ* or *Hoppo*), *Kikusui* (*Chrysanthemum Water*), and *Jisei* (*Two Stars*).[90]

1.3.2 Kyoto in Disarray: the Performers' Search for New Sources of Income

The decade-long *Ōnin bunmei no ran* (Ōnin Disturbances) erupted in the fifth month of 1467 (Ōnin 1), four months after the death of Kanze-dayū Saburō Motoshige. The ensuing war over shogunal succession saw the collapse of the political, economic, social, and cultural order in Kyoto and by extension all of Japan. The conflict led to the eventual downfall of the Ashikaga shogunate and marked the beginning of an era generally referred to as the Sengoku (Warring Provinces or States) period.[91] During this time, new leaders and elites, in their fight for supremacy, emerged in the form of regionally powerful daimyō known as *sengoku daimyō* (daimyō of the Warring Provinces). The war and the concomitant volatile power struggles also impacted the status of nō performers, who had heavily relied on the patronage of the Ashikaga shōgun and his warriors, as well as on the income generated by *kanjin nō* in Kyoto.[92]

---

89 *Bun'an dengaku nō ki*: 712a–17a.
90 The three plays are mentioned, among others, in *Kasuga Wakamiya onmatsuri shukkin dengaku za kiroku*: 176–81.
91 The Sengoku period often refers to the later part of the Muromachi period, specifically from the beginning of the Ōnin Disturbances to the end of the Muromachi *bakufu* in 1573.
92 On the Ōnin Disturbances, see Varley 1967. On Kyoto during this era, see Stavros 2014: 133–50.

With Kyoto in the eye of the storm, everyone who could afford to flee—warriors, aristocrats, monks, and merchants—did. Before long, there were no patrons left to hire performers and no affluent audiences for *kanjin nō*. In addition, smaller shrines and temples were not able to pay their annual tributes to their head institution such that nō performers no longer received their stipends, even if they were hired for *jinji sarugaku*, or "sacred nō" (after the Edo period also read *shinji nō*). In short, the disturbances led to the discontinuation of many performances and depleted the sources of income for nō performers. The few performances that took place in the first year of the conflict were held at the residence of the shōgun Yoshinori, mostly with Kanze-dayū Matasaburō as the main performer. But such events became less frequent as the upheavals grew more brutal. Other nō performances were either canceled or reduced in scale. The *Gohōkōinki* records that due to the fighting in Kyoto only *Shikisanban* (that is, *Okina*) was performed during the yearly *jinji sarugaku* at the *Uji rikyū matsuri* on Ōnin 2 (1468).5.9, instead of the regular five nō.[93]

The precipitous decline of Ashikaga authority and of the Kōfukuji occasioned drastic change for nō performers, as the loss of powerful patrons threatened the foundations crucial to their survival. Their financial distress was so severe that they had trouble assembling the costumes they needed for their performances, and this, in turn, impacted their appearance at Kōfukuji's *takigi nō*. The *Daijōin jisha zōjiki* (*Daijōin's Records of Miscellaneous Matters of the Temples and Shrines*) comments on the participation of Kanze-dayū Matasaburō in the *takigi nō* at Kōfukuji on Bunmei 2 (1470).2.13: "Because of great commotion in the realm it is difficult for *sarugaku* performers to make a living."[94] Nevertheless, the four troupes continued to partake in *takigi nō* until 1474 (Bunmei 6) when Konparu-dayū Shichirō Motouji (Sōin; 1432–1480) called for a boycott, arguing that for several years in a row the performers had not received their rice stipends from the temple.[95]

When the Ōnin Disturbances finally came to an end in 1477 (Bunmei 9), anyone still in Kyoto, most notably the ninth shōgun Ashikaga Yoshihisa (1467–1489; r. 1473–1489) and the daimyō, were keen on displaying their city's return to normalcy. What could be more convincing than a dazzling nō performance to demonstrate the restoration of peace? A large-scale *kanjin nō* was organized at Kyoto's Seiganji in the fourth month of 1478 with Kanze-dayū Saburō Yukishige (d. 1500) as the principal performer, and with Yoshihisa and many daimyō in attendance. But political power had shifted irrevocably, and a number of nō

---

93   *Gohōkōinki* 1: 152.
94   *Daijōin jisha zōjiki* 4: 382b.
95   *Daijōin jisha zōjiki* 5: 450a–b.

performers had chosen to search for new patrons. Kyoto had lost its singular status as the cultural center, and performers increasingly traveled to the provinces in a centrifugal movement, either following old patrons or seeking different audiences in possession of the necessary funds, education, and time to nurture another hobby. They found a suitable target group among the emerging *sengoku daimyō*, and soon Yamato *sarugaku* troupes, formerly concentrated in Kyoto and Nara, expanded their activities into rural areas.

To be sure, performers had always traveled, and it is reported that Kan'ami died on a visit to Suruga Province (present-day central Shizuoka Prefecture) (see ch. 5 *Authors*, 5.2). But in order to cultivate sources of income, some Sengoku period performers relocated to the provinces for extended lengths of time. By the end of the fifteenth century, travel became more profitable. One Hōshō-dayū, for example, traveled to Yamaguchi in Suō Province (present-day southeastern Yamaguchi Prefecture) in 1483 (Bunmei 15) where he was supported by the powerful Ōuchi daimyō clan.[96] In 1484 (Bunmei 16), Usagi-dayū, a kyōgen performer of the Kanze troupe, left Kyoto for Noto Province (present-day northern Ishikawa Prefecture) to visit the Hatakeyama daimyō clan. He then moved on to Harima Province (present-day Hyōgo Prefecture) in 1486 (Bunmei 18), where he found new patrons with the Akamatsu daimyō clan and their retainers from the Uragami clan (Bunmei 15.6.11) (see ch. 9 *Kyōgen*, 9.6).[97] These performers initiated a significant dissemination of nō from the center to the more lucrative periphery where people, in turn, were afforded access to nō performances.

1.3.3 Warriors Onstage: Nō Performances at the Shogunal Residence

Even during the upheavals of the Ōnin Disturbances, nō performances at Ashikaga Yoshimasa's residences were not totally disbanded, and they adapted to the new circumstances by integrating lay performances by the warriors with those by professionals. Probably one of the last performances by Kanze-dayū Matasaburō took place in the shogunal residence in 1470 (Bunmei 2) when he delivered *matsu-bayashi* and performed several nō. Customarily, *matsu-bayashi* were performed during the first month as a part of the New Year celebrations, but the year 1470 was different. The *matsu-bayashi* took place in the third month, and Kanze-dayū was joined onstage by warriors of the Hosokawa clan who held the position of *kanrei* (deputy), one of the highest posts in the Ashikaga *bakufu*.[98] After his retirement in 1473, Yoshimasa regularly enjoyed

---

96 *Daijōin jisha zōjiki* 8: 28b.
97 *Daijōin jisha zōjiki* 8: 28b; *Inryōken nichiroku* 2: 680a, 917b.
98 *Daijōin jisha zōjiki* 4: 400b.

nō performances at his retirement residence at Ogawa in Kyoto. These performances, mostly by Kanze-dayū Saburō Yukishige (d. 1500), were frequently attended by his son and now shōgun Yoshihisa as well as by the emperor Gotsuchimikado (1442–1500; r. 1464–1500). They were not well received by the public. On Bunmei 6 (1474).5.15, Daijōin's head monk Jinson (1430–1508), for example, criticized Yoshimasa as reported in the records of Daijōin: "The shōgun abandons the affairs of state and immerses himself with banquets, as if we were living in peaceful times."[99] What others perceived as mere escapism may in fact have been Yoshimasa's attempt at nurturing his social and political networks and exerting power through such informal gatherings, with nō's popularity serving as camouflage.

That performances at the shōgun's official residence did not cease with the Hosokawa clan's de facto takeover of the *bakufu* also indicates that such events held a symbolic meaning that was well understood. This is also supported by the fact that the end of the Ōnin Disturbances in 1477 did not mean that warriors also stopped performing onstage. One reason for the appearance of these laymen onstage was due to the absence of a sufficient number of nō performers, particularly from the Kanze troupe. The troupe, which had dominated official nō performances, still suffered from financial losses and internal fragmentation.[100] Even after 1493 (Meiō 2), when the most powerful warrior clans, including the Hosokawa and the Ise, forced the tenth shōgun Ashikaga Yoshitane (1466–1523; r. 1490–1493, 1508–1522) to abdicate in a coup d'état from 1492 to 1501 known as *Meiō no seihen* (Political Disturbance of the Meiō Era), nō performances were held as usual at the shogunal residence.[101] On Tenbun 8 (1539).3.23, the Kanze-dayū (Sōsetsu; 1509–1583) and his brother Hōshō-dayū (Ko-Hōshō, or "Little Hōshō," d. ca. 1572) performed at the shogunal residence. The supporting roles were assumed by retainers of the Hosokawa, who belonged to the *bakufu* administration, and of the Ise clan, which held power as the *mandokoro* (chief governing body)—that is, the office of finance and process on fiefs.[102]

The performance of warriors onstage indicates that they were well trained in nō, and that by this time nō had become part of their general education. The

---

99   *Daijōin jisha zōjiki* 5: 479b.
100 Omote 2008: 169–75.
101 See *Gohōkōinki* 2: 993; *Daijōin jisha zōjiki* 10: 449b. The *Meiō no seihen* symbolizes the downfall of the Ashikaga *bakufu*. After 1493 and until 1549, the actual power was in the hands of the Hosokawa, in particular, Hosokawa Masamoto and the warriors of the Ise and Ōdachi clans. See Hall 1995: 127–46. On the relation of the early Muromachi *bakufu* and the daimyō, see, for example, Nelson 1997.
102 *Chikatoshi nikki* 1: 159.

aforementioned Ise Sadayori, a steward in the house office of the Muromachi *bakufu* in charge of etiquette and protocol, writes in the *Sōgo ōzōshi* (*Extensive Notes of [Ise] Sōgo*, ca. 1528):

> It is suitable for young folks to train in bow [shooting], horse [riding], and ball games, furthermore in the way of poetry, the laws of the warriors, in [using the cooking] knives, at least to a certain extent even more so in the present-day fashion of the *ōtsuzumi, kotsuzumi, taiko, fue, shakuhachi*, music, and so on. ... Also, during banquets it is appropriate that the young folks perform a [nō] dance. Such dances during banquets are extremely important.[103]

Warriors trained in nō, especially in the nō chant (*utai*), are already known by the second half of the fifteenth century. What initially began as an entertainment for banquets soon grew into a more organized and formalized practice. Retainers of the Ise clan, for example, regularly gathered for *utaikō*, or "chant assemblies,"[104] where they practiced their nō chants. Some clans such as the Fujita even had a family lineage of *utai* performers, and there are numerous extant *utaibon* (chant books) written by its members (fig. 1.6). The *Fujita Torayori tō fushitsuke ichiban toji utaibon* (*Annotated One-Play Chant Books of Fujita Torayori and Others*), for instance, consists of 197 volumes. The oldest dates to 1523 (Daiei 3) and affords insights into how nō plays were transmitted in the sixteenth century. The warrior custom of performing nō as a part of their cultural activities during the late fifteenth and sixteenth centuries marks another turning point in the history of nō. Conversely, political motives almost always underlay nō performances by warriors, as these functioned either to lend authority to the nominal ruler or to emphasize the positions of those who wielded actual power. It might be argued that the organization of nō performances at the shogunal palace by retainers of the Hosokawa, Ise, and Ōdachi clans mirrored the political power structure of the Muromachi *bakufu* during the first half of the sixteenth century. Clearly, these performances began at the precise moment when the Ashikaga system of rule weakened.

By 1549, Miyoshi Nagayoshi (1522–1564), a *shugodai* (representative of the governor) of Settsu Province (present-day southeastern Hyōgo and northern Osaka Prefectures), had become so influential that his clan successively took over positions in the *bakufu* previously held by the Hosokawa. At the same time, retainers of the Miyoshi also replaced Hosokawa performers during nō

---

103 *Sōgo ōzōshi*: 603b.
104 On the *utaikō* on Bunmei 7 (1475).1.7 and 1.17, see *Chikatoshi nikki* 1: 5, 11; *Tokitsugu kyōki* 4: 140a.

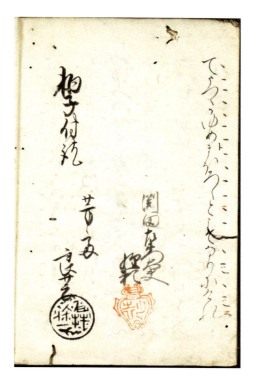

FIGURE 1.6
Chant book (*utaibon*) for *Tenko,* colophon page with seal. Calligraphy by Fujita Saemon-dayū Tsuneyori (dates unknown). Late 16th century. Handwritten book, ink on paper. 20.2 × 13.8 cm. Kōzan Bunko, Hōsei University, Tokyo

performances. In the fourth month of 1552 (Tenbun 21), for example, a performer called Miyoshi—possibly Nagayoshi himself—appeared as *tayū* alongside Kanze-dayū Sōsetsu, while retainers of the *bakufu* and the Ise and Miyoshi clans participated in the chorus.[105] The event anticipates nō's rising popularity among shōguns, daimyō, and warriors in the seventeenth century, when familiarity with nō became essential for a successful career. In any case, it is evidence for the profound connection between nō performances and politics, and subsequently between nō performers and warriors.

1.3.4 Tesarugaku *Performers: Townspeople of Kyoto, Monks, Priests, and Villagers*

Warriors were not the only group actively performing nō. The collapse of the old social order that accompanied the Ōnin Disturbances gave rise to different groups of nō performers. In the fifteenth century, performers who were not organized into one of the above mentioned *sarugaku* troupes were called *tesarugaku,* or "a hand [skilled in] *sarugaku.*" The term included warriors,

---

105   *Tokitsugu kyōki* 2: 465b–66a.

merchants, monks, and priests, as well as *shōmoji* and *onna sarugaku*, and substantiates the popularity of nō not only as a stage performance to be watched and consumed but also as a type of personal refinement to be actively pursued.

This development did not reduce nō to a mere pastime of amateurs, however. *Tesarugaku* troupes of Kyoto townspeople (*machishū*, or "townsfolk"), regardless of their social status, were frequently invited to perform at the imperial palace in Kyoto or maintained close relations with daimyō. *Tesarugaku* performers were only labeled *shirōto* ("amateurs") around the mid-seventeenth century, in contradistinction to the progressive professionalization of the four Yamato troupes.[106]

Among the first documents to employ the term *tesarugaku* was the diary of Jinson who, as noted above, was the head monk of Daijōin. An entry from Chōroku 2 (1458).3.22 states: "People from Kyoto's Shichijō area are summoned to the imperial palace for *tesarugaku* performances to be held a few days from now."[107] Townspeople performing nō for the emperor and his court were not an exceptional occurrence. Ever since the end of the fourteenth century, the court nobility had exhibited a profound appreciation of nō, although they never instigated a regular routine of holding nō performances. This is one likely reason why Jinson was not judgmental about townspeople performing nō at the imperial palace. *Sarugaku* performers were not allowed to participate in these performances since they were regarded as outcastes and prohibited from entering the main imperial palace, a custom that prevailed until the end of the Edo period. In 1427 (Ōei 34), for instance, Mansai, the aforesaid abbot of Daigoji, laments in his diary that a performance by *sarugaku* actors at the imperial palace sponsored by the shōgun Ashikaga Yoshinori, was "inconsiderate."[108] As the mention of *tesarugaku* in Jinson's diary suggests, there was already a well-established custom of townspeople performing nō at the palace before the Ōnin Disturbances, but it was not until their conclusion that the number of *tesarugaku* performers in Kyoto significantly increased. As Sonnō (1432–1514), abbot of Shōren'in, observes in his *Awataguchi sarugakuki* (*Record of Sarugaku at Awataguchi*, 1505): "These days, *tesarugaku* performers reside everywhere in Kyoto."[109] The sheer number of performers hints that there were at least two to three *tesarugaku nō* troupes in every area or district of the city.

The names of some of these townspeople, who were recognized *tesarugaku* performers, have come down to us. That some were referred to as *tayū* implies

---

106 See, for example, *Yoza yakusha mokuroku*: 147.
107 See *Daijōin jisha zōjiki* 1: 359b.
108 *Mansai jugō nikki* 1: 400b. See Ōtani 1991; Ikeda 2012.
109 *Awataguchi sarugakuki*: 725a.

that they assumed leadership of a nō troupe. One of the most famous during the second half of the fifteenth century was Nishikawa Kame-dayū ("turtle leader," dates unknown) from the Shichijō district in Kyoto. The Nishikawa family was active for about forty years, with Kame-dayū's son and grandson inheriting the Kame-dayū title. Another performer called Nakanishi Rokurō lived around Gojō. He went by his *yagō* (shop or house name) Umeshuya ("Plum Liquor Store"), which might indicate that the business produced and sold liquor made from sour plums. The *fudetsukuri* (brushmaker) and kyōgen actor, Kiuchi Yajirō, performed in the residence of the aristocrat Yamashina Tokitsugu (1507–1579) several times in 1544 (Tenbun 13).[110] Moreover, a Shibuya-dayū lived close to the Muromachi district and an Iwa-dayū ("rock" or "stone leader") in Imamachi. The lineage of Shibuya-dayū, which continued for at least four generations until the end of the sixteenth century, is one instance of successful *tesarugaku* performers hired by daimyō in the provinces during the Edo period.[111] In short, townsfolk *qua* performers lived all over Kyoto, sparking competition and rivalry. In 1544 (Tenbun 2), for example, Kiuchi Yajirō filed a complaint with Yamashina Tokitsugu that Shibuya-dayū was chosen for a nō performance at the imperial palace. The urgency of this complaint is borne out by eight or more entries in Tokitsugu's *Tokitsugu kyōki* noting that he intervened on Kiuchi's behalf so that he can perform alongside Shibuya. Unfortunately, the entry for Tenbun 2 (1544).2.2 in the *Tokitsugu kyōki* on the actual performance does not give further details about Kiuchi's participation, although Tokitsugu does mention that Kiuchi dropped by for reimbursement on the tenth day of the same month.[112]

One factor accounting for the popularity of *tesarugaku* troupes was the inclusion of boy and young adult performers. This allowed them to compete with the Yamato nō troupes, and once they garnered a reputation, it was quite likely that they were summoned to the imperial palace. On Bunmei 15 (1483).1.12, the aristocrat Sanjōnishi Sanetaka (1455–1537) comments that the nō performed at the imperial palace by an eight-year-old boy belonging to Kame-dayū's troupe was "unbelievably splendid."[113] The *tesarugaku* troupes not only exploited the handsomeness of young boys but also actively sought to improve their acting skills, turning to performers from the Yamato troupes (mainly the Kanze *za*) as teachers. As a consequence, *tesarugaku* performers

---

110   *Tokitsugu kyōki* 1: 425a.
111   *Yoza yakusha mokuroku*: 172.
112   *Tokitsugu kyōki* 1: 435b–41b.
113   *Sanetaka kōki* 1: 420.

played a decisive role in nō's process of professionalization. Teaching soon became a substantial part of a nō performers' profession and revenues.

The fashion of *tesarugaku* was not limited to the townspeople of Kyoto. Buddhist monks, Shintō priests, and rural inhabitants likewise contributed substantially to the practice of performing nō. An early illustration is the performance of nō songs and dances between sessions of homilies and edifications by the Honganji abbot Rennyo (1415–1499). These seem to have taken root and Honganji subsequently placed a group of specialist monks from its own congregation in charge of nō. During the sixteenth century, this *tesarugaku* group was large enough and skilled enough to perform nō without having to engage outside performers.[114] Located at Ishiyama (in present-day Osaka), Honganji also emerged as a powerful patron of nō performers and of townspeople *tesarugaku*. On Tenbun 15 (1546).6.7 and 6.9, the abbot of Honganji, Shōnyo (1516–1554), noted in his diary that the residents of each of the six neighborhoods within the temple parish created a troupe of young boys who were trained to perform two nō per neighborhood during the *Sengūsai* (Festival of the Shrine Relocation) at Ikutamasha (present-day Ikukunitama Jinja).[115]

Shrine priests and young women also engaged in the practice of nō, as seen in the example of Kasuga Taisha, in which their performances were already recorded for the *Kasuga Wakamiya onmatsuri* in 1349. By the sixteenth century, a group of low-ranking priests of Kasuga Taisha called *negishū* regularly performed nō (also *nanto negishū*, or "Southern Capital Priests," see ch. 9 *Kyōgen*, 9.6). The *negishū* became increasingly popular, and by the second half of the sixteenth century they were hired for *jinji nō* and *kanjin nō* at other shrines and temples.[116]

Given that the Kasuga Taisha had a long and independent tradition of nō, it seems natural that its priests would perform. There are also records of nō performances by villagers in the remote provinces. When the aristocrat Kujō Masamoto (1445–1516) traveled from Kyoto to his Hineno estate in Izumi Province (present-day southwestern Osaka Prefecture), he noted in his travelogue *Masamoto kō tabi hikitsuke* (*Lord Masamoto's Travel Records*) on Bunki 1 (1501).7.13 that the villagers of Funabuchi performed nō during their shrine festival: "[The villager's performance] was in no way inferior to that of performers

---

114 On nō performances at Honganji, see Kagotani 2005: 3–198.
115 *Shōnyo shōnin nikki*: 512b–13a. Shōnyo also notes that Kongō-dayū, Konparu-dayū, Kanze-dayū, Ōkura-dayū, and Miyaō-dayū, among others, paid their respects to the temple during the New Year ceremonies and in return received a rice stipend. *Shōnyo shōnin nikki*: 442a, 495b.
116 Miyamoto 2005b: 180–294.

from Kyoto in its elegance and conduct."[117] A record from Tenbun 17 (1548).12.3 about the hamlet of Sugaura located on the shore of Lake Biwa relates that the villagers purchased the right to assume the position of *gakutō* for the *jinji nō* at Suga Jinja from a Hirowaka-dayū (dates unknown) of the Ōmi *sarugaku*, and that thereafter the villagers performed nō during the shrine's festivals.[118]

These few cases afford a glimpse of the various environments in which nō was performed under the label *tesarugaku*: the places (rural areas, urban centers), occasions (shrine and temple festivals, performances at the imperial palace), and social statuses of performers (Buddhist monks, shrine priests, villagers, merchants) differ significantly. This confirms nō as one of the most prominent and widespread cultural practices of early modern Japan. Moreover, while *tesarugaku* performers were part of a diversification of performers during the fifteenth and sixteenth centuries, they also contributed to the emergence of a stricter distinction between amateur and professional performers from the seventeenth century onward. This eventually pushed them to the margins, reducing them to the status of *shirōto*.

1.3.5 *From Kyoto to the Provinces: Traveling Performers, New Patrons, and Networks*

Kyoto maintained its status as the center of cultural activities, including nō performances, for a time after the outbreak of the Ōnin Disturbances, but things would soon change. The relocation of the political and cultural elites also precipitated a transmission of knowledge, technology, cultural assets, and activities to the provinces. This led to the development of urban centers boasting their own unique cultures around castles such as Kawate of the Toki clan in Mino Province (present-day Gifu Prefecture) or Ichijōdani of the Asakura clan in Echizen Province. This tendency was spurred by the deteriorating power of the Ashikaga shōgun and the rise of *sengoku daimyō* following the Ōnin struggles.

For nō performers, Kyoto's downfall likewise resulted in the loss of lucrative performance opportunities. By the sixteenth century, however, the provinces had become important replacements. Those performers who had previously crowded the city now left in search of new patrons and incomes. According to an entry for Tenshō 13 (1585).2.6 in a diary kept by monks at the Tamon'in sub-temple of Kōfukuji, the only actor from the four Yamato *sarugaku* troupes left in the area who could fulfill the duty of performing *Okina* was a retired Konparu player. The diary laments that "lately the festival's atmosphere

---

117 *Masamoto kō tabi hikitsuke*: 39.
118 *Sugaura monjo* 1: 154a-b.

resembles that of a provincial autumn festival."[119] With the departure of professional nō performers, even the *tesarugaku* townspeople of Kyoto looked to the provinces. There are records as early as the late fifteenth century of *kanjin nō* performances, for example one in Nara on Meiō 2 (1493).8.26 featuring a *tesarugaku* troupe led by Nezumi-dayū ("Mouse Leader") and a troupe led by the son of the head of the Takatsukasa clan guard.[120]

Performers from the nō troupes either relocated to the provinces or began touring the provinces regularly. Kanze-dayū Sōsetsu, for example, visited and performed on Sado Island, as well as in the provinces of Echizen, Tōtōmi (present-day Shizuoka Prefecture), Aki (present-day Hiroshima Prefecture), and Nagato (present-day Yamaguchi Prefecture). When the merchant town Sakai (in present-day Osaka Prefecture) emerged as a new cultural hotspot, performers swiftly resettled there. Sakai not only offered ample opportunities for performances but also the prospect of recruiting affluent townspeople as nō students. Wealthy merchants such as Aburaya Jōtaku (dates unknown) learned nō from Konparu-dayū Shichirō Ujiaki (also Ujiteru, 1489–1571/1572) or from the *kotsuzumi* (shoulder drum) player Miyamasu Yazaemon Chikakata (1482–1556; fig. 1.7).

Other performers relied on the support of individual *sengoku daimyō* families. Hōshō-dayū (d. ca. 1572) attempted to win the favor of the Hōjō clan in Odawara (present-day Kanagawa Prefecture) and Ōkura-dayū Nobushige (d. 1575) visited the Takeda clan in Kōfu Province (present-day Yamanashi Prefecture). Kanze Jūrō (dates unknown), brother of Sōsetsu and from the Ochi-Kanze branch, moved to Sunpu (present-day Shizuoka Prefecture) and found new patrons, first with the Imagawa clan and subsequently with Tokugawa Ieyasu (1543–1616; r. 1603–1605), the first shōgun of the Tokugawa *bakufu*.[121]

This mobility of performers during the sixteenth century created a network of performers and patrons that linked the castle towns of *sengoku daimyō* with the Kinki region. Performers of all kinds were actively courted by *sengoku daimyō*, and their support formed the basis for the Edo-period patronage system. Almost every domain engaged performers, and some *tesarugaku* performers even gave up their original occupations. Shibuya-dayū, for example, had an extended stay with the Shimazu in Kyushu in 1585/1586, during which time he managed to acquire the status of *okakae yakusha* ("hired performer"). He

---

119 *Tamon'in nikki* 3: 404a.
120 *Dajōjin jisha zōjiki* 10: 313a.
121 See *Ōkura Shōzaemon keizu* under References: *Websites of Works Cited* below; *Yoza yakusha mokuroku*: 32, 47.

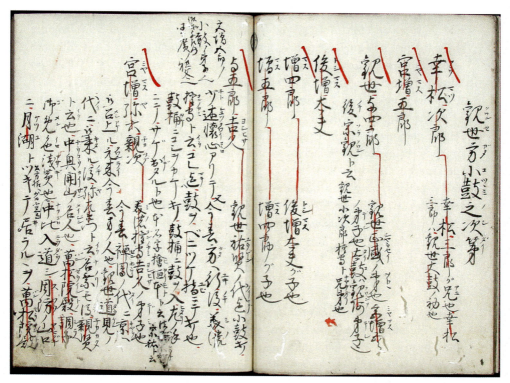

FIGURE 1.7 Entry on Miyamasu Yazaemon Chikakata in the section "On *Kotsuzumi* Players of the Kanze Troupe" (*Kanze kata kotsuzumi no shidai*). From *Catalogue of the Performers of the Four Troupes* (*Yoza yakusha mokuroku*). By Kanze Motonobu (1606–1666). 1653. Handwritten book, ink on paper. 28.7 × 21.6 cm. Noh Theatre Research Institute, Hōsei University, Tokyo

was frequently ordered to the Shimazu mansion in Kyoto where he received an additional stipend.[122]

The patronage of performers from the nō troupes is exemplified by Ieyasu's privileging of Kanze troupe performers. This would prove an important factor in the further dissemination of nō during the Edo period. Kanze Sōsetsu visited Hamamatsu Castle in Tōtōmi Province with his son Kanze-dayū Sakon Motohisa (1536–1577) on Genki 2 (1571).8.21 for the coming-of-age celebrations of Ieyasu's son Matsudaira Nobuyasu (1559–1579). On the evening before the event, Ieyasu, who had trained in nō since he was a child, decided to have an

---

122 Hayashi 2003: 445. Miyamoto 2019: 261–62. Horike, another *tesarugaku* performer, was later hired by the Yamauchi of the Tosa domain (present-day Kōchi Prefecture), and Fukami was hired by the Satake of the Kubota domain (present-day Akita Prefecture). Miyamoto 2021: 392–93.

impromptu performance with Sōsetsu and Motohisa. After this collaboration, Sōsetsu and Motohisa stayed for several years with Ieyasu, who became their greatest patron. During his sojourn at Hamamatsu Castle, Kanze Sōsetsu also annotated *utaibon* for Ieyasu and other *sengoku daimyō*.[123] When on Tenshō 12 (1584).3.3 Motohisa's successor, the Kanze-dayū Tadachika (later Kokusetsu; 1566–1626), performed at Hamamatsu Castle, three generations of Kanze-dayū managed to secure Ieyasu's patronage.[124] In 1586 (Tenshō 14), Ieyasu gave permission for several large-scale *kanjin nō* in his territories in order "to bring Kanze Tadachika's understanding of nō to maturity" by affording him the chance to "watch the performance of those who play for the elites" and take the stage alongside experienced performers.[125] For Kanze Tadachika, these *kanjin nō* offered him the chance to promote himself to the audiences in the provinces of Mikawa, Suruga, and Kai, and to guarantee his position as Kanze-dayū.[126] The intimate relation between the Kanze troupe and the Tokugawa clan described in the biographies of these performers continued throughout the Edo period.

1.3.6 New Audiences, Demands, and Performance Styles

The different types of audiences, performers, and patrons stimulated yet another process of transformation in nō during the sixteenth century. In other words, as nō's social circles expanded, performers adopted a new vocabulary to create novel performance styles, and by doing so strengthened their sense of identity as artists. The effects can be seen in the production of *utaibon*, *tsuke*, or notes on movements, gestures, instruments, or properties (see ch. 7 *Material Culture*, 7.6), and commentaries on and annotations to nō plays, in addition to the development of a flamboyant performance style called *furyū*.

Connoisseurs and patrons of nō began to demand more information about the art, especially concerning the content of plays and the conventions and techniques of performance. On Bunroku 4 (1595).3.26, Yamashina Tokitsune reports in his diary *Tokitsune kyōki* that he was ordered by Toyotomi Hideyoshi's nephew, *kanpaku* (regent) Toyotomi Hidetsugu (1568–1595; r. 1585–1591), to compile the *Utai (no) shō* (*A Selection of Nō Plays*) in collaboration with, among others, the monks Yūsetsu Shūho of Nanzenji, Eiho Yōyū (1547–1602) of Kenninji, the *renga* poet Satomura Jōha (1524–1603), and Torikai Dōsetsu (d. 1602), who

---

123 Motohisa died on Tenshō 5 (1577).1.30 at the Yoshida Castle compound in Mikawa Province (present-day eastern Aichi Prefecture), which was also part of Ieyasu's territory. *Tōdaiki*: 15a, 29b–30a.
124 *Ietada nikki* 1: 181.
125 *Tōdaiki*: 52a. See also *Gowadanki* below under References: Websites of Works Cited.
126 *Tōdaiki*: 52a.

had trained in *utai* with and provided calligraphy for Konparu-dayū Hachirō Yoshikatsu (Gyūren; 1510–1583). Completed around 1600, this is the oldest extant collection of plays complete with commentary and annotations. While based on the Konparu troupe's corpus, the *Utai (no) shō* deeply influenced the standardization of the nō corpus. The compilers assigned *kanji* ideographs to words written in the *hiragana* syllabary for approximately one hundred plays from the Konparu repertory, thus systematizing and codifying the terminology and semantics, and by extension the content of the plays. It is possible, even probable, that the Buddhist associations in nō plays were put into greater relief through such interpretations. This collaborative work between monks, poets, and calligraphers may be considered the product of rivalry over who had the ultimate authority to interpret the content of nō plays.[127] This hypothesis is also supported by the fact that the Kanze troupe made their own *utaibon* public at almost the same time (see ch. 7 *Material Culture*, 7.7).

With the new performance style of the showy *furyū*, performers were now able to relate to a broad social stratum. Kanze Kojirō Nobumitsu (1451/1452–1516), his son Nagatoshi (1488–ca. 1541), and Konparu Zenpō (1454–?) are famous for their extravagant and spectacular productions. Typically, their plays feature a thematic opening, make increased use of stage properties, and display flashier costumes and masks (see ch. 5 *Authors*, 5.6–5.8).[128] These characteristics had a profound impact and greatly popularized nō throughout the country.

1.4 Nō in the Age of Exploration
Patrick Schwemmer

In the sixteenth century, traders and missionaries from Europe arrived in Japan and recorded what they saw, giving us an outsider's view of nō in a social context just before its Edo-period systematization. The Portuguese missionaries Luís Fróis (1532–1597) and "the interpreter" João Rodriguez (1561/1562?–1633) mention nō most often in connection with eating, drinking, and socializing. Fróis reports that: "[d]uring soirées, plays, and tragedies in Europe, one does not normally eat or drink; in Japan, nothing of the sort is done without wine and tapas (*vinho & sacanas*)."[129] Rodriguez, describing palace architecture, moves from banquet halls to kitchens to "rooms [where] at night they have

---

127 *Tokitsune kyōki* 6: 246. See Itō Masayoshi 2013; also *Tokitsune kyōki* 6: 243.
128 On Nobumitsu and *furyū*, see Lim 2012.
129 Fróis 1585: ch. 13, sec. 26.

their songs and entertainments, and places for theatre."[130] As discussed above, even professional actors gave numerous performances "offstage," sometimes even on pleasure cruises "on the rivers or in the fields," as Rodriguez observed.[131] Indeed, Konparu Zenpō (1454–?) lists "singing on boat cruises" (*funa asobi no utai*) among the many types of "house calls" that he was accustomed to make,[132] and paintings survive illustrating this practice (see fig. 1.8).

Even when nō was performed on a stage, it was not in a "nō theatre,"—rather, a stage was built into every mansion "across the atrium or courtyard from the main room."[133] High-ranking spectators sat and watched from this room. Common people were only invited for special performances, at which time they would sit "on mats on the ground in the courtyard," where the seats in most nō theatres are situated today (see ch. 7 *Material Culture*, 7.5; fig. 1.9).

Rodriguez further comments on the economics of nō:

> At the end of each play it is customary for the guests to give gifts of silver, or silk robes, and other valuable things to the actors as a sign of their appreciation, … for this is how these people earn their living, and the author and some others come in procession to receive the gift in the middle of the courtyard, with great reverence and signs of gratitude, draping it over his back if it is a robe.[134]

Most likely the "author" here is a troupe leader: who the author was of a given play was relatively unimportant. Rodriguez also describes *kanjin nō*, perhaps by *tesarugaku* performers:

> At certain spots along the roads, at the entrances to the City, there are enclosures of wood with gates. … Each one who enters pays a certain fee, and with this the actors earn their living, as a decent number of people attend each play. And when it is over they leave and others come in, and another play or performance begins, with rich silk costumes suited to each character. And at the end of each play there is a very funny interlude.[135]

---

130 Rodriguez 1620–1633: bk. 1, ch. 12, sec. 5.
131 Rodriguez 1620–1633: bk. 1, ch. 29, sec. 1. See also the detailed description of pleasure cruises here.
132 *Hogoura no sho*: 384–85.
133 Rodriguez 1620–1633: bk. 1, ch. 12, sec. 5.
134 Rodriguez 1620–1633: bk. 1, ch. 12, sec. 15.
135 Rodriguez 1620–1633: bk. 1, ch. 13.

FIGURE 1.8 Votive tablet (*ema*) for a safe voyage to Đông Kinh in present-day Vietnam. Note the numerous figures in European dress, with faces suggesting Japanese, Indian, African, and European heritage. 1634. Colors on wood. 42.3 × 2.8 cm. Kiyomizudera, Kyoto

Rodriguez knew Toyotomi Hideyoshi followed the warrior custom of keeping performers on staff by alloting them rice stipends (*haitōmai*): the troupe head was "an office, albeit a low and base one, in the house of the ruler (*Cubô*)."[136] Nevertheless, hereditary discipline was still new enough that child actors remained, according to Fróis, "free and uninhibited, smooth and funny."[137]

In all contexts, amateurism was crucial, for nō had a similar place among medieval Japanese warlords and urban commoners to that of golf or yoga among leaders today. Rodriguez notes that "[t]hey put into the hands of the guests, usually the guest of honor, the book of the plays that are being performed, and he sings as he reads." Books were important even for spectatorship: "They will enjoy [a play] more if they look at *utaibon* [the chant book], for

---

136 Rodriguez 1620–1633: bk. 1, ch. 33, sec. 1.
137 Fróis 1585: ch. 3, sec. 14.

FIGURE 1.9 *Illustration of Viewing Nō (Kannō zu)*. Dignitaries (possibly Toyotomi Hideyoshi's entourage) watch from a veranda, others from an inner room, and commoners with various features are seated on the ground in diverse styles of dress. Early 17th century. Eight-panel folding screen, ink and colors on paper. 106.5 × 425.8 cm. Kobe City Museum

they have a great number of these printed books."[138] Such sumptuously printed *utaibon* with calligraphy in the style of Hon'ami Kōetsu (1558–1637) proliferated during Rodriguez's last decade in Japan—many are traceable to the inner circle of the then-ascendant Tokugawa Ieyasu (see ch. 7 *Material Culture*, 7.7).

The Japanese singing that Fróis heard apparently did not feature vibrato, and indeed domestic documents suggest that the elaborate tonal fluctuations we hear in nō today are largely an innovation of the Edo period (see ch. 2 *Performance*, 2.6).[139] Conversely, Fróis' descriptions of pose and gesture are recognizable, with actors walking "stooped down (*debruçado*), looking along the ground as if searching for something they have lost," then "face each other like roosters in a cockfight"—that is, with hips lowered and elbows bent in *kamae* pose (see ch. 2 *Performance*, 2.4).[140]

Meanwhile, in 1613 the Englishman Richard Cocks (1566–1624) arrived with wool, artillery, and other goods to sell in Japan. One day his landlord, the illustrious Chinese trader Li Andreas Dan (d. 1625) invited him to a nō performance by the local lord, Matsura Takanobu (1592–1637), and Takanobu's grandfather.

138   Rodriguez 1620–1633: bk. 1, ch. 29, sec. 1. Rodriguez's stream-of-consciousness memoir was written in his twilight years in China and often mixes information from China and Japan. Although the title of this chapter says that it concerns China, he is clearly flashing back to Japan when he talks about *utaibon* here; what he writes accords well with other sources.
139   Fróis 1585: ch. 13, sec. 16; Sakamoto and Takakuwa 2015.
140   Fróis 1585: ch. 13, sec. 12 and sec. 2.

Cocks, who was in England at the height of Shakespeare's career and clearly interested in the theatre, writes glowingly of the experience:

> The Actors [were] the Kings themselves, with the greatest Noblemen and Princes. The matter was of the valiant deeds of their Ancestors, from the beginning of their Kingdome or Common-wealth untill this present, with much mirth mixed among, to give the common people content. The audience was great, for no house in Towne but brought a Present, nor no Village nor place under their Dominions but did the like, and were spectators. And the Kings themselves did see that every one, both great and small, did eate and drinke before they departed. ... Yet I never saw Play wherein I noted so much, for I see their policie is great in doing thereof, and quite contrary to our Comoedies in Christendome, ours being but dumbe shewes and this the truth itselfe, acted by the Kings themselves, to keepe in perpetuall remembrance their affaires. The King did not send for the Flemmings [the Dutch], and therefore I accounted it a greater grace for us.[141]

---

141 Farrington 1991: 1529. Note that Cocks correctly understood nō spectatorship as one more venue for his business rivalry with the Dutch (in which he would nonetheless emerge the looser).

Cocks knew at first sight the sociopolitical operations of nō: against a background of gift exchange and merrymaking, the ruler makes a display of historical knowledge, cultural accomplishment, and civilizational vision in dance and chant.

1.5 Nō and Political Leaders from the Late Sixteenth to the Early Eighteenth Century
Eike Grossmann and Miyamoto Keizō

1.5.1 Approaches to Nō by Oda Nobunaga and Toyotomi Hideyoshi

Oda Nobunaga (1534–1582), the first of the three so-called "Great Unifiers" of the realm alongside Toyotomi Hideyoshi and Tokugawa Ieyasu, supported performers with stipends and allotments of land. He temporarily revived the *takigi nō* at Kōfukuji with all four troupes participating in 1576 (Tenshō 4) and he may, in fact, have trained in playing the *kotsuzumi*. When he and his armies occupied Kyoto in 1568 (Eiroku 11), successfully breaking the power of the self-proclaimed rulers of the Miyoshi clan and installing Ashikaga Yoshiaki (1537–1597) as the fifteenth shōgun, Nobunaga was involved in the planning of the inauguration celebrations.

As the most influential military leader during the second half of the sixteenth century, Nobunaga was acutely aware of the sociopolitical operations of nō (fig. 1.10). Nobunaga decided that only five plays were to be performed instead of thirteen, and that the first nō should be *Takasago*. The lineup of performers, with Kanze-dayū Sakon Motohisa and Konparu-dayū Hachirō Yoshikatsu, was splendid, but when Yoshiaki suggested that Nobunaga perform the *kotsuzumi* in *Dōjōji*, he declined.[142] There are several possibilities for Nobunaga's refusal: one is that he did not want to stage himself as a vassal of the new shōgun, another that in principle he opposed the idea of warriors performing nō onstage. The latter interpretation is supported by the fact that Nobunaga banned the nō activities of his sons Nobutada (ca. 1555–1582) and Nobukatsu (1558–1630). An entry from 1581 (Tenshō 9) in the anonymous *Tōdaiki* (*Record of the Present Age*, ca. 1620) remarks that Nobunaga saw an enthusiastic engagement in nō as detrimental to becoming an influential and competent ruler. The *Tōdaiki* elaborates and states that this is why Nobunaga had Nobutada's *nō dōgu* (nō props and utensils) transferred to Umewaka-dayū of the Settsu or Kawachi *sarugaku*. Luckily, according to the chronicler, Nobunaga was

---

142 *Shinchō kōki*: 54–55.

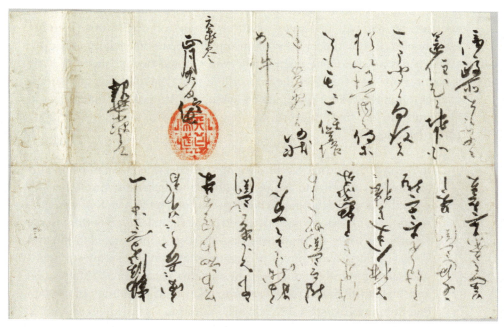

FIGURE 1.10   Handwritten letter with Oda Nobunaga's official seal sent to Kanze Kojirō Motoyori (d. 1573?). 1572 (Genki 3.1.28). Ink on paper. Noh Theatre Research Institute, Hōsei University, Tokyo

unaware that his second son also performed nō. Indeed, Nobukatsu would become a renowned performer.[143]

Toyotomi Hideyoshi likewise recognized the potential nō had for the legitimization of political authority. Staging nō with the political ruler as the main performer became fashionable under Hideyoshi's aegis—a custom that employs subtle strategies in the display of power and the reinforcement of hierarchies. Hideyoshi's successors followed suit in capitalizing on this practice in the same way.[144] While Hideyoshi imitated Nobunaga in sponsoring a five-play staging in the imperial palace with the *tesarugaku* performer Horike only two days after he was proclaimed *kanpaku* on Tenshō 13 (1585).7.13,[145] his interests went far beyond established conventions. In 1591, he had Nagoya Castle built in Karatsu in Kyushu as a base for his military expeditions. Between 1592 and 1598, Hideyoshi undertook an invasion of Korea in a conflict known in Korea as the Imjin War and in Japan as the *Bunroku Keichō* Campaign. Most of the

---

143   *Tōdaiki*: 38b.
144   See Amano 1997; Brown 2001; also Scholz-Cionca 2017a; Scholz-Cionca 2017b.
145   *Uno Mondo nikki*: 534b–35b; *Kanemi kyōki* 3: 65–66.

sengoku daimyō relocated with him to Nagoya Castle from where they supervised attacks, and with few exceptions, they began to concentrate on learning tea ceremony or nō. Almost every daimyō residence in the vicinity of Nagoya Castle had a nō stage. The main castle even boasted two nō stages, turning it into a short-lived center of the nō world in 1593. The following quote from a letter dated Bunroku 2 (1593).1.18 to Kyoto with Hideyoshi's official stamp illustrates the fact that Hideyoshi was not content with merely watching nō performances:

> In Nagoya, the retired regent does not conduct falconry and complains of boredom. In order to escape this ennui, he makes his entertainers do crazy things such as kyōgen. When [his warriors] set foot on Korean soil he wants them to perform nō and kyōgen in the capital there. For this reason, we attach a list of nō properties, and instruct Shimotsuma Shōshin and Toraya Ryūha to make careful preparations and send [the requested items to Nagoya] instantly. Should there be anything else required, Shimotsuma and Toraya will be instructed accordingly. ... Finally, Shimomura Nyūdō and Konparu Hikosaburō Nyūdō, who tarries in Osaka, are to set out for Nagoya immediately. The flute player Sadamitsu Chikuyū is also ordered to come down. Furthermore, *ōtsuzumi*, *kotsuzumi*, and *taiko* players are to be sent as well.[146]

After Hideyoshi began to study nō with the *tesarugaku* performer Kurematsu Shinkurō (dates unknown) in the first month of 1593, he rapidly developed a taste for performing onstage. In a letter from Bunroku 2 (1593).3.5 to his wife Ne, he asserted that he had already acquired sufficient skills to perform ten nō plays and announced that he would perform after his return to Kyoto. He realized this during a performance in the residence of the daimyō Asano Nagayoshi (also Nagamasa; 1547–1611?) on Bunroku 2 (1593).10.2 when the three daimyō—Tokugawa Ieyasu, Hosokawa Tadaoki, and Oda Nobukatsu—appeared in one play each and Hideyoshi himself in two plays as *shite*.[147] This became the new custom with Hideyoshi: roles were distributed during performances so that they mirrored the warriors' hierarchy, and the different settings, including the imperial palace, demonstrated the fact that those onstage were now in power.

---

146 The letter is in the collection of the Fukuoka City Museum (Fukuoka-shi Hakubutsukan).
147 The letter to Ne is in the collection of the Osaka Castle Museum (Ōsaka-jō Tenshukaku). Hideyoshi's stage debut is recorded in *Komai nikki*: 509.

Another example is the three-day performance at the imperial palace in Bunroku 2 (1593).10.5, 10.7 and 10.11, for which Hideyoshi performed as *shite* in four of nine plays, with Konparu-dayū Hachirō Yasuteru as *tsure* in one of them on the first day, in three nō and one kyōgen *Mimihiki* (*Ear Pulling*) on the second, and in five of nine nō on the third day (fig. 1.11). In *Mimihiki*, Hideyoshi pulled the ears of Tokugawa Ieyasu and Maeda Toshiie (1538–1599), two of his highest warriors.[148] It seems beyond doubt that the staging reflected the political status quo. By devoting himself to various cultural activities, and to nō in particular, Hideyoshi—the son of a farmer who initially lacked the educational background expected of a great warrior general—presented himself as a sophisticated leader who was on par with both his peers and the aristocratic court. His actions speak of an attempt to install himself as the uncontested ruler, not simply through brute force but also through cultural savoir-faire. The nō plays Hideyoshi commissioned to celebrate his achievements served this purpose, and they came to be known as *hōkō nō* (Nō for Lord Toyo [Toyotomi Hideyoshi]) (see ch. 4 *Plays*, 4.11). With these celebratory performances, attended by other warriors and aristocrats, Hideyoshi commanded an unsurpassed medium for forcing his vision of power upon them.

1.5.2 Changes in the Patronage of Nō: The Haitōmai System

Like the Ashikaga shōguns, Hideyoshi followed the custom of becoming a nō patron. For the most part, previous shōguns and warriors had focused their support on one or perhaps several performers, but they rarely privileged a single troupe, even though Kanze *za* performers were largely favored. Hideyoshi also preferred individual performers but went beyond precedent when he put into effect rules that significantly altered the organization of nō troupes. These included the introduction of a fixed income in 1597 (Keichō 2) for the four Yamato troupes in a system that was called *haitōmai* (the allotment of rice). It was probably Hideyoshi's greatest contribution to the further advancement of nō. Depending on their ranks, daimyō were required to support the four Yamato *sarugaku* troupes—Kanze, Konparu, Hōshō, and Kongō—through a distribution of rice. In addition to receiving *haitōmai*, the performers were remunerated for every appearance onstage. In reality this meant that the troupes were effectively financed by the daimyō while on duty, in the main for Toyotomi Hideyoshi. The first shōgun of the Tokugawa *bakufu*, Ieyasu, adopted

---

148 *Komai nikki*: 510–12. The *Inishie no o-nōgumi* (*Nō Programs of the Past*) manuscript with a list of the performers for *Mimihiki* is housed in the Miyagi Prefectural Library (Miyagi-ken Toshokan).

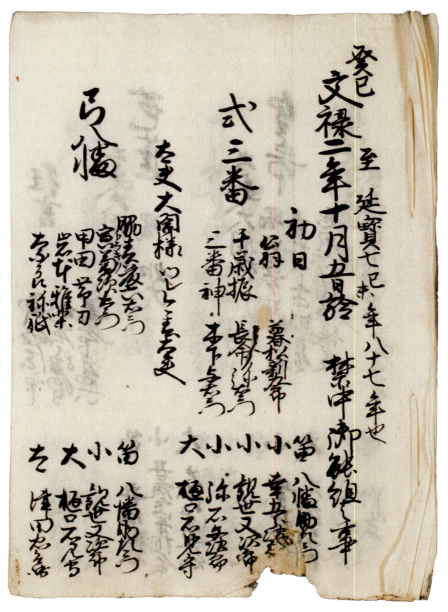

FIGURE 1.11 *Nō Program of the Bunroku Performance at the Imperial Palace* (*Bunroku kinchū nō bangumi*) noting Toyotomi Hideyoshi's performance in 1593. Handwritten program. 1680. Ink on paper. 25.0 × 17.9 cm. Noh Theatre Research Institute, Hōsei University, Tokyo

the *haitōmai* system, and ultimately Hideyoshi's cultural politics influenced the way nō was patronized until the end of the Tokugawa rule in 1868.

The *haitōmai* system was two-sided, however, and this ambivalence profoundly impacted the social structure of nō. On the one hand, the stable financial income allowed performers to devote themselves completely to their art, but on the other, this stability likewise triggered the need to protect what was now perceived as tradition—that is, a standardization process that brought with it a loss of flexibility. This tendency became more pronounced in the centuries to come. With its specific support for certain troupes, the *haitōmai* system forced minor troupes and independent performers to join one of the four Yamato troupes if they wanted to be acknowledged as nō performers. Initially performers of other troupes, for instance, from the Tanba or Yamashiro *sarugaku*, remained with their original troupes while also registering with one of the Yamato troupes. In the end, however, these troupes disappeared one by one. The *haitōmai* system consolidated the position of the four Yamato troupes to the extent that they overpowered other troupes. Moreover, it created an even stronger distinction between professional and amateur performers, and established beyond doubt the troupes as groups of performers under particular daimyō.

1.5.3 *Nō and the Tokugawa Bakufu: The Systematization of the Troupes and the Formation of the Kita Troupe*

After Hideyoshi's death in 1598, Japan faced another period of political transition. Tokugawa Ieyasu emerged victorious from the Battle of Sekigahara (1600), installed himself as the new shōgun (1603), and began an era now referred to either geographically and culturally as the Edo period or dynastically as the Tokugawa period. Ieyasu also supported nō and perpetuated the structures that had developed during the Muromachi period. As a result, warrior patronage continued throughout the Edo period. At the same time, nō troupes went through a process of reorganization whereby nō became an art of professionals, while nō performers not in the official troupes were relegated to the status of students or amateurs.

One important aspect was the return of the Kanze as the foremost nō troupe. Ieyasu, who had basically adopted Hideyoshi's policy of supporting the four Yamato troupes, did not share Hideyoshi's preference for the Konparu troupe. Instead, he installed the Kanze troupe—or, to be precise, the Kanze-dayū—as head performer of the *bakufu* (fig. 1.12). This decision may be interpreted as Ieyasu's attempt to legitimize his leadership by aligning his rule with the Ashikaga shogunate's patronage of the Kanze troupe, thereby suggesting a shared historical lineage. Of course, Ieyasu's personal preferences equally

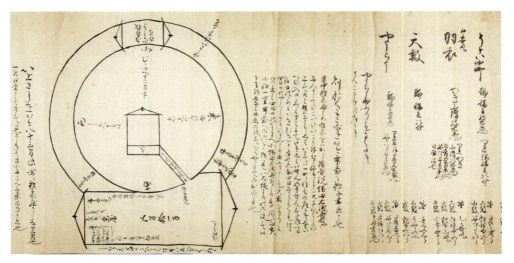

FIGURE 1.12   *Illustration of the Theatre for Kanze-dayū's Kanjin nō in 1599* (*Keichō yonen Kanze-dayū kanjin nō sajiki zu*) sponsored by Tokugawa Ieyasu. By Kanze Jinroku (dates unknown). Early 17th century. Handscroll, ink on paper. 37.5 × 278.9 cm. Noh Theatre Research Institute, Hōsei University, Tokyo

played a role since he had trained with Kanze performers from a young age and was well connected to the troupe.

Another aspect was the all-embracing habitual integration of nō into the political and social life of warriors, which led to its implementation as the *shikigaku* (ceremonial art or state rituals) of the Tokugawa *bakufu*. Besides his own preferences, Ieyasu made clear that the four Yamato troupes, which would soon be consolidated into *ryūgi or ryūha* (stylistic schools), were under *bakufu* jurisdiction. For the three-day nō performance in Keichō 8 (1603) at Kyoto's Nijō Castle that commemorated Ieyasu's proclamation as shōgun, the *tayū* of the four Yamato troupes and their respective successors were ordered to perform onstage.[149] On Keichō 14 (1609).3.26, the four troupes were commanded to relocate their offices from Osaka to Sunpu (present-day Shizuoka City) where Ieyasu resided.[150] The performers, who had taken up office in Osaka after Hideyoshi introduced the *haitōmai* system in 1597, dutifully changed their allegiance and gathered around their new patron. This move was a subtle signal to Toyotomi Hideyoshi's son Hideyori (1598–1615) and his retainers, now residing in Osaka Castle, that his family's influence was on the wane.

149   Although under construction at the time of the performance, Nijō Castle would serve as the Kyoto residence of the Tokugawa shōguns.
150   *Tokitsune kyōki* 12: 56–58; *Tōdaiki*: 149a–b.

With the succession of Tokugawa Hidetada (1579–1632; r. 1605–1623) as shōgun, the *bakufu* patronage of nō intensified. After Ieyasu's death on Genna 2 (1616).4.17, the *tayū* of the four troupes were ordered to relocate to Edo where they were assigned residences in the vicinity of Hidetada's quarters. This moved the performers even closer to the political center, which had both positive and negative results. On the one hand, the exclusive patronage of the *bakufu* meant greater employment and financial security; it also created a dependence on the stability of the Tokugawa's political, economic, and social systems. The most demanding tasks were required of those performers who exclusively served the shōgun and his family. They were, for example, expected to appear during ceremonial events such as the New Year's celebrations or for performances in settings such as evening banquets, and receptions. They equally had to cater to the wishes of the shōgun on a daily basis. In effect, they had to be ready for whatever entertainment the shōgun wanted at Edo Castle, making it almost impossible to take on other commitments.

It was soon obvious that the performers of the four existing troupes would not be able to fulfill all the needs of their patrons in Edo, in the domains, and in urban as well as rural areas, especially since they had not abandoned their other activities, such as *kanjin nō* performances and teaching *tesarugaku* performers and commoners. The increasing demand generated by nō's integration into the *bakufu* rituals of state also contributed to the formation of an additional troupe, the Kita. The first traces of this newcomer troupe began to appear around 1620 (Genna 6). There was no official announcement of the group's founding, which initially consisted of performers from different troupes gathering around an adopted son of Kongō-dayū Yaichi (d. 1605), who for a period was known by the name Kongō-dayū Saburō (1586–1653). Saburō, resigned as Kongō-dayū in favor of Yaichi's son. Although first aligned with the Toyotomi, following the Siege of Osaka Castle in the summer of 1615, he weathered a period without patron or troupe affiliation. He then returned to the Kongō troupe and managed to secure the patronage of Tokugawa Hidetada. Subsequently, he distanced himself from the Kongō troupe and with Hidetada's support he organized a four-day *kanjin nō* in Edo from Genna 6 (1620).8.6 to 8.9. By around 1627, he had changed his name to Kita Shichi-dayū, lending the name Kita to his troupe.[151]

The Kita *za*, although smaller in scale than the four Yamato troupes, was added as the fifth troupe under Tokugawa *bakufu* patronage, and it was decided

---

151 *Yoza yakusha mokuroku*: 46. The *Edo shoki nō bangumi hikae* (*Memorandum of Nō Programs from the Beginning of the Edo Period*) manuscript is housed in the Noh Theatre Research Institute of Hōsei University, Tokyo.

that Kita performers would receive their *haitōmai* share from the Kongō troupe.¹⁵² It was the support by Hidetada and his successor Iemitsu (1604–1651; r. 1632–1651)—especially for Shichi-dayū and the second leader of the Kita *za* Jū-dayū Masayoshi (1624–1665)—that paved the way for the troupe's accomplishments. Many daimyō followed suit and began to integrate Kita performers into their nō patronage. The favoritism toward Kita performers continued until the time of the sixth shōgun Ienobu (1662–1712; r. 1709–1712). Warrior patronage prompted one performer, now only known as Kita-dayū, to advertise his troupe as *buke no shikigaku* (ceremonial art of the warriors) and to use this as a selling point to distinguish his troupe from the four older Yamato troupes. Since the Kita troupe was exempted from attending the *takigi nō* at Kōfukuji, which was still obligatory for the four Yamato troupes, the label *buke no shikigaku* was an important instrument in demonstrating the troupe's uniqueness in competition with the older troupes.

During the Shōhō era (1644–1648), nō performers were ordered to cultivate nō and to protect and preserve the traditional teachings. They were prohibited from any extravagant habits and, moreover, the *shite* troupes were requested to study nō with Kita Shichi-dayū.¹⁵³ This understanding of patronage, with a focus on the preservation of the conventions, encouraged the traditionalization of nō. This did not mean that *tesarugaku* performers instantly disappeared or that all members of the recognized troupes obediently responded. In fact, the sheer number of nō performers coming from the *tesarugaku* or only loosely affiliated to the official troupes allowed for the preservation of a vibrant and multifaceted nō culture throughout the Edo period. But the shogunal measures in effect triggered further systematization. Performance styles became more marked, with *ryūgi* creating lineages, and the differences between "professional" and "amateur" performers became more distinct. One of the main traits of nō until this time—the propensity to develop new styles and to adapt to novel performance contexts—fell into oblivion. Nō became more conservative in outlook as a result. This ultimately led to nō distancing itself from other performance contexts, which enabled competing arts such as the popular *ningyō jōruri* and kabuki to draw larger audiences to their theatres. Seen from another perspective, this conservative tendency can also be seen in a slightly more positive light—that is, the focus on or the invention of a tradition led to performance styles being continuously refined. Consequently, nō gained a rigor and precision that enabled an ever-increasing sophistication and subtlety of expression.

---

152 *Chōshū sarugaku denki*: 164.
153 *Tokugawa jikki* 3: 487b–88a.

1.5.4 Criticism of Excessive Patronage: Restrictions on Performers

The overarching patronage of the Tokugawa *bakufu* included the introduction of the systems of *oheya yakusha* ("private-room performers") during the rule of the fourth shōgun Ietsuna (1641–1680; r. 1651–1680) and *rōkaban* ("hallway attendants") under his successor Tsunayoshi (1646–1709; r. 1680–1709). Ietsuna appointed Kita performers as *oheya yakusha* who were tasked with teaching nō to the shōgun and to the shogunal heir yet to come of age. By 1651 (Keian 4), there was an established custom of organizing shogunal command performances of nō lasting for several days. When daimyō visited another domain, they were almost always entertained with performances of nō, not to mention the sumptuous entertainments coordinated for the shōgun's visits and the daily performances in the shōgun's quarters, in the daimyō residences in Edo, or in their domains. In addition, the shōgun and the daimyō spent considerable time practicing and performing nō. This favored position did not mean that nō performers were beyond reproach. To some retainers, the energy and resources the shōgun and most of the daimyō invested in the cultivation of nō, the patronage of performers, and the gifts of lavish costumes, the purchase of costly *utaibon* or *tsuke* (see ch. 7 *Material Culture*, 7.6, 7.7), and the support of large-scale performances appeared excessive and extravagant.

During the seventeenth century, there were already attempts to limit warrior patronage of nō. One example includes the decrees issued after Ietsuna was proclaimed shōgun on Keian 4 (1651).8.22 by the influential *tairō* ("the great elder," or chief councilor) Sakai Tadakatsu (1587–1662). Tadakatsu's approach to nō was quite similar to Oda Nobunaga's in claiming that "performing *sarugaku* is not appropriate for warriors."[154] He restricted the number of nō performances and regulated the appearance of nō performers at Kōfukiji's *takigi nō*. After Tadakatsu's retirement in 1656 (Meireki 2), this policy was also pursued by other *bakufu* officials, including Sakai Tadakiyo (1624–1681). Under Tadakiyo's command, the distribution of *haitōmai* was changed from rice to coins on Manji 3 (1659).12.11. That same year, it was decided that among the four Yamato troupes, the Kanze troupe could withdraw from *takigi nō*. Again, on Kanbun 2 (1662).6.7, the three remaining troupes were obligated to perform in an alternate system, with one of them skipping attendance every other year.

Most drastically, nō performers were prohibited from carrying swords on Kanbun 8 (1668).5.4. This decree sanctioned 370 nō and kyōgen performers and musicians, while 80 *tayū* performers from families seen as traditionally important were exempt from the ban. The decree also detailed how to travel, how to dress, and even how to behave in a manner deemed appropriate for

---

154 *Meiryō kōhan*: 29a.

performers.[155] The prohibition of carrying swords rendered the performers' status essentially ambiguous. Although by being appointed to *oheya yakusha* they may have been elevated to the warrior rank, effectively they were not regarded as such. This left them in unstable positions especially since payment in coin was less reliable than payment in rice. Once the financial situation of the *bakufu* or the daimyō became dire—as happened from the eighteenth century onward—the performers' incomes were equally threatened. Being excluded from the traditional performances at Kōfukuji likewise deprived the troupes of another potential source of income. Once the *bakufu* implemented these rules, the daimyō in the domains were sure to follow suit. These decrees thus promoted nō's embeddedness as *shikigaku* in the structures of power and made the performers increasingly dependent on the support of both the *bakufu* and the daimyō.

1.5.5 Tokugawa Tsunayoshi and Nō Performers

When Tokugawa Tsunayoshi assumed the office of shōgun in 1680 (Enpō 8), nō performers encountered yet another demanding patron. During Tsunayoshi's long rule, and especially during the Genroku era (1688–1704), cultural production flourished. Commoner culture that had originated in the Kyoto-Osaka region now developed, matured, and thrived throughout Japan. It began to complement the cultural patronage by warriors and the aristocracy: kabuki, *ningyō jōruri*, music, *ukiyo-e* paintings, luxury goods such as lacquerware along with the trappings of a flamboyant lifestyle and a high demand for printed goods were, among other things, products of Tsunayoshi's shogunal reign.[156]

For nō and its performers, this period was accompanied by a tremendous increase in the number of performances for the shōgun, the daimyō, and their respective families (fig. 1.13). Around 1684, the aforementioned hereditary office of *rōkaban* was created, which promoted performers to the warrior rank, in order to be permitted entry into the shogunal palace and residences. The promotion implied that *rōkaban* performers were expected to perform only for the shōgun and his retainers, and were prohibited from traveling and taking the stage in other performances. Until the second half of the eighteenth century when the office was abolished, some hundred nō performers profited from being promoted to *rōkaban*. The *Tokugawa jikki* (*True Records of the Tokugawa*), for example, reports that on Jōkyō 2 (1685).10.27 "the *sarugaku* [performer] Konparu Sankurō was given the rank of a low-level vassal (*go-kenin*) [of the Tokugawa shōgun] and raised to *rōkaban* under his new

---

155   *Ryūei hinamiki* 4; *Tokugawa jikki* 4: 424.
156   See, for example, Jansen 2002: 175–86.

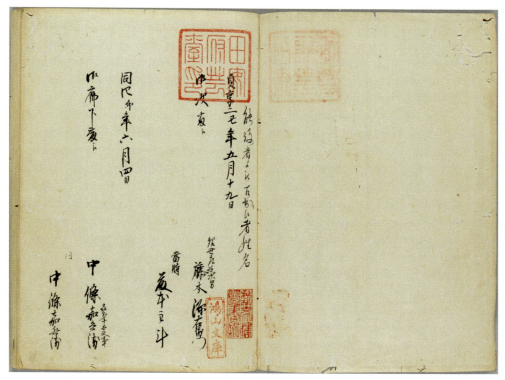

FIGURE 1.13　First page of *List of Names of Nō Performers and Retainers of the Kii Domain Summoned [to Edo]* (*Yakusha Kii hanshi yori meshiidashinin seimei-gaki*). Ca. 1800. Handwritten manuscript, ink on paper. 27.0 × 19.3 cm. Kōzan Bunko, Hōsei University, Tokyo

name Mashita Kurōemon."[157] Conversely, Sakamizu Gorōbei (dates unknown) and his son, two kyōgen performers from Kyoto, refused to enter service as *rōkaban* on Genroku 2 (1689).9.29, leading to their exile by the shōgun.[158]

The coercive nature of the *rōkaban* system inevitably strengthened the *bakufu* influence over nō performers and prevented respective performers from engaging in the regular activities of their respective troupes. If *tayū* or their successors were appointed *rōkaban*, this not only interfered with the organization of a troupe but it could also lead to a troupe's demise. This is precisely what happened to the Kita troupe. When Shichi-dayū Muneyoshi (1650–1731) was named *rōkaban* on Jōkyō 4 (1687).6.4, he was succeeded by Shichi-dayū Umeyoshi (1668–1689) who died only two years later without

---

157　*Tokugawa jikki* 5: 558b.
158　*Tokugawa jikki* 6: 55b. In the Hōei era (1704–1711), Tsunayoshi also established the *tokei no ma ban*, a night watch that was installed in the chambers of his heir Ienobu. More than half of the appointed warriors were performers.

an heir (Genroku 2.5.10). Subsequently, Shichijūrō (d. 1702) from the Kita Gonzaemon family branch was chosen as the fifth *tayū* (Jū-dayū Tsuneyoshi). His promotion to *rōkaban* on Genroku 10 (1697).6.29 once again left the Kita troupe in strife. While the troupe's existence was secured when his brother became Shichi-dayū Nariyoshi (1674–1716), it came at a cost: the extinction of the Kita Gonzaemon family branch.[159]

The comprehensive support by the *bakufu* additionally impacted the nō repertory. Tsunayoshi zealously enjoyed the revival of *haikyoku* ("abandoned plays"; see ch. 4 *Plays*, 4.11) and urged performers to stage rare, at times unusual, plays. The daimyō endeavored to cater to Tsunayoshi's extravagant taste, compelling performers to invest their own resources in an effort to become acquainted with lesser-known plays. On Genroku 7 (1694).2.3, for instance, when Tsunayoshi visited the residence of Yanagisawa Yoshiyasu (1658–1714), he was entertained with four rare nō: *Sakahoko*, *Sumiyoshi mōde*, *Okkake suzuki*, and *Kakkyo*.[160] The effect of warrior patronage on the nō repertory therefore cannot be overemphasized. Their interest triggered a canonization process, the results of which can be seen even today. Most of the nō plays that are now considered standard repertory were favorites of the shōgun or the daimyō. This was especially true of nō used by the performers for teaching their patrons, such as *Hagoromo*, *Aoi no ue*, *Kamo*, or *Takasago*.

Furthermore, Tsunayoshi's patronage of nō sent shockwaves through the nō community, as actors realized that they were no longer in command of the organization of their own troupes. One such instance occurred on Tenna 3 (1683).3.26, when Tsunayoshi ordered the *kotsuzumi* players Kanze Shinkurō Toyoshige (1635–1688) and his son Gonkurō Toyofusa (d. 1707) to perform together with Hōshō Kurō Shigetomo (1619–1685) in *Dōjōji*. When they refused, claiming that tradition prohibited them from performing alongside representatives of other schools, they were immediately banished from Edo. After their pardon three years later in 1686 (Jōkyō 3), Tsunayoshi had them become members of the Hōshō troupe, and they were only allowed to return to the Kanze troupe on Genroku 9 (1696).6.3.[161] Kanze Shinkurō and Gonkurō were not the only performers who experienced this twist of fate. Other performers were also transferred to the Hōshō troupe by Tsunayoshi, no doubt due to his personal preference for the Hōshō troupe. Similar developments can be observed in the domains, where daimyō made their performers change their troupe affiliation on a whim. Such was the case with the Tokugawa in Owari Province

---

159   *Tokugawa jikki* 5: 602a; *Tokugawa jikki* 6: 299b; *Chōshū sarugaku denki*: 191–93.
160   *Ryūkō sōjō nikki* 1: 95. For a list of rare nō performed during Tsunayoshi's time, see Omote and Amano 1999: 117.
161   *Tokugawa jikki* 5: 476b; *Kyōhō rokunen kakiage*: 239a.

(present-day western Aichi Prefecture) and their Konparu performers or with the Maeda in the Kaga domain (present-day southern Ishikawa Prefecture) when they unexpectedly began to hire Hōshō performers.

1.5.6 Daimyō as Performers

Tsunayoshi was in many ways an exceptional patron, and it was most likely because of his influence that nō practice in the domains began to change. While he himself trained in nō and enjoyed performances by nō troupes, he also regularly demanded that the daimyō perform for him. On Jōkyō 3 (1686).4.3, Maeda Tsunanori (1643–1724), for one, made his first appearance on a nō stage in Edo Castle, with little more than a week to prepare his debut.[162] Such sudden demands, as well as Tsunayoshi's favoritism for the Hōshō troupe, were the most probable reasons for the growth and prosperity of the Hōshō branch in the Kaga domain, which is even today referred to as Kaga Hōshō.

Another practice that was institutionalized during the Edo period were the shogunal visits to the Edo residences of the daimyō. These visits were referred to as *o-nari*, and by default they included, among other entertainments, *o-nari nō* ("visit nō"). Tsunayoshi's visits were often announced on short notice, which placed the daimyō under considerable pressure. The forcing of daimyō into the performance of nō meant a growing demand for nō teachers and performers to train with the daimyō. Each domain had its own method of dealing with these demands. In most, the daimyō's retainers had to assume the role of training companions, thereby substantially increasing the number of warriors involved in nō. Sō Yoshitsugu (1671–1694) and Sō Yoshimichi (1684–1718), the daimyō of the Tsushima-Fuchū domain (present-day Nagasaki Prefecture), both trained with Yamada Ichinojō (1636–1717), a Kita troupe performer employed in the Kōfu domain (present-day Yamanashi Prefecture). In order to prepare for performances, the Tsushima-Fuchū daimyō had their retainers learn the instruments as well as train as actors, and it is by no means an exaggeration to say that they formed their own nō group. The retainers were often *kagyōnin*, full-time warriors specializing in fine arts, which extended to being in-house performers, sometimes on a hereditary basis.[163]

The Okayama domain (present-day Okayama Prefecture), conversely, was one of the domains where nō became especially popular during Tsunayoshi's rule. Ikeda Tsunamasa (1638–1714), who became daimyō of the domain in Kanbun 12 (1672), had a nō stage built in his Edo residence in Genroku 7 (1694) and one year later at his Okayama Castle. He gave his stage debut as *shite* in the

---

162   *Tokugawa jikki* 5: 572b.
163   According to the *Kagyōnin no bu* (*Section on In-house Artisans*), a manuscript housed in the Tsushima Museum (Tsushima Hakubutsukan).

play *Miwa* before Tsunayoshi in Genroku 9 (1696). Alongside hired performers, Tsunamasa's page boys served as training partners, and the painter Kanō Santoku (dates unknown) was frequently ordered to partner with him for his nō and kyōgen training sessions.[164]

Following Tsunayoshi's death, the situation of the daimyō and their attitudes toward nō changed slightly. Although the succeeding shōgun, Ienobu (1662–1712; r. 1709–1712), exhibited an equally exuberant addiction to nō, he was less volatile and certainly less taxing. He did not, for example, order the daimyō to perform for him and did not interfere with nō practice in their domains. It was, however, only when Yoshimune (1684–1751; r. 1716–1745) became shōgun in 1716 that the daimyō—and with them the performers—were no longer confronted with outlandish demands.

1.5.7 *Nō Patronage in the Domains:* Okakae yakusha, Machi yakusha, Negi yakusha, *and Merchant Performers*

The enthusiastic patronage of the Tokugawa shōguns encouraged the further dissemination of nō throughout the realm. After the defeat of the Toyotomi clan in 1615 and the uncontested power of the Tokugawa, daimyō started to perform nō openly in order to accommodate the new rulers' tastes. Daimyō in most of the domains committed considerable resources for nō-related activities, in particular, the *tozama daimyō*—those who were not hereditary vassals of the Tokugawa clan and were accordingly seen as "outside daimyō"—such as the Maeda, Date, Shimazu, and Hosokawa. Through their patronage, the daimyō used nō for sociopolitical purposes, and it can be safely conjectured that they tried to prove their loyalty to the Tokugawa *bakufu* by aligning their cultural practices with those of each shōgun. It is difficult to determine with any precision how effective the daimyō's attempts to curry favor with each shōgun were. For the *bakufu*, however, this situation was, at least during economically stable periods, quite convenient since the daimyō who spent their money on performers, masks, costumes, and instruments had few resources left for subversive and seditious activities.

Naturally, the grand-scale exhibition of cultural assets was not restricted to nō. Most daimyō families promoted cultural activities, especially those that could be displayed to great effect. The Date clan, for example, made the tea ceremony and the visual arts their business, frequently making use of these cultural forms in order to entertain the shōgun and showcase their achievements. Daimyō would commission nō plays or have luxurious costumes and costly masks made for shogunal visits. Such spectacles undoubtedly came at

---

164 The *Kanō Den hōkōgaki* (*Kanō Den's Service Report*) manuscript is housed in Ikeda-ke Bunko, Okayama University Libraries (Okayama Daigaku Fuzoku Toshokan).

great expense. Already in the latter half of the seventeenth century, during the rule of the fourth shōgun Ietsuna, daimyō were ordered to reduce these nō performances to staging *hayashi* or *maibayashi* with a single dance or song to be performed with only a few musicians and a smaller chorus. The *shite* was to wear neither costume nor mask.

Throughout the Edo period, various groups of performers were enlisted in the domains. The details of their employment vary from domain to domain and are dependent on many factors, such as the financial situation of the domain and the central government, the amount of support a shōgun was willing to invest in nō, and whether a daimyō had a genuine taste for nō or merely feigned interest to curry favor with the shōgun.[165] Most domains had *okakae yakusha* (also *ote yakusha*, or "performers on hand"), the "hired performers" who were in some cases in service over several generations. *Okakae yakusha* had different backgrounds: they could be performers from one of the five official troupes or come from the *tesarugaku* tradition that flourished in the Kinki region. They received a stipend from the daimyō and performed in annual ceremonies or during the inauguration of a new daimyō. They were likewise active as nō teachers, who often did not reside permanently in the domains, rather only traveled there on specific occasions. This practice had its heyday from the late seventeenth to the early eighteenth century during the rule of the shōguns Tsunayoshi and Ienobu, whose passions for nō encouraged daimyō to enlist performers in a similar fashion. The *Kaisei nō no kinmō zui* (*Revised Illustrated Encyclopedia of Nō*), for instance, records 155 performers active in different domains in the Hōreki era (1751–1764).[166]

Some *negi yakusha* (shrine priest performers) became *okakae yakusha* during the Edo period. A prominent example included the low-ranking priests (*negishū*) mainly responsible for menial duties at Kasuga Taisha in Nara, but who additionally performed nō for the festival at Kasuga Taisha's Mizuya Jinja. The importance these *negi yakusha* had for the domains cannot be overemphasized: there were numerous *negi yakusha* among the *okakae yakusha* from the Hirosaki domain (northern part of present-day Aomori Prefecture) in the north down to Kumamoto domain (present-day Kumamoto Prefecture) in the south. It is virtually impossible to find a domain engaged in the practice of nō that had no *negi yakusha* among its hired performers.[167] According to an entry

---

165   The last few decades have seen an increase in Japanese-language research on Edo-period nō practices in the domains. Early examples are Kajii and Mitsuda 1972; Takemoto 1992. See also Nishiwaki 2005; Iizuka 2009; Aoyagi 2014.
166   *Kaisei nō no kinmō zui*: 157–238. The recent publication of family records of performers in more than forty domains shows that this number actually is only the tip of the iceberg. See Miyamoto 2019; Miyamoto 2021; Miyamoto 2022.
167   Miyamoto 2008c: 58.

in the *Daijōin jisha zōjiki* on Bunmei 10 (1478).4.1, these *negi yakusha* became extremely inebriated at festivals. They appeared in *kanjin nō* in Kyoto during the late sixteenth century, and they even performed several times at the imperial palace, as documented on Keichō 3 (1598).6.8. The document *Nara-zarashi* (*Bleached Cloth from Nara*, 1687) reports that Nara *negi yakusha* comprised more than one hundred performers.[168] One example of a *negi yakusha* who worked as an *okakae yakusha* was Nakamura Sukenoshin Haruhide, a student of Konparu-dayū Motonobu (1629–1703) who was hired in 1691 (Genroku 4) by the Nakatsu domain (present-day Ōita Prefecture) and later by the Nagaoka domain (present-day Niigata Prefecture), where he was listed alongside Konparu troupe performers.

In some domains, such as the Kaga domain and the Shōnai domain (present-day Yamagata Prefecture), the daimyō also relied on the *machi yakusha* (town performers) who lived in the area and could be recruited for performances. Another group whose performance skills were welcomed by the daimyō included merchants, mostly from Kyoto or Osaka, who actively engaged in nō and traveled the domains for business. The custom of merchants training in nō, which started around the end of the fifteenth century in Kyoto and became fashionable in Osaka during the Edo period, fulfilled multiple purposes. On the one hand, the merchants were able to converse with the daimyō and thus create networks that improved their businesses. Ikedaya Zen'emon (dates unknown), a textile dealer from Kyoto, for example, was an official merchant of the Uda-Matsuyama domain (present-day Nara Prefecture) and together with his son performed in several celebratory nō of the domain in 1687 (Jōkyō 4). On the other hand, for the daimyō, these merchants were carriers of information and important components of cultural transfer. By inviting them to perform, the daimyō acquired information without having to travel themselves. The merchants brought with them the latest performance fashions, costumes, and masks, as well as news and gossip. Like the *okakae yakusha* journeying through the domains, their activities supported a cultural and political network, with nō acting as their intermediary.[169]

The close relation between the officially designated merchants of a domain and the daimyō disintegrated toward the mid-eighteenth century when the domains abandoned their traditional suppliers and sought out the cheapest

---

168 *Daijōin jisha zōjiki* 6: 407b. *Oyudono no ue no nikki* 9: 33a. The *Nara-zarashi* manuscript is housed in the *Nara Kenritsu Toshokan Jōhōkan mahoroba raiburarī* (Nara Prefectural Library Information Centre Mahoroba Library); see *Nara-zarashi* below under References: *Websites of Works Cited*.

169 Compare Miyamoto 2005a.

options. Around the same time, general changes occurred in the way performers were hired, as is exemplified by the Hikone domain. During the late seventeenth century, the domain employed fifty performers, but in the first half of the eighteenth century numbers were reduced to two because of its dire financial and political situation. This does not necessarily imply that all daimyō lost interest in nō or that nō was bereft of its significance as a social denominator. On the contrary, in order to guarantee the number of performers needed for the stage, daimyō trained in nō all the more and ordered their retainers to learn nō.

At least for some daimyō the practice of nō was more than a political instrument. During the second half of the eighteenth century, the daimyō of the Kaga domain, the Maeda, had lost their influence, and in their stead the *karō* (chief retainers) ruled the domain. The daimyō Maeda Nariyasu (1811–1884), for instance, performed only symbolic functions and had ample time to indulge in painting, writing, nō, and other pursuits. For Nariyasu, nō came to hold another meaning—namely, that of a performing art for one's own pleasure. When Nariyasu was urged by his *karō* in Tenpō 7 (1836).9.12 to quit his expensive nō training, he complied. But in 1839 (Tenpō 10) he resumed his training and performing, arguing that nō supported and maintained his health.[170]

1.6 Nō Practices and Nō Culture during the Seventeenth and Eighteenth Centuries
Eike Grossmann and Miyamoto Keizō

1.6.1 *The Continuing Role of Kyoto and Osaka as Cultural Centers*
Although troupes were ordered to relocate their offices from Osaka to Sunpu in 1609 (Keichō 14) and then to Edo in 1616 (Genna 2), most performers still maintained residences in Kyoto and Nara and continued to perform in the Kinki region. Between 1607 and 1702, three out of six officially licensed *kanjin nō* by a new Kanze-dayū were held in Kyoto, and the nō performances in honor of the inauguration of the first three shōguns (*shōgun senge nō*) were held at Nijō Castle. A record number of eighty *kanjin nō* by different troupes and performers during the seventeenth century is additional evidence that the popularity of nō among the city's residents was unscathed. This offered performers such as Kongō-dayū Saburō (later Kita Shichi-dayū Osayoshi; 1586–1653), who had not followed the relocation order and found themselves without patrons after the Siege of Osaka in 1615, the opportunity to generate an income even when they were not able to appear onstage. Kongō-dayū Saburō, for example, began

---

170 Kajii and Mitsuda 1972: 168–69, 175–76.

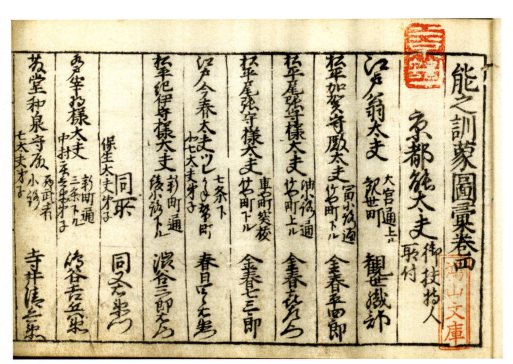

FIGURE 1.14　　List of *nō-dayū* in Kyoto who could be hired as nō teachers. From *Illustrated Encyclopedia of Nō* (*Nō no kinmō zui*). 1687. Woodblock-printed book. 10.7 × 16.1 cm. Noh Theatre Research Institute, Hōsei University, Tokyo

teaching entertainers in Kyoto's pleasure quarters, as did the Konparu troupe *kotsuzumi* player Kō Masayoshi (1539–1626) (fig. 1.14; see ch. 3 *Training*, 3.2).[171]

Kyoto's attraction as a locale for performance and teaching was also one reason that some members of the five troupes declined positions as official performers of the *bakufu*. Kita Sakyō (1606–1682), the oldest son of Kita Shichidayū Osayoshi, and Shindō Isan (d. 1662), a son of the Kanze troupe *waki* performer Shindō Kyūemon Tadatsugu (d. 1653), who established an *utaikō* (chant assembly), were among the most popular figures to stay in the city.[172] Other performers who remained in Kyoto mostly came from the townspeople's *tesarugaku* tradition. They performed at the residences of aristocratic families, such as the Konoe or the Nijō, and at the imperial palace of the emperor Gomizunoo (1596–1680; r. 1611–1629), a great patron of the arts, including poetry, tea ceremony, and painting. He maintained a salon frequented by aristocrats, monks,

---

171　　*Yoza yakusha mokuroku*: 108–10, 136–38.
172　　Omote 1994: 474.

and artists. Nō at the imperial palaces gradually developed traits of the warrior *shikigaku*: performers were invited for the New Year celebrations and seasonal festivals, and their performances were integrated into the coronation of a new emperor (*godai hajime*, or "the beginning of a new reign"). Some performers, such as Shibuya-dayū, the *fue* player Ushio Buzen (dates unknown), and the *kotsuzumi* player Hashi Izu (dates unknown), received stipends, which suggests that at least until Gomizunoo's abdication in 1629 they were employed at the palace in the same manner as performers from the official troupes at the Tokugawa *bakufu*.[173]

During the Edo period, *tesarugaku* performers such as Shibuya-dayū or Horike-dayū, who had already been active during the Sengoku period, were joined by a new generation of performers: affluent city merchants including Tsuruya Shichirōemon (dates unknown), who dealt in fans, and Kobatake Sakon'emon (later Ryōtatsu; 1625–1710), the owner of a dye shop. According to the *Kakumeiki*, the diary of the abbot of Rokuonji (Kinkakuji), Hōrin Jōshō (1593–1668), Tsuruya performed at least eight times at the imperial palaces between 1648 (Keian 1) and 1656 (Meireki 2), either as *shite* in full nō performances or during *utaizome*, the first *utai* of the year. He was also chosen as *nō-dayū* for the celebrations of Tokugawa Ietsuna's proclamation as shōgun on Keian 4 (1651).11.1. Kobatake, however, began to appear onstage on Meireki 2 (1656).5.16 during a large-scale performance at the imperial palace, which was held to celebrate Ietsuna's recovery from illness. The *Kakumeiki* reports on twenty-one of Kobatake's performances until 1667 (Kanbun 7). Tsuruya and Kobatake were later hired by the Ikeda clan of the Okayama domain and the Hachisuka clan of the Tokushima domain (present-day Tokushima Prefecture), respectively.[174]

Through their engagement in nō as either performers or as part of the audience, townspeople were able to establish economic, social, and political networks. While attending performances may have supplemented their study of nō practice, it also served as a status symbol that allowed them to display success and wealth. In the ninth month of 1702 (Genroku 15), for example, Kanze-dayū Shigenori (1666–1716) organized a *kanjin nō* at Kitano. Several tiered seating boxes were built in a circle around the stage. As was the general custom with *kanjin nō*, the box right in front of the stage was reserved for the shōgun Tsunayoshi, who did not attend the performance. The boxes on

---

173 For an *utaizome* by *tesarugaku* performers at Sentō palace on Keian 4 (1651).1.4, see *Kakumeiki* 3: 8. For a collection of materials on performances at the imperial palaces during the early Edo period, see Miyamoto 2005b: 449–558.
174 *Kakumeiki* 2:397; 3:81; 4:57, 65; 6:385. Compare Miyamoto 2005b: 81–117.

the right and left side, which were usually assigned to aristocrats, daimyō, or abbots of important temples, were sold in 1702 to affluent townspeople from Kyoto and Osaka. Among the audience were Mitsui Jōtei II (1641–1702), a member of the Mitsui merchant family, and Kōnoike Zen'emon (1667–1736) from a powerful family of money changers.[175]

Mitsui Jōtei II's father, Jōtei I (1608–1673), even had a nō stage built at his residence for the training of his son. He regularly invited performers to train and perform with his son and on these occasions hosted Kyoto's dignitaries with lavish banquets. Merchants, it turns out, used nō in much the same way as warriors and aristocrats—that is, as a cultural common denominator and networking tool. Jōtei II, who profited from his father's influence, had the opportunity to perform several times at the imperial palace, for example, on Meireki 4 (1658).3.15 and on two consecutive days in the fourth month of 1660 (Manji 3).[176]

While the Mitsui family business developed into a *zaibatsu* (vertically integrated business conglomerate) during the Meiji period (1868–1912) and amassed considerable power until it was dismantled in the 1950s, the Ogata family affords a different perspective on the audience. Ogata Sōken (1621–1687), the owner of Kariganeya, which specialized in designing and producing *kosode*, was a calligrapher of great renown and a patron of the fine arts. He introduced nō to his sons, the Rinpa-school painter Kōrin (1658–1716) and the potter Kenzan (1663–1743), both leading artists in their respective fields. The brothers received training and performed at the Sentō palace and the Nagao Tenmangū, a shrine affiliated with Daigoji, for their *jinji nō*.[177] The examples of the Mitsui and Ogata families demonstrate the existence of a network of townspeople engaged in nō, especially during the Genroku era. A peculiarity of the Kyoto-Osaka region was that townspeople went back and forth between being members of the audience and being performers. This was not the case in Edo.

---

175   If we are to believe Ihara Saikaku (1642–1693), who writes in his fictional account *Nippon eitaigura* (*The Eternal Storehouse of Japan*, 1688) that this was not the first time that all seats for a *kanjin nō* at Kitano by Kanze-dayū Shigekiyo (1633–1687) in the ninth month of 1672 (Kanbun 13) were bought by townspeople of Kyoto, Osaka, and Sakai, among them members of the Ogata family who had made their fortune in garment design. Taniwaki, Jinbō, and Teruoka, eds. 2003: 142. English translation in Sargent, trans. 1959: 101.

176   The *Shōbaiki* manuscript is housed in the Mitsui Bunko. *Bansho hinamiki* in Miyamoto 2005b: 499a–500a; *Kakumeiki* 4: 651–52.

177   *Hirata Motonao nikki* in Miyamoto 2005b: 533a–34a. The *Sanbōin hinamiki* manuscript is in the collection of the Imperial Household Agency. See also Igarashi 2010; Miyamoto 2016. On Ogata Kōrin and nō, see Feltens 2021: 21–25.

1.6.2 Kanjin nō: Large-Scale Nō Performances for Edo Townspeople

In the seventeenth century *kanjin nō* also developed into one of the most popular entertainments in Edo. Miura Jōshin (1565–1644), a writer of popular fiction, even goes so far as to comment in his *Keichō kenmonshū* (*A Collection of Observations in the Keichō Era* [1596–1615]) that "since Edo has been prospering, there is not a single day without a *kanjin nō* performance."[178] While this may be an obvious exaggeration, the statement captures the atmosphere in Edo after the Tokugawa came to power and suggests that people now had more time for leisure activities. During the Edo period, *kanjin nō* served as an umbrella term for various events: *kōgi kanjin nō*, official *kanjin nō* financed by the *bakufu*; *isse ichidai nō* ("once in a lifetime nō," also *ichidai nō*) of the heads of the five troupes; small-scale *kanjin nō* by other performers; and *kishin kanjin nō* ("donation *kanjin nō*" for temples and shrines).[179]

The first recorded *kanjin nō* in Edo took place in 1607 (Keichō 12) on the grounds of Edo Castle. Officially supported by the *bakufu*, it featured Kanze-dayū Tadachika (later Kokusetsu) and Konparu-dayū Yasuteru (1549–1621) performing in a *tachiai* style. For this event, seating boxes were prepared for Ieyasu, the shōgun Hidetada, and the daimyō, but space was also provided for townspeople to attend.[180] Fifteen official *kanjin nō* were held in Edo until 1868, with more than half of them taking place between 1661 and 1673 under the fourth shōgun Ietsuna. For these early *kōgi kanjin nō*, the Tokugawa *bakufu* was eager to maintain the balance between the five troupes and their *nō-dayū* with regards to stage appearances so that no one troupe would outperform the others. Such efforts ceased with Tsunayoshi, under whom most of the official *kanjin nō* were performed by either a Kanze-dayū or a Hōshō-dayū. In order to avoid such favoritism, the *nō-dayū* of each of the five troupes were allowed to apply once for a type of *kanjin nō* that came to be called *isse ichidai nō*. These *isse ichidai nō* functioned as advertisements for nō troupes and were an opportunity to present charismatic performers to a greater public. They usually lasted four to five days, rainy days excluded. Until 1702 (Genroku 15), they were organized only in Kyoto, but the performance by Kanze-dayū Shigenori (1666–1716) in the same year marks the end of this custom. After 1702, the *nō-dayū* held their *isse ichidai nō* in Edo where they were closer to their patrons and were able to

---

178 *Keichō kenmonshū*: 138. On Edo-period *kanjin nō*, see also Groemer 1998a. For a list of Edo-period *kanjin nō* and a detailed introduction of manuscripts, see Miyamoto 2020.

179 For example, In the tenth month of 1674 (Enpō 2), Konparu-dayū held a *kishin kanjin nō* to raise funds for the construction of Tachibanadera in Edo's Mita district. The *Enpō ninen konparu-dayū kanjin nō kakitome* (*Records of Konparu-dayū's Kanjin nō in Enpō 2* [1674]) manuscript is housed in the Noh Theatre Research Institute of Hōsei University, Tokyo.

180 *Tōdaiki*: 99b.

draw a larger audience. They were often held in the vicinity of Edo Castle, typically in front of one of the gates where the performers had sufficient space to construct large temporary theatres.

Several extant manuscripts offer valuable insights into the appearance of these *kanjin nō*. A pair of handscrolls portraying the *Kōka kanjin nō* held in front of the gates of Kanda's Sujikai Bridge by the Hōshō school in 1848 (Kōka 5; fig. 1.15), for instance, show stalls selling sushi, lunch boxes, *sake*, sweets, and programs (see ch. 7 *Material Culture*, 7.5). A large nō stage is depicted along with different types of seats for various ranks of audience members. For the nō performed on Kōka 5.4.22, the handscroll records the biggest audience with 5,300 spectators.[181] Edo's most memorable, and best recorded, *isse ichidai nō* was organized by Kanze Motoakira (1722–1774) in 1750 (Kan'en 3). Claiming that neither his father nor his grandfather had petitioned for their *ichidai nō*, Motoakira applied for fifteen days of performance at the Sujikai Bridge, and the *bakufu* granted his request.[182]

Since nō in this outdoor theatre was only performed on days with fine weather, Motoakira's *ichidai nō* began on the eighteenth day of the third month but lasted until the twenty-third day of the fifth month. During the fifteen stage days, 113 nō (including *Okina*) and 75 kyōgen were performed; Motoakira appeared in forty-four plays. More than five thousand people attended each day, with one exceptional day drawing more than ten thousand spectators. The Tokugawa *bakufu* ordered a record made of the event, and subsequently other *kanjin nō*, which are collected in the three-volume *Kanjin nō ikkendome* (*Records of Kanjin nō Performances*, n.d.). The volumes document every detail: Motoakira's application; drawings of the stage, the program, and the tickets; which daimyō attended; the number of spectators; and a host of other additional information.[183]

1.6.3   Utaikō: *Practicing* utai

Practicing nō, studying with a teacher, purchasing costumes, masks, or instruments—these activities were not easily affordable. Nevertheless, interest in acquiring at least some nō skills was great and led Kyoto residents during the seventeenth century to adopt the practice of gathering in groups known as *utaikō* to study chant, as had been popular among warriors earlier in the first

---

181   For a digitally animated reconstruction of the *Kōka kanjin nō*, see Hōsei Daigaku Edo Tōkyō Kenkyū Sentā, ed. 2019; *Kōka kanjin nō emaki* below under References: *Websites of Works Cited*.
182   *Su-utai yoyo no ato*: 657b–75a.
183   See *Kanjin nō ikkendome* below under References: *Websites of Works Cited*.

FIGURE 1.15 The site of a *kanjin nō* held in 1848 showing the entrance near Sujikai Bridge, the circular seating stalls, and the stage roof. From *Illustrated Handscroll of the Kōka Kanjin nō* (*Kōka kanjin nō emaki*). By Saitō Gesshin (1804–1878). Copy. Meiji period (1868–1912). Folding book (*orihon*), ink and color on paper. 26.3 × 38.8 cm. Kōzan Bunko, Hōsei University, Tokyo

half of the sixteenth century. The popularity of *utaikō* was unabated during the Edo period: townspeople eagerly learned and practiced nō chants together, and still today the study and performance of *su-utai* ("singing nō chants," see chs. 3 *Training*, 3.2; 4 *Plays*, 4.11) continues this tradition. Enjoying this relatively informal pattern of nō training came to be regarded as a refined pastime and a social asset. It led to the appearance of *utaikō* all over the country and to *su-utai* transforming into a variation of nō performance in its own right. The knowledge of *utai* came to be considered essential for one's general education, and *utai* were performed on almost every occasion, including banquets, coming-of-age ceremonies, weddings, and private New Year celebrations (see ch. 7 *Material Culture*, 7.10).

The townspeople of Kyoto were particularly fascinated with the practice of *utai*, and there were dozens of *utaikō* in Kyoto alone. In Kanazawa, the castle town of the Kaga domain, nō chants constantly echoing through the city gave rise to the expression *sora kara utai ga futte kuru* ("*utai* comes pouring down from above")—in other words, everyone in the city was practicing *utai*. *Utaikō* were associated with specific troupes, and they met monthly at temples or shrines. A survey on Kyoto, *Kyō habutae oridome* (*Epilogue on the Silks of Kyoto*, 1689), for example, mentions the *utaikō* of the Fukuō and the Shindō, both *waki* troupes affiliated with the Kanze. The Fukuō *utaikō*, which was established by the *waki* performer Hattori Sōha (also Fukuō Morichika; 1609–1673), met every month on the twenty-second day at Rin'ami, a smaller temple attached to Sōrinji. The *utaikō* of Shindō Isan gathered every seventeenth day at the sub-temple Shōjun'in at Kōdaiji. By the eighteenth century, *utaikō* had developed into institutionalized gatherings with regulations such as the *Asakura shachū utaikō sadame-gaki* (*Regulations for the Participants in Asakura's* [Asakura Rokujirō] *Utaikō*, 1807; see fig. 1.16) or the *Inoue shachū utaikō sadame-gaki* (*Regulations for the Participants in Inoue's* [Inoue Jirōemon] *Utaikō*, 1857).[184] Moreover, the rapid increase of people practicing *utai* during the Edo period created new markets, and the production of chant books (*utaibon*) catered, in particular, to the needs of this group of consumers (see ch. 7 *Material Culture*, 7.7).

---

184 *Kyō habutae oridome*: 360. Manuscripts of the *Asakura shachū utaikō sadame-gaki* and the *Inoue shachū utaikō sadame-gaki* are housed in the Kōzan Bunko at Hōsei University, Tokyo and the Noh Theatre Research Institute of Hōsei University, Tokyo, respectively. The Kanze performers in Kyoto were referred to as *Kyō Kanze* (Kyoto Kanze), mainly because their singing style differed from that practiced by the Kanze troupe in Edo.

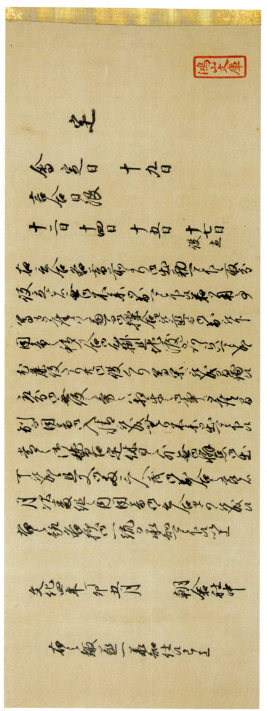

FIGURE 1.16   *Regulations for the Participants in Asakura's [Asakura Rokujirō] Utaikō (Asakura shachū utaikō sadame-gaki)*. First month of 1807 (Bunka 4). Handwritten handscroll, ink on paper. 17.8 (h) cm. Kōzan Bunko, Hōsei University, Tokyo

1.6.4 Tsuji nō: *"Nō at the Crossroads"*

Tsuji nō or *tsuji utai*—"nō at the crossroads"—is another facet of Edo-period nō culture. The use of these terms, and perhaps the appearance of *tsuji nō* performances itself, gained currency due to the custom of mendicants singing *nō utai* by the roadside. These performances belong to the tradition of street entertainment and were particularly popular during the eighteenth and nineteenth centuries. From the late seventeenth to the early eighteenth century, several *tsuji nō* troupes with dozens of members appeared in Edo, Kyoto, and Osaka. In Edo, *tsuji nō* troupes with members named Yamato Gonnosuke or Jū-dayū performed at Sensōji in Asakusa, at the Kanda Myōjin and at Ichigaya Hachiman; in Kyoto, Kaneko Mikinosuke and Saitō Hachijūrō played at the Kitano Tenmangū and in the Shijō-Kawara area; in Osaka, performers including Kanbara Koshirō or Uda Kojirō were active around the Tenmangū and Ikutama Jinja.[185] They often performed in shabby makeshift theatre huts, often hastily erected on the compounds of temples and shrines or on dry riverbeds and crossroads.

The composition of *tsuji nō* troupes was diverse, consisting of former members of nō troupes and nō afficionados. For unknown reasons, well-trained performers also ended up in *tsuji nō* troupes, such as the kyōgen performer Ishikawa Denshirō, who had earlier been hired by the daimyō of the Kishū domain (present-day Wakayama Prefecture and the southern part of Mie Prefecture), and Masuzawa Ukon, who had trained with the Kongō troupe and performed at the imperial palace as well as at Kyoto's Honganji. Under their aegis, the *tsuji nō* troupes developed into full-fledged theatre groups and became serious competitors with the five nō troupes. Their temporary stages, which formerly were open-air stages or roofed with flimsy marsh-reed mats, now became spacious playhouses with nō stages.

With their rising popularity, the activities of *tsuji nō* troupes were closely observed, particularly given that they were not subject to the rules hampering the members of established nō troupes. *Tsuji nō*, for example, freely performed plays such as *Dōjōji*, *Mochizuki*, and *Sekidera Komachi*, while the five troupes were only allowed to do so with permission of the troupe heads. Some *tsuji nō* performers exploited their good looks and refused to wear masks onstage, even for plays normally requiring them. Furthermore, they could invent novel performance styles without fear of official sanction. But most importantly, tickets for large-scale *tsuji nō* performances were sold at a quarter or one-fifth of the price of a ticket for a comparable *kanjin nō* performance. This individual

---

185   Miyamoto 2008a. See Groemer 1998b: 122–26. On street performers between the sixteenth and nineteenth centuries, see Groemer 2016.

artistic freedom, combined with the fact that *tsuji nō* performers began to tour the provinces during the early eighteenth century, prompted the Tokugawa *bakufu* to issue several bans.[186]

How the official nō troupes reacted to *tsuji nō* performers becomes evident when we look at the case of the Sensuke troupe.[187] By 1730 (Kyōhō 15), this troupe, led by the charismatic performer Horii Sensuke (dates unknown), dominated the *tsuji nō* community and did so well until the mid-nineteenth century that it boasted seven generations of "Sensuke" as principal players. The troupe was originally based in Osaka but toured the country from Kanazawa to Kyushu and attracted large audiences, especially in rural areas without nō troupes. Following a hugely successful performance of *Sekidera Komachi* by the Sensuke troupe between 1789 (Kansei 10) and 1801 (Kansei 13 or Kyōwa 1), established nō performers in Kyoto urged their troupes' respective head in Edo to advocate the general prohibition of performances by the Sensuke troupe in Kyoto, Osaka, and Edo. The *tayū* of the five troupes adopted this proposition and filed their own complaint against the Sensuke troupe in 1846 (Kōka 3), which found a precedent in the restrictions imposed on the activities of the *shōmoji* Koinu in the late fifteenth century. The complaint essentially argued that a roofed nō stage and the use of nō costumes was reserved for recognized *nō-dayū* of the five troupes and for these reasons urged the town magistrate of Osaka to prohibit all activities by Sensuke and his troupe. As a result, the Sensuke troupe was banned from performing in all three cities in 1851 (Kaei 4), but they circumvented the prohibition by touring the domains since there was no ruling against performances in the provinces.

When the dust settled, the Sensuke troupe began to resume performances in Kyoto and Osaka. Thanks to the new fans they had gained in the meantime, these were even more popular. In 1855, the troupe once again encountered trouble over a performance in Hirado and ultimately disbanded, with Sensuke VII (dates unknown), already acquainted with kabuki performers and their performance styles, joining the Ebizō kabuki troupe under the name of Ichikawa Baidō. Sensuke, some of his fellow *tsuji nō* performers, as well as kabuki

---

186 See *Maruo nichiroku*, a manuscript housed in the Tatsuno History and Culture Archive, Tatsuno City (Tatsuno Shiritsu Tatsuno Rekishi Bunka Shiryōkan). Compare Miyamoto 2008b. On Shōtoku 4 (1714).3.16, lavish costumes and stage constructions were prohibited for performers who did not belong to one of the five nō troupes. *Tokugawa jikki* 7: 372b–73a.

187 Materials on the Sensuke troupe are scant. The following paragraphs are based on the *Sensuke za ikkendome* (*Notes on the Matter of the Sensuke Troupe*), an official letter exchange from 1855 (Ansei 2). *Sensuke za ikkendome*: 761–68. See also Groemer 1998b: 126–29.

performers, would reappear during the Meiji period (1868–1912) as Sensuke troupe with a nō/kabuki fusion theatre.

1.6.5   Jinji nō *in the Domains*

A simple calculation of the number of temples and shrines at which *jinji nō* were performed regularly, as well as the frequency of performances in most domains reveals how astonishingly buoyant Edo-period nō culture was in the provinces. In Kyushu, for example, shrines such as the Fujisaki Hachimangū and Gion Jinja (present-day Kitaoka Jinja) in the Kumamoto domain, Usa Jingū in today's Ōita Prefecture, Suwa Jinja in Nagasaki, and Kushida Jinja in Fukuoka, maintained a vibrant nō tradition among their parishioners. These shrines were mostly located in urban areas and in domains where daimyō, such as the Hosokawa in Kyushu, showed a strong interest in nō. The daimyō connection to Edo-period *jinji nō*, is also evident in the nō traditions at the Ōnominato Jinja in Kanazawa. Here, shrine parishioners began to perform nō on the shrine's stage in 1604 (Keichō 9) in order to celebrate the victory of Maeda Toshinaga (1562–1614) at the Battle of Sekigahara, and thereafter performed regularly in honor of their daimyō. Indeed, the Kaga domain centered around Kanazawa enjoyed a dynamic nō culture. Even the farmers performed nō as a part of their community's shrine festivals and rites (*matsuri* and *sairei*).

In the village of Kurokawa in the Shōnai domain (present-day Yamagata Prefecture), a nō culture developed that was, and still is, transmitted solely among the villagers. Kurokawa nō's early modern history is well documented, in part because the Sakai clan, who served as the daimyō of Shōnai beginning in 1622 (Genna 8), recognized the farmers' potential as nō performers. Soon after they moved to Tsuruoka Castle, the Sakai became aware of a full-fledged nō tradition in their midst, which they then proceeded to exploit as a source of symbolic power and cultural prestige. This was especially the case after the Hōshō performer Fujino Seizaburō (dates unknown) officially judged Kurokawa's performance of *Takasago*, *Sanemori*, and *Hagoromo* in 1689 (Genroku 2) to be on par with performers of the five official troupes stating that, "[The performers of Kurokawa] are no less [skillful] than Kanze[-dayū]."[188]

Roughly sixty villagers were ordered to perform ten plays for the daimyō in 1690 and were in return presented with costumes and masks. Until the end of the Edo period, the farmers were regularly invited for performances at Tsuruoka Castle, mainly to celebrate a new daimyō or for the *utaizome*. While the villagers, organized into two troupes, continued to perform during their annual festivals at Kasuga Jinja, they also showed a staggering energy when

---

188   *Kurokawa nō shiryō*: 45a. On Kurokawa nō, see Grossmann 2013.

it came to performances outside of a sacred context. Besides ten known performances at Tsuruoka Castle, they toured their domain, particularly around Tsuruoka and Sakata. Extant records suggest they mounted between eight and eleven *kaichō nō*, benefit or subscription performances similar to the *kanjin nō* in Kyoto and Edo. These *kaichō nō* were coordinated by brokers who handled the performer's travel plans and lodgings, the performance space, advertisement, and remuneration. Professional management was obviously necessary: records state that the villagers were able to draw an average audience of 990 people per day over eight to ten days. In addition to performing, they taught nō to the inhabitants of villages in their vicinity and were frequently hired for private performances.[189]

The villagers in rural Kurokawa were farmers with, in effect, their own *ryūgi*. While this may be an exceptional case, it sheds light on the possibilities open to people who were not members of one of the main troupes. It demonstrates how "amateurs" were able to devote themselves to nō and achieve similar results as "professionals" with their *kanjin* performances, private banquets, training, sacred nō, and warrior patronage.

1.7 The Reorganization and Standardization of Nō Practices during the Eighteenth and Nineteenth Centuries
Eike Grossmann and Miyamoto Keizō

1.7.1 *Tokugawa Yoshimune's Patronage and Kanze Motoakira's "Nō Reform"*

In all likelihood, the daimyō of the Kii domain, Tokugawa Yoshimune (1684–1751; r. 1716–1745), did not expect to become the eighth Tokugawa shōgun: he was called to Edo quite suddenly when Ienobu's young son, Ietsugu (1709–1716), died after only four years as shōgun. Following his instatement as shōgun in 1716 (Kyōhō 1), Yoshimune concerned himself with the historical and the theoretical aspects of nō rather than with its performance. The *Tokugawa jikki* even states that Yoshimune "was not fond of *sangaku*." He strictly supervised the education of his son Ieshige (1712–1761; r. 1745–1760) and his grandson Ieharu (1737–1786; r. 1760–1786) to ensure that they were not engrossed in the practice of nō. Although Yoshimune allowed Ieshige to continue his nō training, Ieshige's fascination led Yoshimune to prohibit Ieharu from training altogether.

---

189   Records of Kurokawa's *kaichō nō* are in *Kurokawa nō shiryō* 1959; *Kurokawa mura Kasuga Jinja monjo* 1998. Sakurai Akio lists twenty performances of Kurokawa nō for other individuals in the period from 1813 to 1860. Sakurai 2003: 113–14.

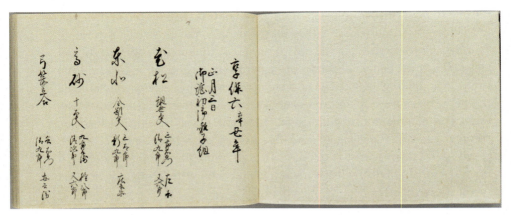

FIGURE 1.17 *Records of Nō Performances* [between 1721 and 1862 at Edo Castle] (*Furenagashi o-nōgumi*). 19th century. Handwritten book, ink on paper. 15.4 × 20.9 cm. Kōzan Bunko, Hōsei University, Tokyo

On Kyōhō 19 (1734).10.8, in a reported conversation with his retainer Shibuya Yoshinobu (1682–1754), he lamented Ieshige's enthrallment with nō.[190] One month later, when Yoshimune learned that Ieshige was scheduled to perform nō for Ienobu's widow, Ten'eiin (1662–1741), he had Ieshige replaced with his second son Tayasu Munetake (1715–1771). As a result, Ieshige never officially performed nō once he became shōgun in 1745 (Enkyō 2).[191]

Yoshimune considered nō a useful representational tool, yet felt that it should never be performed by a shōgun. This does not mean that he was indifferent to nō, but his inclinations greatly veered from the fifth shōgun Tsunayoshi, who had introduced the *rōkaban* system, thereby providing some performers with a stable income. But Tsunayoshi also requested the revival of noncanonical plays, which allowed performers to reevaluate their canon and explore new modes of performance and style. Yoshimune's approach to nō offered a toned-down counterpart to Tsunayoshi's experimental period, and his role in the history of nō can be described as one of accelerating processes of standardization. First, he reversed the excessive ruling of his predecessors: he abolished the hereditary *rōkaban*, minimized the number of performers in the warrior rank, and reduced their stipends. This coincided with the Kyōhō Reforms (Kyōhō 1–Genbun 1 [1716–1736]), which were intended to stabilize the financially stricken *bakufu* through edicts directed at the daimyō in an effort to have them curb their expenditure and to avoid overly luxurious lifestyles.

190 *Tokugawa jikki* 9: 312a.
191 *Tokugawa jikki* 9: 336a–37a. On Yoshimune and nō, see Rath 2004: 123–35. On the *bakufu*'s general policy during this time, see Jansen 2002: 237–54.

Yoshimune also ordered the compilation of the *Furenagashi o-nōgumi* (*Records of Nō Performances* [between 1721 and 1862 at Edo Castle]; fig. 1.17), records of nō performances between 1721 and 1862 at Edo Castle that were organized by the *bakufu*, and requested *kakiage* (reports) from the performers of the five troupes. In the *Kyōhō rokunen kakiage* (*Report of Kyōhō 6* [1721]; fig. 1.18), the *nō-dayū* describe the history of their troupes and their family lineages, list their performers, provide information on authors of nō plays, and much more.

Whether the information provided is true is not crucial since these reports contributed to a general standardization of nō history and established an orthodox way for performers to represent their schools and their art.[192] Another change Yoshimune initiated was the replacement of Kita-dayū with Kanze-dayū as the official *nō-dayū* of the *bakufu*. The only former Tokugawa shōgun who favored a Kanze-dayū was Ieyasu, and Yoshimune's patronage officially announced the return of a Kanze-dayū as leader of the *bakufu* nō community. On Kyōhō 11 (1726).5.21, when Ieshige became shōgun, his *shinan'yaku* (teacher) Kanze-dayū Kiyochika (1693–1747) was promoted to *shōgun nō shinan'yaku* (the nō teacher of the shōgun). Kiyochika was appointed teacher to Ieshige's brother Tayasu Munetake and his son Ieharu in 1758 (Hōreki 8), seven years after Yoshimune's death. Kiyochika's son Motoakira (1722–1774) then followed in his father's footsteps when Ieharu became shōgun in 1760. Motoakira would become the most influential Kanze-dayū in early modern Japan, and his activities and achievements set in motion nō's further development in future centuries (see ch. 2 *Performance*, 2.12).[193]

Motoakira profited from his father Kiyochika's proximity to Yoshimune in setting up his own network within the *bakufu* through which he was able to form connections with three shōguns: Yoshimune, Ieshige, and Ieharu. For his *isse ichidai nō* in 1750 (Kan'en 3), Motoakira was granted the exceptional span of fifteen days for performances instead of the regular four to five, and he performed in as many as forty-four plays. These numbers are evidence of the institutional change that occurred while he was Kanze-dayū: he consolidated control over his troupe by implementing a hierarchical order with one single *nō-dayū*, himself, as absolute authority, and this reveals the first inklings of the *iemoto seido* (head-of-the-school system). In order to assimilate power in his position as the troupe's head, Motoakira employed three strategies.

---

192   *Kyōhō rokunen kakiage*: 211–56. The *Furenagashi o-nōgumi* manuscript is housed in the Noh Theatre Research Institute of Hōsei University, Tokyo.

193   The *Kyōwa ni nen kanze-dayū yuishogaki* (1745) manuscript is owned by the Kanze family (Kanze sōke). For an authoritative collection of essays on Motoakira, see Matsuoka, ed. 2014. For research in English, see Rath 2003: 194–99; Rath 2004: 190–214.

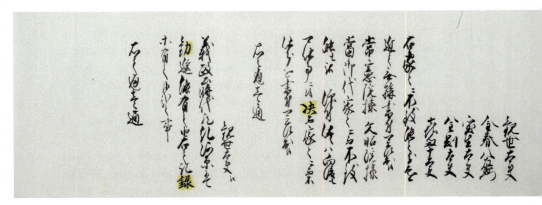

FIGURE 1.18　*Report of Kyōhō 6* [1721] (*Kyōhō rokunen kakiage*). 1721. Handwritten book, ink on paper. 14.5 × 41.5 cm. Noh Theatre Research Institute, Hōsei University, Tokyo

First, annotated copies of Zeami's treatises were distributed to chosen students only, and selected writings such as the *Shudōsho* (*Learning the Profession*, 1430) in 1772 (Meiwa 9) were made available to the general public. Secondly, the *menjō* (licensing) system for amateur students was reinforced, which established a firm connection between the *tayū* in Edo and students in the provinces, and which regulated the performance of *narai mono* ("training pieces") in the sense of mastery pieces; *narai-goto*, specific parts of plays; and sometimes "performance variations" (*kogaki*, or "small letters") outside of training contexts. This practice, which already required the troupe leader's permission, was strengthened by Motoakira with the initiation of a so-called *toritsugi* or intermediary.

When a student in the provinces requested the transmission of a *narai-goto* from the troupe's head, this task was delegated to a student, which meant that all students were connected to the *iemoto*. The licensing system thus reinforced the dependency of disciples on their teachers and concentrated power in the hands of the troupe's leader. The third and last strategy was the standardization of performance practices by defining and reorganizing *kogaki*, as well as by publishing authoritative *utaibon*, in an attempt to categorize, restructure, and codify the repertory of the Kanze troupe.

With the financial and intellectual backing of the *bakufu*, in 1765 (Meiwa 2) Motoakira published his signature work, the *Meiwa kaisei utaibon* (*Utaibon Revised in the Meiwa Era* [1764–1772]; hereafter *Meiwa-bon*), a collection of 210 nō (fig. 19a–b). Although scholars debate the reliability of accounts on details about the evolution of the *Meiwa-bon*, such as those given in the *Kaisei-bon yōkyoku sōan* (*Draft on the Revised Collection of Yōkyoku*, ca. late Edo period), there can be no doubt that the revision was a collaboration between Motoakira,

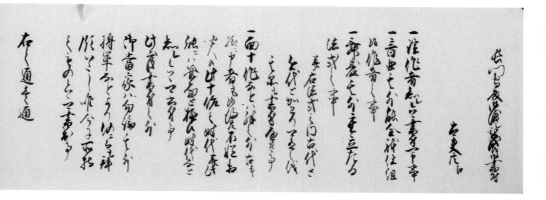

Tayasu Munetake, the poet and philologist Kamo Mabuchi (1697–1769), and the poet Katō Enao (1693–1785).[194] The four aspired to align the wording of literary references in the plays with what they considered the authentic version in their respective source texts, thereby unifying how words were written and, by extension, understood. As such, this work parallels the goals of the sixteenth-century *Utai (no) shō*, but while the latter was projected as a reference work, the *Meiwa-bon* was intended as an authoritative *utaibon*.

What made the *Meiwa-bon* special was the attempt to combine nō texts with musical annotations and directions as to staging, movements, costumes, and properties. In the writing process, new performance practices were created based, its editors would have us believe, on the thorough study of historical materials, be they literary sources or records of customs and manners. This claim naturally suggested that only the performance practices given in the *Meiwa-bon* were accurate and authentic; all other practices, especially those transmitted orally, were flawed. Considering that *utaibon* were among, if not the best-selling publications in the Edo period, the impact of the *Meiwa-bon* was immense. Plays such as Motoakira's *Ume* (*Plum*), for example, were added; others, most notably those popular in the Kyoto-Osaka region, were omitted. Naturally, the publication spawned such controversy that shōgun Ieharu ordered the abolishment of the *Meiwa-bon* three months after Motoakira's death in 1774 (An'ei 3). Although the next Kanze-dayū Oribe Kiyohisa

---

194   See *Kaisei-bon yōkyoku sōan* below under References: *Websites of Works Cited*.

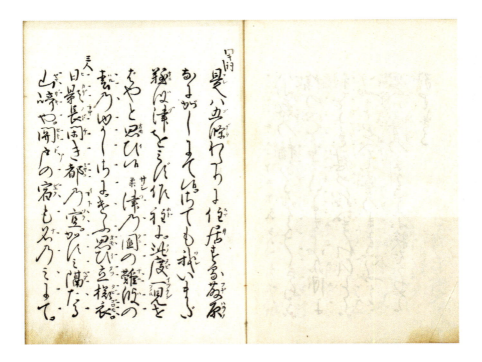

FIGURE 1.19A–B
Utaibon Revised in the Meiwa Era [1764–1772] (*Meiwa kaisei utaibon*): a) first page of *Ume* and b) front cover. By Kanze Motoakira (1722–1774). 1765. Woodblock-printed book. 24.6 × 18.1 cm. Kōzan Bunko, Hōsei University, Tokyo

(1727–1782) announced a "return to the old fashions," the institutional changes initiated by Motoakira endured.[195]

1.7.2 Performances at the Shōgun's Quarters

In 1758 (Hōreki 8), the shōgun Ieshige decided that his son Ieharu, Ieharu's page boys, and other attendants, would receive training to learn *waki* roles, instruments, and kyōgen.[196] Ieharu had his lessons in the shogunal quarters (*nakaoku*, or "middle inner [rooms]") in the central part of Edo Castle, and the carefully selected performers who provided instruction had to submit a pledge prior to entering: "Concerning the training of those present in the inner quarters in *shimai, utai,* and nō, [I/we] shall conduct [my/our] supervision diligently and without favoritism. [I/we] will, at all times, refrain from judging between skilled and unskilled."[197]

Obviously, this pledge was intended to prevent any comparison of the shōgun with his fellow students while he trained as a *shite*. But although Ieharu looked favorably upon nō, this did not include his active participation in official performances before a large audience. Rather, shogunal nō performance in the late Edo period is characterized by a return to private settings, that is *oku nō* (inner nō) in the quarters of the shōgun where only his close relatives, a few daimyō, and trusted advisors were allowed to attend. The custom of the shōgun taking the *oku butai* (inner stage) in private was firmly established during Ieharu's time and also adopted by the subsequent shōguns Ienari (1773–1841; r. 1786–1837) and Ieyoshi (1793–1853; r. 1837–1853). Furthermore, official nō performed for the shōgun, such as his inauguration nō, were still held on the *omote butai* (front or public stage; see ch. 7 *Material Culture*, 7.5), where townspeople were also allowed to attend (fig. 1.20).

The frequency of performances on the *oku butai* depended on the influence of the advisers to the shōgun and the financial circumstances of the *bakufu*. In 1789 (Kansei 1), two years after Ienari became shōgun, the *rōjū* (senior councilor) Matsudaira Sadanobu (1759–1829) was appointed regent, and there are no records of performances at the shogunal quarters until he was driven out of office in 1793 (Kansei 5). In 1799 (Kansei 11), Hōshō-dayū Fusakatsu (1751–1811) and his son Kuniyasu (1769–1809) were appointed Ienari's nō teachers. This

---

195 A harsh critique of the *Meiwa kaisei utaibon* was written by the essayist Kanzawa Tokō (1710–1795), a former officer of the Kyoto city magistrate and Kanze troupe student who recollects the process from development to implementation to abolishment. See *Okinagusa* 2: 1–15.
196 *Tokugawa jikki* 10: 817b.
197 Manuscript in the collection of the Noh Theatre Research Institute of Hōsei University, Tokyo.

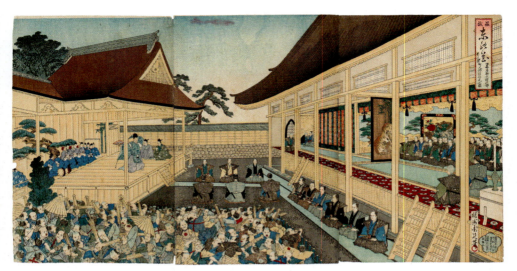

FIGURE 1.20   *Picture of Townspeople Attending Nō (Machiiri nō no zu)* at the Honmaru Goten of Edo Castle. By Yōshū Chikanobu (1838–1912). 1889. Color woodblock print. 36.3 × 71.1 cm. Noh Theatre Research Institute, Hōsei University, Tokyo

comes as no surprise since Ienari came from the Hitotsubashi-Tokugawa family branch that traditionally favored the Hōshō troupe. Naturally, Ienari's son Ieyoshi began training with Fusakatsu in 1806 (Bunka 3), and it was Ieyoshi who came under the spell of nō, once more reviving the practice of *oku nō*. His son Iesada (1824–1858; r. 1853–1858) and the last shōgun Yoshinobu (1837–1913; r. 1866–1867) also appeared onstage with Ieyoshi. In 1851 (Kaei 4), already nearing the end of his reign, Ieyoshi performed almost every month on the *oku butai*, leaving room for speculation about whether his engagement in nō was not in reality a form of escapism.[198] The arrival of Commodore Matthew C. Perry (1794–1858) and his *kurofune* (black ships) in 1853 (Kaei 6) heralded the commencement of even more tumultuous times. In response, the performances at the shogunal quarters ceased.

1.7.3   *Nō in Kyoto and Osaka*

In the eighteenth century, Edo's transition into the new and undisputed cultural center of the realm was almost complete. While the troupes' *nō-dayū* still traveled from Edo to Nara in the early eighteenth century, they soon delegated performances to their students in the Kyoto-Osaka region. Other performers

---

198   *Kyūji shimonroku* 1: 188–89; *Tokugawa shoke keifu* 2: 184a–87b. On this period, see Miyamoto 2009: 36–43.

followed the trail of commodities and the flock of people drawn to Edo, and their activities in Kyoto steadily decreased. This development becomes very clear when we look at the frequency of *kanjin nō* in Kyoto. Records and extant programs indicate that there were eighty or more performances during the seventeenth century, with a *kanjin nō* organized every other year at the very least. By contrast, during the 1730s only four *kanjin nō* took place, and there are no records at all for the time until the end of the Edo period in 1868. This does not mean that nō lost its popularity in Kyoto. Rather, other factors came into play, as Kizaki Tekisō (1688–1766), a merchant from the Obama domain (present-day Fukui Prefecture), writes in his *Shūsui zatsuwa* (*Miscellaneous Tales of Collected Chinquapin Nuts*):

> While the expenses for *kanjin nō* in Kyoto increased around the beginning of the Kyōhō era [1716–1736], the audience dwindled. And on every occasion, the organizers suffered financial losses. It even happened that a performance was canceled halfway through. And yet, day-long training nō (*keiko nō*) sessions were held frequently on the stage of Takeuchi Heishichi's residence.[199]

This report suggests that the costs of organizing a *kanjin nō*, which lasted for several days and was heavily dependent on weather conditions, was no longer covered by the revenues of ticket sales. In turn, the high entrance fees discouraged spectators. But while *kanjin nō* had difficulties drawing larger audiences, smaller performances that operated under the umbrella of "training nō" could be held more often, as they were less expensive to coordinate and guaranteed higher revenues to fewer people. All that was required was a nō stage. The Kita-troupe performer Takeuchi Heishichi mentioned in the passage above had one in his Kyoto residence, which he often rented to other nō performers (see ch. 7 *Material Culture*, 7.5).[200] Apart from *keiko nō*, performances took place on a regular basis at the imperial palaces, at aristocratic residences, and of course at (Nishi) Honganji. There were also *jinji nō* performances at shrines, including the Kamigamo Jinja and the Matsuo Taisha. These performances

---

199   *Shūsui zatsuwa*: 403. *Shūsui zatsuwa* is principally a local history of events, customs, and at times stories from Wakasa in present-day Fukui Prefecture; it also includes information on Kyoto. The last *kanjin nō* in Kyoto appears to have taken place in the eighth month of 1724 (Kyōhō 9). Miyamoto 2020: 20.

200   The *Nō bangumi dētabēsu* by the Research Center of Classic Performing Arts (Koten Geinō Kenkyū Sentā) at Kōbe Women's University (Kōbe Joshi Daigaku) provides information on *keiko nō* in the Kyoto-Osaka region during the nineteenth and twentieth centuries. See *Nō bangumi dētabēsu* below under References: *Websites of Works Cited*.

were supported by several families of performers that all came from Kyoto's townspeople *tesarugaku* tradition and had made nō their main profession: the Nomura and Kawakatsu (Kongō troupe), the Katayama (Kanze troupe), and the Horike (Kita troupe).

As nō lost its momentum in Kyoto, it picked up pace in Osaka. From the eighteenth century onward, performers became increasingly active in Osaka, which by then was a hotspot of popular culture. While *kanjin nō* had ceased to exist in Kyoto and only five large-scale *isse ichidai nō* were held in Edo, there were at least seventy *kanjin nō* in Osaka between 1670 and 1868 (fig. 1.21a–b). Unlike the arrangements in other cities, most Osaka *kanjin nō* were not organized by the *nō-dayū* of one of the five troupes but by other performers, including musicians, *waki*, and kyōgen actors.[201]

This development is mainly related to Osaka's financial and structural environment: ticket purchases for *kanjin nō* were compulsory for Osaka's three city districts of Kita, Minami, and Tenma, each of which was obliged to buy a fixed number of tickets for every performance. For performers, this system provided a secure income, and was complemented by celebratory gifts from the storehouses of Osaka daimyō following a performance. No daimyō wished to appear miserly in the eyes of his peers, and so presents could be lavish. Okada Murao (1875–1911), an Ōkura-school kyōgen performer recollects, that "the profit for a six-day *kanjin nō* was 1500 gold coins (*ryō*)"[202]—a fantastic sum by contemporary standards. The physician Iwanaga Buntei (Shōkisai; 1802–1866) notes in his records on Tenpō 12 (1841).8.16 that *kanjin nō* "began with the intention to show nō to townspeople,"[203] but now for most performers *kanjin nō* were primarily a source of income.

Osaka also had numerous attractive venues ready for performances. Most of Osaka's *kanjin nō* were held on *jōbutai* (permanent stages), perhaps the most distinctive feature of Osaka's nō culture (see ch. 7 *Material Culture*, 7.5). As a part of the city's development plan, nō stages, kabuki playhouses, *sumō* rings, teahouses, and restaurants were built in newly laid-out areas. During the expansion of the Horie district in 1699 (Genroku 12), for example, the *bakufu* approved the construction of three permanent nō stages, and more stages followed in Nanba and Tenma Naramura. Osaka thus became the first city with

---

201 On the development of Osaka into an economic, financial, and cultural center, see, for example, Jansen 2002: 166–86. For a list of *kanjin nō* during the Edo period, see Miyamoto 2020: 16–23.
202 In *Sarugaku kikigaki* (*Oral Recollections of Sarugaku*), a manuscript housed in the Tsubouchi Memorial Theatre Museum, Waseda University (Waseda Daigaku Engeki Hakubutsukan).
203 *Shōkisai nichinchi zakki*: 548b, 553b.

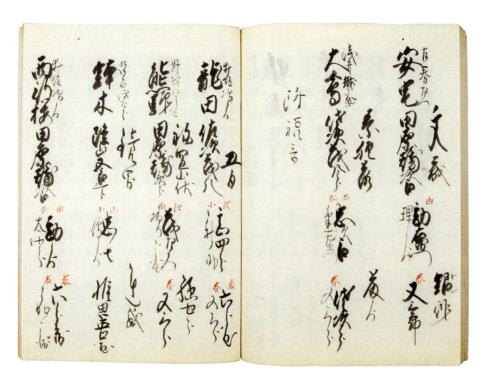

FIGURE 1.21A–B
Complete Records of Kanjin nō and Kanjin kyōgen in Osaka (*Ōsaka kanjin nō narabi ni kyōgen tsukushi roku*): a) program of the fourth and fifth days of the *kanjin nō* in 1760 and b) front cover. Late 18th century. Handwritten book, ink on paper. 24.0 × 17.1 cm. Kōzan Bunko, Hōsei University, Tokyo

permanent stages reserved exclusively for nō performances.[204] The foundation of this type of nō culture was provided by townspeople who started to engage in nō in much the same fashion as the townspeople of Kyoto had.

Up to the end of the Edo period, nō in Osaka prospered with the support of townspeople as both performers and financiers. Many of Osaka's town performers were wealthy merchants who worked in the wholesale trade or as currency brokers, such as the Kongō-troupe performer Kimura Mohei (1816–?) of the Hinoya, a wholesale dealer for Chinese imports, or the currency brokers of the Komeya, Tonomura Heiemon (1741–1788) from the Kanze troupe and of the Izumiya, Isaka Jirōemon (1708–1777) from the Kita troupe. With the nineteenth century, these town performers were in serious competition with performers in Kyoto. They had increased the range of their performances to Kyoto and to Nara, where they appeared at the imperial palace and at Kōfukuji's *takigi nō*.[205] But the involvement of financiers in matters related to nō also affected the decline of Osaka nō culture. When the new Meiji government adopted the gold standard in 1871, it triggered a severe financial crisis for Osaka's merchants. Inevitably, many of the traders and brokers who participated in Osaka's nō culture went bankrupt, and without these affluent patrons, conditions for nō in Osaka rapidly deteriorated.

1.8 The Crisis of Nō in the Late Nineteenth and Early Twentieth Centuries

Eike Grossmann and Miyamoto Keizō

1.8.1 *Nō Performers at Edo Castle and in the Domains*

With the overthrow of the Tokugawa *bakufu* in 1868, the abolishment of the domains, and the establishment of prefectures in 1871, nō encountered yet another existential threat in its long history. For the performers, the introduction of a new system of social classes with *kazoku* (former court aristocracy and daimyō), *shizoku* (warrior families), and *heimin* (commoners) heavily impacted inherited nō practices.[206] With the exception of those with the larg-

---

204 Nakagawa 1995: 42.
205 On performances at the imperial palace, see the *Rappu bangumi* (*Program of Nō Dances*) manuscript in the collection of the imperial library Higashiyama Gobunko; the *Kinri sentō o-nō no ki* (*Record of Nō at the Imperial Palace and at the Residences of Abdicated Emperors*) manuscript in the collection of the Imperial Household Agency Archives and Mausolea Department (Kunaichō Shoryōbu). A transcription of performances at the *takigi nō* is found in Ōmori 1995.
206 On the *bakumatsu* ("end of the *bakufu*") era and the Meiji period, see Jansen 2002.

est domains, the daimyō fell into poverty. Performers who had depended on their patrons faced the same fate. These developments were not entirely unexpected: performers had struggled to make ends meet well before these sociopolitical and economic upheavals.

The decline of nō performances at Edo Castle during the last decade of the *bakufu* is exemplary of the dire situation that faced nō performers. There were approximately three hundred official performers in shogunal service who received their stipends, even if steadily reduced, from the *bakufu* until 1867 (Keiō 3). Since they were also compensated for each stage appearance, a cutback in performances meant financial losses. For most, large-scale performances of full plays preferably on the official nō stage (*omote butai*) at Edo Castle were the only opportunity to perform. According to the *Furenagashi o-nōgumi*, one of the last occasions for nō performers to act on the *omote butai* was in 1862 (Bunkyū 2) when the marriage of shōgun Iemochi (1846–1866; r. 1858–1866) to the imperial princess Kazunomiya Chikako (1846–1877) was celebrated with three days of nō performances (on 2.18, 2.21, 2.23). For several years to come, there were only sporadic performances, if any at all, for the shōgun and his closest acquaintances, and these were smaller in scale as they did not consist of performances of full plays but rather *utai* and *mai*. The last record of a nō performance at Edo Castle dates to Keiō 1 (1865).1.3: an *utaizome* with abridged nō performances.[207]

With the resignation of the shōgun Yoshinobu on Keiō 3 (1867).10.14 and the announcement of the restoration of imperial rule on Keiō 3.12.9, nō performers found themselves without their powerful patrons. On 1868.6.1 (April 1, 1868), they were informed that they had been dismissed from service. They could, however, petition to the new government for acceptance as vassals, and almost two-thirds of the performers made use of this offer.[208] Most performers affiliated with the Kanze school, however, did not approach the Meiji government with a request to enter service, mostly because of their close relations to the Tokugawa clan. Among them were Kanze Kiyotaka (1837–1888), the flute player Morita Hatsutarō (1833–1906), the *kotsuzumi* player Kanze Shinkurō (1817–1888), and the *taiko* players Kanze Sakichi (1815–1874) and Konparu Hiroshige (1830–1896).[209] These performers had to find other ways of making a living, either by abandoning nō or by finding other ways to monetize on

---

207 *Umewaka Minoru nikki* 1: 488b, 489b–91b; *Umewaka Minoru nikki* 2: 53a–b.
208 *Umewaka Minoru nikki* 2: 153b.
209 The five troupes abandoned the honorific title of *tayū* with the collapse of the Tokugawa *bakufu*. During the latter half of the Edo period, the troupes were referred to either as *za* (troupe) or *ryūha/ryūgi* (school). With the Meiji period, *za* was used no longer.

their art. Kanze Kiyotaka, for example, retired from the stage, and took on the commoner name Igaya Chōgorō. He initially lived in Tokyo, then in Shizuoka where he had gone with the last members of the Tokugawa family in 1869 in hope of support. Ultimately, he died there impoverished. By contrast, Konparu Hiroshige moved to Nara in 1868 where he was affiliated with the Kasuga Taisha.[210]

Among the performers who approached the new government were Hōshō Kurō Tomoharu (1837–1917), Kongō Tadaichi (1815–1884), Kita Roppeita XII (1814–1869), Kanze Tetsunojō V (Kōsetsu; 1843–1911), and, also from the Kanze school, Umewaka Rokurō (from 1872 Minoru I; 1828–1909).[211] They stayed in Tokyo, and with Umewaka Minoru I and Kongō Tadaichi as driving forces they established a new performance infrastructure by the end of 1868. Ernest Mason Satow (1843–1929), a diplomat who translated for the British embassy in Japan, writes about a nō and kyōgen performance on the Kongō stage that he attended in the twelfth month of 1868: "The audience consisted entirely of the *samurai* class."[212] In the following year, Kanze Tetsunojō V, Hōshō Kurō, Kongō Tadaichi, and others had their first official appearance as court performers during a banquet for the British crown prince (1869.7.29; July 29, 1869).[213] Their service at the Meiji court did not last long: they were suddenly let go in the eleventh month of 1871. As the nō critic Ikenouchi Nobuyoshi (1858–1934) describes in his *Nōgaku seisuiki* (*Records of the Rise and Fall of the Nō Theatre*), a report on the state of nō during the Edo and Meiji periods:

> Some became tobacco merchants, others purveyors of medicine or even shrine priests, yet others minor bureaucrats or surveyor's assistants; still others found work under gardeners, or glued fans, or whittled toothbrushes. They made a living by whatever means possible, and some were so depleted that they simply disappeared and left their families scattered.[214]

The fact that performers quit nō and kyōgen did result in the extinction of schools, as in the case of the Shindō school of *waki* performers or the Sagi school of kyōgen. Apart from the official performers of the *bakufu*, hired performers in the domains also felt the effects of the transition from the Edo to

---

210 *Umewaka Minoru nikki* 2: 196a–97a. See Miyamoto 2017a: 52–61.
211 *Umewaka Minoru nikki* 2: 196a–97a, 211a.
212 Satow 1921: 397.
213 *Umewaka Minoru nikki* 2: 236a–b.
214 Ikenouchi 1992: 4. See *Umewaka Minoru nikki* 2: 333b.

the Meiji period. Compared to their counterparts in Tokyo, they enjoyed relative stability, which changed only with the establishment of prefectures in 1871. With the resignation of the shōgun in 1868, daimyō were proclaimed *chihanji* (governors of the domains) and for the most part stayed within their domains where they retained an income. In many cases, the former daimyō kept the performers in their service, although it is important to note that their numbers had been reduced significantly after 1854 in an effort to ease economic strains. Being in the service of a domain did not protect performers, however, from facing a variety of fates.

In domains with a distinct nō tradition such as Kaga or Nanbu, those in power continued to practice and perform nō, and not much changed for the performers. Matters were more difficult in other domains. In Satsuma, Chōshū, and Matsushiro, for instance, nō performers were conscripted into militaries in their respective domains and coerced into learning Western marching tunes, with some performers even becoming full-time soldiers.[215] With the abolition of the domains in 1871, the daimyō-turned-governors lost their positions and were relocated to Tokyo. Without the backing of their daimyō, nō performers were left behind and barely managed to survive by teaching *utai* or instruments to city dwellers and former warriors. Small wonder then that the popularity of nō decreased rapidly, and nō traditions gradually vanished from the provinces.

1.8.2 *Experimental Nō and the Search for New Patrons*

The dissolution of the domains in 1871 and the dismissal of "court performers" forced actors to seek out other sources of income once more. Their efforts may be divided roughly into two categories: 1) the experimentation with or implementation of novel performance styles with the aim of making nō more popular, and 2) the more conventional route of teaching, training, and finding substitute patrons. Hiyoshi Kichizaemon (d. 1884), a Hōshō-school *shite* actor, is an example of the first category. He attempted what Gerald Groemer calls "another reinvention of nō"[216] when he formed an unprecedented cross-theatre troupe in Tokyo called *Azuma nō kyōgen* (Nō and Kyōgen of Eastern Japan). He was joined by Fukuō Shigejūrō (1863–1898), head performer of the Fukuō *waki* school, and the Sagi-school kyōgen performer Namekawa Shōsaburō (1820–1903), both former official performers of the *bakufu*, but also by commoners and artists of other traditions. The troupe incorporated elements from *ningyō jōruri* and kabuki, especially its music and dance, into their performances. Like many others engaged in similar experiments, this troupe

---

215 Miyamoto 2017a: 61–66.
216 Groemer 1998b: 132–33.

was fairly popular. Once the novelty had worn off, however, support waned and the troupe disbanded around 1885 with most members leaving the theatre world. Such experimental nō performers found it difficult to return to one of the nō schools, partly because their engagement with kabuki performers was considered detrimental to the art of nō.

Those who fall into the second category attempted to revive the performance contexts of Edo-period nō and reinstate its system of patronage. They initiated their project by organizing small performances on nō stages in their homes and by targeting new elites and the nouveaux riches with their *keiko nō* (training nō). They subsequently ventured into different performance contexts but pursued rather conventional approaches. The activities of Umewaka Minoru I, as recorded in his diary *Umewaka Minoru nikki* (covering 1849–1907) are representative. He had already revived his monthly *keiko nō* when he was dismissed by the Meiji government in 1871. From 1872 onward, he began to coordinate performances at his home, which were open to everyone who could afford to purchase a ticket. Like other performers, such as Kongō Tadaichi or Misawa Seitarō (dates unknown) of the Kita school, Minoru I prepared larger events as well, which he advertised as *kankyo* or *gomen kanjin nō*—that is, "*kanjin nō* officially authorized by the Meiji government" (fig. 1.22). They evoked both Edo-period *kanjin nō* and official support by the current government, with successful performances attracting up to eight hundred spectators per day.[217] Minoru I also traveled to various places as a hired performer. In 1873, for instance, he went to Kasukabe in Saitama Prefecture for a performance of *jinji nō* at the Kasukabe Hachiman Jinja in July and to Odawara in Kanagawa Prefecture in October for a five-day nō performance commissioned by an influential citizen who administered the post station of Odawara along the Tōkaidō highway.[218] Although fairly traditional, the revivalist attempts of established performers such as Umewaka Minoru I proved triumphant. At this point in their history, nō performers managed to survive without the support of any major patrons.

1.8.3 Peers' Nō, the Establishment of the Nōgakusha and the Shiba Nōgakudō

By 1869, the daimyō and the court aristocracy had merged into an elite class called *kazoku*, a hereditary peerage that was abolished only in 1947. Former daimyō were requested to relocate to Tokyo when the prefectures were established in 1871, and there they soon created networks with other members of

---

217 *Umewaka Minoru nikki* 2: 357a–68b.
218 *Umewaka Minoru nikki* 3: 27b–28b, 32a, 35b, 37a–38a.

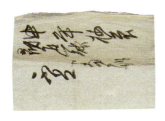

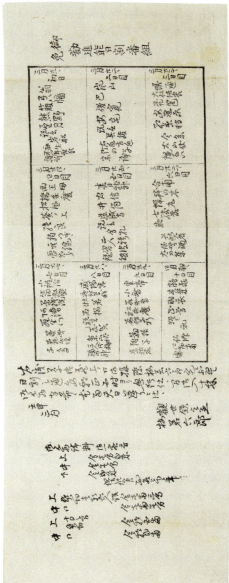

FIGURE 1.22   Daily Program of an Officially Authorized Kanjin nō (Gomen kanjin nō hiwari bangumi) held at Umewaka Minoru's residence in 1872. Late 19th century. Woodblock-printed sheet. 16.2 × 42.2 cm. Noh Theatre Research Institute, Hōsei University, Tokyo

the *kazoku*. The Kazoku Kaikan (Peers' Assembly Hall), a club founded in 1874, provided an outlet for socializing, and nō served the function of a shared social and cultural denominator. This manifested in *kazoku nō* (Peers' Nō), nō for and by the new peerage, which became overwhelmingly popular among the upper classes around the same time. In these circles, nō became conceptualized as a national symbol, which had to be protected and conserved. Members of the *kazoku* had nō stages built in their mansions, trained in nō, and intermittently took the stage themselves in ways similar to the Edo-period nō practices in daimyō residences. The former daimyō of the Kaga domain, Maeda Nariyasu (1811–1884), for example, celebrated the construction of a nō stage in his Tokyo mansion with a luxurious nō performance on April 4, 1875, which was attended by the prominent statesman Prince Iwakura Tomomi (1825–1883).[219]

Iwakura would become a key figure in the further evolution of nō: he exercised a crucial influence on nō's image as a sophisticated accomplishment for the elites. From 1871 to 1873, he had led embassies to the United States and Europe, where, among other things, he was intrigued by opera performances, which he perceived as a social gathering of the political elite. With his return to Japan, he sought to give nō an equivalent function in society and that would elevate it to *the* representative national performing art.[220] After he became president of the Kazoku Kaikan in 1876, he pursued his vision by first creating connections between *kazoku* members—especially from the imperial family—with nō performers.

A nō performance on April 4, 1876, at his residence marked the beginning of *gyōkei nō* (nō attended by a member of the imperial family), and it soon became a regular event at *kazoku* mansions. This first *gyōkei nō* by Umewaka Minoru I, Maeda Nariyasu, and Hōshō Kurō Tomoharu was attended by the Meiji emperor (1852–1912; r. 1867–1912), the emperor's consort Haruko (1849–1914), and the empress dowager Eishō (1835–1897). Within a few years, nō developed into what Iwakura had envisioned. In 1878, a nō stage was built at the Aoyama detached palace where Eishō resided (fig. 1.23); this was matched by the appointment of Hōshō Kurō, Kongō Tadaichi, Umewaka Minoru I, Kanze Kiyotaka, who had moved back to Tokyo in 1875, and the Izumi-school kyōgen performer Miyake Shōichi (1824–1885) as official nō performers (*o-nō goyō-gakari*) by the Imperial Household Ministry (Kunaishō).[221]

Nō and kyōgen performers were in high demand, and many former daimyō were eager to place the performers they had employed during the Edo period in

---

219   *Umewaka Minoru nikki* 3: 132b–34b. On *kazoku nō*, see Kagaya 2005.
220   See Jansen 2002: 355–61; 474–76.
221   *Umewaka Minoru nikki* 3: 225a–b.

FIGURE 1.23   *Illustration of a Nō Performance at the Temporary Aoyama Imperial Palace (Aoyama kari kōkyo onō no zu)* with Umewaka Minoru performing before Emperor Meiji, July 5, 1878. By Yōshū Chikanobu (1838–1912). 1878. Color woodblock print. 36.9 × 74.3 cm. Noh Theatre Research Institute, Hōsei University, Tokyo

prominent positions. The former daimyō Nakagawa Hisanari (1850–1897) and Hosokawa Morihisa (1839–1893) were leading figures in the *kazoku nō* activities. Although the four nō performers appointed by the Imperial Household Ministry were former *bakufu* performers, Miyake Shōichi had initially performed for the powerful Maeda Nariyasu in the Kaga domain and moved to Tokyo during the *kazoku nō* boom in 1874. Other performers followed, including Yamamoto Tōjirō I (1836–1902), a kyōgen performer of the Oka domain (present-day Ōita Prefecture); the *kotsuzumi* player Misu Kingo (1832–1910) (also Oka domain); and Sakurama Banma (1836–1917), a Konparu-school town actor and former *jinji nō-dayū* of the Gion Sha (present-day Kitaoka Jinja) in Kumamoto, Kyushu. Both Tōjirō I and Banma relocated to the capital in 1879.

Under the aegis of the *kazoku*, the Kairakusha (Association for Public Entertainment) was established in 1880, and with it the term *sarugaku* was replaced by the term *nōgaku* as a general reference to both nō and kyōgen. The foundation of this association was a coalescence of several different trains of occurrences and strategic measures. In 1879, Iwakura Tomomi had met Ulysses S. Grant (1822–1885), the former president of the United States (1869–1877), at a banquet, and it is reported that Grant asked whether there was any music native to Japan. Iwakura decided to invite Grant to a nō performance at his mansion on August 7, 1879. The *Iwakura kō jikki* (*Authentic Records of Lord*

Iwakura) notes that this marked the beginning of Iwakura's efforts to "preserve *nōgaku* and to transmit it for eternity."[222]

Whether his exchange with Grant took place as described in the *Iwakura kō jikki* cannot be verified, but two points merit attention: 1) the inquiry about a form of genuine Japanese culture, and 2) the intent to preserve nō and kyōgen as a symbol of Japanese identity. Iwakura and his peers seized on these suggestions, creating a new link—namely, that between nō and Japanese nationalism. The direct result was the formation of the Kairakusha. Besides Iwakura, the founding members included three former daimyō who were great supporters of nō in their domains—Maeda Nariyasu, Ikeda Mochimasa (1839–1899), and Tōdō Takakiyo (1837–1889)—in addition to two former court aristocrats, Kujō Michitaka (1839–1906) and Bōjō Toshitada (1826–1881). By the time the Kairakusha was renamed Nōgakusha (Nōgaku Association) in 1881, it had nearly sixty members, all peers and was financially supported by the empress dowager Eishō.

The Nōgakusha's primary goal was to create an environment where nō and kyōgen could thrive as national performing arts and where the public might experience the superiority of Japanese culture. Its statutes noted that: "The central meaning of the establishment of Kairakusha is the preservation and promotion of the way of the art of *nōgaku*, the construction of a theatre where the public and future generations can be entertained, and advancing the full development of the art."[223] This was realized with the construction of the Shiba Nōgakudō (Nō Theatre) in Tokyo's Shiba Park (see ch. 7 *Material Culture*, 7.5). The grand opening of this nō theatre in April 1881 was celebrated for three days with a *gyōkei nō* for the empress dowager Eishō on the 16th, *kazoku nō* on the 17th, and nō open to the public on the 18th. The main performers were Umewaka Minoru I and Hōshō Kurō Tomoharu, supported by Kanze Kiyotaka, Kongō Tadaichi, and Sakurama Banma. In the years to follow, *gyōkei nō* and *kazoku nō* were performed regularly at the Shiba Nōgakudō under the management of the Nōgakusha. There were also performances at the Shiba Nōgakudō for foreign visitors, such as an event on June 21, 1894, organized for the American operatic soprano Amalia Mignon "Minnie" Hauk (1851–1929; fig. 1.24a–b).

Kongō Tadaichi, Umewaka Minoru I, and Kanze Kiyotaka maneuvered themselves into a difficult position in December 1880 when they signed a notification stating that they would discontinue public nō performances in an effort to avoid the taxes they had to pay for these. They declared that they

---

222 *Iwakura kō jikki* 2: 1674–75. On nō performances for foreign dignitaries, see Kagaya 2005: esp. 230–33.
223 Furukawa 1969: 26.

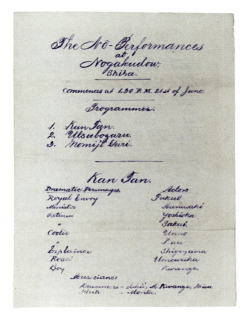

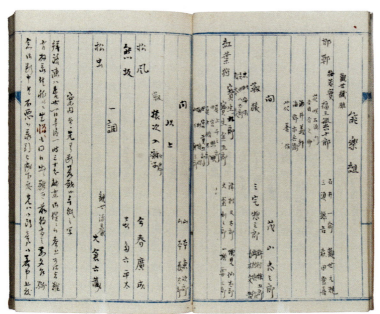

FIGURE 1.24A–B   a) English program for a performance of *Kantan*, *Utsubozaru*, and *Momijigari* at the Shiba Nōgakudō on June 21, 1894, organized for the American operatic soprano Amalia Mignon "Minnie" Hauk and b) record of the performance in the journal of the Shiba Nōgakudō, *News from the Nō Theatre* (*Nōgakudō kiji*). Late 19th century. Ink on paper. (Program) 26.9 × 20.0 cm; (record book) 23.6 × 15.4 cm. Kōzan Bunko, Hōsei University, Tokyo

would only pursue *nō utai shinan*, or "instructing in nō chant." By becoming "nō teachers," they were no longer permitted to organize nō performances for a larger public, only small-scale performances in their mansions for elites that were reportedly free of charge and by this they had officially quit the nō scene. The first monthly nō at the Umewaka mansion after the notification was in January 1881, and it was accompanied by the following announcement: "Today we do not request an admission fee. Instead, we ask for a donation as a gesture of your appreciation."[224] As nō teachers, the performers were able to evade the taxes that came with public nō performances. This declaration is proof that their financial situation must have been dire.

The establishment of the Nōgakusha and the construction of the Shiba Nōgakudō symbolized the assurance of the survival, indeed the restoration, of nō and kyōgen as major performing arts. The support of Iwakura Tomomi and other patrons from the *kazoku*, including the imperial family, promised a glorious and secure future devoted to a sophisticated performing art for the upper classes. At least that is how we might interpret Konparu Hiroshige's move back to Tokyo in order to engage in an active series of performances in the autumn of 1881. With the first performance of the eleven-year-old Kita Chiyozō (later Roppeita XIV; 1874–1971) as official head of the Kita school at the Shiba Nōgakudō in 1884, all five *iemoto* had made their comeback in Tokyo. Nevertheless, the Nōgakusha was unable to make good on its promise. The Association failed to raise sufficient funding to manage the Shiba Nōgakudō, especially after donations from the imperial household ceased in 1898.

Around the same time, the performers, who by then had understood that they depended entirely on a few powerful patrons, made efforts to liberate themselves from the influence of the Nōgakusha. Each school founded its own association, which also operated its own theatre. In 1893, the Kita-ryū Nōgakukai (Kita-School Nōgaku Association), later the Kitakai (Kita Association), was founded along with the Kita Nōgakudō. This was followed by the Hōshōkai (Hōshō Association) and the Hōshō Nōgakudō in 1898, and by the Kanzekai (Kanze Association) and the Kanze Nōgakudō in 1900. These efforts did not mean that the performers distanced themselves from their elite audiences or declined to promote nō's status as national art. Nevertheless, the Shiba Nōgakudō gradually lost its significance, and in 1902 the theatre closed its doors forever. The nō stage itself was transferred to Yasukuni Jinja, where it is still located today.

---

224 The notification is in possession of the Kanze Bunko and can be accessed online. See *Sarugaku haigyō kakumen* under References: *Websites of Works Cited* below; *Umewaka Minoru nikki* 3: 346b–47a.

1.8.4 Nō during the First Sino-Japanese (1894–1895) and Russo-Japanese (1904–1905) Wars

The networks that performers created themselves, or were integrated into, during the Meiji period were not only artistic cliques of nō connoisseurs but also political circles that carried imperialist implications. Iwakura Tomomi and his peers' attempts at reshaping or reinterpreting nō in order to present it as a unique Japanese cultural achievement were intended to project to the imperialist nations of the West, which had forced unequal treaties upon the country, the image of a mature nation that held its own imperialist ambition and potential. Nō performers profited from the patronage of nationalist groups and their ideological backgrounds. The Shiba Nōgakudō afforded them a new and prestigious performance space, enabling them to reach out to diverse audiences and to generate an income. An examination of the period between the First Sino-Japanese (1894–1895) and Russo-Japanese (1904–1905) Wars makes clear that performers' involvement with political matters was neither passive nor innocent. They actively contributed to Japan's militarization and mobilization.[225]

In November 1894, four months after the outbreak of the First Sino-Japanese War, the Shiba Nōgakudō launched a three-day *kanjin nō* in order to collect funds for the war effort. Its announcement declared: "For the unity of the whole nation, which is experiencing a war without precedent, the nō performers have united to demonstrate their 'patriotic spirit.'"[226] The plays for the program were obviously chosen to reflect the era's *zeitgeist*: *Haku Rakuten* (Bai Juyi, 772–846, a poet of the Tang dynasty) describes a competition between the eponymously named Chinese poet Bai Juyi (772–846) and his Japanese rival Sugawara no Michizane (845–903), who possesses the superior wisdom. It ends with Bai Juyi being expelled by the Japanese gods. In *Tōzumō* (*Sumō in China*), a Japanese *sumō* wrestler travels to China where he defeats wrestlers, one after the other. Among the 131 performers who assembled for this staging were Kanze Kiyokado (1867–1911), Konparu Hiroshige, Hōshō Kurō Tomoharu, Kita Roppeita XIV, Umewaka Minoru I, and Kongō Ichijirō Ujishige (1819–1895). They voluntarily played a role in supporting the home front, and for the first time in its history nō displayed a national awareness. The mere number of participants emphasizes the performers' self-perception, as well as their patrons' understanding of nō, as a symbol of Japanese national identity. When the Russo-Japanese War erupted some ten years later, similar *kanjin nō*

---

225 On nō during this period, see Kagaya 2008. See also Miyamoto 2017b.
226 The quote is from the *Gunshi gien kanjin nō hōkoku* (*Report on the Kanjin nō to Raise Money for the War Effort*) manuscript in the Kanze Bunko; see *Gunshi gien kanjin nō hōkoku* below under References: *Websites of Works Cited*.

were organized throughout the country in an effort to offer financial support to the military. Since the Shiba Nōgakudō had already closed its doors, there were no large-scale performances coordinated between the five schools, but each arranged its own fundraising events.

The imperialist ideology that led to the First Sino-Japanese War, and persisted through the end of the Asia-Pacific War (1941–1945), inspired the composition of *shinsaku nō* with propagandistic rhetoric and content (see ch. 4 *Plays*, 4.11).[227] Since their topics were contemporary and catered to the needs and convictions of the times, these plays also came to be known as *jikyoku nō*, or "current situation nō." Some *shinsaku nō* were never performed onstage and were circulated merely as texts, while others were staged as full-fledged nō performances mostly aimed at soliciting donations for the Imperial Army. *Sankan* (*The Three Korean Kingdoms*, 1895) by Takagi Nakaba (1827–ca. 1913), a well-connected nō enthusiast from Osaka, for example, exploits the story of the legendary Empress Jingū (fl. 2nd–3rd c. CE) and her mythic conquest of the Korean Peninsula. The work was never performed onstage. *Mikuni no hikari* (*The Blazing Light of Our Nation*), a straightforward one-scene play, consists of a single *otoko mai* (man's dance) and recapitulates Japan's glorious victory. Written by Mōri Motonori (1839–1896), the former daimyō of the Chōfu domain (present-day Yamaguchi Prefecture), with melody and movements by Umewaka Minoru I, it was performed at Umewaka's mansion during the monthly nō in 1896. Among the *shinsaku nō* that were composed during the Russo-Japanese War were *Washi* (*The Eagle*) by the nō scholar Ōwada Tateki (1875–1910) with melody by Kanze Kiyokado (1867–1911), *Ikusagami* (*The War God*), a *shinsaku nō* of the Kongō school, *Kamikaze* (*Divine Wind*) of the Kita school, and *Takachiho* of the Hōshō school.[228]

Between 1905 and 1945, nō performances by professional actors were also organized in the *gaichi* (Japan's overseas territories), and there was at least one performance by semiprofessional and amateur actors in the United States

---

227 On some of these *shinhisaku nō*, see Kagaya 2008; Smethurst and Smethurst 2008. These *shinsaku nō* were also inspired by Emperor Meiji's short *utai*, "*Seikan eki*" ("Seonghwan Station"), in which he celebrated Japan's victory over Chinese forces in the July 1894 Battle of Seonghwan in Korea. With musical setting (*fushitsuke*) by Umewaka Minoru I, the *utai* turned into a popular war song. *Umewaka Minoru nikki* 5: 302a.

228 On Takagi Nakaba, see Nakao 2013. On *Mikuni no hikari*, see Kagaya 2008: 24–26. Umewaka Minoru I describes the development of *Mikuni no hikari* in several entries of his diary. *Umewaka Minoru nikki* 5: 266a–355b. Two versions of the play are in Tanaka, ed. 1987–1998: 14: 179–85. On *Washi* and *Ikusagami*, see Scholz and Oshikiri 2004: 23–59. *Washi* is published in Tanaka, ed. 1987–1998: 17: 167–79. Takachiho was the supposed location where the legendary Ninigi, the first human emperor in the dynastic line of the sun deity, Amaterasu Ōmikami, descended from the heavens.

(fig. 1.25).²²⁹ With Taiwan colonized (1895) and the Korean Peninsula a protectorate (1910), Japanese settled in the new territories. This led to the formation of large settler communities, most significantly in Manchuria or in cities such as Qinghai and Shanghai. The lives of the colonizers do not seem to have differed greatly from that in Japan, and this included the cultural practices of *nō utai* and *mai* (nō dance). Politically, such communities were instrumentalized for the promotion of Japanese nationalism and the wartime effort, and according to Kagaya Shinko, nō became a "mascot for colonialist expansion" and a means to foster morals among the Japanese colonizers who were the main audience of such performances. As for the performers, it is unclear "whether [they] resisted the use of their art as a means to promote nationalism—and if so, in what way and to what degree."²³⁰

Most of the overseas performances took place in private Japanese residences where the tatami room (*zashiki*) served as a nō stage, or in public halls where a simple, temporary nō stage was installed. More elaborate performances were staged during festivals at shrines established by the Japanese colonizers or during celebrations that were meant to display the power of the "Great Empire of Japan" (Dai Nihon Teikoku). The first performance in the *gaichi*, for example, was held on May 25, 1905, in Keijō (the Japanese name for Seoul), to celebrate the Keifu Railroad (J. *Keifu tetsudō*) that connected Keijō and Busan and the operation of which began in 1908. Kanze Kiyokado, one of the most renowned nō performers of the time, Katayama Kurōsaburō, and others performed a two-day nō on a regular nō stage that was constructed exclusively for this event in front of the city's historical Southern Great Gate (K. Namdaemun, also Sungnyemun). Five months later in the same year, Kita Roppeita XIV performed in Taiwan.²³¹

1.9 Nō from World War I through the 1980s
Eike Grossmann and Miyamoto Keizō

1.9.1 Gentlemen's Nō and Women's Nō in the Early Twentieth Century

During the first decade of the twentieth century the performance contexts and audiences that developed with the Meiji period were firmly established, and both nō and kyōgen performers enjoyed relative stability. They profited

---

229 On performances in Japan's occupied territories, see Kagaya 2001; Satō 2020. On performances in the United States, see Satō 2018.
230 Kagaya 2001: 264–65.
231 Kagaya 2001: 261.

FIGURE 1.25 *Tsuchigumo. Shite*, Nishimura Rakuten (Kanze school). Dedication performance by semiprofessional and amateur actors at the (Higashi) Honganji sub-temple in California (presumably Los Angeles), September 5, 1926. Photo: Kōzan Bunko, Hōsei University, Tokyo

from the unprecedented economic boom that was created by World War I and were able to significantly extend the range of their activities by appealing to yet another target group. While many members of the former elite class (the *kazoku*) who had sponsored them faced impoverishment, men of financial power, most notably *zaibatsu* entrepreneurs and founders, advanced quickly to provide the economic basis of Japan's imperialism and become important political players.[232] These men engaged in *shinshi nō* (gentlemen's nō), and at

---

232 The Meiji period saw the integration of Edo-period and newly founded enterprises into powerful *zaibatsu*, which amassed huge profits with diverse businesses. *Zaibatsu* had begun to show signs of their economic power already in the late nineteenth century and increased their wealth during the brief boom of the WWI economy—that is, the "Taishō Bubble" of 1915–1920. The expansion of military manufacturing as well as the colonization of Taiwan, the annexation of the Korean Peninsula, and the invasion of the Chinese

the same time their wives and daughters began to challenge conservative performance concepts by producing *fujin nō* (women's nō), asserting their equal right to take the nō stage (see ch. 3 *Training*, 3.3). The fact that the wealthy upper class engaged in nō is nothing novel in its history. Affluent merchants from Kyoto had been the pillars of *tesarugaku nō* in the fifteenth century, and financiers had shaped Osaka's nō culture from the late eighteenth century onward. In the Meiji period, this role was taken up by the elites of politically well-connected financial institutions.

The members of the *kazoku* who founded the Nōgakusha in 1880 acknowledged the important social, economic, and political position of these "gentlemen" by granting them membership in 1882. Among the new members were Mitsui Takenosuke (also Takahisa; 1855–1914) and Yasuda Zenjirō (1838–1921), who were immediately appointed administrators of the Nōgakusha.

Mitsui Takenosuke, a scion of the Edo-period Mitsui merchant family, and Yasuda Zenjirō, founder of the *zaibatsu* centered around Yasuda Bank, had already devoted themselves to nō training around 1880. Mitsui trained with Umewaka Minoru I and Yasuda with Hōshō Kurō Tomoharu.[233] By 1910, the old and new financial elites had replaced the *kazoku* as patrons of nō and began to engage in nō in a similar fashion. They enjoyed nō as a form of entertainment, applied themselves enthusiastically to nō training, and performed nō onstage. Some five years later, around 1915, their nō practice was introduced as *shinshi nō*, a creation that carried the freshness of the word *shinshi*, itself coined as a translation of the English "gentleman." The flamboyance of their nō practice is exemplified by the *Tōzai gōdō shinshi nō* (Joint Gentlemen's Nō from Eastern and Western Japan), organized by Tokyo *zaibatsu* entrepreneurs in Osaka on April 17–18, 1915. The event gathered together businessmen from the Kyoto-Osaka region, and all the *iemoto* from Tokyo were also required to travel to Osaka to participate.[234]

At the same time, women claimed a more prominent position in the world of nō. Although women were welcomed as students during the Meiji period, they were not considered suitable as nō performers, and it was not until 1948 that female performers were allowed onstage in professional nō performances. The early twentieth century, however, may be seen as a stepping stone toward this ultimate achievement. Japan's political and social liberalism between 1912 and 1926, which came to be referred to as the "Taishō Democracy," affected

---

mainland also contributed to the thriving of *zaibatsu* conglomerates. See Jansen 2002: 376–77, 528–36.
233 See Miura 2018.
234 The event was repeated on April 7–8, 1917. On *shinshi nō*, see Miyamoto 2013.

the self-perception of male performers, fostered the self-confidence of female performers, and generally changed the organization of nō.[235] The question whether women should be granted permission to perform nō in public became a compelling issue, which was closely related to the Josei Kaihō Undō (Women's Liberation Movement). Aspects of this development, seen from the perspective of Taishō-period nō practice, are briefly introduced here.

Closely related to the practice of *shinshi nō*, upper-class women devoted themselves to nō training and demanded permission to present their skills onstage. Their activities centered around the Osaka scene and were subsumed under the generalized term, *fujin nō*. In 1916, for instance, the Ōsaka Nōgaku Shashinkai (Osaka Nōgaku Photography Association) organized the event, *Fujin yōkyoku hayashi taikai* (Women's Nō and *Hayashi* Gathering), in which women performed *utai* and instrumental music (*hayashi*) from nō plays.[236] In 1921, the performance of *Hyakuman* as a *han nō*, or "half nō," that is just the second half of the play, by Fujita Tomiko (1882–1976), the wife of the head of the Fujita *zaibatsu*, Fujita Heitarō (1869–1940), sent shockwaves through the nō community.[237]

Up to that point, most events with female actors comprised performances of *utai, shimai, hayashi*, or abridged nō, but this changed in the 1920s. One of the most remarkable occurred on May 7, 1922, at the country residence of the socialite Masaoka Kasaburō (1867–1950) on Awaji Island in Hyōgo Prefecture (fig. 1.26a–b). The announcement of the production already seemed to hold great promise. The *Ōsaka Asahi Shinbun* ran a long article on May 5 entitled "Nō and Kyōgen by Only Women, Starting a Revolution in the Nō Community, the Enthusiasm of Osaka's Women's Organizations."[238] The female performers were mainly women from Osaka, among them Masaoka Fuyuko and her two daughters Kayoko and Kana (all dates unknown). No male performers appeared onstage for the four nō, one *maibayashi*, and three kyōgen. Since the event was advertised beforehand, the audience was diverse—islanders from Awaji took their seats next to spectators from Kyoto, Osaka, Kobe, and even Tokyo. Reactions were enthusiastic, spurring discussions about female performers. As a result, *iemoto* from each of the five schools were required to justify and elaborate on the generally extremely conservative attitudes of their respective schools regarding women performing nō onstage.[239]

---

235   Compare Geilhorn 2011: 98–107.
236   "Fujin yōkyoku hayashikai no seikyō": 15; Utai 1916: 20.
237   Itō Maki 2013.
238   Itō Maki 2013: 21.
239   See Itō Maki 2013; Geilhorn 2015.

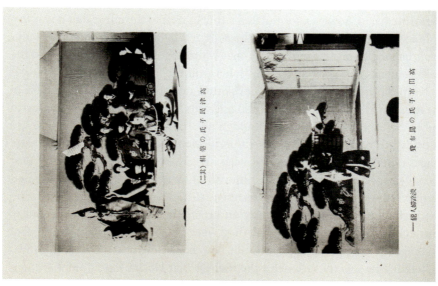

FIGURE 1.26A–B Women's nō (*fujin nō*) on Awaji Island, May 7, 1922: a) *Makiginu*; *shite*, Takatsu Tamiko (Kanze school) and b) (top) the same *Makiginu* performance and (bottom) kyōgen *Koburi*; *shite*, Takada Ichiko (school unknown). Photographs reprinted in *Nōgaku Journal* (*Nōgaku gahō*). Noh Theatre Research Institute, Hōsei University, Tokyo

1.9.2 Disputes about Performance Spaces and Attempts to Popularize Nō in the 1920s and the 1930s

Only two months after the *fujin nō* on Awaji Island, another incident led to controversy over the spaces appropriate for the performance of nō. On July 9, 1922, the Kanze *iemoto* Motoshige (1895–1939) traveled with a group of about thirty performers to Yamagata where he was informed that the performance would not be held at a temporary *nōgakudō* in the city's Daini Kōen (Second Park) as planned. Rather, it was to be moved to the kabuki playhouse Chitoseza. Nō performers had, however, formulated a rule in 1894 to the effect that it was forbidden to stage plays "in [kabuki] theatres, red-light districts, and other inappropriate locations." Accordingly, Kanze Motoshige immediately canceled the performances and left Yamagata with his group.[240]

Nō performances from the Meiji period onward were frequently held in locations without actual nō stages, and this included temporary stages in public halls or other facilities. Although nō spaces had diversified, it was still considered inappropriate to stage a performance on another type of theatre stage, especially those associated with kabuki. For events such as the 1907 Tōkyō Kangyō Hakurankai (Tokyo Industrial Exhibition), nō and kabuki performances were integrated as sideshows. Nevertheless, nō performers unrelentingly persisted in perpetuating an artistic hierarchy and only agreed to participate on the condition that they were the first performers to set foot on stage. If this agreement could not be reached or met, the invitation was rejected. This was the case with the request that Hōshō Kurō Tomoharu perform during the first anniversary celebrations of the Teikoku Gekijō (Imperial Theatre), the first Western-style theatre in Japan, which opened in Tokyo in 1911.[241]

The 1922 controversy about the kabuki stage in Yamagata occasioned a discussion about how nō performers and their supporters envisioned the future of nō. It was argued that performers should actively seek new audiences and that nō should evolve into a form of entertainment with broader public appeal. Nonetheless, in 1925 the *iemoto* of all the schools decided in a "sectional meeting of the heads of the nō houses" (*sōke bukai*) to reinforce the prohibition:

---

240 This regulation was published alongside nineteen others in *Hinode Shinbun* on June 15, 1894. The Yamagata incident was reported by *Yamagata Shinbun* on October 7, 1922.

241 Itō Maki 2000. The performers' dismissive behavior toward kabuki was likely also related to the treatment of kabuki by the Tokugawa *bakufu* during the Edo period and the prejudice that kabuki was a vulgar performance for the masses. This was in contradistinction to nō, which defined itself as an elite form of entertainment. See Shively 2002: 46–47.

"Since nō performances on [kabuki] theatre stages are not a traditional convention, [we] reject them."[242]

Some *iemoto* changed their strict dismissal of other stages after the Great Kantō Earthquake of September 1, 1923, struck the Kantō area (Tokyo was the epicenter). Numerous lives were lost, and those who survived lost their homes and belongings in the ensuing conflagration. Almost all private nō stages in Tokyo were reduced to ash; nō families lost treasured costumes, masks, historical manuscripts, and much more. The challenges of rebuilding in the wake of the disaster were enormous, and the performers agreed to participate in a *yagai nō* (outdoors nō) coordinated by the *Tōkyō Nichinichi Shinbun* on November 30, 1923 (fig. 1.27). This *yagai nō* was advertised as an event to provide comfort to the disaster victims, and it took place on the temporary stage of the Hibiya Yagai Ongakudō (Hibiya Open-Air Concert Hall). It marked the earliest modern nō performance that was not on a nō stage proper. An audience of around ten thousand people attended this spectacle free of charge, and this probably was the first time for many to witness a nō performance. The organizers hailed it as "nō's emancipation from an entertainment of the wealthy class to a performance for the benefit of the general public."[243]

In December 1923, a group of performers, among them Kanze Yoshiyuki (1885–1940) and Ōtsuki Jūzō (1889–1962) who had appeared in this *yagai nō*, founded the Nōgaku Kankōkai (Association for the Enjoyment and Promotion of Nōgaku). One of the Association's goals was the popularization of nō and the reorganization of nō schools. For the *Minshūteki nōgaku taikai* (Grand Assembly of Nō and Kyōgen for the Masses), a performance at Osaka City Public Hall, Association members ignored the rule of not performing on stages other than those reserved for nō, and the revenues were divided evenly among the performers. Discord ensued between the members of the Association and conservative performers. Kanze Motoshige, for example, did not approve of the activities of the Nōgaku Kankōkai and denied them access to nō stages in Osaka, which limited their options for performance spaces and forced them to improvise.[244]

The protectionist reactions of traditionalists notwithstanding, a number of performers worked to overcome nō's conventional framework. The tackling of gender issues and the expansion of the performance space from specialized nō stages to stages in general, alongside attempts to appeal to the general public, all belonged to this fresh vision for nō. At the same time, the performers

---

242   Compare Kanze 1926. See Yokoyama 2015: 129–30.
243   Shimei 1924: 78. See Itō Maki 2008.
244   Tomo 1924: 91–95.

FIGURE 1.27   Outdoor nō (*yagai nō*) organized by the *Tōkyō Nichinichi Shinbun* on November 30, 1923. Photograph reprinted in the *World of Nō* (*Yōkyokukai*). Noh Theatre Research Institute, Hōsei University, Tokyo

were quick in adapting the latest media as a means to disseminate nō further. In 1903, the year gramophone records were introduced in Japan, Hōshō Kurō Tomoharu was among the first to release several recordings of complete nō plays. With the advent of radio broadcasting in 1924, broadcasts of nō were among the most popular programs, and in 1928, the recently constructed Hōshō Nōgakudō—the original stage burnt down in 1923 following the Great Kantō Earthquake of September 1, 1923—was equipped with a radio relay from which nō was broadcasted nationwide several times a year. Through records and radio broadcasts, nō became accessible to audiences not living near a *nōgakudō* or in *gaichi* overseas.[245]

---

245   For a list of nō records distributed between 1903 and 1942, see Satō 2017: 135, 140–43, 146. On radio broadcasting and nō, see Satō 2014.

1.9.3 Nō during the Asia-Pacific War

The Taishō period (1912–1926) was accompanied by a wave of democratization and liberalization that was supported by technical advancements. Performers profited from this environment, which offered fresh opportunities with regard to performance spaces, contexts, and dissemination. But the social and political climate underwent fundamental changes in the 1930s. With the rise of militarism and with military circles exercising steadily more influence over national politics, performers faced new hurdles. They were confronted with nationalist and imperialist criticism, censorship of their repertory, and integration into Japan's wartime mobilization machinery. Perfromers self-censored, composed, and performed patriotic nō (fig. 1.28). Additionally, many were drafted and sent to the front.[246]

In 1938, the first cabinet of Prime Minister Konoe Fumimaro (1891–1945) passed the *Kokka sō dōin hō* (National Mobilization Law), which stipulated that the entire nation must contribute to the war effort. Nō and kyōgen performers contributed through fundraising performances (*kenkin nō*) for the military, holding *hayashi kai* for soldiers wounded on the battlefield and giving benefit performances for families whose members had been sent to war or had fallen in the fighting.[247] Apart from such efforts, most performers were able to conduct their business as usual. There was enough stability to introduce new performance formats aimed at the younger generations. After the Kita school had organized *gakusei shōtai nō* (performances for invited students) in 1926, the other schools followed suit and coordinated student invitation nō throughout the empire. From 1930 onward, the Kansai Daigaku Yōkyoku Renmei (*Yōkyoku* League of Kansai Universities), for example, staged nō and kyōgen events at schools and universities.[248] In 1939, the *iemoto* of the five schools revived the *gobandate* (five-play program) with a performance at Hōshō Nōgakudō, for which they took inspiration from Meiji-period *shiki nō* (ceremonial nō).[249]

---

246 For contemporary primary sources, such as articles from newspapers and journals, see Miyamoto 2017b: esp. 324–39.
247 For example, a *kenkin nō* on July 17, 1937, by the five schools at the Hōshō Nōgakudō, a *hayashi kai* for wounded soldiers at the Kanaoka Hospital for the Imperial Army in 1938, or nō for the families of dispatched and deceased soldiers at the Kudan Gunjin Kaikan (Kudan Soldiers' Assembly Hall, present-day Kudan Kaikan) in 1939.
248 For the events organized by the Kita school, see, e.g., "Nō to kōen no kai" 1926; "Seikō seru 'nō to kōen no kai" 1926; "Nō to kōen no kai suketchi" 1926.
249 See *Yōkyokukai* 1940. During the Meiji period *shiki nō* (ceremonial nō) were held at the Shiba Nōgakudō on June 11, 1899, with *Okina* preceding the four other plays and on November 7, 1903 at Yasukuni Jinja without *Okina* and with five nō plays instead. See *Umewaka Minoru nikki* 6: 192b–93b; *Umewaka Minoru nikki* 7: 62a–63a.

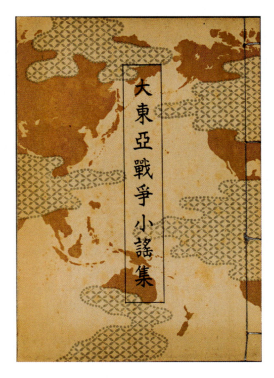

FIGURE 1.28
A Collection of Short Nō Chants on the Greater East Asia War (*Daitōa sensō koutaishū*). 1943. 21.0 × 14.8 cm. Kōzan Bunko, Hōsei University, Tokyo

While the performance in 1939 met with enthusiastic media reception, performers and their activities were under greater scrutiny by the public. For example, five years earlier, in 1934, right-wing circles protested against nō plays that allegedly disrespected the emperor, which prompted the *iemoto*'s decision to remove the plays *Semimaru* and *Ohara gokō* from their repertory. Thereafter, the schools censored their repertory, either by withdrawing plays altogether or by revising inappropriate content. In April 1940, the *iemoto* went a step further when they discussed every single play of their current repertory and revised phrases that might be interpreted as disrespectful of the emperor or the imperial family. In December 1940, it was finally decided to refrain from performing plays such as *Kuzu, Matsuyama tengu, Nue, Uneme,* and *Sesshōseki*, since impersonating a member of the imperial family onstage was likewise perceived as inappropriate (fig. 1.29).[250]

With Japan's attack on Pearl Harbor in 1941, the performers who at that time were organized into the Nōgakukai (Nōgaku Society, est. 1896) developed several war-related formats such as *nōgaku hōkoku* (patriotism nō) or *ian nō to*

---

250 Nakamura 2004.

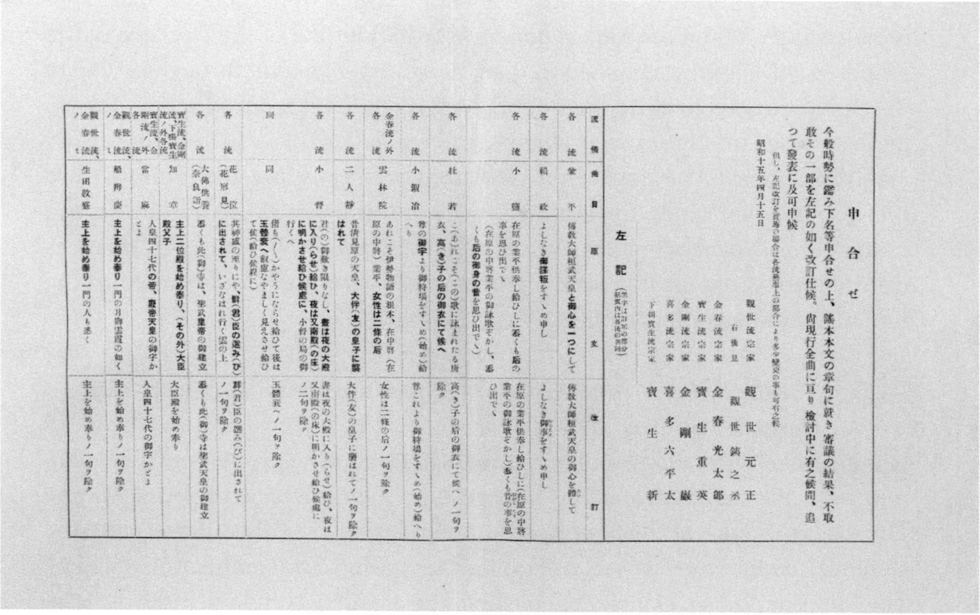

申合せ

今般時勢に鑑み下名等申合せの上、謠本本文の章句に就き審議の結果、不取敢その一部を左記の如く改訂仕候。尚現行全曲に亘り檢討中に有之候間、追つて發表に及可申候

但し、左記改訂を實施の場合は各流藝事上の都合により多少變更の事も可有之候

昭和十五年四月十五日

觀世流宗家 觀世元正
右後見 觀世鐵之丞
金春流宗家 金春光太郎
寶生流宗家 寶生重英
金剛流宗家 金剛巖
喜多流宗家 喜多六平太
下掛寶生流宗家 寶生新

左記（黑字は訂正の部分 括弧内は各流の異同）

FIGURE 1.29 *Agreement on the Revision of the Contents of Nō Plays* (*Yōkyoku shishō kaitei mōshiawase*) representing the five *shite* schools and the Hōshō *waki* school. April 5, 1940. Printed sheet. 26.0 × 41.1 cm. Kōzan Bunko, Hōsei University, Tokyo

kyōgen (relief nō/relief kyōgen). *Shinsaku nō*, some of which were explicitly written for these events, were part of these performances. The play *Chūrei* (*Loyal Spirits*) was written and performed at Kanze Nōgakudō in October 1941 in order to celebrate the appointment of Kanze Tetsunojō VII (1898–1988), Ōtsuki Jūzō, and others as committee members of the Dai Nihon Chūrei Kenshōkai (Great Japan Committee to Exalt the Loyal Spirits), which commemorated the soldiers who had died in battle. The play narrates the encounter between a man praying before a war memorial and the spirit of a fallen soldier who swears to protect his country before vanishing. It was an instant success and was performed throughout Japan.[251]

Stimulated by the positive reactions, the Kanze school concentrated its efforts on the production of *shinsaku nō*. The play *Yoshitsune* was composed by the famous poet Takahama Kiyoshi (1874–1959), *Miikusa-bune* (*The Emperor's Warship*) was commissioned by the Japanese Navy and written by the naval officer Sako Hikosaburō (d. 1944), and Kanze Tetsunojō VII was the *shite* in the premiers of both plays in October 1941 and May 1943, respectively. Records

251 Miyamoto 2017b: 329–39; Smethurst and Smethurst 2008.

of the plays went into sales shortly thereafter, which were then used for radio broadcasts.[252] When the *Kessen hijō sochi yōkō* (Outline of the Decisive Battle Emergency Decree) was issued in 1944, however, *nōgakudō* throughout Japan were either forced to close their doors or to operate on reduced schedules. Nō performances totally stopped when the air raids on Tokyo increased in early 1945, and almost all nō stages were destroyed by the ensuing fires. This was also the case in other cities, for example, with the Nunoike Nōgakudō in Nagoya or the Osaka Nōgakuden. But even during these times of crisis, performances were staged where location and circumstances permitted, for instance, at the Kudanshita Nōgakudō in Tokyo.

1.9.4 The Revival of Nō and Kyōgen in the Postwar Era and Developments through the 1980s

Japan's unconditional surrender to the Allied Powers in 1945 marked the beginning of the Occupation, and performers found themselves on the brink of ruin. The declared goals of the Supreme Commander for the Allied Powers and the General Headquarters were the demilitarization and democratization of Japan. The Meiji-period *kazoku* were abolished, the *zaibatsu* conglomerates dismantled. As a consequence, performers saw their financial infrastructure crumble with the loss of the economic power of their elite patrons.[253] Nevertheless, performers profited from their promotional activities before and during the war, especially from their early use of new media. After the end of the war, they could still rely on a group of supporters—less wealthy but nonetheless devoted—and their efforts to revive nō and kyōgen in the postwar period made use of their connections to a comfortable bourgeoisie that emerged with the country's general recovery. This target group not only comprised fervent theatregoers but included people interested in learning nō. Performers accordingly generated their main income by teaching *utai* or *shimai* to amateurs (see ch. 3 *Training*, 3.1, 3.2).[254]

Postwar nō essentially became the product of the efforts of an upcoming generation of performers who were interested in exploring the possibilities of nō as a traditional performing art in a modern context. In search of nō's potential, performers like Kanze Hisao (1925–1978), along with his brothers Kanze Hideo (1927–2007) and Kanze Shizuo (Tetsunojō VIII; 1931–2000), challenged conventional views and enthusiastically pursued a wide range of performing activities that received great attention. In 1950, Kanze Hisao founded the

---

252 Smethurst and Smethurst 2008; Kagaya 2009: 178–79.
253 On nō and kyōgen during the Occupation, see Kagaya 2009.
254 See Moore 2012.

Nōgaku Runessansu no Kai (Nōgaku Renaissance Society), followed in 1953 by the establishment of the Hana no Kai (Flower Society) by Kanze Hideo and Kanze Shizuo. Both societies traversed school boundaries, roles, and performance genres to pursue multifaceted activities intended to foster a consciousness among audiences and performers alike of nō as a flexible dramatic art and not just a reproduction or reenactment of *kata* (forms).[255] Their program included traditional nō plays, *shinsaku nō*, such as *Takahime* (*The Hawk Princess*) inspired by W. B. Yeats' one-act play *At the Hawk's Well* (1916) (see ch. 8 Reception, 8.3), and the participation in cross-genre collaborations, as in *Pierrot lunaire* (1955) by the avant-garde artist collective Jikken Kōbō (Experimental Workshop), in *Oedipus* (1971), or in Samuel Beckett's *Waiting for Godot* (1973) by Kanze Hisao's group Mei no Kai (Society of Darkness, est. 1970).[256]

Nō of the postwar era was characterized by two diametrically opposed aims: 1) the emphasis on nō as one of Japan's traditional performing arts including an even closer teacher-student relation between performers and trainees, and 2) the desire to reinvent nō as a contemporary dramatic art and to appeal to a broader viewership. In a way, both had reciprocal influence. The construction of the National Nōgakudō in Tokyo in 1983, for example, substantiated the position of nō and kyōgen as a dramatic art but also contributed to the expansion of an audience who enjoyed nō performances without learning nō themselves. With a decline in the number of amateur students, the established system of selling tickets of one's performance to students was threatened. Performers, once again, were forced to rethink nō—its position and its meaning—in contemporary society. The future of nō and kyōgen will be decided by their efforts to respond to the vagaries of the twenty-first century.

References

Akiyama Kiyoko 秋山喜代子. 2003. *Chūsei kuge shakai no kūkan to geinō* 中世公家社会の空間と芸能. Tokyo: Yamakawa Shuppansha.

Amano Fumio 天野文雄. 1995. *Okina sarugaku kenkyū* 翁猿楽研究. Osaka: Izumi Shoin.

Amano Fumio 天野文雄. 1997. *Nō ni tsukareta kenryokusha: Hideyoshi nōgaku aikōki* 能に憑かれた権力者―秀吉能楽愛好記. Tokyo: Kōdansha.

* Amaral Abranches Pinto, João do, ed. 1954. *História da igreja do Japão*. Notícias de Macau. Critical edition of the Lisbon section in Rodriguez 1620–1633.

---

255 See Quinn 1992; Rath 2003.
256 On *Pierrot lunaire*, see Tezuka 2011.

Aoyagi Yuriko 青柳有利子. 2014. *Nanbu han no nōgaku* 南部藩の能楽. Waseda Daigaku Monogurafu 早稲田大学モノグラフ 104. Tokyo: Waseda Daigaku Shuppanbu.

Araki, James T. 1978. *The Ballad-Drama of Medieval Japan*. Rutland: Tuttle.

Averbuch, Irit. 1995. *The Gods Come Dancing: A Study of the Japanese Ritual Dance of Yamabushi Kagura*. Cornell East Asia Series 79. Ithaca: Cornell University East Asia Program.

Awataguchi sarugakuki 粟田口猿楽記. In *Gunsho ruijū* 群書類従 19, edited by Zoku Gunsho Ruijū Kanseikai 続群書類従完成会, 724a–27b. (1932) 2002. Tokyo: Zoku Gunsho Ruijū Kanseikai.

Brown, Steven T. 2001. *Theatricalities of Power: The Cultural Politics of Noh*. Stanford: Stanford University Press.

Bun'an dengaku nō ki 文安田楽能記. In *Gunsho ruijū* 群書類従 19, edited by Zoku Gunsho Ruijū Kanseikai 続群書類従完成会, 712a–17a. (1932) 2002. Tokyo: Zoku Gunsho Ruijū Kanseikai.

Chikatoshi nikki 親俊日記 1. Edited by Takeuchi Rizō 竹内理三. 1967. *Zoku shiryō Taisei* 続史料大成 13. Tokyo: Rinsen Shoten.

Chōshū sarugaku denki 重修猿楽伝記. In *Nōgaku shiryō shūsei* 能楽史料集成 11, edited by Katagiri Noboru 片桐登, 5–209. 1981. Tokyo: Wan'ya Shoten.

* Cooper, Michael, trans. 2001. *João Rodrigues's Account of Sixteenth-Century Japan*. London: The Hakluyt Society. English translation of the Lisbon section in Rodriguez 1620–1633.

Daigoji shin yōroku 醍醐寺新要録. Edited by Daigoji Bunkazai Kenkyūjo 醍醐寺文化財研究所. 1991. 2 vols. Tokyo: Hōzōkan.

Daijōin jisha zōjiki 大乗院寺社雑事記. Edited by Tsuji Zennosuke 辻善之助. 1931–1936. 12 vols. Tokyo: Sankyō Shoin.

Daijōin nikki mokuroku 大乗院日記目録. In *Zoku zoku gunsho ruijū* 続々群書類従 3, edited by Kokusho Kankōkai 国書刊行会, 623–75. (1907) 1978. Tokyo: Kokusho Kankōkai.

* Danford, Richard K., Robin D. Gill, and Daniel T. Reff, trans. 2014. *The First European Description of Japan, 1585*. London: Routledge. English translation of Fróis 1585.

de Poorter, Erika. (1986) 2002. *Zeami's Talks on Sarugaku: An Annotated Translation of the Sarugaku Dangi with an Introduction on Zeami Motokiyo*. Amsterdam: J. C. Gieben. Reprinted in the series Japonica Neerlandica 2. Leiden: Hotei Publishing.

* de Poorter, Erika. 1989. "Nō which is not Nō: The Ritual Play 'Okina'." *Maske und Kothurn* 35, no. 2/3: 21–30.

Farrington, Anthony, ed. 1991. *The English Factory in Japan, 1613–1623*. 2 vols. London: The British Library.

Feltens, Frank. 2021. *Ogata Kōrin: Art in Early Modern Japan*. New Haven: Yale University Press.

Foster, Michael Dylan. 2015. *The Book of Yōkai: Mysterious Creatures of Japanese Folklore*. Oakland: University of California Press.

Fróis, Luís. 1585. *Tratado em que se contem muito susinta e abreviadamente algumas contradições e diferenças de custumes antre a gente de Europa e esta provincia de Japão*. Biblioteca de la Real Academia de la Historia, Madrid, 9/7236, ff. 247–286v.

"Fujin yōkyoku hayashikai no seikyō" 婦人謡曲囃子会の盛況. 1916. *Nōgaku shashinkai* 能楽写真界 11: 15.

Furukawa Hisashi 古川久. 1969. *Meiji nōgakushi josetsu* 明治能楽史序説. Tokyo: Wan'ya Shoten.

Fūshi kaden 風姿花伝. In *Renga ronshū, nōgaku ronshū, haikairon* 連歌論集, 能楽論集, 俳諧論, edited by Okuda Isao 奥田勲, Omote Akira 表章, Horikiri Minoru 堀切実, and Fukumoto Ichirō 復本一郎, 207–91. 2001. *Shinpen Nihon koten bungaku zenshū* 新編古典文学全集 88. Tokyo: Shōgakukan.

Geilhorn, Barbara. 2011. *Weibliche Spielräume: Frauen im japanischen Nō- und Kyōgen-Theater*. Munich: iudicium.

Geilhorn, Barbara. 2015. "From Private *zashiki* to the Public Stage: Female Spaces in Early 20th Century Nō." *Asian Theatre Journal* 32, no. 2: 440–63.

Geinōshi Kenkyūkai 芸能史研究会. 1983. *Kodai chūsei* 古代―中世. *Nihon geinōshi* 日本芸能史 2. Tokyo: Hōsei Daigaku Shuppankyoku.

Gohōkōinki 後法興院記 1–2. Edited by Takeuchi Rizō 竹内理三. 1967. *Zoku shiryō taisei* 続史料大成 5, 6. Tokyo: Rinsen Shoten.

Goodwin, Janet R. 1994. *Alms and Vagabonds: Buddhist Temples and Popular Patronage in Medieval Japan*. Honolulu: University of Hawai'i Press.

Gotō Hajime 後藤淑. 1975. *Nōgaku no kigen* 能楽の起源. Tokyo: Mokujisha.

Gotō Hajime 後藤淑. 1981. *Nōgaku no kigen, zoku* 能楽の起源・続. Tokyo: Mokujisha.

Grapard, Allan G. 1992. *The Protocol of the Gods: A Study of the Kasuga Cult in Japanese History*. Berkeley: University of California Press.

Groemer, Gerald. 1998a. "Elite Culture for Common Audiences: *Machiiri Nō* and *Kanjin Nō* in the City of Edo." *Asian Theatre Journal* 15, no. 2: 230–52.

Groemer, Gerald. 1998b. "Nō at the Crossroads: Commoner Performance during the Edo Period." *Asian Theatre Journal* 15, no. 1: 117–41.

Groemer, Gerald. 2011. "*Binzasara*: Music and Dance at Sensōji in Edo/Tōkyō." *Yearbook for Traditional Music* 43: 37–61.

Groemer, Gerald. 2016. *Street Performers and Society in Urban Japan, 1600–1900: The Beggar's Gift*. London: Routledge.

Grossmann, Eike. 2013. *Kurokawa Nō: Shaping the Image and Perception of Japan's Folk Traditions, Performing Arts and Rural Tourism*. Leiden: Global Oriental.

Hall, John Whitney. 1995. "The Muromachi bakufu." In *Warrior Rule in Japan*, edited by Marius B. Jansen, 91–146. Cambridge: Cambridge University Press.

Hare, Tom, trans. 2008. *Zeami: Performance Notes*. Translations from the Asian Classics. New York: Columbia University Press.

* Hashimoto Hiroyuki 橋本裕之. 2017. *Ō no mai no engekigakuteki kenkyū* 王の舞の演劇学的研究. Tokyo: Rinsen Shoten.

Hayashi Kazutoshi 林和利. 2003. *Nō, kyōgen no seisei to tenkai ni kansuru kenkyū* 能・狂言の生成と展開に関する研究. Tokyo: Sekai Shisōsha.

Heldt, Gustav, trans. 1997. "Saigyō's Traveling Tale: A Translation of *Saigyō monogatari*." *Monomenta Nipponica* 52, no. 4: 467–521.

Hitorigoto ひとりごと. Annotated by Shimazu Tadao 島津忠夫. (1973) 1995. In *Nihon shisō taikei* 日本思想大系 23, edited by Hayashiya Tatsusaburō 林屋辰三郎, 465–76. Tokyo: Iwanami Shoten.

Hogoura no sho 反古裏之書. In *Konparu kodensho shūsei* 金春古伝書集成, edited by Omote Akira 表章 and Itō Masayoshi 伊藤正義, 350–405. 1969. Tokyo: Wan'ya Shoten.

Honchō seiki 本朝世紀. Edited by Kuroita Katsumi 黒板勝美. 1999. *Kokushi taikei* 国史大系 9. Tokyo: Yoshikawa Kōbunkan.

Hōsei Daigaku Edo Tōkyō Kenkyū Sentā 法政大学江戸東京研究センター (eToS), ed. 2019. *Fukugen: Edojō nō butai to kōka kanjin nō* 復元—江戸城能舞台と弘化勧進能. Tokyo: Hōsei University.

Ietada nikki 家忠日記. Edited by Zoku Shiryō Taisei Kankōkai 続史料大成刊行会. 1968. 2 vols. Tokyo: Rinsen Shoten.

Igarashi Kōichi 五十嵐公一. 2010. *Kinsei Kyōto gadan no nettowāku: chūmonnushi to eshi* 近世京都画壇のネットワーク—注文主と絵師. Tokyo: Yoshikawa Kōbunkan.

Iizuka Erito 飯塚恵理人. 2009. *Kindai nōgakushi no kenkyū: Tōkai chiiki o chūshin ni* 近代能楽史の研究—東北地域を中心に. Tokyo: Taiga Shuppan.

Ikeda Michiko 池田美千子. 2012. "Chūsei kōki no sarugaku: tennō, in, Muromachi-dono to no kankei" 中世後期の猿楽—天皇・院・室町殿との関係. *Ochanomizu shigaku* お茶の水史学 56: 19–52.

Ikegami, Eiko. (1995) 1997. *The Taming of the Samurai. Honorific Individualism and the Making of Modern Japan*. Cambridge: Harvard University Press.

Ikenouchi Nobuyoshi 池内信嘉. 1992. *Nōgaku seisuiki: Gekan Tōkyō no nō* 能楽盛衰記—下巻東京の能. Tokyo: Sōgensha.

Imaizumi Yoshio 今泉淑夫. 2009. *Zeami* 世阿弥. Tokyo: Yoshikawa Kōbunkan.

Inoura, Yoshinobu, and Toshio Kawatake. 1981. *The Traditional Theater of Japan*. New York: Weatherhill.

Inryōken nichiroku 蔭涼軒日録 1–2. In *Dai Nihon bukkyō zensho* 大日本仏教全書, edited by Takakusu Junjirō 高楠順次郎, Ōmura Seigai 大村西崖, and Mochizuki Shinkō 望月信亨, 133–34. 1912. Tokyo: Bussho Kankōkai.

Ishii Kōsei 石井公成. 2017. "*Monomane* no rekishi: Bukkyō, warai, geinō" 〈ものまね〉の歴史—仏教・笑い・芸能. Tokyo: Yoshikawa Kōbunkan.

Itō Maki 伊藤真紀. 2000. "Ennō no "jasutisu" o motomete: nōgaku no teigeki shutsuen mondai'" 演能の「ジャスティス」を求めて—能楽の帝劇出演問題. *Taishō engeki kenkyū* 大正演劇研究 8: 70–87.

Itō Maki 伊藤真紀. 2008. "Hibiya yagai nō to 'nōgaku kankōkai' no setsuritsu: taishōki no 'demokurashī nō'" 日比谷野外能と「能楽歓興会」の設立—大正期の「デモクラシー能」. *Bungei kenkyū* 文芸研究 104: 45–68.

Itō Maki 伊藤真紀. 2013. "Nō butai ni agatta joseitachi: Taishō jūichi nen no 'Awaji fujin nō' wo megutte" 能舞台に上がった女性たち—大正十一年の「淡路婦人能」をめぐって. *Engekigaku ronshū* 演劇学論集 56: 21–37.

Itō Masayoshi 伊藤正義. 2013. "*Utaishō* kō"『謡抄』考. In *Itō Masayoshi chūsei bunka ronshū. Dai nikan: Utai to nō no sekai (ge)* 伊藤正義中世文華論集第二巻—謡と能の世界（下）, edited by Sekiya Toshihiko 関屋俊彦, and Inada Hideo 稲田秀雄, 260–70. Osaka: Izumi Shoin.

Iwakura kō jikki 岩倉公実記 2. Edited by Tada Kōmon 多田好問, and Kagawa Keizō 香川敬三. 1906. 2 vols. Tokyo: Kōgōgūshoku.

Jansen, Marius B. 2002. *The Making of Modern Japan*. Cambridge: Harvard University Press.

Kagaya, Shinko. 2001. "Nō Performances in Gaichi." *Asian Theatre Journal* 18, no. 2: 257–69.

Kagaya, Shinko. 2005. "The First Umewaka Minoru and Performances for Guests from Overseas." NOAG 177/178: 225–36.

Kagaya, Shinko. 2008. "Dancing on a Moving Train Nō between Two Wars." In *Nō Theatre Transversal*, edited by Stanca Scholz-Cionca and Christopher Balme, 19–30. Munich: iudicium.

Kagaya, Shinko. 2009. "Nō and Kyōgen during the Occupation." In *Rising from the Flames: The Rebirth of Theater in Occupied Japan, 1945–1952*, edited by Samuel L. Leiter, 175–84. Lanham: Lexington Books.

Kagenki 嘉元記. Edited by Hōryūji Shōwa Shizaichō Hensanjo 法隆寺昭和資財帳編纂所. 1984. *Hōryūji shiryō shūsei* 法隆寺史料集成 5. Tokyo: Wakō Bijutsu Shuppan.

Kagotani Machiko 籠谷眞智子. 2005. *Geinōshi no naka no Honganji: nō kyōgen, cha no yu, hana no bunkashi* 芸能史のなかの本願寺—能・狂言・茶の湯・花の文化史. Tokyo: Jishōsha Shuppan.

Kaisei nō no kinmō zui 改正能之訓蒙図彙. In *Nōgaku shiryō shūsei* 能楽資料集成 10, edited by Omote Akira 表章, 157–238. 1980. Tokyo: Wan'ya Shoten.

Kajii Yukiyo 梶井幸代 and Mitsuda Ryōji 密田良二. 1972. *Kanazawa no nōgaku* 金沢の能楽. Tokyo: Hokkoku Shuppansha.

Kakumeiki 隔蓂記. Edited by Akamatsu Toshihide 赤松俊秀, and Kakumeiki Kenkyūkai 隔蓂記研究会. 1997–2006. 7 vols. Tokyo: Shibunkaku Shuppan.

Kanchūki 勘仲記 1. Edited by Sasakawa Tanerō 笹川種郎. 1917. 2 vols. Tokyo: Nihon Shiseki Hozonkai.

Kanemi kyōki 兼見卿記 3. In *Shiryō sanshū kokiroku hen* 史料纂集古記録編, edited by Hashimoto Masanobu 橋本政宣, Kaneko Hiraku 金子拓 et al. 2014. 7 vols. Tokyo: Yagi Shoten.

Kanmon gyoki 看聞御記 [*Kanmon nikki* 看聞日記]. In *Zoku gunsho ruijū, hoi 2 jō, ge* 続群書類従補遺二上下. (1930) 2000. 2 vols. Tokyo: Zoku Gunsho Ruijū Kanseikai.

Kanze Motoshige 観世元滋. 1926. "Fujin nō to gekijō mondai" 婦人能と劇場問題. *Dai Kanze* 大観世 44, no. 8: 1.

Kasuga Wakamiya onmatsuri shukkin dengaku za kiroku 春日若宮御祭出勤田楽座記録. In *Dengaku, sarugaku* 田楽・猿楽. *Nihon shomin bunka shiryō shūsei* 日本庶民文化史料集成 2, edited by Geinōshi Kenkyūkai 芸能史研究会, 165–81. 1978. Tokyo: San'ichi Shobō.

Keichō kenmonshū 慶長見聞集. Edited by Kondō Heijō 近藤瓶城, 1–283. 1926. *Shiseki shūran* 史籍集覧 10. Tokyo: Kondō Shuppanbu.

Kennaiki 建内記 3. Edited by Tōkyō Daigaku Shiryō Hensanjo 東京大学史料編纂所. 1968. *Dai Nihon kokiroku* 大日本古記録. Tokyo: Iwanami Shoten.

* Kim Inhi 金仁姫. 2015. *Kankoku shishi mai no hen'yō: fūshigeki* 韓国獅子舞の変容：風刺劇. Osaka: Fūeisha.

Kimbrough, R. Keller. 2008. *Preachers, Poets, Women, and the Way: Izumi Shikibu and the Buddhist Literature of Medieval Japan*. Michigan Monograph Series in Japanese Studies 62. Ann Arbor: Center for Japanese Studies, The University of Michigan.

Komai nikki 駒井日記. In *Shiseki shūran* 史籍集覧 25, edited by Kondō Heijō 近藤瓶城, 488–584. 1926. Tokyo: Kondō Shuppanbu.

Kōyōki 迎陽記 1. Edited by Ogawa Takeo 小川剛生. 2011. *Shiryō sanshū kokiroku hen* 史料纂集古記録編. Tokyo: Yagi Shoten.

Kuroda, Toshio. 1996. "The World of Spirit Pacification: Issues of State and Religion." *Japanese Journal of Religious Studies* 23, no. 3/4: 321–51.

Kurokawa mura Kasuga Jinja monjo 黒川村春日神社文書. Edited by Sakurai Akio 桜井昭夫. 1998. Tsuruoka: Tōhoku Shuppan Kikaku.

Kurokawa nō shiryō 黒川能史料. Edited by Kushibiki Mura Kyōiku Iinkai 櫛引村教育委員会. 1959. Kushibiki: Kyōiku Iinkai.

Kyō habutae oridome 京羽二重織留. In *Shinshū Kyōto sōsho* 新修京都叢書 2, edited by Shinshū Kyōto Sōsho Kankōkai 新修京都叢書刊行会, 313–539. 1995. Kyoto: Rinsen Shoten.

Kyōhō rokunen kakiage 享保六年書上. In *Nō* 能. *Nihon shomin bunka shiryō shūsei* 日本庶民文化史料集成 3, edited by Geinōshi Kenkyūkai 芸能史研究会, 211–56. 1978. Tokyo: San'ichi Shobō.

Kyūji shimonroku 旧事諮問録 1. Edited by Shinji Yoshimoto 進士慶幹. 2 vols. 1986. Tokyo: Iwanami Shoten.

Lim, Beng Choo. 2012. *Another Stage: Kanze Nobumitsu & the Late Muromachi Noh Theater*. Cornell East Asia Series 163. Ithaca: Cornell University East Asia Program.

Mansai jugō nikki 満済准后日記. In *Zoku gunsho ruijū, hoi 1 jō, ge* 続群書類従補遺一上下. (1928) 2002. 2 vols. Tokyo: Zoku Gunsho Ruijū Kanseikai.

Masamoto kō tabi hikitsuke 政基公旅引付. Edited by Kunaichō Shoryōbu 宮内庁書陵部. 1961. *Zushoryō sōkan* 図書寮叢刊. Tenri: Yōtokusha.

Matsuo Kōichi 松尾恒一. 1997. *Ennen no geinōshiteki kenkyū* 延年の芸能史的研究. Tokyo: Iwata Shoin.

Matsuo Kōichi 松尾恒一. 2011. *Girei kara geinō e: kyōsō, hyōi, dōke* 儀礼から芸能へ——狂騒・憑依・道化. Tokyo: Kadokawa Gakugei Shuppan.

Matsuoka Shinpei 松岡心平. 2008. "Ushirodo sarugaku no kosumorojī to nō butai" 後戸猿楽のコスモロジーと能舞台. *Nō to kyōgen* 能と狂言 6: 41–45.

Matsuoka Shinpei 松岡心平, ed. 2014. *Kanze Motoakira no sekai* 観世元章の世界. Tokyo: Hinoki Shoten.

Matsuoka Shinpei 松岡心平. 2021. "Ichijō Takegahana kanjin sarugaku to Zeami" 一条竹鼻勧進猿楽と世阿弥. *Zeami* 世阿弥 5: 34–58.

McCullough, Helen Craig, trans. 1988. *The Tale of the Heike*. Stanford: Stanford University Press.

McKinney, Meredith, trans. 1998. *The Tale of Saigyō*. Michigan Papers in Japanese Studies 25. Ann Arbor: University of Michigan Press.

McMullin, Neil. 1988. "On Placating the Gods and Pacifying the Populace: The Case of the Gion *Goryō* Cult." *History of Religions* 27, no. 3: 270–93.

* Meeks, Lori. 2011. "The Disappearing Medium: Reassessing the Place of *Miko* in the Religious Landscape of Premodern Japan." *History of Religions* 50, no. 3: 208–60.

Meiryō kōhan 明良洪範. Edited by Kokusho Kankōkai 国書刊行会. 1912. Tokyo: Kokusho Kankōkai.

Miura Hiroko 三浦裕子. 2018. "Shosei Umewaka Minoru to Yokohama no shirōto deshi: Yokohama yōshinkai o megutte (sono ichi)" 初世梅若実と横浜の素人弟子——横浜養心会をめぐって（その一）. *Musashino Daigaku Nōgaku Shiryō Sentā kiyō* 29: 1–10.

Miyamoto Keizō 宮本圭造. 2005a. "Edo jidai nōgaku hanjōki: daimyō goyō no kyō chōnin, nō wa shōbai no dōgu nari" 江戸時代能楽繁盛記——大名御用の京町人．能は商売の道具なり. *Kanze* 観世 72, no. 11: 48–52.

Miyamoto Keizō 宮本圭造. 2005b. *Kamigata nōgakushi no kenkyū* 上方能楽史の研究. Osaka: Izumi Shoin.

Miyamoto Keizō 宮本圭造. 2008a. "Zoku, Edo jidai nōgaku hanjōki: Nagesen o kou tsuji nō yakusha, bushi ya shōka no nare no hate" 続・江戸時代能楽繁盛記——投げ銭を乞う辻能役者、武士や商家のなれの果て. *Kanze* 観世 75, no. 1: 58–63.

Miyamoto Keizō 宮本圭造. 2008b. "Zoku, Edo jidai nōgaku hanjōki: Sensuke nō no chūgaeri, Kita-ryū no tayū ga manete hyōban o toru" 続・江戸時代能楽繁盛記——仙助能の宙返り、喜多流の大夫が真似て評判をとる. *Kanze* 観世 75, no. 2: 44–49.

Miyamoto Keizō 宮本圭造. 2008c. "Zoku, Edo jidai nōgaku hanjōki: Kasuga naru mizuya ni tsudou negidomo ga, sake ni yoitaru midaremai" 続・江戸時代能楽繁盛記——春日なる水屋に集う禰宜どもが．酒に酔たる乱れ舞い. *Kanze* 観世 75, no. 3: 54–59.

* Miyamoto Keizō 宮本圭造. 2008d. "Kasuga Wakamiya onmatsuri to Yamato sarugaku: 'za' o meguru mondai o chūshin ni" 春日若宮おん祭と大和猿楽—「座」をめぐる問題を中心に. *Nō to kyōgen* 能と狂言 6: 112–21.

Miyamoto Keizō 宮本圭造. 2009. "Zoku, Edo jidai nōgaku hanjōki: shōgun ga nō mau goyo wa taihei no yo" 続・江戸時代能楽繁盛記—将軍が 能舞う御世は 泰平の世. *Kanze* 観世 76, no. 12: 36–43.

Miyamoto Keizō 宮本圭造. 2011. "Shushi-bashiri to 'okina': 'okina' no seiritsu o meguru ni, san no mondai" 呪師走りと「翁」—「翁」の成立をめぐる二、三の問題. *Nihon bungaku shiyō* 日本文学誌要 84: 29–40.

* Miyamoto Keizō 宮本圭造. 2012. "Buke tesarugaku no keifu: nō ga bushi no geinō ni naru made" 武家手猿楽の系譜—能が武士の芸能になるまで. *Nōgaku kenkyū* 能楽研究 36: 29–64.

Miyamoto Keizō 宮本圭造. 2013. "Renzu ga torareta nōgakushi 11: shinshi nō no jidai" レンズがとらえた能楽史 11—紳士能の時代. *Nō to kyogen* 能と狂言 11: n.p.

* Miyamoto Keizō 宮本圭造. 2015. "Yamato no sonraku saishi to nō: Yamato sarugaku no sonritsu kiban" 大和の村落祭祀と能—大和猿楽の存立基盤. *Man'yō kodaigaku kenkyū nenpō* 万葉古代学研究年報 13: 65–92.

Miyamoto Keizō 宮本圭造. 2016. "Rinpa to nō, nō yakusha ni natta kamo shirenai Ogata Kōrin: rinpa o torimaku nō no kankyō" 琳派と能、能役者になったかも知れない尾形光琳—琳派を取り巻く能の環境. *Kanze* 観世 83, no. 2: 22–30.

Miyamoto Keizō 宮本圭造. 2017a. "Bakumatsu ishin o mukaete nō yakusha wa dō natta ka" 幕末維新を迎えて能役者はどうなったか. In *Kindai Nihon to nōgaku* 近代日本と能楽, edited by Miyamoto Keizō 宮本圭造, 39–80. *Nōgaku kenkyū sōsho* 能楽研究叢書 6. Tokyo: Nogami Kinen Hōsei Daigaku Nōgaku Kenkyūjo.

Miyamoto Keizō 宮本圭造. 2017b. "Nō to gunkoku shugi: senji tōseika no nōgaku" 能と軍国主義—戦時統制下の能楽. In *Kindai Nihon to nōgaku* 近代日本と能楽, edited by Miyamoto Keizō 宮本圭造, 307–43. *Nōgaku kenkyū sōsho* 能楽研究叢書 6. Tokyo: Nogami Kinen Hōsei Daigaku Nōgaku Kenkyūjo.

Miyamoto Keizō 宮本圭造. 2017c. "Kanze za to Iga" 観世座と伊賀. *Shimei* 紫明 40: 10–17.

Miyamoto Keizō 宮本圭造. 2019. *Kinsei shohan nō yakusha yuishogaki shūsei (jō)* 近世諸藩能役者由緒書集成（上）. *Nōgaku shiryō sōsho* 能楽資料叢書 5. Tokyo: Hōsei Daigaku Nōgaku Kenkyūjo.

Miyamoto Keizō 宮本圭造. 2020. "Kanjin nō nenpyō" 勧進能年表. In *Kanjin nō* 勧進能. *Subscription (kanjin) noh Performance*, edited by Kokuritsu Nōgakudō 国立能楽堂, 11–23. Tokyo: Kokuritsu Nōgakudō.

Miyamoto Keizō 宮本圭造. 2021. *Kinsei shohan nō yakusha yuishogaki shūsei (chū)* 近世諸藩能役者由緒書集成（中）. *Nōgaku shiryō sōsho* 能楽資料叢書 6. Tokyo: Hōsei Daigaku Nōgaku Kenkyūjo.

Miyamoto Keizō 宮本圭造. 2022. *Kinsei shohan nō yakusha yuishogaki shūsei (ge)* 近世諸藩能役者由緒書集成（下）. *Nōgaku shiryō sōsho* 能楽資料叢書 7. Tokyo: Hōsei Daigaku Nōgaku Kenkyūjo.

Miyoshi tei o-nari ki 三好亭御成記. In *Zoku gunsho ruijū* 続群書類従 23, edited by Zoku Gunsho Ruijū Kanseikai 続群書類従完成会, 234b–49b. (1925) 1975. Tokyo: Zoku Gunsho Ruijū Kanseikai.

Moore, Katrina L. 2012. "Singing in the Workplace: Salarymen and Amateur Nō Performance." *Asian Theatre Journal* 29, no. 19: 164–82.

Nakagawa Katsura 中川桂. 1995. "Kinsei kōki Ōsaka no nō jōbutai" 近世後期大阪の能常舞台. *Geinōshi kenkyū* 芸能史研究 131: 40–53.

Nakagawa Minami 仲川みなみ. 2016. "Tsuina to setsubun gyōji no keisei" 追儺と節分行事の形成. *Denshō bunka kenkyū* 伝承文化研究 14: 83–100.

Nakamura Masayuki 中村雅之. 2004. "Senji taiseika ni okeru tennōsei no hen'yō: 'Semimaru, Ohara gokō jiken' to utaibon kaitei" 戦時体制下における天皇制の変容—「蝉丸・大原御幸事件」と謡本改訂. *Nō to kyōgen* 能と狂言 2: 103–17.

Nakao Kaoru 中尾薫. 2013. "Nōgaku no kindaika to Takagi Nakaba: Sono rireki to nōgaku kairyōron e no nō yakusha no hannō o megutte" 能楽の近代化と高木半—その履歴と能楽改良論への能役者の反応をめぐって. *Machikaneyama ronsō: bigaku hen* 待兼山論叢：美学編 47: 1–25.

Nelson, Steven G. 2008a. "Court and Religious Music (1): History of *Gagaku* and *Shōmyō*." In *The Ashgate Research Companion to Japanese Music*, edited by Alison McQueen Tokita and David W. Hughes, 35–48. Aldershot: Ashgate.

Nelson, Steven G. 2008b. "Court and Religious Music (2): Music of *Gagaku* and *Shōmyō*." In *The Ashgate Research Companion to Japanese Music*, edited by Alison McQueen Tokita and David W. Hughes, 49–76. Aldershot: Ashgate.

Nelson, Thomas. 1997. "Bakufu and *shugo* under the Early Ashikaga." In *The Origins of Japan's Medieval World: Courtiers, Clerics, Warriors, and Peasants in the Fourteenth Century*, edited by Jeffrey P. Mass, 78–90. Stanford: Stanford University Press.

Nihon sandai jitsuroku 日本三代実録. Edited by Kuroita Katsumi 黒板勝美. 2000. In *Kokushi taikei* 国史大系 4. Revised and enlarged edition. Tokyo: Yoshikawa Kōbunkan.

Nishiwaki Ai 西脇藍. 2005. *Okayama hanshu Ikeda Tsunamasa to "nō": Genrokuki no daimyō no seikatsu to nō* 岡山藩主池田綱政と「能」—元禄期の大名の生活と能. Okayama: Kibito Shuppan.

Nō no kinmō zui 能之訓蒙図彙. In *Nōgaku shiryō shūsei* 能楽資料集成 10, edited by Omote Akira 表章, 5–156. 1980. Tokyo: Wan'ya Shoten.

"Nō to kōen no kai" 能と講演の会. 1926. *Kita* 喜多 4: 1.

"Nō to kōen no kai suketchi" 能と講演の会スケッチ. 1926. *Kita* 喜多 6: 2–3.

Nose Asaji 能勢朝次. 1938. *Nōgaku genryū kō* 能楽源流考. Tokyo: Iwanami Shoten.

Ochiai Hiroshi 落合博志. 1994. "Inuō no jidai: *Rokuon'in saigoku gekō ki* no kiji o shōkai shitsutsu" 犬王の時代―『鹿苑院西国下向記』の記事を紹介しつつ. *Nōgaku kenkyū* 能楽研究 18: 101–44.

Ogawa Takeo 小川剛生. 2008. "Kōyōki (kōryaku gan'nen kara ōei hachi nen) honkoku" 迎陽記（康暦元年〜応永八年）翻刻. In *Ashikaga Yoshimitsu ki no Muromachi bakufu shōgun kenryoku ni okeru seiji, bunka no sōgo hokanteki kankei no kenkyū* 足利義満期の室町幕府将軍権力における政治・文化の相互補完的関係の研究, 31–74. Tokyo: Kokubungaku Kenkyū Shiryōkan.

Okada Mitsuko 岡田三津子. 2009. "Enkyoku no bungeisei to geinōsei: enkyoku kara kusemai, yōkyoku e" 宴曲の文芸性と芸能性―宴曲から曲舞・謡曲へ. *Kokubungaku kaishaku to kanshō* 国文学解釈と鑑賞 74, no. 10: 79–88.

Okinagusa 翁草 1–3. Edited by Nihon Zuihitsu Taisei Henshūbu 日本随筆大成編集部, 1–258. 1996. *Nihon zuihitsu taisei* 日本随筆大成 11–13. Tokyo: Nihon Zuihitsu Taisei Kankōbu.

Ōmori Masako 大森雅子, ed. 1995. *Nanto ryō shinji nō shiryōshū* 南都両神事能資料集. Tokyo: Ōfū.

Omote Akira 表章. 1974. "Tōnomine no sarugaku" 多武峰の猿楽. *Nōgaku kenkyū* 能楽研究 1: 25–122. Reprinted in Omote Akira 表章. 2005. *Yamato sarugaku shi sankyū* 大和猿楽史参究, 3–109. Tokyo: Iwanami Shoten.

Omote Akira 表章. 1983. "Kan'ami Kiyotsugu to yūzaki za" 観阿弥清次と結崎座. *Bungaku* 文学 51, no. 7: 35–46.

Omote Akira 表章. 1994. *Kita-ryū no seiritsu to tenkai* 喜多流の成立と展開. Tokyo: Heibonsha.

Omote Akira 表章. 2008. *Kanze-ryū shi sankyū* 観世流史参究. Tokyo: Hinoki Shoten.

Omote Akira 表章 and Amano Fumio 天野文雄. (1987) 1999. *Nōgaku no rekishi*. In Vol. 1, *Iwanami kōza: nō kyōgen* 岩波講座―能・狂言 1, edited by Yokomichi Mario 横道萬里雄, Koyama Hiroshi 小山弘志, and Omote Akira 表章. 8 vols. Tokyo: Iwanami Shoten.

Omote Akira 表章, and Katō Shūichi 加藤周一, eds. (1974) 1995. *Zeami Zenchiku* 世阿弥禅竹. *Nihon shisō taikei* 日本思想大系 24. Tokyo: Iwanami Shoten.

O'Neill, P. G. 1958. "The Structure of Kusemai 曲舞." *Bulletin of the School of Oriental and African Studies* 21, no. 1/3: 100–10.

O'Neill, P. G. 1958/1959. "Translations: The Special Kasuga Wakamiya Festival of 1349." *Monumenta Nipponica* 14, no. 3/4 (October 1958–June 1959): 408–28.

Ortolani, Benito. (1990) 1995. *The Japanese Theatre: From Shamanistic Ritual to Contemporary Pluralism*. Princeton: Princeton University Press.

* Ortolani, Benito. 1997. "To Court and Shrine from the World: *Gigaku* and *Bugaku*." In *Japanese Theater in the World*, edited by Samuel Leiter, 38–42. New York: Japan Society Gallery.

Ōtani Setsuko 大谷節子. 1991. "Kinsei kinri sentō nō ikken" 近世禁裏仙洞能一見. *Geinōshi kenkyū* 芸能史研究 113: 38–49.

Oyudono no ue no nikki お湯殿の上の日記. *Zoku gunsho ruijū, hoi* 3 続群書類従補遺三, edited by Zoku Gunsho Ruijū Kanseikai. (1934) 1995. Tokyo: Zoku Gunsho Ruijū Kanseikai.

Quinn, Shelley Fenno. 1992. "Dance and Chant in Zeami's Dramaturgy: Building Blocks for a Theatre of Tone." *Asian Theatre Journal* 9, no. 2: 201–14.

Piggot, Joan R. 2007. "An Account of the New Monkey Music." In *Traditional Japanese Literature: An Anthology, Beginnings to 1600*, edited by Haruo Shirane, 491–97. New York: Columbia University Press.

Pinnington, Noel J. 1998. "Invented Origins: Muromachi interpretations of *okina sarugaku*." *Bulletin of the School of Oriental and African Studies* 61, no. 3: 492–518.

Pinnington, Noel John. 2019. *A New History of Medieval Japanese Theatre: Noh and Kyōgen from 1300 to 1600*. Palgrave Studies in Theatre and Performance History. Cham: Palgrave Macmillan.

Rath, Eric C. 2000. "From Representation to Apotheosis: Nō's Modern Myth of Okina." *Asian Theatre Journal* 17, no. 2: 253–68.

Rath, Eric C. 2002. "Chanters at the Gate: Ritual/Performing Arts of Fifteenth-Century Japanese Outcasts." In *Medieval and Early Modern Ritual: Formalized Behavior in Europe, China and Japan*, edited by Joelle Rollo-Koster, 175–92. Cultures, Beliefs and Traditions: Medieval and Early Modern Peoples 13. Leiden: Brill.

Rath, Eric C. 2003. "Remembering Zeami: The Kanze School and Its Patriarch." *Asian Theatre Journal* 20, no. 2: 191–208.

Rath, Eric C. 2004. *The Ethos of Noh: Actors and Their Art*. Cambridge: Harvard East Asian Monographs 232. Cambridge: Harvard University Asia Center, Harvard University Press.

Rodriguez, João "Tçuzu." 1620–1633. *História da igreja do Japão*. Biblioteca do Palácio da Ajuda, Lisbon, Jesuítas na Ásia 49-iv-53, ff. 1–181; Biblioteca de la Real Academia de la Historia, Madrid, 9/7237, ff. 1–16, 9/7238, ff. 1–87; Kirishitan Bunko Library, Sophia University, Tokyo, KB 445: 336.

Ryūei hinamiki 柳営日次記 4. In *Edo bakufu nikki* 江戸幕府日記. 1993. Sagamihara: Nogami Shuppan.

Ryūkō sōjō nikki 隆光僧正日記 1. Edited by Nagashima Fukutarō 永島福太郎, and Hayashi Ryōshō 林亮勝. 1969. *Shiryō sanshū (kigai)* 史料纂集（期外）6. Tokyo: Zoku Gunsho Ruijū Kanseikai.

Sakamoto Kiyoe 坂本清恵, and Takakuwa Izumi 高桑いづみ. 2015/12/18. "Hōgaku no senritsu to akusento" 邦楽の旋律とアクセント. Presentation at the "Tōkyō Bunkazai Kenkyūjo mukei bunka isan bu kōkai gakujutsu kōza" 東京文化財研究所無形文化遺産部公開学術講座.

Sakurai Akio 桜井昭夫. 2003. *Kurokawa nō to kōgyō* 黒川能と興行. Tokyo: Dōseisha.

Salz, Jonah, ed. 2016. *A History of Japanese Theatre*. Cambridge: Cambridge University Press.

Sanbōin Kenshun sōjō nikki (Jōwa ninen) 三宝院賢俊僧正日記（貞和二年）. Edited by Hashimoto Hatsuko 橋本初子. 1992. *Daigoji Bunkazai Kenkyūjo kiyō* 醍醐寺文化財研究所紀要 12: 132–59.

Sanetaka kōki 実隆公記. Edited by Ōta Tōshirō 太田藤四郎. 1931–1938. 5 vols. Tokyo: Taiyōsha.

Sargent, G. W., trans. 1959. *Ihara Saikaku: The Japanese Family Storehouse or the Millionaires' Gospel Modernised*. Cambridge: Cambridge University Press.

Satō Kazumichi 佐藤和道. 2014. "Rajio hōsō to nōgaku: chihō ni okeru nōgaku kyōju he no eikyō o chūshin ni" ラジオ放送と能楽—地方における能楽享受への影響を中心に. *Nō to kyōgen* 能と狂言 12: 90–103.

Satō Kazumichi 佐藤和道. 2017. "Media to nōgaku: rekōdo, rajio, tōkī" メディアと能楽—レコード・ラジオ・トーキー. In *Kindai Nihon to nōgaku* 近代日本と能楽, edited by Miyamoto Keizō 宮本圭造, 133–61. *Nōgaku kenkyū sōsho* 能楽研究叢書 6. Tokyo: Nogami Kinen Hōsei Daigaku Nōgaku Kenkyūjo.

Satō Kazumichi 佐藤和道. 2018. "Kindai ni okeru kaigai Nihonjin kyoryūmin to nōgaku" 近代における海外日本人居留民と能楽. *Nō to kyōgen* 能と狂言 16: 70–89.

Satō Kazumichi 佐藤和道. 2020. "1930 nendai dairen manshū ni okeru nōgaku: Manshū tsūrizumu no hatten to ennō ryokō" 一九三〇年代大連・満州における能楽—満州ツーリズムの発展と演能旅行. *Engeki kenkyū* 演劇研究 43: 17–31.

Satow, Sir Earnest. 1921. *A Diplomat in Japan: The Inner History of the Critical Years in the Evolution of Japan when the Ports were Opened and the Monarchy Restored, Recorded by a Diplomatist Who Took an Active Part in the Events of the Time, with an Account of His Personal Experiences during the Period*. London: Seeley, Service & Co., Limited.

Scholz-Cionca, Stanca. 2017a. "The Dancing Despot Toyotomi Hideyoshi and the Performative Symbolism of Power." In *The Scaffolding of Sovereignty: Global and Aesthetic Perspectives on the History of a Concept*, edited by Zvi Ben-Dor Benite, Stefanos Geroulanos, and Nikole Jerr, 186–207. New York: Columbia University Press.

Scholz-Cionca, Stanca. 2017b. "Nō within Walls and Beyond: Theatre as Cultural Capital in Edo Japan (1603–1868)." In *Dramatic Experience: The Poetics of Drama and the Early Modern Public Sphere(s)*, edited by Katja Gvozdeva, Tatiana Korneeva, and Kirill Ospovat, 289–306. Drama and Theatre in Early Modern Europe 6. Leiden: Brill.

Scholz-Cionca, Stanca, and Hōko Oshikiri. 2004. "Der Adler und die Chrysantheme: Nō-Spiele zum russisch-japanischen Krieg." NOAG 175/176: 23–59.

* Schütte, Josef Franz, ed. 1955. *Kulturgegensätze Europa-Japan (1585): tratado em que se contem muito susinta- e abreviadamente algumas contradições e diferenças de custumes antre a gente de Europa e esta provincia de Japão*. Monumenta Nipponica Monographs 15. Tokyo: Sophia Universität.

"Seikō seru 'nō to kōen no kai'" 成功せる『能と講演の会』. 1926. *Kita* 喜多 6: 1.

Sensuke za ikkendome 仙助座一件留. In *Nō* 能. *Nihon shomin bunka shiryō shūsei* 日本庶民文化史料集成 3, edited by Geinōshi Kenkyūkai 芸能史研究会, 761–68. 1978. Tokyo: San'ichi Shobō.

Shigeta Michi 重田みち. 2006. "*Fūshi kaden* no kansei to Zeami no shisō" 『風姿花伝』の完成と世阿弥の思想. *Geinōshi kenkyū* 芸能史研究 172: 16–28.

Shimei Sei 紫明生. 1924. "Hibiya no yagai nō" 日比谷の野外能. *Yōkyokukai* 謡曲界 20, no. 1: 77–80.

Shin sarugakuki 新猿楽記, annotated and translated by Kawaguchi Hisao 川口久雄. 1983. *Tōyō bunko* 東洋文庫 424. Tokyo: Heibonsha.

Shinchō kōki 信長公記. Edited by Kondō Heijō 近藤瓶城, 1–258. 1926. In *Shiseki shūran* 史籍集覧 19. Tokyo: Kondō Shuppanbu.

Shively, Donald. H. 2002. "*Bakufu* Versus *Kabuki*." In *A Kabuki Reader: History and Performance*, edited by Samuel L. Leiter, 33–59. Armonk: M. E. Sharpe.

Shōkisai nichinchi zakki 鐘奇斎日々雑記. In *Nihon toshi seikatsu shiryō shūsei* 日本都市生活史料集成 1, *santo* 三都, edited by Harada Tomohiko 原田伴彦, Yamori Kazuhiko 矢守一彦, Nishikawa Kōji 西川幸治, and Moriya Katsuhisa 森谷尅久, 523–642. 1977. Tokyo: Gakushū Kenkyūsha.

Shoku Nihongi 続日本紀 5. Edited by Aoki Kazuo 青木和夫, Inaoka Kōji 稲岡耕二, Sasayama Haruo 笹山晴生, and Shirafuji Noriyuki 白藤禮幸. 1998. *Shin Nihon koten bungaku taikei* 新日本古典文学大系 16. Tokyo: Iwanami Shoten.

Shōnyo shōnin nikki 証如上人日記. Edited by Uematsu Torazō 上松寅三. 1966. *Ishiyama Honganji nikki* 石山本願寺日記 1. Tokyo: Seibundō Shuppan.

Shudōsho 習道書. In *Renga ronshū, nogaku ronshū, haikairon* 連歌論集, 能楽論集, 俳諧論, edited by Okuda Isao 奥田勲, Omote Akira 表章, Horikiri Minoru 堀切実, and Fukumoto Ichirō 復本一郎, 397–410. 2001. Tokyo: Shōgakukan.

Shūsui zatsuwa 拾推椎話. In *Fukui ken kyōdo sōsho* 福井県郷土叢書 1, edited by Fukui Kenritsu Toshokan Kyōdo Kondankai 福井県立図書館郷土懇談会, 1–470. 1954. Tokyo: Fukui Kenritsu Toshokan.

Smethurst, Mae J., and Richard J. Smethurst. 2008. "Two New Nō Plays Written during World War II." In *Nō Theatre Transversal*, edited by Stanca Scholz-Cionca and Christopher Balme, 31–37. Munich: iudicium.

Sōgo ōzōshi 宗五大草紙. In *Gunsho ruijū* 群書類従 22, 537–626. (1932) 1992. Tokyo: Zoku Gunsho Ruijū Kanseikai.

Stavros, Matthew. 2014. *Kyoto: An Urban History of Japan's Premodern Capital*. Honolulu: University of Hawai'i Press.

Sugaura monjo 菅浦文書. Edited by Shiga Daigaku Nihon Keizai Bunka Kenkyūjo Shiryōkan 滋賀大学日本経済文化研究所史料館. 1960. Vol 1. Tokyo: Yūhikaku.

Su-utai yoyo no ato 素謡世々之蹟. In *Nihon shomin bunka shiryō shūsei: nō* 日本庶民文化史料集成 3: 能, edited by Geinōshi Kenkyūkai 芸能史研究会, 657–84. 1978. Tokyo: San'ichi Shobō.

Tadasugawara kanjin sarugaku nikki 糺河原勧進猿楽日記. In *Gunsho ruijū* 群書類従 19, edited by Zoku Gunsho Ruijū Kanseikai, 717b–21b. (1932) 2002. Tokyo: Zoku Gunsho Ruijū Kanseikai.

Taiheiki 太平記 3. Edited by Hasegawa Tadashi 長谷川端. 2008. *Shinpen Nihon koten bungaku zenshū* 新編日本古典文学全集 56. Tokyo: Shōgakukan.

Takemoto Mikio 竹本幹夫. 1992. "Edo jidai shohan ni okeru nō yakusha no mibun" 江戸時代諸藩における能役者の身分. *Kokubungaku kenkyū* 国文学研究 107: 11–19.

Takemoto Mikio 竹本幹夫. 2009. "Kaisetsu" 解説. In *Fūshi kaden, Sandō: gendaigo yaku tsuki* 風姿花伝・三道—現代語訳付き. Kadokawa Sofia Bunko 角川ソフィア文庫, edited by Takemoto Mikio 竹本幹夫, 383–435. Tokyo: Kadokawa Gakugei Shuppan.

Tamon'in nikki 多聞院日記 3. Edited by Tsuji Zennosuke 辻善之助. 1939. 5 vols. Tokyo: Sankyō Shoin.

Tanaka Makoto 田中允, ed. 1987–1998. *Mikan yōkyokushū zoku* 未刊謡曲集続. 22 vols. Tokyo: Koten Bunko.

Taniwaki Masachika 谷脇理史, Jinbō Kazuya 神保五彌, and Teruoka Yasutaka 暉峻康隆, eds. 2003. *Ihara Saikaku shū* 井原西鶴集. *Shinpen Nihon koten bungaku zenshū* 新編日本古典文学全集 68. Tokyo: Shōgakukan.

"Tēma kenkyū: Tōnomine to sarugaku" テーマ研究・多武峰と猿楽. 2007. *Nō to kyōgen* 能と狂言 5: 79–107.

Terauchi Naoko. 2016. "Ancient and Early Medieval Performing Arts." In *A History of Japanese Theatre*, edited by Jonah Salz, 4–19. Cambridge: Cambridge University Press.

Tezuka, Miwako. 2011. "Experimentation and Tradition: The Avant-Garde Play: *Pierrot Lunaire* by Jikken Kōbō and Takechi Tetsuji." *Art Journal* 70, no. 3: 64–85.

Thornhill, Arthur H., III. 1993. *Six Circles, One Dewdrop: The Religion-Aesthetic World of Komparu Zenchiku*. Princeton: Princeton University Press.

Tian, Min. 2003. "Chinese Nuo and Japanese Noh: Nuo's Role in the Origination and Formation of Noh." *Comparative Drama* 37, no. 3/4: 343–60.

Tōdaiki 当代記. In *Shiseki zassan* 史籍雑纂 2, edited by Kokusho Kankōkai 国書刊行会, 1a–214b. 1912. Tokyo: Kokusho Kankōkai.

Tokitsugu kyōki 言継卿記. Edited by Kokusho Kankōkai 国書刊行会. 1914–1915. 4 vols. Tokyo: Kokusho Kankōkai.

Tokitsune kyōki 言経卿記. *Dai Nihon kokiroku* 大日本古記録, edited by Tōkyō Daigaku Shiryō Hensanjo 東京大学史料編纂所. 1959–1991. 14 vols. Tokyo: Iwanami Shoten.

Tokugawa jikki 徳川実紀. Edited by Kuroita Katsumi 黒板勝美, and Kokushi Taikei Henshūkai 国史大系編修会. 1976. 10 vols. Tokyo: Yoshikawa Kōbunkan.

Tokugawa shoke keifu 徳川諸家系譜 2. Edited by Saiki Kazuma 斎木一馬, Iwasawa Yoshihiko 岩沢愿彦, and Tohara Jun'ichi 戸原純一. 1970–1984. 4 vols. Tokyo: Zoku Gunsho Ruijū Kanseikai.

Tomo Taien 伴苔園. 1924. "Nōgaku Kankōkai yodan" 能楽歓興会余談. *Yōkyokukai* 謡曲界 5: 91–95.

Tonomura Natsuko 外村南都子. 2005. "Sōka to buke shakai" 早歌と武家社会. *Kokubungaku kaishaku to kanshō* 国文学解釈と鑑賞 70, no. 12: 6–13.

Tschudin, Jean-Jacques. 2011. *Histoire du théâtre classique japonais*. Collection Essais. Série "Histoire." Toulouse: Anacharsis.

Tyler, Royall. 1990. *The Miracles of the Kasuga Deity*. New York: Columbia University Press.

Ueki Yukinobu 植木行宣. 2010. *Gion-bayashi no genryū: Furyū hayashimono, kakko chigomai, shagiri* 祇園囃子の源流——風流拍子物・羯鼓稚児舞・シャギリ. Tokyo: Iwata Shoin.

Umewaka Minoru nikki 梅若実日記. Edited by Umewaka Minoru Nikki Kankōkai 梅若実日記刊行会. 2002–2003. 7 vols. Tokyo: Yagi Shoten.

Uno Mondo nikki 宇野主水日記. In *Ishiyama Honganji nikki* 石山本願寺日記 2, edited by Uematsu Torazō 上松寅三, 493–570. 1966. Tokyo: Seibundō Shuppan.

Utai Asako 宇多井浅子. 1916. "Fujin yōkyoku hayashi taikai o mite" 婦人謡曲囃子大会を観て. *Nōgaku shashinkai* 能楽写真界 11: 20.

Varley, H. Paul. 1967. *The Ōnin War: History of Its Origins and Background, With a Selective Translation of The Chronicle of Ōnin*. New York: Columbia University Press.

Varley, H. Paul. 1990. "Cultural Life in Medieval Japan." In *Medieval Japan*. Vol. 3, *The Cambridge History of Japan*, edited by Kozo Yamamura, 447–99. Cambridge: Cambridge University Press.

Wakita Haruko 脇田晴子. 2016. *Chūsei Kyōto to Gion matsuri: ekishin to toshi no seikatsu* 中世京都と祇園祭——疫神と都市の生活. Tokyo: Yoshikawa Kōbunkan.

* Yamanaka Reiko 山中玲子. 1998. *Nō no enshutsu: sono keisei to hen'yō* 能の演出——その形成と変容. Tokyo: Wakakusa Shobō.

Yasutomiki 康富記 1–4. Edited by Sasakawa Tanerō 笹川種郎. 1938–1942. *Shiryō taisei* 史料大成 29–32. Tokyo: Naigai Shoseki.

* Yip, Leo Shingchi. 2016. *China Reinterpreted: Staging the Other in Muromachi Noh Theatre*. Lanham: Lexington Books.

Yokoyama Tarō 横山太郎. 2015. "Doko made ga nō datta no ka?" どこまでが能だったのか？ In *Nōgaku no genzai to mirai* 能楽の現在と未来, edited by Yamanaka Reiko 山中玲子, 115–35. *Nōgaku kenkyū sōsho* 能楽研究叢書 5. Tokyo: Nogami Kinen Hōsei Daigaku Nōgaku Kenkyūjo.

Yōkyokukai 謡曲界. 1940. Vol. 1 (January): 173c–74a.

Yoza yakusha mokuroku 四座役者目録. Edited by Tanaka Makoto 田中允. 1975. *Nōgaku shiryō* 能楽資料 6. Tokyo: Wan'ya Shoten.

Websites of Works Cited

Gowadanki 御和談記. National Archives of Japan. https://www.digital.archives.go.jp/img/1232249.

Gunshi gien kanjin nō hōkoku 軍資義捐勧進能報告, Kanze ākaibu 観世アーカイブ. http://gazo.dl.itc.u-tokyo.ac.jp/kanzegazo/KmView/051/051066001/kmview.html.

Kaisei-bon yōkyoku sōan 改正本謡曲草案. *Kokuritsu Kokkai Toshokan dejitaru korekushon* 国立国会図書館デジタルコレクション. https://dl.ndl.go.jp/info:ndljp/pid/2540821/1.

Kanjin nō ikkendome 勧進能一件留. 3 vols. *Kokuritsu Kokkai Toshokan dejitaru korekushon* 国立国会図書館デジタルコレクション. https://dl.ndl.go.jp/info:ndljp/pid/2605767.

Kanjin nō ikkendome 勧進能一件留. 3 vols. *Kokuritsu Kokkai Toshokan dejitaru korekushon* 国立国会図書館デジタルコレクション. https://dl.ndl.go.jp/info:ndljp/pid/2605767.

Kōka kanjin nō emaki 弘化勧進能絵巻. 2 vols. Noh Theatre Research Institute, Hōsei University, Tokyo. https://nohken.ws.hosei.ac.jp/nohken_material/htmls/index/pages/cate5/kanjin-1.html; https://nohken.ws.hosei.ac.jp/nohken_material/htmls/index/pages/cate5/kanjin-2.html.

Nara-zarashi 奈良曝. 5 vols. 1687. *Nara Kenritsu Toshokan Jōhōkan mahoroba raiburarī* 奈良県立図書館情報館まほろばライブラリー. https://meta01.library.pref.nara.jp/opac/repository/repo/138996/.

Nō bangumi dētabēsu 能番組データベース. Research Center of Classic Performing Arts, Kobe Women's University. https://noh-bangumi.yg.kobe-wu.ac.jp/. Search with 稽古 as keyword or content.

Ōkura Shōzaemon keizu 大蔵庄左衛門系図. The Nogami Memorial Noh Theatre Research Institute of Hōsei University. *Konparu-ke monjo dejitaru ākaibu* 金春家文書デジタルアーカイブ. No. 05/027. https://nohken-komparu.hosei.ac.jp/books/large/1751/1.

Sarugaku haigyō kakumen 申楽廃業各面. Kanze Bunko 観世文庫 online. http://gazo.dl.itc.u-tokyo.ac.jp/kanzegazo/KmView/054/054205001/kmview.html.

Tokyo National Research Institute for Cultural Properties (Tōkyō Bunkazai Kenkyūjo 東京文化財研究所). https://www.tobunken.go.jp/materials/pictweb/227821.html.

Yakushiji shunie hana eshiki 薬師寺修二会花会式. https://yakushiji.or.jp/event/hanaesiki.html.

2
Nō Performance

Edited by Monica Bethe and Diego Pellecchia

2.1 Fundamentals of Nō Performance
Monica Bethe

Nō performances begin with an empty stage and silence. The architecture of the stage establishes a special space distinct from ordinary life. The raised square wood floor protrudes into the audience area. This is the main stage. Four pillars at the corners of the square support a heavy roof, evidence of the stage's outdoor origins. Recessed behind the main stage, the painting of a pine decorates the back panel. A covered bridge connects the main stage with the backstage. Banisters line the bridge, and three pines stand at intervals in front of it. A five-color curtain separates it from the mirror room (*kagami no ma*) where the performers gather before entering the stage.

Sounds from offstage of a flute and drums as the musicians check their instruments (*oshirabe*) announce the beginning of a play. Attendants draw back the curtain or lift it with poles to allow the performers to pass onto the bridge. First to enter along the bridge are the musicians, who seat themselves in front of the painted pine. Chorus members enter from the small side door and quietly kneel in two rows at stage left (right as seen by the audience). If a prop is used, attendants carry it onstage and set it in place.

The sound of the flute pierces the air, drum calls punctuated by sharp beats herald the entrance of the actors. Typically, the supporting actor (*waki*) enters first and his robes reflect the occupation and status of the character: often a Buddhist monk, a Shintō priest, or a minister. Gliding down the bridge that leads to the stage from the left, the actor passes the three pines, and stops near the pillar that marks the edge of the stage proper. Here, the *waki* generally delivers the initial lines. If the *waki* portrays a traveling monk, as is characteristic of many "dream" or "phantom" nō (*mugen nō*), he comments on the places he passes through (a chant section called *michiyuki*), arriving finally at a place central to the story.[1] We as the audience experience with him his ensuing encounter with the main character (*shite*), who usually enters next.

---

[1] The *waki* character is always male and is typically performed by male actors. See chapter 3.3 for a discussion of women actors in nō.

2.1.1 Modular Structure

All performances unfold moment by moment, building a story, developing a theme. In nō, the progression of scenes tends to follow a predictable order. This is because nō plays have a modular structure in which performance modules that are defined by their lyrical, musical, and choreographic forms are assembled into larger modules. These in turn are arranged according to conventions that include methods of adapting to the needs of the storyline. The acts (*ba*), scenes (*dan*), and smaller units, or "segments" (*shōdan*), serve specific dramatic and structural functions. The modules have set musical and choreographic features. For example, the same entrance music or dance sequence recurs in numerous plays. For each instance, however, it is performed in such a way as to evoke the moment within the narrative of the play and unveil its intent by adjusting the timing and rendering to the words of the text or dramatic situation. Knowledge of the conventions provides keys to reading nō performance as action, visual expression, and musical articulation.

The high formalization of every aspect of nō dramaturgy defines it as a genre distinct from other performing arts. The rules, although precise and detailed, allow for flexibility: abbreviation, duplication, reversal, substitution, and variation of dramaturgical units with unlimited possibilities. Aural, visual, and textual markers indicate the beginnings and signal the closures of the scenes, and smaller segments (*shōdan*) that seamlessly follow one into the next to create a fluid progression. In this way, the rules offer a dramaturgical grammar that can be adapted to various situations. Deciphering this intricate multimedia system is one of the challenges, and at the same time one of the pleasures, of nō theatre appreciation.

The smallest working kinetic units are *kata*, which are movement combinations involving various parts of the body. Similarly, the smallest rhythmic units played by each of the three drummers—*kotsuzumi* (small hand drum), *ōtsuzumi* (large hand or hip drum), and *taiko* (stick drum)—are short patterns consisting of drummer's calls coordinated with drum strokes. These kinetic and rhythmic pattern units have names, as do the flute melodies. Chant sections are defined by pitch, style, meter, and method of matching the words to the drum rhythms. The sections on movement (2.4), instrumental music (2.5), and chant (2.5 and 2.6) detail each of their systems separately.

Small units are linked together into larger segments (*shōdan*) that are strung together to compose a scene. In performance, however, dance, rhythm, melody, and drumming fuse into a multifaceted experience in which the players are continually adjusting and interacting to cues built into an integrated system. The section on *shōdan* (2.7) brings these disparate elements together and describes how rhythmic, melodic, kinetic, and poetic arts merge to form the basic segments that constitute the building blocks of the dramatic structure.

2.1.2 Visual Vocabulary

The subtly sculpted masks, worn exclusively by *shite* actors, encapsulate the essence of a nō play, defining characters such as gods, demons, warriors, young beauties, jealous women, distraught mothers, ghosts, etc. The section on masks (2.8) presents their types and manipulation. It is complemented by a section on the history of mask carvers in chapter 7.3. The richly textured costumes stand out against the wood architecture, their sculptural draping encasing the actors in a visual definition of character, gender, and rank. The section on costumes (2.9) introduces the ways a limited number of garment types are layered and draped to represent numerous different stage figures. Further information on costume, fan, and mask production appears in chapter 7.2. Fans are carried by all performers; those for the *shite* help define the character and enhance the movements of the dance. Details about their use, construction and decoration are given in the section on fans (2.10). While the open nō stage jutting into the audience serves as the universal set for all performances, in some plays a larger or smaller prop—a hut, tree, or stool—locates the place more specifically, adding color and redefining space. Props, their types, construction, use, and imagery, are discussed in the section on properties (2.11).

The interpretive power of the props, fans, costumes, and masks is highlighted in the section on variations (*kogaki*, 2.12). Minor changes, such as the substitution of a prop of a thatched hut for one of a palace, can shift the reading of the entire performance. This section also explores how adjusting not only the visual but also the audial and compositional aspects of a performance affect interpretation.

2.1.3 Aesthetic Concepts

The performance of a nō play is an act of collective narration of a story, generally centered around the *shite*, in which all performers, including the musicians and the chorus participate. Actors portray characters, but they do not necessarily utter all the lines of the character (see ch. 4 *Plays*, 4.6). Convention dictates that certain parts of the text are sung by the chorus, which switches between what could be interpreted as third person narration and first person voicing the *shite* or the *waki* lines. In some sections, *shite* and *waki* alternate lines, finishing each other's sentences and blurring the distinction between them. These passages, indeed, all parts of performance, are defined as much by the musical structure as by plot development. The music is not a mere accompaniment but is integral in conveying the feelings of characters and the intent of the text.

Instrumentalists and actors work together to set the pace, modulate the expression, and create the atmosphere unique to a given piece. At the core of this is the timing, from general pacing of a play to specific realization lines and key moments. Two concepts are important for understanding the dynamics. The first, *jo ha kyū*—roughly "formal beginning, elaboration or development, and energetic finale"—is derived from *gagaku* where it refers to a progression of slow to fast sections of a composite piece. In nō, its meaning was extended. Zeami used the concept to discuss the order of plays in a program in his treatise *Kakyō* (*A Mirror to the Flower*, ca. 1418–1424) and the order of scenes within a play in his *Sandō* (*The Three Courses*, 1423). He saw it as reflecting style, complexity, and intensity.

The second is the concept of *ma*, or "space between," a term that may refer both to time intervals, such as between drummer's beats, and to physical space. The implementation of *ma* combined with *jo ha kyū* defines the rendition of each line, segment, and section of the performance. In music, the *ma* is often uneven, beginning slower and ending faster and denser (more drumbeats and more syllables). It can be clipped or elongated. Similarly, the architecture of the stage with a main acting area and a bridgeway leading off to the side creates multiple spaces sensed as closer or more distant. Physical contact between actors is rare. Turning to face another character or taking a single step toward them establishes a connection, whatever the physical distance between them.

This maintenance of distance between performers allows for multiple time frames to coexist. A nō begins in the dramatic present with the entrance of the *waki*, who remains of this world, in this time, for the entire performance. For some nō the *shite* may, however, reside in the timeless world of deities, demons, and spirits, or in the cyclical world with recurring memories of ghosts. For a while, the realm of the *shite* meshes with that of the *waki*, and the audience experiences this transcendent "present" as now.

The evocation of this multilayered reality is greatly aided by the absence of overtly realistic expression: movements vary from abstract to indicative to mimetic. Props, if used, are minimalistic; masks erase the face of the actor, and speech is intoned or chanted. What we know of nō today carries on centuries-old conventions that were reworked and adjusted to the cultural demands of changing times, as outlined in chapter 1 on the history of nō. The process of development of the repertory and stage conventions has resulted in a form in which plays and performance techniques are intrinsically connected, and in which the superfluous has been discarded. In nō, minimalism is not a value in itself but a powerful and economic tool to communicate a broad range of character and stories with just a few elements.

Kurai, or the "gravitas" or "level" of a piece, is a term employed to designate the overall atmosphere of a play.[2] Plays are ranked by their *kurai*: a "light" play

---

2 The character 位 used is also read "*i*" and is the one Zeami employs to describe different levels of performance ability and play type in his treatises *Goi* (*Five Ranks*) and *Kyūi* (*Nine*

moves at a faster pace, while a "heavy" (high *kurai*) is slower, subtler. A play like *Hashi Benkei* about a fight between the oversized Musashibō Benkei and the small but nimble youth Ushiwakamaru (later the Genji general Yoshitsune) progresses at a faster overall tempo and has a simpler text than a play like *Obasute*, which features an abandoned old woman commiserating with the moon. *Obasute* is mostly static. For this very reason, it places great demands on the main actor, who needs to express the depth of the text without relying on movement. It has a very high *kurai* and can only be performed by older master actors.

Plays, or parts of a play with a high *kurai*, are considered to be exceptionally difficult and are normally referred to as *narai mono* (mastery pieces). The word *narai* refers to the esoteric transmission of knowledge that is required to acquire complete skill in an art. In nō, this means the skills needed to perform an especially demanding piece. *Narai* pieces have a high *kurai*, therefore staging them indicates that a performer has reached an advanced expertise in the art. Prescribed performance variants (*kogaki*) usually have higher *kurai* than standard versions.

An actor might choose to perform a play with weightier *kurai* to honor a special occasion, such as an anniversary. *Kurai* refers not simply to tempo but also to the intensity of concentration shared by all those onstage. The drummers and flute player adjust their timing (*ma*) accordingly and how they "ride" (*noru*) the beat according to the *kurai* of a performance. In addition, certain masks that are older, by famed carvers, or best handled by a master, are seen as having greater *kurai*, and some costumes can only be worn by the *iemoto*, or school head. In this way, the *kurai* of a piece and performance is related to theme, tempo, and age of the character as well as to the experience of the *shite* and the economics of the production. More information on the actor's art, training, and the mounting of a performance can be found in chapter 3, *Training, Practice, and Production*.

2.1.4   *Research on Performance*

While the study of nō literature and sources has a long history (see chs. 4 *Plays*; 10 *Research Overview*), much less attention has been paid to performance elements. In modern times, Nogami Toyoichirō (1883–1950) was one of the first to go beyond simply listing what was worn or used in plays to develop a more comprehensive understanding of how elements fit together. This is seen, for instance, in his 1944 *Nōmen ronkō* (*Thoughts about Nō Masks*), in which he collates types of costumes and masks with the types of dances performed, and in

---

Ranks); therefore, it is likely that the present-day use of *kurai* reflects a modern derivative of the older idea of ranks (see ch. 4 *Plays*).

his edited 1944 *Nō no enshutsu* (*Nō Performance*), volume 4 of *Nōgaku zensho* (*The Complete Nōgaku*) that introduces the stage, movement, music, masks, costumes, and properties. The groundbreaking analysis of nō structure based on a combination of textual, musical, and staging characteristics by Yokomichi Mario (1916–2012) and Omote Akira (1927–2010) appeared in the two volumes of Iwanami Shoten's *Yōkyokushū* (*Anthology of Nō Playtexts*) in 1960 and 1963; it set the stage for further study of both texts and performance. In 1971, Frank Hoff (1932–2013) and Willi Flindt summarized his ideas in their section, "The Life Structure of Nō" in *Concerned Theater Japan*. In 1978, Monica Bethe and Karen Brazell (1938–2012) presented the multifaceted interplay of all elements in *Nō as Performance: An Analysis of the Kuse Scene of Yamamba*, and subsequently in 1982 and 1983 they developed a theory of choreography in *Dance in the Nō Theater*. Concurrently, Yokomichi refined his research on performance in his 1987 *Nō no kōzō to gihō* (*Nō Structure and Technique*). More recent studies of aspects of performance, particularly nō music and movement, include Takakuwa Izumi's 2003 and 2015 publications on instrumental music and chant, *Nō no hayashi to enshutsu* (*Nō Instrumental Performance*) and *Nō kyōgen utai no hensen: Zeami kara gendai made* (*Evolution of Nō and Kyōgen Chant: From Zeami until Today*), respectively. In addition, ongoing investigations of movement patterns and their notation at the Noh Theatre Research Institute of Hōsei University in Tokyo has broadened the understanding of kinetic expression.

The publication of a series, *Nōgaku shiryō shūsei* (*A Compilation of Nō Research Materials*), edited by the Noh Theatre Research Institute between 1973 and 1996 made available sixteenth- and seventeenth-century documents on performance. These greatly deepened the understanding not only of historical performance but also of how nō was conceptualized in the past and how this relates to modern performance. Similarly, the National Noh Theatre's exhibitions of costumes, masks, old texts, daimyō collections, and illustrations have enriched the appreciation of nō staging through time. The majority of studies on costumes, masks, and fans treat them as art objects or as historical resource materials; few of these focus, as we do here, on their stage use and interpretive role.

2.2 The Stage
Monica Bethe, Yamanaka Reiko, and Diego Pellecchia

Today, nō and kyōgen are typically performed on a special raised wooden stage (*nō butai*) that protrudes into the area of audience seating and is fitted with a

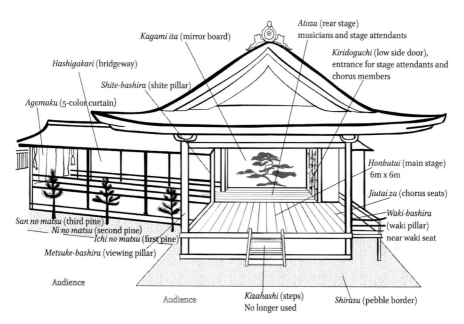

FIGURE 2.1 The parts of the nō stage

cedar-bark roof (fig. 2.1). A covered bridgeway (*hashigakari*) stretches out from stage right, and a strip of white pebbles (*shirasu*) runs along the perimeter of the stage, demarcating the performance area from the audience.[3] Three pines set in the pebbles alongside the bridgeway are a reminder of the time when performances were held on outdoor stages. At the center of the stage are steps (*kizahashi*), which are never used in performances today.

The historical evolution of the contemporary stage is outlined in chapter 7.5. In the late nineteenth and early twentieth centuries, theatre buildings were constructed around existing nō stages. Other theatres were specially built to contain nō stages. Currently, theatre buildings are equipped with dressing rooms, storage rooms for props, costumes, and masks, as well as administrative offices. Details about modern nō theatres and their use are discussed in chapter 3, section 3.4.

The main stage (*honbutai*), a square of about 5.4 meters on each side and about one meter high, is defined by four pillars (*shite-bashira, metsuke-bashira, waki-bashira, fue-bashira*) that stand at its corners and function as reference

---

3   Outdoor stages, mostly in shrines and temples, might have water (e.g., Miyajima, Hiroshima Prefecture), a moss garden (e.g., [Higashi] Honganji, Kyoto), or grass (e.g., Chūsonji, Iwate Prefecture).

FIGURE 2.2 Sketch of the placement of the chorus and instrumentalists

points for the actors during performance. At the back of the stage, the "mirror board" (*kagami ita*), painted with a pine tree, also serves to reflect the sounds toward the audience. Under the stage are earthen jars placed at different angles. These amplify the sound of the performers when they stamp rhythmically.

The *hashigakari* connects the main stage with the mirror room (*kagami no ma*). Actors and musicians enter and exit along this bridge. Still, this is not a simple passageway; it is also a performance area. For example, the main stage may represent the ground in the performance and the *hashigakari* a place above the clouds, or the two areas may each signify separate dwellings.

Musicians, chorus, and stage assistants sit in allocated spots (fig. 2.2). At the side, the eight members of the chorus sit in two rows in the *jiutai za* (chorus area). In the *atoza* ("rear area") in front of the painted pine, the instrumentalists (*hayashi-kata*): *fue* (flute), *kotsuzumi* (shoulder drum), *ōtsuzumi* (hip drum) and *taiko* (stick drum). The *kōken* (stage attendants) sit next to the bridge directly in front of the painted pine.

The mirror room is where the *shite*, who was robed in the dressing room (*gakuya*), puts on the mask and completes the preparation to perform the role to be played. Although there is no curtain between the stage and the audience, a five-color curtain (*agemaku*) separates the *hashigakari* from the mirror room. Each time an actor enters or exits, it is lifted and lowered. This is done differently in accordance with the type of character passing through: quickly

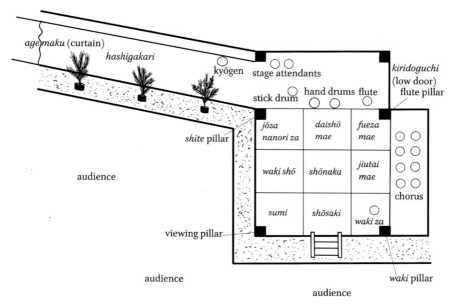

FIGURE 2.3 Top-view sketch of a nō stage with the names of areas and pillars as well as placement of performers

and violently for demons, slowly and gracefully for women and old people. For special effects, the curtain may be raised halfway, so the only part of the figure behind it is exposed, then lowered, and once again lifted for the entrance. The manipulation of the curtain is one element of the performance.

Each part of the stage has a name indicating how the space is used (fig. 2.3). The "*shite* pillar" (*shite-bashira*) marks the *jōza*, or "beginning spot" (also known as the "name-announcing spot" or *nanoriza*) where the actor stops when first entering the stage proper. Characters often give their first speech here. Other areas are known by the performer who most frequently occupies the spot: the supporting actor, or *waki*, sits in the "*waki* seat" (*wakiza*), the chorus in the "chorus area" (*jiutai za*), and the instrumentalists in the "rear area." Each pillar also has a name (e.g., *waki* pillar, flute pillar). The most prominent pillar is at the corner projecting into the audience, and this is called the "viewing pillar" (*metsuke-bashira*). The *honbutai* is divided into nine square sections. The square near the viewing pillar is called the "corner" (*sumi*). In dance sequences, the *shite* often stops at the *sumi* and performs visually striking movements before circling to another area. Other spaces are described as "in front of the hand drums" (*daishō mae*; upstage center), "in front of the flute" (*fueza mae*; upstage left), "in front of the chorus" (*jiutai mae;* center stage left), "center" (*shōnaka*), "front" (*shōsaki*), and "*waki* front" (*wakishō*; center stage right).

All that happens onstage is in full view, whether part of the narrative of the play or merely the placement of an object, the adjustment of a costume, or the strokes of the drummers. The audience sits on two, sometimes three, sides of the stage such that the action is experienced differently depending on where one sits. This is accentuated by the bridgeway: for those seated facing the painted pine an actor recedes into the distance when exiting, while for those on the side near the bridgeway, the same figure advances toward them becoming increasingly palpable. Sections 2.3 and 2.4 discuss the use of space, its fluidity, and multipurposed expressions.

2.3 Performance Conventions
Monica Bethe

2.3.1 Structure of Nō Plays: Acts (ba), Scenes (dan), and Their Spatial Dimensions

Nō plays have a wide range of dramaturgical configurations; however, there is an underlying structure that may serve as a generalized model for a great number of plays. Generally, nō have either one or two acts (*ba*). If they have two, the *shite* actor exits at the end of the first act (*maeba*) and returns, sometimes in a new form (that is, with a different mask and costume), in the second act (*nochiba*). Typically, an interlude (*ai*) featuring a narration or presentation by the *ai kyōgen* separates the first and second acts. In some pieces, the kyōgen actor plays a character in the overall narrative and may appear earlier in the first act.

In addition to this subdivision, it is possible to identify various scenes (*dan*) within each act. In his treatise on how to compose a nō play, *Sandō* (*The Three Courses*, 1423), Zeami conceived of plays as consisting of five scenes, which he delineates according to his concept of *jo ha kyū*: an introduction (*jo*), followed by three sections of development (*ha*), and ending with a conclusion (*kyū*). During the introduction, the first character enters and sets the scene. The first development section begins with the entrance of the *shite*, which often involves a monologue composed of a series of musical passages. In the second development section, the person already onstage (usually the *waki*) and the *shite* converse, ending in a chorus passage. The third development section presents the core story and contains several musical passages. Finally, the concluding scene showcases active movement, frequently a dance to instrumental music succeeded by a highlight dance while the chorus sings.[4]

---

4 Hare, trans. 2008: 152–53.

This tripartite structure—an opening, three development sections, and a finale—was commonly used by twentieth-century scholars such as Sanari Kentarō (1880–1966) and Nogami Toyoichirō (1883–1950) to present the construction of the nō plays in the annotated anthologies they published.[5] In their introduction to *Yōkyokushū* (*Anthology of Nō Playtexts*, vol. 1, 1960), Yokomichi Mario and Omote Akira built on Zeami's five-part structure of a whole nō to propose a model structure for an act consisting of: 1) *waki* entrance; 2) *shite* entrance; 3) dialogue between the *waki* and *shite*; 4) *shite* presentation; and 5) exit.[6] They saw a two-act play as repeating the same structure in modified form. In other words, act 1: 1) *waki* entrance; 2) *shite* entrance; 3) dialogue between the *waki* and *shite*; 4) *shite* presentation; and 5) *shite* exit; interlude; and act 2: 1) *waki* waits; 2) *shite* entrance; 3) dialogue between the *waki* and *shite* (often abbreviated or deleted); 4) *shite* presentation; 5) exit.

In all of the above theories, the idea of flexibility is built into the overall construct. Scenes can be abbreviated, expanded, or repeated. In fact, Zeami already acknowledged in his *Sandō* the possibility of an expansion to more scenes or a contraction to fewer.

Since each scene has a typical choreography, the placement of the actors on the stage can be a key to identifying the scene. A hypothetical progression is presented in figure 2.4a–e. This model is a simplification extrapolated from collating a broad range of nō and seeking a common thread.

In fact, most nō plays do not fit this model precisely. Some, such as *Tadanori* discussed below, conform to it comparatively well, others, especially those in which all of the action is set the present time (*genzai nō*), follow more flexible structures.[7] Nonetheless, the overall flow of entrances, interaction building to a presentation with greater activity, and a concluding scene applies to almost all nō.

The placement of each performer onstage is a key to identifying the scene. Since the stage is viewed from various angles, the placement of actors occurs along multiple axes: parallel to the sides of the stage and along the diagonals between corner pillars. Opening scenes are more static, the performers standing, or sitting, in set areas of the stage—upstage right (*jōza*) to deliver opening speeches, then downstage left (*wakiza*) for the *waki*, and center stage (*shōnaka*) for the *shite*. Action and movement around the stage increases as the scenes progress, with later scenes often focusing on danced narrative or

---

5 Sanari 1930–1931, 1982; Nogami 1949–1951, 1971.
6 Yokomichi and Omote 1960, vol. 1: 13–27; Hoff and Flindt 1973: 210–56.
7 Variant structures are most commonly found in early nō of the fourteenth century before the "mature" form of nō was developed and in later theatrical (*furyū*) nō of the later fifteenth and sixteenth centuries.

FIGURE 2.4A   *Waki* entrance. The *waki* enters along the bridge and stands at the *jōza*. If there are several *waki*, they line up in the middle of the stage. Generally, the *waki* tells his name and mission. He sings a travel song (*michiyuki*), mentioning various places on his way to a specified destination. This sets the place and circumstances for the play. He then takes a seat at the *wakiza* in front of the chorus

FIGURE 2.4B   *Shite* entrance. The *shite* enters along the bridge and may deliver the first lines here. The actor then stands at the *jōza* to recite a monologue that sets the tone and often evokes an inner psychological atmosphere

FIGURE 2.4C *Waki* and *shite* dialogue (*mondō*). The *shite* at the *jōza* and the *waki* at the *wakiza* are situated along the diagonal axis of the stage. As the *waki* questions the *shite* about the place or a special object, poem, or incident, the *shite* at times faces forward, at times turns to address the *waki*

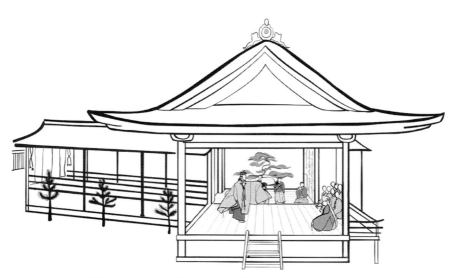

FIGURE 2.4D *Shite* presentation. While the *waki* listens and watches, the *shite*, through the chorus, narrates the key story of the play. Often, particularly toward the end of a play, this includes a dance to instrumental music followed by more dance to narration

FIGURE 2.4E Exit. After a final scene, usually danced, the *shite* stamps, generally at upstage right, to signal the end of the play. The *shite* exits along the bridge. In silence, the rest of the performers leave, first the actors, then the musicians and chorus members

dance to instrumental music during which the actor circles the stage, moves along its vertical, horizontal, and diagonal axes, and pauses here and there to perform significant gestures.

The dimensional impact of the square stage jutting out into the audience enhances the sense of immediacy. Action near the viewing pillar projects intimacy and proximity. Here, the character may look longingly at the moon, mime donning a lover's garment, or enact a poignant death scene. A return to the upstage area creates a sense of distance, at times accompanied by words indicating travel or retreat, at other times marking a closure to a sequence of movements. The *shite* addresses the *waki* along the diagonal.

The bridgeway, while mainly a passageway for entrances and exits, might be used to dramatic effect. Action on the bridge may signify a change in place, such as stepping outdoors or indoors, or moving aside to have a private conversation. In the process of a dance, retreating down the bridge adds distance, expanding the performance area, and is often followed by a sudden swift return to the stage. When, for instance, the malicious spirit of a resentful woman battles with monks in plays such as *Aoi no ue* and *Dōjōji*, the spirit is forced to retreat along the bridge almost to the curtain, where it gathers energy, swiftly strikes out and pushes the monks back down the bridge to the stage proper. In the dramatic representation of the heavenly maiden's ascent up the mountains and beyond into the sky in a variant performance of the play *Hagoromo*, the *shite* recedes down the bridge, then rushes back to the stage proper with accelerating speed, only to glide down the bridge again and vanish behind the curtain (see sec. 2.12).

2.3.2 Categorization of Nō Plays
2.3.2.1 Gobandate

The nō repertory includes a wide variety of plays with a broad spectrum of characters, both human and nonhuman, the latter being deities, demons, ghosts, sprites, animals, and spirits of plants. Some nō are slow, ponderous, and subtly delicate, others are flashy and action-packed.

Today, plays are grouped following the "five categories system" (*gobandate*, table 2.1), described in detail in chapter 4.2. It serves as a useful reference for content and character types but also, by extension, for costuming, masks, and musical expression. Simply, first category nō plays feature the appearance of a Shintō deity. Their presentation is formal, stately, and celebratory. Second category nō mostly present characters from the epic *Heike monogatari* (*The Tale of the Heike*) and narrate the fate of warriors who fought decisive battles. Third category plays focus on female characters, who often appear as ghosts remembering the trials of their love lives. The lyrical texts and sonorous music complement flowing dance movements. Fourth category plays encompass a range of topics, characters, and dramaturgical expression. They include plays set in present time with humans interacting with humans, such as the reunion of parent and child, stories of filial piety or lord-vassal loyalty, and men or women influencing a change of heart in an authoritarian character through dance or song. Fourth category plays also feature spirits or humans bent on revenge and the enactment of myths. Fifth category plays tend to be quick-paced, dynamic, and highly theatrical, such as staging the vanquishing of an evil spirit. Others present the demons, devils, and strange beings in an ambiguous or benevolent light.

TABLE 2.1   The five categories of nō plays

Gobandate category	Japanese name	English name
1st category (*shobanme mono*)	*waki nō/waki mono*	Deity plays
2nd category (*nibanme mono*)	*shura nō/shura mono*	Warrior plays
3rd category (*sanbanme mono*)	*kazura nō/kazura mono*	Woman plays
4th category (*yobanme mono*)	*zatsu nō/zatsu mono*	Miscellaneous plays
5th category (*gobanme mono*)	*kiri nō*	Finale plays

2.3.2.2 *Mugen nō* and *genzai nō*

Twentieth-century scholars looking at patterns of structure and staging conventions in nō posited a different standard for categorization. They grouped nō into *mugen* ("dream" or "phantom") *nō* and *genzai* ("present time") *nō*. In *mugen nō*, the main character has otherworldly aspects and may be a ghost or a god who often appears to the *waki* as in a dream. These plays are structured around a tale told by the *shite*. In *genzai nō*, the main character is a human alive in the narrative present. Naturally, not all nō fit perfectly into any single category, with some plays combining elements from more than one. A more detailed discussion of the literary conventions that underlie these two classifications appears in chapter 4.5.

2.3.2.3 *Mugen nō*: Spirits, Ghosts, and Gods

Typical *mugen nō* have two acts with the *shite* appearing "in disguise" in the first act as an ordinary human. At the end of the first act the *shite* hints at being a nonhuman, then disappears. After an interlude during which the *shite* changes costume and possibly mask, the *shite* reappears in the second act revealed in the character's "true" form as god, ghost, or demon.

The warrior play *Tadanori* exemplifies a typical *mugen nō* structure. The Heike warrior Tadanori was an aspiring poet and a seasoned warrior who died during the Battle of Ichinotani at Suma Bay in 1184.[8] The famed courtier-poet Fujiwara no Shunzei (1114–1204) included a poem by Tadanori in the imperial anthology *Senzai wakashū* (*A Collection of Waka of One Thousand Years*, 1187) but because the whole Taira clan was by this time declared an "enemy of the court," the poet is listed as anonymous. This disturbs the ghost of Tadanori so that when a monk (*waki*), who was formerly one of Shunzei's retainers, and his companions (*waki tsure*) break their journey to admire a cherry tree on the shore of Suma Bay, Tadanori's ghost appears in the guise of an old man (*mae shite*) and requests that his name be put to his poem (fig. 2.5a). The poem goes: "Traveling late I lodge beneath this tree. Tonight, the cherry blossoms are my host." He asks the monk to spend the night, promising to reappear and tell his story. In the second act, the *nochi shite* reappears dressed as a warrior and narrates how, when the Taira fled the capital, he slipped away in order to ask Shunzei to include his poem. Tadanori's ghost then relates his final battle when the Genji warrior Okabe no Rokuyata, who, having cut off Tadanori's head (fig. 2.5b), discovers a strip of paper in his quiver inscribed with his poem

---

8 The Genpei War (1180–1185), fought between the Heike (Taira) and Genji (Minamoto) clans, ended in the demise of the former. The story of their struggles is told in *The Tale of the Heike*; see Tyler 2012.

FIGURE 2.5A–B *Tadanori*: a) *mae shite* (old man) and b) *nochi shite* (ghost of Tadanori), Takahashi Norimasa (Hōshō school, both roles). 2021.7.17. Hōshō Nōgakudō
PHOTOS: YOSHIKOSHI STUDIO

that serves to identify him. By the end of the play, the monk and his retinue have indeed spent the night under the cherry tree that marks Tadanori's grave. They pray for his repose.[9]

Tadanori: Scene by Scene

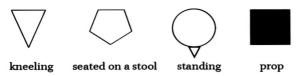

kneeling   **seated on a stool**   **standing**   **prop**

FIGURE 2.6–2.25   Key to the marking in the stage diagrams below. The initials for the role are inside the icons: "S" for *shite*, "W" for *waki*, "WT" for *waki tsure*, "k" for *kyōgen*, and "Ko" for *kokata*

Act 1

Scene 1. *Waki* Entrance

Shidai instrumental music and *shidai* chant. A monk (*waki*) accompanied by travel companions (*waki tsure*) explains that he is a former retainer of the courtier-poet Fujiwara no Shunzei (fig. 2.6a–b). He and his companions are traveling from the capital to the west and arrive at Suma Bay.

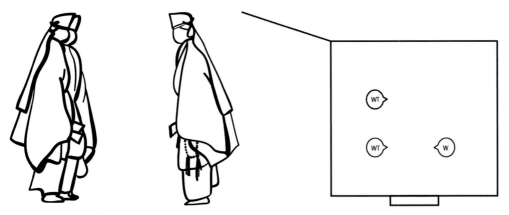

FIGURE 2.6A–B   *Tadanori*: a) *waki* and *waki tsure* entrance and b) stage placement for the *waki* entrance scene

---

9 For a translation of the play, see Tyler 1992: 260–76.

Scene 2. *Shite* Entrance

Issei instrumental music. An old man from Suma Bay appears (fig. 2.7a–b). After describing his hard life of hauling sea brine and collecting firewood from the mountain, he quotes a poem and then goes to pay homage to a blossoming cherry tree (not represented onstage).

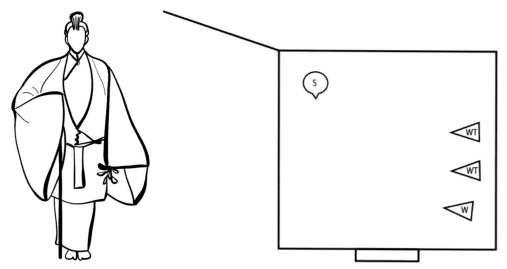

FIGURE 2.7A–B   *Tadanori*: a) *shite* entrance and b) stage placement for the *shite* entrance scene

Scene 3. *Waki-shite* Dialogue

The *waki* questions him about his work and the place (fig. 2.8a–b). An argument about mountain work and sea work is settled and parallels are drawn to the mountain cherry now on the shore.

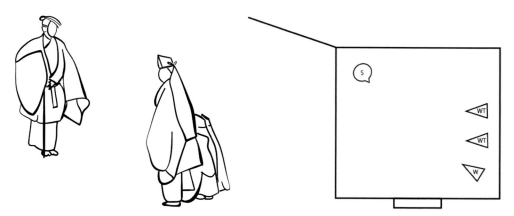

FIGURE 2.8A–B   *Tadanori*: a) *waki-shite* dialogue and b) stage placement for the *waki-shite* dialogue scene

Scene 4. *Shite* Story/Presentation-Exit

The old man invites the monks to shelter under the cherry, just as expressed in a poem by the warrior-poet Tadanori. Then, revealing he is actually the ghost of Tadanori (fig. 2.9a–b), he disappears.

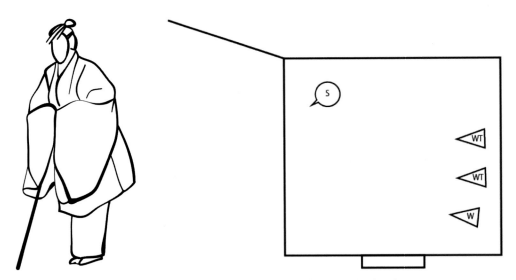

FIGURE 2.9A–B   *Tadanori*: a) *shite* presentation and b) stage placement for the *shite* presentation scene

Scene 5. Interlude (*ai kyōgen*)

A villager (*ai kyōgen*) explains to the monk that Tadanori's poem about the cherry tree was included anonymously in a poetry anthology. He also describes Tadanori's last battle with Okabe no Rokuyata. During the interlude the *shite* changes costume backstage, and mask in the mirror room.

Act 2

Scene 6. *Waki*-Waiting Song (*machiutai*)

Waki and *waki tsure* settle on the grass under the blossoms and wait for dreams (fig. 2.10a–b).

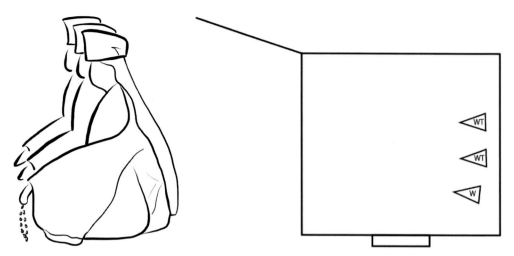

FIGURE 2.10A–B   *Tadanori*: a) *waki* waiting and b) stage placement for the *waki*-waiting scene

Scene 7. *Shite* Entrance (Act 2)

Appearing in the dream of the *waki*, the ghost of Tadanori claims he cannot rest in peace while his poem remains anonymous (fig. 2.11a–b). He asks the *waki* to appeal to Fujiwara no Teika (1162–1241), the son of the imperial anthology compiler Shunzei, to correct this.

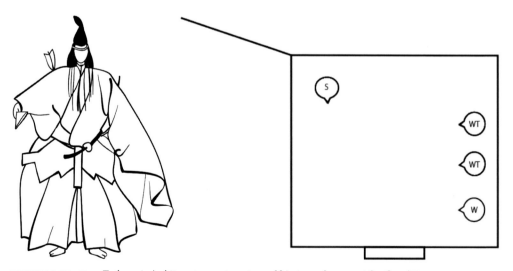

FIGURE 2.11A–B   *Tadanori*: a) *shite* entrance in act 2 and b) stage placement for the *shite* entrance scene in act 2

Scene 8. *Shite* Narrative Dance (*sageuta-ageuta* Section)

The ghost tells of Tadanori's final days and last battle, underscoring the narration with gesture and movement (fig. 2.12a–b). After requesting that his poem be included in the imperial anthology, he joins the battle at Ichinotani. Missing the escaping boats, he turns to fight Okabe no Rokuyata. They grapple. Rokuyata cuts off his arm, then his head. Seeking to identify his foe, Rokuyata discovers a poem paper in Tadanori's quiver and reading it confirms Tadanori's identity. The *shite* performs both characters, shifting seamlessly from one to the other.

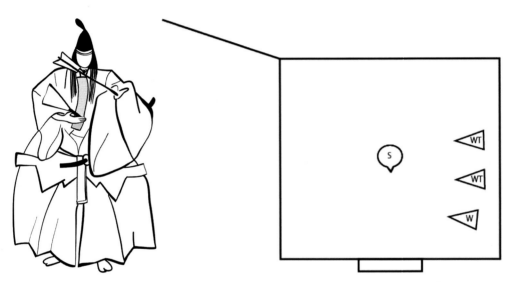

FIGURE 2.12A–B   *Tadanori*: a) *shite* dance and b) the *shite* moves around the stage miming the narrative

Scene 9. *Shite* Final Dance and Exit

After a short dance to music, the *shite* returns to the role of the ghost of Tadanori. Still moving about the stage and gesturing, the *shite* addresses the *waki* through the chorus, requests prayers, and tells the *waki* that they have now enacted the poem since they have spent the night together under the cherry tree (fig. 2.13a–b).

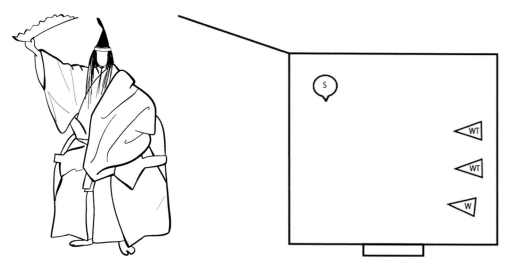

FIGURE 2.13A–B   *Tadanori*: a) *shite* final dance and b) the *shite* returns to the *jōza* before exiting

2.3.2.4   *Genzai nō*: Human Drama in the Narrative Present

While *mugen nō* often evoke a past transporting the viewer through time and memory, *genzai nō* are firmly set in the narrative present and proceed in chronological order. For this reason, *genzai nō* have a far more varied scene arrangement. To explore this in detail would require the analysis of a range of fourth and fifth category plays, such as revenge plays, lost-child plays, loyal retainer plays, and plays about military figures, vanquishing demons, and lovers' relationships. This section looks at one type of *genzai nō* to demonstrate how its structure differs from a standard *mugen nō* such as *Tadanori*.

Miidera, a "crazed person" (*monogurui*) play, presents a mother wandering in search of her child, who was stolen by slave traders. In nō, characters labeled as "crazed" are in a troubled state of heightened emotion. This unstable state spurs them to erratic actions, to the inversion of the socially accepted, and to unconventional activities, including dancing in the streets.

The play opens with the mother (*shite*) praying at a temple (fig. 2.14a). She receives an oracle interpreted as a suggestion that she go to the temple Miidera. She does so on a full-moon night. Once there, she manages to gain entrance into the temple, even though women are forbidden. After hearing the famous bell being rung, she grabs the bell rope and rings it herself. The monks and a young boy have been admiring the moon, but now the boy recognizes the woman as his mother, and they are finally united.

In *Miidera*, the first act is truncated, eliminating the *waki* entrance, substituting an exchange with the *ai kyōgen* for a dialogue with the *waki*, and

FIGURE 2.14A–B *Mīdera*: a) *mae shite* (mother praying for an oracle) and b) *nochi shite* (mother ringing the temple bell in the *Kane no dan*, or "Bell Scene"), Kongō Hisanori (Kongō school, both roles). Performance September 8, 2017. Kongō Nōgakudō, Kyoto

PHOTOS: HALCA UESUGI

skipping the presentation scene. In contrast, the second act is expanded with extra scenes. The second *ai kyōgen* takes a central role in moving the plot forward. The highlight bell-ringing scene (fig. 2.14b) is preceded by a kyōgen scene. Visual and musical interest increase with each scene until the reunion of mother and child, which in its low-keyed simplicity may appear anticlimactic. Having two *ai kyōgen* roles (*ado ai* and *omo ai*) and integrating the *ai kyōgen* role into the plot as an indispensable character are uncommon features, but not unique.

One aspect of the crazed state in lost-child plays is the upturned ending. While most nō build an increasingly complex texture leading to a final climactic scene, lost-child plays end in a denouement. The frenzied craze evaporates into normalcy when mother and child are reunited. A look at the construction of *Miidera* will elucidate how the scenes were arranged to suit this alternative trajectory of intensity and to facilitate the unfolding of the story.[10]

Miidera Scene by Scene

Act 1

Scene 1. *Shite* Entrance

The mother (*shite*) comes onstage in silence. At the temple Kiyomizudera, the mother prays to the bodhisattva Kannon to help her find her son, Senmitsu (fig. 2.15a–b). She sees an oracle in her dream.

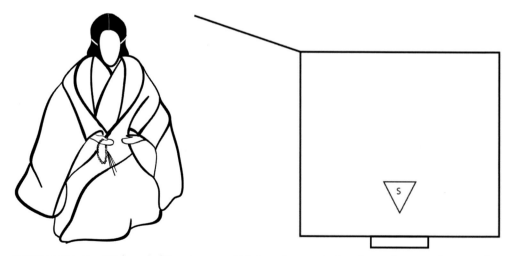

FIGURE 2.15A–B *Miidera*: a) *shite* entrance and b) stage placement when the mother prays for an oracle

---

10 Translations of *Miidera* include Kato 1998; Bethe and Emmert 1993.

Scene 2. *Shite-Ado Ai Kyōgen* Dialogue

The mother relates the oracle (fig. 2.16a–b) that she saw while dreaming to the temple gatekeeper (*ado ai*). He interprets the message as auspicious, saying that she should go to Miidera in Ōmi Province because the words include "*ō*," written "*au*," meaning "to meet," and "*mi*," meaning "to see." She sets out, both exit.

FIGURE 2.16A–B *Miidera*: a) *shite-ado ai* dialogue and b) stage placement for the *shite-ado ai* dialogue

Act 2

Scene 3. *Waki* Entrance

The head monk of Miidera (*waki*) enters with other monks (*waki tsure*) and a child (*kokata*). He introduces himself and his young acolyte (fig. 2.17a–b). They await the setting of the sun in anticipation of a clear full moon. This self-introduction, followed by a poetic passage about the landscape, typifies *waki* entrance scenes, which normally would begin the first act.

FIGURE 2.17A–B *Miidera*: a) *waki* entrance and b) stage placement for the *waki* entrance

Scene 4. *Waki* and *Omo Ai Kyōgen* Dialogue

The temple servant (*omo ai*) and head monk comment on the moon. The monk then asks the servant to perform for the acolyte (fig. 2.18a–b). He does, but is distracted by noise from outside and discovers it is a crazed woman. The monk refuses to let the woman in, but the servant is so tempted that he allows her to pass on the sly.

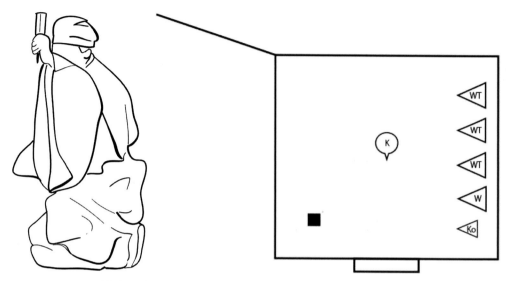

FIGURE 2.18A–B   *Miidera*: a) *omo ai* presentation and b) stage placement for the *omo ai* presentation

Scene 5. *Nochi shite* Entrance

The mother travels along the bridge to Miidera (*michiyuki*; fig. 2.19a–b). Distraught with thoughts of her lost child, her confused mind incites her to perform an anguished dance (*kakeri*). She then rambles on about gusty winds as she nears the temple and arrives at the main stage. The travel song and anguish dance create an early highlight scene with erratic music and movement.

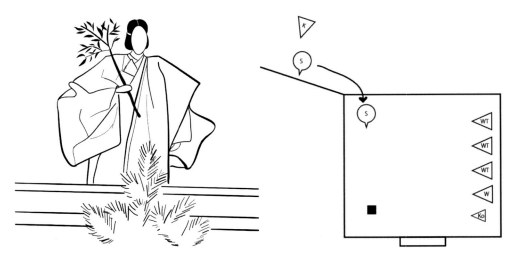

FIGURE 2.19A–B   *Miidera*: a) *nochi shite* entrance and b) stage movement for the entrance of the *nochi shite*

Scene 6. *Waki-shite* Coincidental Monologues

Waki and *shite* utter separate speeches, not a dialogue. In alternating passages, the monks at downstage left and the mother at upstage right (fig. 2.20a–b) gaze at the moon and in separate soliloquies wax lyrical about its beauty above the lake waters.

FIGURE 2.20A–B   *Miidera*: a) *shite* monologue and b) stage placement for the *shite-waki* monologues

Scene 7. *Shite* and *Omo Ai* Dialogue

The servant rings the late-night bell (fig. 2.21a–b). The mother is drawn to it, hits the servant from the back and demands to ring it herself. The text details the beauty of various bell sounds and related stories. The mimetic actions of the *omo ai* in this added interlude-like scene function to lighten the mood.

FIGURE 2.21A–B *Miidera*: a) servant ringing bell and b) stage placement for the kyōgen bell ringing

Scene 8. *Shite* "Bell Scene" (*Kane no dan*)

In the *shite* "Bell Scene" (fig. 2.22a–b; see also fig. 2.14b), the monk tries to prevent the mother from ringing the bell, but she prevails, quoting a Chinese precedent. While she rings the bell, she lists other examples of bell ringing related to Buddhism. This highlight scene full of poetry has a special mimetic section that focuses on interaction with the bell prop. Although in the previous scene the *omo ai* mimed ringing the bell, here the *shite* actually pulls on the bell cord of the small bell in the tall bell-tower prop.

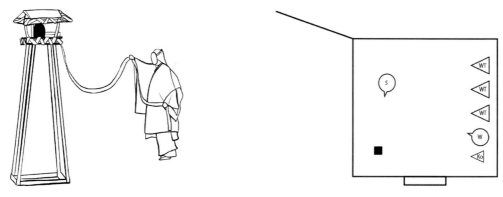

FIGURE 2.22A–B *Miidera*: a) *shite* bell scene and b) stage placement for the *shite* bell scene

Scene 9. *Shite* Narrative (*kuse* Section)

In a continuum of action flowing out of the bell scene, the mother eventually kneels at center stage while the chorus for her sings a long litany of bells and their implications. She grows more coherent, ending with an account of the beauty of the bell resounding over the lake and her solitary search for her child (fig. 2.23a–b).

FIGURE 2.23A–B   *Miidera*: a) *shite* narrative and b) stage placement at the end of the narrative

Scene 10. Reunion: *Shite, waki, kokata*

Narrative gives way to acting. The acolyte asks the monk to question the mother about her identity. Both mother and child recognize each other. After the boy reveals that he was taken by slave traders, the monks are convinced (fig. 2.24a–b). The tolling bell has brought parent and child together and has brought sanity to the mother's mind. With normalcy now returned, the visual excitement of the preceding scenes dissolves into a quiet ending.

FIGURE 2.24A–B   Miidera a) shite *kokata* reunion and b) placement for the reunion scene

Scene 11. Exit Scene
The reunited mother and child leave together and return home (fig. 2.25a–b).

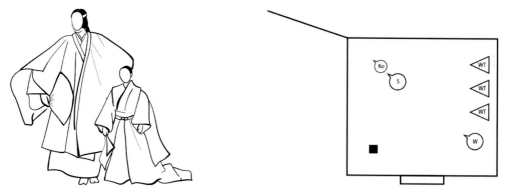

FIGURE 2.25A–B   *Miidera*: a) *shite* and *kokata* exit and b) stage placement for exit scene

Location is treated differently in *Tadanori* and *Miidera*. The absence of elaborate sets makes possible shifts in location, established primarily through the text and verbal reference. In *Tadanori* and many *mugen nō*, the *waki* travels to a place at the beginning of the play. This establishes the site of the rest of the performance. In *Miidera*, however, there is a change of place between the first and second acts, from Kiyomizudera in Kyoto to Miidera on Lake Biwa. While the *waki* remains at Miidera, the *shite* is seen approaching the temple at the end of a long walk over the mountains. Such alterations in setting between the first and second acts occur frequently in *genzai nō* but rarely in *mugen nō*.

The system for modifying the structure of a nō play includes doubling scenes, deleting scenes, and reversing their order, such as the *shite* entering before the *waki*. Expansion, contraction, and other manipulation of the structure occur in units—that is, in whole scenes or segments. This flexibility allows for a wide variation that is adjusted to the needs of each text and storyline, yet also builds on the basic units of the system. Nō set in present time that follow a chronological progression often have less rigid structures.

2.3.3   *Progressions*

The models presented here move from simple introductions of individual characters to their interaction. This then turns to aural description and visual enactment—in other words, the progression goes from simple to complex, from single voice to increasingly multilayered voices. The dialogue gives way to chorus recitation. Speech mutates to poetry and song. The instruments add further musical dimensions. This progression from formal introduction to content elaboration to a final flourish follows a similar trajectory as the concept of *jo ha kyū* (formal beginning, interesting development, flashy finale). As will be discussed in subsequent sections of this chapter, the progression from slow to fast, from simple to complex, from still to active informs all aspects of performance. The progression is cyclical, *jo ha kyū*, and back to *jo*, and cumulative. The methods of variation introduced above provide a fluid and flexible formula that retains the fingerprint of a model structure but permits the adjustment to the needs of the story, text, and performance.

2.4 Movement
Monica Bethe with Diego Pellecchia

As the five-colored curtain is lifted, a character comes into view. In a beautifully sculpted costume, the character moves down the bridge, the upper body steady while the feet slide along the polished floor boards, pristine white *tabi* socks accentuating articulated steps. The movements in nō are highly condensed. They seem still yet in motion, suspended yet grounded, flowing yet clearly punctuated.

In the sense that the actors stand, sit, walk, leap, or stamp with controlled precision, fully aware of every part of their bodies at all times, the entire nō performance might be seen as formalized, minutely prescribed choreography. This movement is integrally tied to the lyrics and to the instrumental music. In a complete staging of a play the text is delivered by actors (performers enacting characters) and by a chorus. The actors' movements are timed to the sung text; the *shite* faces forward while the *waki* speaks and then pivots toward the *waki* at times when addressing him. These small movements serve to enhance the meaning, although for the most part they are not overtly mimetic. This holds even for long sections of the performance that are largely static. Such scenes focus on the recitation of monologues or of descriptive passages, rather than on movement. The stillness allows the audience to envision the places described as the character narrates travels through various landscapes. During a dialogue scene, even these slight movements are deeply impactful.

As the plot develops and the dramatic tension intensifies, more movements are added to the words. These movements highlight specific passages, thus providing visual and kinetic dimensions to the recitation. Such movements rarely represent the actions of a character in a realistic manner (that is, "as they would appear in real life"). A number are close enough to "real-life" actions to appear as stylized versions of them, while the most frequently used movements, although basically abstract, are sufficiently reminiscent of daily actions to evoke associations when correlated to the lyrics. These gestures—arm movements combined with steps and stamps—are codified into modules called *kata* ("forms" or "patterns"), which in turn are connected to create sequences that, when strung together, constitute the choreography of a play.

2.4.1   Fundamentals: Kamae *and* hakobi

The root of all action and non-action is the basic stance (*kamae*) and the walk (*hakobi*) that originates from the *kamae*.

2.4.1.1   Basic Stance (*kamae*)

With straight back, chin pulled in, arms at the side somewhat away from the torso, the basic stance (fig. 2.26) acts as a central axis from which all movement arises and to which all movement returns. The upper body maintains this stance even while the feet slide along the boards, pivot, back up, or stamp. The torso remains static as the arms rise and fall, or make circular motions. There is a stillness within motion from which the energy of the actor emanates.

FIGURE 2.26
Basic stance: *kamae*

FIGURE 2.27   Sliding step: *hakobi* or *suriashi*

2.4.1.2   Walk (*hakobi*)

The verb *hakobu*, here in nominative form *hakobi*, means "to carry." It refers to the walk that is characterized by sliding the feet along the stage boards and thus the style called *suriashi*, or "sliding step." For this, the actor slides one foot forward along the floor, briefly lifts the front of the foot, and then shifts the weight onto the forward foot, releasing the back foot so it can slide forward (fig. 2.27). The upper body is kept at a constant height, which creates a sense of the figure gliding through space. Rotating the feet turns the torso, shifting the view of the mask. Pivoting to face another actor engages the characters in direct address with one another.

The stillness of the stance and the fluidity of movement keep the mask at a consistent angle. Since the mask severely restricts peripheral vision, the sliding step also has practical implications. The actor maintains foot contact with the floor, feeling the slight gaps between the wooden boards of the floor, which helps navigation to the various areas of the stage. *Kamae* and *hakobi* are performed differently depending on the character. In addition, small variations distinguish each of the *shite* and *waki* stylistic schools (*ryūgi*). Also, individual actors might have distinctive styles, with divergences that include how the hips are angled, the extent to which the knees are bent or straightened, and the height and curvature of the arms at rest.

Role types require adjustments in the *kamae* and *hakobi* that reflect gender, age, and, in some cases, occupation. For a woman's role, the knees are less bent, the arms closer to the body, the toes straight forward, and the steps smaller. For a strong deity or mighty warrior, the knees are bent, the arms higher at rest, and the toes turned out, such that when the actor stops with one foot forward, the body is at an angle to the direction of the motion. This gives an impression of strength similar to the stance in Japanese martial arts. Although modern practice has presumably changed from that of the fifteenth century, this distinction in stance, which determines the style of all movement generated from it, was already delineated in Zeami's *Nikyoku santai ningyō zu* (*Figure Drawings of the Two Arts and the Three Modes*, 1421; see ch. 6 *Treatises*, 6.2).[11]

2.4.2 *Basic Movement Modules:* Kata

As noted above, the modules that constitute the basic vocabulary of movement combine arm and foot actions. These movement modules that form the kinetic language of nō, and today referred to as *kata*, have names or identifying descriptions. They have been passed down from generation to generation of actors through practice and training within the context of pieces. They are never taught as isolated movements divorced from the words and music.

Most *kata* do not have an intrinsic "meaning" separate from their context as matched to the lyrics. To the uninitiated viewer, *kata* may appear as abstract movements, sometimes interspersed with a few recognizable gestures. This is

---

11   Hare, trans. 2008: 139–49.

because, first and foremost, *kata* do not aim at providing a true-to-life imitation of the narrated passage, and secondly, their very abstractness allows for multiple interpretations and uses. The ambiguous semantics of *kata* elicit the active participation of the audience, who fills the gap between lyrics and movement. On the other end of the spectrum, a few of the gestures are closer to their "real-life" counterparts and therefore immediately recognizable even by the nonspecialist. As will be explained in more detail below, the choreography of a nō play loosely mixes both kinds of *kata*.

2.4.2.1   Example: *Kata* and the Spectrum of Expression

Kata range from a single stamp to complex arm movements combined with steps forward, backward, or shifting directional orientation. To execute almost all *kata*, the torso is held still, the arms are used as single units that extend to the end of the fan, and the feet slide along the boards in *suriashi* style.

Perhaps the most ubiquitous *kata* is the "forward point" (*sasu*) involving lifting the right arm, which holds the fan, up to the front until it is almost level with the shoulder and the fan points forward. When combined with stepping forward, it is called *sashikomi* in the Kanze school and *shikake* in other schools (fig. 2.28a–b). Renditions of the forward point include varying the number of steps, the height of the point position—for example, higher when pointing at the moon, lower when pointing at a nearby river—and the timing of execution. Stylistic variations reflect school (*ryūgi*) traditions and adjustments for expression of mood and type of role.

The same *kata* may be performed differently depending on the scene and the character. Zeami in his *Nikyoku santai ningyō zu* broadly grouped the styles of performing *kata* into Martial (*guntai*), Woman (*nyotai*), and Aged (*rōtai*).[12] For a woman's role, he stipulated that one "cast force aside."[13] In modern performance, the actor keeps the arms somewhat lower, even in the final point position of a *sasu* or *sashikomi*, and moves with suspended flow. The toes point forward when walking. For the martial mode, which is used not only for warriors in battle scenes but also for demons and strong gods, Zeami stated the movements as, "With force as Substance, make the intent intricate."[14] Today, the actor's more powerful execution involves withholding and releasing energy. A point pattern ends with the point usually higher than for a woman's role and the torso at an angle. This "half-shifted" (*hanmi*) position is a direct result of

---

12   Zeami suggests that all roles are a combination or variation on the basic three modes. Hare 1986: 131–224.
13   Hare, trans. 2008: 143.
14   Hare, trans. 2008: 144–45.

FIGURE 2.28A–B   The forward point pattern: a) woman's mode, fan open (left) and b) martial mode, fan closed (right)

the warrior's *kamae*, with toes turned out. If the right foot ends in front pointing forward, the left toes remain pointed "out" in relation to the right, thereby shifting the torso orientation to the left. Conversely, the torso is angled to the right when the left foot is forward. One might also see the woman and martial modes as two contrasting articulations of *jo ha kyū* timing: slow beginning, gaining speed, final position, and then back to the beginning: the woman's movements tend to be gentle, inwardly focused, and elegant, while the strong and dynamic actions of the warrior in battle, vigorous god, or demon are typically sharp, angled, and definitive. The modulation of this wave-like, circular flow creates the style of the dance. The grace, power, and tempo with which a movement is performed, as well as its juxtaposition to the words being chanted, express the mood and evoke the meaning.

The *hiraki* ("open") pattern (fig. 2.29a) generally follows the forward point and serves to complete the movement in order to return to the basic stance. The *hiraki* involves taking three steps backward while spreading both arms out to the side. In the martial mode, the steps are larger when stepping back, the feet set at an angle, and the arms raised higher (fig. 2.29b). In this way, the same

FIGURE 2.29A–B   The *hiraki* pattern: a) woman's mode (left) and b) martial mode (right)

kata can be adjusted for each character. Style and timing become major means for interpretation.

The same pattern can express a range of "meanings," even within one play, when correlated to the text. In *Tadanori*, for instance, the forward point occurs four times in Kanze-school choreography. First, when Tadanori goes back to the capital to request that his poem be included in an anthology, the *sashikomi* underscores the intensity of his desire. Performed to the words, "[I returned] to beg my poem be published," it has no specific meaning beyond emphatic action. Secondly, during a description of the Battle of Ichinotani, when Tadanori is seeking to board a boat and escape with the others of his clan, he looks back and sees the enemy approach. While the chorus identifies the enemy as, "a man from Musashi Province," the actor [Tadanori], raising his arm, takes a step toward where the enemy would be. Although Tadanori's adversary Okabe no Rokuyata does not appear onstage, pointing toward him evokes his presence in an implicative action. Thirdly, after the description of Tadanori's death and Rokuyata's discovery of his poem written on a paper attached to one of his arrows, the actor [now as Tadanori's ghost] faces the *waki*. He advances, pointing, and says, "[I waylaid you] to tell this tale." Here, the *sashikomi* is a direct address and close to mimetic action that shifts the scene to the dramatic present. And finally, quoting Tadanori's poem, "Traveling late, I lodge beneath this tree; tonight the blossoms serve as host," the forward point is performed to the words "beneath this tree." Indicating the tree, which is not represented by a prop, references the central motif or image of the play. The same movements have been utilized to intensify a feeling, to evoke a presence, to address a person, and to point to a tree that exists only in the imagination of the audience. Abstract *kata* like the forward point may also function as choreographic indicators—that is, to mark the beginning of a sequence of movements, as will be discussed below.

2.4.3   Analysis of Kata Types (Movement Modules)

It is important to state at the outset that, as with other elements in nō, there is no unified, official way to categorize *kata* into types. Performers learn the movements in context and may not concern themselves with the theory behind the practice. Indeed, a classification of *kata* types is one of the least studied aspects of nō performance. Two major works in the field are by the Japanese scholar Yokomichi Mario and the American scholars Monica Bethe and Karen Brazell.[15] Both studies describe the bodily movements and consider the *kata* within the context of their use, focusing on the extent to which it is abstract or referential and whether it carries a specific mimetic meaning. Bethe and Brazell also coordinate this with the function of *kata* within the choreography.

Yokomichi suggests a categorization of nō movements into two types of units or *kata* in more conventional nō parlance: "basic blocks" (*kiso tangen*) and "special blocks" (*tokutei tangen*). He considers the "basic blocks" to be those *kata* with no univocal meaning. By contrast, "special blocks" are movements that have a univocal meaning. Following a subdivision shared by other Japanese scholars, Yokomichi's subdivision is largely based on the semantic value associated with each movement. In fact, there is a broad gray area here, as the meaning of a large group of *kata* is not fixed but depends on the words of the text they accompany.

Bethe and Brazell offer a more complex categorization of *kata*, whereby *kata* belong to one of two main groups: "ground patterns" and "design patterns."[16] Ground patterns are more frequently performed and lay the groundwork for most dance sections, performed both to chant and to instrumental music, in which they are abstract elements delineating the choreographic structure.

---

15   Yokomichi 1987: 261–80; Bethe and Brazell 1982: 52–68; 1983: 28–136.
16   For charts of the basic ground and design patterns and their uses, see the website JPARC.online.

These ground patterns can also carry a contextual meaning when performed concurrently with words or phrases, as seen in the use of the "forward point" above. Design patterns, instead, are performed less frequently, usually at highlight passages of the play, and tend to carry more concrete meaning. In addition, design patterns are further classed as "abstract, dance-like" movements, which are closer to ground patterns in that their relationship with meaning is ambiguous, and "mimetic" movements, whose appearance is closer to 'real-life' gestures. As a result, the latter directly denote meaning. Bethe and Brazell also categorize patterns by their kinetic traits, such as "foot patterns," "fan-centered patterns," or "body-centered patterns." While Yokomichi's approach was largely semiotic, Bethe and Brazell's categorization combines phenomenological analysis (what part of the body is involved in the movement) with semiotic analysis (about the relationship between movement and meaning) and formal analysis (the frequency of occurrence and structural role within the choreography).

These attributes for categorizing *kata* place them on a sliding scale between simple and complex, abstract and realistic, ambiguous and univocal meaning. Yet another attempt at clarifying the various types and uses of *kata* was proposed by Konparu Kunio (1926–1984). He places them on two vectors. One runs from pure dance through descriptive patterns and dramatic *kata* and the other from abstract movements through symbolic patterns to realistic ones.[17] Here, we have used the Bethe-Brazell terminology as it fits most easily into the following discussion of choreography.

2.4.3.1   Ground *Kata*

This category contains *kata* such as standing/sitting, step back/forward, moving around the stage, turn, jump, or stamp. The majority of ground *kata* recur often within a piece, such as the forward point discussed above, *hiraki* (opening), *sayū* (left-right pointing sequences; fig. 2.30a), and *uchikomi* (circling the fan from back to front over the head; fig. 2.30b). Movements in this category can be considered as ground patterns because they are frequently performed and because they have no exclusive semantic use. In addition, a core set of these *kata* are used for formal purposes within the choreographic structure. Similarly, the different ways of holding a fan outlined below often have no semantic meaning in connection with the narrative but have formal purposes in choreography.

Customs govern how these basic *kata*, which inform the framework for all dances, are strung together in series and how they function as "grammatical" indicators. For instance, the "*sayū-uchikomi-hiraki*" series involves one step to

---

17   Komparu 1983: 217–19.

FIGURE 2.30A–C   The series of *kata*: a) *sayū* ("left-right"); b) *uchikomi* ("overhead circling point"); and c) *hiraki* ("open").

the left raising the left arm, one step to the right raising the right arm (fig. 2.30a), followed by circling the fan over head to a front point while taking one step forward (fig. 2.30b), and then spreading the arms and stepping back in an open pattern (fig. 2.30c). This frequently occurs at the end of a dance or the end of a section within a dance. The larger version of the same arm movements—the "*ōzayū-uchikomi-hiraki*" series—involves multiple steps in each direction and occurs in the middle of a dance just after an internal break.[18] While these are not the exclusive uses of these two series of *kata*, they typify how ground patterns create a grammar of choreography.

2.4.3.2   Design *kata*

Design *kata* occur less frequently than ground *kata* and tend to be associated with more specific meanings. These *kata* are added to fill out the framework of a dance or to highlight a moment in the narrative. Although they are less abstract and therefore less versatile than ground *kata*, design *kata* do not necessarily have a univocal meaning, as evinced in the *kata* called *hane ōgi* ("feather fan"; fig. 2.31a). The *hane ōgi* pattern belongs to a core group of design *kata* that are centered on fan manipulation, most of which have names that include the word *ōgi* ("fan"), such as *makura ōgi* ("pillow fan"; fig. 2.31b) and *maneki ōgi* ("beckoning fan"). With *hane ōgi*, the open fan is held in the right hand across the chest so it rests on the left upper arm, and then it is swept out and to the

---

18   A common occurrence for the *ōzayū* sequence is following the single *shite* line, or *ageha*, in a *kuse* dance.

FIGURE 2.31A–C   Design patterns: a) *hane-ōgi* (feather fan); b) *makura-ōgi* (pillow fan); and c) *shiori* ("weeping")

right until the arm is extended to the right. The action can be repeated to create a sense of the wind blowing (e.g., in *Hagoromo* to the words "fluttering in the beach breezes"). The large diaphanous sleeves worn by the dancer billow with the gesture, evoking a sense of wind and flight. The same action, however, is used in *Nonomiya* to suggest brushing dew from a fence.

Not all design *kata* are named. A large number of actions, thought of as *kata*, are merely indicated by describing the movement involved. These include mimetic actions, such as scooping water or shouldering a heavy object, methods of handing objects like sticks or hats, the manipulation of the large sleeves that might be twirled around the arm or thrown over the head like a veil, and head movements focused on the mask. Yet another group of design *kata* are more overtly mimetic, as seen in *shiori* ("weeping"), which can signify dejection and crying (fig. 2.31c).

The martial *kata* also belong to this group: striking and slashing with a sword or manipulating a halberd. Some go beyond the realistic, like "grappling" (fig. 2.32a), which evokes two people locked in combat by crossing both arms. Both in full performance and in the recital version of warrior's dance, the fan substitutes for a shield in the *kata* for "setting the shield" (fig. 2.32b). This precedes unsheathing a sword, which in a fully costumed performance may be a sword hand prop, but in the *shimai* version, a fan replaces the sword (fig. 2.32c).

2.4.4   *Dances and Their Choreographies*

Certain sections of a play emphasize movement and are referred to as "dances." If the dances accompany song, they are *shimai*. If they are performed to longer instrumental passages, they are called *mai* or *mai-goto*, and when the instrumental accompaniment is shorter or more dramatically explicit, they are

FIGURE 2.32A–C   Martial patterns: a) grappling (*ryōte o kumiawase*); b) setting the shield; and c) striking the enemy (*utsu*)

called *hataraki* or *hataraki-goto*. These danced sections involve moving around the stage from area to area while performing *kata*. To create a choreographed dance, the *kata* are strung together in predictable series performed at stipulated areas of the stage. In order to understand fully the modular conventions that govern movement and dance in nō, they must be considered within the greater context of text and music.

2.4.4.1   *Shimai*: Dances to Song

There are three main types of dances to sung text (*shimai*): *kuse, dan mono*, and final dances (*kiri*).[19] Of the three types, *kuse* dances, performed during the narrative *kuse* section (see sec. 2.7), have the most formal structure. The dancer begins the *kuse* dance with a closed fan (fig. 2.33a), and circles the stage (fig. 2.34a). In the middle of the dance he or she opens the fan (fig. 2.33b) while singing a single line (*age-ōgi* or *ageha*), zigzags across the stage to the front (fig. 2.34b). The *kuse* dance ends with extending the hold of the fan (fig. 2.33c) and circling the stage again (fig. 2.34c).

Dan mono refers to another type of danced narrative section. *Dan* sections center on a specific image, sometimes involving manipulation of a prop, such as the ringing of a temple bell in the "Bell Scene" (*Kane no dan*) in *Miidera*

---

19   *Kiri* for final dances is only one of several types of final dances, which are more accurately referred to by their various musical structures.

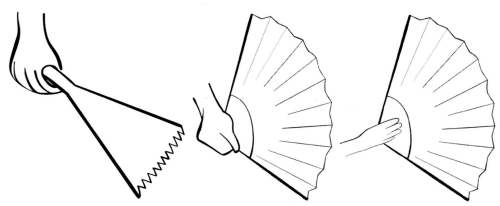

FIGURE 2.33A–C Fan holds marking sections of a *kuse* dance: a) closed for first circling; b) opened in the middle; and c) extended for closure

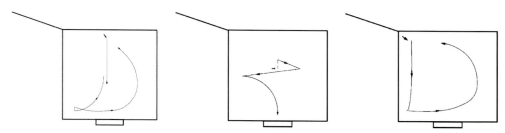

FIGURE 2.34A–C Movement around the stage during a *kuse* dance: a) *kuse* opening left circling; b) middle *sayū* zigzag; and c) closure left circling with fan extended

discussed above in section 2.3. The choreographic structure of a dan is adjusted to the enactment of the scene and thus less prescribed than that of the *kuse*. The music also is less regulated, although it is similar to *kuse* in that it is sung by the chorus to the accompaniment of the two hand drums.

Technically, final dances, loosely referred to as *kiri*, go by a number of names differentiated by the rhythm of the chant and drums—for instance, final dances to *ōnori* chant are indicated as *noriji*. The final dances enhance the climax of the performance. The fan is open from the beginning and design patterns are used extensively. Although the final dances tend to begin and end with one of a select number of standard opening and closure series, their choreographic structure is very loosely defined. Text and imagery dictate the movement more than formal structure.

Warrior plays, for example, generally end with a scene in the warrior's hell, the Asura realm (*shuradō*) of continuous battle or with a retelling of a battle that incorporates a combat scene. The patterns for sword fighting mimic the martial arts: setting the shield, striking, and stabbing (see fig. 2.32a–c). Because, however, a single actor performs all the roles, some of the *kata* represent combat figuratively by combining the actions of both defender and attacker. In *Tadanori*, for instance, Tadanori grapples with his adversary Rokuyata, is knocked off his horse, has his arm cut off, and is then beheaded. Crossing the arms above the head indicates the two warriors struggling as they grapple on horseback. Twirling and sinking to the ground suggests Tadanori falling off his horse. Letting the arm go lax evokes the act and result of severing the arm. Raising the arm above the head and allowing the point of the fan to drop backward indicates beheading Tadanori (see fig. 2.5b).

2.4.5 *Progression of Choreographic Elements within a Play*

Section 2.3 introduced the idea of cumulative progressions, and in choreography this progression moves from stillness to motion, from simple movement around the stage to complex strings of *kata*. One of the most basic choreography modules is the left circling of the main stage. It is standard for the *shite* to make the first small circling during the first chorus chant (*shodō*). Fuller renditions of this left circling serve as openings and closures to *shimai* and *mai*.

As outlined above regarding standard *kuse*, circling or zigzagging across the stage, pointing or stamping, and changing the fan hold form the framework of the choreography. Within the context of the poetic narrative, these basic ground patterns, which form the structure, might also express the text when juxtaposed with the chant.

At specified places in the choreographic structure referential design patterns can be added to enliven the movement and underscore the text. These more dynamic patterns are inserted sparingly in dances that appear earlier in the play, such as the *kuse*, and more frequently in the final dances ending the play, where they heighten the interest and intensity. In the standard Kanze-school version of *Hagoromo*, for instance, the *kuse* has thirty-three lines of text but only three design patterns (9 per cent), while the final dance (*kiri*) has fifteen lines of text and eight design patterns (53 per cent) that specifically underscore the text. Of the eight, five occur in succession linked in the middle by one ground pattern (see below). The *kiri* describes the heavenly maiden showering presents on mankind and then taking leave, her feather mantle fluttering in the breeze as she rises over the pine beach and ascends against the background of distant mountains.

Text and translation	Dance patterns
Shippō jūman no takara o furashi Showering jewels and treasures	design pattern *maneki ōgi*: bring both hands from head down to the front
Kokudo ni kore o hodokoshi tamō To bestow on the domain	design pattern: kneel holding out the flat fan as if presenting the treasures
Saru hodo ni toki utsutte Meanwhile, the time has come	functional ground pattern: circle left, also suggests the passage of time
Ama no hagoromo Heavenly feather robe	left hand to right shoulder indicates garment (preparation for *hane ōgi*)
Urakaze ni tanabiki tanabiku Fluttering and billowing in sea breezes	design pattern *hane ōgi*: left arm swings out to the left and back fluttering the fan
Mio no matsubara Mio pine grove	design pattern *kakae ōgi*: nestle the open fan in the crook of the arm, look out at pines
Ukishima ga kumo no floating island, clouds on	mask manipulation, *omote tsukai*: look up to the left then right
Ashitaka yama ya Fuji no takane Mount Ashitaka and Mount Fuji's high peak	design pattern *ue e sasu*: stepping back, point high at peak

2.4.6 Long Dances to Instrumental Music (mai)

The dances performed to instrumental music (*mai*) form an audio-visual highlight in a nō play, expressing in sound and movement the atmosphere of piece without the support of text. Although these long instrumental dances go by many names—the slow, quiet *jo no mai*; the medium-paced *chū no mai*, and so forth—they are all based on the same choreographic and musical structures. Yet this uniformity is almost imperceptible due to the differences in costume, style of movement, and rendition of the music. Two long instrumental dances that do not include the word "*mai*" in their name are *gaku* evoking a *bugaku* court dance and *kagura* evoking a dance of a Shintō shrine maiden. Although these two pieces have their own distinctive melodies, their basic choreographies are the same as for *mai*, except for a few details and the handheld objects. *Gaku* increases the number of stamps and the dancer holds a Chinese-style

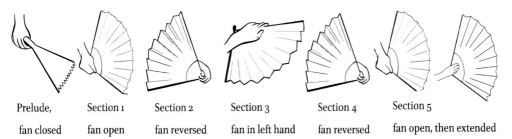

| Prelude, fan closed | Section 1 fan open | Section 2 fan reversed | Section 3 fan in left hand | Section 4 fan reversed | Section 5 fan open, then extended |

FIGURE 2.35   The fan holds marking the sections of a *mai*: prelude: closed; section 1: open; section 2: reversed; section 3: in the left hand; section 4: reversed; and section 2: opened in right hand, then extended

round fan (*tō-uchiwa*). *Kagura* includes a distinctive bowing pattern and the dancer holds a Shintō purification tool, a stick with folded paper strips (*gohei*).

The choreography of the *mai* shares numerous similarities with that of the *kuse*. The standard *mai* has five sections (*dan*), and each is distinguished by a fan hold (fig. 2.35). These are altered at the junctures where one section links to the next. Each change of fan hold occurs at a specific spot on the stage: open fan at stage center; the first backward-held fan at stage left; left-hand fan at downstage right; and so forth (fig. 2.36). The middle sections of the instrumental dances (sections 1, 2, and 3) also have short passages called *oroshi* where the music slows, and the dancer stays in place. These *oroshi* are accentuated with stamps and sleeve manipulation.

True to the rule of abbreviation and expansion, the five sections of a standard *mai* can be shortened to two or three sections, or extended to as many as thirteen (see sec. 2.12). Today the number of sections is usually decided before the performance, but in the past a change in the way the fan was held and the position of the actor onstage served to notify the musicians of the *shite*'s wish to skip or repeat sections. This convention is apparent in the different ways the stylistic schools abbreviate the dance. The Kanze school skips the second section, going from the first section with open fan to the downstage right corner (rather than left) and takes the fan in the left hand (rather than reversed hold) to start the third section. Conversely, the Kita and Kongō schools skip the third section, going directly from the second to the fourth, both with the fan in the reverse hold.

2.4.7   *Short Dances to Instrumental Music* (hataraki)

Hataraki, or *hataraki-goto* are also dances to instrumental music but shorter and less formalized than the *mai*. Some are decorative, like the *iroe* ("color dance"), others add expressive emotion, like the *kakeri* that portrays the anguish of a

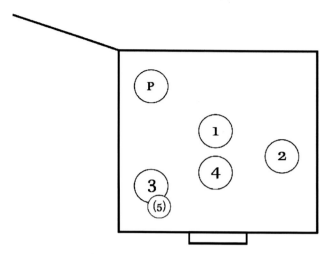

FIGURE 2.36 Placement on the stage where each *mai* section begins: prelude plus sections 1–5. Depending on the *shite* school, the placement of the beginnings of the sections can vary; section 2 may begin further back, and sections 4 and 5 are combined in the Kanze school

mad woman or of a warrior fallen into hell, and still others embody the power and vitality of a deity or demon, like the *mai-bataraki*. In addition, some are enactments integral to the narrative. Pieces incorporating realistic action dramatizing an event include the exorcism (*inori*), the *kirikumi* featuring a clash of swords in a fighting scene, and special *kakeri* that enact scenes specific to a single play (for the types of *hataraki*, see sec. 2.7).[20]

Composed of one or two sections, the *hataraki* dances begin with a left circling and continue variously. Unlike the *mai*, in which the dancer follows the matched rhythms set by the musicians, the dancer normally sets the pace with the drummers following him and the flute playing in "free rhythm" (*ashirai*) for all short instrumental dances except the *mai-bataraki*.

At their most dramatic, *hataraki* are highly mimetic. An example is the *kakeri* in the nō *Utō*. Here the ghost of a hunter returns and recounts his love of hunting. In particular, he relished hunting the chicks of the *utō* bird nesting on the beach. The dance enacts sneaking up on a nest of chicks, striking at them with a stick, watching as baby birds scatter, retreating to the bridge, while

---

20 This categorization loosely follows that outlined by the flute player Morita Mitsukaze (1829–1966) in Morita 1980: 79.

following their flight and then cautiously closing in on the nest as they resettle, this time hitting the mark.

2.4.8 Movement and the Costumed Performance

In full performances, the masks, costumes, and properties influence movement. The small eye holes of the mask restrict the vision, which explains the need for a very stable stance, securely grounded like the *kamae*, the gliding step (*suriashi*) that keeps the body steady, and the helpfulness of pillars that guide the dancer as he moves about the stage.

Garments wrapped tightly around the legs force the actor to walk with smaller steps, while the broad divided skirts allow for larger movement. Bulky layered draping adds volume to the figure, and enables broader movements. Broad diaphanous sleeves billow as the figure circles the stage or moves his arms, breathing life and grace into simple gestures. When closed, the fan serves as an extension of the arm, when opened its ever-shifting angles accentuate the action presenting glimpses of imagery and color while punctuating the gestures. Through these devices, minimal movements get maximum expressive power.

Properties placed in the upstage area push the choreography to the front and those placed at downstage center foreshorten the stage use. Crossing the invisible line created by the placement of a prop, such as in *Matsukaze* when the *shite* circles around the pine prop at downstage center, breaks a choreographic convention and thus carries an element of surprise. Similar containment and expansion of stage use is seen in *Kantan*, when the *shite* dances as he dreams on a magic pillow. He performs the movements of the instrumental dance on the one-mat platform that serves as his bed. Then, suddenly, he steps down from the mat, still dancing: the space expands as he enters fully into the dream world (see sec. 2.12).

2.5 Music[21]
Takakuwa Izumi with Monica Bethe

Here we begin by introducing each of the instruments and their role in the performance. This leads to a step-by-step discussion of the underlying system that informs the way the instruments play together and how their rhythms interlace with the sung text. The distinctive voicing techniques of nō chant used to color

---

21   The authors are indebted to Andrea Giolai, Lecturer at the Institute for Area Studies, Leiden University for his careful reading and comments on the two music sections.

the narration are also described. Finally, the section turns to notation systems and the relationship between notation and what is actually sung or played.

Nō music combines a chanted text (*utai*) with instrumental accompaniment (*hayashi*). The chant has various styles, ranging from song to stylized speech. The instruments consist of three drums (two hand drums and a stick drum) and a transverse flute (*fue*, also known as *nōkan*). The large and small hand drums (*ōtsuzumi* and *kotsuzumi*) play in tandem through much of the performance, creating a rhythmic fabric that correlates loosely or tightly with the chant. They can also play alone or with the flute. In any given nō, the stick drum (*taiko*) plays only limited passages, and in about half the repertory does not play at all.

Each of these musical elements is at times heard singly, at times in overlapping layers. The distinct voices of the chorus chanters intermingle, but do not conform to strict harmonic principles. The rhythms of the individual elements seem to diverge and converge. The instruments do not simply accompany the chanted passages, but are an essential part of the narrative. Guided by neither director nor conductor, playing from memory without a score, the musicians, actors, and chorus must be in constant dialogue with each other to develop the musical soundscape.

The musical dialogue, which generates the fabric of sound and energizes the performance, depends on the manipulation of small predefined rhythmic and melodic units. These are strung together in systematic ways to produce longer passages, much in the same manner as the *kata* patterns in dance are combined to form recurrent series of patterns, which in turn create a choreography. As a result, the mix of voices, calls, drumbeats, and flute may sound baffling to the unaccustomed ear. In fact, nō music, like other aspects of its performance, is highly systematic and guided by basic structural indicators for openings and closures, and include recurrent progressions. These rules aid the memory and make possible the flexibility that includes duplication, omission, exchange, and substitution.

2.5.1 *Instruments*
2.5.1.1   Transverse Flute (*nōkan* or *fue*)

The *nōkan* (fig. 2.37) is a transverse flute with seven finger holes. The bamboo body (the finger holes and mouthpiece excluded) is reinforced by winding around it a string fashioned from the outer bark of the cherry tree. Red lacquer is painted around the mouthpiece and each finger hole. It also has a metal fitting at the head end, which is often decorative, and serves to balance the weight.

FIGURE 2.37   *Fue* or *nōkan* with its lacquer case
PHOTO COURTESY OF THE TOKYO NŌGAKU HAYASHIKA KYŌGIKAI

The greatest distinguishing feature is the bamboo tube (*nodo*, literally "throat"; fig. 2.38a–b) that is inserted between the mouthpiece and the first finger hole and constricts the passageway. The insertion of the *nodo* makes it impossible for the *nōkan* to play a Western scale. It is not clear why or when the *nodo* was initially inserted in the flute, but its presence produces a sharp timbre and reduces the number of overtones. Consequently, the flute plays base notes textured by one overtone that is not a true octave. No two flutes are tuned exactly alike, however, resulting in dissonance when multiple *nōkan* play together.

The *nōkan* does not play in harmony or to the same rhythm as the chanted *utai*, even when playing at the same time. Instead, it colors the atmosphere of the scene at discrete intervals. Nonetheless, the flute player never improvises the melody. This style of playing is called *ashirai*, and the various melodic progressions are given identifying names. For instance, to embellish the *shōdan* segment called *ageuta* (high-pitched song; see sec. 2.7), the flute plays three prescribed melodies at set places: a *takane* (high tune), a *naka no takane* (mid-high tune), and a *kote* (short notes). The number of lines in an *ageuta* differs depending on the play, and these may be chanted in diverse styles—slowly or vigorously—as fits the content. The flute complements the *ageuta* chant by changing its tempo and adding embellishments, all within the framework

FIGURE 2.38A–B The process of making a *nōkan*: a) the *nodo* to be inserted inside the *nōkan* between the blow hole and the first finger hole is seen here above the disassembled flute and b) the *nodo* inserted in the lower portion of the *nōkan* before slipping it into the upper portion. After assembling the *nōkan* into a single piece, it will be bound with thread and lacquered such that it will no longer be able to be separated into its parts. Private collection

of the three patterns mentioned above. Similar short flute passages occur in a number of *shōdan* segments, including the *kuse* and the entrance song known as *issei*.

For sections that have no chant and during which the performer dances to instrumental music (*mai*), the *nōkan* takes the lead, and both the drums and the flute play a coordinated rhythm. As described in sec. 2.7, the actual correlation of rhythms differs according to the type of dance. The melodies are set to scales, or modes (*chō*), the names of which are borrowed from the Chinese nomenclature used for *gagaku* modes. The most common nō flute mode is *ōshiki chō*, in which the tonic *ōshiki* is approximately equivalent to A in the Western scale. *Banshiki chō* is higher pitched, with a tonic roughly equivalent to B in the Western scale (for a discussion of the mood associations evoked by the characteristics of each *chō*, see sec. 2.12).

2.5.1.2   Hand Drums: *Ōtsuzumi* and *Kotsuzumi*

The *ōtsuzumi* (also *ōkawa*; fig. 2.39a), a large hand drum (also hip drum), and the *kotsuzumi* (fig. 2.39b), a small hand drum (also shoulder drum), have an hourglass-shaped wooden body. The drumheads at either end are made of skin and lashed to the body with hemp ropes before each performance. The horsehide skins are clamped to an iron frame. While the skins of the *ōtsuzumi* must be dried over a brazier before each performance, those of the *kotsuzumi* need to be kept humid and pliable so they can produce several pitches depending on how tightly the player squeezes the lashing ropes. The *kotsuzumi* player will often blow moist air on the skins or wet them with a finger during performance to keep them pliant.

The *ōtsuzumi* and *kotsuzumi* function as a pair, playing together to construct the rhythmic patterns (see fig. 2.5). Broadly speaking, the *ōtsuzumi* takes charge of the odd number beats that form the rhythmic framework and the first half of the phrase, while the *kotsuzumi* governs the even number beats and the last half of the phrase. The sounds of the drums are represented aurally with the onomatopoeic words "*po*," "*pu*," "*chi*," and "*ta*" for the four most common sounds produced by the *kotsuzumi* and "*chon*" for the sound made by the *ōtsuzumi*.[22] In drum scores, each sound is noted with a symbol (table 2.2).

While the *ōtsuzumi* produces a sharp sound with little variation and establishes the foundation of the rhythm, the *kotsuzumi* plays ornamentation between the *ōtsuzumi* beats using variations in timbre and rhythm. The contrast of these roles, coupled with the wet, changeable sounds of the *kotsuzumi* and the dry, sharp sound of the *ōtsuzumi*, is frequently seen as analogous to the Chinese concept of yin and yang—yin is dark, wet, and feminine, yang is light, dry, and masculine.

Equally as important as the sounds of the drums are the drummer's calls (*kakegoe*) that precede the drumbeats. These visceral utterances serve to keep the performers together by marking the beats ("*yo*" beats 1 and 5, "*ho*" before other beats, written "*ya*" and "*ha*" in the Japanese scores and pronounced somewhere between the two vowels). Other drummer's calls ("*yoi*" and "*iya*") establish the larger rhythmic structure by indicating cadences and breaks (table 2.3). The style of the drummer's calls is modulated to the moment, at times low and guttural, at times strident and clipped. In this way, the calls complement the content of the play and do much to evoke the atmosphere. The drummer's calls greatly influence the impact of the rhythmic pattern. Although the number of rhythmic patterns is limited, the same patterns can

---

22   Two additional *kotsuzumi* sounds, "*tsu*" and "*pen*," are rarely used.

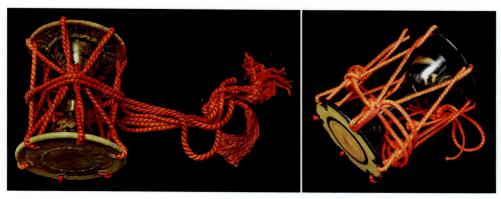

FIGURE 2.39A–B   Hourglass-shaped hand drums: a) the assembled larger *ōtsuzumi* and b) the assembled smaller *kotsuzumi*
PHOTOS COURTESY OF THE TOKYO NŌGAKU HAYASHIKA KYŌGIKAI

TABLE 2.2   The sounds produced by the two hand drums with their aural and visual representations

Kotsuzumi	⊙ *po*: tightening the cords before beating while releasing them produces a varied resonance	• *chi*: softer, hit with two fingers on the rim ⊖ *pu*: the lowest note	■ *ta*: a short clack on the rim
Ōtsuzumi	Δ strong *chon*	○ weak *chon*	

TABLE 2.3   The drummer's calls and their functions

Yo (or ya)	**Ho (or ha)**	**Yoi**	**Iya**
Basic (Before the first and fifth beats)	Basic (Before all other beats)	Special (Signals a change is close)	Special (Highlights closures and transitions)

be adapted to evoke distinctly different atmospheres by modifying the way the calls are voiced and fine tuning the way the intervals (*ma*) between beats are manipulated. Formal deity nō, vigorous warrior nō, and gentle, lyrical women's nō all utilize the same recurrent drum patterns. In addition, the same patterns are played in chant and instrumental dance sections.

The drum patterns are conceived as fitting into a theoretical eight-beat metrical unit (*yatsu-byōshi*). Most of the basic patterns span a single eight-beat metrical unit, although more complex ones extend over sixteen or more beats, and some are truncated to four beats. The schematic representation of this metrical unit can be seen in score 2.1. Here, the solid lines indicate the downbeats, while the dotted lines mark the upbeats and play an important role in the distribution of the syllables of the chant. Drummers' calls also start on the upbeats in preparation for the actual drum strokes on the downbeats. The *taiko* plays on both upbeats and downbeats. The score begins with the upbeat before 1 because many of the vocal and drum patterns start on the upbeat before the first downbeat. It should be noted that Japanese drum instruction books use a schematic representation of the eight-beat unit, drawn vertically in accordance with Japanese writing conventions that read from top to bottom, right to left.

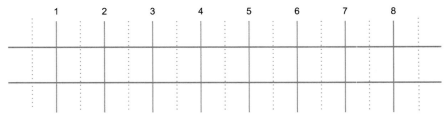

SCORE 2.1 Horizontal (left to right) schematic rendition of the eight-beat metrical unit underlying both the chant and the drumbeats

Some hand-drum patterns are sparse, with strokes on only a few beats in the metrical unit, others are denser with drumbeats throughout the unit. The two basic styles are referred to as *mitsuji* ("three-beat"; score 2.2) and *tsuzuke* ("continuous beat"; score 2.3), based on the names of the *kotsuzumi* patterns played. The chant rhythms are matched differently to the drumbeats for these two styles, as dealt with in greater detail below.

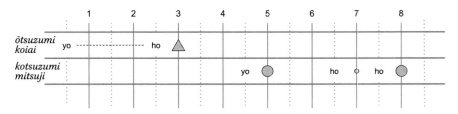

SCORE 2.2 Sparse hand-drum ground pattern: *koiai* (*ōtsuzumi*) and *mitsuji* (*kotsuzumi*)

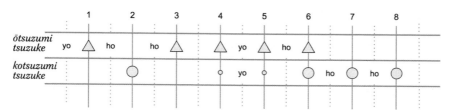

SCORE 2.3   Dense hand-drum ground pattern: *tsuzuke* in both *kotsuzumi* and *ōtsuzumi*

2.5.1.3   Stick Drum (*taiko*)

The *taiko* (fig. 2.40) employed in nō has two skins lashed together at either end of a barrel-shaped body.[23] The top skin has an extra circular padding in the center where the sticks hit the surface. When played, the drum is suspended on a low frame. It is played with two sticks, one in each hand, striking the skin from above. The right hand usually plays on the downbeats, while the left hand strikes on the upbeats (score 2.4). Playing on both the upbeats and downbeats contrasts with the two *tsuzumi*, which beat primarily on the downbeats. Thus, the *taiko* strengthens the sense of a regular rhythm, creating the feeling of an even pace. As with all nō music, however, the tempo accelerates and retards to intensify the mood or mark closures and transitions between sections.

Capitalizing on these characteristics, the nō repertory only uses the *taiko* for some plays, specifically when evoking a nonhuman world, and then just for certain sections. For instance, in the deity play *Takasago*, the *taiko* does not play in the first half when the *shite* and *tsure* perform the roles of an old couple appearing in human form. It does enter, though, in the second half when the *shite* plays the deity of Sumiyoshi. In nō, when the second half enacts a prayer for the deceased, such as in the warrior plays *Tomonaga* and *Sanemori*, the *taiko* performs solely during the section of the religious service.

The same applies to the inclusion of the *taiko* accompaniment for instrumental dances (*mai*; see secs. 2.4, 2.7). The *taiko* does not play for the *jo no mai* dance in nō featuring aristocratic women, such as *Izutsu* and *Nonomiya*, but it does play for the *jo no mai* danced by spirits of plants, as in *Kakitsubata* and *Saigyōzakura*, for foreign characters, and for the heavenly maiden in *Hagoromo*. There are some exceptions where other concerns outweigh the trajectory of human/nonhuman. In the play *Bashō*, for instance, although the *shite* is the

---

23   The folk *taiko* is set vertically on a pedestal and hit from the side, while the large *taiko* played in *gagaku* court music is hung from a frame and struck from the side with a padded stick.

FIGURE 2.40 The stick drum (*taiko*) set on its stand with the sticks resting underneath
PHOTO COURTESY OF THE TOKYO NŌGAKU HAYASHIKA KYŌGIKAI

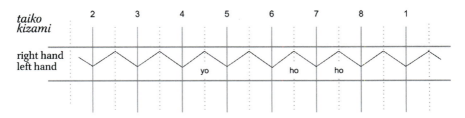

SCORE 2.4 The basic *taiko* pattern (*kizami*): downbeats are played with the right hand, upbeats with the left. Generally, the *taiko* patterns begin on what corresponds to beat 2 of the standard metrical unit

spirit of a plantain, the *jo no mai* has no *taiko* accompaniment, presumably to emphasize the strong Buddhist flavor.[24]

---

[24] The inclusion or absence of the *taiko* provides a window into understanding how medieval people understood the plays.

2.5.2 *Vocal Music* (utai)

Nō is a poetic musical drama in which chant is responsible for the narration of the story and for its emotional impact. Although the nō text has "spoken" sections, most of the text consists of "song." In fact, the word *uta* means both "song" and "poem," traditionally recited to a melodic formula, and is contained within the word for nō chant: *utai*. In actual rendition, *utai* covers a range of melodic styles, and even the spoken sections follow a set pattern of tonal shifts. The types of melody and rhythm used for *utai* are important musical elements for the expression of the content. They also define the segments (*shōdan*) that constitute the structural building blocks of a play. Poetic sections of nō chant adhere more or less strictly to standard lines of 7 + 5 syllables, which are sung in diverse styles ranging from melody to recitative. Most of the chanted sections, except those in stylized speech, have drum accompaniment.

Two basic rhythmic conventions are employed to coordinate the chant with the drum rhythms. In the first, known as *hyōshi awazu* ("noncongruent" or "unmatched" rhythm), the rhythms of the chant and drums do not correlate exactly. While the chanters and musicians begin and end the passage together, they are only loosely correlated between the start and finish. In the second, *hyōshi ai* ("congruent" or "matched" rhythm), the syllables chanted by the actors or chorus are tightly matched to the drumbeats, with both melody and drums following the eight-beat metrical unit.

Nō chant and instrumentation are performed according to a preestablished system, in which the flexibility of its rules requires performers to be attending to each other, sometimes following another's lead, sometimes spurning changes in tempo or intention. This type of communication is only possible because nō performers know all the elements. Actors study all the instruments, while instrumentalists have to memorize the chant (see ch. 3 *Training*, 3.1).

2.5.2.1 Unmatched or Noncongruent Chant and Instrumentation (*hyōshi awazu*)

The performers constantly listen and adapt to each other during the *hyōshi awazu* sections in which the chant is not tightly bound to the eight-beat metrical unit played by the drums. For these, the drummers have to measure the speed they play their stipulated patterns, expanding or contracting the patterns in coordination with the chant, a technique called *mihakarai* ("watchful pacing"). For instance, the instructions might be, "play pattern A in a loop until XYZ words in the song." The drummers might repeat A three times, twice, or possibly four times, depending on how long it takes the actor or chorus to complete their passage. Sometimes, to make sure the chant and closure drum patterns end at the same moment, the drummers might contract two patterns into one, playing the first half of A and joining it to the second half of B. This adjustment is not scripted but depends on the impromptu execution of the play. This, however, is not improvisation since the specific patterns they play are set and paced according to rules. It is precisely because the type and sequence of the patterns follow such rules that "unmatched" rhythmic coordination is possible. Similarly, the chanter must be aware of the patterns being played by the drums, and time the song to match the part that is supposed to correspond to a given part of the chant.

A variety of signals allows the performers to communicate with one another. The shift to a new type of pattern, for instance, may be signaled by a higher pitched drummer's call or by a change in the pattern—that is, from repeating A to a closure pattern. Once one drummer switches to the next pattern, the others follow suit. Alternatively, actors might extend syllables to signal a slowing in the pulse.

There are two styles of chant employed for *hyōshi awazu* passages. The more common style, *sashinori,* is a kind of recitative in which each line, sung mostly on a single pitch, starts slow, quickens in tempo, and then ends with an extended, often modulated, syllable (score 2.5). *Sashinori* passages generally preface longer passages in congruent rhythm. Variations of *sashinori* melodies that have more melismas include the *issei* and the *kuri* (see sec. 2.7 for their definitions). The other style of chant in noncongruent rhythm, *einori,* is used to render classical Japanese poetry and incorporates numerous extended syllables and melismatic turns. The noncongruent songs framing instrumental dances are in *einori*. In this way, the style of singing *hyōshi awasu* passages is determined by their position within the performance as a whole.

2.5.2.2 Congruent or Matched Rhythms in Both Chant and Drums (*hyōshi ai*)

As noted above, the matching of the syllables of the chant to the drums marking the eight-beat metrical unit is known as *hyōshi ai*. Three main methods are

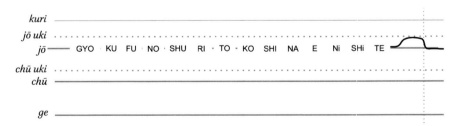

SCORE 2.5 *Sashinori. Yowagin* mode in unmatched rhythm (*hyōshi awazu*). *Hagoromo sashi* before *kuse,* line 2

employed to match the syllables to the eight-beat metrical unit: *hiranori* (plain match), *ōnori* (whole-beat match) and *chūnori* (half-beat match).[25]

2.5.2.2.1 Plain-Match Chant (hiranori)

The most common match of the congruent rhythmic systems seen in every play is *hiranori* (score 2.6). Much of the nō text is written in poetic lines of twelve syllables (7 + 5), and for *hiranori* these twelve syllables are distributed unevenly over the eight beats (sixteen half-beats) of the basic rhythmic measure. The first hemistich of seven syllables stretches from the upbeat to beat 1 through beat 5 with three caesuras or extensions of the voicing of a syllable. The second poetic hemistich is evenly distributed from beat 5.5 through 7.5, one syllable per half-beat. In modern practice, the model for most schools of nō is that the singer begins just before the first beat of the unit and fits in two syllables per beat, with caesuras over beats 1, 3, and 5.

This model is modified in various ways to incorporate poetic lines that have either more or less than twelve syllables and melismatic demands. For instance, delaying the initial syllable is used when the first hemistich of poetry is less than seven syllables. To fill the gap, the last syllable of the previous line is extended. Score 2.7 illustrates a 4 + 5 syllable distribution, and in these cases, the *ōtsuzumi* often strikes the drum on beat 1 while uttering a call that extends to the half-beat before the chant begins. It is also possible to extend the eight beats when there are too many syllables and to shorten the eight beats to either six or four beats when the text is only half a line (seven or five syllables rather than twelve). As such, the eight-beat metrical unit permits adjustments in length and usage.

The two hand drums accompany *hiranori* song. When the drums beat on almost all eight beats, the singing basically uses the standard extensions on the beats 1, 3, and 5 described above.[26] This is called *tsuzuke utai* after the name of the continuous (*tsuzuke*) drum pattern. For passages in which the *shite* chants, or which have a quiet, descriptive, or narrative tone, the hand drums often play on only a few of the beats in the eight-beat metrical unit to allow the words being chanted to resonate more clearly. These typically are matched with the *koiai* and *mitsuji* pattern shown in score 2.8. Accompanied by sparse drum strokes, the singers can render the syllables with almost even spacing in a style called *mitsuji utai* (three-beat chant). Thus, within the parameters of *hiranori*,

---

25 In Kanze-school *utaibon*, *hiranori* is labeled as "*ai*" (matched), *ōnori* as "*noru*" (ride the beat), and *chūnori* is treated as a variation of *hiranori*.

26 In the past, the arrangement of syllables among the eight beats differed, and even today there is variation between the *shite* schools.

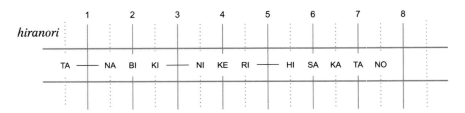

SCORE 2.6 *Hiranori*. Twelve syllables distributed over sixteen half-beats

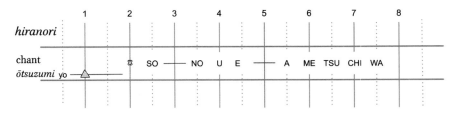

SCORE 2.7 *Hiranori* with a short first half-line. The *ōtsuzumi* begins the line with a drummer's cue

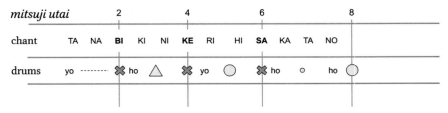

SCORE 2.8 *Mitsuji utai*. Even syllable distribution and sparse drum accompaniment. Compare with score 2.6.

it is possible to chant the same line of text in two different ways. The first (*tsuzuke utai*) uses standard extensions on beats 1, 3, and 5 (syllables 1, 4, and 7), while the second (*mitsuji utai*) eliminates those extensions.

The key to the ability of chanters and drummers to synchronize, whether in *tsuzuke utai* or *mitsuji utai*, or other congruent rhythmic systems, is the *komi*, an internal mental marking of the even-numbered beats (beats 2, 4, 6, and 8) in the eight-beat metric unit. For the drummers, the *komi* is a silent muscular contraction (noted in the score 2.8 with an "x") preceding the drummer's call announcing the drum stroke. The chanters similarly take a mental *komi* at the beginning of a phrase and add stress to the syllables that come on the even beats. The drummers' cues on beats 2, 4, and 6 correspond to the third, sixth, and ninth syllables of the chant. As long as the *komi* of chant and drums match up, the exact correspondence for the actual drumbeats is of little concern.

When performing a slow piece, the players take their cues with a deep *komi*, and when performing a fast piece, they clip the cue so that it is short and sharp. Breathing plays a key role in marking *komi*. Especially in chorus singing, in which all members sing in unison, the chorus leader's breathing between phrases cues the rest of the chorus as to how to sing the following phrase. Listening to each other's breath is essential for actors, musicians, and chorus to follow the same rhythmical intention. The performers come together mentally on the even beats, but the audial effect of the drummer's hand hitting the drum is heard on the following odd beats. This cycle lies at the core of nō music: the silent intervals (*ma*) between the drumbeats play an important role.

Since the drumbeats in *mitsuji utai* are few and the drummers' calls are long, the length of the calls can easily be adjusted to the chant. This flexible *mitsuji utai* style chant, which is closer to natural speech, is also used when singing without instrumental accompaniment. Because long passages in *mitsuji utai* can become tedious, the two types of drum patterns—sparse and continuous—generally alternate, with the singers adapting the distribution of the syllables according to the drum patterns. There tends to be more sparse patterns at the beginning of a *hiranori* segment, while toward the end there are more continuous patterns, which add intensity and lead to special closure patterns.

One interesting aspect of nō music is that the performers intentionally avoid the use of evenly spaced intervals between the beats even when the song, drums, and flute follow the same eight-beat metrical unit. As a result, one does not sense a regular beat, and in fact, following a mechanical beat is considered amateurish or artistically inferior. Within the conventional limitations, performers shorten or extend the time-space between the beats. The amount of elasticity in rendering a passage differs by school, as well as by individual performer, and may change with each performance.

2.5.2.2.2 Whole-Beat Match Chant (ōnori)

The most regular of all nō rhythms is *ōnori*, whereby seven syllables are distributed one syllable per beat over eight beats, with one beat for taking a breath (score 2.9). Because the *taiko* normally accompanies *ōnori* song, and the *taiko* patterns by convention begin on beat two, *ōnori* song also begins on beat two. When, however, there are more than eight syllables (*ji-amari*), two syllables might be packed into one beat, or vice versa, but when there are fewer than eight (*ji-tarazu*), one syllable might be extended for one-and-a-half or more

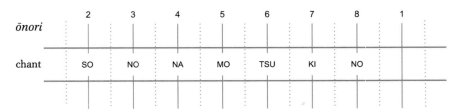

SCORE 2.9 Ōnori. The basic seven-syllable line. *Hagoromo noriji*, last section, line 3

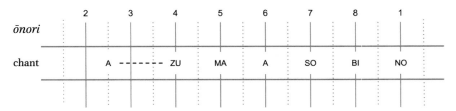

SCORE 2.10 Ōnori. A seven-syllable line with the first syllable a half-beat delayed for rhythmic variation. *Hagoromo noriji*, last section, line 1

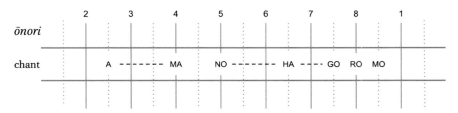

SCORE 2.11 Ōnori. A seven-syllable line with the first and third syllables extended and the last four syllables packed into three-and-a-half beats. *Hagoromo noriji*, last section, line 14

beats so as to fit the syllables into the framework of the eight-beat metrical unit. Similar extensions and contractions might also be used to create rhythmic variation in seven-syllable lines (see scores 2.10, 2.11).

Dance-centered sections and scenes depicting supernatural events are often chanted in *ōnori*. Perhaps the use of more rhythmical chant to express the out-of-the-ordinary reflects an understanding that people in their everyday activities do not move to a regular pulse. When the stick drum joins the ensemble, it adds an extra dynamic, thereby creating a magnificent atmosphere. Examples of *ōnori* methods of matching the syllables to the beats are noted in scores 2.9–2.11.

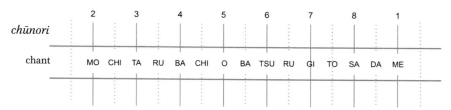

SCORE 2.12 *Chūnori*. Syllables are distributed one on each half beat

2.5.2.2.3 Half-Beat Match Chant (chūnori)

The end of warrior plays, when characters depict their sufferings in the Asura warrior hell, and the end of revenge plays (*shūshin mono*, a sub-division of the fourth category) are sung at a faster pace. This style came to be called *chūnori* by the early nineteenth century (score 2.12). In this style, fifteen syllables are distributed over eight beats (fifteen half-beats), with a silent half-beat for a breath. Although there are very few lines with fifteen syllables, the fundamental rule of two syllables per beat is kept and produces a clipped, forceful song.

When composing a nō play, the playwright considers whether the passage is to be in *hiranori*, *chūnori*, or *ōnori* and adjusts the syllable count accordingly. For the same basic content, the use of the 7 + 5 syllable count of Japanese poetry would create a natural flow, but eight-syllable lines would be appropriate for a passage presenting a dance performance or an otherworldly setting. Packing fifteen syllables into a line would raise the intensity of the scene.

2.5.2.3 Modes of Voice Production

Nō chanters pull their chins back and allow their voices to reverberate in the chest and abdomen, producing a vibrato emanating from the depth of the body. The way actors use their voices changes somewhat according to the role: *shite* roles typically require a more somber and slower enunciation; *tsure* sing in a lighter, quicker, and slightly higher pitched voice, while *waki* may minimize vibrato to emphasize the words. The individual differences among actors, however, defies strict characterization. Pitch reflects character types, rather than gender, and the level of intensity or excitement. As a result, a *shite* playing a female role may sing at a lower pitch than the *waki* performing a man. It is important to note that nō actors do not seek to imitate voices in a realistic way. For example, a male nō actor performing a woman will sound unmistakably male. As with other aspects of nō aesthetics, chant does not seek to imitate reality; instead, it aims to suggest states of mind through association.

Modern *utai* distinguishes between the "soft voice," or melodic scale (*yowagin*), and the "strong voice," or dynamic scale (*tsuyogin*). Characters of women and old people appearing in calm, quiet scenes employ the melodic scale, while gods, demons, and strong figures chant in the dynamic scale.

2.5.2.3.1   Characteristics of yowagin

Many features of nō chant, such as the limited number of tones, the pentatonic scale, the set ways the tones are strung together, the indication of the initial tone for each song segment, and the predetermined end tones, can also be found in other medieval Japanese musical arts, including Heike *biwa* (lute) narration and Buddhist narrative songs (*kōshiki*).

Nō chant is essentially restricted to the tone intervals in the fundamental pentatonic scale. It is important to state at the outset, however, that unlike Western classical conventions, nō chant does not conceive of absolute pitch. The tones are relative to each other and depend on the pitch that the *shite* or chorus leader establishes. This base pitch may also shift as the singing progresses. In addition, rules govern the progression of tones in the scale.

The *yowagin* scale has three main tones—*jō on* (high), *chū on* (middle), and *ge on* (low)—each separated by a perfect fourth and connected by intermediary tones (score 2.13). The tones have distinctive singing styles. Passages that are more songlike tend to be in the upper register with the high tone as a nuclear tone and the melody moving up and down around it. Passages that are more narrative are generally set in the middle register with the middle tone as its nuclear tone and the melody moving between middle and low. Higher than *jō on*, the tone *kuri* (highest note) has a special voicing called *nabiki*. Rising to *kuri* lays emphasis on the words, often expressing strong feelings or sorrow.[27]

The limited number of tones might suggest simplicity, but in actuality by controlling the use of the breath to change the tone level, the quality of voice, the amount of vibrato, and manipulating the intervals (*ma*) between syllables, the song is minutely modulated to evoke the scene.

2.5.2.3.2   Characteristics of tsuyogin

Tsuyogin notation differentiates four tones: *jō on*, *chū on*, *ge no chū on* (above-low tone), and *ge on*. In present practice, however, the upper two are essentially the same pitch, as are the lower two (score 2.14). Consequently, the rising from "middle" to "high," although marked in the notation, is indecipherable to the ear (score 2.15). Descent from high to middle is simulated by increasing the intensity of the vibrato to produce the sense of rising pitch immediately preceding notation of a down shift (score 2.16). This creates the illusion

---

27   The Hōshō school uses another pitch above *kuri* called *kanguri*, or "high *kuri*."

```
kuri ─────────── kuri
jō uki ·········· above high
   jō ─────────── high
chū uki ·········· above middle
   chū ─────────── middle

   ge ─────────── low
```

SCORE 2.13 *Yowagin* tone names and relationships

```
   chū & jō ─────────── middle & high

ge & ge no chū ─────────── low & above low
```

SCORE 2.14 *Tsuyogin* pitch names and their relationships

```
chū (middle) ────────▶ jō (high)

   ge (low) ────────▶ ge no chū (above low)
```

SCORE 2.15 *Tsuyogin* "ascending" stays on the same pitch, with a change in breath support

```
        jō (high) ─────╱── chū (middle)

ge no chū (above low) ─────╱── ge (low)
```

SCORE 2.16 *Tsuyogin* "descending" is preceded by an increase in intensity and a broadening of vibrato that is sensed as a rise in pitch

of descent when the chant returns to the preceding tone. The same principle holds for movement between "above low" and "low," except that *ge no chū on* uses a softer exhalation than *ge on*. Thus, the retention of notations like "high" or "middle" are used, not to indicate pitch levels, but rather to mark changes in breath support that incidentally result in micro sliding shifts in pitch. The near total lack of clear pitch distinctions that characterizes *tsuyogin* leads to its relative flattening. It is seen as a method for transmitting the force and the meaning of the words. At times, the two singing styles are combined or alternate with each other, such as in crazed scenes where the shifts in voicing reflect the complex, disturbed psychological state of the singer.

2.5.2.3.3   Comparison of yowagin and tsuyogin

Scores 2.17 and 2.18 compare two similarly modulated lines, one in *yowagin*, the other in *tsuyogin*. In both cases, the first line, which begins on beat 2, rises to *kuri*, and the second ends with a melisma (*chūmawashi*).

2.5.2.3.4   Spoken Sections (kotoba)

The "spoken" (*kotoba*) passages are not voiced like everyday speech, but have a standardized form of recitation (score 2.19). At one point in each written line, there is a symbol resembling a check mark, known as *okoshi* (✓). Up to this check, the voice rises gradually. After the check, the second syllable is stressed, rising in pitch, after which the pitch curves down. The contours differ for male and female roles (score 2.10). Depending on the role, the strength of the stress (rise) varies, and in some schools the stress is shifted to a later syllable. In any case, at one or two places in each spoken line, there is a stressed syllable, and this becomes the highpoint of the tempo and the pitch for that particular phrase.

2.5.3   Notation (gakufu)

The notation for nō chant appears as "sesame-seed"-like marks (*goma-bushi*) to the right of the words of the text. The *goma-bushi* can be horizontal, rise to the right, or descend to the right. In certain instances, this reflects a melodic movement up or down, but the direction of the *goma-bushi* is generally unrelated to the melody in the *yowagin* mode, at least in the Kanze-school *utaibon* (chant books; fig. 2.41).

In the *utaibon*, the small characters at the beginning of some lines of text mark changes in the nuclear tone, such as 上 (*jō*) "high" for singing focused around the high tone (*jō on*), 中 (*chū*) for singing on the middle tone, and 下 (*ge*) for starting on the low tone. Shifts of tone within the line include a rise to the high *kuri* pitch, which is marked with クリ (*kuri*), シオリ (*shiori*), or 入 (*iri*) depending on the style of melisma. Other notations for tonal movement are ハル (*haru*) for rising up to *jō on* and a variation of 下 (*sage*) to note descent down one nuclear tone.

Tone notation is neither absolute nor consistent across schools, and some schools do not indicate the intermediary tonal shifts. For complex melismas, special marks are used, or the shape of the *goma* combines two "sesame seeds" into one, such as a horizontal plus vertical hook, a visual representation of the tonal movement where an extended vowel descends one tone (*mawashi*). For the complex *yuri* pattern, which has extended, repetitive modulations, there is no visual mark for the movement of the sound. Rather, it is abbreviated to a simplified sign, differing slightly with each school of nō.

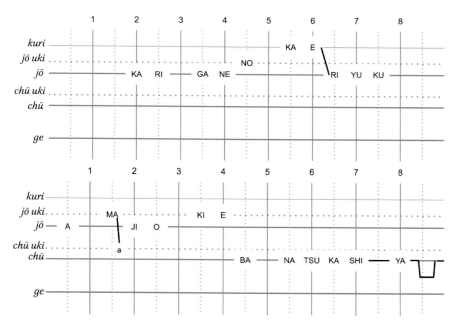

SCORE 2.17 *Yowagin* (melodic) mode in matched rhythm (*hyōshi ai*). *Hagoromo, shite ageuta*, lines 4 and 2

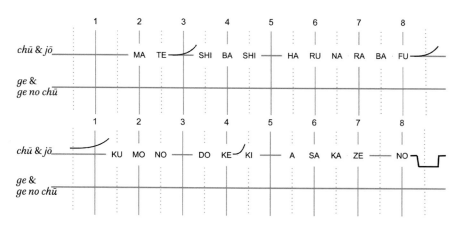

SCORE 2.18 *Tsuyogin* (dynamic) mode in matched rhythm (*hyōshi ai*). *Hagoromo, waki ageuta*, lines 4 and 2

Although an identical notation system is used for both *tsuyogin* and *yowagin*, it is read differently in each mode. As noted above, because the heavy vibrato of *tsuyogin* collapses pitches so that "high" and "medium" are heard as the same, indications like "up" (rise to the next higher nuclear tone) or "down" reflect shifts in dynamics more than actual changes in pitch. There is a

kore wa hitoritaru koromo nite sōrō hodo ni ↙ *torite kaeri sōrō yo*

SCORE 2.19   *Kotoba* (speech) inflection. Typical *waki* intonation for a standard line. *Hagoromo*, dialogue with *shite*

sore wa tennin no ✓   *hagoromo to te*

SCORE 2.20   *Kotoba* (speech) inflection. Typical intonation for a female character. *Hagoromo*, dialogue with *waki*

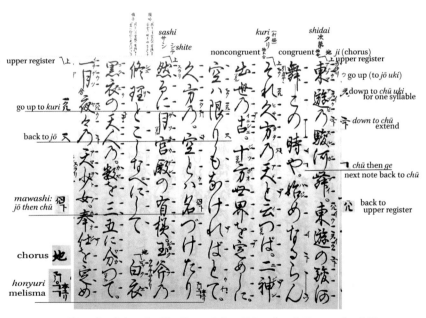

FIGURE 2.41   Chant book (*utaibon*) by Kanze Sakon (Motoshige). Kanze school. *Hagoromo* (*shidai-kuri-sashi*). From *Anthology of Kanze-School Chant Books* (*Kanze-ryū taiseiban utaibon*). Tokyo: Hinoki Shoten, 1931

distinction, however, between *chū* and *ge*. Here, the adjustment in breath support results in a slight distinction in pitch. Various other ramifications make it challenging to sing a piece without having learned the ins and outs of the notation system.

Some sections of the text have no *goma* next to the words; instead, there is a single check mark-like symbol placed somewhere in each sentence. These are the spoken (*kotoba*) sections and the check indicates the break after which the voice rises (see above).

2.5.3.1 Notation for Rhythm

More problematic is the rhythmic notation in the *utaibon*. Since the rhythm is set by the tacit understanding of the performers, markings are kept to the minimal necessary markings, such as the places where the singing begins from a nonstandard beat, or where the rhythmic system shifts from *hiranori* to *ōnori*. The lack of obvious rhythmic indication makes reading an *utaibon* difficult for the beginner.

Relying on an insider's knowledge to make sense of the notation is not limited to nō. As with other traditional Japanese arts, knowledge must be acquired directly from the master in a one-to-one oral transmission. Instead of being used in training, notation was passed on after a piece was learned, as a certificate, or for the teacher to write in notes about details. This equally applies to dance choreography. In fact, many old *utaibon* only have the lyrics without *goma* notation. Because this awareness still persists, notation is limited to memory cues for the performers, even when the notation is printed for general use.

2.5.3.2 Lack of a Comprehensive Score

Although *utaibon* have some notation for the melody and rhythm of the song they lack notation for the for the instrumental music or the choreography. Performers often add their own notations to the printed *utaibon*. Some books for beginners feature excerpts of the *utai* and include notation of the *kata* for the movement. Other books note the drum patterns next to the *utai*, and still others write out the flute melody or list the flute patterns to be played with the singing. There is no total score, however, that shows all of them.

One reason such a score does not exist is that each performance member (*shite, waki, kyōgen, fue, ōtsuzumi, kotsuzumi, taiko*) belongs to one of several stylistic schools (*ryūgi*), all with variant traditions governing the details of how or which patterns are performed. These details match up differently when specific *ryūgi* gather for a given performance. To produce a score that includes all these variations would not only be an enormous task, it would also be practically impossible.

Nō performers learn each other's parts so they have knowledge of how everything fits together. For each staging, they check out the patterns played by the others who will perform with them. Taking note of the points that diverge from previous performances turns out to be more practical than looking at an enormous composite score. The repertory for nō is set, and the performers have much of it memorized. One explanation why they might not feel hampered by having only their own score is that it is easy to foresee the patterns due to the structure of nō being based on building-block units assembled into larger units.

2.5.4 Ensemble Music for Dances to Instrumental Music (mai/hataraki)

2.5.4.1 Long Instrumental Dances (*mai*)

Mai refers to a group of dances performed to instrumental music, the choreography of which has been discussed in sec. 2.4. The names of these instrumental dances reflect the type of character performing (see sec. 2.7). While the *mai* types appear quite different when performed, in fact the slow, graceful *jo no mai* (women's dance), the vigorous *otoko mai* (man's dance), and the quick-tempo *kami mai* (deity dance) all share the same basic flute melody matched to the beat and incorporate identical drum patterns.

The basic flute melody consists of four lines set to the eight-beat measure that are repeated in a cycle (score 2.21). By adding embellishments and changing the style of playing, it is adapted to gentle refined dances or energetic dynamic dances. When practicing their parts, nō performers intone the flute melody with a solfège (*shōga*), in which syllables are used to represent the melody and rhythm. This solfège serves as a base for the drummers and dancer, who sing the tune in their minds. The scores in 2.21 use that solfège to write out the flute melody for two contrasting *mai*, the *otoko mai* and the *jo no mai*. Although the notes are the same for both forms, their tempos and the way the notes match the beat differ, that is the way the *ma* is implemented. While *jo no mai* has long extended notes that bridge the pulse, *otoko mai* rides the beat, creating an impression of great energy. In score 2.21, the circles signify breath breaks, usually on beat 2. The syllables in the solfège (indications of the melody) are almost identical. For the *jo no mai*, however, they are bunched together and followed by long extensions; for the *otoko mai* they are spread out and generally fall on the up and down beats.

Instrumental dances consist of multiple sections (*dan*), as described in section 2.4. Each section of the dance has a set number of repetitions of the basic melody, and this may vary depending on the *shite* school. The ends of each section are marked by closure patterns, including the drummer's calls *"yoi"* and *"iya."* A transition melody opens each new section. If there is a switch in basic pitch (that is, from *ōshiki chō* to *banshiki chō*) or style, it usually occurs at the transition from section to section. Although the musical structure of all these dances is fundamentally the same, their performance lengths differ. For

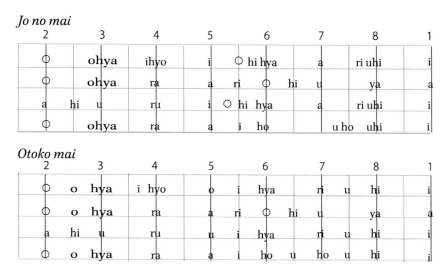

SCORE 2.21 Basic flute repeat used for dances to instrumental music (*mai*): *jo no mai* (top) and *otoko mai* (bottom)

instance, the *kami mai* may take eight minutes to perform, the *jo no mai* up to fifteen. Also, since the costume and mask are character-appropriate, these dances appear as totally distinct to the audience.

Some of the instrumental dances have more mimetic characteristics that figure more specifically in the narrative. Built around recurring flute patterns, the melodies for these are unique to each piece. *Gaku* evokes the music for *bugaku* by making the odd number beats strong, the even number beats weak, and alternating strong and weak. With this method, *gaku* expresses a sense of foreignness distinct from indigenous Japanese music. In *kagura*, which imitates the music for Shintō ritual dances, the flute plays a *yuri* pattern with trills—represented in solfège as a quick succession of notes "*ra-ra-ra.*"

2.5.4.2   Short Instrumental Dances (*hataraki*)

Shorter dances to instrumental music known as *hataraki* ("action dances") typically add a dramatic element. These instrumental pieces vary from the simple *iroe* with flute repetitions and unmatched drums, to the dramatic *inori* (exorcism) that switches back and forth between intense syncopation and a more even beat, reflecting the waxing and waning of the relative power of the vengeful spirit versus the monks trying to quell it. For most of these *hataraki* pieces the music is noncongruent, and the musicians adjust their tempos to the movements of the dancer. Table 2.10 in section 2.7 outlines the various types of short instrumental dances and their musical characteristics.

2.5.4.3 Entrance and Exit Music

The musicians play solo or ensemble passages before characters enter, as characters exit, and during onstage costume changes. These passages create atmosphere, herald appearances, and provide a premonition of the stage action. When the drums play alone, even if they are playing "in rhythm," they extend their calls and to fill in *ma*. When they play noncongruent rhythms, the drummer's calls can be long and dominant.

To begin a play, the two hand drums often play alone, with occasional flute embellishment. The music accompanying a *waki* entrance suggests his status: a minister enters to formal music played by the two hand drums (*shidai*) and begins with a formal song (*shidai*), while a nameless traveling monk may enter to a flute solo (*nanori-bue*) and immediately announce his name and destination (*nanori*) in unaccompanied prose. As a rule, human figures, including those in "dream" or "phantom" nō who appear in the form of women or old men, enter to music where both flute and hand drums play noncongruent rhythms. For a wide variety of living and supernatural characters the hand drums play more rhythmically, but the flute melody is noncongruent.

For entrance music in the second act, the flute frequently plays the whole passage along with the two hand drums. The quality of the drummer's calls, the spacing of the beats, and the rendering of the flute passage all contribute to the evocation of a mood that heralds the character. The *taiko* joins the ensemble when a stately deity, spirit of a plant, or ghost of an aristocrat enters. In this case, the drums play with the beat, but the flute melody is not matched to their rhythms. When, however, the character is a demon, beast, or malicious spirit, the fast, energetic *hayafue* is played, and all the instruments match their rhythms to the eight-beat metrical unit. For the entrance of an exotic figure, like the Chinese wine-loving creature in *Shōjō*, beat emphasis is shifted, suggesting something foreign (e.g., *sagariha*).

Instrumental interludes may also bridge sections in a performance. In *Hagoromo*, for instance, there is an onstage costume change (*monogi*) when the *shite* retires to the rear and attendants place the feather robe (a *chōken*) on her. During the costume change, the hand drums and flute fill this time of suspended action with music timed so it ends when the costuming is completed. Occasionally, instrumental music also accompanies exits before an interlude between acts. The slow, stately *raijo* exit music switches after the *shite* has disappeared to lighter and faster music announcing an *ai kyōgen*, who represents a deity from a subsidiary shrine. The musicians lighten their calls and beats to accompany the kyōgen deity dance that follows.

2.5.5 The "Weight" of Performance (kurai)

At the root of the expressive capacity of nō lies the concept of *kurai* (see sec. 2.1), which could be loosely translated as "rank" or "gravitas." In musical terms, *kurai* refers to overall tempo and pitch. The "weightier," higher-ranking, masterful *kurai* pieces are performed slowly with long intervals between beats, and the pitch of the *utai* and the drummer's calls is low. Conversely, the tempo and general pitch for beginner pieces are relatively faster and higher. A variant performance of a beginner piece might raise its *kurai* and as a result slow down the tempo.

It should be noted, however, that no matter what the *kurai* of a piece, the basic musical patterns remain the same and just because a piece is designated as "masterful" does not necessarily imply it is especially complicated. Although special patterns might be inserted in one section, fundamentally all nō are performed with the same melodies and rhythmic patterns. It is the realization of these patterns—the particular emphasis and coloring—that demands a master's touch.

2.6 The History of Nō Chant
Takakuwa Izumi with Monica Bethe

Nō chant as practiced today differs from earlier times in melodic contours, rhythmic details, and diction. Without recordings of chants from the Edo period (1603–1868) and earlier it is impossible to verify conclusively the nature of nō chant in the past, but research into early plays, extant texts with notation in Zeami's hand, and later *utaibon* (chant books) provide indications of some vectors of change.[28] Furthermore, over the last six to seven hundred years, shifts have occurred in the pronunciation and intonation of the Japanese language. The evolution of nō voicing and rhythmic techniques paralleled the spoken language.

2.6.1 Historical Changes in Styles of Vocalization

Zeami discusses singing techniques and styles in a number of his treatises. His earliest dealing specifically with music, the *Ongyoku kuden* (*Oral Instructions on Singing*, 1419; see ch. 6 *Treatises*, 6.2),[29] identifies two types of singing: *ō no koe* and *shu no koe* that are paired with the anhemitonic and pentatonic scales

---

28 Takakuwa 2015. This section summarizes some of the content in her book.
29 Hare, trans. 2008: 81–95. Zeami also discusses singing in *Go-ongyoku jōjō* (*Articles on the Five Sorts of Singing*) and *Go-on* (*Five Sorts of Singing*); Hare, trans. 2008: 224–37, 238–415.

of *ryo* and *ritsu*, respectively. He describes *ō no koe* as *ryo*, "the voice of joy, the voice of breath exhaled," and *shu no koe* as *ritsu* "the voice of sadness, the voice of breath inhaled."[30] He goes on to say that to sing in the celebratory style (*shūgen*) one uses a "... strong singing voice. This is a disposition toward the voice of *ryo*. A strong voice swelling with *ki* [supported breath] should meet the standard for breath exhaled." In contrast, a softer style (*bōoku*) uses *shu no koe* and "... gently hold[s] back the *ki*. It is at heart soft and frail. The essence of the inhaled voice is to hold the *ki* gently. This is the standard for *ritsu*, a disposition to tenderness."[31] In the same text, Zeami calls voices that combine the two "doubly proficient." Interestingly, the distinction in voice production applies to *utai* as sung today in as much as different voice mechanisms are used together to produce a straight, full voice and a restrained voice. Alternating the two produces a complex sound texture. Variations in methods of voice production characterize each of the *shite* schools.

There is no clear correspondence, however, between Zeami's *shu no koe* and the "melodic mode" (*yowagin*) that uses a tonal scale (see sec. 2.5) and his *ō no koe* and modern practice of the "dynamic mode" (*tsuyogin*).

Japanese traditional music uses pentatonic scales with five whole note pitches in the octave. Although around the beginning of the seventeenth century, other forms of Japanese music began to use various intermediary half tones, nō chant remained essentially restricted to pitches in the fundamental pentatonic scale (score 2.22). This is the basis for the *yowagin* with its three central tones set at intervals of a fourth. It is important to state at the outset, however, that, unlike Western classical conventions, nō chant does not conceive of absolute pitch. The pitches and their modulation are closely related to methods of voice production.

Studies in deciphering Zeami's system of musical notation are relatively recent.[32] Despite the inconsistencies of usage and unfamiliar symbols in Zeami's ten extant holographs (*jihitsu nōhon*), it is possible to identify beginning and ending pitches, movement up or down, and syllables that are drawn out or have a melisma. Analysis of Zeami's holographs reveals that, compared with plays predating Zeami, his own are built on clearly structured modular units, each with a distinct poetic format and rendered with an overall

---

30 Hare, trans. 2008: 85.
31 Hare, trans. 2008: 85.
32 Gamō 1992 and Mochizuki 1998 predated Takakuwa's seminal book of 2015.

SCORE 2.22 The basic *yowagin* scale set on a Western staff. Since there is no absolute scale, only relative tones, the specific note allocation here is arbitrary

consistency in melodic movement.[33] As a playwright-composer, Zeami fit the words to the musical units, which he arranged according to the demands of the piece.

Documents from the late sixteenth century provide more concrete details about pitches and the melodic movement. *Jinkaishō* (*Dust and Dregs*, 1583), a book on chant theory, includes examples from *utai* where pitches are marked using graphs taken from Buddhist chant (*shōmyō*).[34] Combining these with notation in the earliest printed *utaibon*, the *Kurumaya utaibon* (1601), written by the Konparu-school disciple Torikai Dōsetsu (d. 1602), scholars have reconstructed aspects of Momoyama-period (1573–1603) *utai*.[35] Although the Momoyama-period core pitches—low (*ge*), middle (*chū*), and high (*jō*)—are set a fourth apart like those used today, the movement from pitch to pitch differs from current practice (score 2.23). More specifically, while today's descent from "high" to "middle" involves first rising to "upper'" (*jō uki*) and then going down a major fifth, during the Momoyama period the contour generally did not rise, but rather went down in steps, through "above middle" (*chū uki*) (score 2.24). Similarly, present-day movement goes directly from "middle" to "low," except for the special effect known as *kuzushi*, but in the Momoyama period, the melody passed through "above low" (*ge no chū*). Again, the highest note, *kuri*, was a whole fourth above "high." In addition, the *utaibon* notation indicates more modulation than contemporary practice, suggesting a more songlike effect.

During the Edo period, the schools diverged from each other. The *Yoza yakusha mokuroku* (*Catalogue of the Performers of the Four Troupes*, 1653) mentions that in the past the Konparu *utai* was closer to the Kanze style, but recently

---

33 Takakuwa 2015: 33–34.
34 *Jinkaishō* 1583.
35 Omote 1988–1997.

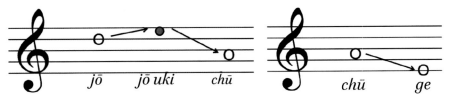

SCORE 2.23A–B   Modern-day movement a) from "high" (*jō*) to "middle" (*chū*) first rises to "above high" (*jō uki*) and then descends a major fifth and b) from "middle" (*chū*) to "low" (*ge*)

SCORE 2.24A–B   Momoyama-period melodic movement from a) "high" (*jō*) to "middle" (*chū*) descends in steps through "above middle" (*chū uki*); and b) from "middle" (*chū*) to "low" (*ge*) descends in steps through "above ge" (*ge no chū*)

had changed dramatically. Both the Konparu and Hōshō schools developed melodic modulation distinct from the other three schools.[36]

In *utaibon*, sesame-seed-like notations (*goma-bushi*) are placed to the right of syllables. Originally, the *goma* indicated rhythm and melodic movement: rising *goma* for ascent, horizontal *goma* for a steady pitch, and downward *goma* for descent. Research has shown that melodic inflection was greater in the Momoyama period than in the present day.[37] Particularly in sections sung in noncongruent rhythm (*hyōshi awazu*), such as the recitative *sashi* (see sec. 2.5) chanted today mostly on the "high" (*jō*) pitch, it was found that they were formerly sung with more up and down movement. This, studies suggest, mimics the intonation of Kyoto speech during the Muromachi and Momoyama periods.[38] Over time, the directional value of the *goma-bushi* became less precise. In the early twentieth century, when the schools revised and updated their *utaibon*, each school consolidated some of the changes slightly differently.

Modern *tsuyogin* is based on variations in intensity of breath support, collapsing the pitches "middle" and "high" to the same tone (see sec. 2.5). This style dates to the early twentieth century. As noted above, already in Zeami's

---

36   Quoted in Takakuwa 2015: 67.
37   Takakuwa 2015: 97.
38   Sakurai 1965.

lifetime some distinction was made between a softer style voice (*shu no koe*/*bōoku*) production and a stronger style (*ō no koe*/*shūgen*), but both styles of voicing still used the same musical scale at least until the early seventeenth century. The term *tsuyogin* first appeared in *utaibon* at the end of the seventeenth century. Yet, even in the early nineteenth century this *tsuyogin* continued to distinguish pitches. The process of flattening the distinction between "middle" and "high" occurred over time. Gradually, more emphasis was placed on the support strength for the vocalization with the result that the vibrato expanded, and the difference between pitch levels was minimalized until the present style of *tsuyogin* prevailed.

2.6.1.1   Historical Changes in the Rhythmic Systems

It is generally acknowledged that in early Japanese music the syllables of the text were not matched to the beats. This is directly related to shifts in Japanese language. Before the fourteenth century, Japanese mixed long sounds and short sounds and did not give each syllable equal vocal weight as is the practice today. Equal stress for each syllable began sometime between the fourteenth and sixteenth centuries. The popular songs known as *sōka* (also pronounced *sōga*) that preceded nō used a style of rhythmic singing similar to *hiranori* as it was sung in the Muromachi period: syllables were matched to the downbeats while some vowels were lengthened to extend over the upbeats (score 2.25). Matching syllables to the downbeats strengthens the rhythmic impact of the song (on *sōka*, see ch. 1 *History*, 1.1).

Other performing arts following nō did not incorporate *hiranori*, and since *sōka* died out rather early, *hiranori* became a rhythmic style unique to nō in Japanese music.

The actual rendering of *hiranori* became more flexible with time. In its model form, with some syllables extended and others not, the words become distorted. During the Edo period, greater emphasis was placed on the audience's understanding of the lyrics. This in turn influenced the way *hiranori* was sung: shifting the extended syllables so the loud *ōtsuzumi* "chon" on the first third and fifth beats did not compete with the enunciation of the syllable aided clarity to the words and also allowed for some leeway in phrasing.[39]

2.6.2   *The Evolution of the Chorus* (jiutai)

Despite having a six-hundred-year continuous performance history, nō as chanted today would probably sound very unfamiliar to Zeami. One other aspect of performance that he would not recognize is the eight-person chorus

---

39   Takakuwa 2015: 95–97.

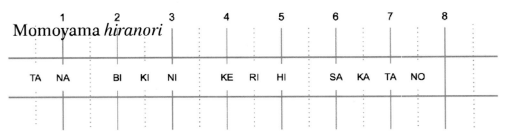

SCORE 2.25 Muromachi-period style *hiranori* (compare with score 2.6)

seated at stage left.[40] The ideograph used to indicate the chorus lines in Zeami's holographs reads 同 (*dō*), suggesting all the actors sang together. In addition, sixteenth-century nō stages did not have the extra extension for chorus seats. Illustrations indicate that an unspecified number of extra actors sat behind the instrumentalists. The *waki*, seated in the *waki* seat, served as leader, facing the rear at an angle in order that the chanters at the back could see and hear his chant. By the late fifteenth and sixteenth centuries, with the rise of the more theatrically dramatic *furyū nō* (see ch. 5 Authors, 5.6, 5.7), the *waki* often had to be at center stage, possibly also dance. This led to the introduction of a chosen chorus leader (*jigashira*) and eventually to a standard number of chorus members.

2.7 *Shōdan*: the Building Blocks of Nō
Monica Bethe and Takakuwa Izumi

As described above in section 2.3, nō plays typically have one or two acts made up of a sequence of generally predictable scenes. The scenes in turn are constructed of strings of smaller named units, each characterized by their musical, poetic, and choreographic form, and by their type of narrative content. Some of their names, such as *shidai* and *ageuta*, already appeared in Zeami's writings. In fact, Zeami refined and systematized the composition of nō by assembling units to build a piece,[41] and recasting earlier plays into these named units. Pieces created after Zeami's time retained this convention, although some modern nō are an exception.

---

40   Takakuwa 2015: 228, 229, is based on studies by Omote 1985 and Fujita 2000.
41   Takemoto 2013: 31, Zeami outlines various methods of structuring nō in *Sandō*. Hare, trans. 2008: 150–64.

The twentieth-century scholar Yokomichi Mario referred to these subunits collectively as *shōdan* ("small *dan*").[42] *Shōdan* are the building blocks of nō, through which the performers identify the contours of melody, rhythm, drumming, and movement. Most *shōdan* are noted in modern *utaibon* as well as in some printed texts, including a number of translations. Their various aural textures evoke a flow of shifting styles of expression.

2.7.1 Types of shōdan

Yokomichi Mario divided *shōdan* into three main groups: chanted text (*utai-goto*), purely instrumental (*hayashi-goto*), and silent (*shijima-goto*).[43] *Utai-goto* (e.g., *nanori*, *sashi*, *kuse*) have prescribed verbal, melodic, rhythmic, and kinetic characteristics rendered either with or without the instruments playing. *Hayashi-goto* include entrance and exit *shōdan*. These may be played by two or three drums with or without the flute. The rhythms may be loosely or strictly tied to the eight-beat metrical unit. *Hayashi-goto* also refers to the various instrumental dances (*mai* and *hataraki*) as well as to stage action with no chant. *Shijima-goto* examples include onstage costume change for male roles as well as silent entrances and exits. Table 2.4 summarizes the types of language and rhythmic systems that are combined to define *shōdan*.

After categorizing the types of *shōdan*, Yokomichi noted typical progressions of *utai-goto* within given scenes: some start with a formal opening and after that they tend to follow the order from speech to melody, from non-congruent rhythm (*hyōshi awazu*) to congruent rhythm (*hyōshi ai*), from low-pitched to high-pitched song, from single to multiple voices. The musical elements increase as the nō performance progresses and often, just when music reaches a climax, the scene ends and the next scene begins, returning to a simpler format. A similar gain in complexity also occurs on a broader scale from scene to scene, incrementally adding aural texture and progressing from little movement to flowing dance, thus gradually building a multilayered, multivalence expression.

The first scene of *Tadanori*, introduced previously in section 2.3, provides insight into how these progressions work (table 2.5). The *waki* enters to instrumental music in unmatched rhythm (*shidai* music). Standing at the *jōza*, the *waki* begins with a preamble—that is, with a short formal poem in strict meter matched to the drumbeats (*shidai* chant). He then introduces himself in a spoken passage (*nanori*; no drums), after which he prepares to set off on a trip. This is a segment in a recitative style (*sashi*) in which the drums enter with loosely

---

42 Omote and Yokomichi 1969: 13–18; Hoff and Flindt 1970 [1973]: 225–28.
43 Yokomichi 1987: 329–48.

TABLE 2.4 Types of language and rhythmic attributes that define *shōdan*

Types of language	Speech, free verse, strict verse, recited poems
Types of chant rhythms	1) Arhythmic
	2) Loosely flowing
	3) Matched to drum rhythms following a basic eight-beat metrical unit
Types of instrumental rhythms	1) Loosely adjusted
	2) Matched to a basic eight-beat metrical unit

TABLE 2.5 The progression of *shōdan* in the opening scene of *Tadanori*

Shidai entrance music	Noncongruent (*ashirai*) drums, intermittent flute
Shidai chant	Single voice, set meter, congruent rhythm with drums
Nanori	Single voice, spoken, prose, no drums
Sashi	Single voice, free verse, noncongruent drums
Sageuta	Several voices, strict meter, congruent drum rhythms
Ageuta	Several voices, strict meter, congruent drums, intermittent flute, symbolic movement

coordinated rhythms. Next, with his companions (*waki tsure*) he describes his travels to the West in strictly metered poetry matched with the drumbeats, first sung in the lower register (*sageuta*) and subsequently in the higher register (*ageuta*). The flute enters intermittently during these passages: a step forward and back marks the end of the trip.

In this way, nō music assembles *shōdan* of various kinds into scenes (*dan*) to produce an act (*ba*) and a play (*kyoku*). The same units are used for warriors and for beautiful women in love stories, for pieces that are the preserve of the *iemoto*, and for pieces performed by novices. The number of commonly used units is few.

Shōdan are performed with preset melodies and rhythmic patterns. These are slowed down or sped up, the pitch raised or lowered, the tone strengthened or softened. The rhythms may have a clear or barely distinguishable pulse; the intervals between the beats (*ma*) may be lengthened or shortened to convey the atmosphere and emotional tenor of the piece. Such variations build the interest of nō and make each play, each performance, unique.

2.7.2 Shōdan *with Chanted Text* (utai-goto)

A nō text is chanted in an array of styles, which in turn define the various *shōdan*. Stylized speech (*kotoba*) is prose. It has no set rhythmic structure and is almost never accompanied by the drums. The recitative (*sashinori*) is poetry but sung with little melodic movement and with natural flow of words unmatched to the drums. For the poetic, melodic *shōdan*, chant and drum rhythms are matched according to the system outlined in section 2.5. They are further categorized by tonal register—that is, by whether they are centered on the higher pitches like an *ageuta* or on the lower pitches like *sageuta*. These *shōdan* are also differentiated by poetic structure (number of lines, repetition of lines, and syllable count). In addition, *shōdan* have prescribed choreography, including non-movement, and some include short flute passages.

Tables 2.6–2.8 cumulatively introduce the variables that make up the fabric of nō chant: types of prose and poetry with their linguistic rhythm conventions (counted in syllables to a line) and methods of matching the song with the instruments.

TABLE 2.6   Types of language found in nō

Poetry	Rhythmic	Strict 7 + 5 syllable count
		Irregular 7 + 5 syllable count (many exceptions)
		Syllable count adjusted to whole beat or half-beat rhythms
Poetry	Arhythmic	Loosely 7 + 5 but articulated like prose
Prose	Speech	*Naribun*: more formal speech; sentences end in classical verb forms
		Sōrōbun: more informal speech; sentences end in *sōrō*

TABLE 2.7   Types of rhythm found in nō (see also sec. 2.5)

Congruent *ai* and *noriji*	*Hiranori*	7 + 5 syllables spread over 16 half-beats, hand drums only
	Chūnori	15 syllables spread over 16 half-beats, hand drums only
	Ōnori	7 or 8 syllables matched to whole beats, hand drums and *taiko*
Noncongruent (*awazu*)	*Sashinori*	Intoned speech with slight embellishment, flexible drum rhythm
	Einori	Melismatic extensions, flexible drum rhythm timed to end together

TABLE 2.8 Types of chant *shōdan* by their name designation with correspondence between language, rhythmic systems, and musical register

Shōdan name	Poetic structure	Rhythm/chant
Shidai	7 + 5, 7 + 5, 7 + 4	*Hiranori*
Ageuta	7 + 5, first and last repeated lines	*Hiranori*, high register
Sageuta	7 + 5	*Hiranori*, low register
Rongi	7 + 5	*Hiranori*
Kuse	Irregular syllable count, but 7 + 5 base	*Hiranori*, low → high register
Issei	7 + 5	*Einori*, melismatic
Jō no ei	7 + 5	*Einori*, melismatic
Sashi	Loose poetry	*Sashinori*, recitative, high → middle
Kuri	Loose poetry, often in parallel Lines	*Sashinori*, melismatic
Chūnori ji	Irregular syllable count	*Chūnori*
Ōnori ji	Irregular syllable count	*Ōnori*
Nanori	Prose	*Kotoba*
Katari (*waki*)	Prose	*Kotoba*
Katari (*shite*)	Prose	*Kotoba* → *sashinori*
Mondō	Prose/semipoetic	*Kotoba* → *sashinori*

2.7.2.1   *Ageuta*

Ageuta ("high-pitched song") is a chant section appearing in many plays in various places. The *ageuta* is sung in *hiranori*. It begins on the high pitch *jō on*, and uses the same poetic system based on syllable count (in nō 7 + 5 syllables is standard) as in Japanese *waka* poetry (5 + 7 + 5 + 7 + 7). The model *ageuta* begins with a half-line, followed by a repetition of the first line as seen in the example below, and the last two lines also repeat. Variations may omit one or both repetitions. These stipulations for its composition were essentially set during Zeami's lifetime. Zeami often placed the *ageuta* song units as the final song of a series of *shōdan* making up a *dan*. Typically, the first *ageuta* occurs as the last *shōdan* of the *waki* entrance scene, which generally presents traveling, as set out in the example of *Tadanori* given above. In *Hagoromo*, the fisherman Hakuryō (*waki*) sets out with his companions for the pine woods of Mio. The first *ageuta* describes the scene as he approaches Mio:

Kaze mukō	Winds afar
Kumo no ukinami/tatsu to mite	Clouds adrift. Look at those waves!
[*uchikiri* drum passage, flute plays *takane*]	

Kumo no ukinami/tatsu to mite	Clouds adrift. Look at those waves!
Tsuri sede hito ya/kaeru ran	Men, going home without a catch?
Mate shibashi/haru naraba	But, stay, for spring has come
Fuku mo nodokeki/asa kaze no	The morning breeze blows gently
[*uchikiri* drum passage, flute plays *naka no takane*]	

Matsu wa tokiwa no/koe zo ka shi	Whispering through the evergreen pines
Nami wa oto naki/asa nagi ni	Waves are soundless in the morning calm
Tsuribito ōki/obune ka na	Fishers swarm out in small boats
Tsuribito ōki/obune ka na	Fishers swarm out in small boats
[flute ends *kote* pattern]	

Here, all the lines are composed of 7 + 5 syllables, except the first half-line and the fifth line (5 + 5). The short drum passage, *uchikiri* ("break beats"), between the repeat of the opening line is standard. The second *uchikiri* marks an internal break: the song has gone from the high tone (*jō on*) to the highest tone (*kuri*), and down to the middle tone (*chū on*). After the break, the melody returns to *jō on* and the passage ends on the low tone (*ge on*). The framework of tonal shifts is predetermined, but where they occur is adjusted to the text. Since the fishermen are robust, they sing in the dynamic *tsuyogin* mode.

Hakuryō discovers a feather robe on a branch of one of the pines. The heavenly maiden (*shite*) calls out pleading for its return. When Hakuryō refuses, the maiden becomes desperate, saying she cannot reascend to the moon. Her desolate state culminates in another *ageuta*, this time sung in the melodic *yowagin* mode to a slower tempo. Otherwise, it has the same format as outlined above for the fisherman's *ageuta*.

Often *ageuta* also come at the end of a *shite* entrance scene, and in nō with two acts, the *waki*-waiting song (*machiutai*) is usually in the *ageuta* style. All types of roles and all manner of content can be fit into the single *ageuta* format, which is adjusted to express a range of roles and content.

2.7.2.2   *Kuse*

While *ageuta* can appear several times within a play, a *kuse* occurs, with a few exceptions, only once. Its form derives from another medieval performing art, the *kusemai* (*kuse* dance), which Zeami's father and mentor, Kan'ami (1333–1384), is said to have incorporated into nō. The segment in nō known as *kuse* is defined as a long narrative *shōdan* with "broken" or irregular 7 + 5 syllable lines (*haritsubun*) of poetry set to *hiranori* rhythm. It has a strong narrative element and a clear kinetic, melodic, and drum structure.

A standard *kuse* is composed of three stanzas (*setsu*). The first stanza begins in the lower register, the second in the middle register, and the third in the upper register. Some *kuse* double this structure. Not only are the opening pitches set and the general melodic movement predictable but the hand-drum patterns for each stanza are also standardized. *Kuse* can be seated (*i-guse*) or danced (*mai-guse*). For a danced *kuse*, the opening, middle, and closure movements follow a set sequence of patterns as outlined in section 2.4, and some of these patterns are timed to specific drum patterns. Another defining characteristic of the *kuse* is that although the chorus sings the body of the *kuse* text, the actor sings the opening line of the third stanza (*ageōgi/ageha*).

A *kuse* is often preceded by *shōdan* in noncongruent rhythm: *kuri* and *sashi*. For the *kuri*, the drums play with unmatched rhythm, the song has many ornamental notes and finishes with a long drawn-out melisma known as *yuri*. This chant *yuri* is matched by the flute playing a *yuri* pattern, which consists of a long trill that closes on the low note *ryo*. The combination of decorative elements creates a sense of rhythmic and melodic complexity, which is finalized by the drums playing an *uchikiri* pattern to bridge into the simpler recitative (*sashi*) follows. Then, a clear pulse in the drums matched with the low-pitched song marks the beginning of the *kuse shōdan*.

Zeami placed the *kuri-sashi-kuse* scene in the center of his *mugen nō* (dream nō). Generally, for *kuse* in the first act (*maeba*) of a nō, the *shite* is seated at stage center, but for *kuse* in the second act (*nochiba*), the *shite* dances to the words. In *Hagoromo*, after the heavenly maiden retrieves her feather robe from the fisherman Hakuryō, the actor performs a series of dances, of which the *kuse* is central. It follows the standard format of being introduced by a *kuri* and *sashi* and is composed of three stanzas.

It is possible to break some *shōdan* into even smaller units. As noted above, *kuse* are comprised of three stanzas. The third of these stanzas can be combined with other *shōdan* to produce a new *shōdan*, as seen in the "*kurui*" (crazed) dance in *Hanagatami*, which presents a scene of heightened emotion that incorporates drum patterns from stanza three of a *kuse* and some movements based on the *kuse* patterns. Devices like these allow for the creation of new, derivative *shōdan*.

2.7.3 *Instrumental shōdan* (hayashi-goto)

Instrumental *shōdan* include longer and shorter dances to music, purely instrumental passages, including entrance and exit music, and also music played during onstage costume changes.

2.7.3.1   Long Instrumental Dance (*mai*) *shōdan*

As discussed above in sections 2.4 and 2.5, the dances to instrumental music without chant are called *mai*. These pure dances heighten the atmosphere with nonverbal emotive expression. Flowing out of the narrative, often framed by a poem, the *mai* bring melody, rhythm, and movement to the fore. Far from being mere performative decorations, *mai* are essential to the development of a play's narrative. *Mai*, like other *shōdan*, serve as building-block units in the composition of a full performance. They generally form an audiovisual highlight just before the final dance to song at the end of a play. More rarely *mai* function as highlight scenes in the first act, coming after or as a substitution for a *kuse*.

Mai go by various names that reflect the type of role. The slow, graceful *jo no mai* is performed by beautiful women, such as the heavenly maiden in *Hagoromo*, or by ghosts of women and the spirits of plants, some of which are male. The quick-tempo *kami mai* (deity dance) is reserved for strong male gods, and the vigorous *otoko mai* expresses the power of warriors in *genzai nō* and other male roles that do not employ masks. Long instrumental dances with more mimetic characteristics do not include the word *mai* in their names. Rather, they are referred to by the genre they evoke: *gaku* (dances to court music), *kagura* (Shintō dance), *kakko* (drum dance), and *shishi* (lion dance). Table 2.9 begins with the *mai* and is expanded to include the more dramatically specific dances to instrumental music. All dances are performed by the *shite* unless indicated otherwise.

TABLE 2.9   The main types of long instrumental dances and their characteristics

Dance name	Description	Examples
Jo no mai	Character type: female, rarely male. Slow, refined dance. Free rhythm opening (*jō*), usually 3 *dan*. With or without *taiko*.	*Eguchi*, *Izutsu* (without *taiko*), *Hagoromo* (with *taiko*)
Shin no jo no mai	Character type: deities appearing as elderly males and courtiers. Long, slow preface that speeds up in later sections. 3 *dan*. With *taiko*.	*Oimatsu*, *Ugetsu*
Chū no mai	Character type: various types of *shite*, *tsure*, *kokata*, both male and female. Medium tempo. 3 *dan*. If the character is a female deity *chū no mai* is normally performed in the *tennyo no mai* (celestial maiden dance) variant. With or without *taiko*.	*Atsumori* (Kanze school), *Matsukaze*, *Yuya*, *Shōjō*. As *tennyo no mai*: *Kamo*

TABLE 2.9 The main types of long instrumental dances and their characteristics (*cont.*)

Dance name	Description	Examples
Haya mai	Character type: ghosts of noblemen, enlightened women. Strong, elegant, with increasing speed. 3, 5, 8, 13 *dan* versions. It can be performed in the *banshiki* or *ōshiki* version. With *taiko*.	*Banshiki chō* (higher flute pitch) version: *Tōru, Ama. Matsumushi* (in *ōshiki* lower flute pitch version)
Otoko mai	Character type: men who are alive in the narrative present. Fast, dynamic, masculine. 3 or 5 *dan*. Without *taiko*.	*Ataka, Ashikari, Kosode Soga*
Kami mai	Character type: young gods. Very fast, vigorous. 3 or 5 *dan*. With *taiko*.	*Takasago, Yumi yawata, Awaji, Yōrō*
Ha no mai	Character type: female. Short dance performed after *jo no mai* or *chū no mai*. 2 *dan*. With or without *taiko*.	Without *taiko*: *Nonomiya, Matsukaze*. With *taiko*: *Hagoromo, Kochō*
Kyū no mai	Character type: mostly female characters. Fastest tempo. With or without *taiko*.	Without *taiko*: *Dōjōji, Momijigari* (*chū no mai* shifts to *kyū no mai*) With *taiko*: *Awaji* (Konparu, Kongō schools)
Kagura	Character type: female deities, Shintō priestesses (*miko*)—*shite* or *tsure*. Melody reminiscent of Shintō music (*kagura*). Graceful, but with wide sleeve movements. A Shintō wand (*gohei*), used by shrine priests, is used instead of the fan, though it may be replaced by the fan after *dan* 3. Usually 5 *dan*, but can be shorter if the *tsure* dances it (*kagura-dome*). With *taiko*.	*Tatsuta, Miwa, Makiginu*
Gaku	Character type: Chinese men, strong gods. Music evoking an exotic atmosphere. Round *uchiwa* fan replaces folding fan. Imposing, elegant. 5 *dan*. Normally with *taiko*.	With *taiko*: *Kantan, Tsurukame, Shirahige, Kiku jidō* (*Makura jidō*) Without *taiko*: *Tenko, Fujidaiko, Umegae*

TABLE 2.9   The main types of long instrumental dances and their characteristics (*cont.*)

Dance name	Description	Examples
Kakko	Character type: youths, lay monks. Begins as *chū no mai* and switches into special music later. Imitates playing drum hung at waist, drumsticks substitute for the fan. Without *taiko*.	*Jinen koji, Kagetsu*
Shishi	Character type: *shishi* (mythical lions) or a man performing a *shishi* dance. Has a unique music and choreography.	*Shakkyō, Mochizuki, Uchitō-mōde*
Midare (1)	Character type: *shōjō*, a mythical creature fond of *sake*. Has a unique music and choreography.	*Midare* variant of *Shōjō*
Midare (2)	Character type: heron, performed by a boy or elderly person. Has a unique music and choreography.	*Sagi*
Ranbyōshi	Character type: woman entertainer seeking revenge. Played by the *kotsuzumi* in solo coordinated with the dancer's steps.	*Dōjōji, Uchitō-mōde*

2.7.3.2   Short Instrumental Dance (*hataraki-goto*) *shōdan*

Shorter instrumental dances are either momentary embellishments, such as the *iroe*; closely tied to the narrative, acting out the story nonverbally, such as the *inori* (exorcism); or the *kakeri* in *Utō* that dramatizes the hunting of beach chicks (see sec. 2.4). The major *hataraki shōdan* are consolidated in table 2.10.

2.7.3.3   Entrance Music and Other Instrumental *shōdan*

Instrumental passages that herald the entrance of a character or accompany an exit are also standardized pieces and have *shōdan* names (table 2.11). Although there are as many different characters as there are nō, there are only a few types of entrance music, some played in the first act, others in the second. As with all aspects of nō, a single form serves as a vessel that can be modulated, and molded to express the desired image. The entrance music sets the atmosphere giving the audience a premonition of the character that will appear. In some plays, music also accompanies the first act exit and entrance of the *ai kyōgen*. Instrumental *shōdan* may also bridge sections in the performance,

TABLE 2.10 The main types of short instrumental dances and their characteristics

Dance name	Description	Examples
Mai-bataraki	Character type: strong gods, dragon gods, *tengu*, vengeful ghosts. Powerful, vivacious. 2 *dan*. Flute congruent.	*Funa Benkei, Chikubushima, Kamo, Kurama tengu, Momijigari, Kokaji*
Kakeri	Character type: crazed women, warriors in hell, other. Erratic shifts in tempo. Flute noncongruent. Without *taiko*.	*Sakuragawa, Tsunemasa, Yashima*
Iroe	Character type: various types of women. Decorative. One left circling. Flute noncongruent. Generally, without *taiko*.	*Kakitsubata, Sakuragawa, Sotoba Komachi, Funa Benkei, Yōkihi*
Kirikumi	Character type: male warriors in *genzai nō*. Sword fighting scene. 2 *dan*. Flute noncongruent. With *taiko*.	*Shōzon, Eboshi-ori*
Inori	Character type: vengeful spirits. Exorcism. Strong shifts in tempo, special patterns evoke the fight between monk and *shite*. 3 *dan*. Flute noncongruent. With *taiko*.	*Dōjōji, Aoi no ue, Adachigahara* (*Kurozuka*)
Tachimawari	Character type: various types of men and women. Circling of the stage, adjusted to each play. Flute noncongruent, drums ride rhythm. With or without *taiko*.	Without *taiko*: *Kayoi Komachi, Hyakuman, Tadanori, Shari, Daie*. With *taiko*: *Yamanba*

TABLE 2.11 The main types of entrance and exit music, their use and characteristics

Entrance and exit music type	Act	Description
Shidai	Act 1	Performed by large and small drum, with sporadic flute. Flute plays *hishigi*. Followed by a *shidai* song. Tempo and style varies depending on the character.

TABLE 2.11 The main types of entrance and exit music, their use and characteristics (*cont.*)

Entrance and exit music type	Act	Description
Issei	Act 1 or 2	Performed by the two hand drums, with, sporadic flute. Prefaces the entrance of a variety of living characters as well as ghosts and spirits. Generally followed by an *issei* song.
Nanori-bue	Act 1	Solo flute free rhythm, announcing single waki, who then sings a *nanori* passage.
Deha	Act 2	Two hand drums and *taiko*, accompanied by the flute. Variable tempo, style and format depending on the character role.
Hayafue	Act 2	Hand drums and *taiko* matched to the flute melody. Very fast and vigorous. Introduces dragons, warriors, and crazed spirits.
Sagariha (*watari-byōshi*)	Act 2	Two hand drums, *taiko*, and flute. Begins phrases on the first beat rather than the second (typical of *taiko* pieces). Paced, expectant. Introduces supernatural characters.
Raijo	Exit act 1, kyōgen entrance	Two hand drums and *taiko*, with flute. Slow, formal stately for the exit of a *tengu*, spirit, or deity followed by light quickened music for the entrance of a subsidiary god (kyōgen).
Hayatsuzumi	Hurried act 1 exit in *genzai nō*. Hurried kyōgen entrance	Large drum and small drum play fast beats anticipating excited activity.
Ashirai nakairi	End of act 1	Two hand drums playing unmatched rhythms. Adjusted to the character role and scene, such as for crazed woman roles (*kyōjo*).
Okuri-bue	End of act 1	Solo flute exit music played at the end of act 1 in *mugen nō*.

such as when the *shite* goes to the rear upstage area so that the attendants can change or adjust their costumes.

2.7.4 Silent *shōdan* (shijima-goto)

A nō performance flows seamlessly from one *shōdan* to the next, from one scene into another without pauses or clear delineations. Sometimes the action happens in silence. For instance, some plays begin with the character walking onto the stage in silence. When there is a costume change for a female role, the instruments play softly, but for a male role this is executed in silence. Finally, the silence that falls after the last drumbeat leaves the audience momentarily suspended between illusion and reality, while the actors walk offstage followed by the musicians and chorus.

2.8   Masks
Monica Bethe

Masked and costumed, the *shite* entering along the bridge embodies a visual expression of the character. The mask provides the figure with emotive depth. At first, the character is sensed from afar, but as the *shite* rounds the pillar and stops at the name-announcing spot (upstage right), the features of the mask come into full view. With movement and stillness, the mask takes on life, its countenance apparently mirroring the shifting feelings of the character. This expressive capacity emerges from within the sculptural modeling and is amplified by the wig and costume that frame it.[44]

Training prepares the actor for wearing a mask. The severely restricted vision through the small mask eye openings requires actors to keep a stable stance with a low center of gravity. The gliding walk (*hakobi*) and still torso of the stance (*kamae*) allow actors to move smoothly. They learn to rely on their feet to navigate the stage, sensing the floorboards beneath them. The stance and gliding walk also serve to keep the mask at a constant angle. When this angle is altered by leaning the torso slightly forward, for instance, the mask tilts somewhat forward, changing the angle at which it is seen. Minimal movements bring the mask alive with the shifting light and shadow. In this way, the expression of the masks is integrally tied to the movements that bring them alive. The same style of movements governs roles played without masks (*hitamen*), which include all the *waki* roles, most *ai kyōgen* roles, and male *shite* roles for plays in real time (*genzai nō*).

---

44 For a description of mask making and mask carvers, see ch. 7, secs. 7.2 and 7.3, respectively.

2.8.1 Categories of Mask Types and Mask Names

To perform the canon of about 240 nō plays, some eighty to ninety different mask types are necessary. Each mask type has specific iconographic characteristics and a name (e.g., Magojirō, Kurohige, Dōji). Most of these named mask types can be used in a variety of plays representing a range of characters. A large number of the third category (women) plays, for example, can be performed with the same young woman's mask. Likewise, several of the second category warrior plays can utilize the warrior-courtier mask called Chūjō.[45]

A simple grouping of masks divides them on a scale of human to nonhuman into old men (*jō*), men (*otoko*), women (*onna*), ghosts and spirits (*onryō*), and supernatural beings, including gods and demons, and mythical beasts (*kijin*). Separate from these five are the masks used in the ritual *Okina* (*Shikisanban*). As the following discussion will make evident, this categorization summarized in table 2.12 is neither exclusive nor exhaustive.[46]

TABLE 2.12 Mask categories and examples

Mask category	Examples (mask names)
Okina	Okina (Hakushikijō), Sanbasō (Kokushikijō), Chichinojō, Enmei Kaja
Old men	Kojō, Asakurajō, Maijō, Ishiōjō, Shiwajō, Sankōjō
Men	Dōji, Jidō, Jūroku, Chūjō, Heita, Kantan otoko, Kasshiki, Semimaru, Yoroboshi, Kagekiyo, Shunkan
Women	Fukai, Komachi, Ko-omote, Magojirō, Masukami, Rōjo, Shakumi, Uba, Waka onna, Zō onna
Spirits	Deigan, Hashihime, Hannya, Ryō no onna, Yase otoko, Yase onna, Yamanba
Gods, demons, beasts, and sprites	Tobide, Tenjin, Kurohige, Akujō, Beshimi, Shishiguchi, Shikami, Yakan, Shōjō

---

45 It is unclear when mask types began to receive specific names, but presumably the process began with generic names for generic roles: *oni* masks to portray demons, haggard masks for suffering ghosts, women's masks for female roles, and so forth. On the history of mask makers, see sec. 7.3.

46 For a comprehensive listing of masks types and discussion of classification methodology, see the section on nō masks on the website JPARC.online.

2.8.2 Many Masks for One Character, Single Masks for Many Characters

Each *shite* school has its own rules for mask use. For the role of the heavenly maiden in *Hagoromo*, for instance, the Kanze and Kongō schools stipulate Zō onna (fig. 2.42), whose serene yet detached expression reflects the maiden's celestial origins. The remote sublimity distinguishes this mask from other young women's masks.[47] The Kanze actor may also select Waka onna—their standard mask for young women's roles—to emphasize the humanity of the heavenly maiden. A more intimate impression is seen in the youthful Ko-omote mask (fig. 2.43), which the Kita and Konparu schools use and which is an alternative choice for a Kanze or Kongō actor.

These masks all share the general characteristics of young women's masks: black hair parted down the middle with a few individual strands running along the side of the face, shaved eyebrows repainted high on the forehead (a cosmetic practice of the era), reddened lips, and blackened teeth (another cosmetic practice). The details vary, however, to evoke distinct impressions. Zō onna is the most remote, with unsmiling lips, less fleshy cheeks, thinner eyebrows, and horizontal brushstrokes for the ground that deemphasize the contours of the sculpting. Ko-omote's fuller cheeks, heavier chin, pert mouth, and fuzzy eyebrows give an impression of youthful ingenuousness. These differences are produced, in part, by the balance of the eyes, nose, mouth, cheeks, and so on within the overall contours. The triangle formed by the eyes and mouth is smallest for Ko-omote, the distance between the pupils the shortest. This concentrates the features toward the center of the face and highlights the full cheeks suggestive of youth. Zō onna's eyes are set slightly farther apart; her mouth is a bit wider, the cheeks almost flat.

In *Hagoromo*, when the heavenly maiden realizes that she may never get her feather robe back and thus may be locked on earth permanently, she begins to lose her celestial powers and breaks down weeping. This scene inspired a variant of Zō onna with a more troubled expression called the "crying Zō" (Nakizō). The Hōshō school often uses Nakizō and another variant, Fushikizō, as their standard mask for all young women's roles.[48] In contrast, the Konparu and Kita schools employ Ko-omote for the same roles, and this reflects an acting style that is more straightforward and direct. Choosing a mask to wear for *Hagoromo*, then, is on the one hand stipulated by the *shite* school tradition and on the other a tool for interpretation of the role (see sec. 2.12).

---

47 Zō onna is used for female deities or heavenly beings, such as the *nochi shite* in *Yoshino tennin, Ukon, Seiōbō, Saoyama, Ema, Miwa, Tatsuta*, as well as the enlightened Chūjōhime in *Taema*.

48 The elegant refinement of Fushikizō resonates with Hōshō performance style, which incorporates a unique extra high note, *kanguri*, in the melodies and places special emphasis on melismatic renditions.

FIGURE 2.42 Zō onna mask (sub-name: Aioi Zō). Attributed to Ōmiya Yamato (d. 1672). 17th century. Colors and gesso on wood. Tessenkai collection

FIGURE 2.43 Ko-omote mask (sub-name: Sawarabi). By Kodama Ōmi (d. 1704). 17th century. Colors and gesso on wood. Tessenkai collection

The choice of mask for *Hagoromo* speaks of another aspect that both controls and blurs the line of classification of nō mask types. The heavenly maiden does not belong to our everyday human experience, but rather to the supernatural world where we encounter deities, demons, ghosts, and celestial beings. Such encounters generally occur in a dream context (*mugen nō*) and involve an initial dissemblance as a normal human followed by a revelation of their more-than-ordinary "true" form. Masks for these other-than-human beings differ in essential details from masks depicting humans.

2.8.3 *Masks Representing Humans or Ghosts in Human Disguise*

Masks of humans (or their ghosts) are realistically portrayed. They are slightly smaller than an adult male face, light to tan in color, with fleshed-out features and rounded contours. Each age and gender has a specific iconography. For instance, all women's masks have hair parted in the center. Straggly loose

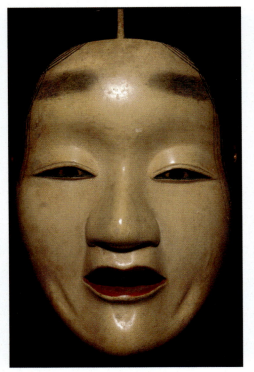

FIGURE 2.44
Shakumi mask. Attributed to Deme Zekan (d. 1616), actually by Shinagawa Motomasa (dates unknown). 17th century. Colors and gesso on wood. Tessenkai collection

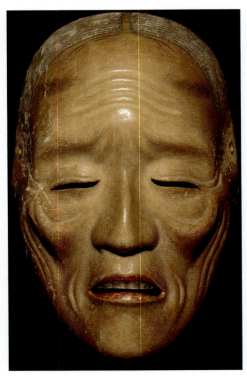

FIGURE 2.45
Uba mask. By Deme Tōhaku (1633–1715). 17th century. Colors and gesso on wood. Tessenkai collection

strands suggest agitation. Eyebrows are shaven and redrawn high on the forehead. Age is expressed in increasingly gaunt faces. The eyes droop, the lips get thinner and begin to turn downward, and the hair turns gray. The straight-cut square pupils of the young women's masks lend them a quiet look and their downturned eyes focus inward. The middle-aged women (Fukai and Shakumi; fig. 2.44) have very slightly curved pupils set in heavy-lidded eyes, an indication of their experiences of life and suffering. The old woman, Uba (fig. 2.45), is so sight-challenged that her half-closed eyes form slits, a trait that, ironically, enables the actor to see better.

Youths have loose hair and bangs, sometimes trimmed, as for the acolyte Kasshiki. The Dōji mask (fig. 2.46) represents an eternally youthful person who has drunk the elixir of long life. Adult men have their hair pulled back as if in a topknot. Aristocratic men like Chūjō (fig. 2.47) have a black line across

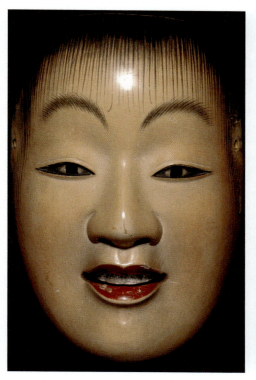 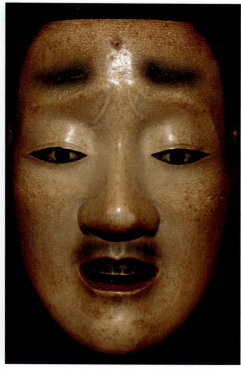

FIGURE 2.46
Dōji mask. 17th century. Colors and gesso on wood. Tessenkai collection

FIGURE 2.47
Chūjō mask. By Iseki Kawachi Ieshige (d. 1657). 17th century. Colors and gesso on wood. Tessenkai collection

their upper foreheads to indicate where the courtier's hat rests. The middle-aged mask Heita (fig. 2.48) worn by victorious warriors has round eyes and a dynamically painted mustache and eyebrows that express the strength and vigor of the characters portrayed (e.g., Yoshitsune in *Yashima*). For old men's masks, such as Kojō (fig. 2.49), horse hair is implanted into the mask at the upper sides with the strands twisted together and tied with a cord at the center so that it blends with the old man's wig. The old men's masks have ears, unlike most other masks of humans. Other realistic aspects include hair implanted to create a beard, and in some cases for a mustache (e.g., Waraijō). A distinction is made between old men's masks donned for the first act, typically in first and second category plays, and old men's masks for the second act in which they perform a dance (e.g., Maijō, Ishiōjō, Shiwajō). While the former characters are in human guise, the latter are deities and consequently rendered less realistically.

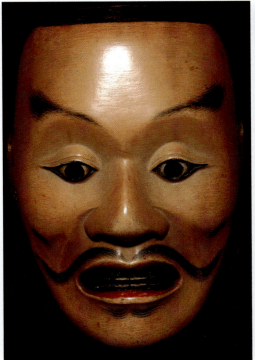
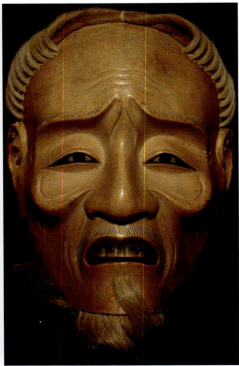

FIGURE 2.48
Heita mask. By Kodama Ōmi (d. 1704). 17th century. Colors and gesso on wood. Tessenkai collection

FIGURE 2.49
Kojō mask. Late 17th–early 18th century. Colors and gesso on wood. Tessenkai collection

2.8.4 *Masks of Nonhuman Characters*

In contrast to these masks for characters with human appearances, those for supernatural beings and ghosts in a heightened emotional state (vengeance, jealousy, extreme suffering) have more stylized, exaggerated features. Most have visible upper and lower teeth, the tips of which are either white or gold imparting a strong impression. Coloring is often more intense, sometimes red, sometimes gold. Most have gold eyes, since gold implies the supernatural nature of the characters associated with these masks. For some, the irises of the eyes and teeth are painted gold, while for very supernatural figures, the whole mask may be painted gold, and copper fittings set over the eyes and teeth.

In nō masks, the shape of the eyelids (from thin almond shapes to rounds), the shape of the pupils (slits, squared, or rounded), and the presence or absence of gold (painted or metallic insert) contribute to the impact onstage. Among the women's masks, Deigan ("Gold Eyes"; fig. 2.50) has pupils that are slightly rounded with gold painted onto the whites of the eyes. Onstage, the eyes seem

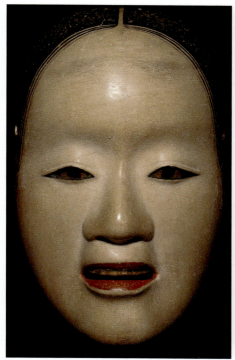

FIGURE 2.50
Deigan mask. Traditionally attributed to Zōami (dates unknown). 16th century. Tessenkai collection

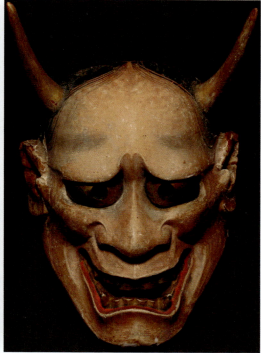

FIGURE 2.51
Hannya mask. By Iseki Kawachi Ieshige. 17th century. Tessenkai collection

to flash momentarily. The presence of gold, minimal as it is in Deigan, indicates that the figure is a more-than-ordinary being. The Deigan mask is used for several very different types of characters. On the one hand, it can be worn by celestial beings, such as the enlightened daughter of the dragon god in *Ama*. Here, the gold suggests her supernatural aspect. On the other, Deigan is a choice for female spirits in emotional disarray, such as the living ghost of Lady Rokujō in the first act of *Aoi no ue*, who is bent on retribution and in the second act transforms into a serpentlike character wearing a Hannya mask (fig. 2.51). The Hannya mask's round metallic eyeballs and perfect circles for pupils carry a fierce intensity accentuated by the gold-fanged gaping mouth and horns but modulated by the troubled ridges above the eyes. The high delicate eyebrows and parted, straggly hair are remnants of her femininity.

A similar range can be seen in the eyes of male masks: the more fantastic and powerful, the rounder the eyes. Examples with huge gold eyes include Tobide, donned by powerful deities, Kurohige (fig. 2.52), used for dragon gods;

FIGURE 2.52
Kurohige mask. Traditionally attributed to Shakuzuru (dates unknown). Late 16th century. Colors and gesso on wood, gilt copper eyes. Tessenkai collection

FIGURE 2.53
Chōrei Beshimi mask. 17th century. Colors and gesso on wood, gilt copper eyes. Tessenkai collection

Beshimi (fig. 2.53) worn for *tengu*, demons, and bandits; Shishiguchi representing mythical lions; and Shikami a type of malicious being (fig. 2.54). Masks of the Akujō type (fig. 2.55) can be utilized to represent a powerful dragon king and are also appropriate for wronged persons seeking retribution, such as the old gardener in *Aya no tsuzumi*.

Tobide and Beshimi are employed for the diametrically opposed roles of deity and demon, nonetheless they traditionally form a pair, one with wide open mouth, the other with clenched lips. Their prototypes are some of the oldest among nō masks.

Suffering ghosts, revengeful wraiths, and vigorous gods have rings of gold inserted for the irises of the eyes, lending each a different type of out-of-the-ordinary ambience. For Yase otoko (fig. 2.56), a ghost suffering in hell and seen in plays such as *Fujito* and *Utō*, the downturned eyes almost hide the gold rings, while the angular rendering of his skeletal bone structure emphasizes

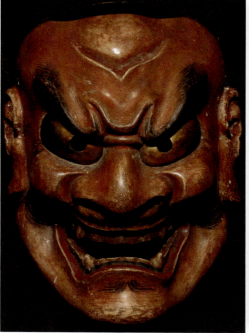 

FIGURE 2.54
Shikami mask. By Deme Chōun (dates unknown). 18th century. Colors and gesso on wood, gilt copper eyes. Tessenkai collection

FIGURE 2.55
Hanakobu Akujō mask. 18th century. Colors and gesso on wood, gilt copper eyes, implanted moustache and beard. Tessenkai collection

his anguish. In contrast, Mikazuki (fig. 2.57) looks straight forward, his gold-rimmed eyes bright with energy suitable for the vigorous god of Sumiyoshi who appears in the second act of *Takasago*.

Typical of the ambiguities inherent in nō renditions, the borderlines between human and nonhuman are not always clear. Over time, some of the masks designed to represent humans were adopted for other roles. The Kantan mask is a case in point. First created for the role of a Chinese commoner in search of enlightenment who experiences a dream of glory as he sleeps on a magic pillow in the play *Kantan*, the mask also came to be used for the character of the Sumiyoshi deity in *Takasago*. The ambivalent expression of concern in the furrows between the eyes lies hidden behind a headband when the actor is dressed as the deity. Revealed instead is the strength and masculinity apparent in the lower half of the mask. Although not as vivid as Mikazuki, the power of the god is fully evident and given an extra element of humanity.

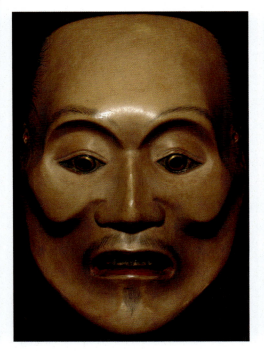

FIGURE 2.56
Yase otoko mask. By Kodama Ōmi (d. 1704).
17th century. Colors and gesso on wood. Tessenkai collection

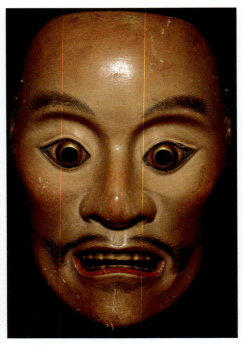

FIGURE 2.57
Mikazuki mask. By Deme Tōhaku (1633–1715).
17th century. Colors and gesso on wood. Tessenkai collection

2.8.5 Okina Masks: Bridging the Human and the Sacred

The masks used for the ritual *Okina* (also known as *Shikisanban*) appear at once otherworldly and intimately human. These three masks—Okina (also Hakushikijō, or "White Old Man"; fig. 2.58); Sanbasō (also Kokushikijō or "Black Old Man"; see fig. 9.9); and Chichinojō ("Old Man Father"; fig. 2.59)—plus a fourth called Enmei Kaja, form a group that in their origins predate nō by well over a century.[49] Zeami treats the performance of *Shikisanban* as the origin of his art and the basis for nō performance. Even today, it is staged every New Year during celebratory occasions and in shrines around the country (see ch. 4 *Plays*).

---

49 Legend attributes an Okina mask to the hand of the seventh-century Prince Shōtoku. The earliest example known is an Okina mask in the Ethnological Museum in Berlin; recent infrared photography has revealed it has an inscription dated 1278. Otani 2016: 3–36 (English).

FIGURE 2.58
Okina (Hakushikijō) mask. Traditionally attributed to Fukurai (dates unknown). 15th–early 16th centuries. Colors and gesso on wood, hemp eyebrows and cords. Tessenkai collection

FIGURE 2.59
Chichinojō mask. Traditionally attributed to Fukurai (dates unknown). 12th–early 16th centuries. Colors and gesso on wood, hemp eyebrows and cords. Tessenkai collection

Okina is a ritual extolling the peace of the nation, the fertility of the land, and long life. The white Okina mask (Hakushikijō), with its hemp or rabbit-fur circular eyebrows, detached chin (*kiri-ago*), and joyful face sculpted with stylized wrinkles, is all smiles, a benevolent godlike old man who blesses the land.[50] The black Sanbasō mask (Kokushikijō), whose dance awakens the earth and mimics the growing plants, is similarly sculpted, but his eyebrows and mustache are made of implanted hair. The "Old Man Father" (Chichinojō) differs from the other two, mainly in that his almond-shaped eyes slant upward. The abstract rendering of furrows in the forehead and cheeks on all three masks contrasts with the more realistic treatment of other old men's masks, as seen in the Kojō mask discussed above.

50   Masks with severed or dangling chins can be found in Korea, China, and Indonesia, suggesting foreign origins that were then adapted.

All three Okina masks have been carved from a single block of wood, but their chins were then cut off in downward slants from the corners of the mouth to the rim of the mask. Holes were bored in the lower cheeks and chin such that the chin could be reaffixed by tying it on with a hemp cord. In performance the jaw jiggles slightly, particularly when the performer is speaking or being very active. Despite this device and the unrealistic eyebrows, these joyful masks personify an intimacy that surpasses realism, yet remains very human.

2.8.6 *Donning the Mask, Becoming the Character*

Nō masks are handled with special reverence and this is especially the case with the treatment of the Okina masks in the *Okina* performance.

Before a performance of *Okina*, the masks to be worn are set on an altar and worshipped as the embodiment of deities (*shintai*). *Sake* and salt piled in a white conical mound are set before the masks. The performers, who have all undergone ritual austerities, gather in front of the altar to share the same *sake* cup and uncooked rice and to scatter some salt for purification. Sounds and sparks from a flint stone used to purify the *hashigakari* and stage can be heard coming from the mirror room (*kagami no ma*).

The performance begins with a mask-box carrier presenting a lacquer box containing the masks. The *shite* who will perform Okina enters barefaced and bows at stage center or center front and then retires to upstage left.[51] During a purification dance by an unmasked character called Senzai, the *shite* opens the box, venerates the mask, and lifts it to his face, so that an assistant can tie it in place. Once masked, he is thought to have become one with the deity within the mask and the dance is thus performed by the deity. After he finishes, he retires to the same spot, removes the mask, honors it, and replaces it in the box.[52]

The ritualized veneration of the mask presented onstage in *Okina* points to its special position among nō masks. The idea of the mask having a spirit that enters the actor and performs through that person, harks back to shamanistic performance and can be seen in other Asian traditions. Today, each nō performer has a personal take on just what the ritual implies.[53]

---

51 There are a number of interpretations concerning the identity of recipient of this dedication and the bow: the shōgun, the audience, or the North Star. Teele 1986: 93–103.
52 Today, Chichinojō (fig. 2.79) is used only in special performances, most notably at Shintō shrines.
53 Historically, there have also been differing interpretations. See Pinnington 1998: 492–518.

For all other nō performances, paying reverence to the mask before donning it is incorporated into the dressing process and done in the mirror room just beyond the curtain that separates backstage from the bridgeway leading to the stage proper. Contemplating the masked image in the mirror, the actor seeks to become one with the role. The mask serves as a vehicle for its embodiment. Or, conversely, the actor functions as a vehicle for the embodiment of the character that resides in the mask.

2.8.7   Use of the Mask Onstage

As outlined at the beginning of this section, the mask's expressiveness emerges from the stance and overall body movements within the context of the costumed character. Rather than having set facial expressions at this or that angle, the mask's rounded or angled contours seem to come alive as an extension of the body movements. The fluid, minimal, or sharp motions enhance the mask's evocative power.

Only a few movement patterns (*kata*) apply specifically to mask manipulation. Leaning forward a small amount angles the mask down (*kumorasu*, "cloud the mask"), the inward curve of the body accentuating a sense of sadness. Stretching the torso and lifting the head slightly angles the mask upward (*terasu*, "lighten the mask"), which is felt to convey joy or relief. Turning the head somewhat to the left and then to the right is called "using the mask" (*omote o tsukau*). This action can assume a range meanings, such as searching for something or looking around at a vista as in the final dance of *Hagoromo* when the heavenly maiden holds up the fan mirroring the view of Mio Bay and the sea and steps forward while looking right and left. It is as if the maiden is surveying the area before taking flight into the sky. The more dynamic, stylized masks of supernatural beings, such as deities and demons, gain intensity with vigorous movement and sharp head turns (*omote o kiru*, "cut with the mask"). The circular metallic insets for eyes seem to jump about as the head jerks to the side.

In deciding on a mask to use for a performance, an actor considers not only its artistic excellence but more importantly its impact from a distance. The choices may differ if the performance is indoors or outdoors, with modern lighting or torchlight. The mask selection should also match both the occasion and the level of the performer. Certain masks require a veteran master's art and are therefore seen to have a higher *kurai*.

2.9 Costumes
Monica Bethe

The nō actors draped in voluminous silhouettes of rich silks stand out luxuriously against the austere wood and painted pine of the nō stage. Adding color, texture, and line, enhancing the movements and catching the mood, the costumes take on the role of scenery and stage set as well as defining characters. For those familiar with traditional Japanese attire, the types of garments and the way they are draped indicate the identity of the character; their patterns and colors can add interpretive overtones. Many of the costume types are derived from garments worn by the military aristocracy or commoners in the sixteenth century (see ch. 7 *Material Culture*, 7.2). Monks, ministers, and other living male characters tend to be dressed similarly to people in corresponding occupations. By contrast, deities and demons wear bold, flashy garments that do not imitate real-life outfits, but instead express their superhuman powers. This blend of "real" and "otherworldly" runs through the conventions of nō.

Each costume consists of an assemblage of garments layered one on the other. These combinations are prescribed by tradition and are noted at the beginning of the modern *utaibon* (chant books). Although there are only twenty or so main types of garments, different combinations and draping result in a number of variations, representing the nuanced variety of characters appearing in nō and kyōgen. Broadly speaking, these can either belong to the living, present human world (men and women of all ages and occupations), or to the world of supernatural beings (deities, demons, goblins, dragons, animals, and spirits). Ghosts lie somewhere in between, sometimes dressed as they did when alive, sometimes transfigured into vengeful creatures. While several of the garment types are worn in both nō and kyōgen performances, simply stated, silk costumes dominate nō performance, while bast-fiber (hemp or ramie) garments are emblematic of kyōgen costumes (see ch. 9 *Kyōgen*, 9.4).

The garments used in nō and kyōgen are grouped into five categories: 1) inner robes (*kitsuke*) tailored similarly to the box-sleeved, "T"-shaped kimono that were known as *kosode* ("small sleeve") until the late nineteenth century; 2) outer, upper robes with broad, usually double width, open sleeves (*ōsode*); 3) the sleeveless (*sodenashi*) variants of broad-sleeved garments; 4) several types of pleated trousers (*hakama*); and 5) accessories including hairbands, waist sashes, fans, and headgear (table 2.13, fig. 2.60a–e). Two or more of these garments draped in specified ways are assembled to create outfits (*idetachi*).

TABLE 2.13 Types of nō and kyōgen costume garments

Garment type	Description	Techniques	Garment names
Kosode ("Small sleeve")	"T"-shaped kimono with square sleeves sewn up at the cuff. All the same tailoring. Types are distinguished by weave and patterning technique. Outer garment or undergarment for female roles. Undergarment for male roles.	Woven: plain color, plain weave; stripes; checks; float patterning. Surface design: stenciled gold leaf; embroidery.	*karaori* *atsuita* *noshime* *surihaku* *nuihaku*
Ōsode ("Large sleeve")	Outer, upper "jackets" worn by men and women with broad, usually double-width sleeves open at the cuff. Many cuts with different tailoring.	Silk: plain weave; gauze weave; patterned satin weave; patterned twill weave. Bast fiber: stenciled or hand-drawn paste-resist dyeing.	*mizugoromo* *chōken* *kariginu* *happi* *suō* *hitatare*
Sodenashi (Vests)	Sleeveless variations of "large-sleeve" garments.	Silk: patterned satin or twill weave. Bast fiber: stenciled or hand-drawn paste-resist dyeing.	*sobatsugi* *kamishimo* *kataginu*
Hakama (Pleated trousers)	Skirtlike trousers with several pleats in front and two panels in the back. Broad and bulky in the back or slimmer *hakama* style.	Silk, stiffened in the back to form a bulge: ribbed plain weave; patterned weave. Bast fiber, slimmer, ankle bound and extra-long variations: stenciled or hand-drawn paste-resist dyeing.	*ōkuchi* *hangiri* *sashinuki* *naga-bakama* *han-bakama* *kukuri-bakama*
Accessories	Headgear, hairbands, waist sashes, and handheld objects, such as fans, rosaries, and swords.	Woven, embroidered, lacquered, carved, papered, and so forth.	*kanmuri* *eboshi* *kazura obi* *koshi obi* *ōgi*, and so forth

FIGURE 2.60A–E   Examples of nō costumes from each category: a) *kosode* "small sleeve"; b) *ōsode* "broad sleeve" (e.g., *happi*); c) *sodenashi* "sleeveless" (e.g., *kataginu*); d) *hakama* "pleated trousers" (e.g., *ōkuchi*); and e) accessories (e.g., *eboshi*)

2.9.1   Layering Costumes and Creating Outfits

To understand how these few garments are combined to create some eighty types that are further identified through details like headgear and handheld props, it is important to note that character roles in nō are to a large extent generic: minister, village woman, traveling monk.[54] The costumes reflect these general types. In other words, the same outfit, indeed the very same garment, can be worn in numerous plays to represent a spectrum of people. This generality makes possible the gradual disclosure of identity, a key aspect of most *mugen nō*. In the play *Izutsu* (see ch. 4 *Plays*, 4.5), for instance, the *shite* in the first act is a local woman. Only after considerable discussion with a traveling monk (*waki*) and after her narration of how two neighboring children played

---

54   A number of nō anthologies include compendium of costume outfits. The second volume of Yokomichi and Omote, 1969: 478–88, illustrates eighty-three nō outfits and twelve kyōgen outfits.

FIGURE 2.61
Standard woman's costume in act 1. *Karaori* in straight *kinagashi* draping

around a well and eventually married, does the local woman reveal she is the ghost of the woman in the story.

A closer look at her outfit serves to discuss key aspects of costuming and to introduce a few basic costumes. In the first act, the local woman wears a *karaori*, a brocaded "small-sleeve" *kosode*, over a *surihaku*, a satin *kosode* decorated with gold- or silver-leaf stenciled patterns. Although the character is that of a villager, the costume for the role is made of silk with elaborate, colorful woven patterning that in real life could only be worn by the aristocracy. She also sports a richly embellished undergarment. This is standard for *shite* women appearing in act 1 and *tsure* women, regardless of their social status. The *karaori* would be draped to hang straight from shoulder to ankle (*kinagashi*; fig. 2.61) with the collar spread at the shoulders. Binding the garment at the hips with a cord or narrow sash follows the fashions of the late sixteenth century.

Karaori are woven with elaborate, multicolor designs (floated weft patterning on a twill foundation weave; fig. 2.62a–b). These gorgeous robes are often lauded as the quintessential nō costumes because of the sophistication of their designs and weaving techniques. The feminine designs tend to be taken from nature—flowers, birds, butterflies—or to reference court life, such

FIGURE 2.62A–B   a) *karaori* with autumn flowers and grasses and b) detail showing the woven float design. Edo period. 19th century. Silk twill foundation with silk and gold thread supplementary patterning. 172.3 (l) × 147.3 (w) cm. The Metropolitan Museum of Art, Edward C. Moore collection, Bequest of Edward C. Moore, 1891. Public domain

as court carriages for outings. For young characters, the designs include red (*iroiri*, "with color") while for older characters they lack red (*ironashi*, "without color"). Seasonal associations may guide the selection for a performance, for example, the red *karaori* with a design of autumn flowers and grasses shown in figure 2.62 would be appropriate for the autumnal setting of *Izutsu*.

The *shite* in *Izutsu* wears a long black wig (*kazura*) bound in a ponytail at the nape of the neck and a young woman's mask (see sec. 2.8). A long narrow sash or hairband (*kazura obi*), which runs over the wig but under the mask, is tied decoratively at the back of the head. The headband for the village woman in *Izutsu* should have a gold-foil ground and embroidery including red (fig. 2.63). The under collar should be white. The *shite* carries an offering branch and holds a string of crystal prayer beads.

In act 2 of *Izutsu*, the *nochi shite* returns as the ghost of Ki no Aritsune's daughter and dressed in the robes left by her lover. As the *nochi shite* dances the slow, elegant *jo no mai*, the robe's "blossom sleeves swirl like snow." The diaphanous elegance of the *chōken* that represents this robe derives from its open gauze weave. Typically, *chōken* have large medallion-like designs brocaded in gold or silk threads placed across the chest and upper back; they are

FIGURE 2.63 Headbands (*kazura obi*). Late 18th century. Embroidered chrysanthemum scroll on a gold silk satin ground and clematis scroll over stenciled gold leaf (*surihaku*) on silk satin. 3.2 (h) × 122.6 (l) cm. The Metropolitan Museum of Art, Purchase, Gift of Mr. and Mrs. Teiji Ito, by exchange, 1984. Public domain

balanced with lighter scattered motifs in the lower portion (fig. 2.64a–b). She also wears Narihira's black lacquered courtier's cap (*uikanmuri*; fig. 2.65) with a long "tail" that symbolizes his rank as a government official. During the final dance in *Izutsu*, the *nochi shite* thus attired in her lover's "robe and headdress" peers into the well that formed the center of their budding affair years before and sees his image merge with hers.

Although the costume change in *Izutsu* appears to be a simple donning of an outer robe and hat, in fact, it also involves a total substitution of the inner robes. The stiff *karaori* is rather bulky as an undergarment, so the slimmer *koshimaki* outfit (*koshi*: waist, *maki*: wrap; fig. 2.66) consisting of softer-weave garments (generally satin) is used. These are the *surihaku* ("imprint gold leaf"; fig. 2.67a–b) with gold- or silver-leaf stenciled patterns worn as an undergarment and the *nuihaku* (embroidered gold leaf) with embroidery in addition to the metallic-leaf patterns worn over it (fig. 2.68a–b). The *nuihaku* is draped folded down at the waist. Only the hem and a bit of the collar of the outfit are visible under the *chōken*. In other plays, such as *Hagoromo*, the shite wears a *koshimaki* outfit from the beginning. The glossy white *surihaku* glitters with the reflection of gold patterning, while the folded-down *nuihaku* "skirt" displays pictorial designs embroidered on richly dyed glossy fabric.

2.9.2 *Same Garment, Different Draping*

With a limited vocabulary of costumes types, combinations and draping become important signifiers. The *karaori* introduced above, for instance, can be draped in four different ways to indicate different activities and rank. A woman doing manual labor, like punting a boat, as the *tsure* does in *Eguchi*,

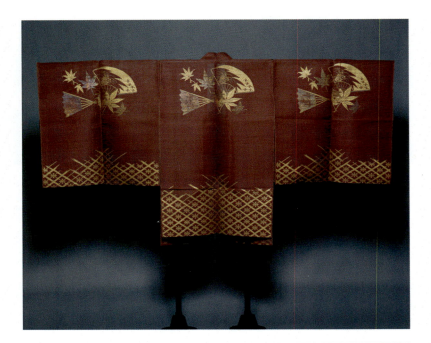

FIGURE 2.64A–B   a) *chōken* with fans and maple leaves in gold and silver on a purple gauze weave and b) detail. 18th century. Purple ribbed gauze with supplementary gold thread patterning. 107.3 (length at center back) cm. RISD Museum, Gift of Miss Lucy T. Aldrich. Public domain

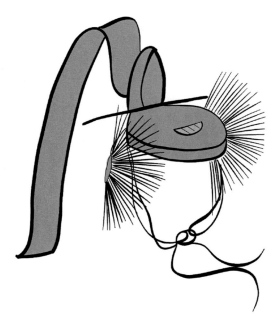

FIGURE 2.65
Uikanmuri courtier's cap

FIGURE 2.66
Koshimaki draping with a *surihaku* inner robe exposed above and an embroidered *nuihaku* folded down at the waist so that the sleeves hang over the hips

has the right sleeve of her *karaori* slipped off (*nugisage*) for ease of movement (fig. 2.69a). A dancer might don a *karaori* as an outer garment over a *koshimaki*, tucking it up at the waist (*tsuboori*; fig. 2.69b). A very high-ranking court woman, like the Chinese court lady Yang Guifei in *Yōkihi*, wears a gorgeous *karaori* over broad pleated trousers (*ōkuchi*; see fig. 2.77a) that give the figure stature (fig. 2.69c). The drunken creature portrayed as a red-faced youth in *Shōjō* also wears a *karaori* tucked up in *tsuboori* style over broad pleated trousers, in this case with brocaded pattern (*hangiri*).

A wider range of characters are dressed in the broad, open-sleeved *mizugoromo* (traveling jacket). These roles are distinguished by the texture and pattern of the weave as well as by draping. *Mizugoromo* come in several variations. Most common are monochrome plain-weave *mizugoromo*, like that worn by the traveling monk (*waki*) in *Izutsu* (fig. 2.70a), whose sober, simple garb befits a mendicant. His plain *mizugoromo* is bound with a damask waist sash (*koshi obi*) tied such that its ends hang down in front. His inner robe (*kitsuke*) is a

FIGURE 2.67A–B   a) *surihaku* with Chinese bellflowers and b) detail. 18th century. Gold- and silver-leaf stenciled design on silk satin. 173.4 × 142.4 cm. The Metropolitan Museum of Art, Purchase, Joseph Pulitzer Bequest, 1932. Public Domain

FIGURE 2.68A–B   a) *nuihaku* with design of chrysanthemum sprigs and flower-filled hexagon lattice and b) detail. 18th century. Silk embroidery and gold-leaf stenciled pattern on blue silk satin. 124.4.cm (length at center back) cm. RISD Museum, Gift of Miss Lucy T. Aldrich. Public domain

monochrome plain-weave silk *kosode* called a *noshime*. Finally, his folded cloth hat (*sumibōshi*, also read *sunbōshi*), fan decorated with a simple ink painting, and prayer beads unequivocally define him as a Buddhist monk.

A similar monochrome, plain-weave *mizugoromo* is employed for the outer garb of the old man (*mae shite*) in *Tadanori* (see sec. 2.3; ch. 4 *Plays*, 4.5; fig. 2.5a). What distinguishes his outfit from those of the monks he encounters (*waki* and *waki tsure*) is that he wears a mask (Asakurajō or Waraijō), carries a walking stick, and dons an old man's wig (*jōgami*) rather than a cloth monk's hat.

The monochrome *mizugoromo* worn by the deity appearing as an old man in *Takasago* (fig. 2.70b) is belted over broad pleated trousers (*ōkuchi*). Striped *mizugoromo* distinguish the attire of the *yamabushi* mountain ascetics. Loosely woven *mizugoromo* with displaced wefts (fig. 2.71a–b) suggest poverty, frailty, or age, and may thus be used as the garb of suffering ghosts, including the hunter in *Utō*, the fisherman in *Fujito*, and the centenarian Ono no Komachi in *Sekidera Komachi* and *Sotoba Komachi*. While men wear the *mizugoromo* belted, women allow it to fall free from the shoulders (fig. 2.70c; also fig. 2.14b).

FIGURE 2.69A–C   *Karaori* draping examples: a) *nugisage*; b) *tsuboori* over *koshimaki*; and c) *tsuboori* over *ōkuchi*

FIGURE 2.70A–C *Mizugoromo* draping examples: a) traveling monk outfit: *mizugoromo* jacket over a *noshime*, *sumibōshi* hat and rosary; b) *mizugoromo* worn over *ōkuchi* for an old man's role; and c) *mizugoromo* worn unbelted for a woman's role

2.9.3 Lined and Unlined Garments

Other examples of ways weave structure and texture serve to distinguish roles types are the broad-sleeved jackets, *happi* and *kariginu*. Both garment types come in two varieties: lined and unlined. The lined examples (*awase*) use a dense fabric with a satin, twill, or plain-weave foundation and woven patterning, while unlined examples (*hitoe*) are fashioned from patterned gossamer fabrics of simple gauze (*sha*), ribbed gauze (*ro*), or self-patterned gauze (*monsha*). The lined and unlined versions create such different stage effects that they are not interchangeable.

2.9.3.1 Happi

Happi have double-width open sleeves, collars running straight down rather than in a V, and no side seams but strips of cloth at the hem connecting the front and back center panels. Unlined *happi*, such as might be worn for the *nochi shite* in *Tadanori* (see sec. 2.3), are reserved for more refined roles, typically defeated warrior-courtiers of the Heike clan, famed for their music and poetry. In contrast, powerful victorious warriors, including the ghost of Yoshitsune in *Yashima*, may wear lined *happi* (fig. 2.72). Lined *happi* often have large, strong patterns in gold or silver set against a dark ground and combined with equally bold patterned pleated trousers (*hangiri*; fig. 2.73). The volume and contrasting colors of the design against the background create a dynamic

FIGURE 2.71A–B a) *mizugoromo* with displaced wefts and b) detail. 19th century. Blue plain-weave bast fiber, ramie warp and hemp weft. 110.2 (length at center back) × 163.8 (w) cm. The Metropolitan Museum of Art, Purchase, Friends of Asian Art Gifts, 2002. Public Domain

effect. Demons (*Ōeyama*; fig. 2.74a), menacing animal spirits (*Sesshōseki*), dragon gods (*Chikubushima*), and vengeful ghosts (*Funa Benkei*; fig. 2.74b) can wear lined *happi* belted over *hangiri* pleated trousers. Differing mainly in the size of patterns, draping and accessories, the *happi* combined with *hangiri* is also used for bandits (Kumasaka in *Eboshi-ori*) and Chinese immortals (*Kiku jidō*; fig. 2.74c).

2.9.3.2 Kariginu

A similar distinction between rarefied roles (unlined) and vigorous roles (lined) informs the use of the round-collared *kariginu* jacket (fig. 2.75a–b). During the Heian period (794–1185), this silk "hunting cloak" served as a courtier's informal jacket. The cord lacings at the cuffs of the broad, open sleeves are a remainder from when the cuffs were bound at the wrist while hunting. The round collar with overlapping front panels retains a feature of Chinese court garb adopted by the Japanese for official costumes, such as the *hō* and *sokutai*, and is thus indicative of high rank. In the Kamakura period (1185–1333), the military aristocracy adopted the *kariginu* as formal wear.

In first category deity plays, the *waki* in the role of a court envoy, minister, or Shintō priest, wears a lined *kariginu* over *ōkuchi* (fig. 2.76a). Patterns and

FIGURE 2.72   Lined *happi* with *tomoe* design. 19th century. Gold paper thread patterning on blue silk satin. 102 (length at center back) cm. RISD Museum, Gift of Miss Lucy T. Aldrich. Public domain

FIGURE 2.73   *Hangiri* pleated trousers with leaf design. 19th century. Gold paper thread pattern on a green satin ground. 82.2 (l) cm. RISD Museum, Gift of Miss Lucy T. Aldrich. Public domain

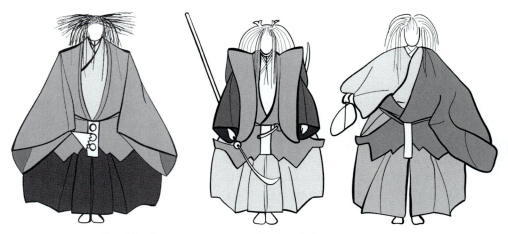

FIGURE 2.74A–C   *Happi* draping over *hangiri* examples: a) with sleeves down for a demon b) with sleeves hiked up for the vengeful ghost in *Funa Benkei;* c) with the right sleeve slipped off (*nugisage*) for a Chinese immortal youth

colors tend to be refined. *Shite* roles of ministers are also dressed in similar outfits. By contrast, the ghosts of elegant courtiers, such as Minamoto no Tōru in the play *Tōru* and the courtier-poet Ariwara no Narihira in *Unrin'in* don unlined *kariginu* (fig. 2.76b). The gossamer weave, soft colors, and small motifs evoke sophistication and lend these characters of the past an ethereal grace.

Spirits of aged trees (*Yugyō yanagi*, *Saigyōzakura*) also wear unlined *kariginu*. The semitransparency of the gauze weave heightens the sense of elegant timelessness. Long, loose off-white hair (*shirotare*) framing a pale old man's mask (Maijō, Shiwajō, or Ishiōjō) fill out the image.

In this way, *kariginu* outfits present a progression from living men to ghosts, gods (fig. 2.76c) and *tengu* (fig. 2.76d) through altering one or another element of the ensemble: wig, mask, headdress, fan, and type of pleated trousers. Patterns and color contrasts also come into play. Shintō deities wear lined *kariginu* with large bold patterns, often in gold or silver, and frequently set against contrasting dark grounds. Deities like the Thunder God in *Kamo* match the dynamic patterns in their lined *kariginu* with equally eye-catching gold patterning on their *hangiri* pleated trousers. Long, shaggy bright red hair (*aka-gashira*), and the gold Tobide mask with gaping mouth and large round eyes conjure the image of a powerful deity.

Less august figures wearing lined *kariginu* are the *tengu*, supernatural creatures who fly through the sky and inhabit mountain peaks. *Tengu* are ambivalent characters: on the one hand, they are portrayed as testing the monks' Buddhist faith (as in *Zegai*) or as kidnaping children (as it is narrated in *Kagetsu*). On the other, they are also capable of acts of kindness (as in *Daie*). The large round cap (*ōtokin*) that *tengu* wear atop their shaggy red or white wig (*shiro-gashira*) suggests their connection with *yamabushi* ascetics, while their distinctive feather fan indicates their affinity with the natural world.

2.9.4 Same Role, Several Variables

Although for most roles the garments that compose an outfit provide little choice, for some roles, such as warriors, there is greater latitude. The *nochi shite* in *Tadanori*, for instance can be dressed in any one of a number of under *kosode* combined with a choice of outer jacket.

The transformation of the old man, who appears in act 1 (see above), into the ghost of the warrior-courtier-poet Tadanori in act 2 requires a full costume change: in size from slim to broad, in color from somber to bright multichromatic, and in texture from smooth to varied. Simplicity is replaced by complexity. The volume is formed by the pleated trousers (*ōkuchi*; fig. 2.77a–b), their broad, stiffly ribbed back panels given a large tuck when placed on the actor to fashion a hump. These trousers may be white, red, or another color, and they may have small woven patterning.

The choice of *kosode* undergarments for the *nochi shite* role in *Tadanori* encompasses a range from the those deemed masculine to those associated with female roles. The *atsuita*, worn as an undergarment for the majority of male roles including gods and goblins, has brocaded patterning on a twill

FIGURE 2.75A–B a) lined *kariginu* with ginkgo leaves, feather fans, and pines over a fence-weave lattice and b) detail. 19th century. Gold paper thread pattern on a purple satin ground. 142.2 (length at center back) cm. RISD Museum, Gift of Miss Lucy T. Aldrich. Public domain

FIGURE 2.76A–D *Kariginu* draping examples: a) minister: lined *kariginu*, *ōkuchi*, *eboshi*, and lacquered hat; b) courtier: unlined *kariginu*, *sashinuki* pantaloons, and *uikanmuri* courtier's hat; c) vigorous deity: lined *kariginu* folded under at the collar (*emon* draping), *ōkuchi*, *tō-kanmuri* Chinese court hat, and *kurotare* wig; and d) *tengu*: lined *kariginu*, *hangiri*, round *tokin* cap, shaggy wig (*kashira*), and *hane ōgi* (feather fan)

ground and is thus similar to the *karaori*, except that the patterns tend to be geometric and bold in contrast to the floral designs on the feminine *karaori*.[55] An *atsuita* therefore fits the image of Tadanori as a valiant warrior. He is, however, also a sensitive poet and elegant courtier. To emphasize this side of his character, an actor might prefer to dress him in a more delicate (read feminine) attire and has the choice of either a *karaori* or even the softer embroidered satin *nuihaku*. In between these gendered garments is the *atsuita-karaori*, which has bold but not necessarily geometrical designs and was created specifically for warrior-courtier roles.

Over the *kosode*, the actor has a choice of wearing either a male broad-sleeved unlined *happi* jacket or a *chōken*, otherwise worn as a dancing cloak by women. It will be remembered that both these garments are tailored from a diaphanous gauze weave. Although the constructions of the *happi* (fig. 2.78a) and *chōken* (fig. 2.78b) are different, on a warrior figure, both are draped in a like fashion. They are belted at the waist with the right sleeve slipped off, rolled up, and tucked in at the back (fig. 2.79a–b). Once draped, the final effect of these two garments is similar. Figure 2.5b shows Tadanori dressed in a *chōken* draped over an *atsuita*.

FIGURE 2.77A–B   *Ōkuchi*: a) pleated in front and made of two large stiff, ribbed panels in the back and b) back view showing the large tuck

---

55   Some *atsuita* are woven with checks and lack brocaded patterns.

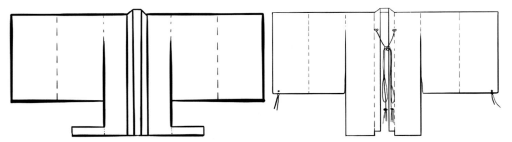

FIGURE 2.78A–B   Construction of outer jackets: a) *happi* and b) *chōken*

FIGURE 2.79A–B   Warrior-courtier attire: a) in an unlined *happi* over an *atsuita* or *atsuita-karaori* and *ōkuchi* and b) in a *chōken* over an *atsuita-karaori* or *nuihaku* and *ōkuchi*

Completing the outfit for Tadanori are a young man's mask (Chūjō; see fig. 2.47), a black lacquered cap (*nashiuchi eboshi*), a white headband (*hachimaki*), long flowing black hair (*kurotare*) and a waist sash (*koshi obi*) to bind the outer garment. The fan has a depiction of the sun setting over waves, a reference to the demise of the Heike clan toward the end of the twelfth century.

The long, curved sword (*tachi*) lashed to the actor's waist is unsheathed while enacting Tadanori's final battle and death.

In summary, similar garments can be worn for quite different roles, yet their combinations and draping create identifiable characters. Often the distinction lies in small details and accessories. Patterning and color coding also play a part. For instance, the *nochi shite* in the second acts of both *Izutsu* and *Tadanori* might don a *chōken*, but it is likely, although not stipulated, that the aristocratic woman in *Izutsu* would wear a purple or red *chōken* with a floral pattern in gold. Conversely, it would be appropriate to dress the role of the warrior-courtier Tadanori in a green or blue *chōken* with large, evenly distributed motifs.

2.9.5 Everyday Clothing Onstage

2.9.5.1 Matched Suits (*suō, hitatare, kamishimo*)

The costumes for roles of samurai and daimyō—roles that are central to kyōgen and frequent in fourth category *genzai nō*—correspond to sixteenth-century samurai dress, even though their origins reach back to at least the thirteenth century, and they continued to be worn throughout the Edo period. Matched suits (*suō*; fig. 2.80; *hitatare*; fig. 2.81a–b) consist of a broad-sleeved upper jacket over matching pleated trousers or over *ōkuchi*. Their construction differs only slightly, such as in the presence (*hitatare*) or absence of sleeve tassels. The *kamishimo* ("upper and lower") is an abbreviated matched suit with a "shoulder wing" vest and either ankle-length or long trailing trousers (fig. 2.82). It is worn for roles of townsmen.[56]

These matched suits and the separate winged vest (*kataginu*, see ch. 9 *Kyōgen*, 9.4) are woven from hemp or ramie bast fibers and decorated with dyed designs that are generally created by applying a resist paste through stencils or drawing with it freehand and then dyeing the cloth (indigo, black, and brown are the most common colors). Some, such as the *hitatare* in figure 2.83a–b, have painting in delineated areas.

2.9.6 Donning the Costume

When selecting a costume, the actor follows the stipulations of the stylistic school for the basic garment types. For most plays, color and pattern are largely a matter of choice, either by the mature actor or by a superior like the *iemoto*. Factors in choosing a design focus more on density, size of motif, and contrast

---

[56] The same kind of outfit is also used by the instrumentalists and by some chorus members for special performances.

FIGURE 2.81A–B *Hitatare* draping examples: a) military elite in matched top and trailing trousers (*naga-bakama*) and b) official in matched suit jacket with *ōkuchi* trousers

FIGURE 2.82
Townsman in *kamishimo* vest and trailing trousers (*naga-bakama*)

FIGURE 2.80
Commoner in *suō* top and trailing trousers (*naga-bakama*) decorated with the same pattern

FIGURE 2.83A–B   a) *hitatare* (matched suit) of jacket and trousers (*han-bakama*) with cranes and long-tailed tortoises over undulating vertical lines filled with flowers and b) detail. 19th century. Paste-resist dyed and painted on plain weave bast fiber, probably ramie. (Jacket) 102.9 (l) × 209.2 (w) cm; (*hakama*) 101.6 (l) × 91.4 (w) cm. The Metropolitan Museum of Art, Purchase, Friends of Asian Art Gifts, 2002. Public domain

with the background color than on the specific meaning attached to the motifs, although seasonal considerations are important.

Actors do not dress themselves, but rather are dressed by two or more stage assistants (*kōken*) working in tandem as they layer, belt, and secure each garment in succession. Standing in thin white undershirt and leggings, which serve to absorb perspiration, the actor first wears an additional white silk robe padded with cotton wool (*dōgi*). All of this constitutes the basic underwear on top of which costumes are layered. The actor may add silk and cotton wadded pillows as padding in the abdomen region. Once the inner collars are in place, the inner robe (*kitsuke*) is draped over the shoulders, the left lapel is placed over the right, and the garment secured with sashes at the waist.

Next are the pleated trousers (*ōkuchi* or *hangiri*), if worn. Cords threaded through holes at the top of the stiff back panels are pulled tight and tied to form a tuck that creates a hump (see fig. 2.77b). The front half of the trousers is tied to the actor's hips over the waist sash. A forked wooden frame is slipped into the waist sashes at the back, and the back half of the trousers are lifted up and set on the frame before securing the back with the attached sashes that are then tied at center front.

Finally, either a broad-sleeved jacket or a *kosode* used as an outer cloak (*tsubo-ori* style), may be placed over the other garments and either allowed to hang free or bound at the waist. The process of draping the garments on the actor's body—taking a tuck here, a temporary stitch there—creates a sculpture in fabrics. Dressed, the *shite*, seated in the mirror room, receives his mask, wig, hairbands, and headdress. The order in which these are donned depends on the construction of the wig. Fully attired, the actor focuses on the image he will bring to life onstage.

2.9.7   Manipulating the Costume

The actor's movements are influenced by the costumes: *kosode* restrict the size of steps, while pleated trousers, permit larger, more forceful leg movements. The square sleeves of *ōsode* (also *hirosode*) garments conceal the hands but exaggerate even small gestures.

When the *shite* dances, the broad sleeves of these jackets are given special play, flowing with the movement, shimmering in shifting lights. Certain gestures are designed to capitalize on these effects. At key places in a dance, the *shite* may flip a sleeve up so it rests on the arm (*sode o kakeru*). Or the actor may twirl the sleeves around one or both arms (*sode o maku*) or float the sleeve upward such that it falls over the head like a veil (*sode o kazuku*).

2.10   Fans
Diego Pellecchia

Similar to other elements of performance, fans can be examined from the point of view of their inherent materiality or for their symbolic values. Fan designs—delicately rendered figures, colorful flowers, or bold abstract patterns—identify the character type, but they also transcend physical appearance to signify something other. The fan is transformed when opened, closed, flipped, and circled. Moreover, it functions to transform the reality with which it is connected. Like the mask, whose gaze virtually materializes what the character sees, the fan in its manipulation urges the audience to visualize what is otherwise invisible: from distant mountain peaks to a horde of enemy warriors, from the mercy of Buddha to the longing for a lost love. As such, it is a powerful means of interaction between audience and performers.

Characters carry folding fans that spread at the tip even when closed (*chūkei*; fig. 2.84a). These fans have two main functions. The first is descriptive, since the fan design complements the costume, thus contributing to defining or suggesting the identity of the character. The second is narrative: the fan is an expressive tool, allowing the actor to perform a story. Movements bring the fan to life: whether lifting the arm or circling it around, the fan gives the gesture extra breadth, shaping its trajectory in space. The fan also serves as a mimetic tool, representing a sword, a bow, an arrow, a cup, or a pillow, as the context demands.

The fan is also utilized to signal key points in the progression of a play. All nō performances begin with the fan closed. When movement turns to dance, as for instance in the middle of a *kuse* section, the fan is opened to reveal its full design. Closing the fan is often the last gesture actors perform before leaving the stage. As discussed in section 2.4, the various ways in which the fan is held typify given dance sections and help to visualize the structure of the choreography.

Codified uses of the fan are not restricted to the actors. Each performer carries a fan, as this is an integral part of traditional kimono attire. These close-tipped fans (*shizume ōgi*) are smaller than those used for characters. As they enter, the drummers, chorus, and stage attendants have their own small fans tucked in their *obi* sashes or *hakama*. When they are seated, they place their fans on the stage according to set rules. Chorus members place their fans in front of them at the beginning of a performance. Just before singing, they carefully pick up the fan with both hands and, in the case of a full performance, hold them vertically in their right hands, to the left of their right knees. At the end of a chant section, they place the fans back on the floor, indicating their "inactive" status. Different ways to hold the fan when seated depend on the formality of the performance instance and may vary from school to school. In a full nō performance the chorus will hold the fan vertically, while during the performance of a *shimai* or a *maibayashi*, they would hold it with the tip touching the stage, or resting on the knees, held with both hands.

Taiko drummers place the fan to their right, while the *kotsuzumi* and *ōtsuzumi* drummers have them behind their stools. Flute players lay the fan to their right with one open leaf and rest the instrument on it when they are not playing.

2.10.1   Fan Types and Main Features

The basic structure of the *shizume ōgi* is similar to that of a standard Japanese fan that folds completely shut. Bamboo sticks join at one end and are fastened together with a rivet. Arc-shaped papers folded into ten leaves fit onto the pointed ribs of the sticks. The size, head shape, and other details vary from school to school. *Shizume ōgi* are utilized in actors' practice or in recital-style performances such as *shimai* or *maibayashi*, when the performer is dressed in kimono and *hakama* and does not wear a mask. For these performances, the

FIGURE 2.84A–B   *Chūkei* fan: a) closed and b) open displaying a painting of a phoenix. Pigments and gold on paper, bamboo. Noh Theatre Research Institute, Hōsei University, Tokyo

fan can substitute for certain handheld properties. Kyōgen actors also carry *shizume ōgi*.

Chūkei (fig. 2.84a–b), seen exclusively in full performances for *shite*, *tsure*, *kokata*, *waki*, and *waki tsure* roles, have fifteen leaves. The ribs holding the leaves are slightly bent so the outer tip of the fan spreads like a partially open fan even when the fan is folded shut. *Chūkei* are beautifully ornamented and are considered of a higher rank (*kurai*) than *shizume ōgi*.

As with costumes and masks, the decoration on a fan indicates the nature of the character carrying it. One way of categorizing them is according to the role type. Different kinds of fans are used for Okina, gods, old men, warriors, adult men, boys, old women, young women, mad women, and demons (table 5.14). This distinction generally follows the categorization of the *gobandate* repertory (see sec. 2.3; ch. 4 *Plays*, 4.2), although certain character types, such as the old man, may appear in different play categories.

The bamboo sticks and guard may be left untreated (*shiro-bone*, or "white sticks") for characters of deities and men alive in the narrative present or may be coated with dark lacquer (*kuro-bone*, or "black sticks") for women, spirits, ghost warriors, or demons. This subdivision follows the principle of *yin* (negative, female, dark, death) versus *yang* (positive, male, bright, life).

Fans can be further subdivided in two large groups: those with colorful illustrations on a gold leaf background and those with black ink drawings on a

TABLE 2.14 Types of fans categorized by character and decorative style

Role type	Background	Frame	Description
Okina	Gold	White	Colorful. Motifs: Mount Hōrai with auspicious animals and plants (cranes, turtles, pines, bamboo).
Deities	Gold	White	Colorful. Motifs: auspicious designs, such as phoenixes and paulownia, peacocks and bamboo, cranes, and turtles.
Old men	White	White	Monochrome ink. Motifs: Chinese deities, immortals, or sages, plants, and birds.
Warriors	Gold	Black	Colorful. Motifs: sun setting in the sea, without or with red *tsuma* (losing warrior), sun rising behind pine branches, with blue *tsuma* (winning warrior).
Old women	Gold	Black	Colorful, without red. Motifs: flowers, plants, birds, and water.
Women	Gold	Black	Colorful, with red. Motifs: flowers, scenes of Chinese court life, and Chinese deities.
Men	Gold or white	White	Two main types: 1) colorful on gold background, with large design. Frequent motifs: waves, birds, fish, plants, and moon; 2) black ink on white background. Frequent motifs: birds, fish, grass, moon.
Mad women	Gold	Black	Colorful, detailed design.
Demons	Gold	Black	Colorful, bold design. Flowers or abstract patterns.
Boys	Gold	Black	Similar to women. Frequent motifs: flowers.

white background. A frequent feature of colorful *chūkei* fans is the inclusion of cloud designs (*unkei*) at the bottom, and colored embellishments (*tsuma*) at the top left and right of the paper. *Tsuma* can be red (*tsuma beni*) for young characters or blue (*tsuma kon*) for older characters, following the "with or without color" (*iro iri/iro nashi*) convention that also applies to costumes.

The illustrations on fans range from detailed, realistic designs, used for refined characters such as deities or women to abstract, bold patterns that appear on fans for demons or men. Some fans may have different designs on the front and back, although they are usually semantically linked. Other fans have the same design on both sides. In the latter, the verso design mirrors the front in a technique known as *uchinuki* such that the fan displays the same left-right design regardless of how it is held.

Two kinds of non-folding fans are used in special cases. The first is the round Chinese-style *tō uchiwa*, which is made with a wooden frame covered with red lacquer and a silk surface decorated with various motifs. This fan is primarily reserved for plays set in China such as *Kantan*, *Kiku jidō*, or *Sanshō*, the special variation being *Tamura*. The second is the *ha uchiwa*, which is made with a lacquered stick into which long falcon feathers (*ha*) are inserted. This type of fan is exclusively the domain for *tengu* characters in plays such as *Kurama Tengu*, *Zegai*, or *Kuruma-zō*.

2.11 Properties
Monica Bethe

The main method of establishing place and evoking scenery in nō is through allusion generated by the words and actions, yet in some plays, stage properties (*tsukurimono*) aid the imagination. Following an aesthetic that also applies to other aspects of performance, nō theatre properties do not aim at a realistic representation of a place or an object. Rather, properties are visual poetry, functioning like figures of speech in which a part of an object is used to refer to the whole. They suggest an object by replicating, for example, its shape but not its size, or by showing only a part of it and letting the viewer imagine the rest.

Nō properties are minimal structures, normally consisting of a simple bamboo frame wrapped with strips of white or colored cloth (*bōji*). They are sometimes encased with fabric, and can sport a symbolic pine, cherry, or willow branch. They include huts, caves, graves, carriages and carts, gates, wells, trees, platforms, boats, and small props, including buckets, musical instruments, and spinning wheels.

Nō properties can be grouped into two types: 1) essential props, that is, architectural structures that are onstage the entire performance, set the scene, and become the focus of activity, and 2) occasional props brought out for use in a single scene where they focus the action. Often smaller, these are taken off the stage after they are no longer needed.[57]

---

57   Yokomichi 1987: 100.

2.11.1   *Essential Props*

The essential nō props are minimal structures employed for multiple purposes. These might be further categorized by form and placement on the stage. Taller structures representing mounds, graves, and huts, particularly when covered with cloth, obscure what is behind them, and therefore are placed upstage, typically in front of the hand drums. Lower frame structures, such as cubes and cones supporting a symbolic object, are often placed downstage. Platforms can be positioned variously and may have added structures on top or decorative elements, such as large flowers, attached to them.

2.11.1.1   Large Props Placed Upstage Set the Scene

More sizable props are placed on the stage before the performance proper begins and removed after the performers leave the stage at the end. They serve as scenery, taking up space and defining its use, and also act as symbolic representations of objects central to the text. A bamboo frame with a square base and vertical poles held in place at the top provides, for example, a skeletal structure for mounds, caves, and huts. Additions and modifications are made to suit the needs of each play. One of the simplest is the prop for *Miwa*, a diagram of which is illustrated in the Konparu-school book, *Ōkura-ryū tsukurimono hiroku* (*Ōkura-School Secret Records on Properties*; fig. 2.85).[58]

When the prop is brought onstage in *Miwa*, it is covered with a cloth. The two cedar branches attached to the front poles identify it as Mount Miwa, known for its cedar trees and its Shintō shrine. In the interlude of the play, a villager notices a garment hanging on the prop. It turns out to belong to the *waki*, the priest Genpin, and to have a poem freshly inscribed on it by the deity of Miwa. Later, the cloth covering the prop is lowered and removed to reveal the Miwa deity in female guise therein. The folded white paper strips, now visible, mark the structure as a sacred spot. During the second act, the narration describes the story of the sun deity Amaterasu Ōmikami shutting herself in the heavenly cave and then being coaxed out of hiding. For this enacted passage, the prop takes on the imagery of the narration and functions as the cave within that tale. The simplicity of the structure makes possible layered imagery and shifting symbolism.

Attaching small identifying embellishments to the basic bamboo frame of a prop changes its character. A roof creates a hut. Gourds and moonflowers

---

58   I have chosen to illustrate this section with historical drawings that serve as references to the building of props because this provides insight into how the props are constructed. It is also noteworthy that the props have essentially not changed since the time of these Edo-period drawings.

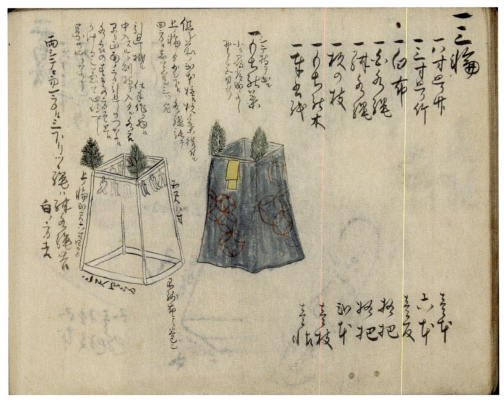

FIGURE 2.85   The shrine prop for *Miwa*, covered and unveiled. *Ōkura-School Secret Records on Properties* (*Ōkura-ryū tsukurimono hiroku*). 1849. Colors and ink on paper. Noh Theatre Research Institute, Hōsei University, Tokyo

(*yūgao*) growing on a lattice that lifts indicate the dilapidated dwelling of Lady Yūgao in the play *Hajitomi* (also read as *Hashitomi*; fig. 2.86 left). Rough branches filling in the walls establish the home of the old woman who turns out to be a monster in *Kurozuka* (Kanze name *Adachigahara*; fig. 2.86 right). Minimal and suggestive, these props complement the text, lending an extra layer of visual reality.

Mound props use the same frame, but have rounded tops. In *Teika*, a vine known as the *teika kazura* grows up the framework and spills over the upper portion. For *Saigyōzakura* (see fig. 2.96), a similarly shaped framework has dangling cherries branches, and the prop for *Yugyō yanagi* has weeping willow branches streaming down its sides. These extra embellishments make the prop symbolic of the play, and reference the action and the text.

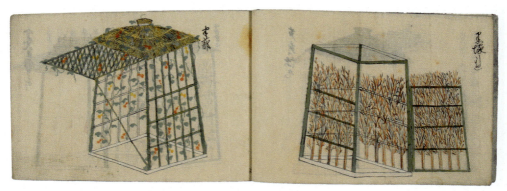

FIGURE 2.86   Props for *Hashitomi* (left) and *Kurozuka* (right). From *Illustrations of Nō Stage Properties* (*Nō tsukurimono zu*). 17th–19th centuries. Colors on paper. Noh Theatre Research Institute, Hōsei University, Tokyo

Often these large props in the upstage area function as alternative settings for *shite* entrances or exits. A character hidden within a curtained structure could start chanting from inside. In this case, the character is heard before being seen. Whether the draped cloth is slowly lowered or swiftly removed evokes the mood as the figure is revealed. Dynamic variations of entrances from inside a stage property include a rock that splits open to disclose a malevolent spirit in *Sesshōseki*, a fallen bell that when lifted releases a snake figure intent on revenge in *Dōjōji*, and a spider web ripped open as an aggressive spider emerges in *Tsuchigumo* (fig. 2.87).

2.11.1.2   Smaller Props Placed Downstage Center

Smaller low props set at center downstage draw the focus of the action to the front. The wooden frame indicating a well in the play *Izutsu* (see Part 4, 5; fig. 2.88) serves as an example. Action and text gradually draw attention to the prop. First a wandering monk (*waki*) takes note of the well as a marker of the place, the temple Ariwaradera, once the home to the great lover Ariwara no Narihira. Then a village woman (*shite*) offers flowers at it. She focuses her attention on the well during the narration of a story, recounting how as children Ki no Aritsune's daughter played with her future husband, Ariwara no Narihira, around the well that stood between their houses. They would peer into its water, side by side, sleeve on sleeve. His marriage proposal is a poem about the well, which becomes a mantra recapitulated in the final scene of the play when the ghost of Ki no Aritsune's daughter, now dressed in her lover's raiments, peers into the well and sees not herself but her lover's reflection. Their

FIGURE 2.87   *Tsuchigumo.* A spider emerges from its web, casting web filaments at its adversary. *Nochi shite*, Yamai Tsunao (Konparu school). March 19, 2016. Yokohama Nohgakudō
PHOTO: TSUJII SEIICHIRŌ

identities fuse into an inseparable single image. In this way, textual and kinetic imagery accumulate around a prop, coming together in a final moment when the *shite* has physical contact with the prop.

2.11.1.3   Platforms for Multiple Purposes

Platforms (*ichijōdai*) create a miniature stage on the main stage.[59] Some twenty centimeters high, the top surface has the dimensions of one tatami mat (approximately 182 × 91 cm), and can be set almost anywhere, either singly or several side by side. Other properties can be added to platforms: some have symbolic tress, like the cherry trees in *Arashiyama* (fig. 2.89) or oversize flowers, such as chrysanthemums in *Kiku jidō* or peonies in *Shakkyō*. Some have tools (hammer and anvil in *Kokaji*) or other significant objects. When the actors mount the platforms, they enter a different space: in *Shakkyō* the

---

59   The name *ichijōdai* translates literally as "one *jō* platform," where a *jō* is a unit corresponding to one tatami mat.

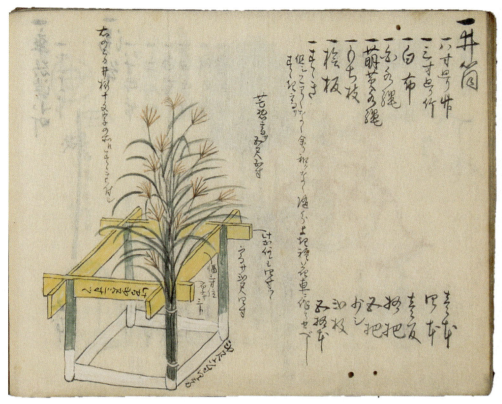

FIGURE 2.88   The well prop for *Izutsu*. From *Ōkura-School Secret Records on Properties* (*Ōkura-ryū tsukurimono hiroku*). 1849. Colors and ink on paper. Noh Theatre Research Institute, Hōsei University, Tokyo

paradise realm of the bodhisattva Monju (Skt. Mañjuśrī) on the other side of the stone bridge where lions dance among peonies and in *Kokaji* the smithery where the fox deity helps forge a sword.

The platform in *Kantan* serves as a bed, throne, and palace (see 2.12). *Kantan* features a young man, Rōsei, in search of enlightenment. When he stops at an inn, he takes a nap in a bed. The prop consists of a platform with canopied bedposts (see fig. 2.98). The pillow he lays his head upon induces a dream where he experiences fifty years of being emperor with all the entertainment that accompanies royalty. During the dream the bed becomes his throne, and all manner of people come to pay him homage. He begins to dance, performing all the movements within the limited space on the platform, now perhaps a palace room. The dream world expands—the dance flows out onto the full stage and down the bridge. Suddenly, the innkeeper comes to wake the man.

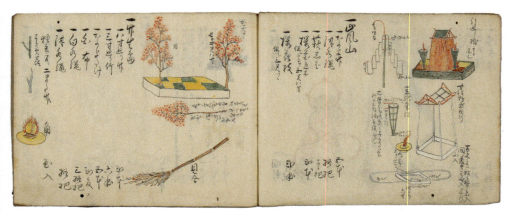

FIGURE 2.89   The platform with cherry trees attached used in *Arashiyama* (left) and the platform with a shrine and dedicatory lanterns used in *Shirahige* (right). From *Ōkura-School Secret Records on Properties* (*Ōkura-ryū tsukurimono hiroku*). 1849. Colors and ink on paper. Noh Theatre Research Institute, Hōsei University, Tokyo

The dream broken, Rōsei speeds from the bridge across the stage and takes a flying leap, landing horizontally "in bed" with his head on the pillow. The palace vanishes, fifty years evaporate, the prop returns to being a bed.

The above examples demonstrate that the very simplicity of the props makes possible multiple uses and fluid references within a play. As has been discussed in the sections on movement, costumes, and other elements of performance, layered imagery, transformation, and seamless shifts in place characterize nō dramaturgy and echo the poetic narrative conventions of the art.

2.11.2   *Props That Add Interest*

Some props bring color and tangibility to a performance, but are less essential in the sense that the *shite* does not interact with the prop. Variant performances (*kogaki*; see sec. 2.12) may add or delete these props. For instance, the prop for *Hagoromo*, like the well in *Izutsu*, is a low bamboo frame (square in some schools, conical in others) supporting a pine tree. At the beginning of the play, the pine prop, laden with the heavenly maiden's feather robe that she removed to go bathing, is brought onstage and placed at downstage center. The audience sees the central imagery before they hear the opening entrance music: questions, curiosity, and anticipation precede the action. As the fishermen (*waki, waki tsure*) enter, the pines along the bridgeway and the pine prop stand between the viewer and action, creating a sense of looking in through the setting of Mio's pine-lined bay.

After his companions have been seated, the fisherman Hakuryō (*waki*) goes up to the pine and discovers the wondrous robe. This passage forms the high point of the *waki* entrance scene. He picks up the robe and retires to his seat.

Although reference to the pines at Mio recurs several times later in the play, in a sense the pine prop has done its duty once the *waki* removes the robe. For this reason, an alternative staging has the robe draped over the railing near the first pine (closest to the stage) and dispenses with the pine prop. Without the prop, more extensive use of stage space is possible when the heavenly maiden dances.

2.11.3   Occasional Props

Some props are only placed onstage for a specific scene and then removed when no longer needed. These can be large vehicles. In *Yuya* or instance, the courtesan Yuya steps into a covered oxcart traveling through the streets of the capital. The elaborate carriage enhances a colorful highlight scene (fig. 2.90).

Smaller props similarly highlight single scenes. Miniature brine carts are used in *Matsukaze*. A thread winder adds realism to a scene in *Adachigahara* (fig. 2.91), and in *Tōru* an old man mimes dipping water with pails he has slung over his shoulders. All these temporary props manipulated by the *shite* enhance the scene and add visual interest.

2.11.4   Costume or Stage Property?

In some plays, the *shite* enters holding a prop that identifies the character's profession or activity: pails to scoop water (*Kamo*, *Matsukaze*), a bundle of plum twigs (*Tadanori*), or a rake (*Takasago*). These objects from nature as well as manmade items, such as tools (fig. 2.92), weapons, or pieces of clothing, do not shift reference, accumulate associations, or change shape. They are often set down and removed after the entrance scene.

Other handheld objects are used throughout the performance and thus might be considered a part of the costume. While most characters carry a fan,

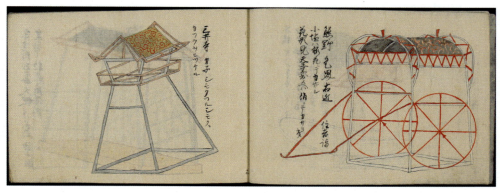

FIGURE 2.90   The bell tower used in *Miidera* (left) and the cart used in *Yuya* (right). From *Illustrations of Nō Stage Properties* (*Nō tsukurimono zu*). 17th–19th centuries. Colors on paper. Noh Theatre Research Institute, Hōsei University, Tokyo

FIGURE 2.91　*Adachigahara* (*Kurozuka*). The old woman winding threads. *Mae shite*, Umano Masaki (Kanze school). Performance September 2, 2014. Yarai Nōgakudō
PHOTO: KOMAI SŌSUKE

FIGURE 2.92　Handheld tools indicating profession or activity. From *Illustrations of Nō Stage Properties* (*Nō tsukurimono zu*). 17th–19th centuries. Colors and ink on paper. Noh Theatre Research Institute, Hōsei University, Tokyo

certain roles require special items. Blind or old characters walk with sticks; male or female demons attack with "T"-shaped wands (*uchizue*); warriors draw their swords or flail halberds; and crazed women carry branches of bamboo grass.

Conversely, garments can serve as props. We saw earlier how the feather robe in *Hagoromo* was found on a tree, retrieved, argued over, returned, and donned to complete the identity of the heavenly maiden, and finally to enhance the dance. In *Matsukaze*, a similar robe is a keepsake from a lover, which the *shite* fondles and then by putting it on effectively becomes one with her lover.[60]

In *Jinen koji*, a child donates a garment to a lay monk so that he will say prayers for her deceased mother. In *Aoi no ue*, a *kosode* robe placed at downstage center represents the ailing Lady Aoi whose presence is felt throughout the performance. The garment becomes the center of focus and a magnet for the action.

While in *Aoi no ue* the robe substitutes for a living person, in *Utō* the ghost of a hunter rips off his sleeve so it can be used as proof of his identity. In addition, his lacquered conical hat (*kasa*) becomes a prop when a traveling monk sets it up as a stupa altar and recites prayers before it. Then, as the hunter's ghost reenacts his lifetime occupation of hunting baby birds, the hat turns into their nest (see sec. 2.4). In the hell scene that follows, sharp blood tears of the parent birds rain down on him, forcing the hunter's ghost to pick up the hat and use

---

60　Possession by the spirit in the robe is the theme of *Futari Shizuka* in which a woman is made to discover and then wear a robe that once belonged to the deceased Shizuka Gozen. Her dance is shadowed by the ghost.

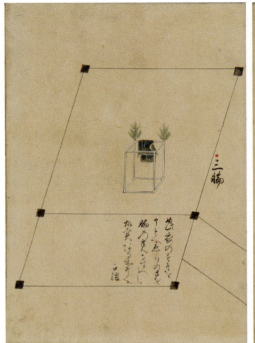 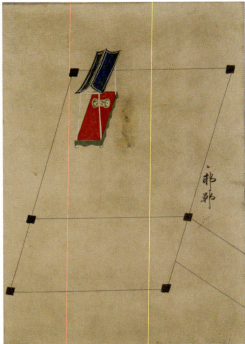

FIGURE 2.93   *Miwa* (left) and *Kantan* (right). From *Stage Illustrations* (*Butai no zu*) by Shimotsuma Shōshin (1551–1616). 1573–1603. Colors and ink on paper. Noh Theatre Research Institute, Hōsei University, Tokyo

it to cover his head. Finding it useless, he discards it, sending the hat whirling across the stage. From stupa, to nest, to ineffective head cover, the hat finally turns into a swirling vortex, a symbol of spinning despair.

2.11.5   *Building the Props and Transmission of the Art*

Traditionally, most prop structures are put together just prior to performance and taken apart after it. Today, the larger frameworks might be only partially dismembered. Assembling the prop for a play is one of the many preparatory jobs done by the *shite* actor. Building the prop often begins with going outdoors to collect the vines, cherry branches, willows, or reeds. When out of season, artificial plants can be substituted. Oversized paper flowers are created for fantasy scenes, like the peonies and chrysanthemums used in *Shakkyō* and *Kiku jidō*, respectively. Young actors learn backstage jobs as well as the duties of the *kōken* in carrying the props onto the stage and removing the enveloping cloths (see ch. 3 *Training*, 3.4).

Each school has its own notebooks on prop construction that detail dimensions and techniques (see ch. 7 *Material Culture*, 7.6). As the images in this chapter testify, a considerable number of prop manuals from the Edo period have survived. They note the size, materials, and methods of making props, along with how to vary them for different plays. Perhaps the oldest extant illustrations of props are in the *Butai no zu* (*Stage Illustrations*; fig. 2.93) by Shimotsuma Shōshin (1551–1616), which pictures the props on schematic drawings of the stage.[61] Interestingly, these sixteenth- or early seventeenth-century props are remarkably similar to those still employed today.[62]

2.11.6 Property Location and the Imagination

The placement of a prop and its manipulation helps designate the stage space. The use of boat props serves as an example of how its placement establishes areas of water in the mind's eye. The simplest boat prop is a square frame with rounded extensions.[63] In *Shunkan*, messengers from the capital bring a boat to the end of the bridge, announcing that two of the three exiles have received a reprieve and can return to the capital. The reprieved men step into the boat and shove off down the bridgeway, leaving their companion, Shunkan, to bemoan his fate deserted on Devil's Island (fig. 2.94a). In *Eguchi*, a riverboat loaded with entertainers is brought to upstage right (placement varies), marking a corner of the stage as water (fig. 2.94b). In *Funa Benkei*, the boatman (an *ai kyōgen*) runs onto the stage carrying the boat with himself inside the central frame and sets it down in front of the chorus (fig. 2.94c). Benkei, retainers, and Yoshitsune step inside the frame to board the boat. As the boatman rows them out to sea, the entire stage swells with the waves whipped up by a sudden storm. Seeking vengeance, the ghost of Taira no Tomomori skirts over the waters, his prancing steps seemingly kicking up the sea froth. If the *shite* wears divided skirts (*hangiri*) decorated with images of large waves, the garment reinforces this watery image.

In *Sakuragawa*, a mother looking for her lost child, Sakurago (Cherry-Blossom Boy), is so crazed that she tries to scoop him up in her net along

---

61 Shimotsuma: 162–256. Figure 2.95 *Miwa* on page 228, *Kantan* on 198.
62 Reference to props by Zeami testifies to their use, although not their forms. In *Zeshi rokujū igo sarugaku dangi* (*Talks on Sarugaku by Zeami after Sixty*; also *Sarugaku dangi*) or instance, he is quoted as saying that for the performance of *Aoi no ue*, Inuō entered in a carriage, even though its appearance is not described. Early attempts at greater realism include the use of real horses at a Tōnomine performance.
63 Other boats build on this structure, adding a pavilion (*Eguchi*), or sails (*Tōsen*), or clappers to frighten off birds (*Torioibune*).

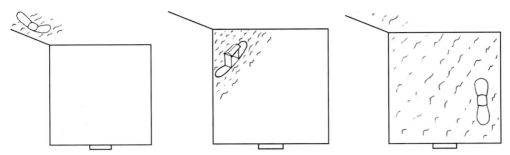

FIGURE 2.94A–C   a) *Shunkan*: the stage is an island, the bridgeway the sea; b) *Eguchi*: riverboat near the shore; and c) *Funa Benkei*: the boat at sea

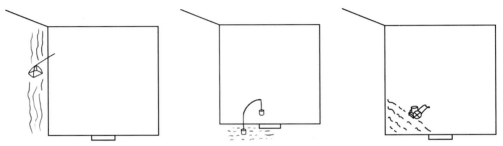

FIGURE 2.95A–C   a) *Sakuragawa*: netting cherry blossoms; b) *Tōru*: dipping buckets to collect water; and c) *Matsukaze*: collecting brine by the seashore

with the cherry petals that float by in a stream that meanders by stage right (fig. 2.95a). In *Tōru*, an old man dips his buckets off the front of the stage as if to haul up water (fig. 2.95b), and in *Matsukaze*, the girls collect brine in buckets placed downstage left—the ocean seems to be splashing over the stage boards (fig. 2.95c).

2.11.7   *Visible and Invisible Presence*

In nō, the lack of painted scenery illustrative of the setting allows for shifting perspectives with multiple realities. While the text evokes the scene, the action, song, and instrumentation realize the words. Word-images couched in sound, movement, and costume flow through the mind, conjuring up chains of connected thought-pictures to create a narrative. In this sense, are props truly necessary? What does their presence or absence contribute? Three plays featuring cherry trees—*Saigyōzakura*, *Sakuragawa*, and *Tadanori*—present three different answers.

For *Saigyōzakura* a large hut structure set up stage center and strewn with blossoming cherry branches establishes the place (fig. 2.96). The *shite* remains

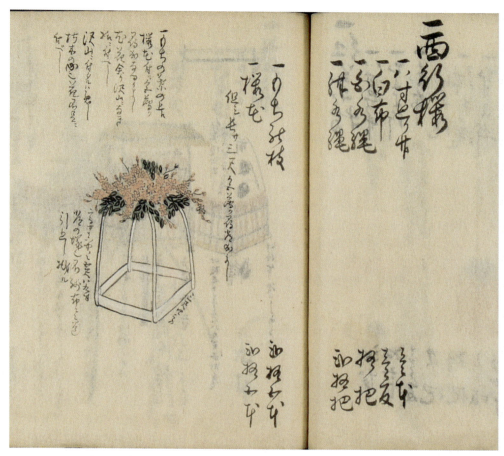

FIGURE 2.96   The unveiled cherry-tree prop in *Saigyōzakura*. From *Ōkura-School Secret Records on Properties* (*Ōkura-ryū tsukurimono hiroku*). 1849. Colors and ink on paper. Noh Theatre Research Institute, Hōsei University, Tokyo

inside the structure for the first half of this one-act play. During the opening scenes Saigyō (*waki*) speaks of the beautiful cherry blossoms, and reluctantly admits visitors to his garden. He then composes a poem accusing the tree of disrupting his solitude. After the crowd has left, the cloth covering the tree prop is removed and an old man—the tree spirit—emerges from within the prop. He admonishes Saigyō and defends the blossoms as innocent. The centrally placed prop presents a constant reminder of the tree's presence and also makes possible an onstage entrance revealing the spirit from within the tree. The characters in *Saigyōzakura* belong to another time-space. The poet Saigyō encountering the spirit of the cherry tree places the experience in a fantasy world, and the prop lends this visionary world a necessary tangible solidity.

In *Sakuragawa* (Cherry-Blossom River), as the mother tries to scoop up cherry petals from Cherry River thinking they might be her son, the mind's eye envisions cherry trees lining the river bank. The petals are floating on the water and whirling in the breeze, a movement caught in the frenzied scooping action of the net. Neither tree nor blossoms are tangibly represented except by the net. Yet, the addition of a realistic net deepens the intimacy and pathos of the mother's predicament.

In *Tadanori*, a monk (*waki*) stops on his pilgrimage to admire a cherry tree (see sec. 2.3) and ends up spending the night under it, thereby enacting the central poem of the play: "Traveling late I lodge beneath this tree. Tonight, the cherry blossoms are my host." During the performance, the tree is remarked on, prayed at, sat under, pointed to, and referenced, situating it just beyond the front of the stage on the audience's side. Although a dominant presence, the tree has no material visual form. With its roots in a narrated storytelling tradition of blind musicians singing episodes from *The Tale of the Heike*, this second category nō play requires no prop.

2.12   Interpreting Conventions for Standard and Variant Performances
Yamanaka Reiko

2.12.1   *Interpreting Standard Performances*

The staging of a nō play is based on conventions inscribed in tradition. Knowledge of performance techniques, such as movement, timing, and the general aesthetic aspects of a piece, is passed down from parent to child, from teacher to disciple within each performance group. Since this knowledge is shared by all performers, the production of a play does not require a director. Perhaps the closest to the role of the director would be the *shite*, the actor performing the lead role and around whom the play is generally centered (see ch. 3 *Training*, 3.4).

Young *shite* actors who are still in training perform according to the instructions they receive, singing and dancing as they are taught, and wearing costumes and masks chosen by their teacher. There is very limited room for individual choice. With age and experience, however, the actor has greater latitude of expression, which allows for interpretation of the various conventional aspects of performance.[64] This signals that the performer has gained the

---

64   The discussion here is in the context of *shite* actors, but the interpretation of a piece involves all the performers working together; *waki*, musicians, and kyōgen players may also instigate interpretive elements.

ability to interpret, yet the range of selection is not boundless: performers cannot act totally at their own discretion. Even high-ranking performers are constantly being observed by those well versed in the conventions and aesthetics of nō and whose judgment will influence their decisions.

The sections on movement (2.4) and music (2.5) explained that the system for writing down choreography and music leaves room for interpretation, as the actor may adjust timing and style to his or her discretion. Actors exploit the indeterminateness of the notations to express their personal understanding of the piece. Moreover, the choice of mask and costume for a performance involves selecting among alternatives that will reflect an actor's image of the piece (see secs. 2.8, 2.9). For some plays, several mask types may be designated, but even when only one type is listed, individual masks within a type have subtle distinguishing features.[65] Moreover, while garment types are set for costumes, in most cases the colors and patterns are left unspecified. The generality of these indications permits a surprisingly wide range of character interpretation even within the same stylistic school (*ryūgi*). Obviously, the choice of mask and costume will also greatly depend on what is available for an actor at any given performance (see ch. 3 *Training*, 3.4).

In addition to the aesthetic choices described above, plays can be modified to adjust to the needs of the event in which they are staged. For example, a play may be performed in an abridged version to shorten the overall time in a performance for school children or for an inexperienced audience. This entails skipping certain segments (*shōdan*) of a play that do not impact the narrative. These deviations from the "standard," follow rules and are built into the flexible, modular system for staging nō plays. They testify to the extent that nō, although a traditional art, is able to adapt to the occasion, changing its form for the benefit of the audience.

The impulse to create performance variants did not begin recently. Zeami, who perfected the foundation of nō that shaped its development into the form that we know today, explained the importance of adapting the performance to the demands of the occasion and adjusting it to the place and to audience tastes. In his 1430 *Zeshi rokujū igo sarugaku dangi* (*Talks on Sarugaku by Zeami after Sixty*; hereafter *Sarugaku dangi*), which collects his comments and critiques on performance, Zeami says: "As for the play *Sumidagawa*, the beginning has not so much color, so the traveler may wear broad pleated trousers. In

---

65 Conventions are constantly being revised. For example, current Kanze-school conventions for the play *Nonomiya* stipulate that the mask of the *shite* can be Waka onna, Fukai, or Ko-omote. In contemporary practice, however, Fukai is no longer used.

the beginning of *Ukai* [the main role] is unmasked and wears a bamboo hat. This is as it is in the countryside. It must depend on the circumstances."⁶⁶

Here Zeami is stressing the point that, because the opening portion of *Sumidagawa* is quite subdued, the character of the traveler might be dressed in *ōkuchi* (see fig. 2.77a–b) that stand out on the stage, rather than in an ordinary *suō* (see fig. 2.80). He also refers to the costuming of the cormorant fisherman in the first half of *Ukai*, mentioning that the choice of costume should depend on whether the performance takes place in a rural or urban setting.

In *Sumidagawa*, a mother in search of her lost son eventually finds his grave, where she chants a *nenbutsu* prayer that awakens the child's spirit. Zeami and his son Motomasa, the author of the play, had different opinions as to whether the ghost of the dead son should actually appear onstage. There is a famous episode in which Motomasa insisted that it is impossible to perform the piece without having the child actor appear, and Zeami replied that "one should try things like that and adopt what is effective. If one does not try, it is difficult to know what is good or bad."⁶⁷ Envisioning variations of the performance of *Sumidagawa* began almost as soon as the idea of staging began to develop and before the choreographies became fixed. In more recent times, both versions of the performance have been staged.⁶⁸

2.12.2   *Prescribed Performance Variants* (kogaki)

During nō's long history, there were individuals, particularly head performers, who were extremely interested in expressing their own interpretation of various plays or in showcasing their own abilities and polished techniques. The variations in performance born of their efforts were not limited to the choice of costume and mask, however, but equally extended to include numerous examples of significant alterations, such as increasing or reducing the number of actors, imposing extensive cuts of the texts, and changing the instrumental dances.

Noteworthy among these innovators, Kanze Motoakira (1722–1774) created close to two hundred variants during his tenure as the Kanze-school *iemoto*. Compared with other *iemoto*, this number was extraordinary, yet his interest in variant performances was not unusual for the period. By the mid-eighteenth century, the *iemoto* of every nō school were securely established in their statuses under the Tokugawa *bakufu*, which oversaw the nō repertory. The writing of new pieces was halted, and performers repeatedly staged the canon of set

---

66   de Poorter (1986) 2002: 117.
67   de Poorter (1986) 2002: 92.
68   Yokomichi et al. 2009: 11–14.

pieces. As a result, audiences saw the same plays time and time again. Under these circumstances, it was inevitable that the extant repertory would undergo refinement. The reason why performers produced so many variants, which were then passed down and continually refined, lay in the desire to find new ways to perform a set repertory. Other factors were the creative ambitions of nō actors and the reception by an expert audience that could fully appreciate and enjoy such experiments. As these new conventions were transmitted in the form of performance variants, they were given names and began to be indicated in play programs with small letters next to the title of the play, the earliest examples appearing already in the late sixteenth-century collection of nō programs, *Nō no tomechō* (*Shimotsuma Shōshin's Record of Nō Programs*; fig. 2.97). This practice gave rise to the term *kogaki* ("small letters") to connote a performance variation.

The *kogaki* in the modern repertory are the result of past innovations that were not discarded as one-time individual interpretive efforts, but rather became part of the conventions of a school. Today, most plays have a "standard" way of being performed and one or more *kogaki*.[69] *Kogaki* increase the range of variations the audience can enjoy, even within a relatively restricted repertory. As a result, performers must learn multiple ways of performing the same play. Generally, performers are allowed to stage a *kogaki* only after they have done the standard version of a play at least once. *Kogaki* are seen to be of a higher rank (*kurai*) than the standard versions of a play. Permission to perform a *kogaki* is granted by the head of the school or, in some cases, by the leader of an important subgroup of performers.

A considerable number of *kogaki* incorporate special passages that require extra study, and for the performers these are classed as *narai* (mastery pieces). *Kiyotsune*, for instance, has a *kogaki* called *Koi no netori* (*Tune of Love*), in which the flute plays a long solo piece introducing the entrance of Kiyotsune's ghost, who appears in his wife's dream. This is understood as *narai* for both the flute player and the *shite* actor, but not for the other musicians. Similarly, a variant set in the *banshiki* musical mode, which only affects the instrumental dance, would be viewed as *narai* for the musicians and dancer, and does not apply to the *waki*. The level, or difficulty, of the *narai* may also differ from role to role.

Generally, *kogaki* variants are performed less frequently than the standard version of a play. Reasons for this include their being of a higher *kurai*, their necessitating additional study, and that the supporting performers might

---

69 Although the most evident types of performance variant are identified as *kogaki*, there are some performance variants that certain *ryūgi* do not consider *kogaki*. The number of *kogaki* for each play reflects the popularity of a play; rarely performed plays may not have any *kogaki*.

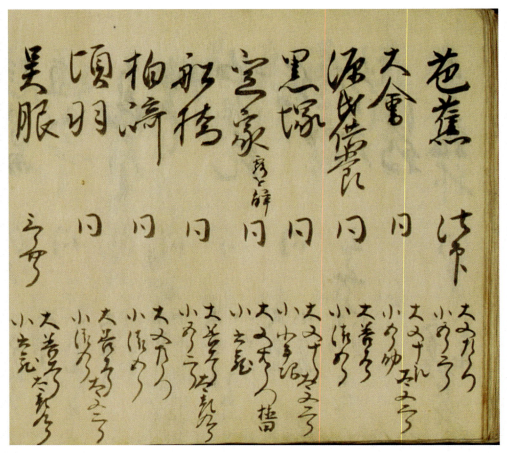

FIGURE 2.97　A nō performance program from 1602, with the variant performance of *Teika* in small letters under the title (fifth from the right). From a *Shimotsuma Shōshin's Record of Nō Programs* (*Nō no tomechō*). Between 1588 and 1612. Ink on paper. Noh Theatre Research Institute, Hōsei University, Tokyo

command higher performance fees, thereby raising production costs. Since *kogaki* are more demanding or more spectacular, they draw interest for their distinct characteristics. Their rarity value makes them appropriate for special performance events.

Not all *kogaki* were created several hundred years ago. Numerous *kogaki* were composed at the beginning of the Meiji period when nō was experiencing hard times. Also, *kogaki* from the late Edo period were enriched with new or additional devices and performed frequently to increasingly wider audiences. For example, the early Meiji head of the Kongō school, Kongō Tadaichi (1815–1884), is celebrated for having invented the stage devise of the "spider web" (*kumo no ito*) in which rolls of thin white paper are hidden in the actors' sleeves. The *shite* in *Tsuchigumo* hurls this at his adversary and snarls him in a web of fine filaments (see fig. 2.87). This began as a performance variant in the Kongō school, yet it was so successful that other schools soon adopted it, creating a new standard for the performance of the play. In addition, during the early Meiji period, Umewaka Minoru I (1828–1909), who performed frequently in Tokyo, experimented with diverse techniques staging numerous *kogaki* performances in order to further enhance the enjoyment of the audiences of that time.

After World War II, the famous actor Kanze Hisao (1925–1978) devoted time to researching how nō might be performed "as theatre." He discovered early *kogaki* and reconsidered the performance of nō in innovative ways. Scholars, as well as performers, held study groups that resulted in the reenactments of old performance conventions, in the composition of new nō, and in collaboration with other theatre arts. The endeavors of Umewaka Minoru IV to pursue the further possibilities of nō performance are also noteworthy.

2.12.3   Types of kogaki

The current repertory has around 750 *kogaki*, which range from radical alterations, such as altering the gender of the *shite* role or eliminating an entire section of text, to modifying the visual impression by changing the mask, costume, or prop, revising the choreography, or altering the audial effect by adjusting the instrumental music. Some involve only minor modifications, including relocating an area on the stage where action takes place.[70]

2.12.3.1   Variations in Text: Cutting, Adding and Shifting

The text of a play may be cut, added, or changed, and this frequently involves an entire large section rather than a single line or two. This might be done in an effort to shorten the performance time when it is necessary to adapt a play to the general length of time or the overall balance of an event. Mostly, however, it occurs in order to achieve a desired performance effect.

Certain scenes or elements may be deleted so as to focus on a specific theme within a play. For example, in *Uneme*, the main character is the ghost of a lady-in-waiting who served the emperor in ancient times. The play treats two themes: the faith in the Kasuga deity, who bestows blessings and brings peace to the country, and the story of the lady-in-waiting, who upon losing the emperor's love drowns herself. In order to concentrate on the plight of the

---

70   This count includes both *kogaki* that occur in all five schools, such as Senbō in *Tomonaga*, and those that go by the same name in several nō plays, such as *Kutsurogi*.

drowned woman, the *Minaho no den* variant deletes the scenes in which the first theme is treated. This involves extensive cuts: in the first half, the *shite* entrance scene is cut and in the second half, the sections (*kuri-sashi-kuse*) recounting the origin story of the Kasuga Taisha are eliminated. Other textual cuts might be made to place greater weight on dance or music.

The deletion of lines or scenes does not undermine the understanding of the story, however. Rather, extraneous descriptions, poetic divergences, or secondary themes tend to be cut. Variations emphasizing the visuals of a play are often greeted with enthusiasm by the general public. Although there are only a few such examples, sometimes the text has been amended to accommodate the demands of a person in power. For instance, when *Utō* was performed in front of a hunt-loving feudal lord, the words for the scene in which a hunter falls into hell and is chased by birds and wild beasts, were moderated.[71]

2.12.3.2   Variations in Dances to Instrumental Music without Accompanying Text

Besides altering the text, variants may amend the instrumental dance, which is considered to be one of the highlights of a play. On the one hand, such sections may be lengthened, shortened, or modified to increase their interest, or to balance other parts of the play. On the other, the type of instrumental dance might be changed entirely. A long instrumental dance (*mai*), for instance, might replace a short action piece (*hataraki*). Examples include the *Omoide no mai* (*Recollection Dance*) variant of *Kashiwazaki*, the *Hōraku no mai* (*Sacred Offering Dance*) variant of *Hyakuman*, or the *Setsugekka no mai* (*Snow-Moon-Flower Dance*) variant of *Yamanba*.

In plays that normally contain a *mai*, the number of sections that compose the instrumental dances can be augmented to prolong the dance. In the Kongō school, *Jūnidan no gaku* (*Twelve-Section Gaku*) variant of *Kantan*, for example, the standard five sections of the *gaku* dance are supplemented to accommodate eight sections, which are further subdivided to make the count twelve. One interpretation suggests that this represents the twelve months of the year. More simply put, the variant answers a desire to extend the *gaku* into a longer dance. Likewise, the Kanze-school variant of *Tōru*, *Mai kaeshi* (*Dance Repeat*), has ten sections and changes the flute mode. The variant *Jūsandan no mai* (*Thirteen-Section Dance*) of *Tōru* has thirteen sections and markedly increases the tempo. Both the *Tōru* variants introduce musical devices to keep up the interest of otherwise repetitive dances.

---

71   Itō 1982: 409.

The choreography of instrumental dances, which are unaccompanied by text, is abstract. Its movements do not imitate real-life actions or objects, and generally the same choreography can be used in multiple plays. Some performance variants, however, insert realistic or symbolic acting related to the narrative of the play. This often incorporates action on the *hashigakari* bridgeway, an area that is normally not used for *mai*. For instance, in the middle of the instrumental dance, the *shite* might go down the bridgeway and gaze out into the distance as if listening to the thundering waterfall (*Ataka*), or look down and view the area below, entranced by the wild array of blooming iris at the edge of a pond (*Kakitsubata*). Or, the *shite* might regard a loved one seated on the stage proper and perform a weeping pattern, indicating that while the dance is in celebration of the lover's release, the *shite* is in fact lamenting their separation (*Funa Benkei*).

A similar device is seen when a simple action piece substitutes for *mai*. Inserting a *hataraki*, such as the *Iroe no den* (Color Dance Piece), when originally there was none, was popular during the late Muromachi period, and some of these have remained in the repertory to the present day. Most entail circling the stage once, but at times a concrete action related to the theme of the play is set in the middle of the circling. For example, in the *Ukai* variant *Shinnyo no tsuki* (*Moon of the Ultimate Truth*), the *shite* goes to the bridge in the middle of the *hataraki* and performs looking up at the moon, a symbol of Buddhist enlightenment.

For plays that normally include an action piece, the *hataraki* might be lengthened and imbued with more realistic patterns. This is seen in the *Amayo no hataraki* (*Rainy Night Hataraki*) variant of *Kayoi Komachi* in which the action piece is extended by adding mimetic gestures, such as holding a rain hat in both hands, then lifting it for protection against rain before dropping it, to symbolize the character roaming about in the dark night. The device of going down the bridgeway during a variant performance is frequently employed in action pieces. Since *hataraki* have a simpler structure than *mai*, the focus for variant performances is on highlighting walking to or along the bridgeway. For this, the instrumental accompaniment often includes marked shifts in tempo.

The above examples represent performance variants in which dances are deliberately expanded. The opposite holds for variants where the *mai* or *hataraki* is altered by reducing the number of its sections or eliminating the dance altogether. As noted above, *Tōru* has variants that extend the dance through the addition of sections. There are, however, other variants eliminating the *mai* and replacing it with a simple *iroe* or *tachimawari* stage circling. These are referred to as *Mai-bataraki no den* (*Action Piece Variant*) in the Kanze school and *Yūkyoku* (*Pleasure Piece*) in the Konparu, Kongō, and Kita schools.

There are a number of reasons why a dance is shortened in a performance variant. In the *Murasame-dome* (*Light Shower Ending*) variant of *Yuya*, the dance stops mid-way to represent that, within the play's narrative, it has started to rain. In the *Muchū suibu* (*Dream Dance*) of *Kantan*, the dance is abbreviated to indicate it happens within a dream. In the *Aoyagi no mai* (*Green Willow Dance*) variant of *Yugyō yanagi*, each of the sections of the *mai* is likened to one of the four seasons but is interrupted at the time of young willows. In the *Wagō no mai* (*Joined Dance*) of *Hagoromo*, several dances are executed in sequence. Some pieces normally featuring the slow *jo no mai* totally dispense with the dance, as in the *Hayahiraki no den* (*Early Ending*) variant of *Tokusa* (*Scouring Rushes*) and the *Tamasudare* (*Jewel Curtain*) variant of *Yōkihi*. The main reason behind these abbreviated variant performances is to reduce the performance time. During the Edo period, a nō event was required to finish before sunset, and therefore nō performed in the latter part of the day, in particular, have numerous variants for the purpose of shortening their performance time.

The producers of events today choose which variant to perform in advance, but in the past, when performers competed with each other for artistry, the variants may have been used as a way to outshine a rival. With a quick onstage cue, performers could signal a change in the performance. There were also times when things had to be decided suddenly, such as the timing when sunset approached. One such cue was to open or close the fan. For the short congratulatory play (*shūgen nō*) taking place at the end of the day, the entrance of *shite* from behind the curtain with his fan already open meant that the instrumental dance would be cut. Conversely, if there was extra time, the shite could close the open fan at the end of a *mai* to signal that the dance would continue (*maikaeshi*).

The musical scale of the flute playing an instrumental dance piece changes in some variants. Frequently, the base pitch of the standard scale, known as *ōshiki chō*, is raised slightly to *banshiki chō*. *Jo no mai* and *gaku* have variations known as *banshiki jo no mai* and *banshiki gaku* respectively. In exceptional cases, the standard *ōshiki chō* scale is lowered to *sōjō chō*.[72]

Old transmission documents identify the correlation between the musical scales and the five agents theory (*in'yō gogyō*), a five-fold conceptual view of cosmic correspondences between the basic natural elements (fire, water,

---

72 The *chō* (modes or scales) in nō are derived from *gagaku*, which names the scales by their final pitch: *Ōshiki chō* on what corresponds approximately to A in the Western tonal system, *banshiki chō* with a base note of B, *sōjō chō* on G, and *hyōjō chō* on E. In nō pitch is relative rather than set.

wood, metal, earth) and the seasons, directions, colors, and so forth.[73] In this scheme, *banshiki chō* is the scale of water and night, *sōjō chō* of spring, and *hyōjō chō* of autumn. *Banshiki chō*, in particular, is frequently coupled with water themes. In the *Takinagashi* (*Cascade*) variant of *Ataka* and the *Suiha no den* (*Waves*) variant for *Yōrō*, the *otoko mai* and *kami mai*, respectively, shift the mode of later sections of the dance to *banshiki chō*. Similarly, for the *Amayo no Hataraki* variant, the *hataraki* is changed to *banshiki chō* due to the link with both rain and night.[74]

2.12.3.3   Variations in Masks, Costumes, and Wigs

Some variations involve changing the mask, costume, or wig of the *shite*. A special mask may be adopted instead of a more frequently used one. In the *Shiro-gashira* (White Shaggy Wig, also read *Hakutō*) *kogaki* of the play *Kokaji*, the *nochi shite*, in addition to wearing a white wig rather than red one, uses the large, gold-painted Ōtobide mask in lieu of the standard, reddish Kotobide mask. The costume is also all-white with gold designs instead of the standard colorful one. Normally, supernatural beings such as demons or *tengu* have shaggy red wigs, but alternatively a black or white shaggy wig can be selected, thereby signifying an alteration in the way the character is portrayed. A white wig might represent power and wisdom. Conversely, a black wig, also used to depict human characters, might imbue the character with a more human dimension. Essentially, the color white expresses a higher *kurai* of a character. The different color wig indicates the extra-ordinariness of the variant and usually comprises other changes. The tempo of the entrance music and the chant switches, parts of the text might be abridged, and adjustments might be made to the *hataraki*.

2.12.3.4   Entrance and Exit Scenes

Enhancing the entrance of the *shite* is one method of creating variation. This might involve a costume shift, or a change in the entrance music. In addition, rather than the *shite* entering through the curtain as usual, the character can appear from inside the prop, or the curtain might be raised only halfway to provide a preview of a part of the costumed character and then lowered before being fully raised for the real entrance.

Special entrances feature alterations in the music to reflect the mood of the variant. A character known for his love of flutes might enter as if he were

---

73   The five agent correspondences are mentioned, for instance, in the 1537 *Fue no ki* (*Flute Record*) and 1548 *Sōtekishō* (*Flute Pieces*). See Yamanaka 1985: 31–44.

74   Yamanaka 2001: 87–88.

playing the flute, or listening to the sound of a flute (*Kiyotsune*). A living spirit might be drawn to the stage by the sound of the catalpa bow twanged by a shaman (*Aoi no ue*). A young warrior's ghost might appear drawn by the sound of the drums in a Buddhist service (*Tomonaga*). These variants are often secret transmissions for the instrumentalists.

Other forms of variation are applied to the ending of a piece. The chorus might stop singing before the *utai* text is finished (*Kataku-dome, Kasumi-dome*), creating an unexpected ending that leaves the interpretation up to the audience or a lingering sense. Then, for *kogaki* with particularly heavy *kurai*, the instruments might play on even after the chanting has stopped. Unlike the lingering effect left from an abrupt ending, the extended music evokes a sense that the performance is not yet over. Alternatively, the *shite* might exit through the curtain while the chorus is still chanting and the *waki* watching the vanishing figure (*waki-dome*).

The above demonstrates that *kogaki* concern a range of aspects of the performance. These changes, however, cannot be applied arbitrarily. A person of authority would initially have made the change, which was then accepted by others, and ultimately recorded as a convention of that particular school. The majority of the variants involve the performance of the *shite*, but some relate to the *waki* or kyōgen, while others to the music played by the instrumentalists. It is also important that all the performers know how to adjust their parts, even when the alterations center on performance other than their own.

2.12.4 *Analysis of Performance Variants*

Like other forms of theatre, the impact of a performance depends on how the story and its characters are interpreted. Should one use a mask with a gentle appearance or one with a sharp expression? How to decide the colors of the costumes? Such details make a difference, and with *kogaki* the general impression of the performance changes radically. This is evident in the *kogaki* for the plays *Kantan* (secs. 2.4, 2.8, 2.11), *Hagoromo* (secs. 2.3–2.5, 2.7–2.10), and those invented by Kanze Motoakira for the play *Uneme*, as discussed below.

2.12.4.1   Kantan

Kantan is set in ancient China. Its main protagonist is a man in search of enlightenment who sleeps on a special pillow and dreams of becoming the emperor. In his dream, fifty years have passed since his enthronement, and special celebrations are being held at court. The standard production of the play presents, through nō conventions, the magnificence of his (dream) life at court, as described in the text. This is depicted onstage in such a manner as to be easily understood and carry visual appeal. The prop representing the imperial palace is placed on a one-mat platform covered with a gorgeous

FIGURE 2.98   *Kantan*. The roofed bed placed on a platform that transforms into a palace; Rosei holds up the *Kantan* pillow. *Shite*, Kano Ryōichi (Kita school). Performance June 26, 2021. Kita Nōgakudō, Tokyo
PHOTO: ISHIDA YUTAKA

brocade (fig. 2.98). A child actor in the role of palace page and ministers enter the stage to the stately *shin no raijo* music, usually performed to accompany the entrance of high-ranking characters, such as emperors. The *shite* performs a full five-section *gaku* dance. This begins on the palace platform, but in the middle of the dance he steps down from the platform onto the stage proper.[75]

Among the *kogaki* for *Kantan*, the *Waraya* (*Thatched Roof*) variant highlights the insubstantial essence of the magnificence described in words: court life is but a dream and the palace is nothing more than a country inn. In this variant, the one-mat platform is not covered in brocade, and the prop on it does not represent a palace (*miya*)—instead, it is a thatched-roof structure (fig. 2.99). The dancing page and ministers do not enter to *shin no raijo*; they appear inconspicuously while the chorus sings. The *gaku* is shortened and, together with the dance sung immediately thereafter, is performed entirely on the platform. Rather than seek visual interest, the performance underscores the inner mind of the protagonist, emphasizing the ephemerality of the world

---

75   Both the *shin no raijo* entrance and the *gaku* are the same as performed by Emperor Gensō in *Tsurukame*, also set in China.

FIGURE 2.99 *Kantan, Waraya* variant with thatched roof. From the series *One Hundred Nō Dramas* (*Nōgaku hyakuban*). By Tsukioka Kōgyo (1869–1927). 1922. Printed colors on paper. University of Pittsburgh

around him through the contrasting images: the lavish dance at court mentioned in the text and the protagonist dancing in a small, shabby hut. In recent times, however, new versions of this *kogaki* have been staged that have aimed at increasing the visual interest by having the *shite* step out of the thatch-roof prop in the middle of the *gaku* and enter his dream world as in a standard performance.

2.12.4.2 Hagoromo

In *Hagoromo*, the main character is a maiden who needs to retrieve her feather robe in order to be able to return to her heavenly home. This kind of character can be portrayed variously. Should the focus be on her divinity, therefore presenting her as an august celestial being from a realm far beyond that of human beings? Or should she be depicted as an innocent young maiden? These choices can be expressed through the selection of mask and costume. The celestial maiden donning the Zō onna mask (see fig. 2.42) imparts a more forceful expression than the sweeter impression exuded by the Ko-omote mask (see fig. 2.43). Furthermore, the choice of the emblem on top of the crown—crescent moon, phoenix, white lotus flower, or pink peony—greatly influences the maiden's countenance (fig. 2.100).

Hagoromo variants place emphasis on different themes in the text, which describes the beauty of the scenery of the pine groves at Mio Bay and states that the heavenly maiden's dance is the origin of the *suruga mai* performed at the imperial palace (Suruga, present-day central Shizuoka Prefecture). The standard performance conveys the pastoral scene of a celestial maiden whose descent to earth has lent the landscape a paradisiac beauty.

Alternate performance styles, however, appeal directly to the senses by deleting a large portion of the explanatory text in order to depict a sublime and inaccessible heavenly maiden. In this case, the *jo no mai* dance can be performed in *banshiki chō*, which being pitched higher enhances the sense of the music emanating from high above.

2.12.4.3 Uneme

An example of a variant by Motoakira is the *Minaho no den* variant of *Uneme*, in which substantial cuts were made to focus on the lamenting woman who had drowned herself. Though it displays Motoakira's genius in choreography and dramaturgical presentation, none of the techniques were necessarily new to nō: Motoakira adroitly arranged extant performance practice.

In the *Minaho no den* (Minaho Transmission) variant of the scene in which the drowned spirit of *Uneme* appears in the pond, the *shite* enters bent over

FIGURE 2.100 *Hagoromo*. Zō onna mask and white lotus crown. *Shite* (heavenly maiden), Kongō Tatsunori (Kongō school). Performance September 8, 2017. Fushimi Inari Shrine
PHOTO: FABIO MASSIMO FIORAVANTI

and shrouded with a *noshime* (a kind of plain-colored kimono) draped over the head. The actor stops on the bridge and bends down. This type of *shite* entrance is used for roles of jealous women wearing a Hannya mask, ghosts of men who have descended into hell, or invisible demons who suddenly appear. Motoakira applied this technique to the entrance of a beautiful woman, creating the impression that she had floated up from the depth of the waters. Again, the *shite* does not perform any of the standard stamps during the *jo no mai*, but instead bends down. At the break between sections of the dance, the *shite* momentarily sits. None of the standard sleeve manipulations are employed. She does not stamp because she is on water; she does not flip her sleeves because they are drenched. These rather realistic devices may be subtle, but they are dramatically evocative. The movements of the *shite* bending and leaning forward or opening the fan to point slowly to the right and left, are envisioned as if seen nebulously through water. This type of experimentation continues to the present day. Later additions of the *Minaho no den* include a version where the music of the *jo no mai* scale is changed to *banshiki chō* so as to evoke the water setting. In another version, the main character goes down the bridge in the middle of the dance to gaze upon the pond where she drowned. These have become standard elements in the modern versions of this variant.

2.12.4.4   *Kogaki* Today

Today the impetus to forge new variants derives not only from a wish to find innovative ways to please the audience but also from historical research and a subsequent interest in reviving extinct versions. For instance, in the *Sarugaku dangi* Zeami describes a performance of *Aoi no Ue* in which the actor Inuō (Buddhist name Dōa) entered in a broken-down carriage accompanied by a *tsure*. Reenvisioning that performance has led to a new variant. Similarly, an old version of *Yoroboshi* with different characters from the modern play has been newly staged based on the text written in Zeami's hand.

Due to the prevalence of *kogaki* for the majority of popularly performed plays, actors today have a wide choice of performance styles. Some of the *kogaki*, like the *Wagō no mai* (Kanze) and *Banshiki* (Kongō) variants of *Hagoromo* are actually performed more frequently than the standard version and may in the future cease to be considered *kogaki*. Indeed, just what is considered standard and what is seen as a *kogaki* depends in part on decisions made by each stylistic school. For example, during a highlight scene in *Ataka*, the *shite*, Benkei, "reads" an appeal for donations from a blank scroll, in a long recitation called "Kanjinchō." Originally, this recitation was done in unison with other characters, but today all the schools have Benkei recite it alone. Interestingly, though, only the Kanze school still indicates this solo recitation format as the *kogaki*, *Kanjinchō*, and as a result all Kanze-school performances of *Ataka* have *Kanjinchō* written in small letters next to the title.

In this way, *kogaki* have changed over time and within stylistic schools. What once were innovations have become standard. Despite being based on time-tested traditions and a closely calibrated system, nō performance is continually being reassessed and revised. Actors today adjust and adapt their performances, and this creative process will continue as an ever-evolving response to the times.

2.13 Underlying Principles of Nō Dramaturgy
Monica Bethe

The description of the various elements of nō performance—the stage and its use, movement, music, props, masks, costumes, fan, and variations—has highlighted underlying themes that inform all levels of this traditional theatre form. The following section offers a review of such elements.

2.13.1 *Modular Units and Systems*

Modular units work as building blocks that are assembled based on prescribed rules, yet nothing is fixed, and any detail can be adjusted. The smallest blocks are *kata* (patterns). In dance these are combinations of gestures and foot movements, in music combinations of drum strokes and calls or short melodies, in masks the profile measurements and outlines of the sculptural shape, and in garments the repeat pattern units.

These blocks are simple and recurrent. As each repetition is in a new context—following a different sequence, being performed at a different tempo or with a different nuance, or a visual pattern being rendered with the colors combined differently—the patterns appear novel rather than monotonous. Gestures take on new meanings in the context of the words, and music gains impact by accentuating text. The same music and choreography performed slowly and gently or executed with sharp clarity produces dances so divergent that the uninitiated would not recognize their commonality. Masks come alive with movement and are reinterpreted by costume and wig. Out of a simple, restricted vocabulary emerges an expression with infinite variety.

The modular units are assembled according to a system. The basic model moves from simple to complex, from single voice to multiple voices, from slower to faster, adding visual, audial, and textual imagery to engender a cumulative multivalence experience. Still, this progression is not linear, but rather a series of waves of circular units. Moreover, the basic model is only a model. It is continually reworked through abbreviation, expansion, elimination, enhancement, simplification, and other alteration. Each school has its own conventions, further enriching the variety.

The modular system applies to all levels of performance, from the rendering of a single line and the construction of a *shōdan* section to the composition of a play. Altering the established form within the conventions of the modular system lays the groundwork for the composition of new nō and forms the basis for envisaging variant performances (*kogaki*).

2.13.2 *Practice the Form, Perform the Moment*

The implications of the modular system for learning and in performance are manifold. The building-block structure facilitates learning: mastery of one piece lays the foundation for learning others. It also streamlines memorization and aids retention, such that many professionals are able to perform some hundred pieces on demand. Instrumentalists can conceptualize a piece in terms of the number of repetitions of ground patterns and the placement of cadence or other distinctive patterns. Dancers mentally mark the extras that embellish a preset sequence of movements; costumes and props use identifying details to distinguish similar outfits and structures. When the vocabulary is given, the details stand out. Exceptions define uniqueness.

On one level, in performance, the modular system eliminates the need for a director and numerous rehearsals. In general, a single dress rehearsal, not necessarily of the whole piece, suffices. On another level, the modular system encompasses interaction between performers. Sections in free rhythm are based on the musicians and actors adjusting to each other (*mihakarai*, "watchful pacing"). Sections with a defined rhythm incorporate cues for rhythmic shifts. The parts are independent yet linked. The intensity felt in performance is created in some measure by the alert focus required of everyone onstage to respond to each other. Timing is integral to expression. Rather than keeping a steady beat, moments are matched within a flexible parameter. Just how a syllable of text, a drum stroke, or a gesture fills the space shapes the articulation. Subtle differences, nuances of voicing, and shadows shifting the mask's features have a strong impact.

2.13.3 *Minimalism, Multiplicity, and Fluidity*

The simpler the form, the greater its potential range of meaning. Gestures are basic, props are minimalistic, drum strokes are limited in kind, sparse in execution. Set in the fabric of the performance, however, against the imagery and words of the text, these simple forms take on complex and mutable implications. One pattern, section, or action moves seamlessly to the next in a flowing progression of *shōdan*. Similarly, the bare stage enables fluidity of space definition, with the same spot being first outside, then inside, first a beach and then a mountain. Shifts in scenery arise from the words and may be indicated by minimal gesture or movement. The props often aggregate imagery. Characters share lines, completing each other's sentences and merging in the voice of the chorus.

The blurring of roles in nō works toward a unity of expression. Each of the performers has an image of the piece based on training, understanding of the text, experience, and tradition. Although the images carried by each individual may be different, in a successful performance they merge to form a total vision that is completed in the audience's mind.

At the same time, the merging of characters is also seen in the use of double identities conveyed in costume, text, and musical nuances: the god of Miwa (male), for instance, appears in *Miwa* in female guise but "dressed as a man." In *Matsukaze* and *Izutsu*, by contrast, a woman puts on her lover's robe and takes on his presence, while in *Futari Shizuka* this doubling is played out as spirit possession. In *Yamanba* the *shite*, at once an old woman, a demon, and an enlightened being, encounters her impersonator. In the second act, they are said to perform for each other, one striking the drum for the other to dance. It is the drummers at the rear and the chorus at the side, however, who carry the narrative and bring the stage action into a unity that overrides the ambiguities of subjective, objective, first and third person. Ambiguity here needs no resolution, as the simple nō patterns allow for multiple images to coexist and build a unified impact.

2.13.4 *Transformation and Revelation*

Certain nō, in particular those classified as "dream" or "phantom" nō (*mugen nō*), present the illusion of normalcy (the *shite* is a woodcutter or village woman) in the first act and a revelation of the true form (a deity, demon, or ghost) in the second act. Between the two acts, the transformation from illusionary form to real form is effected in a change of costume, and often also of mask. This outward expression is mirrored in alterations of music and style of movement. Yet, the basic patterns remain a constant in tying these disparate visions together as two aspects of a single nō world.

In a one-act nō such as *Hagoromo*, the transformation, symbolized by an onstage donning of the heavenly maiden's feather robe, is a completion or restoration. In the eyes of a doubting Hakuryō fisherman, however, it is a confirmation that the woman confronted was not an ordinary villager, but rather a celestial being. He, and the audience, experience the fusion of this world, our world, and the world beyond. It lingers in his gaze at her vanishing figure and in the trailing notes of the musicians.

2.13.5 *Centrality of Text*

While the modules provide tools for composition and performance, it is the particulars that give each play its unique expression. The choice of words, the turns of phrase, the development of scenes, and the interaction of characters on the one hand and the matching of melody, rhythm, mask, costume, and properties to that text on the other make each performance a "once only" event. Although the words are composed with a poetic rhythm in mind, the chant cannot exist without the text. Likewise, movement and dance take on meaning in response to the text. In this sense, the words are the foundation upon which the performance is built, and these words, phrases, sentence structures reflect the Japanese language and its poetic traditions.

References

Amano Fumio 天野文雄. 1995. *Okina sarugaku kenkyū* 翁猿楽研究. Osaka: Izumi Shoin.

Anno, Mariko. 2020. *Piercing the Structure of Tradition: Flute Performance, Continuity, and Freedom in the Music of Noh Drama*. Cornell East Asia Series. Ithaca: Cornell University East Asia Program.

Bethe, Monica, and Karen Brazell. 1978. *Nō as Performance: An Analysis of the Kuse Scene of Yamamba*. East Asia Papers Number 16. Ithaca: Cornell University China-Japan Program.

Bethe, Monica, and Karen Brazell. 1982, 1983. *Dance in the Nō Theater*. Vol. 1 (1982): *Dance Analysis*; vol. 2 (1983): *Plays and Scores*; vol. 3 (1983): *Dance Patterns*. East Asia Papers Number 29. Ithaca: Cornell University China-Japan Program.

* Bethe, Monica, and Karen Brazell. 1989, 1990. "The Practice of Noh Theatre." In *By Means of Performance: Intercultural Studies of Theatre and Ritual*, edited by Richard Schechner and Willa Appel, 167–93. Cambridge: Cambridge University Press.

* Bethe, Monica, and Richard Emmert, trans./eds. 1992–1997. *Noh Performance Guides*. *Matsukaze* (1992); *Fujito* (1992); *Miidera* (1993); *Tenko* (1994); *Atsumori* (1995); *Ema* (1996); *Aoi no ue* (1997). Tokyo: National Noh Theatre.

Bethe, Monica, and Richard Emmert, with Gus Heldt. 1993. *Guide to Noh: Miidera*. Tokyo: National Noh Theatre.

* Bethe, Monica, Nagasaki Iwao, Susan Anderson Hay. 1992. *Patterns and Poetry: Nō Robes from the Lucy Truman Aldrich Collection at the Museum of Art, Rhode Island School of Design*. Providence: Rhode Island School of Design.

* Bohner, Hermann. 1959. *Nō: Einführung*. Tokyo: Deutsche Gesellschaft für Natur- und Völkerkunde Ostasiens.

Brazell, Karen, ed. 1998. *Traditional Japanese Theater: An Anthology of Plays*. New York: Columbia University Press.

de Poorter, Erika. (1986) 2002. *Zeami's Talks on Sarugaku. An Annotated Translation of the Sarugaku Dangi with an Introduction on Zeami Motokiyo*. Amsterdam: J. C. Gieben. Reprinted in the series Japonica Neerlandica 2. Leiden: Hotei Publishing, 2002.

Fujita Takanori 藤田隆則. 2000. *Nō no taninzū gasshō (korosu)* 能の多人数合唱(コロス). Tokyo: Hitsuji Shobō.

Fujita Takanori 藤田隆則. 2010. *Nō no nori to jibyōshi: rizumu no minzoku ongaku gaku* 能のノリと地拍子：リズムの民族音楽学. Tokyo: Hinoki Shoten.

Gamō Satoaki 蒲生郷昭. 1992. "Nihon no ongaku riron ni okeru 'chū' ni tsuite" 日本の音楽理論における「中」について. *Geinō no kagaku* 20: 1–32.

* Gellner, Winfried. 1990. *Die Kostüme des Nō-Theaters*. Stuttgart: Franz Steiner Verlag.

* Griffiths, David. 1998. *The Training of Noh Actor and The Dove*. Vol. 2 of *Mask: A Release of Acting Resources*. London: Routledge.

* Hare, Thomas Blenman. 1986. *Zeami's Style: The Nō Plays of Zeami Motokiyo*. Stanford: Stanford University Press.

Hare, Thomas Blenman (Tom), trans. 2008. *Zeami: Performance Notes*. Translations from the Asian Classics. New York: Columbia University Press.

Hoff, Frank, and Willi Flindt. 1973. *The Life Structure of Noh: An English Version of Yokomichi Mario's Analysis of the Structure of Noh*. First published in *Concerned Theater Japan*, vol. 2, nos. 3/4 (1971).

Itō Masayoshi 伊藤正義. 1982. "Matsui-ke zō myōan shutaku utaibon shikigo hikae" 松井家蔵妙庵手沢謡本識語控. *Kokubungaku kenkyū shiryōkan chōsa kenkyū hōkoku* 国文学研究資料館調査研究報告 3: 185–207.

Jinkaishō 塵芥抄. 1583. Author unidentified. https://kokusho.nijl.ac.jp/biblio/100275941/1?ln=ja.

Kato, Eileen. 1998. "*Miidera.*" In *Traditional Japanese Theater: An Anthology of Plays*, edited by Karen Brazell, 158–78. New York: Columbia University Press.

* Keene, Donald. 1966. *Nō*. Tokyo: Kodansha International. Reprinted as *Nō and Bunraku: Two Forms of Japanese Theatre*. 1990. New York: Columbia University Press.

* Khanh Trinh, ed. 2014. *Theatre of Dreams, Theatre of Play: Nō and Kyōgen in Japan*. Sydney: Art Gallery of New South Wales.

Komparu, Kunio. 1983. *The Noh Theater: Principles and Perspectives*. New York: Weatherhill/Tankosha.

* Malm, William P. 1959. *Japanese Music and Musical Instruments*. Rutland: Charles E. Tuttle Co.

Mochizuki Ikuko 望月郁子. 1998. "*Zeami jihitsu nōhon* (Hōzanji zōhon) ni okeru kigō "○" no bunpu to sono kinō" 世阿弥自筆能本(宝山寺蔵本)における記号○の分布とその機能. *Nishōgakusha Daigaku ronshū* 二松学舎大学論集 41: 71–93.

Morita Mitsuharu 森田光春. 1980. *Morita-ryū ōgiroku* 森田流奥義録. Tokyo: Nōgaku Shorin.

Morita Toki 森田都紀. 2018. *Nōkan no ensōgihō to denshō* 能管の演奏技法と伝承. Kyoto: Shibunkaku Shuppan.

* Nakamura Yasuo 中村保雄. 1996. *Nōmen: bi, kei, yō* 能面：美・形・用. Kyoto: Kawara Shoten.

Nogami Toyoichirō 野上豊一郎. 1944. *Nōmen ronkō* 能面論考. Tokyo: Koyama Shoten. Reprinted in Nogami Toyoichirō, ed. 1979, 1994. *Nō no enshutsu* 能の演出. *Nōgaku zensho* 能楽全書 4. Tokyo: Sogensha.

Nogami Toyoichirō 野上豊一郎. 1949–1951, 1971. *Kaichū yōkyoku zensho* 解註謡曲全書 1–6. Tokyo: Chūō Kōronsha.

Omote Akira 表章. 1985. "Nō no dō(on) to ji(utai)" 能『同(音)』と『地(謡)』. *Kokugo to kokubungaku* 国語と国文学 62, no. 4: 1–17.

Omote Akira 表章. 1988–1997. "*Kurumaya utaibon shinkō*" 車屋謡本新考. In *Nōgaku kenkyū* 能楽研究 13–21; also *Hōsei Daigaku Bungakubu kiyō* 33 法政大学文学部紀要 33.

Ōtani Setsuko 大谷節子. 2016. "Kōan gannenmei Okina men o meguru kōsatsu: nōmen kenkyū no shatei" 弘安元年銘翁面をめぐる考察－能面研究の射程 / "A Study of the Oldest Extant Old Man's Ōtani 'Okina-men' 1278." In *Nōmen o kagaku suru: sekai no kamen to engeki* 能面を科学する－世界の仮面と演劇 / *A Scientific Approach to Nō Masks: World Masks and Performance*, edited by Kobe Joshi Daigaku Koten Geinō Kenkyū Sentā 神戸女子大学古典芸能研究センター, 3–36. Tokyo: Bensei Shuppan.

* Perzyński, Friedrich. 1925. *Japanische Masken: Nō und Kyōgen*. 2 vols. Berlin: Verlag von Walter de Gruyter & Co. Abridged English version: Stanley Appelbaum, trans./ed. 2005. *Japanese Nō Masks with 300 Illustrations of Authentic Historical Examples*. New York: Dover Publications.

* Pinnington, Noel J. 1998. "Invented Origins: Muromachi interpretations of *okina sarugaku*." *Bulletin of the School of Oriental and African Studies* 61, no. 3: 492–518.

Sakurai Shigeharu 桜井茂治. 1965. "Zeami no nōgakusho to akusento: Muromachi jidai no akusento shiryō to shite" 世阿弥の能楽書とアクセント—室町時代のアクセント資料として. *Kokugakuin zasshi* 國學院雜誌 66: 59–72.

* Salz, Jonah, ed. 2016. *A History of Japanese Theatre*. Cambridge: Cambridge University Press, 2016.

Sanari Kentarō 佐成謙太郎. (1930–1931) 1982. *Yōkyoku taikan* 謡曲大觀. 7 vols. Tokyo: Meiji Shoin.

* Schneider, Harald. 1983. *Das Japanische Nootheater; Spielpraxis und Spielumfeld unter Ausschluss der Noomusik*. Munich: Knecht-Druck.

Shimotsuma Shōshin 下間少進. *Butai no zu, butai shō* 舞台之図, 舞台抄. In *Shimotsuma Shōshin shū* 下間少進集 1, edited by Nishino Haruo, 161–274. 1973. *Nōgaku shiryō shūsei* 能楽資料集成 1. Tokyo: Wanya Shoten.

* Suginomori Hisako 椙杜穹才子, ed. *Nō o irodoru ōgi no sekai* 能を彩る扇の世界. 1994. Tokyo: Hinoki Shoten.

* Takakuwa Izumi 高桑いづみ. 2003. *Nō no hayashi to enshutsu* 能の囃子と演出. Tokyo: Ongaku no Tomosha.

Takakuwa Izumi 高桑いづみ. 2015. *Nō kyōgen utai no hensen: Zeami kara gendai made* 能・狂言謡の変遷―世阿弥から現代まで. Tokyo: Hinoki Shoten.

* Takemoto Mikio 竹本幹夫. 1978. "Tennyomai no kenkyū" 天女舞の研究. *Nōgaku kenkyū* 能楽研究 4: 93–158.

* Takemoto Mikio 竹本幹夫. 1999. *Kan'ami, Zeami jidai no nōgaku* 観阿弥・世阿弥時代の能楽. Tokyo: Meiji Shoin.

* Takemoto Mikio 竹本幹夫. 2013. "Nō no kōzō to gihō ni okeru yōshiki no seiritsu o megutte" 能の構造と技法における様式の成立をめぐって. *Kokubungaku kenkyū* 国文学研究 169: 25–37.

* Takeda, Sharon Sadako, and Monica Bethe. 2002. *Miracles and Mischief: Noh and Kyōgen Theater in Japan*. Los Angeles: Los Angeles County Museum; Tokyo: Agency for Cultural Affairs, Government of Japan.

* Tanba Akira. 1974. *La Structure Musicale du Nō*. Paris: Klincksieck.

* Tanabe Saburōsuke 田辺三郎助. 1981. *Nōmen* 能面. Tokyo: Shōgakukan.

Teele, Rebecca, ed. 1986. *Nō/Kyōgen Masks and Performance* (Mime Journal 1984). Claremont: Pomona College.

Tyler, Royall, trans./ed. 1992. *Japanese Nō Dramas*. Penguin Classics. London: Penguin Books.

Tyler, Royall. 2012. *The Tale of the Heike*. New York: Viking Books.

Yamanaka Reiko 山中玲子. 1985. "Tenmon ninen Nakamura Shichirōzaemon Nagachika okugaki fue densho: honkoku to kaidai" 天文二年中村七郎左衛門長親奥書笛伝書―翻刻と解題―. *Nō kenkyū to hyōron* 能研究と評論 13: 31–44.

Yamanaka Reiko 山中玲子. 2001. "Banshiki no narai to kogaki no seiritsu" 「盤渉」の習いの小書の成立. *Nōgaku kenkyū* 能楽研究 25: 65–102.

Yokomichi Mario 横道萬里雄 and Omote Akira 表章, eds. 1960, 1963. *Yōkyokushū* 謡曲集. 2 vols. *Nihon Koten bungaku taikei* 日本古典文学大系 40, 41. Vol. 40 (1960); vol. 41 (1963). Tokyo: Iwanami Shoten.

Yokomichi Mario 横道萬里雄. 1987. *Nō no kōzō to gihō* 能の構造と技法. *Iwanami kōza: nō kyōgen* 岩波講―座能・狂言 IV, edited by Yokomichi Mario 横道萬里雄, Nishino Haruo 西野春雄, and Hata Hisashi 羽田昶. Tokyo: Iwanami Shoten.

Yokomichi Mario 横道萬里雄. 2002. *Nō ni mo enshutsu ga aru* 能にも演出がある. Tokyo: Hinoki Shoten.

Yokomichi Mario 横道萬里雄 and Yamanaka Reiko 山中玲子, and Matsumoto Yasushi 松本雍. 2009. *Nō o omoshiroku miseru kufū: kogaki enshutsu no rekishi to shosō* 能を面白く見せる工夫：小書演出の歴史と諸相. Tokyo: Hinoki Shoten.

Websites for Performance

Invitation to Nohgaku. https://www2.ntj.jac.go.jp/unesco/noh/en/.
Japanese Performing Arts Research Consortium (JPARC. online). https://jparc.online/.
Noh as Intermedia. https://noh.stanford.edu/.
The-noh.com: https://www.the-noh.com/.

3

Training, Practice, and Production

Edited by Diego Pellecchia and Yamanaka Reiko

Numerous Japanese or English language publications to date are dedicated to the history, plays, or performance conventions of nōgaku, yet few studies focus on its current state. Writing in a contemporary context is a challenging task due to the ever-evolving nature of theatre. Even in a traditional art like nōgaku, the continuous flow of new information can make it difficult to capture a definitive picture of the present moment. This chapter attempts to portray the world of nōgaku today, considering not only the training of professionals, the preparation and rehearsal process, the various phases in the production of a performance event but also the socioeconomic aspects of the relationship between professionals, amateurs, and audience.[1]

3.1 Introduction
Diego Pellecchia and Yamanaka Reiko

With the advent of the Meiji Restoration in 1868, the system that supported nō throughout the Edo period (1603–1868) was dismantled, and nō ceased to be performed as ritual entertainment. In the years that followed, the activities of numerous groups of professionals were discontinued, placing the survival of their tradition at risk (see ch. 1 *History*, 1.8). During this period, an increasing number of wealthy amateurs who studied with actors and musicians became the new patrons of nō. Their commitment and dedication were so strong that, in some cases, their descendants became professionals, thus establishing new lineages of actors that continue to be active today. While the financial patronage of nō theatre performers transitioned from the aristocratic class to the emergent bourgeoisie, the underlying social framework governing the art form remained largely unchanged.

Similarly, the system that governs the production and consumption of nō today retains elements of its past. Nō is still a "family business," in which

---

[1] The editors are grateful to nō performers Arimatsu Ryōichi, Kanze Yoshimasa, Noguchi Takayuki, Obinata Hiroshi, Ōshima Teruhisa, Takeda Munenori, Takahashi Norimasa, Udaka Tatsushige, and Zenchiku Daijirō for their generous assistance.

masks, costumes, and theatre buildings as well as the planning and mounting of a performance are managed directly by the actors, often without the support of a production office. Nō and kyōgen performers are individual freelancers belonging to specialized groups not bound by contracts with companies or theatres. While all professionals operate within the same market, and therefore may be seen as competing against each other, the way performances are produced typically emphasizes mutual support. For example, actors taking part in professional performances are not selected through auditions; instead, they are assigned roles according to seniority and rank, often on a rotating basis. This system is supported by the Nohgaku Performers' Association (Nōgaku Kyōkai), to which all performers must subscribe in order to operate as full-fledged professionals.

A nō kinship group is generally called a "family of professionals" if the tradition has been passed down through the same lineage for several generations. Performers who are born into these families benefit from inheriting the assets and fame associated with their name. Yet, the ability of a performer needs to be demonstrated onstage: those who do not uphold the expectations that come with their "family brand" are likely to become unpopular with both audience and critics. Performers who are not born into these families but wish to become professionals will need to build their career from the ground up. Furthermore, the passage of tradition within such groups privileges male heirs. Although their presence has been increasingly acknowledged since the Meiji period, female nō performers are still far from being accepted as equals to their male counterparts (see sec. 3.3).

Nōgaku was designated by the Japanese government as an "Important Intangible Cultural Property" (*jūyō mukei bunkazai*) in 1957. It was declared as a Masterpiece of the Oral and Intangible Heritage of Humanity by UNESCO in 2001 and subsequently inscribed in the Representative List of the Intangible Cultural Heritage of Humanity in 2008. Despite these national and international distinctions, actors and theatres receive no significant subsidy from public institutions. Their finances depend almost entirely on the support of patrons, who are frequently both audience members and amateur practitioners. This has become an increasingly serious issue because, since the burst of Japan's economic bubble in the early 1990s, nō seems to have lost much of its appeal as a status symbol. Today the nō audience is aging and shrinking, as younger Japanese have shifted their interests toward other cultural products, thus posing a serious threat to the survival of the art in future decades. Recently, having realized the need to develop a new fanbase, nō performers are making efforts to reach a broader audience through educational initiatives, collaborations with other art forms, and through digital technologies and social media.

3.1.1 Groups of Performers

During Zeami's time, nō performers formed troupes comprised of different specializations, including *shite*, *waki*, musicians, and kyōgen actors. It was not until the beginning of the seventeenth century that performers formed groups of specialists referred to as *ryūgi* (stylistic school).[2] This was part a process of standardization that occurred in the Edo period and became the foundation of the system we know today.

At present, there are five *ryūgi* of *shite* actors (Kanze, Konparu, Hōshō, Kongō, Kita), three schools of *waki* actors (Takayasu, Fukuō, Hōshō), and two schools of kyōgen actors (Ōkura, Izumi). *Hayashi* musicians comprise three schools of *fue* (the nō transverse flute, also called *nōkan*; Issō, Morita, Fujita), four schools of *kotsuzumi* (shoulder drum; Kō, Kōsei, Ōkura, Kanze), five schools of *ōtsuzumi* (hip drum; Kadono, Takayasu, Ishii, Ōkura, Kanze), and two schools of *taiko* (stick drum; Kanze, Konparu). Performers specialize only in one of these arts, and therefore their only professional affiliation is with one school. *Waki*, *hayashi*, and kyōgen are collectively referred as the *san'yaku* ("three roles") to distinguish them from *shite* actors.

It should be noted that *ryūgi* with different specializations may use the same name. For example, there are *ryūgi* called Kanze for *shite*, *kotsuzumi*, *ōtsutsumi*, and *taiko*. Schools with the same name do not always perform together, however. While the shared nomenclature implies historical affiliations among these schools, in contemporary practice they operate independently and are not bound to perform exclusively with each other.

Ryūgi are organized according to a structure in which a single performer, known as *iemoto* or *sōke* (literally "origin/foundation of the house/family"), is the main representative of the tradition.[3] The so-called "*iemoto* system" is often represented as a pyramid, with the *iemoto* (often translated as "Grandmaster") at the top, professionals below him, and amateurs occupying the bottom. We propose an alternative model, however, represented in table 3.1 in which we wish to show how knowledge of nō originates from the *iemoto*, and spreads outward in layers that are further removed from him. Its components are separated, yet they maintain various degrees of connection between them.[4]

---

2   Here "school" is used as in "school of thought." "School" is a free translation of the word *ryū* 流 (literally "flow" or "current"), indicating the continuous flow of a tradition shared by a group of practitioners; it does not denote an educational institution, such as a drama academy or a conservatory, with a team of instructors teaching a unified curriculum in classrooms.
3   For an introduction to the notion of *iemoto*, see Hsu 1975; Nishiyama 1982.
4   For an extensive analysis of the nō and kyōgen society, see Shimazaki and Shimazaki 2004.

TABLE 3.1   A representation of the current structure of the nōgaku social system

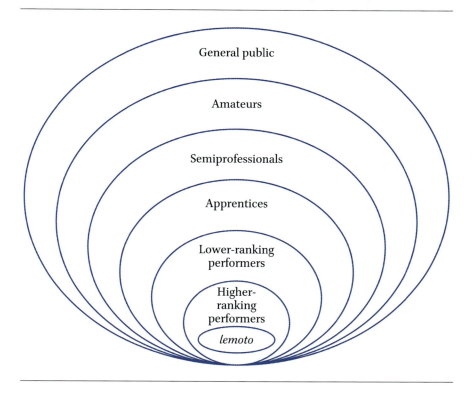

The *iemoto* family line, from which each school takes its name, is the highest ranking within the *ryūgi*. Among the exclusive powers of the Grandmaster are the rights to authorize performances, to revise and publish scripts, or to grant teaching licenses. Leading positions such as the *iemoto* are hereditary and until now have prioritized male heirs. Usually, this role is inherited by the eldest son of the current *iemoto*, who assumes the title of *waka sōke*, or "Young Grandmaster," until receiving his father's title. It is not uncommon, however, for *iemoto* family lines to die out. In that case, a male performer from another family within the same *ryūgi* is likely to be chosen to assume this position.

Despite his central role, the *iemoto* is not the only repository of knowledge within a stylistic school. Around him are the heads of other families of professionals, in turn hierarchically structured, with families with older lineages at the center and more recently constituted families around them. For the sake of brevity, in this chapter we will refer to any such family (or groups of families) as "subgroups." While the *iemoto* retains the overall authority over the institution, each *ryūgi* is in turn composed of smaller clusters of performers, each of which has an important family at its core, around which gravitate individual performers or newly formed families. This results in a complex and varied assemblage of different traditions that follow the same conventions, while at the same time retaining particular styles.[5] Although subgroups within the same school are independent, they nonetheless share the same repertory of plays and conventions, including chant and dance style, as well as training and performance curricula.

It is common practice that perspective actors born into prominent families of nō professionals study with the *iemoto*. Being a direct disciple (*uchideshi*) of the *iemoto* confers a status from which the actors and their families will benefit throughout their careers. In large *ryūgi*, this practice ensures that even powerful and relatively independent families receive training from the same source, thus maintaining a degree of artistic consistency across members of the same school. This system may vary depending on the size and history of the school, making it difficult to provide a treatment of this topic that applies to all cases.

One distinctive feature of nō is how members of the cast prepare for a performance. There is no extensive, collective rehearsal period. Instead, actors and musicians train separately and meet onstage for a single "dry run" of the play.[6] This is possible because the performance text of a nō play, comprised of lyrics, music, choreography, and other staging conventions, is part of a fixed canon currently consisting of about 240 plays, almost all of which are shared across all *ryūgi*. Unlike other theatre traditions, in which the same play may be staged daily over a period of weeks, nō performances are one-off events, never repeated over consecutive days.[7] Nō performers must understand all aspects of the staging of a play in order to be fully functional within this system. This type of comprehensive knowledge is achieved through a dedicated and highly focused study of the nō arts, as well as a constant exposure to nō from a very young age. All performers also master other nō arts in which they do not specialize. For example, *shite*, *waki*, and kyōgen actors learn how to play the instruments, while *hayashi* musicians must study nō chant. Although the performers and the stylistic schools to which they belong remain independent, the professional network they form is highly integrated.

---

5   A factor further complicating this is the practice of adoption across schools.
6   For *Dōjōji*, it is customary to do two rehearsals (*shita mōshiawase* and *mōshiawase*).
7   Tours overseas are an exception. For technical reasons, actors may perform the same play with the same cast in different locations.

3.1.2   The Nohgaku Performers' Association

The Nohgaku Performers' Association (Nōgaku Kyōkai) was established in September 1945. In 2011, it was registered as a public interest incorporated association (*kōeki shadan hōjin*). As of May 2023, it had 1,057 associates (see table 3.2). The aims of the Association are to preserve the tradition of nō and kyōgen, ensuring its transmission and fostering collaboration among its members. Among its principal endeavors are the organization of performances for the education of the artists, the production of public events and outreach activities, and the preservation and utilization of performance-related data, including the management of the image rights of the associates. The Association sponsors activities aimed at supporting young actors and musicians, as seen in the Osaka Yōseikai and the Nagoya Ikuseikai.

The Association also seeks to provide administrative support to performers, most of whom do not have staff to assist them, allowing them to concentrate on their artistic work. Concurrently, the Association offers to support performers who, as will be explained below, cannot expect to generate income exclusively from performance revenues. This support is materialized, for example, through opportunities for members to advertise their teaching activities on the Association's website.

3.1.3   The Demographics of Nō Professionals

Nō performers had been supported by the central government since the late sixteenth century. When the site of the government moved from Kyoto to Edo (present-day Tokyo) at the beginning of the seventeenth century, the main groups of performers followed. Meanwhile, other families continued to serve the feudal lords in the provinces, both in the Kyoto-Osaka region and in other areas (see ch. 1 *History*, 1.6). The relocation of the core performer units from central Japan to Edo represented a significant shift in the principal location of the nō world. This shift is also reflected in the demographic distribution of nō professionals today.

The Nohgaku Performers' Association is divided into eight groups: Tokyo, Nagoya, Hokuriku (the region including the major cities of Niigata, Kanazawa, and Fukui), Kyoto, Osaka, Kobe, Kyushu, and "Other." The great majority of the associates are active in the Tokyo area, which alone accounts for almost as many members as those of all the other regions combined. The second largest center for nō activities is the Kyoto-Osaka area. Currently, the *iemoto* of the Kanze, Hōshō, and Konparu schools are based in Tokyo. Kongō is the only school whose *iemoto* is based in Kyoto. As of 2023, the Kita school does not have an *iemoto*, and stages its regular performances in Tokyo, even though certain members are also active in other regions of Japan (tables 3.2–3.5).

TABLE 3.2   The various schools of nō and kyōgen divided by specialization

Shite-kata	Kanze (346)	Konparu (92)	Hōshō (142)	Kongō (59)	Kita (46)	685
Waki-kata	Takayasu (11)	Fukuō (13)	Hōshō (24)			48
Fue-kata	Issō (11)	Morita (41)	Fujita (4)			56
Kotsuzumi-kata	Kō (28)	Kōsei (9)	Ōkura (17)	Kanze (6)		60
Ōtsuzumi-kata	Kadono (9)	Takayasu (10)	Ishii (10)	Ōkura (10)	Kanze (2)	41
Taiko-kata	Kanze (14)	Konparu (17)				31
Kyōgen-kata	Ōkura (72)	Izumi (64)				136
Total						**1,057**

Note: The number in round brackets () indicates the number of professional practitioners for each school. The column on the right indicates the total for each specialization.
SOURCE: THE NOHGAKU PERFORMERS' ASSOCIATION. MAY 2023

TABLE 3.3   The nōgaku professional population registered at the Tokyo branch of the Nohgaku Performers' Association

Shite	Kanze (174)	Konparu (68)	Hōshō (70)	Kongō (18)	Kita (27)	357
Waki	Takayasu (2)	Fukuō (4)	Hōshō (15)			21
Fue	Issō (11)	Morita (10)	Fujita (1)			22
Kotsuzumi	Kō (10)	Kōsei (5)	Ōkura (8)	Kanze (6)		29
Ōtsuzumi	Kadono (5)	Takayasu (8)		Ōkura (4)		17
Taiko	Kanze (6)	Konparu (6)				12
Kyōgen	Ōkura (25)	Izumi (35)				60
Total						**518**

SOURCE: THE NOHGAKU PERFORMERS' ASSOCIATION, MAY 2023

The presence of specialized schools allows for different combinations. For instance, *shite* actors in the Kanze school could perform with *waki* from the Fukuō, Hōshō, or Takayasu schools, with *kotsuzumi* players in the Kō, Kōsei, Ōkura, or Kanze schools and so forth. Due the substantial dissimilarities in texts and performance conventions between actor schools, however, it is very unusual that members from the various schools who perform the same role type (e.g., *shite* or *waki*) appear together in the same play.

As explained earlier, *ryūgi* are not represented uniformly across the country, and as a result casting combinations are partly determined by the availability

TABLE 3.4 The nōgaku professional population registered at the Kyoto branch of the Nohgaku Performers' Association

Shite	Kanze (59)	Konparu (4)		Kongō (20)	83
Waki	Takayasu (5)		Hōshō (2)		7
Flute		Morita (4)			4
Kotsuzumi	Kō (8)		Ōkura (1)		9
Ōtsuzumi			Ishii (7)		7
Taiko	Kanze (1)	Konparu (2)			3
Kyōgen	Ōkura (23)	Izumi (4)			27
Total					**140**

SOURCE: THE NOHGAKU PERFORMERS' ASSOCIATION, MAY 2023

TABLE 3.5 The nōgaku professional population divided by area

Nōgaku Performers' Association branch	Registered members
Tokyo (main branch)	519
Nagoya	81
Hokuriku	67
Kyoto	140
Osaka	130
Kobe	38
Kyushu	68
Other (*honbu atsukai*)	14

SOURCE: THE NOHGAKU PERFORMERS' ASSOCIATION, MAY 2023

of the performers in a particular locale. For example, as of May 2023 fifty-nine Kanze actors, twenty Kongō actors, and four Konparu actors are registered with the Kyoto branch of the Nohgaku Performers' Association. In fact, most performances happening in Kyoto are hosted either by Kanze or Kongō actors at their respective theatres. In addition to the five Takayasu and two Hōshō school *waki*, Fukuō actors may be hired from nearby Osaka.

3.1.4   Who Qualifies as a Professional Nō Performer?

Nō professionals are called *nōgakushi* ("masters of nōgaku"). Although the line separating professionals and amateurs might at times be blurry, members of the Nohgaku Performers' Association, whose main source of income is through performing and teaching, are generally considered professionals by their peers and the public. After having accumulated sufficient experience, nō performers are designated as Holders of Important Intangible Cultural Properties (*jūyō mukei bunkazai sōgō shitei hojisha*) by the Agency for Cultural Affairs (Bunkachō), thus entering the Japan Nōgaku Association (Nihon Nōgakukai). Being a member of a family of *nōgakushi* facilitates the path to becoming a professional performer, if technical and artistic requirements are satisfied. Today, those who are not born into this world often begin practicing at university clubs or as amateurs. While some may later transition into professionalism or semiprofessionalism, extra effort might be necessary to prove their commitment to the art. Despite their efforts, achieving elevated status within the hierarchical structure of nō society may remain an elusive goal.

There is no formal restriction against the participation of women in official performances, although their activities are in reality quite limited. Furthermore, men are preferred for the hereditary transmission of professional titles such as *iemoto*. There is also a small number of non-Japanese practicing nō at different levels, but even those who have been trained sufficiently to receive a teaching license do not pursue a professional career.[8]

3.2   Training
Diego Pellecchia and Yamanaka Reiko

The focus of this section on the training of *shite* actors is explained by the fact that *shite* actors constitute the great majority of professional nō performers. Their education includes the broadest range of skills, encompassing knowledge of chant, instrumental music, and dance, as well as masks, costumes, and stage properties. Moreover, as will be touched upon below, *shite* actors are also the producers of most nō events, thereby placing them at the core of their professional world.

In nō, as in other traditional Japanese arts, training sessions are called *keiko*, a word that can be translated literally as "thinking about the old," a reminder of how the knowledge that is transmitted or practiced does not rest solely on the efforts of a single individual, but rather derives from tradition as collective knowledge passed down through generations. The word *keiko*, often preceded

---

8   Rebecca Teele Ogamo (Kongō school) is the first and, to date, only non-Japanese member of the Nohgaku Performers' Association.

by the honorific "o" (okeiko), is invariably used both for lessons with a teacher and for individual practice sessions.

Nōgaku is registered as a UNESCO Masterpiece of the Oral and Intangible Heritage of Humanity. But to say that nō is passed down exclusively by oral transmission (kuden) would be inaccurate, as much of the knowledge is acquired through a process of imitation that does not necessarily involve verbalization. "Learning by doing" is a key aspect of Japanese pedagogy, and expressions such as karada de oboeru (learning through the body) or mi ni tsukeru (fixing on the body) are frequently used to indicate that knowledge learned through experience is embodied, rather than acquired intellectually.[9] In tandem with oral and corporeal transmission, nō performers employ a variety of texts to support their training and preparation for a performance (see ch. 7 Material Culture, 7.6, 7.7). The core knowledge of nō is experiential, and therefore access to knowledge depends on the direct contact with a teacher, who equally provides access to the social world of nō. This system aims to ensure that knowledge is not disseminated outside a close-knit circle of committed individuals. As a result, nō often appears as an esoteric art form that is relatively inaccessible to the broader public.[10]

Transmission typically occurs in one-to-one interactions between teacher and student. A master-actor may have numerous students, who, in turn, learn from a single instructor for each of the disciplines they are studying. As noted above, to become full-fledged performers, trainees cannot focus solely on their specialization but must also learn the other nō arts. For example, shite actors specialize in chant and dance, but education in musical instruments is also part of their curriculum. Since the education of new generations of performers who will ensure the continuation of the tradition is considered a shared responsibility of the professional community, actors and musicians on the path of professionalism are not required to contribute financially to their training.

In the early training stages, teachers are physically present during training to provide a model that students imitate, but with time, as trainees acquire an increasingly wide performance vocabulary, direct meetings with instructors become shorter and less frequent. Lessons then transition into opportunities to receive feedback and corrections on the skills and techniques they have honed through independent practice.

---

9   For further exploration of this subject, see Singleton, Brown, and Pea, eds. 1998.
10   See Morinaga 2005.

3.2.1 *Childhood*

Children born into professional households, or children of semiprofessionals who are constantly exposed to nō from a very young age, start their training as soon as they can walk. Traditionally, they perform their first dance excerpt (*shimai*) around the age of three, after which time they begin to appear as *kokata* (child actor). At this stage, the pedagogy does not focus on the fundamentals of chant and dance as units that can be utilized in other pieces, but on the specific role they are meant to perform. Rather than learning how to read chant books or memorizing names of movement routines, children are encouraged to just imitate the teacher (fig. 3.1).

Many children make their first stage appearance as *kokata* in the "flower-viewing" scene in *Kurama tengu*. In this play, a group of children stands in line on the *hashigakari* bridgeway, facing the audience, then enters the main stage area, sit for some time, and finally exits. These are relatively simple tasks, but learning to follow instructions, going onstage in costume, and interacting with other actors is a formative experience that has a strong impact on their education.

At age five, a trainee may appear in longer *kokata* roles, such as the child in *Hyakuman* or Minamoto no Yoshitsune in the plays *Funa Benkei* and *Hashi Benkei*, which demand the memorization of both movement and text. Once they enter elementary school, children are in full control of their bodies, and are able to concentrate for longer periods. They begin to perform dance pieces and learn increasingly complex roles. It is also a common practice for children born into families of professionals to take the *shite* role in short plays like *Shōjō*, *Kagetsu*, or *Kiku jidō* (*Makura jidō*) without wearing a mask. Generally speaking, the age at which a child starts acting in full plays depends on the development of each individual, but also on the scheduling of performances requiring such role by actors affiliated with the child's circle.

Children often cease performing these *kokata* roles in the later years of elementary school. This moment is marked with the participation in a performance featuring a role requiring complex actions and/or dances. These include the son who takes revenge on his father's murderer in *Mochizuki* or Yoshitsune in *Eboshi-ori*. In some schools, *Eboshi-ori* is considered the *kokata* graduation piece par excellence. When the *kokata* is the designated successor of an important family, a performance of *Eboshi-ori*, which requires a large cast and is expensive to stage, may be organized specifically for this purpose.[11]

---

11   Children of *waki*, kyōgen, or musicians may also take part in performances as *kokata* since the children of *shite* actors are not always available.

FIGURE 3.1   Kita-school actor Ōshima Teruhisa training his son Iori at a student's private practice space. 2021
PHOTO: FUKAZAWA NOZOMI. COURTESY OF ŌSHIMA TERUHISA

3.2.2 *Puberty*

As children's voices undergo change during adolescence, they normally take a break from performing onstage. During this phase, they shift the focus of their training to learning how to read chant books (*utaibon*) and choreography (*katatsuke*) books. They also start to study how to play musical instruments and practice the fundamentals of dance: *kamae* (basic stance) and *suriashi* (sliding walk). Around age fifteen or sixteen it is common to perform one's first role as a *shite* with a mask (*hatsu omote*). Typically, this period corresponds to a more intense phase in the regular school curriculum, as well as to the occasional youthful resistance to parental pressure. Even within professional households, some children quit training entirely at this time.

3.2.2.1   *Uchideshi* (Live-in Apprentices)

Children born into a family of practitioners will be taught by a parent, grandparent, or other relatives within the family. This applies first and foremost to the sons of the *iemoto*, who will eventually inherit the title and become leaders of the school. It is not uncommon, however, for the young members of high-profile subgroup families to study with the *iemoto* as *uchideshi* (live-in apprentice). Similarly, the head of a subgroup family will train his own children but may also accept children from other families as *uchideshi* or even students who do not belong to a family of practitioners. *Uchideshi* training customarily takes between five and eight years, although the exact length depends on the instructor. There is no formalized or unified curriculum that can be applied to all students. Trainees mainly practice with their teacher, but they might also be instructed by their seniors (*senpai*), who watch over their progress while coaching them backstage.

The regimen for live-in apprentices is rigorous. In the past, it was assumed that all *uchideshi* would live in the same house as their instructor, although in recent years many are *kayoi*, or "commuting," apprentices, living close to the master's residence or training space. *Uchideshi* do not receive any monetary allowance, although accommodation and food expenses may be covered by the teacher. They must report to their instructor every day in the morning and in the evening. Their daily routine also includes cleaning the stage, the dressing room, and the entrance of the house (fig. 3.2). In some cases, *uchideshi* may take care of the amateur students coming to study with their master, serving tea, and singing chorus parts during their lessons.[12] In short, the *uchideshi* must be available whenever needed, be it for menial chores or for performance-related duties. In exchange, they can use the stage for training, when available. This an added advantage since not all professional actors have free access to a nō stage.

Uchideshi are expected to adjust to the schedule of their instructor. They will study with them when possible and train alone when they are busy—in other words, training depends entirely on their availability. In effect, the apprentice is exposed to as much nō as possible and is required to absorb its various aspects in all possible situations. For example, the apprentice will be able to memorize a great number of pieces (typically chant and dance excerpts) while coaching amateur students. When there are multiple *uchideshi* training with the same actor at the same time, it is common for a junior apprentice to be coached by a senior, who is to be consulted first before asking the master directly. This system is also a chance for more experienced individuals to reflect on what they have learned as they share their knowledge with the newcomers.

Throughout the apprenticeship, students frequent the residence or training space of musicians, with whom they study the instruments. During this period, students are involved in performances as *ji utai* (chorus) chanters, *kōken* (stage

---

12   In the case of the Hōshō school, the Suidōbashi stage is not used for amateur training, so *uchideshi* do not need to assist with these kinds of activities.

FIGURE 3.2 A student of Kanze Yoshimasa polishing the stage of the Yarai Nōgakudō, Tokyo. 2021
PHOTO: YAMANAKA REIKO

FIGURE 3.3 Kongō-school actor Sōmyō Tadasuke preparing the *tsukurimono* for the play *Kanawa* in the "mirror room" of the Kongō Nōgakudō, Kyoto. 2020
PHOTO: UDAKA SANAMI

assistant) or *gakuya-bataraki* (assistant working backstage)—apprentices tend to costumes, masks, and properties before and after a performance (fig. 3.3). They also start to take *tsure* (secondary) roles, often wearing mask and costumes, a precious opportunity considering that these are not used in regular training.

3.2.2.2   Milestone Plays

The training of a nō professional is a lifetime commitment. There are plays that are customarily staged at turning points in the career of a performer, marking the advancement of technique and experience. In particular, young actors must take the lead role in challenging plays such as *Shakkyō*, or *Dōjōji* in order to be considered fully independent artists. The first time an actor takes on such a piece is called *hiraki* or "opening."

The actor's age and the order in which these plays are presented in public depends on the school. In the Kanze school, for instance, an actor first performs the role of Senzai in *Okina*, then *Shakkyō*, *Midare* (a variation of *Shōjō*), and finally *Dōjōji*. The Konparu school follows a similar order: *Shakkyō*, *Midare*, and *Dōjōji*. As a preparation for *Dōjōji*, actors perform a play featuring an exorcism (*Aoi no ue* or *Adachigahara*) and a play in which the *shite* executes an acrobatic movement on a platform, such as *Kantan*. In the Hōshō school, the order is *Shakkyō*, *Kurozuka* (*Adachigahara*), *Dōjōji*, and *Midare*, while the Kongō school has *Midare*, *Shakkyō*, *Dōjōji*, and *Mochizuki* as the standard *hiraki*. This order may also vary. In the Kita school, the role of the *shishi*, the mythical lion appearing in *Shakkyō*, is given particular relevance, so the order becomes *Midare*, *Dōjōji*, and *Shakkyō* (as *tsure*). Exceptions to this rule apply to the sons of a *iemoto*, who typically start performing *hiraki* plays earlier. They can take the lead role in *Sagi* or the role of Senzai in *Okina* when they are still children.

Waki actors and kyōgen actors, as well as musicians also have plays that are considered in the same way. The Izumi school of kyōgen actors, for example, considers the role of the mask-bearer in *Okina* or *Nasu no Yoichi no katari*, the special *ai kyōgen* of the nō play *Yashima*, as milestone roles (see ch. 9 Kyōgen, 9.5).

3.2.2.3   Beginning as an Amateur

The chapter thus far has centered on the life of actors born into nō families. There are cases of school students or university students, however, who start their practice as amateurs by participating in extra-curricular clubs, and then develop into full professionals. Today, actors from any background can take the main role in a play, as long as they have completed the traditional training and can demonstrate that they have the requisite skills to be recognized as a professional. There are some disadvantages in starting as an amateur, such as not having access to an in-house training stage, masks, costumes, instruments, choreography books, and musical scores, which those born into a family of professionals may inherit.

3.2.2.4 Studying at the Tokyo University of the Arts

The Traditional Japanese Music Department at the Tokyo University of the Arts (Tōkyō Geijutsu Daigaku) was founded in 1912 by Ikenouchi Nobuyoshi (1858–1934), one of the great nō scholars of the Meiji period and himself a teacher at the university, which has since developed a special program comprising practice and theory of the nō arts: *shite* chant and dance (Kanze and Hōshō schools), *fue* (Issō school), *kotsuzumi* (Kō school), *ōtsuzumi* (Takayasu school), *taiko* (Kanze school), and kyōgen (Izumi school). The successful completion of study and graduation from this department does not automatically result in becoming a professional in any of these specialties. In order to become a professional, it is necessary to be affiliated with a nō expert and to train as an *uchideshi*. Ultimately, permission to become an independent professional must be granted by the *iemoto*.

3.2.2.5 Yōseikai Training

The Nōgaku Yōseikai ("*Nōgaku* Training Program") was established in 1954 for the purpose of supporting the education of perspective *san'yaku* performers (*waki*, musicians, and kyōgen), whose population is smaller in comparison with *shite* actors. The Tokyo chapter of the Nōgaku Yōseikai closed in 1987 but the Kyoto and Osaka branches, both founded in 1964, continue their activities, including the training of *shite*.[13] Similar programs also exist in other provinces, for example, the Ikuseikai in Nagoya. The source of funding for these programs may vary: the Kyoto Nōgaku Yōseikai is subsidized by the Japan Arts Council and other local patrons, while the Osaka Nōgaku Yōseikai and Nagoya Nōgaku Ikuseikai are supported directly by the local branches of the Nohgaku Performers' Association.[14]

Students enroll in these *yōseikai* free of charge through the recommendation by their teachers, although an entrance exam is mandatory. The *yōseikai* aims at providing young performers, typically in their teens and twenties, with training and opportunities to perform onstage in addition to their usual practice. *Shite* actors in the Kyoto Yōseikai, for instance, are able to study *hayashi*

---

13   Hata 1989: 89.
14   The Japan Arts Council (Nihon Geijutsu Bunka Shinkōkai) is a section of the Agency of Cultural Affairs, a special body of the Japanese Ministry of Education, Culture, Sports, Science, and Technology (MEXT).

instruments at no cost, as well as chant and dance under the supervision of an instructor who is usually an experienced professional in their school but not necessarily their usual teacher.

The repertory studied during *yōseikai* training is performed in a series of public, free-of-charge events aimed at showcasing the progress of trainees. These are chances for the trainee to share the stage with other young performers from different *ryūgi* while being supervised by their seniors. The program also seeks to give actors and musicians the opportunity to play important roles (e.g., *shite* or chorus leader) that they are otherwise not entitled to perform in more official events. Performers typically graduate after finishing a training period between five and seven years, though they may rejoin the program as coaches.

3.2.2.6 The National Noh Theatre Training Program

In response to the dwindling number of nō performers, in particular, *waki*, kyōgen, and musicians, the National Noh Theatre in Tokyo (est. 1938; hereafter NNT), funded by the Japan Arts Council, launched a program (*san'yaku kenshū*) in 1984 that offered training in the three arts (*waki*, one of the four instruments, kyōgen; fig. 3.4). The program reached its twelfth iteration in 2023. The duration of the program spans six years—three years of basic training, plus three years of specialized training with full-fledged professionals. The classes, which also include lectures, take place daily from the morning to the afternoon, with observation of performances on the weekends. Following graduation, students will keep studying and working with their instructors. It has been pointed out that while the training program is more systematic than traditional *keiko*, the fact that each student is coached by a multitude of teachers can be confusing for students.[15]

Although originally open only to men, this program is now accessible to women, too; the only requirements are graduation from middle school and that the participants are under the age of twenty-three.[16] Participation in the program does not require previous knowledge of nō. There is no tuition fee, and scholarships are also available.

---

15 Hata 1989: 105.
16 Hata 1989: 106.

FIGURE 3.4 National Noh Theatre call for applications to the 2020 training program in the three arts (*san'yaku kenshū*)
IMAGE COURTESY OF THE NATIONAL NOH THEATRE, TOKYO

3.3 Female Performers in Nō
Barbara Geilhorn

Women dancing nō, known as *sarugaku* until the Meiji period, were first mentioned in the program of the *Kasuga Wakamiya onmatsuri* (Kasuga Wakamiya Grand Festival) in Nara in 1349.[17] Even the opening performance of *Okina*, usually the reserve of male actors, was performed by a woman, a practice that nowadays is hardly imaginable. Female performers at this festival were priestesses at Shintō shrines (*miko*), not women specializing in *sarugaku*, which was instead the case with *onna sarugaku* ("women's *sarugaku*") that became increasingly popular in the fifteenth and sixteenth centuries. As the expression *onna sarugaku* suggests, male performers were considered the norm. The small, independent *onna sarugaku* troupes, which also participated in *kanjin nō* (subscription nō) events and even performed at the shogunal palace, comprised both men and women. It seems that women performed without masks in both male and female roles, while men focused on music and kyōgen (see ch. 1 *History*, 1.3).[18] In his diary, *Kanmon nikki* (*Diary of Things Seen and Heard*), Prince Fushimi no Miya Sadafusa (1372–1456) writes about a performance in 1432: "They can absolutely compete with Kanze or other *sarugaku* troupes."[19] It appears that the novelty, as well as the beauty of women dancing *sarugaku*, attracted large audiences.

With the beginning of the formalization of nō as the shogunate's official theatre (*shikigaku*) in the early Edo period, *onna sarugaku* fell into decline. Despite the Edo period's rigid social structure, which widely excluded women from performing in public, women continued their activities in niches beyond the realm of nō as *shikigaku*. For example, there were courtesans singing and dancing nō (*yūjo nō*), a practice that can be traced back to the end of the Muromachi period. The *Yoza yakusha mokuroku* (*Catalogue of the Performers of the Four Troupes*, 1653) reports on performances by well-known courtesans being an attraction in Kyoto's Shijō Kawaramachi licensed pleasure quarters. The *kotsuzumi* musician Kanze Motonobu (1605–1666) complained that courtesans had been taught the *ranbyōshi* dance, which is central to particularly demanding plays (*omonarai*), such as *Dōjōji*, and requires personal instruction by a senior performer as well as permission to be performed. Motonobu's

---

17 Nose 1938: 355–67; O'Neill 1958/1959.
18 Wakita 2001: 209–10.
19 *Kanmon gyoki* 2:63.

statement suggests, however, that at least some of these courtesans had a great command of nō.[20]

Novels such as Ihara Saikaku's *Kōshoku ichidai otoko* (*The Life of an Amorous Man*, 1682) describes courtesans performing nō for their customers or chanting *utai* with them.[21] Female attendants at the imperial palace, and in the houses of daimyō and aristocrats also studied nō and kyōgen. At a time when *su-utai* (nō chant without musical accompaniment) was enjoyed by broad sections of the population this should come as no surprise. In Nagoya, for example, *onna mai* ("women's dances") were popular during the late Edo period. Again, it is important to note that performances by women are designated as "dance" (*mai*) and thus marked as deviating from standard nō. In the Edo period, there was the remarkable case of a woman with the Buddhist name Chisei (1676–1759), who took the lead of the Fukuō school of *su-utai* in the Kyoto area after her husband's death.[22] She issued licenses or granted members the right to use the name of the school for nearly four decades.

In the early Meiji period, performances by an exclusively female cast (*onna shibai*, or "women's theatre") became popular in all theatrical genres. In *teriha nō*, for instance, a mixture of nō and kabuki that emerged in Osaka around 1850, it was not unusual for female actors to appear onstage.[23] Itinerant troupes also performed in Tokyo and remained popular until the beginning of the twentieth century. The allocation of roles between men and women seems to have been similar to *onna sarugaku*, although women also acted in kyōgen.

In the late nineteenth and early twentieth centuries, nō practice regained popularity with higher aristocrats and other members of the elite, among them an increasing number of female amateurs.[24] In Tokyo, women like Iwakura Chisako (1861–1922), daughter-in-law of the statesman Iwakura Tomomi (1825–1883), practiced *utai*, *shimai*, and *kotsuzumi* (see ch. 1 *History*, 1.8). Gradually, this trend spread across the social classes, but the nō scholar Ikenouchi Nobuyoshi (1858–1934) believed that two young girls of a middle-class family in Matsuyama were the first to restart women's activities in nō in 1883–1884.[25]

The increasing number of female practitioners provided an opportunity for women born into nō families to take the steps toward a professional career by principally teaching female amateurs. Yamashina Akiko (1876–1972), the eldest

20   *Yoza yakusha mokuroku*: 109.
21   *Kōshoku ichidai otoko*: 244–46; Hamada 1964: 227–28.
22   Amano 1992.
23   Matsumoto 1941: 369.
24   Geilhorn 2015.
25   Nishino 1992: 7.

daughter of Yamashina Tokujirō (1849–1927), head of one of the most prestigious families within the Kanze school, is a case in point.[26] She performed as *shite* and played the *kotsuzumi* and *taiko* on her family's nō stage. Beginning in 1908, she supervised a group of female amateurs, Yamashina Women's Performance Group (Yamashina Fujinkai), which was the first of its kind in Tokyo. At a time when performing in public was not considered appropriate for women, Yamashina was exceptional. In contrast, it soon became acceptable for women to teach amateurs since they conformed to prevailing notions of female gender roles.

Despite the increasing numbers of female actors in all forms of performing arts during the late nineteenth and early twentieth centuries, women onstage were nonetheless transgressing social norms of female behavior. This is reflected in the controversies during this time regarding the appearance of female actors (*joyū mondai*, or "actress problem") in contemporary and classical theatre, including kabuki.[27] Furthermore, the image of the female actor was still linked with the geisha profession, as the boundaries between performance and prostitution had been fluid since the medieval period. Traveling performers, such as the *asobime* or *shirabyōshi*, also engaged in prostitution, and the first permanent theatre buildings in the Edo period were placed in the licensed pleasure quarters. In Meiji-period nō, the naturalization of female roles (the representation of women by female actors only) was not an issue and women performing male roles was inconceivable, even though cross-dressing was an important selling point for having female actors in other genres. Rather, the debate focused on general issues such as questioning the artistic value of female roles when performed by women, with discussions centering on the suitability of the female body and voice to dance and sing nō.

In this historical context, the pioneering figure Tsumura Kimiko (1902–1974) made her debut in the play *Hagoromo* in 1921 in Korea, which was a Japanese colony from 1910 to 1945.[28] Interestingly, she was not born into a nō family. Even though she performed with a group of amateurs and not on a regular nō stage, the event was considered taboo-breaking for women. Tsumura even ventured to take the *shite* role in *Ataka*, a play in which the protagonist is Musashibō Benkei, a particularly "masculine" character, customarily performed without a mask (*hitamen*). This is one reason that even today *Ataka* has been widely perceived as unsuitable for a female actor. Tsumura was expelled from the Kanze school in 1921, and her activities were systematically hampered. She was one

---

26 Aoki 2003.
27 Kano 2001: 15–35.
28 Kanamori 1994.

of the first women to perform some of the most difficult plays, such as *Sotoba Komachi* in 1964 and *Ōmu Komachi* in 1971. Tsumura established the nō troupe Ryokusenkai and even composed *shinsaku nō* ("newly created nō"; see ch. 4 *Plays*, 4.11).

In the late 1930s, the attitude of leading critics and performers toward women in nō began to change. The first step on the way to public approval was achieved when the *iemoto* of all schools of *shite* agreed to allow women onstage in 1936.[29] In 1939, women were able to train as *shite* at the predecessor of the Tokyo University of the Arts.

As noted above, the nō community has been a strictly homosocial environment since the Edo period: social relations in nō develop hierarchically along constructed kinship lines (*giseiteki na kazokuteki ketsugō*)[30] and are defined as between male individuals.[31] While nō is widely transmitted from father to son, the position of performers in the imagined family tree does not necessarily correspond to their blood relationship. Forms of salutation such as *anideshi* ("older brother" disciple) between members of the same group hint at this fact, and performers without family relations to nō are integrated in these constructed kinship lines as well. The role of women in nō conforms to that within a traditionally patriarchal Japanese family—in other words, support the stage careers of male family members and hopefully give birth to male heirs. This deeply conservative perception of gender roles is one reason why female professionals born into nō families are the minority. Although young girls receive training comparable to that of their brothers, by the time of puberty they receive less support and encouragement to pursue a professional career.

In most cases, female performers come from outside the nō community and begin studying nō during their student years, and as a consequent they miss significant years of training. While this can be overcome by personal endeavor, it is nevertheless poses a severe handicap. In addition, the number of graduates from the training programs at the Tokyo University of the Arts and the NNT are too few to make a change in the number of (not only female) performers, and not all schools of nō are represented. Moreover, many female students quit their professional careers shortly after graduation because of the lack of future prospects. Women, and to a lesser degree men, might opt to become semiprofessional and only teach amateurs without performing on the professional stage. As the term "semiprofessional" indicates, this is accompanied by a

---

29 Itō 1997: 80.
30 Shimazaki and Shimazaki 2004: 445.
31 Geilhorn 2017: 29–30.

lower social status within the nō community. Nevertheless, for women this has been the easiest path for a career in nō since the Meiji period.

Women have been formally accepted as professional performers since the admission in 1948 of the first three women to the Nohgaku Performers' Association (Nōgaku Kyōkai): Maruyama Tokie (1911–1989), Yamashina Yaji, and Yotsuya Chiyoko (1923–?).[32] As of January 2022, 164 of the 1,082 Association members are female, a total of 15 percent. There are, however, clear differences between categories of performers and musicians or between schools. There are female performers in all *shite* schools, but this does not apply to all performer types: there are no *waki* and only two female kyōgen actors. Similar to the case of Tsumura Kimiko assuming the leading role in *Ataka*, women are not accepted as *waki* or *ai kyōgen*, since both feature male characters that are performed without a mask. Thus, the conditions of women performing nō differ significantly between roles, schools, groups, or even location. For example, the absence of professional performers in the countryside might give women better opportunities to perform than in large cities.

There are few taboos remaining for female actors, yet not all schools of musicians permit women to perform the plays that mark significant stepping stones in a nō actor's professional career, such as *Dōjōji*. *Okina*, which is enacted on special occasions, such as the first performance of the New Year, is also off-limits to women, even though there have been instances of women dancing *Okina* in the medieval period. While the exclusion of female actors from dancing this role does not necessarily impact their careers, women are "symbolically" excluded from this community of professionals and are not even allowed backstage to participate in this play.

In July 2004, the first twenty-two female actors were designated Holders of Important Intangible Cultural Properties (*jūyō mukei bunkazai sōgō shitei hojisha*), formally acknowledging them as experienced performers. The recipients are entitled to appear in the monthly performances organized by the NNT in Tokyo, which has further responded by launching the series "Performed by Female Actors" (*Josei nōgakushi ni yoru*) in 2007, thereby opening their performance series to women. The recipients were exclusively *shite*, and were relegated to a newly created women-only performance format. This marks a consequential step in the policy of the NNT regarding female performers, but the program's future is still uncertain.

The situation of female performers in the NNT is symptomatic of the overall situation of women in nō, in particular, and in Japanese society, in general. Although in theory women are accepted, they are nonetheless relegated

---

32   Kanamori 1994: 201.

to marginalized positions. Remarkably, all three classical forms of Japanese theatre—nōgaku, bunraku, kabuki—privilege the separation of aesthetics by gender. In nō, male performers are still considered the norm, and this represents the most difficult obstacle for female performers to overcome. This becomes apparent in the expressions *josei nōgakushi* or *joryū nōgakushi* (female nō performers), which do not have a male equivalent such as *dansei nōgakushi* (male nō performer). The male norm also refers to the body and voice of performers and applies to male and female roles alike. Unlike kabuki, the hyperfeminine representation of women is does not apply to nō (there are no categories such as soprano or baritone as in Western classical music). In fact, the voice quality and pitch of female figures does not fundamentally differ from their male counterparts, but opponents of women performing on the professional nō stage nonetheless state that the comparatively higher pitch of the female voice is not suitable for performing nō. Similar arguments are leveled against female musicians. They refer to the calls (*kakegoe*) produced by drummers as a constitutive element of the rhythmic structure of nō music. All told, the arguments against female participation in nō have barely changed since the Meiji period. But for both male and female performers the acquisition of the singing voice appropriate for nō is a question of training. Young performers generally lack this quality of voice, which is produced when breathing from the lower abdomen (*hara*); rather, nō suits the mature voice with its deeper and richer sounds (see ch. 2 *Performance*, 2.5, 2.6). Consequently, male *and* female performers develop full voices with age, experience, and training.

Generally, the conditions of women on the nō stage have improved remarkably during the last decades thanks to the efforts of female performers, who have reached a high technical and artistic level. Moreover, the number of young female professionals born into nō families is slowly on the rise. Nō performances by women have the potential of expanding the interpretation of plays based on their individual and gendered experience, thereby adding novel dimensions, depth, and richness to this classical performing art. In recent years, some female musicians also succeeded in regularly performing onstage, most notably the flute player Hattanda Tomoko (Issō school), who graduated from the training program at the NNT or *kotsuzumi* player Ōyama Yōko (Ōkura school), who decided upon a career in nō during her student years.

Despite these advances, reservations against female participation remain largely unchanged and impediments to a career in nō for women still exist.

While there is little open discrimination, women continue to be excluded through the enactment of more subtle strategies. Female performers, for example, are often relegated to the "women-only" corner, which reinforces the notion of nō as a male-only art and at the same time manifests the lower social status of women therein. Although there are exceptions, to date female performers have frequently been excluded from the male chorus. The difference in pitch between the sexes serves as a pretext for this practice, and some schools still provide "women-only" programs for female professionals.[33] These casting policies reduce the opportunity of women to perform and severely hamper the effort of women to develop the voice quality necessary for nō. In addition to the events hosted by their respective schools, some senior female actors produce their own performance series. Yet, programs focused on female performers bear the risk of marginalization. To overcome the all too often practice of separating performances by gender, in 2010, Uzawa Hisa (fig. 3.5), one of the first female Important Intangible Cultural Properties of the Kanze

FIGURE 3.5 Uzawa Hisa in *Sagi*. Hōshō Nōgakudō, Tokyo. January 17, 2021
PHOTO: HAFUKA SHIGERU

33   Geilhorn 2008: 114–15. Yamashina Yaji and Yotsuya Chiyoko are also known as Keiko and Chizuko, respectively.

school, launched a highly innovative performance series, *Josei jiutai ni yoru* (*Accompanied by a Female Chorus*) with an all-female chorus to accompany a male performer dancing the lead role.[34] Women have made great strides to break into the male domain of nō, but in order to affect real change they will need to establish (and disseminate) the idea of nō as an art that transcends gender.

3.4 Practice and Production
Diego Pellecchia and Yamanaka Reiko

3.4.1 *Individual Preparation*

All performers scheduled to take part in a performance, be they *shite*, *tsure*, musicians, *waki*, or chorus members belong to distinct practice groups and train individually. As nō is based on a fixed repertory, with established conventions that dictate each aspect of performance, extended group rehearsals are, technically speaking, unnecessary (see ch. 2 *Performance*, 2.13). Performers meet for a single rehearsal session called *mōshiawase*. This section will explore the phases leading to the *mōshiawase* and up to the actual performance. It should be noted that each kind of performer may prepare differently; here, we will look specifically at the case of a *shite* actor, introducing the tools and spaces used in training.

A *shite* actor's preparation for the performance of a full nō play rests on three main elements: the role to be played, the general experience of the actor, and the degree of familiarity with the work. First, the preparation for a play depends on what role the actor will take: a *shite* or *tsure* role necessarily calls for the practice of movement and dance, while singing in the chorus only requires chant. Second, younger or inexperienced actors will train more frequently with their teacher; adult or fully independent actors typically train by themselves until the *mōshiawase*. Finally, the preparation for a play that is only rarely staged demands extra memorization and more research than a commonly performed play. The standard preparation for a *shite* role could be subdivided into the following four phases described in more detail below: preexisting knowledge, memorization of the text and chant practice, modular memorization of the choreography, and the *mōshiawase*.

3.4.1.1 Tools

As chant is the foundation of training, the *utaibon* (chant book) is indispensable in the preparation of a play. If the actor is sufficiently experienced, the

---

34 Geilhorn 2017: 33–34.

utaibon will be enough to learn how to sing a play in accordance with the patterns played by the musicians. Even contemporary chant books are not exhaustive scores, however, and need to be complemented by practical knowledge of the music to be interpreted.[35] Actors often add musical notations of the drums to passages that can be executed differently. In doing so, the actor gradually creates a personal library of texts combining the script with knowledge acquired from training and stage experience.

In situations where an actor has never portrayed the role of *shite* in a play, not even in a dance excerpt such as *shimai* or *maibayashi*, they must consult choreography notes (*katatsuke*). While printed chant books and *katatsuke* for *shimai* are commercially available, *katatsuke* for performing nō plays are created by either adding indications of *kata* (choreographic units) to the printed *utaibon*, or by transcribing the script and choreography by hand. Just like annotated chant books, *katatsuke* will form a collection of personal documents handed down from teacher to apprentice, from generation to generation. These books are usually kept secret and are only made available to the initiated as needed. When actors begin to prepare for the role of *shite*, or in some cases of *tsure*, they can copy the *katatsuke*, which will become their principal source of written knowledge. Like chant books, the annotations on *katatsuke* are not exhaustive, hence they are open to interpretation. The actor preparing for a new play may compensate the vagueness of the *katatsuke* by asking a teacher or a senior actor with experience in a certain role. It is not uncommon for actors to learn different interpretations of a choreography and then elaborate with their own.

More recently, audiovisual recordings are used by trainees to facilitate the memorization of pieces. These could be audio recordings of *mōshiawase* in which the actor participated in another role, or video recordings of a staged performance. Furthermore, video tutorials on how to perform dances are increasingly available online, yet these are geared toward amateur practitioners, not professional actors. Nonetheless, videos can serve as aids for those parts of the *katatsuke* that are unclear.

3.4.1.2 Spaces

Shite actors with access to a nō stage use it to rehearse, but any square surface that permits sliding one's feet when walking is suitable for practice. Some actors might have a practice stage or simply a room with a wooden floor in their house, others might rent a separate space. Mirrors are not strictly necessary but are found in some spaces. Actors do not wear costumes and masks in training;

---

35   Chant books differ from school to school. Some, such as those of the Hōshō school, are geared to amateur practitioners, offering more commentaries or instructions for chant and dance.

therefore, nō stage pillars are not required for reference in this context. Rather, they rely on their knowledge of the play to imagine where the other actors would stand or sit onstage in the actual performance. Furthermore, stage properties are generally not employed in training, except in some cases for the platforms (*ichijōdai*), which can be used to practice particularly demanding or potentially dangerous movements such as climbing steps or jumps.

3.4.2   Preexisting Knowledge

For adult actors, the preparation for a play begins before the role is decided. It is likely that actors are already familiar with the play: they may have been involved variously in other productions of the same piece and in several different capacities. If they have sung in the chorus for the play, they would have already memorized the text and, therefore, the musical score. They may also have watched the performance from backstage or from the stage while serving as stage assistant and would be acquainted with the entrances and exits, costume changes, positioning of properties, and other aspects of the staging. During the *mōshiawase*, they might have heard senior actors give advice and discuss diverse aspects of the play. Or, they might have performed excerpts from the play as *shimai* or as *maibayashi*, giving them practical, firsthand knowledge of part of the *shite* chant and, most importantly, of the *kata* performed by the *shite*.

Even in instances when the play is rarely performed, and the actor has no direct experience of taking any role in it, dramaturgical and performance conventions permit actors a degree of flexibility. This allows them to guess how a certain role should be performed and to associate it with more familiar plays. It could be argued that what most characterizes a play are not the details of the story, but rather the role type enacted by the *shite* (i.e., warrior, god, madwoman). This in turn will determine all aspects of the staging, from mask to costume combination, from posture and movement to the kind of instrumental dance to be executed. Ultimately, the preparation for a specific play starts at the very beginning of an actor's life and progresses through the accumulation of knowledge and experience.

3.4.2.1   Chant and Dance Practice

The preparation for participation in a play, regardless of the role, starts with the memorization of the chant. A well-prepared actor will remember the lines of all the roles, including those of the *waki* (also printed in the *utaibon*) and of the *ai kyōgen*, if there is a scene in which he interacts with the *shite*. Moreover, since chant is inextricably linked with music, actors should have the capacity to sing while concurrently internalizing the drum and flute music, as this is necessary to understand the *ma*, the rests between sentences (see ch. 2 *Performance*, 2.5).

Once the chant is memorized, *tachi-geiko*, the practice of actors adding movement to the chant, can begin (fig. 3.6). At this stage actors would have

FIGURE 3.6 *Shite* actor Kanze Yoshimasa preparing for a performance. Yarai Nōgakudō, Tokyo. 2021
PHOTO: YAMANAKA REIKO

FIGURE 3.7 Kyōgen actors Ōkura Noriyoshi, Ōkura Yatarō, and Zenchiku Daijirō preparing for the revived play *Kakuregasa*. Ōkura Kichijirō's practice space. 2017
PHOTO: YAMANAKA REIKO

a mental image of the play in all its parts, and therefore it is possible to practice alone. Dressed in kimono and *hakama* (a type of pleated wide trouser), they go through the parts they perform, perhaps skipping or abbreviating sections such as long instrumental sequences. Kyōgen actors follow a similar training process (fig. 3.7). Except for young actors preparing for their first masked role (*hatsu omote*), masks are generally not used in training. There are various reasons for this, including reducing the risk of accidentally damaging precious masks during training. Actors become accustomed to wearing masks through onstage performance, thus justifying the need to take numerous *tsure* roles during and even after their apprentice years. This also points to how masks are considered as having a symbolic value that exceeds that of a mere stage property.

Instrumental dance sections (*mai*) can be practiced by uttering *shōga*, a solfège that reproduces the sound of the flute, while dancing. If the play involves one or more *tsure*, or a *kokata* interacting with the *shite*, it may be necessary to organize collective practice sessions involving the other roles. When the actors have memorized both chant and movements, they may ask a senior to watch them in order to receive feedback. The process of preparing for a *shite* role therefore consists of the study of the play and a combination of different types of knowledge, some of which are acquired in part before the period of training begins. The actor resorts to both memory and imagination in the construction of the role.

3.4.3 *The* Mōshiawase

A few days before the actual performance, the *shite*, *waki*, musicians, members of the chorus and stage assistants assemble for the *mōshiawase*, a single, partial run through without masks and costumes. The purpose of this is to ensure that what they have practiced separately will fit well together. This is particularly important because of the combinations of styles that might be encountered onstage. As actors and musicians belong to different schools and train separately, it may be necessary for them to check passages that otherwise could be interpreted variously depending on the *ryūgi*. For example, *kotsuzumi* musicians of the Ōkura or Kō schools might play a different pattern for the same chant passage from the same play.

The *mōshiawase* is also crucial because of the possible staging variations that may be adopted. Besides conventional variants (*kogaki*), some parts of the play might be modified depending on the performer's individual interpretation. For instance, *shite* and musicians could opt for a different number of repetitions of drum patterns in an entrance music sequence (see ch. 2 *Performance*, 2.5).

During the *mōshiawase* participants may wear informal cotton kimono and *hakama* and might bring scores or chant books onstage that they can refer to when not engaged in performance (fig. 3.8). Apart from plays in which the interaction of the *ai kyōgen* with the other characters is crucial to the development of the action, kyōgen actors do not take part in the *mōshiawase*. Introductory sections featuring a solo narration by the *waki* may also be skipped because they do not involve an interaction between characters. With these cuts taken into account, the play is usually rehearsed in a single run. At the end of the rehearsal, the *shite* returns to the stage where they receive or exchange (depending on seniority) opinions with the musicians, the chorus leader (*jigashira*), or the main stage assistant (*hon kōken*).

Most significantly, the *mōshiawase* constitutes the only chance when the actor can make final adjustments before the actual performance. These may be stage directions or suggestions given by the *shite* or by other senior members of the cast on how to perform certain passages that are open to interpretation. As noted above, chant books and other scores used by the performers are

FIGURE 3.8   Kongō-school actor Udaka Michishige as *shite* in the *mōshiawase* of the play *Tōru*. National Noh Theatre, Tokyo. 2012
PHOTO: FABIO MASSIMO FIORAVANTI

not exhaustive; instead, they offer minimal indications that can be interpreted varyingly. Since nō plays are staged only once, for an actor, the performance day of a certain play could be the first and last opportunity to partake in the staging of a given play.

Nō performances do not require light, amplification, projections, or stage technicians, resulting in the *mōshiawase* being a rather intimate session while at the same time maintaining the rigor and tension that is always visible on a nō stage. Because there are no directors or conductors in nō, authority and responsibility are distributed according to role and rank. Although the *shite* is the fulcrum of performance, the presence of a more senior performer will shift the center of authority to them. In any case, the adjustments suggested following the rehearsal are the result of an exchange of ideas rather than instructions from a single individual. After the rehearsal, the performers will have only a few days to absorb and put into place what they may have learned during the *mōshiawase* before the day of the performance.

Considering the preparation process that has been described, it may be said that nō is "over practiced" as much as it is "under-rehearsed." Professionals dedicate their entire lives to the study of their art, continuously practicing the same repertory of plays, which in turn consist of a limited set of preset choreography modules or musical patterns. At the same time, they only meet for a single, partial rehearsal. For seasoned performers, the repertory becomes second nature, rendering a longer process of collective rehearsals unnecessary. Young performers, however, will be motivated to study hard to prepare for what will be their only chance to rehearse with the rest of the cast. This peculiar preparation system is also a way to preserve the "freshness" of the encounter between performers, and the positive tension that is generated as a result.

3.4.4 *The Performance Day*

On the day of the performance, apprentices or other trainees reach the theatre early. They make sure that the stage properties that were used during the *mōshiawase* are in place or ready to be employed. Masks, costumes, fans, and other accessories are taken from the storage room and lined up on the shelves in the room reserved for the *shite*. The backstage of a nō theatre consists of a series of contiguous rooms fitted with nothing but tatami mats and low tables. Even though all rooms look alike, they are assigned to different types of performers. That closest to the mirror room (*kagami no ma*) is occupied by the actor performing the role of *shite* or *tsure*. The other rooms are used by other performers, in order of proximity to the mirror room: *shite* actors acting as chorus or as *kōken*, *waki*, and kyōgen. The room farthest from the mirror room is occupied by the musicians. The duties of *shite* trainees include the setting up of the charcoal brazier necessary to dry the drumheads of the *ōtsuzumi*, often in a location near the room used by the musicians. Since drying the skin drumheads takes up to several hours depending on the season, the *ōtsuzumi* player or their assistant is often the first musician to reach the theatre.

Etiquette is strictly respected backstage at the *nōgakudō*. For example, upon arriving the theatre, performers visit the rooms where actors and musicians may already be preparing, in order to greet them. When meeting for the first time in the corridor that connects the various rooms, it is customary to kneel to the ground, not just bow while standing. The manner in which actors sit in a room also reflects hierarchy, with older actors taking their places at the back of the room, while trainees will be closer to the entrance.

Most performers will reach the theatre about one hour or ninety minutes before the beginning of the performance. The three drummers need some time to assemble their drums, which they always bring completely or partly disassembled. *Shite*, *waki*, and kyōgen require time to put on their costumes, although this is done as late as possible due to their heaviness and bulkiness. Actors also help each other in donning their respective costumes. This is unlike other forms of traditional theatre, such as kabuki, in which specialists prepare the costumes and dress the actors. Some assistants to the *shite* appear onstage, and trainees of *waki* and kyōgen may also accompany actors with whom they are associated to assist them with "backstage work" (*gakuya-bataraki*). This includes costuming or operating the five-color curtain (*agemaku*) and small side sliding door (*kirido*).

Depending on the performance venue, costumes might either be personally transported by the *shite* actor, or securely packed in suitcases and shipped via express courier. Masks, which are traditionally preserved in silk bags enclosed within wooden boxes, are usually transported in cases separate from other items. The actor in the role of *shite* is often directly responsible for their transport and will carry them in a handheld cubic suitcase.

Among the most important tasks of the actors in the role of *shite* is to check the mask they will use. Each *shite* actor has a set of fabric or paper pads called *men ate* that are attached to the back of the mask with glue or, recently, double-sided adhesive tape. Actors apply the pads and check that the mask has the desired angle when put on. After this, they change into their costume undergarments, and prepare to be dressed. Once the actor has donned all parts of the costume, including the wig, they sit on a stool, ready to move to the mirror room. No other dressed character is allowed to sit backstage. This is a phase of transformation, during which the *shite* typically does not speak unless they need water or a towel, and for this reason at least one stage assistant remains on standby to attend to the requirements of the *shite*. Meanwhile, the *waki* and kyōgen actors get dressed.

The *shite* moves to the mirror room and sits in front of the mirror. All members of the cast assemble in the room and in the adjacent corridor and salute the *shite* before taking their places. At this stage, the *shite* only responds with a light bow, a gesture that affirms their central role both onstage and backstage. The chorus assembles in the room behind the *kirido*, while the musicians sit in the mirror room and play the tuning sequence (*oshirabe*). At their signal, the curtain is pulled to one side, and the musicians enter the stage through the *hashigakari*. As the flute player reaches the "*shite* pillar" (*shite-bashira*), the *kirido* slides open, the chorus members enter the stage and take their place.

The lights go out in the mirror room as the first actors, usually the *waki* (sometimes the *tsure*), stand behind the curtain, ready to command that it be lifted. The *shite* typically dons the mask as late as possible. Before doing so, they look at it and bow to it. Then, a stage assistant will tie it behind the head, checking the height (*o-atari*) and tightness (*oshimari*) of the knot with the *shite*. The transformation complete, the *shite* is left alone to contemplate the image reflected in the mirror, listening to the sounds coming from the stage.

Finally, the *shite* stands behind the curtain, before uttering "*omaku*" ("the curtain"), which signals to the two stage assistants to lift the five-color curtain using two long bamboo poles.

3.4.5 *Production*

In nōgaku, performers do not form troupes or companies, neither are they are bound by contracts with an agency or manager. Rather, they are individually engaged for one-off events that are usually arranged by other nō performers, usually *shite* actors. A nō performance typically features one or more nō plays, accompanied by one kyōgen play, as well as by excerpts performed in recital style, such as *shimai*. The following section introduces five kinds of performance format: *ryūgi*-sponsored series, self-sponsored, NTT productions, amateur recitals, and commissioned. The organizational and managerial aspects of a performance, including booking, payments, and advertisement, depend on the type of event.

The art production of staging a play is fairly straightforward. It consists of choosing the play, deciding the variant (see ch. 2 *Performance*, 2.12), and selecting a cast. Each *ryūgi* performs the same repertory in a unique style, and as a result the combination of performers belonging to various schools will affect the aesthetics of a performance. Yet, casting is not always an artistic choice, but rather a matter of availability, convenience, or custom.

3.4.5.1 Economics of Production

Shite actors may appear onstage in different capacities (*shite, tsure, ji utai, kōken*) and in various kinds of performance events. Each of these are distinct engagements for which they receive a range in the level of remuneration (or in some cases, none at all).[36] The type of event also determines the fee that will be paid to the performer. The lowest paid jobs are the *ryūgi*-sponsored series, which are organized to showcase various actors on a rotating basis; the low fees therefore reflect the spirit of mutual support that underpins the performers' establishment. By contrast, the highest paying jobs are amateur recitals and commissioned events. The farther from the center of the professional community, the higher the fee. It should be noted that the standard remuneration, determined by the Nohgaku Performers' Association, also depends on the

---

36   There are also a number of *shite* actors who have received an official license to teach by the *iemoto* and are active as professional teachers, mostly as instructors of *utai* (nō chant), but who do not take part in stage activities. Though licensed, many of these are not members of the Nohgaku Performers' Association, therefore blurring the distinction between the professional and the amateur.

region, with differences between Tokyo or Kyoto-Osaka area. Fees have also changed in the past and they will probably continue to change in the future. Performance fees do not provide sufficient earnings for most nō performers, who resort to teaching amateurs in order to sustain their livelihood. From a fiscal point of view, they are freelance artists, not bound by contracts with a company or a theatre.

Shite actors produce the majority of nō performance events, which may not necessarily be a remunerative enterprise if revenues depend solely on ticket sales. An important function of a performance in which these *shite* producers will appear in the main role is as the promotion of their own activities—in other words, spectators enjoying the performance may become supporters, may purchase tickets to other events, or may begin study with them, thus becoming a relatively stable source of income.

Waki actors are constantly hired to perform *waki* and *waki tsure* roles. For some, this generates a sufficient source of income. Sometimes *waki* also teach nō chant to amateurs, but, unlike *shite* actors, they do not teach dance, and their practice groups are generally smaller. The situation of kyōgen actors is similar to *shite* actors, although independently sponsored kyōgen performances are fewer than the ones organized by *shite*, and kyōgen actors are frequently hired to play in *shite*-sponsored performances. Kyōgen actors often teach non-professionals in order to support their own activities. Musicians are employed by *shite* and sometimes by kyōgen actors to perform in their events. They, too, teach amateurs. The study of drums necessarily entails learning the chant section that the instruments accompany, and this results in amateurs often studying both forms.

3.4.5.2   *Ryūgi*-Sponsored Series

Each *shite* school produces a series of performances, are referred to as *teiki* or *teirei* ("regular") since they occur on a regular, usually monthly basis (table 3.6). *Shite* school subgroups also produce regular events, such as the *Tessen kai teiki kōen* (Kanze Tetsunojō subgroup, held monthly), the *Umewaka kai teishiki nō* (Umewaka Minoru subgroup, every two months), the *Kyūkokai teiki kōen* (Kanze Yoshiyuki subgroup, monthly), or the *Katayama teiki nō* (Katayama Kurōemon subgroup, monthly). Each of these events typically features two or three nō plays and one kyōgen with the possible addition of short *shimai* dances. To be recognized by the Nohgaku Performers' Association as a "regular" series, there must be at least four events a year. These are usually held at the main *nōgakudō* managed by the school. Today, the Konparu school does not have a representative *nōgakudō*, and their regular performances are held

TABLE 3.6 Main performance series produced by the five schools of *shite* actors

School	Event name	Location	Frequency
Kanze	*Kanze-kai teiki nō*	Kanze Nōgakudō, Tokyo	Monthly
Konparu	*Konparu-kai teiki nō*	National Noh Theatre, Tokyo	7 times annually
Hōshō	*Tsukinami nō*	Hōshō Nōgakudō, Tokyo	Monthly
Kongō	*Kongō teiki nō*	Kongō Nōgakudō, Kyoto	10 times annually
Kita	*Kita-ryū jishu kōen*	Kita Nōgakudō, Tokyo	Monthly

Note: Data from 2022

at the NNT. Unlike other schools, which have their main performance series in Tokyo, the Kongō school holds theirs in Kyoto, where the *iemoto* is based.

It is impossible for large schools to have all their actors appear onstage in only twelve occasions. To compensate for this, the Kanze and Hōshō schools organize two series, distinguished as "junior" and "senior." The former includes, for example, the *Araiso nō* (Kanze) series or the *Go'un-kai* (Hōshō) series. As actors performing in "junior" series become more experienced, they will be upgraded to the "senior" series when a place becomes vacant with the retirement or death of an older actor.

Kyōgen schools and their subgroups also produce series showcasing kyōgen plays. These are staged less frequently than *shite ryūgi*-sponsored performances. Izumi- or Ōkura-school events usually occur four or more times a year. Typically, kyōgen performances are organized and performed by single kinship groups, such as the Nomura family (Izumi school) or the Shigeyama family (Ōkura school). Families also produce events with group members associated with a family who are not necessarily blood relatives, such as the *Yorozu kyōgen* series, produced by the Nomura Man subgroup of the Izumi school. In recent years, new types of performance produced by young actors are becoming increasingly popular, as seen in the *Ōkura goke kyōgen*, which features young actors from the five families (*goke*) of the Ōkura school, or the *Tachiai kyōgen*, in which young actors of the Izumi and Ōkura stage plays on the same day.

In *ryūgi*-sponsored series, the program for a particular year is usually decided about one year in advance. The general principle according to which series of events are planned is that of assuring a variety of both repertory and performers. Although repertory and staging conventions are fixed, performance variants and individual styles transmitted in the different schools and families allow for a great variety of combinations. Factors to be considered when scheduling performances include seasonality, popularity, and on how often plays have been performed in past series. In cases when two or more nō plays are performed on the same day, the organizer will choose plays based on diversity, attempting to balance play category, theme, *kurai* ("weight" or "gravitas"), running time, and other aspects of performances. Generally, an annual program tends to mix common and rare plays, trying to satisfy the occasional theatregoer and the connoisseur spectator. One additional reason for staging less well-known plays is to keep their memory alive among performers, so that the senior actors who have performed them can share their experience with younger actors. Certain plays, which are still considered in the current repertory (*genkō kyoku*), may be revived after long periods of not being performed. Especially difficult plays, such as those classified as *omonarai* (e.g., *Dōjōji* or *Obasute*), are not included in regular event series.

One purpose of *ryūgi*-sponsored events is to highlight actors belonging to the same performance group, giving each a chance to appear onstage before an audience of loyal subscribers. In the case of a series produced by a *shite ryūgi* or subgroup, the leader (e.g., the *iemoto*) decides on the assignment of the roles and the hiring of *waki*, musicians, and kyōgen. The *shite* and *tsure* roles are appointed on a rotating basis, but that also depends on experience and seniority. It is important to avoid having actors take the same role in the same play twice. As a rule, the organizers ensure that actors capable of performing *shite* roles appear, albeit in capacities that are appropriate to their experience. While seasoned actors are often given the roles of chorus leader and main stage assistant, younger actors tend to serve in the front row of the chorus or work as backstage assistants. The inclusive nature of this system permits the audience, usually composed of regular subscribers, to appreciate a range of abilities, from the spontaneous freshness of an inexperienced young performer to the refined elegance of an elderly one.

Producers also make sure that *waki*, musicians, and kyōgen performers are proportionately represented, with a balance between younger and older artists. These are not chosen based on the individual preferences of the producer, but rather on relationships already established with the *shite* group that has hired them and may depend on the regional availability. For example, Kyoto-based *shite* actors tend to engage musicians in the area comprising Osaka, Kyoto, and Nagoya (see table 3.5).

Kyōgen actors are hired to perform the *ai kyōgen* role within a nō play and to stage independent kyōgen plays between two nō. Usually, the *shite* group producing the event communicates which nō play will be performed and will settle on one *ai kyōgen* and one *hon kyōgen* (independent kyōgen play). In this case, the kyōgen group receiving the request will decide on the kyōgen play, the performers, and who will be the *ai* in the nō. In a second scenario, the organizing group only requests a specific actor to take the main kyōgen role (also called *shite*) in the *hon kyōgen*, but lets the kyōgen actors decide everything else. In a third scenario, the *shite* group sends a request detailing the play and all cast members. The producer will also relay which kyōgen was done in the previous months in order to avoid repetition. *Hon kyōgen* in *shite*-organized events are normally around twenty to twenty-five minutes long. Like nō, *hon kyōgen* are chosen according to seasonality.

The handling of costumes and masks depends on specific agreements within the group of *shite* actors. In most instances, the actors borrow costumes and masks from the affiliated group arranging the performance, although this may not apply to actors with an especially precious mask and costume collection, such as that of Umewaka Minoru IV and Kanze Tetsunojō IX. In the past, *shite* families owned costumes for both *shite* and *waki*, but today *waki* and kyōgen actors tend to bring their own. Large and small properties are kept in the theatre storage rooms and managed by *shite* actors, who are responsible for preparing them, usually before the rehearsal, and who disassemble them following the performance.

Since *ryūgi*-sponsored performances are a chance to showcase the achievements of its members, *shite* actors involved in these events do not receive any remuneration for their performance. On one hand, their work is understood as a duty; on the other, their participation provides opportunities to take the *shite* role without having to bear production costs individually, which is the case of self-sponsored series.[37]

Shite actors are also responsible for selling tickets to the *ryūgi*-sponsored events in which they participate. Each actor has a quota to sell, which may depend on what role they take: actors taking the *shite* role in a certain performance may be allotted a greater number of tickets. Depending on the arrangement between the organizer and the performers, they may be expected to personally supplement any unsold tickets. Actors typically sell tickets to their amateur students, who may in turn advertise the performance to others or purchase additional tickets for friends and relatives. Aficionados often purchase annual subscriptions, for which they receive the tickets to all the performances and sometimes added perks. The subscription system ensures the organizing group a relatively stable annual income. It is estimated that around 70 percent of the tickets for regular series are generally secured through this system, while

---

37 In regular series produced by a performer group, the actor taking the *shite* or *tsure* role may be asked by the organizer to pay a "participation fee," although this depends on the case.

the remaining 30 percent can be purchased independently by occasional spectators either through the theatre's booking system or at the door.

3.4.5.3　Self-Sponsored Events

Individual nō performers may produce self-sponsored events that can be occasional or repeated every year—that is, less than four times a year in accordance with the regulations of to the Nohgaku Professionals' Association. Self-sponsored events often consist of one or two nō plays, one kyōgen play, and other excerpts, and are also used to stage *hiraki* plays, or to celebrate important anniversaries.

Hayashi musicians produce independent events in which they invite *shite* and *waki* actors to perform full plays chosen by them that are especially interesting from a musical standpoint, such as the Hirotada no Kai by the *ōtsuzumi* player Kamei Hirotada of the Kadono school or the Kyoto-based nō musicians' group Dōmei kai. There are likewise performance series produced by *waki* actors, such as the Kenshū kai by Obinata Hiroshi of the Hōshō school, and in these the *waki* actor often chooses plays in which the *waki* role is particularly dominant. Kyōgen actors, too, also organize self-sponsored performance series, such as the Chū no Kai produced by Shigeyama Chūzaburō.

Self-sponsored events are produced by the individual performer who will take the main role in them. With a *shite*-sponsored performance, the actor arranging it will have relative freedom regarding the choice of play to be staged, though younger actors may need to seek permission to perform from elders or from the *iemoto*, especially if the play has a high *kurai*, as is the case with *omonarai* plays. Actors typically use independent events to stage especially challenging plays, sometimes performing them with performance variants (*kogaki*). Newly written nō plays (*shinsaku nō*), or revived nō plays (*fukkyoku nō*) are also often staged on such occasions.

The actor is also free to choose the cast outside the practice of rotation and inclusivity that is privileged in the regular series. It is not uncommon, however, for a *shite* to involve the *waki*, musicians, and kyōgen with whom they have established a relationship in different performances. Independent performance casting choices are deliberate, and they may signify the mutual friendship or trust between artists.

Independent events may feature a *hon kyōgen* with a thematic relation with the nō play. For example, if the nō play poetically depicts a woman's lament over unrequited love, the kyōgen may comically portray the complex relations between husband and wife. The kyōgen *Kane no ne* may be chosen to accompany *Dōjōji*, as the central motif of a bell is present in both pieces. Another pairing is the kyōgen *Kaminari*, featuring a thunder god with a backache, performed alongside the nō *Kamo*, which centers on the rain-sending deity Wake ikazuchi. If the *shite* organizing the event owns the necessary masks and costumes, they are usually free to use them, otherwise they may need to borrow them from another actor or family.[38] Depending on the budget of the producer, new costumes or masks may be purchased on this occasion for special anniversary events or for *shinsaku nō*.

Self-sponsored events tend to be more expensive undertakings for the producer. For example, all *shite* actors belonging to the same group as the producer, must be paid. *Waki*, musicians, and kyōgen charge a fee set by the Nohgaku Performers' Association, which is usually higher than that paid in regular series.[39] Furthermore, the plays in these performances tend to be of a higher *kurai* or they feature performance variants for which *waki*, musicians, and kyōgen charge additional fees. Depending on the situation, the *shite* may also have to pay the rental of the theatre hall, costumes, and masks. Conversely, the organizer will retain all ticket sales revenues in self-sponsored events, in addition to any possible external funding. Actors often form connections with a funding body or location, such as a theatre hall or temple, and regularly perform there. Often these connections are exclusive—that is, the same actor will perform at a certain event every year.

The actor producing the event is also responsible for selling tickets, without being able to enforce a quota on other actors. Again, ticket sales depend largely on the amateur students of the organizer, who might have an even greater responsibility in filling the theatre. While this may be relatively easy for established actors with a large number of followers, it may prove challenging for emerging actors. The success of this kind of event depends on the ability of the actor to create a support group, typically by teaching amateurs or through outreach activities that can include workshops or lectures.

3.4.5.4 Kyōgen Self-Sponsored Events

Hon kyōgen performances differ from nō performances in that they mostly require the presence of actors belonging to the same specialization (i.e., they do not require the presence of *waki* and musicians).[40] Kyōgen self-sponsored events may feature exclusively kyōgen plays, or both kyōgen and nō plays. Kyōgen plays chosen on these occasions may too long to be performed

---

38 The fact that masks and costumes owned by actors can be used freely is not to be taken for granted. Depending on the case, actors may be asked to borrow masks and costumes from the *iemoto* or other high-ranking family.

39 An exception is represented by actors designed as a Living National Treasure (*ningen kokuhō*), whose fees are more expensive, regardless of the performance type.

40 Some plays, such as those belonging to the *waki kyōgen* category, feature musicians.

alongside nō plays in events organized by *shite*. Which *hon kyōgen* plays to perform with the one or more nō plays is generally decided after the selection of the nō. Sometimes nō and kyōgen plays are thematically related, as in *shite* self-sponsored events.

Like nō, the kyōgen repertory is subdivided into categories. When several plays are staged on the same day, they are presented in the order of *waki kyōgen*, followed by *daimyō kyōgen*, *Tarō Kaja mono*, and so on. A play with many characters appearing simultaneously onstage would conclude the day. Recently, events tend to have plays that share the same theme, such as *sake*, relationships between a man and woman, or medieval poems. It has become customary that, if a play with *ashirai* (music) is going to be staged, musicians are also asked to perform instrumental pieces (*su-bayashi*).

3.4.5.5 National Noh Theatre Events

The state-owned National Noh Theatre (NNT), part of a system of national theatres managed by the Japan Arts Council, normally produces four performance events every month. In addition, a special performance is produced on the last Saturday or Sunday of months with five weekends.

Since the NNT is independent from performer groups and associations, its producers seek to adopt an equal stance toward the various schools. Members from all over the country are invited to perform, and schools are represented proportionally according to their size. Consequently, *shite* from the Kanze school, by far the largest *shite* school, tend to have the greatest representation onstage. While parity is emphasized, *waki*, musicians, and kyōgen actors graduating from the NNT program are given special consideration when a play is cast. Fees are paid from the NNT's own budget, in accordance with the standard established by the Nohgaku Performers' Association.

The NNT produces the following types of events:

1. Regular series (*teirei kōen*): every first Wednesday and third Friday of the month. The program consists of one nō and one kyōgen. Plays are chosen among those that are easily accessible to a non-specialized audience;
2. Popularization series (*fukyū kōen*): every second Saturday of the month. The program consists of one nō and one kyōgen. These performances are preceded by explanations of the plays and the salient features of their staging;
3. Special series (*tokubetsu kōen*): every fifth Saturday or Sunday. The program consists of two nō and one kyōgen. Very challenging plays are chosen, and usually the cast is composed of famous performers. Tickets for these tend to be more expensive than usual; special series performances are staged exclusively in those months with five weekends;

4. Themed series (*kikaku kōen*): they generally take place on the fourth week of the month and may occur on different days. Plays are chosen based a selected theme with the aim of raising the interest of the audience by approaching nō from multiple perspectives. The theme may also influence the choice of other plays performed in this month, in particular, the "special series" plays. The emphasis is not so much on the difficulty of the play or to the level of the performers but rather on the topic chosen. For example, April 2018 was dedicated to plays related to the monk-poet Saigyō (1118–1190), as this year corresponded to the 900th anniversary of Saigyō's birth. Both the April special series performance on the fifth weekend of the month and the themed series performance focused on plays related to the poet.

In addition to the above, the NNT also produces the following:

1. Special themed series (*tokubetsu kikaku kōen*): these events are not held regularly. Plays chosen are newly written or revamped. In some cases, nō or kyōgen plays are staged together with other genres;
2. Kyōgen events (*kyōgen no kai*): every fourth Friday of the month. These events focus on kyōgen, with three plays staged in every performance;
3. Nōgaku appreciation classes (*nōgaku kanshō kyōshitsu*). These are special events for students, generally taking place on weekdays in June, with morning and afternoon programs. Nō and kyōgen plays easily accessible to first timers are preceded by explanations of the pieces;
4. "Discover Noh & Kyōgen" series. These events target non-Japanese audiences. Information materials such as synopses and explanations are provided in various languages.

The calendar timeline for the year 2019 (from April 2019 to March 2020) serves as a reference for how performances are produced at the NNT:

- November 2017: drafting the program: which plays will be performed, and which main performers star in them. For newly written or revamped plays, an additional six-month advance may be necessary;
- December 2017–January 2018: NNT directors finalize the program;
- February or March 2018: NNT producers consult with a committee of specialists, generally composed of scholars;[41]
- April 2018–August 2018: NNT producers contact the performers and finalize the line-up for each play.

---

41 Since the National Noh Theatre is government funded, the supervision of a committee ensures that the selection of plays and performers is without bias.

3.4.5.6 Amateur Recitals

Shite, musicians, and kyōgen actors also produce public recitals for their amateur students, typically taking place once a year. Depending on the number of students, these events can last from the morning until the evening, featuring several *su-utai*, *shimai*, *maibayashi*, or even complete nō plays. As large amateur groups can include dozens of members, recitals can last up to eight hours. Because these are amateur events, entrance is free of charge, as stipulated by the regulations of the Nohgaku Performers' Association. Production costs are absorbed entirely by the amateurs participating in the event. One of the peculiarities of this kind of recital is that professional performers appear onstage together with amateurs. For example, an amateur taking the *shite* role in a *shimai* could be accompanied by a chorus of professionals. In the case of amateurs performing full performances, professional musicians, *waki*, and kyōgen actors will be hired. Amateur events are organized and supervised by professionals for their amateur students. In these performances, amateurs have the opportunity to mingle with professionals onstage, a luxury requiring high fees for the professionals.

3.4.5.7 Commissioned Events

On some occasions, external individuals or institutions, including local civil or religious organizations, television networks, newspapers, or schools, commission a performer, usually a *shite* actor, to arrange a performance event or a series of events. These might cater to a broader, more popular audience, and thus may feature easily accessible plays with familiar stories or characters, such as *Hagoromo* or *Funa Benkei*. For these kinds of commissioned events, the fees requested by the performers can be up to three times higher than those of *ryūgi*-sponsored and self-sponsored performances, making them the most remunerative for professionals. By contrast, events organized by groups of researchers and critics, such as the Hashi no Kai (1980–2003), or by newspaper companies as part of their cultural activities, such as Nikkei Noh (by the Nihon Keizai Shimbun), aim to provide high-quality performances by carefully selecting outstanding performers and plays.

3.4.6 Performance Venues

3.4.6.1 Nōgakudō

Most nō performances are staged at *nōgakudō*, buildings that, as explained above, often belong to, and are managed by *shite* actors. Dedicated buildings of this kind appeared after the Meiji Restoration of 1868, when, following a trend that had already emerged in the previous Edo period, the wooden nō stage topped with roof was placed within a theatre hall building. In the early twentieth century, lighting and Western-style seating were also introduced (see ch. 7 *Material Culture*, 7.5).

A typical *nōgakudō* hall is a simple square or rectangular hall in which the wooden stage structure occupies the bottom right of the hall, with the *hashigakari* stretching along the left wall (see ch. 2 *Nō Performance*, 2.2). The only direct connection between the stage and backstage are the curtain (*agemaku*) and the *kirido*, a small, low door at upstage left. There are no wings, lifts, trapdoors, or orchestra pit. This, along with the architectural features of the nō stage itself, makes the *nōgakudō* less versatile than other kinds of theatre halls.

The stage architecture of a *nōgakudō*, regardless of theatre venue, is essentially the same. Differences can be found in the design of the pine tree invariably painted on the *kagami ita* ("mirror board") backdrop. The area behind the *hashigakari* can also vary, sometimes imitating outdoor architectural elements, as can the stage size. The *hashigakari* is the one component that diverges the most in terms of length, usually between 11 and 13 meters (the NNT stage is almost 14 meters). Correspondingly, the three small pine trees positioned between the pillars along the bridgeway can be in pots or planted in the *shirasu* narrow bed of white pebbles that runs around the stage. When the bridge is very short, only two pines are installed. The stage is a flat surface, approximately 1 meter above the floor of the front rows in the audience.

The configuration and size of the audience seats may differ. Today, most theatres have armchairs. The smaller, private residential theatres described below may still have tatami mats and cushions. And while some theatres have a balcony that extends to face both stage front and side, in modern *nōgakudō* fitted with chairs, the seating area is often inclined toward the stage to facilitate the view. Seats are arranged in three main sectors: front (*shōmen*), side (*waki shōmen*), and corner (*naka shōmen*). The first row is about 2 to 3 meters from the stage; at the back of the hall some theatres have smaller booths, vestiges of the stage design from earlier periods. In addition, some theatres may also have a balcony along one or more sides of the hall. Complementing these primary sections, certain theaters may also feature a balcony, which can extend along one or multiple sides of the hall.

Modern nō stages feature light rigs under the stage ceiling, with additional rigs fitted against the theatre walls. Many theatres have a single light setting employed throughout the performance event, illuminating both stage and seating areas. In some theatres it has become standard practice to dim the lights on the audience seating area before the play begins. Nevertheless, lights on stage are fixed, uniformly illuminating all of the performance area. There are no projectors, and since nō performances are not amplified, nō halls do not have powerful speaker systems. Amplification is generally reserved for voice

FIGURE 3.9   The National Noh Theatre stage and seating area. A monitor displaying summaries and subtitles is lodged on the back of each seat
IMAGE COURTESY OF THE NATIONAL NOH THEATRE, TOKYO

announcements, although select performances may be recorded for archival or commercial use. The minimal audio and light requirements mean that there is no visible audio or light mixer in front of the stage. Some theatres have a booth for light switching or spoken announcements. Likewise, theatres are often only fitted with simple permanent video-recording equipment. Today, backstage cameras connected with monitors allow actors to see what is happening onstage. For example, a monitor is installed in the small room behind the *kirido*, prompting stage assistants when to open and close the low sliding door during performance. In the past, this was done by peeking through the lattice of the sliding door or by opening it slightly. This method can still be employed to make sure that the opening of the door is synchronized with the exit of the performers.

Unlike other traditional theatres, such as those for opera or bunraku, *nōgakudō* usually do not have subtitle or surtitle equipment. An exception to this is the NNT, where small screens displaying multilingual subtitles are lodged on the back of each seat (fig. 3.9). New systems for providing explanations of performances through handheld devices have been recently developed.

Finally, the *nōgakudō* staff normally consist of a few office workers who take care of administrative work and booking management. Additional staff may be helpers or cleaners.

3.4.6.2 *Ryūgi*-Managed Theatres

Most *shite* schools have established foundations and associations, such as Public Interest Incorporated Associations (*kōeki shadan hōjin*) or General Incorporated Associations (*ippan shadan hōjin*). These groups manage the theatres and the collections of costumes and masks. Different from individuals, associations and foundations are legally permitted to receive grants and donations.

Some *nōgakudō* belong to and are managed by the associations representing the five *shite* schools, and presently they include the Kanze Nōgakudō (Ginza, Tokyo), the Kyoto Kanze Kaikan (Okazaki, Kyoto), the Hōshō Nōgakudō (Suidōbashi, Tokyo), the Kongō Nōgakudō (Nakagyō-ku, Kyoto), and the Kita Nōgakudō (Meguro, Tokyo). The Konparu school holds its regular events at the NNT. Most *nōgakudō* are managed directly by *shite* actors. *Waki*, musicians, or kyōgen actors may own private stages for practice or research purposes, but they rarely own halls for public performances.[42] As noted above, this reflects the central role of *shite* groups in the production of a performance. Subgroups in each school also manage private halls, as seen with the Ōtsuki Nōgakudō in Osaka, managed by the Ōtsuki family (Kanze school), or the Yarai Nōgakudō in Tokyo, owned by the Kanze Yoshiyuki family line.

Privately owned *nōgakudō* are typically used as the primary venue for the regular performances of the groups that own them, be they an *iemoto* or a subgroup. It is also possible, however, for other nō performers to book them. Occasionally, these nō stages are rented for performances other than nō and can range from classical Japanese music to contemporary experimental performances. Educational events for schools or other groups are also held here, and rental prices in these instances usually depend on whether the producer of the event is a member of the Nohgaku Performers' Association. Prices for members tend to be lower.

---

42 Kyōgen actors of the Yamamoto Tōjirō lineage own the Suginami Nōgakudō, where they host public kyōgen performances.

3.4.6.3   Private Residential Stages

It is not uncommon for nō actors to have stages built in their residences. While some are simple platforms that reproduce the surface of the stage and are mostly used for private practice and occasionally amateur recitals, others are complete structures, designed for public performances. These may also be referred to as *nōgakudō*. Examples of this kind of *nōgakudō* are the Ōshima Nōgakudō in Fukuyama, Hiroshima Prefecture, owned by the Ōshima family (Kita school), or the Kawamura Nō Butai in Kyoto, owned by the Kawamura family (Kanze school), the latter of which still retains its traditional seating of tatami mats instead of Western-style seating.

3.4.6.4   Third-Party (Private or Public) Nō Stages

Some *nōgakudō* are owned by local or national administrations, or by companies. Examples include the National Noh Theatre in Tokyo (state-owned), the Cerulean Tower Nōgakudō (Tōkyū Corporation, Shibuya, Tokyo), the Toyota City Concert Hall–Nohgakudo (Toyota Municipality), or the Nagoya Noh Theater (Nagoya Municipality). These venues can be large or small, and they host performances by any school since they are not owned or managed by *shite* actors.

3.4.6.5   Other Venues

Temples, shrines, outdoor temporary stages, theatre halls, and banquet halls in hotels may be equipped with a permanent nō stage that is often used for different kinds of performances or rituals. Nō is also performed on temporary stages, erected for a specific performance, and on modern proscenium-arch theatre stages, over which is laid a platform recreating the surface of a nō stage and its *hashigakari*. But nō can be performed virtually anywhere as long as actors have a smooth surface upon which they can slide their feet. An exception are the performances known as *shiba nō*, which are performed on the lawn and therefore reminiscent of ancient performance forms.

3.4.7   *Nōgaku Theatregoing*

As discussed above, a single nōgaku event normally comprises multiple performances, possibly with the addition of excerpts such as *shimai* or *maibayashi*. Most nō performances take place on weekends, often on Sunday afternoons, but there are also all-day and evening events. The average length of an afternoon event is between four and five hours; in the evening they can be as short as two hours. All-day performances are less frequent and may be up to eight hours long.

3.4.7.1   Advertisement

Compared with other forms of theatre, nō productions are not advertised broadly and usually not outside circles of enthusiasts. While posters or pamphlets for special performance events might be seen at public locations, including temples or municipal halls, regularly scheduled and privately sponsored performances are seldom marketed broadly. Traditional, yet commercially managed kabuki, promotes its performances with TV commercials or even vans with large placards. Nō and kyōgen base most of their advertisement activities on leaflets that can be found at the nō theatres, public buildings, or universities. Sometimes patrons hang a poster for a performance outside their homes or shops as a means to show support for specific actors.

Nō advertisements rarely feature the faces of performers. Unlike kabuki, whose actors regularly appear in blockbuster films and television commercials, it is not customary for nō actors to use their physical appearance or charisma to attract the general audience. With the exception of highly renowned individuals occasionally covered in newspapers, the names and faces of most nō actors are unknown to those who are not frequent nō theatregoers. Moreover, nō advertisements may be difficult to understand for people unfamiliar with nō, as they often do not have photos, but abstract or decorative designs with indirect references to the plays they advertise (see fig. 3.9).

That said, in recent years, there has been a greater push to disseminate nō to a broader public through the internet and social media. Groups of performers have websites to publicize their activities. Blogs or social networks are valuable tools for sharing updates, often enriched with photographs or videos. Some performers, especially young actors and musicians, also take advantage of online video streaming channels such YouTube to showcase their training classes or to advertise forthcoming performances.

Despite these developments, currently there is no official single site that spectators can consult to find information about nō performances. Some websites are maintained by enthusiasts, such as the privately sponsored *the-noh.com* or *Nōgaku kōen jōhō*, and they provide a performance calendar divided by region. In both, performance information is based on text rather than visuals. Furthermore, as most of these websites are only in Japanese, it can be challenging for non-Japanese speakers to locate performance information online. In recent times, however, there have been growing efforts to provide foreign audiences with information in English about performance schedules.

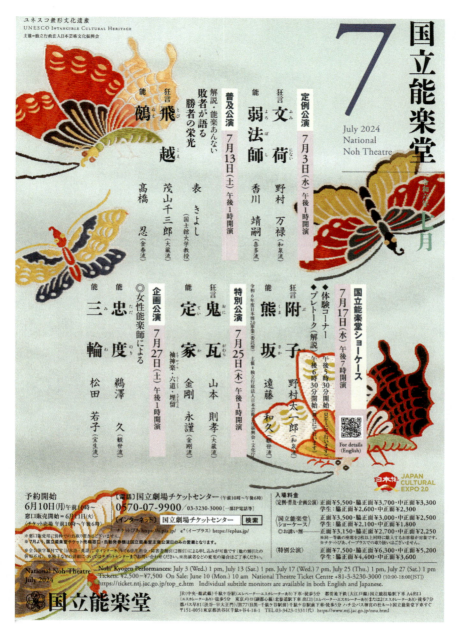

FIGURE 3.10   National Noh Theatre monthly performance series. July 2024
IMAGE COURTESY OF THE NATIONAL NOH THEATRE, TOKYO

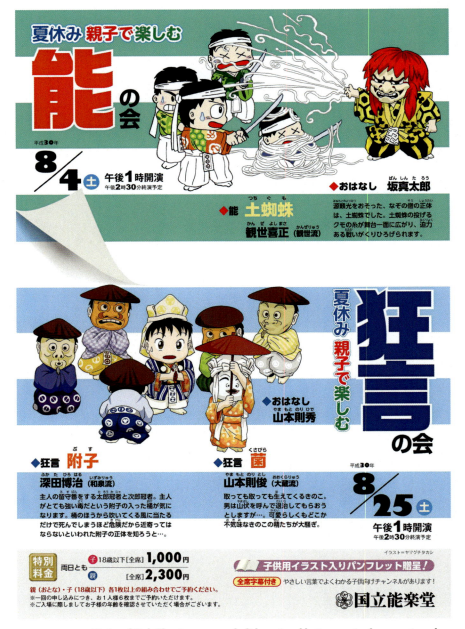

FIGURE 3.11   National Noh Theatre summer holiday nō and kyōgen series for parents and children. August 2018
IMAGE COURTESY OF THE NATIONAL NOH THEATRE, TOKYO

3.4.7.2 Tickets and Seating

Ticket prices depend on the performance. As of 2023, the average price for a regular performance is around 5,000 yen. Tickets for special events, such as the performance of a *hiraki* play (e.g., *Dōjōji* or *Obasute*), which normally features high-ranking performers, may cost up to 10,000 yen or more, depending on the seating area. With very few exceptions, tickets can only be purchased for the entire performance day, and not just for a single play within the program. Students are generally entitled to a discount.

Some events are sponsored by institutions such the Japan Foundation or the Japan Arts Council, thus the comparatively lower ticket prices. Tickets to NNT productions are usually cheaper than those for performances produced by individual performers. Arranged in ascending order of cost, the options available are: front seats, side seats, middle seats, and balcony seats. Some events may have a range of price tiers depending on the proximity of the seats to the stage.

3.4.7.3 Purchasing Tickets

There are a number of ways to buy tickets, depending on the performance. As venues and producers are often separate entities, there is no centralized booking system. Many regular nō theatregoers subscribe to a yearly program, and subscriptions might give patrons perks such as extra tickets or discounts. It is possible to subscribe to diverse performance types, from school-sponsored events to performance series. While it is customary for amateur students to purchase subscriptions or tickets to the performances in which their instructors are involved, regular spectators may also buy tickets this way. Amateur students may purchase several of them in advance, which they sometimes resell to acquaintances. They often attend as many of their teachers' performances as possible and may buy tickets for shows they are unable to attend, gifting them to friends or relatives to support their mentors financially.

In recent times, performers have started advertising their events online and providing email addresses for ticket requests. This is particularly convenient for spectators with no direct connection with the actor-producers, especially because advance sales are cheaper than tickets sold at the door. Most booking requests are received via email, with paper tickets either mailed to a physical address or picked up at the theatre entrance. Increasingly, event organizers have implemented an online system that allows audience members to pick their own seats. In most cases, it is also possible to purchase the ticket from the *nōgakudō* ticket box. For sponsored performances, the sponsoring body, for example, a municipal office or a temple, might take care of promotion and ticket sales.

3.5 The Role of Amateur Practitioners
Diego Pellecchia and Yamanaka Reiko

Enthusiasts have enjoyed singing and dancing nō since the fifteenth century. Nō was not a mere pastime, but a form of "cultural distinction."[43] In the latter half of the Muromachi period, amateur practice became increasingly popular among members of the warrior class, who would perform nō during ceremonies or banquets (see ch. 1 *History*, 1.5). Perhaps the most celebrated of this group was Toyotomi Hideyoshi (1537–1598), who was particularly passionate about nō: he wrote and acted in plays celebrating his military victories that were staged during grandiose pageants (see chs. 1 *History*, 1.5; 4 *Plays*, 4.11). During the Edo period, nō was part of a samurai's cultural education, but thanks to the circulation of printed *utaibon* it became popular among commoners as well. Hundreds of plays were written by amateurs during this era, although the majority were only meant to be chanted.

During the early years of the Meiji period, with the sudden loss of their patronage base due to the dismantling of the daimyō system, nō performers discovered a new source of income in the emerging middle-class. Nō became a popular leisure activity among the educated bourgeoisie, including women, who were finally allowed to study nō but not to perform in public (see chs. 1 *History*, 1.9; 3 *Training*, 3.3). This increase of amateur practice continued until World War II, when performers were drafted into the army, and most stages were destroyed in the Allied bombings.

During the postwar economic revival, nō practice was revived as an important educational activity, not only for the office worker but also for the "prospective good wife." The amateur population peaked during the "leisure boom" of the 1970s and the 1980s when traditional cultural pursuits were promoted by governmental institutions such as the Agency for Cultural Affairs and the Japan Foundation as part of the reconstruction of national identity.[44]

With the burst of the economic bubble in the early 1990s, the size of the amateur population started to shrink, a worrying trend that continues to this day. Younger generations might regard it as an obscure or boring pastime for the elderly, or even as a negative status symbol. A survey conducted at the NNT in September 2012 revealed that only 6 percent of the audience was under thirty, while 65 percent was between sixty-five and eighty.[45] Since amateurs play the crucial role of advertising and disseminating nō to potential new

---

43 Bourdieu 1984.
44 Cox 2003: 161.
45 Horigami 2014: 232–36.

audiences, their declining numbers pose a serious threat to future new generations of professionals and to the survival of the art.

3.5.1 Amateur Performers Today

In the world of nōgaku, amateurs are first and foremost disciples of a professional performer. This is radically different from amateurs in other performing arts, who may study under a professional but whose activities are completely independent from their teacher. The practice of nō is considered an "art of the way" (*geidō*), a concept implying the devotion to a traditional art in a relatively closed environment in which students learn under the guidance of an expert, often a professional practitioner. In these arts (e.g., tea ceremony, flower arrangement, calligraphy), the amateur practitioner often forms an exclusive, lifelong relationship with a single teacher, lasting until they are physically unable to continue their training. Although amateur students advance, gradually acquiring certificates that prove their skill and commitment, for most of them this subordinate position remains immutable and is a defining characteristic of their artistic and social identity.[46]

Diverse motivations attract people to amateur nō practice. It is safe to say that the vast majority do not study to become "art producers," but rather to become better "art consumers"—that is, to acquire tools that will allow them to achieve a deeper appreciation of performance. Being able to sing along silently, to recall a sequence of movements, or to predict the ending of a musical pattern produces in the informed spectator what Anne Ubersfeld has dubbed the "pleasure of understanding."[47] Another major motivation for engaging in nō is the chance to gain exclusive insights into the life of a professional by frequenting his or her training space, and, in the process, strengthening their sense of belonging to the community of practice. What is more, amateurs not only train but can even perform together with high-ranking artists, an aspect unthinkable in other classical Japanese arts.

Nō amateurs engage in what may be called "serious leisure"—in other words, they invest a great amount of time and money in an art that, for the vast majority, will never become a profession.[48] More elderly amateurs may also practice for the added benefit of light physical training and memory exercise. In addition to university students, the number of retirees and stay-at-home

---

46 See Moore 2014; Pellecchia 2017.
47 Ubersfeld 1982: 132.
48 Stebbins 1982.

parents who practice nō is particularly high, as the requisite time commitment may be unsuitable for individuals in full-time employment.[49]

3.5.1.1 The Training of an Amateur

Most amateurs train with *shite* actors, as this offers insights into both dance and chant. A smaller cohort of amateurs learn from *waki* actors. There are also considerable numbers of amateurs studying with kyōgen actors or musicians. The pedagogy of amateur practice is fundamentally the same as that for professionals—that is, it is largely based on observation, imitation, and repetition (fig. 3.12). While *shite* amateurs can learn both chant and dance, it is not uncommon to study either one or the other. Lessons typically take place two or three times a month for about thirty minutes. This time is not spent rehearsing together with the teacher or with other students, but rather demonstrating what they have studied individually, receiving corrections, and

FIGURE 3.12 *Shite* actor Kanze Yoshimasa teaching an amateur student. Yarai Nōgakudō, Tokyo. 2021
PHOTO: YAMANAKA REIKO

---

49 Moore 2014.

gathering information or materials to be learned by the next lesson.[50] Drawing on a more traditional pattern of practice, students are not allotted a specific timeslot; instead, they gather at the *keikoba* and will have their lesson on a first-come-first-serve basis. It could be that a student ends up waiting in the lesson room, chatting and socializing with other members, or quietly observing the training of other fellow students before their turn. This aspect of amateur practice is preferred by many amateurs, who do not necessarily visit a teacher solely for the purpose of training, but also to enjoy the interaction with their peers. Teachers may also receive their students "by appointment," which has the advantage of optimizing the lesson time. This, however, can limit any social interaction between peers.

Amateur *shite* actors customarily begin by learning short *utai* or *shimai* sections (in some cases as short as a minute). As training continues, the pieces become longer and more complex. Since nō performance is essentially modular, it is possible to start by studying short choreographies with a few basic movements, which may constitute the foundation of extended, more intricate routines. It is also not unusual for students of chant and dance to also learn how to play an instrument, providing a better understanding of music, allowing them to perform *maibayashi* or even complete performances with costume and mask.

Study materials may vary depending on the teacher. Chant books (*utaibon*) authorized by the *iemoto* or musical scores are available for purchase in shops or online. *Shite* schools also publish *shimai katatsuke*, in which *kata* are added to the portions of chant corresponding to the *shimai*. Actors and scholars have also published a considerable number of manuals on how to practice nō chant or music, sometimes even including CDs or DVDs. Recently, actors and musicians have also begun to post brief tutorial videos online that are used more for advertisement, rather than as study materials. Although these sorts of explanatory resources abound, it is hard to imagine that a student could master techniques without training directly with a professional.

University clubs differ from other amateur practice in that students tend to meet more frequently to learn from older students, and only occasionally with teachers. Students may interrupt their practice after graduation due to family or job commitments, although they may resume training later in life, or during retirement. University club students meet several times a week, and *keiko* sessions can last numerous hours. Materials, as well as traditional costumes, belong to the club and are shared by the members; training fees are generally very low.

---

50   Although it is not the norm, some performers may also offer group lessons.

3.5.1.2 The License System

As amateurs advance in their training, they are expected to purchase official permissions (*menjō*) in order to study or to perform a certain piece in a public event. Licenses are produced by the *iemoto* but are requested and acquired through the teacher. These are ranked according to difficulty (*kurai*) and tend to be more expensive the higher the level. Licenses are not necessarily acquired through an evaluation of the amateur's skills. Instead, they are mostly assigned according to seniority: they do not certify ability as much as they testify to the commitment of the amateur. Furthermore, the way the license system works depends on the school. Presently, this system has become relatively loose, and amateurs are not always requested to purchase a license every time they perform a piece.

Some schools permit particularly skilled or committed amateurs to purchase "instructor licenses." The holders of such licenses may not be as active as full professionals but are officially allowed to teach. Some may also become members of the Nohgaku Performers' Association, formally making them "professionals," although their actual activities are closer to those of a "semi-professional," as they support themselves with daytime jobs rather than with nō-related work.

The license system, also common in other Japanese traditional arts, serves two main functions. First, it controls the diffusion of knowledge through official channels, thus reinstating the central authority of the *iemoto*. Second, as the price of these licenses can be as high as several hundred thousand yen, this system provides the *iemoto* with a significant income in that each time a certain piece is performed by an amateur, a fee is paid directly to him (the in-between teacher may also retain a sum). In this sense, the license system functions as a form of taxation. The ability to control the teaching rights of its affiliates also contributes to maintaining the consistency in the style transmitted within a school. While the licenses are important for the existence of the *iemoto* system, the high fees may be seen as an obstacle to practice, especially by those who are approaching nō for the first time.

3.5.1.3 Amateur Recitals

In addition to training, amateurs are expected to participate in recitals along with other members of the same group. Such events are arranged by the teacher and may feature other professional performers, depending on the program. Most amateur recitals include excerpts from plays, such as *su-utai*, *rengin*, *shimai*, or *maibayashi*, though in some cases full-scale nō plays are also performed.

Recitals, occurring several times a year or only once in a few years, provide amateurs a platform to showcase their progress. The performance represents the culmination of the study of a specific piece, and upon its completion, the student usually moves onto a new piece. For the instructor, recitals serve as a promotional platform for their individual endeavors. Given that participation entails the payment of a fee to the organizing instructor, such events may also act as a substantial revenue stream. Such fees vary according to the type of performance: a *shimai*, for example, will be much lower than taking the *shite* role in a full play. This cost is separate from the licensing fee.

In addition to participation fees, amateurs are expected to cover all production costs of their performances, from stage rental to advertisement, from costume and mask rental to the fees of the professionals they employ. They may also be asked to purchase a specific license to perform a certain piece, such as *maibayashi*, or a full play performed with masks and costumes. The average cost of performing a full-scale nō as *shite* may range between 1,000,000 and 3,000,000 yen, although these figures can greatly increase depending on factors such as venue, status of the musicians and other performers, and the specific requirements of the plays such as costumes and masks. And finally, as it has already been mentioned, since only members of the Nohgaku Performers' Association are entitled to be paid, entrance to amateur recitals is always free of charge.[51]

If the *shite* role in a full-scale nō play is taken by an amateur, most of the chorus members, as well as *waki*, kyōgen and instrumentalists will be professionals. If, instead, the amateur is a *kotsuzumi* player, all other performers, including the *shite*, may be professional. Even high-ranking professionals may appear onstage together with amateurs. A *kotsuzumi* amateur may hire all the performers necessary to stage a full nō, for instance, and have an established *shite* actor in the main role. This constitutes an important financial investment, but one that many committed amateurs are willing to make. In the case of long recitals, the same professionals might be asked to act consecutively through a full-day performance. This is a particularly useful activity for young performers, not only because they are paid to perform but also since they utilize this type of event to memorize a considerable number of pieces. Full-scale performances with an all-amateur cast are extremely unconventional.

University clubs hold events once or more annually, often featuring the performance of a complete play. Participation fees to university club recitals are considerably lower than those paid by regular amateurs because of the relatively low fees charged by the teachers, the donations from alumni, or the financial support from the university. For example, for a club member performing the *shite* role in a full nō performance with professional musicians may cost

---

51   Yanagisawa 2012.

between 100,000 and 150,000 yen. In order to involve more students and to cut costs, other roles, such as the chorus and stage assistants, are taken by other students. Since a great many university club members are now women, it is not unusual to see events of this kind in which the cast is principally women.

3.6 Kurokawa Nō
Eike Grossmann

The performance of nō and kyōgen is not the exclusive domain of professionals or amateurs who train with them. There are also several communities throughout Japan with active nō and kyōgen performance traditions that primarily rely on their own members. The majority of these performance traditions originated in the Edo period and profited from nō's enormous popularity, which effectively crossed socioeconomic barriers (see ch. 1 *History*, 1.6). Among the extant performance traditions are *Shingai nō* (Miyama, Fukuoka Prefecture), *Nōgō no nō kyōgen* (Motosu, Gifu Prefecture), *Ōnominato Jinja shinji nō* (Kanazawa, Ishikawa Prefecture), and *Kurokawa nō* (Tsuruoka, Yamagata Prefecture). Although geographically diverse, they share certain characteristics, one being that at least once a year several nō and kyōgen are performed by shrine parishioners (*ujiko*) who, in their spare time, participate in their village's shrine festivals (*matsuri* or *sairei*). That individual traditions of nō performances should be embedded in religious contexts and performed by amateurs without obvious connection to one of the five established nō schools was one of the main reasons that these traditions came to be regarded as folk performing arts (*minzoku geinō*). While the folk elements in these traditions are clearly evident, they are also connected to the world of professional nō, as illustrated in the example of *Kurokawa nō*.[52]

During 2014, around 210 of the 230 *ujiko* households of the Kasuga Jinja in Kurokawa engaged in the performance of nō and kyōgen, indicating that an estimated 140 male members of the community performed onstage regularly. They either trained as *maikata*—that is, as nō actors—starting with *waki* roles and then progressing to *shite* roles, as *hayashi-kata*, musicians, or as *kyōgen-kata*, kyōgen actors. The residents claim that their concept of *maikata*

52　An overview on folk performing arts and folklore research in Japan is given in Thornbury 1997. On *Shingai nō*, see Sakamoto and Miyamoto 2015. On *Kurokawa nō*, see Grossmann 2013; on *Kurokawa nō* after the Edo period, see Sakurai 2003: 186–216. *Nōgō no nō kyōgen* is transmitted in sixteen households and performed once a year at Nōgō Hakusan Jinja. *Shingai nō*, with around sixty participants, is connected to the Hōman Jinja, where four nō and two kyōgen performances are held annually.

preserves a performance style from before actors begin to specialize in either *shite* or *waki* roles. From an ethnographical standpoint, the progression from *waki* to *shite* roles can be viewed as a rite of passage by which young boys are introduced to and progressively integrated into the community. This interpretation is supported by the fact that Kurokawa's Kasuga Jinja serves as a shrine guild (*miya za*), within which two nō guilds exist: the *kami za* (upper guild) and *shimo za* (lower guild). Each guild is led by a *nō-dayū*, which residents endeavor to preserve as a hereditary office and which is organized according to a relatively strict age hierarchy.

Kurokawa residents have a remarkable 540 nō and about forty kyōgen plays in their repertory, which is divided unevenly (and without overlaps) between the two nō guilds. They perform about fifty different nō on a regular basis, among them *Kanemaki* (Bell Wrapping), a supposedly older version of the play *Dōjōji*, and a handful of kyōgen. Originally, the residents did not use chant books (*utaibon*) and solely relied on oral transmission. In the twentieth century, they successively integrated self-annotated versions of Kanze and Hōshō school *utaibon* into their training practice.

The residents maintain a demanding schedule of training and perform up to twenty times a year. Nō and kyōgen are staged during four shrine festivals at the Kasuga Jinja: the *Kinensai* ("Spring Festival," March); the *Reitaisai* ("Annual Shrine Festival," May); the *Niinamesai* ("Harvest Festival," November) with two nō and one kyōgen; and the popular, large-scale *Ōgisai* ("Fan Festival," February). The *Ōgisai* is an all-night performance of usually five nō and four kyōgen held in two private residences (fig. 3.13)—recently in the respective community halls of each guild—followed by nō, kyōgen, and competitions at the shrine the next day. In 1984, the residents, together with the municipality office of the former Kushibiki district created the *Suien no nō* ("Nō on Water"), an outdoor "torchlight" or "firelight" nō (*takigi nō*) that takes place in July. They also created a candlelight nō (*rōsoku nō*) in 1994 in response to the enormous number of visitors to the February *Ōgisai*. The candlelight nō also intended to raise the interest of residents who were not connected to the performance and festival tradition.[53]

Kurokawa, like many other rural villages in Japan, faces various challenges: a declining birth rate and a rapidly aging population; a depopulation of rural

---

53 Although *rōsoku nō* was suspended during the COVID-19 pandemic, the residents created a YouTube channel called "Kurokawa rōsoku nō," which made available well-made teasers showing the residents practicing during their daily work breaks, and a recording of the kyōgen *Chidori* and the nō *Shishi* performed during an event held at the Kasuga Jinja in December 2021.

FIGURE 3.13   Kurokawa resident performing as *shite* in *Dōjōji*. February 1, 2006, private house, Ōgisai
PHOTO: EIKE GROSSMANN

areas; the difficulty of opening up to newcomers and in recruiting new participants; and most notably, the refusal to admit female performers despite ongoing discussions. These challenges severely impact the realization of the festivals and the transmission of the performance tradition. Kurokawa residents have managed to transmit their tradition uninterrupted since the seventeenth century, proving itself resilient to changes and adapting to an ever-changing lifestyle.[54] The aforementioned festivals suspended the performance of nō in 2021 due to the COVID-19 pandemic—a drastic measure given that nō continued to be performed even during World War II. How the COVID-19 pandemic will affect nō and kyōgen in Kurokawa in the future will only become evident with time. At least for now, it seems that for the *Ōgisai* in 2023 the residents of Kurokawa returned to their pre-pandemic mode of nō performances.

54   In 2018 and 2019, Kurokawa residents participated in a study using motion capture to digitize their nō dances, one of the many attempts to secure a transmission of *Kurokawa nō*. Tamamoto and Tō 2020.

3.7 Recent Developments and Future Perspectives
Diego Pellecchia and Yamanaka Reiko

The world of nō is constantly in flux. The manner in which professionals, amateurs, and audiences interact, the economic models of nō groups, and how knowledge of nō is transmitted inside and outside of the nō community—all these elements have undergone change throughout its long history. Nō as we know it today is the result of a process of transformation that began with the dismantling of the shogunal system that sponsored nō as "ritual entertainment" during the Edo period.

Once extremely popular among both the elite and the middle-class, nō seems to have lost much of the social value as a cultural status symbol and finding new young people who are interested in the art is a challenge. Until the early 1990s, nō was a common hobby among male white-collar workers and their wives. Amateurs would regularly buy tickets, contribute monthly fees, and provide other forms of financial support. Payments would be made even if one could not participate in lessons or recitals. Today, however, it has become more common for students to pay only for the classes they actually attend. While previously old and new students would have had more chances to interact during longer practice hours, nowadays younger professionals tend to teach "by appointment," catering to the needs of the individual. As a result, the former sense of community fostered among students has weakened, sometimes disincentivizing them to support their teacher financially. As a significant proportion of regular nō theatregoers are themselves amateurs, a decline in the amateur participant base consequently leads to a reduction in the overall spectator count. Ticket sales have generally decreased, impacting on the economic capability of professionals, and therefore on the amount of money that can be invested in the purchase of masks, costumes, and fans, for example. The artisans making such products are suffering from declining orders, forcing them to sell their work at lower prices.

Fewer people today will decide to pursue a career as a nō professional because of the grim reality of economic uncertainty. In 1988, just before the burst of the economic bubble, the total population of the Nohgaku Performers' Association was 1,433—35 years later, in 2023, it was 1,057.[55] Many *uchideshi* apprentices today do not actually live with their teachers, but "commute" to the practice space and consequently they are becoming further distanced from the "centers of knowledge." Small *ryūgi*, in particular, are suffering from a paucity of young members, a problem that may not only jeopardize the transmission

---

55   Hata 1989: 93.

of knowledge but also the quality and number of performances. The awareness of economic instability and the concern for the future has gradually become a catalyst for change. In recent years, performers have begun to diversify and extend their markets through the use of new communication channels that did not exist a few decades ago. The activities of nō performers were strictly regulated until after World War II: starring in a film, in a television show, or even in a nō performance featuring a member belonging to a different school could result in a ban from the *iemoto* and ostracism from the professional community. Today, however, such rules seem to have been loosened. Nō performers now appear to be freer than ever, judging by the instances of collaborations between nō performers and pop musicians, nō events in which actors from different *shite* schools appear in the same play, or hybrid experiments involving other art forms. The Ginza Six stage, home to the Kanze school, is utilized for performances other than nō, as are many other important *nōgakudō*. Performances also take place in locations that previously were considered unsuitable for nō performance. For example, the Suigian restaurant in Tokyo has a nō stage, and there are other similar venues in which nō is offered as a "cultural experience." While this may appear as a form of touristy commodification of the art that has emerged from economic necessity, it may also serve as a form of advertising for the younger actors taking part in these shows.

Various attempts are being made in an effort to attract new types of audiences. The Nohgaku Performers' Association is disseminating nō in elementary and middle schools. Actors and musicians travel to provincial areas where they teach children and schoolteachers about nō and demonstrate their art in classrooms or in auditoriums. Performers make use of the latest available technologies, advertising via social networks, creating YouTube advertisements for workshops and public events, utilizing subtitles and earphone guide systems. As Japan is experiencing a spike in the number of foreign tourists, more nō events are catering to international audiences, with multilingual subtitle systems and other materials being made available.

Japanese society is currently undergoing scrutiny regarding issues of gender discrimination. The *sumō* establishment, for example, has been heavily criticized for not permitting women to step into the *dohyō* wrestling ring. In nō, too, women still suffer various forms of discrimination, which is often explained by the fact that nō is an art created to be performed by the male body. With more women being trained as professionals, however, it seems that the world of nō has finally begun to recognize their efforts, even though greater effort is needed to allow women to rise higher in the social hierarchy by appearing in more important performance events.

As the number of foreigners interested in nō increases, it is only natural that some will want to practice nō. But will they be accepted by the community of nō professionals, even if their interest and technical capability exceeds the amateur level? Since the 1970s, foreigners have studied nō in Japan under the guidance of professional actors and musicians. None, however, have become fully professional performers, even though the presence of non-Japanese practitioners could stimulate new types of performers and draw international attention. And this begs the question of whether the system of selection of professionals should change to a system of auditions rather than one based on seniority and hereditary transmission?

Change will not come easily. The diverse traditions of nō, including the precious costume and mask collections, have survived for centuries thanks to the hereditary transmission that characterizes the *iemoto* system. Clearly, this is not a matter of "genetic preservation"—during the art form's long history families adopted members from outside—as much as it is an attempt to avoid the potential disintegration of their cultural patrimony into smaller independent entities. This does not necessarily justify the patrilineal nature of the of the *iemoto* role, however, or the fact that women are greatly underrepresented.

During the COVID-19 pandemic, the restrictions imposed on performing arts had severe repercussions: nō and kyōgen performances were canceled, postponed, or shortened.[56] Other adjustments affected the format of the performance, such as the chorus having to wear face masks or cutting back the number of its members. The forced suspension of performance and teaching activities of actors and musicians took its toll on their physical and mental well-being. The consequences of such restrictions on the economics of nō was dire. Cancellations and the reduced seating capacity resulted in a significant loss of ticket revenues. The teaching of amateurs was also impacted, with older students suspending or ceasing to practice altogether.

The challenges posed by the pandemic prompted positive responses, one notable example being that performers resorted to various forms of relief funding to create audiovisual contents. Popular online streaming platforms such as YouTube were quickly populated by videos, ranging from demonstrations to full performances. Video streaming is often supported by foreign language subtitles, rendering such content accessible to viewers outside Japan. This was a substantial contribution to the otherwise scarce number of audiovisual materials on nō and kyōgen available internationally. Still, there are aspects of performance that can only be appreciated when experienced in the context of an "offline" event, in which audience and actors share the same space/time. This is all the more meaningful in the case of nō, in which plays are only staged for a single performance event. The advancement in digital technologies is urging

---

56 For the results of a survey about the effects of the COVID-19 pandemic on nōgaku in 2020, Toyoshima 2021; Pellecchia 2021; Yamanaka 2023.

actors to reconsider how to communicate their art outside the usual circle of connoisseurs.

During its centuries of history, nō has faced many hurdles. It has survived because of its ability to morph into new forms while maintaining its fundamental aesthetics and repertory. Should nō open its doors to globalization and commercialization, perhaps simplifying its language and performance conventions, or should it prioritize its current production methods? Should it embrace new communication technologies, or should it preserve its traditional, esoteric ways of working? Perhaps it is this tension between preservation and innovation that will allow the art to evolve without betraying its "true nature." Either way, it appears that the future of nō will depend on its ability to adapt to its ever-changing audience and on the efforts by performers in nurturing a meaningful path forward.

References

Amano Fumio 天野文雄. 1992. "Kyō kanze fukuō ke no Chisei ni—sono jiseki no ni, san" 京観世福王家の智清尼—その事蹟の2, 3. *Geinō* 芸能 8: 14–20.

Aoki Ryōko 青木涼子. 2003. "Onna ga nō o enjiru to iu koto: Tanimura Kaneko to Yamashina Akiko no baai" 女が能を演じるということ：谷村甲子と山階明子の場合. *Gakugekigaku* 楽劇学 10: 1–18.

* Bethe, Monica, and Karen Brazell. 1990. "The Practice of Noh Theatre." In *By Means of Performance: Intercultural Studies of Theatre and Ritual*, edited by Richard Schechner and Willa Appel, 167–93. Cambridge: Cambridge University Press.

Bourdieu, Pierre. 1984. *Distinction: A Social Critique of the Judgement of Taste*. Cambridge: Harvard University Press.

Cox, Rupert. 2003. *The Zen Arts*. London: Routledge.

* Emmert, Richard. 1987. "Training of the Nō Performer." *Theatre Research International* 12, no. 2: 123–33.

Geilhorn, Barbara. 2008. "Between Self-Empowerment and Discrimination—Women in Nō Today." In *Nō Theatre Transversal*, edited by Stanca Scholz-Cionca and Christopher Balme, 106–22. Munich: iudicium.

Geilhorn, Barbara. 2015. "From Private zashiki to the Public Stage—Female Spaces in Early 20th Century Nō." *Asian Theatre Journal* 32, no. 2: 440–463.

Geilhorn, Barbara. 2017. "Women in a Man's World: Gender and Power in Japanese Noh Theatre." In *Women in Asian Performance: Aesthetics and Politics*, edited by Arya Madhavan, 28–38. London; New York: Routledge.

Grossmann, Eike. 2013. *Kurokawa Nō: Shaping the Image and Perception of Japan's Folk Traditions, Performing Arts and Rural Tourism*. Leiden: Global Oriental.

REFERENCES

Hamada, Kenji, trans. 1964. *The Life of an Amorous Man by Ihara Saikaku*. Rutland: Charles E. Tuttle Company.

* Hare, Thomas Blenman. 1999. "Try, Try Again: Training in Noh Drama." In *Teaching and Learning in Japan*, edited by Thomas Rolen and Gerald LeTendre, 323–44. Cambridge: Cambridge University Press.

Hata, Hisashi. 1989. "Nōgaku ni okeru kōkeisha yōsei no genjō" 能楽における後継者養成の現状. *Geinō no Kagaku* 芸能の化学 17: 87–108.

* Horigami Ken 堀上謙. 2009. *Nō no shūseki kairo* 能の集積回路. Tokyo: Tachibana Shuppan.

Horigami Ken 堀上謙. 2014. *Nōgaku jōhō omote ura* 能楽情報表裏. Tokyo: Nōgaku Shorin.

Hsu, Francis. 1975. *Iemoto, the Soul of Japan*. Cambridge: Cambridge University Press, Shenkman.

* Ishiyama Sachiko 石山祥子. 2009. "Minzoku geinō wa 'tabi' o suru: Kurokawa nō shimo za pari kōen o meguru shosō" 民俗芸能は「旅」をする—黒川能下座・パリ公演をめぐる諸相. *Bunka/Hihyō* 文化/批評 1: 245–60.

Itō Maki 伊藤真紀. 1997. "Nō to josei (Meiji-ki) ni tsuite" 能と女性（明治期）について. *Taishō engeki kenkyū* 大正演劇研究 6: 71–80.

Kanamori Atsuko 金森敦子. 1994. *Joryū tanjō: nōgakushi Tsumura Kimiko no shōgai* 女流誕生：能楽師津村紀三子の生涯. Tokyo: Hōsei Daigaku Shuppankyoku.

Kanmon gyoki 看聞御記 [*Kanmon nikki* 看聞日記]. In *Zoku gunsho ruijū, hoi 2 jō, ge* 続群書類従補遺二上下. (1930) 2000. 2 vols. Tokyo: Zoku Gunsho Ruijū Kanseikai.

Kano, Ayako. 2001. *Acting Like a Woman in Modern Japan: Theatre, Gender and Nationalism*. London: Palgrave.

* Kelly, William K. 1990. "Japanese No-Noh: The Crosstalk of Public Culture in a Rural Festivity." *Public Culture* 2, no. 2: 65–81.

Kōshoku ichidai otoko 好色一代男. In *Ihara Saikaku shū* 井原西鶴集 1, edited by Teruoka Yasutaka 暉峻康隆 and Higashi Akimasa 東明雅, 15–250. 1996. *Shinpen Nihon koten bungaku zenshū* 新編日本古典文学全集 66. Tokyo: Shōgakukan.

Matsumoto Kamematsu 松本亀松. 1941. *Nō kara kabuki e* 能から歌舞伎へ. Tokyo: Yōkyokukai Hakkōsho.

* Martzel, Gérard. 1982. *La fête d'Ogi et le noh de Kurokawa*. Paris: Publications orientalistes de France.

Moore, Katrina L. 2014. *The Joy of Noh: Embodied Learning and Discipline in Urban Japan*. Albany: State University of New York (SUNY) Press.

Morinaga, Maki Isaka. 2005. *Secrecy in Japanese Arts*. New York: Palgrave Macmillan.

Nishino Haruo 西野春雄. 1992. "Ikenouchi Nobuyoshi: Nōgaku shinkō no shōgai" 池内信嘉：能楽振興の生涯. In *Ikenouchi Nobuyoshi ten: nōgaku e no gyōseki o tataeru* 池内信嘉展：能楽への業績を讃える, edited by Nankai Hōsō Sanpāku Bijutsukan, 3–17. Matsuyama: Nankai Hōsō Sanpāku Bijutsukan.

Nishiyama Matsunosuke 西山松之助. 1982. *Iemoto no kenkyū* 家元の研究. Tokyo: Yoshikawa Kōbunkan.

Nōgaku Kyōkai. "Nōgaku Kyōkai ni tsuite." https://www.nohgaku.or.jp/about.

Nose Asaji 能勢朝次. 1938. *Nōgaku genryūkō* 能楽源流考. Tokyo: Iwanami Shoten.

O'Neill, P. G. 1958/1959. "The Special Kasuga Wakamiya Festival of 1349." *Monumenta Nipponica* 14, 3–4 (October 1958–June 1959): 408–28.

Pellecchia, Diego. 2017. "Noh Creativity? The Role of Amateurs in Japanese Noh Theatre." *Contemporary Theatre Review* 27, no. 1: 34–45.

* Pellecchia, Diego. 2019. "Time in Noh Theatre Performance and Training." In *Time and Performer Training*, edited by Mark Evans, Konstantinos Thomaidis, and Libby Worth, 43–49. London: Routledge.

Pellecchia, Diego. 2021. "Kyōto no nōgaku ni okeru korona ka no eikyō: genjiten de no kōsatsu" 京都の能楽におけるコロナ禍の影響：現時点での考察. *The Bulletin of the Institute for Japanese Culture, Kyoto Sangyo University* 京都産業大学日本文化研究所紀要 26: 153–58.

* Rath, Eric. 2004. *The Ethos of Noh: Actors and Their Art*. Cambridge: Harvard East Asian Monographs 232. Cambridge: Harvard University Asia Center, Harvard University Press.

Sakamoto Ikkō 坂本一光 and Miyamoto Satoshi 宮本聡. 2015. "Henka o ikiru nōmin nō. Kurokawa nō to shingai nō no konnichiteki keishō" 変化を生きる農民能．黒川能と新開能の今日的継承. *Kyūshū Daigaku Daigakuin kyōikugaku kenkyū kiyō* 九州大学大学院教育学研究紀要 17: 1–21.

Sakurai Akio 桜井昭夫. 2003. *Kurokawa nō to kōgyō* 黒川能と興行. Tokyo: Dōseisha.

Shimazaki Minoru 島崎稔 and Shimazaki Miyoko 島崎美代子. 2004. *Nōgaku shakai no kōzō* 能楽社会の構造. Tokyo: Reibun Shuppan.

Singleton, John, John Seely Brown, and Roy Pea, eds. 1998. *Learning in Likely Places: Varieties of Apprenticeship in Japan*. Cambridge: Cambridge University Press.

Stebbins, Robert A. 1982. "Serious Leisure: A Conceptual Statement." *The Pacific Sociological Review* 25, no. 2: 251–72.

Tamamoto Hideo 玉本英夫 and Tō Ei 唐栄. 2020. "Kurokawa nō no dejitaruka o tōshita minzoku geinō no odori keishō no shin shuhō" 黒川能のデジタル化を通した民俗芸能の踊り継承の新手法. *Tōhoku kōeki bunka daigaku sōgō kenkyū ronshū* 東北公益文科大学総合研究論集 37: 87–97.

Thornbury, Barbara E. 1997. *The Folk Performing Arts: Traditional Culture in Contemporary Japan*. Albany: State University of New York (SUNY) Press.

Toyoshima, Mizuho 豊島瑞穂. 2021. "Atarashii jidai no nōgaku: IT MATTERS! (9)" 新しい時代の能楽：IT MATTERS! (9). *Nōgaku taimuzu* 能楽タイムズ 828, 3.1, no. 6.

Ubersfeld, Anne. 1982. "The Pleasure of the Spectator." *Modern Drama* 25: 127–39.

Wakita Haruko 脇田晴子. 2001. *Josei geinō no genryū: kugutsu, kusemai, shirabyōshi* 女性芸能の源流——傀儡子・曲舞・白拍子. Tokyo: Kadokawa Sensho.

Yamanaka Reiko 山中玲子. 2023. "Koronaka to nōgaku" コロナ禍と能楽. In *Kiki to nōgaku* 危機と能楽, edited by Nakatsuka Yukiko 中司由起子, Fukazawa Nozomi 深澤希望, Miyamoto Keizō 宮本圭造, Yamanaka Reiko 山中玲子, 87–122. *Nōgaku kenkyū sōsho* 能楽研究叢書 8. Tokyo: Nogami Kinen Hōsei Daigaku Nōgaku Kenkyūjo.

Yanagisawa Shinji 柳沢新治. 2012. *Nō kyōgen no mikata tanoshimikata* 能・狂言の見方楽しみ方. Tokyo: Yamakawa Shuppansha.

Yoza yakusha mokuroku 四座役者目録. Edited by Tanaka Makoto 田中允. 1975. *Nōgaku shiryō* 能楽資料 6. Tokyo: Wan'ya Shoten.

Websites of Works Cited

Japan Arts Council (Nihon Geijutsu Bunka Shinkōkai). https://www.ntj.jac.go.jp/.

(nō-kyōgen) Nōgaku kōen jōhō 能楽（能・狂言）公演情報. http://nohgaku.fan.coocan.jp/.

The Nohgaku Performers' Association. https://www.nohgaku.or.jp/.

The noh.com. https://www.the-noh.com/.

"Kurokawa Rōsoku Nō" 黒川蝋燭能, YouTube channel. https://www.youtube.com/channel/UCbMNeJXycGyudQzrP1HvXdw.

4
Plays: Their Conventions and Backgrounds

Edited by Tom Hare, Takeuchi Akiko, Michael Watson, and Yamanaka Reiko

4.1   **Introduction**
        Takeuchi Akiko

The majority of nō plays in the current repertory were created between the late fourteenth and sixteenth centuries. This corresponded to a period when the samurai culture of Japan's eastern provinces began to impact the long-established court culture of the capital; when Pure Land Buddhism and Zen flourished and interest in (Shintō) *kami* worship increased, leading to interactions at a more profound level between religious practices and the various forms of literature and art; and when the popularity of a new poetic genre of *renga* (linked verse), which required a deeper knowledge of classical literature, reached its zenith. After a relatively peaceful period, however, Japan entered a new era of civil war and social upheaval with the devastation of the capital during the *Ōnin bunmei no ran* (Ōnin Disturbances, 1467–1467). The development of nō plays during this cultural, social, and religious watershed in Japanese history—one of its most fertile—reflects the myriad influences of literature, the arts, and belief systems. Together they would be absorbed into the fabric of nō plays through theatrical conventions that would come to characterize the genre.

The eleven sections in this chapter are arranged so as to facilitate the reader's gradual understanding of the conventions, intertextuality, and cultural backgrounds of nō plays. "Categories of Nō Plays" (4.2) examines several different approaches in the categorization of nō plays, thus demonstrating the diversity and the patterns of the subjects in nō as well as how these subjects are handled in the plays themselves. "Sources of Nō Plays" (4.3) introduces the wide range of materials that provided the plots for many nō plays, while "Nō and Its Belief Systems" (4.4) discusses the variety of religious beliefs dealt with in nō plays and treatises. "Reading Nō: *Mugen nō* and *Genzai nō* (*monogurui nō*)" (4.5) presents a few models for the construction of nō plays using examples from representative plays, with particular emphasis on "dream" or "phantom" nō (*mugen nō*) and "present-time" nō (*genzai nō*). The sections, "Aspects of Time and Character Relations" (4.6), "Stylistics and Poetics" (4.7), "Narration and Ambiguous Voice" (4.8), "Religious and Political Allegory in Nō" (4.9), and "Medieval Commentaries and Nō Theatre" (4.10) all explore the particular styles of nō texts. The final section, "*Bangai kyoku* and *Shinsaku nō*: Noncanonical Plays and Modern Nō Plays" (4.11), offers an overview of plays that are not part of the current performance repertory, with a particular focus on plays from the late sixteenth century onward. It thus sheds light on the development of nō from the establishment of the traditional repertory and conventions until the present day.

4.2 Categories of Nō Plays
Yamanaka Reiko (Translated by Steven Nelson, contributions by Takeuchi Akiko and Michael Watson)

The generally accepted image of nō as a drama of stillness and deep feeling is not borne out by the enormous variety in content and structure that typifies the hundreds of nō plays composed over the centuries. This section will first examine the question of how only a limited number of plays came to make up the current repertory. It will then introduce several different approaches to the categorization of nō plays that enable us to grasp the range of themes, characters, and structures that constitutes this theatrical genre.

4.2.1 *The Number of Plays in the Repertory*
Numerous nō plays were written from the Muromachi period (1336–1573) onward, and especially until the sixteenth century, many of these were staged only to be forgotten afterward. For this reason, it is not easy to give an estimate of the total number of plays written in the early period. Seven hundred and ten plays are included, however, in *Iroha sakusha chūmon* (*Nō Plays and Their Authors in Iroha Order*), a list of plays (*nayose*) compiled in the late sixteenth century, when nō had already become regarded as a "classical" performing art. During the seventeenth century under Tokugawa shogunal rule, each of the nō schools organized the plays in their own repertory, provided the shogunate with lists of the plays that they performed, and took responsibility for managing the staging and transmission of these plays to establish a classical canon.

The repertory of plays performed today is much the same as that handed down from the Edo period (1603–1868). Of the approximately 240 plays currently performed, 120 are staged regularly. Since the Edo period, very few new compositions have entered the repertory, and the pieces performed nowadays are mostly from before the end of the sixteenth century. This is not to suggest that new plays were not being composed, only that they did not enter the canon. Plays that were once, but are no longer, performed are known as *bangai kyoku*, or "noncanonical pieces." The same term is also applied to the large number of plays by literati (*bunjin*) conceived as a type of entertainment, rather than for actual performance. Nō plays written from the beginning of the Meiji period (1868–1912) are known as *shinsaku nō* ("newly created nō"). *Shinsaku nō* have generally been written to be performed, but in many cases such plays have been staged only once (see sec. 4.11).

4.2.2   Types of Main Characters

The plot of a nō play usually revolves around its main character, the protagonist, who is central in determining the principal theme and structure of the work. Nō plays tend to depict humans who are the tragic victims of fate, and these contrast heart-warming dramas of everyday life that are the province of kyōgen plays (see ch. 9 *Kyōgen*, 9.2). Some of the most common types of characters and classic plots are:
- Human spirits:
  - Plays featuring the spirits of elegant men and women who appear in works of classical literature. Through recitation, song, and dance, they recall their memories of a famous scene from the story;
  - Plays featuring the spirits of commanders who died in battle. They reenact their final moments and ask for salvation;
  - Plays featuring the spirits of those suffering in hell. They recollect the events that led to their present agony, asking for salvation.
- Deities, demons, and other nonhuman spirits:
  - Plays in which a deity appears and gives blessings of peace to the world;
  - Plays in which a female deity dances a sacred dance;
  - Plays in which a spirit of a plant or blossom appears and performs a dance;
  - Plays in which a supernatural creature, such as a demon or *tengu* goblin, reveals its power or is vanquished.
- Living persons:
  - Plays based on an episode from a well-known narrative about a beautiful woman or the portrayal of her aged figure;
  - Plays in which a man and woman, or a parent and child, are reunited after being separated;
  - Plays featuring a poet or artist who demonstrates his or her talents;
  - Plays in which a warrior demonstrates his loyalty in battle;
  - Plays set in China that depict a scene from a famous story.

4.2.3 Zeami's Classification of Nō Plays

Explanations of the typology of nō plays, the types of main characters, and performance methods can be found in Zeami's writings on nō. In the "Monomane jōjō" ("Notes on Dramatic Imitation") section in his first treatise *Fūshi kaden* (*Transmitting the Flower through Effects and Attitudes*, 1400–ca. 1418), Zeami (1363 or 1364–1443?) discusses the costuming and acting techniques for roles portraying women (aristocrats, ordinary women, performers), old men, adult males not wearing masks, deranged persons, monks, warrior spirits in the Asura warrior hell (J. *shuradō*), gods, demons, and Chinese figures.[1]

In his work on the composition of nō plays, *Sandō* (*The Three Courses*, 1423), Zeami categorizes plays in terms of three modes (*fūtei*): the Aged (*rōtai*), the Woman's (*nyotai*), and the Martial (*guntai*). In addition, he discusses plays dealing with clerics and mad people and differentiates between demons whose form is demonic but whose intent is human and thus exhibit a more intricate style, and demons whose intent is demonic and thus have a style marked by violent movement. He cites examples of celebrated plays representing these modes, and at the same time advises against the last type of demon.

The Aged mode includes deity plays such as *Takasago* and *Oimatsu* and those with an aged male protagonist such as *Tōru* or *Aridōshi*, while the Woman's mode is typified by plays such as *Matsukaze*, *Hyakuman*, or *Ukifune*, as well as by plays such as *Higaki* in which the *shite* represents an aged female spirit. Illustrating the Martial mode are plays, including *Michimori*, *Tadanori*, or *Kiyotsune*, that feature *shite* who are commanders of the Heike (Taira) clan and are killed in the Genpei War (1180–1185). Plays with lay monks such as *Jinen koji* or those with mentally unstable characters (*monogurui nō*) are categorized by Zeami as pieces of charismatics (*yūkyō*), while plays such as *Koi no omoni* or *Kayoi Komachi*, which show humans who have become demons in hell, are considered as plays of "intricate movement" (*saidōfū*).[2]

In his late work *Go-on* (*Five Sorts of Singing*, ca. 1429), Zeami states that he has "provisionally divided the art of singing into five different classes": *shūgen* ("celebratory"; "the sound of peace and contentment"), *yūkyoku* ("elegant expressiveness"), *renbo* ("love and longing"), *aishō* ("grief and suffering"), and *rangyoku* ("a superlative singing voice").[3] These classifications are based on the kinds of melody or vocal articulation, but the style of singing has a very close connection with the lyrical content—that is, the words. Many of Zeami's examples of *shūgen* are therefore from first category plays (*shobanme mono*) in which a god offers blessings for beneficent rule on earth. Plays representative of

---

1 Hare, trans. 2008: 31–37.
2 Hare, trans. 2008: 154–63.
3 Hare, trans. 2008: 8, 224–415.

yūkyoku portray scenes of beauty and refined sentiment, while those described as *renbo* are love stories, and *aishō* comprise nō plays that lament tragic fates or the transitoriness of life and death. Unlike the other four categories, the term *rangyoku* is not used to suggest a particular category of play. Instead, the category is positioned at a level higher than the other four, referring to a sort of "virtuosity" in singing.[4]

4.2.4 The Five Categories of Nō (gobandate)

Gobandate, or "five categories," is a classification system of nō plays based on the type of role acted by the *shite* or by the type of play more generally. The first category is known as *shobanme mono*, while the second, third, fourth, and fifth categories are known respectively as *nibanme mono, sanbanme mono, yobanme mono*, and *gobanme mono*, all with the suffix *-me mono* used for ordinal numerals. These terms have led to the idea that first category plays are to be performed first in the program, with second category plays performed next, and so forth, although this is not necessarily the case. When these five categories originated is not clear, but a closer look at the role types and play types of the five categories might be instructive before an explanation of their beginnings (see ch. 2 *Performance*, 2.3).

4.2.4.1 First Category Plays (*shobanme mono*): Deity Plays

In *shobanme mono*, a god appears and bestows blessings on the well-governed realm. In some rare examples, the blessing is directed toward an individual. This category is also known as *waki nō* or *waki mono*, indicating that it is the play performed after *Okina*.[5] In most cases, the *shite* is a young male god or a god who assumes the form of an old man, but there are also of female gods and dragon gods. Plays in this category include *Takasago, Oimatsu, Kamo, Chikubushima*, and *Ema*.

4.2.4.2 Second Category Plays (*nibanme mono*): Warrior Plays

The *shite* is the spirit of a warrior who has died in battle. In most cases, the material for these plays is drawn from the *Heike monogatari* (*The Tale of the Heike*), a tradition of narratives that describe the twelfth-century conflicts between the Genji (Minamoto) and the Heike (Taira) families (see sec. 4.3). The spirit recounts how he fell in battle, begging for salvation from the hellish realm of the warring titans (Skt. Asura; J. *shuradō*). The category is also

---

4 Hare, trans. 2008: 8, 298.
5 These plays are not about *waki* roles. The character for "*waki*" means "side" and thus *waki nō* is performed at the "side" of *Okina* and the *waki* character is the "side" role in relation to the *shite*, who has the main role.

known as *shura mono* or *shura nō*, and often translated as "warrior plays." It subsumes numerous significant works of Zeami such as *Atsumori*, *Sanemori*, and *Tadanori*. In *Tomoe*, the main character is a female warrior. *Nibanme mono* also include three examples of plays, such as *Tamura*, which end in victory rather than death in battle.

4.2.4.3   Third Category Plays (*sanbanme mono*): Woman Plays
The *shite* may be a spirit of a cultured person who appears in classical literary works, including the *Genji monogatari* (*The Tale of Genji*) or the *Ise monogatari* (*The Tales of Ise*) (see sec. 4.3). Other types of *shite* in this category may be the spirit of a plant or flower, the living form of a beautiful woman, or an old woman who was once a great beauty. Elegant songs and slow dances like *jo no mai* or *chū no mai* are the highlights of many plays. In a few exceptional cases the *shite* represents a male, as in *Saigyōzakura* and *Yugyō yanagi*, which feature the spirit of an old tree, or the plays *Unrin'in* or *Oshio*, which feature the beautiful Heian courtier-poet Ariwara no Narihira (825–880). Plays in this category are also referred to as *kazura mono* or *kazura nō* ("wig plays" or "wig nō," respectively), with representative works being *Higaki*, *Izutsu*, *Kakitsubata*, *Matsukaze*, *Nonomiya*, and *Yuya*.

4.2.4.4   Fourth Category Plays (*yobanme mono*): Miscellaneous Plays
This category, sometimes called *zatsu nō* or *zatsu mono* ("miscellaneous plays"), comprises plays that do not fit into the first, second, third, or fifth categories. A typical plot type is *monogurui nō* ("crazed person" nō) in which a parent and child, husband and wife, or lovers are separated and are finally reunited after having wandered in search of them. Another plot type focuses on protagonists who display their ability in one of the medieval performing arts. Also in this category are plays about living warriors who demonstrate their loyalty or courage. In all these cases of "present-time" nō (*genzai nō*), the protagonists are living persons, with the plot driven by dialogue. *Hanjo*, *Hōkazō*, *Hyakuman*, *Jinen koji*, *Kosode Soga*, and *Sumidagawa* are examples of this type.

The fourth category additionally subsumes a great variety of other plot types: a female god dances a sacred dance or *kagura*, a woman is transformed into a demon through feelings of jealousy or anger, a spirit of a man or a woman who has descended into hell appears. Select plays based on Chinese tales also belong to this category. *Aoi no ue*, *Fujito*, *Kanawa*, *Kayoi Komachi*, *Miwa*, *Motomezuka*, *Sanshō*, and *Tenko* are illustrative of these plot types.

4.2.4.5   Fifth Category Plays (*gobanme mono*): Finale Plays
Plays in this category are performed last in a one-day program and thus their name *kiri nō* or "finale nō." The protagonists include the spirits of demons and

animals, *tengu* or *yōsei* (spirits), as well as heroes who defeat demons.⁶ Also included are plays involving a fast dance (*haya mai*) featuring male aristocrats or emperors whose spirits appear from heaven, or bodhisattvas or female dragon deities. Demons and *tengu* differ greatly from bodhisattvas and heavenly deities, but as the variety in the protagonist types suggests, the classification is not based on character or outward appearance, but rather on what kind of play makes for a suitable end to the day's program. Examples of the former group include *Nomori*, *Ōeyama*, *Sesshōseki*, *Shakkyō*, *Shōjō*, *Tsuchigumo*, and *Zegai*, while *Ama*, *Taema*, and *Tōru* are illustrative of the latter.

4.2.4.6   The Origins of the Five Categories

As noted above, the circumstances that led to the establishment of the five nō categories are not well understood. Some guides to nō incorrectly explain the categories as being based on Edo-period performance practice, claiming that a formal program began with *Okina* followed by five nō plays, one for each category, with four kyōgen plays performed between the nō.

Official records of the Edo period show, however, that the formal arrangement of programs consisted of *Okina* followed by four nō plays and two kyōgen. A first category play was followed by a kyōgen, then a second category play and another kyōgen. Next there was a third category play. This was not followed by a kyōgen, but by a nō play from the fourth or fifth category. The program ended with a celebratory nō (*shūgen nō*) consisting either of the second half of a first category play or sometimes a celebratory play of another category, such as *Shakkyō* and *Shōjō*. The example here is the program of a nō performance held on the nineteenth day of the eleventh month in 1775 in celebration of the official appointment of the ninth shōgun Tokugawa Ieshige (1712–1761; r. 1745–1760):

> *Okina*
> > First nō: *Naniwa*: a first category deity play (fig. 4.1)
> > First kyōgen: *Ongyoku muko* (*The Musical Son-in-Law*)
> > Second nō: *Sanemori*: a second category warrior play (fig. 4.2)
> > Second kyōgen: *Kaki yamabushi*
> > Third nō: *Bashō*: a third category play (fig. 4.3)
> > Fourth nō: *Tsuchigumo*: a fifth category play (fig. 4.4)
> > Celebratory piece: the second half of *Kureha*: a first category deity play⁷

---

6   *Tengu* are usually evil mountain spirits; see Wakabayashi 2012: xiii–xvi.
7   "Shōgun senge nō bangumi" (将軍宣下能番組), a manuscript owned by Nō Theatre Research Institute of Hōsei University, Tokyo.

FIGURE 4.1 *Naniwa*. From *An Illustrated Model of Nō* (*Nō on'ekagami*), vol. 1. By Kanō Shunko (d. 1726). Late 17th or early 18th century. Album (*orijō*), ink and color on paper. 42.2 × 48.5 cm. Noh Theatre Research Institute, Hōsei University, Tokyo

FIGURE 4.2 *Sanemori*. From *An Illustrated Model of Nō* (*Nō on'ekagami*), vol. 1. By Kanō Shunko (d. 1726). Late 17th or early 18th century. Album (*orijō*), ink and color on paper. 42.2 × 48.5 cm. Noh Theatre Research Institute, Hōsei University, Tokyo

FIGURE 4.3 *Bashō*. From *An Illustrated Model of Nō* (*Nō on'ekagami*), vol. 1. By Kanō Shunko (d. 1726). Late 17th or early 18th century. Album (*orijō*), ink and color on paper. 42.2 × 48.5 cm. Noh Theatre Research Institute, Hōsei University, Tokyo

FIGURE 4.4 *Tsuchigumo*. From *An Illustrated Model of Nō* (*Nō on'ekagami*), vol. 2. By Kanō Shunko (d. 1726). Late 17th or early 18th century. Album (*orijō*), ink and color on paper, 42.2 × 48.5 cm. Noh Theatre Research Institute, Hōsei University, Tokyo

It is also worth noting that when the hereditary heads (*iemoto*) of the nō schools presented the shogunate with a record of plays in their repertory, only the lists of first and second category plays corresponded to the present-day classifications of plays. There is much variation in how the other kinds of plays are classified, suggesting that the categories were not as well defined as they are today. Some scholars point instead to the way that nō chant books (*utaibon*) were very frequently printed during the Edo period, with five plays of different genres bound together in a single volume. Again, however, there is no conclusive proof that the five category system originated in this way.

This system of classification is not very precise, but it is convenient to use, allowing us to assign each of the currently performed plays to one of the five categories. Nowadays, five nō plays are rarely performed on a single day, yet the categories are helpful in delineating the characteristics of nō plays. Moreover, the order of plays within a program still tends to follow the old system, even when only two plays are performed.

4.2.5 Mugen nō *and* Genzai nō

The distinction between *mugen nō* ("dream" or "phantom" nō) and *genzai nō* ("present-time" nō) is another important form of classification, although it is not as useful as the five category system. In very early nō, the dramatic plot was created through the dialogue of characters representing living persons. *Mugen nō* has a different structure, depicting the state of mind and feelings of a central character. This new structural type is thought to have been established by Zeami and perfected by his son-in-law Konparu Zenchiku (also Ujinobu, 1405–ca. 1470).[8] It should be noted, however, that the term *mugen nō* did not originate with Zeami. The term was first employed in the early twentieth century in a radio broadcast explaining nō, and was later adopted by scholars (see ch. 10 *Research*, 10.4).[9]

4.2.5.1   *Mugen nō*

Mugen nō are structured around a tale told by the *shite*. The following outlines the common structure of *mugen nō*:

1. A traveler such as a monk or imperial messenger (*waki*) makes a journey to a certain place where he encounters a person residing there (*mae shite*, *shite* in the first act). They exchange words;

---

8 See Quinn 2005; Atkins 2006.
9 For details and reference to Japanese scholarship on the origins of the term, see Pellecchia 2021: 5.

2. The local person gives a detailed account of a story related to the place, then disappears after hinting that he or she is the very person described in the story;
3. While the *waki* waits, the same person reappears (*nochi shite*, *shite* in the second act), this time in his or her real form, and performs a dance that reenacts the events of the past.[10]

The *mae shite* and the *nochi shite* have distinct guises, with differing costumes and masks, but in most cases, they represent the same person. Initially, these *mae shite* appear in disguise before the *waki* and relate the events of the tale in third person, as if they have no personal connection with the story. In the second half of the play, the spirit of a human reappears in his or her past form, while the spirit of a demon or god is revealed in its true form.

The structure of *mugen nō* can be summarized as the appearance of a supernatural being who discloses memories of the past. Through this structure, the play is freed from the limitations of actual space and time: only what the protagonist wants to remember is depicted onstage in a direct appeal to the audience (see sec. 4.5; ch. 2 *Performance*, 2.3).

4.2.5.2 Genzai nō

Not all nō plays are *mugen nō*. There are many nō plays with characters who are people living in the dramatic present, involved in events that unfold in real time onstage. Such nō plays are known as *genzai nō*, or "present-time" nō. *The Tale of the Heike* provides source material for typical *mugen nō* second category warrior plays that showcase the ghosts of warriors who have perished in battle, yet there are also numerous *genzai nō* based on this classic war tale (*gunki monogatari*), such as *Kogō*, *Ohara gokō*, *Shunkan*, and *Yuya*. Just as Euripides and Racine dramatized famous episodes of Greek literature, these *genzai nō* extract various scenes from *The Tale of the Heike* and build the nō play around them.

In addition, there are quite a few plays adapted from the legends related to Minamoto no Yoshitsune (1159–1189), such as *Ataka* and *Eboshi-ori*, or describing the vendetta of the Soga brothers, such as *Kosode Soga* and *Youchi Soga* (see sec. 4.3). In these nō, scenes that express the spirit and loyalty of warriors in battle or as they exact revenge describe the bravery and strategies of the hero, and at times, too, the emotions of a bereaved family.

---

10   It should be mentioned that there are plays in which the spirit is understood to be an apparition seen by the traveler. In many others, the spirit appears only in the traveler's dream. It is often not possible to determine the point in the playtext where the dream begins.

Different from *mugen nō*, *genzai nō* do not have a set structure. The protagonists of many *genzai nō*, especially Zeami's "crazed person" plays (*monogurui nō*), convey deep feelings through poetry in much the same way as *shite* in *mugen nō*. The powerful portrayal of feelings is the result of much ingenuity in creating the texts for the plays (see sec. 4.5; ch. 2 *Performance*, 2.3).

4.3 Sources of Nō Plays
Takeuchi Akiko

Most nō plays rely on famous classical tales, military epics, religious narratives, and poems as sources (*honzetsu*) for their plots. This section offers an overview of representative materials that served as basic plots for nō drama, but it might be instructive initially to clarify a few significant issues on the relationship between nō plays and their sources.

Firstly, these sources are generally adapted rather freely for nō drama. Zeami advocated the importance of being faithful to his original sources, yet he always added new perspectives when dramatizing them. The *mugen nō* structure that he established was a device that allowed playwrights to present a familiar story in a new light, as a well-known historical or fictional episode is retrospectively retold and reenacted through the subjective recollection of a ghost or a spirit (see sec. 4.5). It was a technique that involved at once being "faithful to the source" while also "fresh to the eye," two qualities that Zeami attributed to good nō in his treatise *Fūshi kaden*.[11]

Secondly, most of these source materials survive in a large number of variant texts, even though many are now lost. It is therefore often difficult to work out exactly which version of the original material was directly consulted by a playwright when producing a particular nō play. When drawing upon a literary classic or a story already familiar to the playwright, as well as to the audience, it is possible that a specific written text was not necessarily referenced.

Thirdly, even in the case of plays that do not seem to derive from any known source (*tsukuri nō*), playwrights usually create the main plot by expanding or building upon celebrated literary topoi. For example, in Zeami's *Hanjo*, a heartbroken courtesan becomes deranged and wanders to the capital. Holding a fan—her lover's keepsake—she laments being abandoned like a fragile fan in the autumn. In her derangement, she dances amid the crowds at the Kamo Shrine, where her lover finds her. The play ends with the couple's reunion. While this plot is the playwright's invention, it was nonetheless developed from the

---

11   Hare, trans. 2008: 58.

poetic trope of the "autumn fan," a metaphor for an abandoned woman that originated in a Chinese poem composed by the consort Ban (ca. 48–ca. 6 BCE) who lost the affections of the Chinese emperor Chengdi (51–7 BCE). This metaphor was adopted by numerous later poets, before eventually becoming a favored poetic motif in both China and Japan.

Finally, a single play may have several "sources," each of which is related to the play's dramatic development to various degrees. The main plot of the nō play *Atsumori*, for instance, is based on a noted episode from *The Tale of the Heike*, while the allusions to *The Tale of Genji* strongly suggest a link between the play's protagonist Atsumori, the ghost of a young man at the site of a great battle, and Shining (Hikaru) Genji, the epitome of the court culture and the protagonist of the canonical *Genji* tale. The play is also peppered with citations from a number of Japanese and Chinese poems and Buddhist texts.

Japanese poetry, *The Tales of Ise*, *The Tale of Genji*, and as just mentioned, *The Tale of the Heike*, were rich sources of inspiration for the main plots in nō plays. It should be noted, however, that diverse sources operating at different textual levels of a play create intertextual complexity, which is one of the most essential characteristics of nō drama (see sec. 4.7).

4.3.1 *Japanese Poetry and Its Commentaries*

It might seem strange that *waka*, a Japanese poetic form comprising just thirty-one syllables, provided plots for many nō plays. While an individual *waka* is too short to contain much narrative development, the considerable number of *waka* textbooks (*kagakusho*) circulating during the medieval period offered detailed explanations of the circumstances behind the creation of famous poems and popular poetic topoi, and these explanations were generally imaginary rather than grounded in any historical fact. In form, these *waka* commentaries often resemble collections of episodes that allegedly gave rise to poems and poetic themes. *Aridōshi*, *Ashikari*, *Funabashi*, *Matsura*, *Miwa*, *Motomezuka*, *Nishikigi*, *Obasute*, and *Utō* are among the plays that draw upon these anecdotal *waka* commentaries.

Occasionally, the plot of a play was taken directly from a specific *waka* without referencing an existing anecdotal poetic commentary, as can be seen in the plays *Akogi*, *Saigyōzakura*, *Tokusa*, and *Yugyō yanagi*. *Saigyōzakura*, for example, centers on a celebrated *waka* by a prominent monk-poet, Saigyō (1118–1190):

hana min to	Flowers! Do let's look!—
muretsutsu hito no	And on they come,
kuru nomizo	Amateurs in droves.

atara sakurano	Ah, lovely blossoms,
togani ha arikeru	This is all your fault![12]

In the play, Saigyō's quiet mountain refuge is frequented by noisy crowds wishing to view the cherry blossoms. He composes the above *waka* that blames the blossoms for attracting these annoying visitors. The spirit of the cherry tree appears, objects to this unfair accusation, and celebrates the splendid beauty of cherry blossoms with a dance. It is possible that Zeami consulted an anecdotal commentary that is today lost, but it is also quite possible that he invented this plot based on the *waka* itself. Imagining a story behind a short *waka* poem or poetic exchange was an essential element of literary creativity.

The most canonical of the many *waka* collections was the *Kokin wakashū* (*A Collection of Ancient and Modern Poems*, 905–913/914), the first imperial anthology of *waka*. Its "Kana Preface" (*kana jo*) was much revered by later generations as the first treatise on Japanese poetry. Medieval commentaries provided highly allegorical interpretations of almost each phrase in this text, including anecdotes that were the source of numerous nō plays (see sec. 4.10), including *Awaji*, *Fujisan*, *Kawazu*, *Matsumushi*, *Naniwa*, *Ominameshi*, *Takasago*, and *Uneme*.

Takasago is the most representative example of this type. The play centers on a famous line from the "Kana Preface": "The pines in Takasago and Sumiyoshi seem to be growing together (*ai oi*)." The original meaning is that these two pine trees seem to be growing together with humans, signifying the intimate bond between nature and humankind. Yet, the *Kokin wakashū jo kikigaki: sanryūshō* (*Lecture Notes on the Preface to the Kokin wakashū: Selected Comments from the Three Schools*),[13] an extremely influential commentary on the "Kana Preface" in the medieval period, noted that the pine tree of Takasago stands for the ancient period that witnessed the compilation of the first Japanese anthology of poetry, the *Man'yōshū* (*A Collection of Myriad Leaves*, 8th c.). The pine tree of Sumiyoshi, by contrast, stands for the later reign when the *Kokin wakashū* was compiled. According to this allegorical reading, their "growing together" means that these two different eras are one and the same, as the flourishing of poetry gives rise to a society that is identical to the ideal past.

The nō play *Takasago* dramatizes this allegorical interpretation. In the play, the spirits of the pine trees of Sumiyoshi and Takasago first appear as an old

---

12 Tyler, trans./ed. 1992: 219.
13 Aside from *Takasago*, plays that reflect allegorical interpretations presented in the *Kokin wakashū jo kikigaki: sanryūshō* include *Awaji*, *Ominameshi*, *Matsumushi*, *Naniwa*, and *Sekidera Komachi*.

couple, who "grew (old) together." In the second act, the spirit of the Sumiyoshi pine tree reappears as the Sumiyoshi deity, who was revered as the deity of poetry. After elucidating the allegorical meaning of the phrase from the "Kana Preface," the god bestows his blessings on the reign and its people through dance, thus visually embodying onstage how the arts effect a peaceful world.

4.3.2 The Tales of Ise *and Ise Commentaries*

The tenth-century *The Tales of Ise* is among one of the most canonical texts in Japanese classic literature.[14] In medieval literary circles, it was considered almost as an esoteric religious text, with various commentaries offering allegorical readings on the work (see sec. 4.10). According to those commentaries, each of the 125 episodes in the *Ise* tales signifies a certain phase in the life of the Heian-period courtier-poet Ariwara no Narihira, who was equally renowned for his many love affairs. Aside from specifying the names of the personages in those episodes, who are, in *Ise*, referred to merely as "a man" and "a woman," the commentaries state that Narihira was in fact the avatar of the bodhisattva of song and dance (*kabu no bosatsu*) as well as the deity of male-female sexual union. His amorous liaisons with various women were thus an expedient means (*hōben*) toward enlightenment. These commentaries were once a part of secret teachings but became common knowledge among a broader audience by Zeami's time.[15]

Nō plays that draw upon *The Tales of Ise*, such as *Izutsu, Kakitsubata, Oshio*, and *Unrin'in*,[16] assume the *mugen nō* structure, in which a ghost or a spirit retells a celebrated episode from the *Ise* story to a traveler and reveals its "true" meaning as explained in the commentaries. The Zenchiku-attributed play *Kakitsubata*, for example, is based on episodes 7, 8, and 9, in which Narihira, on his way into exile in the eastern provinces, stops at Yatsuhashi in Mikawa Province (present-day eastern Aichi Prefecture), where he admires iris flowers (*kakitsubata*) blooming by a marsh. He composes a famous *waka* citing his longing for a love he has left behind in the capital. The medieval commentaries treat this eastern journey as an allegory for Narihira being forcibly detained in Higashiyama on the eastern periphery of the capital following the revelation of his affair with the high-ranking consort of the emperor, Lady Nijō. In this reading, the iris flowers symbolize Lady Nijō, the place name Yatsuhashi (Eight

---

14 See Bowring 1992; Mostow and Tyler, trans. 2010.
15 See Klein 2002.
16 *Unrin'in* was later revised drastically (especially its second half) in the middle to late Muromachi period, as a result of which it lost most of its references to this allegorical reading.

Bridges) refers to Narihira's long relationships with eight different women, and the name of the province Mikawa (Three Rivers) signifies his notable affairs with three high-ranking women, one of whom is Lady Nijō. Similarly, all proper nouns and poetic phrases in the episodes are treated as allegories.

The play *Kakitsubata* stages this allegorical reading. In Yatsuhashi, where the iris flowers are in full bloom, a traveling monk encounters a woman who tells him that this was the very place where Narihira paused on his journey into exile. She then reveals her identity as the spirit of the iris, donning Lady Nijō's court robe and Narihira's headdress. She thus resembles Lady Nijō, and at the same time, represents the union between Narihira and the Lady Nijō. In this androgynous appearance, the spirit reenacts Narihira's life, journey, and his numerous liaisons with women. She also praises him as the deity of yin and yang (*in'yō no kami*), who saved women through his affairs, and as the bodhisattva of song and dance, who brought salvation to plants like her through his *waka* (see sec. 4.9).

4.3.3   The Tale of Genji

Another canonical work of classic Japanese literature, *The Tale of Genji*, was equally a rich source for nō drama. Many nō plays showcase its female characters, principally in the form of spirits, as can be seen in *Aoi no ue* and *Nonomiya* (featuring Lady Rokujō) as well as with *Hajitomi* and *Yūgao* (featuring Lady Yūgao), *Ochiba*, *Tamakazura*, and *Ukifune* (each featuring a lady known under the sobriquet of the title). By contrast, only two plays in the current repertory of the five nō schools have the Shining Genji as their protagonists: *Suma Genji* and *Sumiyoshi mōde*.

Given the exceptional length, complexity, characters, and episodes in the original narrative, the number of nō plays based on *The Tale of Genji* is relatively small. Moreover, they were mainly composed by Zeami's successors.[17] This is mostly due to the difficulty in accessing the entire text of the original *Genji* narrative. Except for the financially and culturally privileged, people in Zeami's time acquired knowledge of *The Tale of Genji* primarily through digests of it or from *renga* manuals dealing with the literary connotations of poetic idioms that were prevalent in the medieval period (see sec. 4.7). This explains why a number of *Genji*-related nō plays were written by highly literate members of the samurai class, and not by professional nō playwrights. The fragmented understanding of the original text among early nō playwrights is further attested to by *Aoi no ue*, one of the earliest plays based on *The Tale of Genji*. It dramatizes a celebrated episode in the original narrative—that is,

---

17   See Goff 1991 for translations and discussions of fifteen plays based on *The Tale of Genji*.

the attack on Lady Aoi, Genji's principal wife, by the spirit of his former lover, Lady Rokujō. The play diverges significantly from the original narrative, especially with the ending when the spirit of Lady Rokujō is finally appeased by the monk's prayer. In the original, however, the spirit succeeds in killing Lady Aoi and continues to torment Genji's other wives.

Another factor that hindered the creation of nō based on *The Tale of Genji* was the challenge in having female characters dance in the play. Most of the major female characters in *Genji* are noblewomen, who were not supposed to dance in real life. Zeami produced numerous plays in which female deities, professional female dancers, or deranged female characters perform a dance at a climactic moment in the play, and thus the dances of female characters became part of the theatrical conventions of nō. It was only after this innovation that female characters could perform dances without any social or dramaturgical justification.

An exemplar of post-Zeami *Genji nō* is *Nonomiya*, composed by Zeami's son-in-law Zenchiku. At the end of the play, the ghost of Lady Rokujō performs a tranquil, meditative dance that neither serves a clear purpose in the plot nor is justified by her social status. The play depicts Genji's last visit to Lady Rokujō at a remote "shrine in the fields" (*nonomiya*) on an autumn night, with frequent textual citations from the original narrative. It also gives a very detailed account of the episode of the "Battle of the Carriages" from chapter 9, "Heart-to-Heart" (*Aoi*), in the *Genji* tale that eventually ends with Lady Rokujō's vengeful action against Lady Aoi. The play thus testifies to Zenchiku's familiarity with the textual source, which was quite exceptional for nō playwrights of this period.[18]

4.3.4 *Martial Narratives*

Some 30 percent of all the nō plays composed during the Muromachi period draw upon war tales, and these include *The Tale of the Heike*, *Taiheiki* (*The Chronicle of the Great Peace*, late 14th c.), *Heiji monogatari* (*The Tale of Heiji*, 13th c.), *Jōkyūki* (*The Record of Jōkyū*, 13th c.), *Soga monogatari* (*The Tale of the Soga Brothers*, 14th c.), and various narratives relating to Minamoto no Yoshitsune and his retainers, such as the *Gikeiki* (*The Chronicle of Yoshitsune*, 14th–15th c.).[19]

---

18 For more details on the use of *The Tale of Genji* in nō, see Goff 1991; Yamanaka 2008b: 81–87.

19 Takemoto 2000: 185. Martial plays are translated and discussed in Shimazaki 1987; Shimazaki 1993; Oyler and Watson 2013.

Undoubtedly the most influential of these was *The Tale of the Heike*, which recounts the war between the Heike (Taira) and the Genji (Minamoto) clans in the late twelfth century. Vividly illustrating the rise and the fall of the Heike and the tragic fate of those caught up in the conflict, *The Tale of the Heike* was widely enjoyed, both through oral storytelling and in many variant written forms. It provides stories for more than 10 percent of the plays in the current nō repertory, including most of the second category *shura nō* or *shura mono* plays about the ghosts of warriors, a category that assumed its present form through Zeami's far-reaching reforms.

Before Zeami, *shura nō* presented the ghosts of warriors as demonic figures who were tormented in the hellish warrior realm (Skt. Asura; J. *shuradō*). Zeami altered this in order to meet the artistic demands of the patrons of the art, shōguns, and high-ranking samurai who emulated court culture. With its focus on aristocratic accomplishments, such as music and poetry, and on human aspects of the warriors, *The Tale of the Heike* was well matched to the new representation of warriors that Zeami sought to achieve in his revised form of *shura nō*. The seven *shura nō* that can be firmly attributed to Zeami—*Atsumori, Kiyotsune, Michimori, Sanemori, Tadanori, Yashima*, and *Yorimasa*—all draw from the *Heike* tale.[20] These plays highlight the human side of the warriors: their artistic sophistication, their anguish or resignation to their tragic fates, or their affection toward their loved ones. These plays are made elegant through frequent references and allusions to classic poems and tales, as mentioned above relating to the play *Atsumori*.

In his *shura nō*, Zeami did not make use of the *Taiheiki*, another epic war tale that describes the political and military machinations of the power struggle between the emperor Godaigo (1288–1339) and the shogunal powers in the fourteenth century. It is not clear why Zeami did not make use of this source. Perhaps he avoided it because of the work's overly realistic depiction of brutality of war or perhaps the tale was too close in time and therefore too politically sensitive to be staged. By contrast, *The Tale of the Heike* retells a conflict that took place two centuries earlier in a manner that romanticizes the historical figures in such a way that they are almost fictionalized. It could even be argued that the creation of warrior-spirit nō based on *The Tale of the Heike* forged the way for *mugen nō* drawn from *The Tale of Genji*, in which a ghost of a fictional character appears before a monk to ask for religious salvation.[21]

Aside from the *shura nō*, most nō plays based on war tales are *genzai nō*, in which the main event unfolds in the dramatic present through interactions

---

20 *Michimori* is an earlier play that was largely remade by Zeami.
21 Yamanaka 2008b: 89–90.

between the living characters. These include many plays dealing with Minamoto no Yoshitsune and his retainers, second in number only to those based on *The Tale of the Heike*.[22] Yoshitsune also appears in the *Heike* story as a prominent general on the victors' side, but the diverse legends about him and his followers that developed following its completion concentrate on other periods of his life, either incidents from his youth or in the aftermath of the Genji victory over the Heike. Most Yoshitsune-related nō plays are grounded in these popular legends that portray him as an innocent hero tragically deceived by politically cunning enemies. The *Gikeiki* is the most notable collection of such narratives related to Yoshitsune and his retainers, although it never served as direct source material for nō.

These Yoshitune plays can be divided into several types: those spotlighting him as an agile, aspiring young boy (e.g., *Eboshi-ori, Hashi Benkei, Kumasaka, Kurama tengu*); those depicting his narrow escape with his followers after their victory against the Heike clan and the subsequent false accusations of betrayal by his own brother, the shōgun Minamoto no Yoritomo (e.g., *Ataka, Funa Benkei, Settai, Shōzon*); those portraying the difficulties suffered by his lover Shizuka, a famous *shirabyōshi* dancer, after he left her behind (e.g., *Futari Shizuka, Yoshino Shizuka*); and those featuring Yoshitsune's individual retainers and their families (e.g., *Nishikido, Tadanobu*).

4.3.5   *Religious Narratives and Other Religious Materials*

Plays that dramatize the narratives related to Japan's creation myths are *Furu, Gendayū, Kusanagi, Mimosuso, Orochi, Tamanoi,* and *Unoha*. Rather than drawing directly from the two compilations of Japanese mythology, the *Kojiki* (*A Record of Ancient Matters*, 712) and the *Nihongi* (*The Chronicles of Japan*, also *Nihon shoki*, 720), these plays usually reflect the common medieval understanding of these myths in interpretations collectively referred to as *chūsei Nihongi* (medieval-period *Nihongi*).

Origin tales and stories of miracles connected to shrines, temples, and deities were popularly enjoyed in the medieval period through oral preaching, sometimes with the help of illustrated handscrolls and mandalas. They were also the inspiration for the nō plays *Ama, Dōjōji, Enoshima, Kusenoto, Seiganji, Taema,* and *Unomatsuri*, to name a few, which dramatized the legends of particular temples and shrines.

A deity featured in a number of nō plays is Hachiman (or Yawata), also called the Great Bodhisattva Hachiman (Hachiman Daibosatsu). He is said to be an

---

22   For an overview of plays related to Yoshitsune and his retainers, see McCullough, trans. 1966: 36–66.

avatar of the Amitabha (J. Amida) Buddha, who was believed to have appeared in this world as the Japanese emperor Ōjin. His mother, Empress Jingū, was imagined to have conquered the Korean Peninsula when she was pregnant with the future emperor. She is enshrined along with Ōjin in the Hachiman shrines located throughout Japan. Empress Jingū's legendary expedition to the Korean Peninsula and the Hachiman deity's special protection of the nation, including during the attempted Mongol invasions of Japan in 1274 and 1281, are detailed in various narratives such as *Hachiman gudōkun* (*Exegesis of Hachiman Legends for the Ignorant and Children*, late 13th–early 14th c.) and *Hachimangū junpaiki* (*A Record of Pilgrimages to Hachiman Shrines*, latter half of 13th c.). In addition, countless illustrated handscrolls were created and used in preaching at Hachiman shrines across the country.

As the guardian deity of the Genji clan (the Ashikaga were a branch), and the god of war and archery, Hachiman was especially revered by the third shōgun Ashikaga Yoshimitsu (1358–1408; r. 1368–1394) and his successors, who were patrons of the arts during Zeami's lifetime. Not surprisingly, these narratives provided the source material for numerous plays, such as *Hakozaki*, *Hōjōgawa*, *Kashii*, *Yawata yumi*, and *Yumi Yawata*, in which the Hachiman deity or his mother, the Jingū deity, offer benedictions to the current regime.

Besides Hachiman, another deity worshipped by the Ashikaga shogunate was Tenman Tenjin, the deification of Sugawara no Michizane (845–903). A distinguished poet, scholar, and politician, Michizane was believed to have become a fierce, vengeful spirit after his death in exile. Legends about Michizane, some of which were depicted in illustrated handscrolls produced for Tenjin shrines, served as sources for plays such as *Dōmyōji*, *Kanshōjō*, *Oimatsu*, and *Raiden*, as well as for earlier nō plays that are today lost, as can be seen in Zeami's account in *Sarugaku dangi*.[23]

There are a number of nō plays from the latter half of the Muromachi period that exhibit a clear tendency for scenes that are visually appealing and spectacular. They also take up religious themes in ways that were previously uncommon. For example, audiences' increased interest in unique religious services in the provinces is reflected in plays (e.g., *Mekari*, *Hitachiobi*), which represent local Shintō practices in Hitachi and Nagato Provinces, present-day Ibaraki and Yamaguchi Prefectures, respectively.[24] Others aimed at representing the visual images found in religious illustrated handscrolls and mandalas

---

23   See Scholz-Cionca 1991 for German translations and discussions of plays featuring Sugawara no Michizane.
24   Yamanaka 1996: 14.

(*Arashiyama, Nakifudō*) and other esoteric religious services (*Kōso, Kurokawa, Ningyō*).²⁵

4.3.6 Other Sources
Aside from the sources mentioned above, many other short tales were widely known in the Muromachi period. They were transmitted orally, for instance, through preaching, and in written form as in illustrated books and handscrolls, and in various collections of short tales such as the thirteenth-century *Jikkinshō* (*Miscellany of Ten Maxims*) and *Senjūshō* (*Tales of Renunciation*). They also served as sources for nō plays, including *Eguchi, Sesshōseki,* and *Zegai*.

Nō plays also frequently adopt Chinese themes.²⁶ *Chōryō, Shōkun,* and *Yōkihi,* for example, were so named after the historical Chinese figures Zhang Liang, Wang Zhaojun, and Yang Guifei, respectively. The main plot of the play *Kantan* can be traced back to a famous Tang-dynasty tale *Zhenzhong ji* (*Record within a Pillow*). It appears that nō playwrights only rarely consulted original Chinese sources, and generally these themes had already been long familiar in Japan through literary renditions. The medieval war narratives such as the *Taiheiki*, for instance, often retell Chinese anecdotes as comparable precedents for events in Japan. Nō plays usually turned to those domestic versions as their sources.

4.4 Nō and Its Belief Systems
Tom Hare and Takahashi Yūsuke

Various religious beliefs and practices have impacted the origins and the development of nō. This section presents them in a range of contexts, beginning with the beliefs and legends particular to performers of *sarugaku*—that is, early nō and kyōgen. It will then discuss the roles of gods, as well as the placation of spirits and ghosts, and examine the manifestations of religious devotion in nō plays before looking at the relation between Zen Buddhism and nō performance and theory.

4.4.1 Beliefs Particular to Sarugaku *Players in the Formative Period*
What types of beliefs were held by the creators and early performers of *sarugaku*? An answer to this question requires a consideration of matters such

---
25 Texts survive of all these plays, but today only *Mekari* and *Arashiyama* are currently performed.
26 Yip 2016.

as the sanctity of *Okina* or *Okina sarugaku*, the representation of gods and demons onstage, and the use of demon masks within a historical and religious setting.

4.4.1.1   *Okina* as Sacred Ritual and the Celebratory Character of Nō

Okina (also known as *Shikisanban*; see ch. 1 *History*, 1.1), which is today performed mainly at the New Year or on special occasions, holds a special place in the nō repertory, and its mask is viewed as a sacred object (see ch. 2 *Performance*, 2.8). From its beginnings in the thirteenth century, it has been associated with New Year rituals, agricultural rituals, and ancestor cults. Zeami regarded it as the foundation of *sarugaku* performance, and it has been handed down since that time, albeit with some changes in performance elements.

Many aspects of *Okina* are also seen in other nō plays. For instance, *Okina* has a strong incantatory quality grounded in celebration in which an old man, the Okina, delivers prayers for peace in the world and stability throughout the realm. Nō drama overall retains a strongly commemorative character. First category plays, in particular, include similar prayers for peace and prosperity. In addition, the singing of auspicious passages from certain plays as short songs (*koutai*) has been practiced since the Muromachi period. Another way the celebratory essence of nō is retained is in the custom of closing a program of plays about the quelling of ghosts and demons with the auspicious song "Senshūraku" from the end of the play *Takasago*.

The *Meishukushū* (*Collection Illuminating the Indwelling Deity*, ca. 1460s) (see ch. 6 *Treatises*, 6.4) written by Konparu Zenchiku, is the most prominent text since the Muromachi period to extol the sanctity of the Okina, asserting that the old man who appears in *Okina* should be regarded as the god of *sarugaku* performance, and a manifestation of various other buddhas and gods. Accordingly, on the first of each month, they made obeisance to the *Okina* mask and to the sacred image (*miei*) of the god of performance wearing a courtier's *suikan* outfit, a monk's surplice (J. *kesa*; Skt. *kaṣaya*), and a tall *eboshi* hat, and carrying a *hinoki* cypress fan and rosary. There is no question that the development of Okina as the god of performance is connected to the belief that the *Okina* mask itself was sacred. There are, in fact, numerous miracle tales handed down since the medieval period in which manifestations of deities and buddhas occur in the form of old men, evidence that people's imagination was occupied with the idea of manifestations of sacred beings.

Many riddles surround the origins of *Okina sarugaku*, but one thread leading to the answer to such riddles is to be found in the *shushōe* ritual (see ch. 1 *History*, 1.1) and festival held from the first to the seventh day of the New Year in the Jōgyō Hall at Myōrakuji, a Tendai-lineage temple in Tōnomine in Nara

Prefecture. (The Jōgyō Hall is a Buddha Hall with Amida Buddha at the center.) During the Muromachi period, the *shushōe* at Myōrakuji served to welcome the guardian deity Matarajin. On the third night of the New Year, a monk would appear before the portable shrine housing the Matarajin wearing an *Okina* mask and chanting lines from an early version of the mnemonics of the instrumental music for *Okina* as performed in nō. Then once again, on the fifth night of the New Year, a monk wearing the *Okina* mask would chant a *saimon* (a Buddhist hymn or praise song) before the Matarajin. The *Meishukushū* makes reference to the ritual and the mask, and it is possible that the Myōrakuji rite, with a monk performing in the *Okina* mask, is one of the forerunners of the nō *Okina*. The celebratory character of *Okina* is also related to the Buddhist rituals of the *shushōe* and their New Year prayers for peace.

4.4.2 *The* Okina *Mask and Belief in the* Kōjin

The *Meishukushū* also records religious observances centered on demon masks on the twenty-eighth day of each month, a day devoted to the propitiation of potentially dangerous demigods. These demigods appear first in documents of the eleventh century with a double character as *kōjin* (disruptive and dangerous deities), who must be propitiated as evil gods but who could bestow great benefits if brought under control. Zeami, in fact, mentions them in his treatises. In "Shingi ni iwaku" ("Divine Purport"), chapter 4 in his *Fūshi kaden*, Zeami writes that after the legendary founder of *sarugaku*, Hata no Kawakatsu, had transmitted his art to his descendants, he floated away to the coast of Sakoshi in Harima Province (present-day Hyōgo Prefecture) and became a *kōjin* in the form of a vengeful deity. Since he was worshipped as a god, however, the province prospered. Moreover, Zenchiku records in *Meishukushū* that Hata no Kawakatsu was himself a *kōjin* but was known as "*Sarugaku no miya*" or "The *Shukujin*." He goes on to quote a passage in scripture to the effect that Okina should be worshipped as such a *kōjin* because he will then become a buddha (specifically a *Tathagata*).

Belief in the *kōjin* was not restricted to Zeami and Zenchiku, but appears to have been widespread among the performers of Yamato *sarugaku*, and one can infer a yet older tradition of such beliefs. In *Meishukushū*, Zenchiku touches upon the unity of the *kōjin* and Kangiten (a Japanese version of the Indian Hindu deity Ganesha), and it seems that he went so far as to perform offices for Kangiten on Mount Inari. Kangiten is regarded as the benevolent version of the obstacle deity Vinayaka, and by the middle of the twelfth century, a doctrine emerged in which Kangiten is seen as identical to the *kōjin*.

In the time before the development of *Okina sarugaku* from the late Heian to the early Kamakura period (twelfth to thirteenth centuries), *sarugaku* players participated in the *shushōe* festivals and rituals of State Buddhism carried out at the New Year. On the last day of the *shushōe*, the *tsuina* ritual was performed to assure peace and stability in the world by chasing away demons. The demons in question were identified as Vinayaka, and it was possible that *sarugaku* players performed this role. The "Divine Purport" in Zeami's *Fūshi kaden* recounts a legend about the origin of *sarugaku* in India, where an attempt to prevent the historical Buddha Shakyamuni from delivering a sermon is thwarted by means of performance. By turning the malevolent potential of *kōjin* toward the beneficence of Buddha, *sarugaku* performers expressed their belief that performance could symbolically transform the whole world for the better.

4.4.3 Gods in Nō

As noted earlier, the plays that best exemplify an auspicious or celebratory character are those of the first category, in which a god appears and bestows blessings upon the nation or narrates the founding of a shrine or temple. Examples of such plays are *Takasago*, in which the god Sumiyoshi Myōjin makes himself manifest at the Sumiyoshi Shrine in Osaka before the *waki*, a priest from the Aso Shrine in Kyushu, to dance a *kami mai* (deity dance); and *Naniwa*, set in the Osaka area in the village of Naniwa, in which Wani (the *nochi shite*) and the female deity Konohana Sakuyahime (the *nochi tsure*) appear before a retainer of the imperial house and perform a dance recalling courtly *bugaku* to rejoice in peace in the realm. Or there is *Arashiyama*, in which the gods Komori Myōjin, Katsute Myōjin (*nochi tsure*) and Zaō Gongen (*nochi shite*) appear and present a short vigorous dance called *mai-bataraki*. All these plays are characterized by energetic performances to honor the current reign, cast out demons, afford protection to the people, and bless the nation. This reflects the fact that nō was nurtured into being within the cultural context of shrines and temples (see ch. 1, *History*, 1.1).

In medieval Japan, the belief in the gods was intimately negotiated with Buddhist thought such that the gods appearing on the nō stage are different in certain respects from the gods of Shintō as conceived today. Among first category nō, for instance, in the play *Chikubushima*, the *nochi tsure*, Benzaiten, a transformation of the Hindu female deity Sarasvati, and the *nochi shite*, a dragon god, together express the syncretic deity Uga-Benzaiten. The iconography of Uga-Benzaiten includes the image of an aged dragon god on top of the head of a female deity. Another example is the play *Yōrō*, the last act of which emphasizes the unity of the Shintō god manifest as the *nochi shite* with a Buddhist bodhisattva Yōryū Kannon, a version of Avalokitesvara (J. Kannon). This is a clear representation of the fusion of Buddhist and Shintō belief typical of medieval Japan.

In the play *Makiginu*, the *shite* is a female shaman possessed by gods of the Kumano Shrine, but at the climax of the piece, several buddhas and bodhisattvas are manifested through them. This mirrors the medieval Japanese doctrine of *honji suijaku* (the earthly manifestation of transcendent deities), whereby the Shintō gods were considered avatars of transcendent buddhas. In another play, *Miwa*, the god who gives the play its name appears before a Buddhist monk to request release from suffering, exemplifying a pattern in folk legends about suffering gods that is traceable to the eighth-century practice of constructing small Buddhist temples alongside Shintō shrines to alleviate the distress of the deity. In the eleventh to twelfth centuries, the belief that the gods were avatars of buddhas became widespread, as evinced in the play *Makiginu*, but the earlier belief that a suffering god might seek relief from a Buddhist monk did not disappear. In nō, then, belief in the suffering god and the god who was the avatar of a buddha coexisted in parallel versions. It is possible to find examples of each type of god in plays in the nō repertory.

4.4.4 Offerings to the Dead and the Placation of Spirits in Nō

There are a great number of plays in nō in which the main character, the *shite* as a ghost, appears onstage in search of salvation. This is a major characteristic of nō as a dramatic genre. In second category nō plays (*shura nō*) featuring the spirit of a warrior as the principal character, there are often scenes in which this character complains about the suffering he experiences in the Asura realm. In Japanese, this *shuradō* (literally "Path of Asuras") is one of the six paths into which an individual can be reincarnated after death, the others being those of heavenly beings, human beings, animals, hungry demons, and denizens of hell. The Path of Asuras is a world of ceaseless torture by the sword, and was conceived as the inevitable fate of a warrior who had killed others. Zeami lived around two centuries following the Genpei War, but the ghosts of warriors killed in those wars were still believed to appear on occasion. In 1414, for example, there were rumors circulating that the spirit of Saitō Bettō Sanemori (1111–1183) had appeared to a monk of the Ji lineage of Buddhism at the place in Shinowara in Kaga Province (present-day southern and western Ishikawa Prefecture) where Sanemori had been killed. This is thought to have been the source of the nō play *Sanemori*. During this period, the placation of the spirits of warriors fallen in battle was a major social concern, thus the spirit of Sanemori seeks salvation from the monk in the play bearing his name. Zeami created *shura nō*, and he explained that it was desirable to compose these plays in such a way that there would be a connection with the beauty of the natural world, season by season, and music and poetry. But the fact that even within this context an account of suffering in the Asura realm should find a conventional place speaks to the importance of the religious background for such plays.

There are other plays in which spirits, who did not die on the battlefield, remain in this world because of lingering emotions and attachments. From a Buddhist perspective, in which an individual aims to achieve release from the cycle of reincarnation through the Six Paths in order to achieve Buddhahood, this obsession with or clinging to the worldly has negative connotations. Nonetheless, the appearance of the spirits of the deceased and the recounting of their memories of life were regarded in themselves as important means toward the placation of the spirit. It is this very recollection and recounting that become the focal point of the drama in many nō plays about ghosts, and in most cases, the plays revolve around the quest for Buddhist salvation through the revelation of events during life. It should be noted, however, that even fictional characters from literary works such as *The Tales of Ise* and *The Tale of Genji* seek religious salvation in nō plays, just like the spirits of actual historical figures.

4.4.5   *Shamanism and Spirit Possession*

In chapter 2, "Monomane jōjō" ("Notes on Dramatic Imitation"), in his *Fūshi kaden*, Zeami discusses the madness resulting from the separation of parents from their children or spouses from each other and touches upon characters who have gone mad because of their possession by supernatural beings. In premodern Japan, gods and spirits were believed to possess humans and to make oracular pronouncements through them. There are plays in the nō repertory based on such supernatural possession.

During an encounter with the shrine priest in the play *Futari Shizuka*, for example, a woman who has come to the Katte Shrine in Yoshino to offer freshly plucked herbs to the gods suddenly undergoes an uncanny change in appearance due to her possession by the spirit of Lady Shizuka. In the play *Sotoba Komachi*, the aged Komachi is possessed by the spirit of her erstwhile suitor, Lesser Captain Fukakusa (Fukakusa no Shōshō). In some plays, such as *Aoi no ue*, *Makiginu* and *Utaura*, professional shamans take to the stage. *Aoi no ue* depicts a female shrine priest who strikes a catalpa bow while intoning a magical *waka* poem in order to call forth the vengeful spirit of the royal consort, Lady Rokujō. A female shaman in *Makiginu* is possessed by a series of gods from Kumano, while in *Utaura*, a shaman is possessed by a spirit as he dances the *Jigoku no kusemai*, or "Kuse Dance about Hell." In these cases, madness itself, entailing the wild manifestations of spirit possession during a deranged state and the starkly contrasting return to psychological normalcy, becomes the focal point of the drama.

4.4.6   *Esoteric Religion*

There are numerous nō plays in which an evil spirit plays a central role, with *Aoi no ue* a representative example. In most plays that feature such an evil spirit, an ascetic typically appears in order to quell and chase the spirit off by deploying his rosary beads and intoning the mantra of the most prominent of the Five Heavenly Kings, Fudō Myōō (Skt. Acala). In *Aoi no ue*, for instance, a holy man from Mount Hiei is summoned to save Lady Aoi, who has been attacked by the evil spirit of Lady Rokujō. He calls upon the Five Heavenly Kings, chanting the mantra of Fudō Myōō, and succeeds in quelling the vengeful spirit. This pattern can be observed in many plays, among them *Dōjōji*, *Zegai* and *Adachigahara*. In *Funa Benkei*, the general Minamoto no Yoshitsune finds his sword to be of no use against the angry spirit of the dead Heike warrior, Taira no Tomomori, who has emerged from the sea. Ultimately, it is his retainer Benkei who manages to send the evil spirit away with prayers to the Five Heavenly Kings, a further demonstration that the medieval Japanese believed in the existence of a world that could only be controlled through esoteric magic.

4.4.7   *Manifestations of Religious Devotion in Nō Plays*

In addition to the placation of a range of angry spirits, a number of nō plays offer expiation or comfort to the deceased who are trapped in attachment to their past lives. The ground for such expiation frequently draws upon belief in the efficacy of the *Lotus Sutra* (J. Hokekyō), in the chanting of Buddha's name (*nenbutsu*), or in the compassion and mercy of buddhas (often Amida) and bodhisattvas (often Kannon). Plays such as *Ama*, *Hyakuman*, and *Sumidagawa* focus on beliefs related to Pure Land Buddhism, not in a strictly sectarian sense, but more broadly embracing devotionalism as exemplified in Tendai Buddhist thought or in the practices of charismatic movements such as the Ji lineage, as noted above regarding the play *Sanemori*.

4.4.7.1   Devotion to Amida Buddha in the Play *Taema*

In *Taema*, the mechanics of devotion inform the play in both plot and structure. The work draws on the story of Chūjōhime, a pious eighth-century court lady and relates how she took a strict vow never to leave her grass hut in the hills west of Nara until she had seen Amida Buddha firsthand. Legend recounts how she spent day and night reciting the *nenbutsu*. One evening an old nun appeared to her, and when Chūjōhime asked who she was, the nun replied, "What a silly question! You've been calling for me all along, so here I am." Chūjōhime's vow had been fulfilled. This tale is recounted to the *waki*, himself a devotee of *nenbutsu*, and two fellow monks (*waki tsure*) by a mysterious old nun (*shite*) who is accompanied by a female companion (*tsure*). The entourage of the *waki* are on pilgrimage and have made their way to the temple Taema where they encounter both the *shite* and *tsure*.

The chorus praises the wondrous tale of Chūjōhime at this point and asks why the old nun and her companion have turned up at the temple at this particular time. They say they have come to perform a religious rite, at which point "a brilliant light flashes, flower petals rain down from the sky, a wondrous fragrance fills the air, music resounds, and the two women mount purple clouds and disappear into the heavens." In the last act of the play, Chūjōhime appears as a bodhisattva offering the *waki* and the audience a splendid vision.[27]

Written by Zeami, *Taema* follows a relatively orthodox structure, but it is noteworthy that the structure reinforces the tale of Chūjōhime and her miraculous encounter. The *waki* and his companions pursue their devotional rounds, thereby echoing the Chūjōhime of legend, while the *shite* and *tsure* appearing before them are avatars of Amida and Kannon.[28]

4.4.7.2   Devotion to the Bodhisattva Kannon in *Morihisa*

Other plays are more literal enactments of miracles attributed to Buddhist faith. The play *Morihisa*, for example, begins with a conversation between the *shite*, the warrior Morihisa, and the *waki*, Tsuchiya Saburō, a lower-ranking retainer of the Kamakura shogunate. Morihisa asks to be taken to Kiyomizudera, a temple in the hills east of Kyoto, and once there, he delivers the following lines:

MORIHISA (*shite*) [*sashi*]
 Glory to Kanzeon [Kannon] of great love and compassion,
 bounteous as the grass are the blessings of his holy vow
 such that a single prayer, a lone appeal to his name, inspires confidence.
 So how could the affinity of long devotion fail to prove true?
 Yet all the same, how sad to think of parting![29]

The final line alludes to the tension in the plot, because Morihisa, having been condemned to death, is being taken to Kamakura to meet his fate. Much of what follows traces his journey, with the imminent execution overshadowing

---

27 For a translation of *Taema*, see Rimer 1970.
28 This is not merely a coincidence; it is coded into the text at one point when the author echoes his own name in the chant of the *tsure*: *hachiman shoshōgyō kai ze-Amida to mo* 八万諸聖教皆是阿弥陀とも. The character *ze* in this text is not the same as that in Zeami's own name, but the chant contains the same kind of pun one finds in other plays by Zeami, so we can read the pun as a devotional statement by the author.
29 Yokomichi and Omote, eds. 1960: 413. All the translations in this section are by Tom Hare, unless otherwise indicated; see Quinn 2013: 355.

poetic references to the places passed on the journey. Arriving in Kamakura, Morihisa asks that the execution be carried out immediately, but Tsuchiya informs him it will take place the following morning. Morihisa then requests to be left alone to chant a passage from Buddhist scripture extolling the virtues of the Bodhisattva of Compassion, Kannon. Included among those virtues is escape from royal condemnation, something the *waki* notes with surprise since he has by now developed a degree of empathy for his prisoner. The undaunted warrior Morihisa renounces hope for any such escape himself, saying he chants the sutra so as not to be consigned to warrior hell after his death.

Morihisa sleeps and upon waking recounts that he has had a miraculous dream. Tsuchiya announces that the cock has crowed, and it is time to go to the execution grounds. Morihisa follows his orders in expectation that he will soon die. He chants the name of Kannon, but as the executioner raises his sword to strike he is blinded by a light emanating from the sutra Morihisa holds: the sword has been split into two. Tsuchiya stops the execution and reports the events to the shōgun. Morihisa is then summoned to retell what transpired in his dream. In it, he saw an old man in scented vestments carrying a crystal rosary who announced that he had appeared on account of Morihisa's extraordinary devotion: "Have no fear, for I have come in exchange for your life."[30] At this point, Morihisa awoke from the dream. The shōgun admits that he, too, had the same dream that morning. Morihisa is spared and does a dance (*otoko mai*, or "man's dance") to celebrate the miracle.

4.4.7.3 A Miraculous Reunion Effected by Kannon

A similar use of dreams appears in another play eulogizing faith in Kannon, but from a different social context. The play, *Miidera*,[31] belongs to the genre of plays about lost children and their distraught parents (see ch. 2 *Performance*, 2.3). It opens with lines of the *shite* praising Kannon in the hope of recovering a lost child. After this scene, the mother leaves the stage, and this is followed by a scene in which the *waki* and his companions, monks from the temple Onjōji, explain that they are en route to the temple Miidera with a lost child who has appealed to them for help. Their reason for the trip is that this is the night of the most celebrated full moon of the year, and they wish to join the crowd there.

The mother, meanwhile, announces that she has had a dream telling her to go to Miidera. She arrives there and becomes the center of attention in her distraction at having lost her child. At Miidera, she asks for permission to ring

---

30 Yokomichi and Omote, eds. 1960: 421; see Quinn 2013: 373.
31 A translation of *Miidera* by Eileen Kato is found in Brazell, ed. 1997: 158–78.

the great bell. At first, the *waki* tries to chase her away, but she persuades him to let her proceed. What follows is the acclaimed "Bell Scene" (*Kane no dan*), characterizing the sound of the bell as the voice of Dharma.

The child who has accompanied the monks notices the woman ringing the bell and singing. He asks the *waki* to inquire about her and discovers that she is from the village of Kiyomigaseki. Upon hearing this, the child recognizes the woman as his mother. The *waki* remains suspicious, but the child and mother both press their case, and claim they have been reunited on account of the bell. The play ends happily with their reunion.

4.4.8 *Buddhism and Social Action*

Buddhism is not all meditation, ritual, and devotion. Counted among the great Buddhist figures in Japanese history were influential leaders of movements for social change and the betterment of people's lives. This, too, is reflected in the plots of nō plays, such as the work *Jinen koji*, whose *shite* is a *koji*, or "lay monk."[32]

4.4.8.1 Lay Monk Jinen Rescues a Slave

An introductory passage explains that the lay monk Jinen has undertaken a series of sermons at the temple Ungoji in the hills east of Kyoto. This is the final and particularly important day, and as Jinen delivers his sermon, the gift of a beautiful *kosode* ("small sleeve") kimono is brought to his attention. A young girl has offered the kimono in exchange for prayers to assist the rebirth in paradise of her parents. Jinen and the assembled crowd are all moved to tears by such devotion.

The scene then changes. The *waki*, a slave trader, explains to the audience that he has been in the capital buying slaves, and that one of them is a girl of fourteen or fifteen. The day before she had asked permission to leave her captivity temporarily. He had allowed this, but now wonders whether she went to Ungoji to pray for her parents. He asks his companion, the *waki tsure*, to go in search of her. The *waki tsure* identifies her in the crowd and attempts to take her away. The villager objects, but he is intimidated and eventually lets her go with the slave traders. He tells Jinen about the incident, who concludes that she has sold herself into slavery to buy the very kimono that she offered him for prayers. Jinen sees this as an opportunity to show the difference between good and evil, and immediately breaks off his sermon to go after the girl. He locates the slave traders and the girl just as they are pulling away from shore

---

32 For translations, see Ueda, trans. 1962 (*Jinen the Preacher*); Tyler 1978a (*Layman Selfsame*); Shimazaki 1998 (*Jinen koji*).

at Lake Biwa. He detains them and argues for the girl's release. The slave traders initially refuse to give her up, but Jinen distracts them in a series of clever verbal disputations. Finally, in exchange for the performance of some dances for which he is celebrated, they release the girl.

At first glance, the plot of *Jinen koji* might appear as an excuse to have an attractive young actor exchange witty dialogue and perform some masterful dancing, but its focus on a monk's beneficence points to a broader social concern. This is echoed in other plays in the repertory and in the texts of plays no longer performed, in which people with religious convictions work for the betterment of humankind, while in other plays, social evils are exposed in the performance (e.g., *Yura no minato no kusemai*, "The *Kusemai* at Yura Bay").[33]

4.4.9 Zen Buddhism and Nō: Performance and Theory

The link between nō and religion has frequently focused on Zen, and this is not surprising since nō originated in the late fourteenth- and fifteenth-centuries when intellectual life in Japan was deeply embedded in the language of Zen. Nonetheless, the mid-twentieth-century enthusiasm for Zen sometimes led to characterizations of the Japanese visual and performance arts from all eras as somehow expressing the "spirit" of Zen without substantive support for such assertions. Zen is clearly relevant to the backdrop against which nō evolved, but it is important to clarify how such a relationship is articulated.

4.4.9.1 Zen in the Plot

In a superficial sense, Zen plays a role in certain nō plays as a plot device. In some, characters are identified as Zen monks (e.g., *Zenji Soga*),[34] and Zen dialogues are used to further the development of a given story. One of the most representative examples of this is the play *Hōkazō*.[35]

The *shite* in *Hōkazō* is a young man, Makino Kojirō, whose father was killed in a quarrel with Tone Nobutoshi. Resolved to take his revenge, but reluctant to face Tone alone, Kojirō appeals to his elder brother, who had been given to a Zen temple as a child. The brother readily agrees but wonders how they will catch the enemy unawares. They decide to take advantage of the contemporary craze for "performer monks"—the *hōkazō* of the title. The brothers disguise themselves as *hōkazō* and approach Tone at Mishima, where he seeks refuge from his nightmares. Tone is suspicious since they do not have the vestments conventionally worn by monks. In fact, they only carry a flat fan inscribed in

---

33   *Yura no minato no kusemai* is translated in Hare, trans. 2008: 373–77.
34   Sanari 1954: 3:1689–98; Nonomura and Ōtani 1978: 491–93.
35   Sanari 1954: 4:2435–52; Nonomura and Ōtani 1978: 451–54.

Chinese and a staff. In response to Tone's question of their claim to be monks, Kojirō replies that "The fan in motion produces a fresh breeze, when still it represents the unclouded moon: the unclouded moon and a fresh breeze reside between movement and stillness and serve our religious discipline in recalling to us that all dharmas are the product of the mind in action."

Tone, satisfied with this response, then asks about the bow and arrows carried by one of the brothers: "What kind of priestly implement is a bow!" he says, to which the elder brother replies, "The bow takes the form of the passage of time, representing the sun and moon and the secret Dharma of the nonduality of the pure and the impure." Later he adds: "We shoot with bows undrawn and arrows unloosed, neither hitting our target nor missing it." Tone then continues and questions the brothers' Zen lineage and practice. They respond by citing Zen claims to a lineage outside the sutras that does not subsist in language. As the brothers answer his each and every question, they edge closer and closer to their revenge. The discourse of Zen is thus used ingeniously as a plot device and generator of dialogue. At one point, the esoteric guardian king, Aizen Myōō is also invoked, demonstrating the play's catholic approach to the reuse of religious material for dramatic ends.

In *Hōkazō*, Zen appears as a pretext to allow the brothers to advance their vendetta, and if there is religious or quasi-religious importance to the play, it is not clearly related to Zen, but rather to the fact that the two brothers exact their revenge as an act of filial duty. Once they have accomplished their goal, its significance as an example of filial piety is summed up in a final line, "To attack the enemy of one's parents comes from a deep commitment to filial piety, and for this their names will live on for countless generations." Whether such sentiments can be interpreted as religious or ideological would depend upon the definition of "religious" in this context, but nevertheless it does not provide much support for a substantive connection between Zen and nō.

4.4.9.2 Enlightenment as a Theme in *Sotoba Komachi*

More persuasive engagements with Buddhist doctrine can be found in other plays, however, most notably in the celebrated early work, *Sotoba Komachi*,[36] attributed to Kan'ami and revised by Zeami.

Sotoba Komachi is one of five plays in the modern repertory in which the great tenth-century poet, Ono no Komachi, plays a central role. Here, she is an unattractive old crone, unrecognizable from the legendary beauty of her youth. As she leaves the capital, where she is now despised, she sits down, exhausted, on what she thinks is an old block of wood. Before long, a pair of monks (*waki* and *waki tsure*) approach her, berating her for sitting on a fragment of a sacred

---

36   *Sotoba Komachi*, Yokomichi and Omote, eds. 1960: 81–88.

Buddhist statue (characterized as a stupa in the play). They tell her to move along, but in the dialogue that follows she reveals that her spiritual depth is far greater than theirs:

MONK (*waki*) [*mondō*]
    You there! Derelict! What you've set yourself down on ... a stupa, the very form of Buddha? Get away from there and go somewhere else to rest.
KOMACHI (*shite*)
    How good of you to point out that an image given the Buddha's form is a blessed object ... yet I don't see any words inscribed here, or any carving to reveal a form. It's nothing but a rotting stump as far as I can see.
MONK [*kakeai*]
    Though moldering deep in the wilderness, no tree can hide if yet it blossoms bears, how much less a tree graced with Buddha's face!
KOMACHI
    Though myself of no account, just a buried stump, there are yet blossoms in this mind of mine, so why not take them as my offering?[37]

A debate on doctrine follows, in which Komachi challenges the monks, engaging in a deeper level of spiritual discourse. This frustrates them and leads them to ask her, "If you have such an enlightened mind, why then haven't you forsaken the world?" to which she responds, "As if it were in mere appearances that the world should be forsaken!—no, giving up the world is a matter of the mind!"

Such an assertion is not the sole domain of Zen. It resonates with the psychological emphasis characteristic of Buddhist thought generally, but it is clear that Komachi takes a more specifically Zen-oriented approach. The dialogue between her and the monks demonstrates the significance of nonduality. She then alludes to the *Platform Sutra of the Sixth Patriarch* (C. *Liuzu Tanjing*, a central text of Chinese Chan [J. Zen] Buddhism) in quoting the celebrated poem with which the sixth patriarch Huineng makes manifest his enlightenment. By this time, Komachi has the monks entirely in her control:

MONK (*waki*) [*kakeai*]
    Enlightenment
KOMACHI (*shite*)
    Never was a tree

---

37   Yokomichi and Omote, eds. 1960: 84; see translation by Herschel Miller in Shirane, ed. 2007.

MONK
   The bright mirror
KOMACHI
   Never had a stand.
CHORUS [*uta*]
   For it's true: "Fundamentally, there is no 'thing'."
   So then, there is no distance between Buddha and the rest of us.[38]

Is the employment of Zen in *Sotoba Komachi* fundamentally different from what was seen in *Hōkazō*? The answer to such a question will depend on how one approaches the notoriously thorny question of what Zen is in the first place. On the one hand, the scriptural allusion is clear and Komachi defeats the monks at their own game—they acknowledge as much themselves—so the connection of *Sotoba Komachi* to such a legacy is stronger than in *Hōkazō*. Interestingly, however, this is not the end of the play. In what follows, the monks question Komachi about her clothing, and she tells them about it in a way that both links it to priestly vestments and distinguishes it from them, primarily by reference to her dire poverty. In the most striking scene after the "Zen dialogue," she goes mad, possessed by her frustrated suitor, Lesser Captain Fukakusa (Fukakusa no Shōshō). This leads to the denouement of the play, in which she acts out his agony and frustration in courting her, only to die before his love is consummated. The play concludes with Komachi's expression of a hope for enlightenment, even with the entanglements of passion.

Zen, or not? Despite Komachi's spiritual discernments and insights, she seems very far from enlightenment in the last act of the play. At the same time, if Zen's claims about nonduality are taken seriously, then the snares of passion in the play might indeed be seen as simply one more version of enlightenment. This would accord with the antinomian and deconstructive Zen of a figure such as Ikkyū Sōjun (1394–1481), himself a great fan of nō performance.

4.4.9.3   Zen, Training, and Aesthetic Theory

The use of Zen in nō plays is only one aspect of its relation to nō more generally. The place Zen holds in training, performance, and the vocation of the actor must also be considered when looking at the relation between nō and Zen. The most cogent materials for such an examination are found in Zeami's treatises, but his son-in-law Konparu Zenchiku was also deeply interested in Zen and discovered inspiration there for his recondite discourses on performance.

---

38   Yokomichi and Omote, eds. 1960: 85. The *Platform Sutra of the Sixth Patriarch* has been variously translated; here, the authors have relied on Yampolsky (1967) 1978.

Zeami's approach to training is frequently cast in the discourse of Zen, with generous use of paradox, including "formless form" or "patternless pattern." Such characterizations are not merely rhetorical sleights, but gestures toward aesthetic attainments that are not readily apparent or explicable in visual or aural terms. Beyond the visual and aural, Zeami posits a realm of mental or cognitive pleasure that cannot be clearly explained or accounted for logically. Is he merely borrowing from the rhetoric of Zen to explain something more immediate to his performance strategies, or is he, indeed, emulating Zen in its insistence on "a transmission apart from the teachings that does not subsist in language"?[39]

Again, the answer to such a question will depend on how one interprets the practice of Zen and what is appropriate to it. Purists may find the very notion of performance alien to the meditative focus of Zen practice, but for generations of Zen practitioners, especially in the Rinzai lineage, performance has had its own integrity, whether inside or outside of monastic life.

It might be helpful to consider a specific passage from Zeami's writings to come to a better understanding of this problem, as from his text *Kakyō* (*A Mirror to the Flower*, ca. 1418–1424):

> What I mean by "don't forget your initial intent in old age" is that life has its term, but performance should have no bounds. Having mastered each particular style in its time, you then learn those forms of expression appropriate to old age; this is your initial intent in old age. Since this is the initial intent in old age, your earlier performances entail retrospective intent. I have said that from fifty on, "there is no better method than to do nothing." That one should undertake in old age to do something as difficult as making a method of doing nothing—doesn't that amount to initial intent?[40]

This passage signals a change in how Zeami regards the problem of "nothing," a change that must have a close relation to his increasing deployment of Zen rhetoric. He had already noted this in his earliest and most famous text, *Fūshi kaden*, but in that text his meaning was that actors of advanced age had little to offer audiences and should gracefully restrain their stage presence in favor of their heirs. In this "restatement," however, doing something by doing nothing is difficult and is representative of the boundlessness that Zeami aspires

---

39 不立文字、教外別伝. Although traditionally attributed to Bodhidharma, there is no reliable textual source linking this couplet to him. It is, however, widely quoted among Chan (Zen) texts.

40 Hare, trans. 2008: 125.

to in nō performance. It again reflects the heavily psychological orientation of Buddhism generally, and perhaps Zen in particular.

The above observations relate most directly to performance and training, but there is also a similar predisposition toward paradox in Zeami's aesthetic theory. He speaks, for instance, of a level of performance that is "wondrous" (*myō* 妙): "There where the path of language is of no avail, where one cannot fathom the principle, and the operations of the mind founder; *that* is wondrous."[41] Or, again, in discussing lofty levels of attainment in performance, he can speak of "The Effect of the Wondrous Flower: Silla, midnight: the sun is bright" (see ch. 6 *Treatises*, 6.3).[42]

It is noteworthy that Zeami attributes the first of the above two quotations to the otherwise unknown text *The Tendai Interpretation of "Wondrous"* (*Tendai myōshaku*). That this is specified as "Tendai" rather than Zen might give some pause, but in such a context, it should be remembered that most patriarchs of Zen began their religious lives in Tendai (C. Tiantai) monasteries, and that among their earliest and most practical meditation manuals were those produced by the Chinese Tiantai monk, Zhiyi (538–597).

Even those who are enthusiastic about a purported relation between Zen and nō should probably step back from too strict a sectarian identification. If the discourses Zeami used with some Zen connections are mostly Rinzai, then it is worth pointing out that he was buried in a temple of the Sōtō Zen lineage, and, as we saw above, it is Tendai he refers to for his most prominent engagement with the wondrous.

4.5 Reading Nō: *Mugen nō* and *Genzai nō* (*Monogurui nō*)
Yamanaka Reiko (Translated by Steven Nelson)

The texts of nō plays were written for performance. They are divided into several scenes (*dan*), each of which consists of combinations of smaller units (*shōdan*). Together these constitute the standard format of a nō play. The individual functions of the *dan* and *shōdan* units have been largely fixed since the time of Zeami. Subsequent playwrights created texts based on these rules. Audiences familiarize themselves with the rules in order to enhance their appreciation of nō works (see ch. 2 *Performance*, 2.3, 2.7; ch. 3 *Training*, 3.3). In addition, a nō text can contain diverse styles of language, ranging from conversational speech and everyday colloquialisms to verse passages that are imbued with highly elaborate rhetoric (see sec. 4.7). Music and rhythm also

---

41   Hare, trans. 2008: 186.
42   Hare, trans. 2008: 193.

vary according to these differences in textual styles, reflecting variously how prose or verse is employed, or whether the language is sinified (Chinese in origin) or native Japanese.

Here we will examine how nō texts mirror the underlying structure of nō plays, focusing on textual development, first in *mugen nō* ("dream" or "phantom" nō) and then in *monogurui nō* ("crazed person" nō), one of the major types of *genzai nō* ("present-time" nō). This section expands upon the section "Performance Conventions" (2.3) in chapter 2 of this publication, which presents nō structures typical of *mugen nō* and *genzai nō* and concentrates on visual and choreographic elements.

4.5.1 Mugen nō

Mugen nō, or "dream" or "phantom" nō, usually comprises two acts. In the first act, a supernatural being such as a ghost, spirit, or deity (*shite*), appears in the guise of a local to a traveler (*waki*) and relates a story that occurred in that place long ago before disappearing. In the second act, normally set at night on the same day, the character appears to the traveler once again, this time in his or her true form, but vanishes before dawn. Between the two acts there is an interlude during which a local person (*ai*, played by a kyōgen actor) recounts the background to the story. The following examines the textual characteristics of typical *mugen nō* structure from its opening to its end.

4.5.1.1 The Appearance of the *waki*

A *waki* character generally appears first. The vast majority of *waki* characters are men who are on a journey, such as a minister heading somewhere at the emperor's behest or a monk visiting various regions of Japan. *Mugen nō* scenarios follow a basic form in which a *waki* character arrives at some significant place, where he meets someone related to the place. Whatever the manner of this first appearance, once onstage, the *waki* delivers a *shōdan* called *nanori* (a naming passage) in which he addresses the audience with information such as who he is, where he is now, and what he is going to do. In *Izutsu*, a third category woman play by Zeami, for example, the *waki* is a monk journeying around Japan who recounts:

MONK (*waki*) [*nanori*]
> You have before you a monk who is seeing all the provinces. Lately I visited the southern capital, and now I am on my way to Hatsuse. Someone told me, when I inquired, that this temple is called Ariwara Temple. I will go to it and have a look.[43]

---

43 Tyler, trans./ed. 1992: 124; here with modifications.

He then visits Ariwara Temple (Ariwaradera), which is associated with Ariwara no Narihira and his wife, the daughter of Ki no Aritsune. The *waki* is praying for the repose of this couple's spirits when the *shite*, a woman, appears.[44] This speech by the *waki* involves no complex rhetoric. Addressing the audience, he establishes the setting of the nō work in plain, everyday speech.

There are also many cases in which the *waki*, after appearing and introducing himself, sets off on a journey. Such passages are based on a rhetorical form known as *michiyuki*, which is also known in other genres of classical Japanese literature. A *michiyuki* is a verse in 7 + 5 syllables that indicates sites along the journey from departure to destination by weaving in *uta makura*, the names of geographical locations often used in *waka* poetry, typically associated with specific feelings or images. This verse form is also laden with rhetorical elements such as *kakekotoba* (pivot words) and *engo* (associated words), techniques that have their roots in *waka* poetry. In the following example from *Tadanori*, a second category warrior play by Zeami, the *waki* travels from Miyako (the capital) to Ichinotani in Suma, a place where a battle between the Genji (Minamoto) and the Heike (Taira) once took place (fig. 4.5). Expressions in italics are *uta makura*:

MONK (*waki*) and COMPANIONS (*waki tsure*) [*sashi*]
    Then off past *Their Majesties' South-west Villa*,
    farewell to *Miyako*, and over the hills
    to *Yamazaki*!
    Tollgate Station, now only a name,
    cannot detain us: as travelers will,
    we press on, weary, worn with the cares
    of our sad, soiled world, across *Akuta River*,
    through *bamboo-grass brakes at Ina*, and on
[*sageuta*]
    to where the moon in *Koya Pond*
    so deep and clear, lodges, radiant.
[*ageuta*]
    That dreary wind sighing through the reeds,
    that dreary wind sighing through the reeds,
    we fain would ignore,
    who once renounced sorrow, yet hear it too,

---

44 Some nō plays begin with a *waki* monk's announcement of his resolve to discover the identity of a person who pays daily visits to a place where he is undertaking religious observances (e.g., *Kayoi Komachi* and *Higaki*).

below *Mount Arima*: nowhere to hide
in this vale of tears. Folly fills the mind
with vain dreams that only fade
when distant bells from *Naniwa*
ring in the dawn. And now we pass on
to *Naruo*. Beyond the sands
dance far waves, and little boats sail by
dance far waves, and little boats sail by!⁴⁵

FIGURE 4.5 Map of the route taken by the monk in *Tadanori* as he travels from the capital to Ichinotani in Suma

---

45 Tyler, trans./ed. 1992: 267–68; layout modified and italics added.

The *waki* then adds a *tsukizerifu*, a conventional expression to declare that he has reached his destination, the distant shore of Suma:

MONK (*waki*) [*tsukizerifu*]
   Having come so swiftly, we have already reached the shore at Suma. Let us rest a while and look at the cherry blossoms.[46]

In plays like *Tadanori*, the *waki* hardly moves onstage during the *michiyuki*. He merely makes an abbreviated gesture of walking. Although the nō stage remains the same as before with no stage scenery to indicate place, the announcement of the *waki*'s arrival (*tsukizerifu*) describes the locality he has reached. It indicates whether it is in the mountains or by the sea, whether it is a lively festival scene, or whether it is the time of year when cherry blossoms are in full bloom as opposed to when there is a heavy snow fall (see sec. 4.6).

4.5.1.2 The Appearance of the *shite*

Once the place and season in the play have been established, the *shite* appears onstage. The *shite* explains his or her circumstances and feelings while at the same time creating a picture of the surrounding scenery. In Zeami's works, there are many instances in which these descriptions also function as expressions of emotions. In *Izutsu*, for example, the *shite* speaks of an old, ruined temple in autumn, suggesting an inner nostalgia and yearning, which becomes clearer in the following passage when she reveals that she has long been waiting to be saved by the Buddha (see sec. 4.7). The source story (*honzetsu*) for *Izutsu* is from episode 23 of *The Tales of Ise*:

> Once upon a time, a young boy and girl would often play together by a well in their village. As they grow up, they become bashful and do not see each other as much as before. All the same, neither of them accepts the arrangements their parents try to make for their marriages. Eventually, the young man attaches a poem to a love letter he writes to the young woman. The young woman sends a poem in reply. Their love matures and they are married. For a while, the two live happily together, very much in love, but eventually the man takes a mistress in another village called Takayasu, and starts visiting her secretly. His wife does not resent him for that, but she worries about his safety when he goes away to visit the mistress. She composes a poem, saying, "When the night falls, white waves break on the shore, yet will you still go off all alone?" When the man hears

---

46   Tyler, trans./ed. 1992: 268; layout modified.

the poem, he understands how much pain he has caused her and breaks off the affair with the woman in Takayasu.

This source story spans many years, and if Zeami had merely wished to reproduce one of its scenes, an autumn setting is not imperative: it could have been spring, summer, or winter. Yet, Zeami used the setting of a ruined temple on an autumn night to symbolize a woman who has waited years and months for the man she loved, living only with the memories after his death and hoping for salvation from the Buddha.

4.5.1.3 Exchange between the *shite* and *waki*

The *waki* next addresses the *shite*. There begins an exchange in dialogue form known as a *kakeai*. The language of this exchange starts as everyday conversational speech before shifting to 7 + 5 syllable verse. The *shite*'s identity and the story of the place gradually become clear through the *kakeai* dialogue between the two characters, which the *shite* and *waki* initially deliver as lines in entire sentences. As the pace of their exchange quickens, their lines shorten to build a momentum until finally the chorus takes over. In effect, the identities of the *shite* and *waki* merge to tell the story.

In the case of *Izutsu*, the *waki* asks the *shite* her identity and if she has anything to do with Narihira. The *shite* evades this question, answering that Narihira was called "a man of old" even when he was alive, so there is no way that he could have acquaintances or relatives in the present.[47] As she gazes at the scenery with an expression of longing, however, the chorus describes the sight of the ruined Ariwaradera, which recalls Narihira's family name of Ariwara. The chorus sings of a tall old pine tree, weeds growing on graves, and grasses swaying like a person's beckoning hands. The sight of the ruin, covered with thick grass and moistened with autumnal night dew, is recounted not as something frightful, but rather as an image overflowing with sentiment that evokes past memories and yearning. The sight of an ancient temple on an autumn night is a poetic motif that is often used in Chinese poetry and Japanese *waka*:

CHORUS [*ageuta*]
　The name, at least, is with us still,
　While Ariwara Temple, his own, grows old
　while Ariwara Temple, his own, grows old,

---

[47] Ariwara no Narihira was nicknamed "a man of old" because in *The Tales of Ise*, many sections start with the phrase "A long time ago, a man ...".

and a pine springs from the mound's grasses.
Seek him here, then, by a grave
nodding with grasses in full plume
that call to mind what times now gone?
Wild, wild the weeds,
deep, deep the dews
that moisten the ancient grave.
O, it is true! Out of the past,
his present trace holds my love still
his present trace holds my love still.[48]

A typical pattern in exchanges between *shite* and *waki* characters is for the *shite* to rebut something said by the *waki* (see sec. 4.6). This type of rebuttal is often a highlight of works belonging to the *monogurui*, or "crazed person," category. In the case of *mugen nō*, the exchange between the characters is frequently indirect. Nonetheless, it performs the function of creating a literary world that relates to the work's setting or theme and offers the audience a shared understanding of a select set of images. The response of the *shite* to a simple remark by the *waki* transports the *waki* and the audience to a realm where a knowledge of classical literature is taken for granted.

In *Tadanori*, for example, the *waki* monk addresses the *shite*, an old man he has met in the hills of Suma, and inquires if he is someone who works in the mountains. The *shite* answers that he is an *ama*, a person who makes a living by collecting seaweed and other products from the sea. The *waki* then asks why he is not at the coast; this appears to be a reasonable point. But the *shite* rebuts this by stating that he must burn the seaweed that he collects, which requires him to collect firewood in the mountains. The significance of this line is in the fact that the "smoke of burning [seaweed to collect] salt" is a motif that is often used in *waka* poetry. This part of the text is laden with expressions from chapter 12, "Suma," in *The Tale of Genji*, with which medieval poets, as well as writers of *waka* and *renga*, would have been familiar (see sec. 4.7). Compare this with *Izutsu*, in which the dialogue focuses more on describing subtle and beautiful sentiments than on artful exchange. Nevertheless, a trace of rebuttal is evident in the line about "a man of old."

4.5.1.4 The Story of the *shite* and the Disappearance from the Stage
The first act of a *mugen nō* culminates with the *shite* recounting the source story central to the play's plot. In many cases, this retelling takes place in a part known as the *kusemai*, which combines three *shōdan* units called *kuri*, *sashi*,

---

48 Tyler, trans./ed. 1992: 127; layout modified.

and *kuse*. The *kusemai* involves retelling a source-story episode in the form of a rhythmically complex chant that is not restricted to 7 + 5 syllable meter. The episode is often taken from classical literary works such as *The Tales of Ise* or *The Tale of Genji*. Alternatively, in nō plays in which the *shite* is a deity, the *kusemai* recounts the origins and history of the deity's shrine. *Shura nō*—plays about the spirits of fallen warriors—are exceptions to this rule. Zeami's treatise, *Sandō* (*The Three Courses*, 1423), contains instructions about moving the *kusemai* to the second act, and that *The Tale of the Heike* should be followed closely if the protagonist is from the Genpei War.

In *Izutsu*, the *shite*, whose part is voiced in performance by the chorus, retells episode 23 from *The Tales of Ise*, but she does it out of order. She first narrates the story of her husband's affair with the woman in Takayasu, then delves deeper into the past to relate how her childhood playmate later became her lover. As she recalls the past, she is reminded of her longing and the experience of waiting for him.

Similar examples of recalling memories out of chronological order exist in other nō plays. In *Hajitomi*, the *shite* Yūgao initially recounts her memory of the last dawn she spent with Shining (Hikaru) Genji, and then she remembers the first time they met. In addition, there are also many cases in which episodes evoked by characters in nō are told in a slightly different manner than narrated in source-story texts. In *mugen nō*, the conventions of realistic time and place disappear, and the *shite*'s memories are selective and associative such that all the twists and turns of a long love affair, for instance, can be set aside. A specific memory that a woman has of her lover, a memory that she has long cherished, can become the focus of what she describes to the audience.

These narratives are usually delivered in the third person; the episodes are at first related as events that occurred to someone long ago at the given location. The account is so detailed, however, that the *waki* becomes suspicious and asks the *shite* about his or her identity. This often develops into a *rongi shōdan*, in which the *shite* and the chorus chant alternately. In this case, the chorus chants in place of the *waki*. During the *rongi*, after which the *shite* suddenly disappears, various facts come to light. These may include the revelation that the *shite*, who has until then seemed to be an ordinary man, woman, or elderly person living in the area, is actually the protagonist of the source-story episode. In some plays, he or she died many years in the past but has returned from the underworld as a ghost. In others, he or she is a god disguised as a human.

4.5.1.5   *Ai* (Interlude)

As the *shite* disappears from the stage (*nakairi*), a character living in the area moves onstage from the *hashigakari* bridgeway and begins a standardized dialogue with the *waki*. This character, referred to as an *ai*, is played by a kyōgen actor. The *waki* informs the *ai* of his encounter with a mysterious figure and asks if there is anything he might know. The *ai* is able to give a detailed account of the same episode as that described in the first act of the work, showing that the incident is widely known by people in the area. After giving the *waki* some advice, the *ai* leaves the stage. In plays in which the *waki* is a monk, the *ai* requests that he should pray for the spirit of the *shite*, while in first category deity plays, the *ai* suggests that the *waki* stay and wait for the deity to appear. While the summary given in the interlude is usually identical or similar to the account of the episode given in the first act, the plain prose of the version delivered by the *ai* helps deepen the audience's comprehension.

In deity plays, there are cases when a deity subordinate to the main deity of the shrine (*shintai*) appears between the acts, to announce the manifestation of the main deity in the second act and to perform a dance.

4.5.1.6 The Wait of the *waki*

The second act of a *mugen nō* often takes place in the dreams or imagination of the *waki*. While delivering a *machiutai* ("waiting chant"), the *waki* waits for the *nochi shite* (*shite* of the second act) to reappear. Although some plays clearly indicate that their second acts take place in dreams, others leave it ambiguous as to whether events are occurring in a dream or in reality. The three examples here demonstrate that the *waki* is dreaming (*Izutsu*), praying for the spirit of a dead person (*Atsumori*), and waiting for a deity to appear (*Takasago*):

– *Izutsu*:

> MONK (*waki*) [*ageuta*]
> The night hour grows late:
> above the temple hangs a moon
> above the temple hangs a moon
> to restore the past: with robe reversed,
> I prepare to dream, and, briefly pillowed,
> lie down upon a bed of moss
> lie down upon a bed of moss.[49]

– *Atsumori*:

> RENSHŌ (*waki*) [*ageuta*]
> Then it is well: to guide and comfort him
> then it is well: to guide and comfort him,

---

49 Tyler, trans./ed. 1992: 130; layout modified.

> I shall do holy rites, and through the night
> call aloud the Name for Atsumori,
> praying that he reach enlightenment
> praying that he reach enlightenment.[50]

- *Takasago*:

> TOMONARI (*waki*) and COMPANIONS (*waki tsure*) [*ageuta*]
> Takasago!
> Our light craft under all sail
> Our light craft under all sail
> slips out with the moon
> rising, the flood-tide swells
> foam round Awaji Isle,
> thunder upon Naruo
> far behind us now, for we skim on
> to Sumiyoshi where we soon put in
> to Sumiyoshi where we soon put in.[51]

In this excerpt from *Takasago*, the *waki* and his companions describe their sea travel from Takasago to Sumiyoshi. In other first category nō, in which the *waki* is described as remaining in the same place, he does not meet the deity in his dream. Instead, the work plainly shows him waiting for the deity's miraculous manifestation. Additionally, when the kyōgen actor in a deity play is the deity of a subsidiary shrine, there is no *machiutai* from the *waki* and the *shite* comes onstage immediately.

4.5.1.7 From the Appearance of the *nochi shite* to the Climax

The setting for the second act thus established, the *nochi shite* comes onstage. Unlike the *mae shite* (the *shite* of the first act), the *nochi shite* appears in his or her true form and chants sonorously, providing his or her name and identity, and explaining his or her motivation for coming before the *waki*. In some plays, such as *Tadanori*, the identity of the *nochi shite* is already clear, and this information is hence abbreviated.

In contrast to the first act, the second act does not have many prose lines; most of the lines are in the form of 7 + 5 syllable verse (see ch. 2 *Performance*, 2.7):

---

50 Tyler, trans./ed. 1992: 44; layout modified.
51 Tyler, trans./ed. 1992: 290; layout modified.

– *Izutsu*:

> LADY (*shite*) [*sashi*]
> Fickle they are,
> or so people say,
> these cherry blossoms,
> who have yet been pining
> for one rare all year round.
> Yes, that poem being mine as well,
> they call me, too, the Pining Lady.[52]

– *Tadanori*:

> TADANORI (*shite*) [*sashi*]
> I am ashamed! Here where death took me,
> a dream recalls my form into vision,
> real as waking. My heart roams once more
> the past, that old tale I shall tell you now:
> for this my spirit, transformed, has come.
> [*kudoki*]
> But O, in this deluded world
> rife with wrongful clinging
> why, I ask, did he range my poem
> among such exalted company
> in the *Senzaishū*,
> yet, alas, invoke imperial censure
> and give the poet as 'Anonymous'?
> That supreme disappointment binds me still.[53]

– *Atsumori*:

> ATSUMORI (*shite*) [*ge no ei*]
> Across to Awaji the plovers fly,
> while the Suma barrier guard sleeps on;
> yet one, I see, keeps nightlong vigil here.
> O keeper of the pass, tell me your name.

---

[52] Tyler, trans./ed. 1992: 130; layout modified.
[53] Tyler, trans./ed. 1992: 273; layout modified.

[kakeai]
    Behold, Renshō: I am Atsumori.[54]

The structures of the second acts of nō exhibit more variation than the first acts. The initial acts of first category nō and of works such as *Izutsu* and *Nonomiya*, for example, have *kusemai* that relate episodes from the source-story text. In such plays, the *nochi shite* performs a long instrumental dance. This instrumental dance flows into a concluding poetic passage highlighted with gesture, movement, and instrumentation to create a climactic finale.

The composition of *Izutsu* has numerous aspects in common with the compositions of deity plays. After the above passages, the *shite* says that many years have passed and that her robe is a memento of her late husband. This is followed by the *issei* chant by the chorus and then the beginning of the *jo no mai* dance by the *shite*:

LADY (*shite*) [*sashi*]
    I take upon me that same robe
    Narihira left me,
[*issei*]
    O shame! To dance the Man of Old,
CHORUS
    blossom sleeves swirling snow.[55]

It is common for *issei* chants that directly precede a dance to feature words such as "snow" or "flower petals" as figurative references to the fluttering movements of sleeves. There are also a number of examples in which the first five syllables of a *waka* poem are sung, the dance begins and ends, and the entire *waka* is sung once again. This is believed to have something to do with the fact that *shirabyōshi mai*, the form of dance from which the long instrumental nō dance form *jo no mai* derives, was a style of dance that accompanied *waka* singing (see ch. 2 *Performance*, 2.4).

In *Izutsu*, the chorus does not sing a preexisting *waka*. Rather, an original verse related to the work's theme is used in the *waka* pattern of 5-7-5-7-7 syllables with the final line repeated: "*Koko ni kite / mukashi zo kaesu / ariwara no, / terai ni sumeru / tsuki zo sayakeki, tsuki zo sayakeki*":

---

54 Tyler, trans./ed. 1992: 44–45.
55 Tyler, trans./ed. 1992: 131; layout modified.

LADY (*shite*) [*waka*]
  Come hither now, I bring again
  the days of old; in Ariwara
CHORUS
  Temple's well, round and clear,
  a radiant moon shines
  a radiant moon shines.[56]

This verse conjures up the sight of the well and the deep-seated emotions it evokes for the *shite* when she sees the bright moon reflected in its depths, as it was once ages ago. This was where she had played with her childhood friend, where she had lived with him after their marriage, and where she managed to avoid its breakup over his affair with the woman of Takayasu.

After this, the chorus performs a chant that is somewhat semantically ambiguous, especially in the Japanese original, which could describe either the *shite*'s reminiscence of old memories associated with the scenery of the Ariwaradera or the sight of the *shite* and the scenery in the eyes of the *waki* monk. In other words, the chant leaves it unclear as to who or what the grammatical subject is (see sec. 4.8). The *shite* dances to this chant. The last *shōdan uta* starts with the *shite*'s monologue "*Mireba natsukashi ya*" ("There before me, and so dear!"), and the chorus takes over the rest:

CHORUS [*uta*]
  I see myself, yet still I love him!
  Departed lover in phantom form,
  a flower withered, all color gone,
  but fragrant yet, Ariwara
  Temple bell tolls in the dawn:
  an ancient temple, loud with pines
  where the wind sighs. Plantain-leaf frail,
  the dream has broken into waking,
  the dream breaks into day.[57]

At first, the chorus seems to speak for the feelings of the *shite*. This shifts to a depiction of a fading phantom. The tolling of the temple bell announces the coming dawn, while the sounds of wind blowing through pine trees and the flapping of thin, wind-torn plantain leaves wake the monk from his dream.

---

56 Tyler, trans./ed. 1992: 131; layout modified.
57 Tyler, trans./ed. 1992: 131–32; layout modified.

The trajectory of lyricism versus narrative varies with the type of play. For instance, a *kusemai* in the second act is a trait in nō plays in which *shite* characters are female ghosts (e.g., *Eguchi*, *Tōboku*, *Uneme*). In the case of warrior plays (*shura nō*), the instrumental dance tends to be short, with a mimetic replay of a battle forming the highlight. This usually draws on passages from *The Tale of the Heike*. The second act of a warrior play hence features a recitation dance, a *katari mai*, "narrative dance," which in many cases takes the form of a *kusemai*. Here, the main character retells the episode as he dances, often with some of his words voiced by the chorus. Warrior nō thus have expanded second acts.

The endings of *mugen nō* deviate widely depending on the style and mood of the work. Plays like *Izutsu* end with the *waki* waking up from a dream, while others end with the *shite* disappearing after requesting that the *waki* pray once more for the repose of his or her spirit. This ending is common among warrior plays. At the end of *Tadanori*, for example, the ghost asks for prayers to comfort him in the afterlife:

CHORUS [*uta*]
>These blossoms, O monk, drew you on
>to seek lodging here, because I wished
>that you should hear my tale.
>For this I detained you and ended the day.
>Now you know me beyond a doubt,
>the flower again shall seek its root.
>Guide my shade, comfort me, I pray!
>A tree's sheltering boughs you made your inn,
>and, yes, the blossoms were your host![58]

First category deity nō generally end with a deity blessing the world with peace and prosperity, as seen here in the concluding chorus of the second act of *Takasago*:

CHORUS [*rongi*]
>"A Thousand Autumns" brings peace to all,
>'Ten Thousand Years' makes life long
>While, touched by the wind,
>the Paired Pines sing, inspiring tranquil joy
>the Paired Pines sing, inspiring tranquil joy.[59]

---

58   Tyler, trans. 1992: 276; layout modified.
59   Tyler, trans. 1992: 292; layout modified.

The figure of the Sumiyoshi deity dancing onstage is evoked by the names of ceremonious and auspicious *gagaku* dances, "A Thousand Autumns" (*Senshūraku*) and "Ten Thousand Years" (*Manzairaku*). *Takasago* thus ends with the Sumiyoshi deity bestowing a benediction of tranquility, longevity, and conjugal happiness.

The above has examined the typical structure pattern of *mugen nō*, with some examples of representative plays. Adhering to this basic pattern, playwrights could draw upon an almost unlimited resource of possible protagonists, ranging from characters from works of classic literature—most notably *The Tale of Genji* and *The Tale of the Heike*—to the spirits of plants and trees. Numerous *mugen nō* plays simply followed this set pattern, and as a result they closely resembled each other. Many of these mediocre plays gradually ceased to be performed and were ultimately removed from the repertory.

There are, however, greater differences among those plays by Zeami, who established the *mugen nō* structure. In addition to *Tadanori*, Zeami created many other warrior plays that depict members of the Heike clan as having refined sentiments and elegant tastes. All of these works follow the general framework of *mugen nō*, yet no two plays have an identical structure: *Kiyotsune* is a one-act play, for instance, while in *Atsumori*, the *shite* performs an instrumental dance in the second act. Another example of deviation from the set pattern is *Nonomiya*, a highly praised woman play attributed to Zeami's artistic successor Zenchiku. Its first act is strikingly similar to Zeami's *Izutsu* in terms of its structure and mood, but the second act diverges substantially from *Izutsu*, thereby contributing to the play's most distinctive allure.

Explanations of the typical structure of *mugen nō* often lead to the misunderstanding that every *mugen nō* adheres to exactly the same pattern, but this is not the case. Although they share a basic structural framework, a closer look at the most highly esteemed *mugen nō* reveals considerable differences, with various means adopted to achieve a particular artistic goal.

4.5.2 Monogurui nō: *A Case Study of* Genzai nō

In classical Japanese, the verb *kuruu* (the base form of the suffix *-gurui* of *monogurui*) means both "to lose one's senses" and "to do a performance of some sort." It appears that in medieval Japan, those in heightened states who were moved to sing and dance by the things they saw and heard were identified as "performers." As a performing art, nō exploited this view of understanding madness and depicted "crazed" figures as particularly amenable to performance.

Works of the *genzai nō* category, which cover a broad range of themes, differ from *mugen nō* in that their actors portray living human beings, and the storyline unfolds onstage in real time through interactions between them.

Discernible to a degree among the diverse types of *genzai nō* are certain patterns of plot construction in *monogurui nō* ("crazed person" nō), even though the stories tend to unfold freely in response to the subject matter of the work, much the same as in modern Western drama.

The following examination discusses the patterns in the plot construction of *monogurui nō*, in which someone has been separated from a loved one—child, spouse, or lover—and finally meets (or fails to meet) them after a long, extensive search. It introduces different scene and character types, as well as rhetorical features, that characterize *monogurui nō*.

4.5.2.1   First Act (*maeba*): Depicting Separation

Monogurui nō can be in one or two acts. In a two-act work, the reason for the crazed state of the *shite* character is set out in the first act, and the *shite* is already in this state when he or she appears in the second act. While a typical cause for this heightened emotional state is separation from a loved one, the separation itself is not portrayed. Rather, a letter arrives that informs the *shite* of a separation that has already taken place: from a child informing a parent of his or her intention to cut ties, to renounce the world, and to take Buddhist vows, as in the plays *Kashiwazaki* and *Sakuragawa*, or from a lover stating that he has been summoned to the capital to be enthroned as emperor, as in *Hanagatami*. The letter eloquently sets out the feelings of its writer, but the difference in time between when it was written and when it is read means that the recipient has no way of preventing the sender from leaving. It is precisely this emotional shock that causes the *shite*'s crazed state of mind.

A model structure in these sorts of plays is for the letter to be chanted by the *shite* in a *shōdan* called *fumi* ("letter section") in recitative style similar to a *sashi* (see ch. 2 *Performance*, 2.7). This leads into a section sung by the chorus that conveys the feelings of the *shite*, during which the *shite* quietly leaves the stage. Earlier works tend to give more detail about the separation, and have a longer *fumi*, but the first acts of Zeami's works of this type tend to be abbreviated. One of Zeami's later works, *Hanagatami*, begins after the separation of the lovers. A prince living in Echizen Province (present-day Fukui Prefecture) has suddenly been summoned to the capital to be enthroned. Unable to bid farewell to the local woman he loves dearly, he leaves her a letter and a flower basket, which a messenger delivers. The scene of her reading the letter and leaving the stage is depicted in the following, compact fashion:

LADY (*shite*) [*fumi*]
   Although a descendant of Emperor Ōjin,
   I was not one who might expect to gain the throne,
   yet since my lineage derives from the Great Goddess Amateru

> I have paid daily reverence to Ise.
> Thus, it may be through her divine blessing
> that I have been chosen by members of the court
> and invited to lofty eminence above the clouds.
> Just as the moon in its course will come around once more
> in autumn, shining on fields of ripened grain,
> so just have faith
> that the moonlight that has shone upon your sleeves will do so again,
> though for a time it may be hidden by the clouds.
>
> CHORUS [*sageuta*]
>> His words written as traces on paper,
>> left behind as I am, so miserable!
>
> [*ageuta*]
>> Even living with my lord
>> this mountain village was a lonely place,
>> this mountain village was a lonely place.
>> Now I remain alone, the spring moon passes
>> indifferent to my plight, the wind in the cedars
>> blows through the pines, and scatters the flowers;
>> How fondly I remember the flowers that were here,
>> in my lord's basket. The basket and his letter
>> I clutch to my breast as I return to my village,
>> I clutch to my breast as I return to my village.[60]

Hanjo, another of Zeami's late works, is more economical in facilitating the separation and does not employ the letter convention. Instead, a *kyōgen* actor appears onstage as the madam of an inn at Nogami in Mino Province (present-day Gifu Prefecture). In the introductory *nanori* section, the madam complains that one of her girls, Hanago, has stopped receiving other guests since falling in love with an aristocrat from the capital, Lesser Captain Yoshida, a client with whom she has exchanged fans as a pledge of their love. She calls the *shite*, Hanago, and instructs her to leave immediately. The *shite* laments her fate in the short *sashi*-like *kudoki* section, and leaves the inn during the following chorus section. In terms of both its *shōdan* structure and the departure of the *shite* from the stage as the chorus sings of her feelings and actions, *Hanjo* closely resembles *Hanagatami*, albeit with a much shorter first act:

---

60   New translation by Steven Nelson. A summary of *Hanagatami* is in Waley 1921: 221–23; complete translation in French in Sieffert 1979: (2) 205–20.

HANAGO (*shite*) [*kudoki*]
   O the world does play us false,
   and always will; yet many sorrows
   break her days' swift flow—she whom fate
   bends to be a woman of the stream.
CHORUS [*sageuta*]
   Now I go wandering,
   knowing nothing of what lies ahead;
   robe wet with weeping,
[*ageuta*]
   Nogami I abandon and set forth
   Nogami I abandon and set forth
   along the Ōmi Road—to him, perhaps,
   that cruel man—for since he left,
   dew forever lingers on my sleeves.
   O that I might vanish with my grief!
   O that I might vanish with my grief![61]

4.5.2.2   Setting the Venue of the Second Act

The short first act moves quickly to the second because there is no interlude (*ai*) to function as a bridge as in two-act *mugen nō*. Although *mugen nō* portray the experience of an individual character (the *waki*) in the span from afternoon to night, the second act of a two-act *genzai nō* occurs at a different place and at a later date.

Common venues for the second acts of *monogurui nō* are crowded places, including celebrated temples and shrines, festivals, and spots famous for their cherry blossoms. Chance encounters of people who have been separated transpire where people congregate. At the beginning of the second act, the child or the lover who has left or been separated from the *shite* comes to a location of this type. Analogous to the appearance of the *waki* in the first act of *mugen nō*, with the announcement of the *waki*'s identity and a journey to the place where the work is set, the second acts of *monogurui nō* start with a figure. This can be as a monk who has taken in a child (often as a disciple), a newly enthroned emperor (e.g., *Hanagatami*), or a courtier in search of his lover (e.g., *Hanjo*), who appears onstage, introduces himself with, when applicable, the child accompanying him. These figures then make their way to a thronged venue.

---

61   Tyler, trans./ed. 1992: 111; layout modified.

4.5.2.3 Expansion of the Entrance of the *nochi shite*

The *shite* (as *nochi shite*, or *shite* of the second act) then reappears, already suffering from the crazed state of mind occasioned by the separation dealt with in the first act. This emotionally disoriented state is coupled with a second function of entertainer or performer—specifically, in singing passages from famous *waka* poems or descriptions of the *shite*'s feelings in the high vocal range of the *issei* section. Sometimes the *shite* replies to taunts from children positioned peripherally who are not actually seen onstage; sometimes the *shite* performs a series of movements known as a *kakeri*, an indication of the *shite*'s disturbed state of mind.

4.5.2.4 Lines That Trigger the Crazed Performance

It is common for the crazed figure in the *shite* role to be well known at the site of the performance, rather than just a passerby.[62] Local people would know how to goad the crazed figure into giving a performance. They generally do this in order to have the *shite* perform for the *waki* and those accompanying him, who have just happened to turn up at the venue. The *shite* of *Sakuragawa* is the mother of a lost son and is driven into her mad performance when told that mountain gusts are sweeping the cherry blossoms from the trees. Hanago, the *shite* of *Hanjo*, is teased, but answers with her wits about her, before being set off on her performance by the mention of a fan associated with a celebrated Chinese lady:

GENTLEMAN (*waki*) [*mondō*]
  You, the mad girl! Why are you not raving today? Come, rave and entertain us!
HANAGO (*shite*)
  You are too cruel! Why see there!
  Those boughs, till now, had looked firm enough,
  yet at the wind's touch, one leaf falls.
  For once I have my wits, you gentlemen
  would have me rave. It is you, I think,
  the wild wind turns. That flying autumn leaf
  spins my heart away to storms of love.
  O please, do not ask me to rave!

---

62 There are, of course, exceptions. The *shite* of both *Kashiwazaki* and *Miidera* appear suddenly in temple scenes, while the *shite* of *Sumidagawa* comes to the banks of the Sumida River for the first time. In the latter case, the *shite*'s reputation precedes her, as a traveler who arrives before her mentions her madness explicitly.

GENTLEMAN
> Well, what have you done with Lady Han's fan?[63]

Mountain gusts and cherry blossoms, and Lady Han's fan are stock literary phrases, but what triggers an extended crazed performance can vary. The *shite* of *Hanagatami*, for example, begins hers when her lover's flower basket is knocked to the ground, while the *shite* of *Sumidagawa* starts hers when the ferryman answers her question about the birds on the river in a way that betrays his ignorance of classical literature. In every case, the crazed figure is good with words, countering the *waki*'s statements with objections that display a knowledge of the classics.

4.5.2.5 Pretending Not to Recognize Someone

While it might strike us as unnatural for two people long separated not to know each other when they are in the same place, this trope is common in *monogurui nō*. Some plots provide an explanation, such as that one of the characters has changed so dramatically as to be hardly recognizable, or that one character hesitates to acknowledge the other because of what the people assembled there might think. A lost child may point out his or her parent to its new protector, who then waits for the right moment to talk to the crazed parent. In any of these cases, this is a dramaturgical means of delaying the reunion until the performance of the crazed character onstage has finished.

4.5.2.6 Narration-Like Chorus of the Denouement

The conclusions in *mugen nō* are often depicted from the perspective of the *waki*—the breaking of dawn, as in *Izutsu*, *Saigyōzakura*, and *Yashima*, or the disappearance of a ghostly figure or deity, as in *Nonomiya* and *Yorimasa*. In *genzai nō*, however, the conclusion generally shifts to a narration-like tone, with a passage sung by the chorus. Directed at the audience, this announces the conclusion of the work from a third-person perspective, and usually adds instructive or moral commentary that praises the virtue of filial piety or Buddhist teachings. Two such examples, the concluding chorus of *Hyakuman* and *Miidera*, have crazed mothers who are ultimately reunited with their lost sons. In *Hyakuman*, the chorus praises the benevolence of Amida Buddha. The ending part of *Miidera* extols the filial piety of the son that will bring prosperity to the family, thus summarizing the sequel that will happen after this mother-child reunion:

---

63 Tyler, trans. 1992: 115; layout modified.

- *Hyakuman*:

 CHORUS [*kiri*]
 Think on this and see the lesson
 think on this and see the lesson:
 the Buddha here enshrined to all beings
 ever has been father;
 thus Dharma-might which has joined
 mother and son is blessed indeed.
 All hopes fulfilled ride we the highway
 back to our Sovereign's Seat in perfect joy
 back to our Sovereign's Seat in perfect joy.[64]

- *Miidera*:

 CHORUS [*kiri*]
 And thus, they set forth for home together.
 And thus, they set forth for home together.
 Mother and child united forever,
 their house prosperous, their happiness great.
 Blessed are the virtues of filial piety!
 Blessed are the virtues of filial piety![65]

4.5.2.7 Other Types of *Genzai nō*

As mentioned above, diverse themes are handled in *genzai nō*. Aside from the *monogurui nō*, there are plays in which a medieval performer becomes the central character and puts on a performance for an audience. In others, a living warrior displays loyalty and valor in battle or takes revenge on an opponent employing wisdom and bravery. Many plays that dramatize celebrated revenge tales and legends related to Minamoto no Yoshitsune represent this latter type. These subcategories of *genzai nō* other than *monogurui nō*, however, do not exhibit the well-defined patterned structure that is observed in the cases of *mugen nō* and *monogurui nō*. While structures vary greatly from play to play, reflecting the wide range of themes and source materials, a few loose patterns are apparent in these plays that *mugen nō* and *monogurui nō* both share. The play's climax is again located in the latter half, for example, in the dance of the *shite* or a fierce battle scene. A character's long journey is expressed by short

---

64 Tyler 1978b: 129; layout modified.
65 Bethe and Emmert, eds. 1992–1997 (1993): 177; layout modified.

michiyuki chanting and a few steps onstage. In terms of style and rhetoric, a character may describe his or her own actions in the third person, and the chorus often takes over the part of one of the characters. This ambiguity of grammatical person can be seen in *mugen nō* and *genzai nō*. In fact, it is one of the characteristics of nō that differentiate it from modern Western theatre (see sec. 4.8).

4.6 Aspects of Time and Character Relations
Paul S. Atkins

4.6.1 *Compression and Expansion of Time*

The distinctive quality of nō dramaturgy that intersects with performance practice is its peculiar way of handling time, mainly by compressing it. For example, in the play *Takasago*, the *waki*, a Shintō priest from Aso Shrine in Higo Province (present-day Kumamoto Prefecture), announces that he has never seen the capital (Kyoto) and intends to visit there, stopping along the way at Takasago (in present-day Hyōgo Prefecture). The distance between the two locations is about five hundred kilometers as the crow flies. Accompanied by two attendants, he embarks on a journey by sea:

PRIEST (*waki*) and ATTENDANTS (*waki tsure*)
   In traveling attire,
   Along the road to the capital as it stretches far away,
   Along the road to the capital as it stretches far away,
   We set our minds to go today, and ride the coastal waves.
   The ship's course lies across calm seas, and in the spring's soft breeze,
   "How many days have we come now, how many days ahead?"
   I wonder. Wandering here beneath the white, far-ranging clouds,
   Far still, I thought, but here is Harima Bay.
   We have come the long, long way to Takasago Coast.
   We have come the long, long way to Takasago Coast.[66]

In the preceding lines, the *waki* was in the middle of a stock lamentation of the length of the journey when they arrived, almost suddenly. He was musing, almost ironically, "How many days have we come now, how many days ahead?" In dramatic terms, the answer to both questions is zero.

---

66   Hare 1986: 72; layout modified; see Tyler, trans./ed. 1992: 281.

This sung passage is followed immediately by the remarkable statement, "Having hurried, we have arrived at Takasago Coast in the Province of Harima."[67] This is a stock phrase that might escape our notice, but if we read it closely, the playwright (Zeami) seems to be winking at his own quick handling of the trip.

The compression of a long journey into a minute or two is a standard conceit in nō dramaturgy, and similar lines may be found in a number of other plays. For example, the same way of depicting journeys from the western provinces to the capital is seen in *Motomezuka*; from Kazusa Province (present-day Chiba Prefecture) to the Shirakawa Barrier (in present-day Fukushima Prefecture) in *Yugyō yanagi*; from the capital to Obasuteyama (in present-day Nagano Prefecture) in the play of the same name; and a trip of several days length from an undisclosed point of departure to the Michinoku region in *Nishikigi*. One of the longest voyages is that taken by the sorcerer who sails to the Land of Immortality (C. Penglai; J. Hōrai) in *Yōkihi*. Of course, not all *waki* travel long distances: some stay where they are (*Kayoi Komachi*, *Dōjōji*), while others make day trips (*Semimaru*, *Ashikari*, *Nonomiya*). But all journeys, regardless of the distance, take up the same amount of time in the world of the play.

4.6.1.1   The Special Case of *Kantan*

A sophisticated variation of this tendency is found in the nō play *Kantan*, where the compression of time is essential to the narrative. The play is about a young man in China in search of enlightenment. He stops at an inn in the village of Handan (J. Kantan), where he is offered the use of a magic pillow by the innkeeper. While his meal is being prepared, the young man dozes off, only to be awakened by an imperial messenger who summons him to court. The young man then embarks upon an illustrious fifty-year career as a distinguished courtier. His career comes to an abrupt end when the innkeeper taps him on the shoulder to rouse him for dinner. The glory and fame were but a dream, half a century passing in the span of time it took to boil some millet. This realization inspires the young man to firmly reject the pursuit of fame, power, and wealth.

The illusory nature of worldly goals is clearly the theme of *Kantan*; however, the play also has something to say about the nature of time. Even if the young man had actually done the things he dreamed about, he might have felt that the time had passed all too quickly. Everyone has had this experience, and it teaches us that time is not something measured, but felt. *Kantan* shows an

---

67   Itō, ed. 1986: 2:284. All translations are by the author, unless otherwise indicated; see Tyler, trans./ed. 1992: 281.

explicit awareness of the relative "elasticity" of the subjective appearance of time. Toward the end of the play, the chorus sings, "Thus the hours pass, and the seasons come and go, / and the glory of fifty years is gone. / It was really the span of a dream ..."[68] Not only does the play enact the compression of time, it comments upon it as well in a metacommentary.

Nō is also performed in stop-motion. The characters can freeze time through such aspects of performances as the *jo no mai*, one of the slowest dances in the performance repertory, which lasts about twenty minutes. These dances typically begin with a few phrases sung by the *shite* and the chorus, and then are performed mainly to musical accompaniment only. The action of the dance is not generally mimetic. Therefore, they do not drive the play forward, although they do express deep feeling. In this way, the play stops as we enter the internal emotions of the *shite*.

Nō texts and performance techniques slow down, speed up, and stop dramatic time. This acknowledges our experience of time as elastic. It is also entirely consistent with the general tendency of nō to avoid overt mimesis. The compression of long journeys into a few moments could be avoided by playwrights simply by starting the action at the end of the journey instead of at the beginning. But audiences must have wanted to hear travel described poetically, and enjoyed the wordplay on place names that always accompanied such descriptions. Actors, too, who frequently toured and were deeply familiar with the rigors of travel, might have valued these sections. Moreover, there was no need to make the scenes more realistic. Nō seeks instead a deeper kind of mimesis, one that is internal and emotional, rather than external and physical, through its portrayal of characters onstage.

4.6.2   The Role of the *waki*

The *waki* has various functions in a nō play. On the one hand, in many *genzai nō* ("present-time" nō) plays, he may actually be one of the major characters (e.g., Sotsu no Ajari in *Tanikō*). On the other, there is a tendency to regard the *waki* in a *mugen nō* play as a mere listener of the ghost's recollection of the past. In fact, the *shite* and *waki* are strangers (sometimes tied by fate) at the beginning of the play, but through dialogue they come closer to each other (also physically onstage). In questioning the *shite* and listening to the answers, he serves as the audience's representative, asking the same questions of a mysterious stranger that the audience might pose. The *waki* can also play a role in the action, praying for the enlightenment of a character who is suffering the bonds

---

68   Itō, ed. 1983: 1:359; see Tyler, trans./ed. 1992: 141.

of attachment. The *waki* may have some previous connection to the *shite*, as seen with the monk Renshō, formerly Kumagai Naozane, in *Atsumori*.

The *shite* enters and engages in a dialogue with the *waki* in a number of plays. These encounters often produce something more than an exchange of information; there is sometimes real tension or animus between the *waki* and the *shite*. The *shite* frequently rebukes the *waki* for his obtuseness, lack of sensitivity, or even haughtiness.

4.6.2.1 The Ignorant *waki*

In the play *Teika*, the *waki* is a traveling monk, a very common identity for a *waki*. He is journeying with some colleagues from the north country in order to visit the capital for the first time. A sudden shower forces the group to take cover in an abandoned pavilion, whereupon they encounter the *shite*, a woman who is actually the ghost of Princess Shokushi (d. 1201). She begins their interaction by accosting them:

SHOKUSHI (*shite*)
> I say, reverend monks, why do you stop at that shelter?

MONK (*waki*)
> We simply stopped to wait out this sudden shower. By the way, what is this place called?

SHOKUSHI
> It is known as the "Pavilion of Sudden Rains," and it has a history. I addressed you in this way because I thought you might perhaps have known what it meant when you stopped here.[69]

Although the princess's ghost addresses the monks in respectful language, even using the double honorific *-sasetamō*, she subtly criticizes their ignorance by pointing out that they know less about the place than she had expected.

Princess Shokushi lets these monks off easy in comparison to other characters. In *Kakitsubata*, the *waki* is again a traveling monk who stops at Yatsuhashi in Mikawa Province, a place renowned for its irises since their depiction in *The Tales of Ise*, and encounters the spirit of the irises in the figure of a young woman. As the monk stops to rest, he is accosted by the spirit in language very similar to that used by Princess Shokushi in *Teika*: "I say, reverend monk, for

---

69   Itō, ed. 1986: 2:344; see 241–42 in the full translation of the play *Teika* by Hiroaki Sato in Sato and Watson 1981.

what purpose do you take your rest at that marsh?"[70] Like the other monk, this one has no idea where he is; he saw some pretty flowers and decided to rest there. The spirit of the irises is not so forgiving. She explains to him where he is and how famous the site is, and concludes by exclaiming "Oh, what an unsophisticated traveler!"[71]

4.6.2.2 The Snobbish *waki*

The conflict between *waki* and *shite* can almost seem hostile. In *Atsumori*, the *waki* is Renshō, a Buddhist monk and former warrior who once went by the name of Kumagai Naozane. The *shite* in the first act is a young man cutting grass, revealed later as the ghost of Taira no Atsumori, whom Renshō killed in battle. It is quite natural for Atsumori to resent Renshō, but the manner in which he does it is unusual. Renshō hears the young man playing a flute, an instrument played by Atsumori while he was alive. He comments: "How touching! For people such as you, that is a remarkably elegant thing to do! Oh, yes, it is very touching." The youth replies: "It is a remarkable elegant thing, you say, for people like us to do? The proverb puts the matter well: 'Envy none above you, despise none below'."[72] Although Renshō means to complement the young man, his surprise at hearing a humble grasscutter playing the flute is interpreted as snobbishness by the touchy *shite*. We know, however, that the grasscutter is not actually of humble birth—he is the ghost of Atsumori, a son of the elite military Taira clan. Atsumori's reproach is insincere.[73]

Just as soon as Atsumori reminds him of the proverb, Renshō changes his view, and accepts Atsumori's criticism. This reconciliation in the first act is followed by a much deeper one in the second, in which Atsumori forgives Renshō for killing him, thereby releasing himself from the horrific ordeal of existence in the Asura realm (J. *shuradō*).

There is a similar tendency, even more pronounced and protracted, in *Sotoba Komachi*. In this play, a monk (*waki*) and his companion are traveling from Mount Kōya to the capital and stop to rest in a forest of pine trees in Settsu Province (present-day southeastern Hyōgo and northern Osaka Prefectures). There they spot an old, shabby-looking woman sitting on a wooden Buddhist

---

70 Itō, ed. 1983: 1:260. For this passage, see the translation of *Kakitsubata* by Susan Blakeley Klein in Brazell, ed. 1988: 67.
71 Itō, ed. 1983: 1:260; see Brazell, ed. 1988: 67–68. A similar expression appears in the play *Fuji*.
72 Tyler, trans./ed. 1992: 40.
73 Curiously, this encounter reverses their roles on the battlefield. In their fatal encounter, Atsumori refuses to reveal his name, as he felt Naozane's social status was not high enough for him to make a worthy enemy. It is he who was the snob.

relic, and they rebuke her: "How now, you beggar there! That place where you are sitting—do you know that you are profaning a stupa, the form of Buddha's body? Get up from there; go rest some other place!"[74] The woman later reveals herself to be the famous poet Ono no Komachi and prevails over the monks in a debate over Buddhist doctrine.

The monks' reactions are totally justifiable, as Komachi is in fact committing sacrilege by sitting on the stupa. The positions she takes are contrary to common-sense practice but justified by esoteric concepts in Buddhist philosophy (see sec. 4.4).

4.6.2.3   Reconciliation of *waki* and *shite*

As we have seen, the *waki* and *shite* in *mugen nō* are more than interlocutors. A dramatic tension often exists between them. Yet this tension is always relieved before the main part of the play—the ghost's retelling of the past—begins to unfold. In *Atsumori*, after the grasscutter points out Renshō's error, he immediately acknowledges it. At the end of *Sotoba Komachi*, the monks recognize Komachi's acute understanding of Buddhist belief and the depth of her insight. This reconciliation is sometimes accomplished linguistically through phrases uttered by the *waki* such as "How true, how true" (*ge ni, ge ni*) and "that makes sense" (*kotowari nari*). In the case of the ignorant *waki*, the *shite* follows up his or her rebuke with an explication of the facts the *waki* needs to know, and he acknowledges the importance of the place and appreciates it.

A consonance is also accomplished formally by the allocation of dialogue to the *shite* and *waki*. The statements they make—for example, in *Atsumori*, about how culture transcends class—are not uttered by one character or the other, but in close alternation. The *shite* and *waki* finish each other's sentences and by doing so seal their newfound agreement. After all, in cases in which the *shite* is a suffering ghost and the *waki* a traveling Buddhist monk, the *shite* needs the intercession of the *waki* to release him or her from the torments of the afterlife and lead him or her into enlightenment and freedom from painful rebirth.

This brief section has proposed a rethinking of the role of the *waki* in *mugen nō* solely as a representative of the audience. In many cases tension, or even conflict, arises between *waki* and *shite*. It would be going too far to characterize them as protagonist and antagonist because the tension usually dissipates quickly, and the conflict never becomes a force that drives the plot. The *waki* remains the deuteragonist.

---

74   Translation by Herschel Miller in Shirane, ed. 2007: 941.

4.7 Stylistics and Poetics
Takeuchi Akiko

Nō plays are renowned for their ample use of rhetorical devices, such as *kakekotoba* (pivot words), *engo* (associated words), *makura kotoba* (pillow words), and *jokotoba* (preface phrases), as well as their intertextual weaving of classical citations and allusions. In the past, nō plays were even dismissed as mere patchworks of classic texts, with no literary value of their own. A more careful examination reveals, however, that nō plays employ classical rhetorical devices and intertextuality to create distinctive literary styles and dramatic effects. The writer Mishima Yukio (1925–1970) succinctly remarked on the nō plays by Zeami: "They are almost impeccable as poetic drama. The networks of associations by means of pivot words and pillow words, which at a first glance may seem meaningless, in fact have a profound significance."[75] This section will explore how these rhetorical devices and deeply incorporated intertextuality comprise the distinctive "style" of nō texts.

4.7.1 Citations and Allusions

Nō's high intertextuality and rich rhetoric can be attributed to the fact that it developed within a cultural milieu dominated by literary forms of *renga*. This highly performative and collaborative form of poetry was ubiquitously enjoyed across the social classes in medieval Japan. It required participants—including the audience, the playwrights, and the performers of nō—to have a wide breadth of knowledge of Japanese and Chinese canonical poems and tales, as well as their poetic associations. It is thus quite natural that nō should be strongly influenced by the poetic genre of *renga*, not only in terms of aesthetic ideals but also for its diction, rhetoric, and intertextuality.

Let us first examine the citations of poems within nō plays. In his treatise on playwriting, *Sandō* (*The Three Courses*, 1423), Zeami urges the reader to cite Japanese and Chinese poems suitable for a play's mood. If a play is set in a place with deep historical or literary associations, Zeami emphasizes the importance of citing a poem related to its setting at the play's climax.[76] This is true of most nō plays: poems are cited throughout the course of the drama, not only at its climax. These poems may or may not be directly related to the play's locale. Furthermore, these poems sometimes appear in full, but often only parts of them are cited.

---

75 Mishima 1975: 536–37. All translations are by the author, unless otherwise indicated.
76 Hare, trans. 2008: 153–54.

One example is *Nishikigi*, a *mugen nō* by Zeami. The play takes place in the village of Kefu, deep in the mountains in the northern provinces at the height of autumn. The story draws upon the legends of *hosonuno* ("narrow cloth") and *nishikigi* ("brocade tree"), which are tokens of unrequited love in the region and familiar poetic tropes. It is thus no surprise that poems referring to the two legends are quoted extensively in the play. In addition, the play also cites poems in Japanese and Chinese that lament unrequited love or describe desolate autumn mountain scenery. Many of these citations are fragmentary, quoting only part of the poem, whether they are related to the legends or not. Since these poems were common literary knowledge in medieval Japan, it was enough to use only half of a poem, or even just a few phrases, to conjure up an image in the audience's mind. The degree of understanding must have differed greatly, however, depending on the cultural background of the audience.

The same is true regarding citations of other types of text. Nō plays draw on expressions from classic tales from the Heian period (794–1185), such as *The Tale of Genji* and *The Tales of Ise*, and diverse religious texts, such as Buddhist sutras and famous oracles of deities. The citations vary in length and the degree to which they are relevant to a play's dramatic developments. Moreover, those from Heian tales tend to be especially fragmented in nō. Numerous *renga* manuals widely circulated in medieval Japan included lists of conventional associations of poetic words, many of which were based on their use in Heian tales. Due to the conventionalization of poetic associations, a single word or phrase was sufficient to evoke a celebrated scene from *Genji* or *Ise* tales. Thus, these fragmented citations of Heian prose narratives may be more aptly called "allusions."

An example of the use of such citations, or allusions, is *Tadanori*, a warrior play by Zeami that is based on *The Tale of the Heike*. The protagonist is the ghost of Tadanori, a high-ranking member of the Heike (Taira) clan and devoted poet who died at the 1184 Battle of Ichinotani in Suma. Zeami depicts this warrior-poet not as a denizen of *shuradō*, the hellish realm of never-ending battle, but as an elegant court noble who tragically met a bloody death. The play emphasizes how he was devoted to composing poetry until the very end of his life and even afterward, for Tadanori's ghost appears to a traveling monk who visits Suma, asking him to save his posthumous name as a poet.

The play directly quotes many lines from *The Tale of the Heike*. At the same time, it frequently alludes to chapter 12, "Suma," in *The Tale of Genji*, one of the most renowned in the tale. It features the protagonist Shining (Hikaru) Genji during his self-imposed exile on the remote, desolate seashore of Suma. The play's depiction of the surrounding scenery is studded with well-known words and phrases from the Suma chapter, such as "remote from any village" (*sato banare*), "mountains close behind" (*ushiro no yama*), "village in a mountain" (*yamazato*), "what is called firewood" (*shiba to iu mono*), and "young cherry tree" (*wakagi no sakura*). The background scene is thus portrayed as a highly poetic landscape, strongly associated with aristocratic culture, rather than a bloody battlefield. The same technique is used in another of Zeami's warrior plays, *Atsumori*, which suggests an analogy between Atsumori, a young courtier of the Heike who loved music and died in battle in Suma, and Shining Genji, who, as noted, was also exiled from the capital to this remote seashore (see sec. 4.3).

4.7.2   Rhetoric That Creates Continuity

Aside from these citations from classical texts, nō plays make extensive use of rhetorical devices that are widely employed in *waka* and *renga*, such as preface phrases, pillow words, pivot words, and associated words (*jokotoba, makura kotoba, kakekotoba,* and *engo*, respectively). Additionally, alliteration, which is not commonly seen in *waka* and *renga*, frequently appears in nō. Pivot words and associated words, in particular, are used not only as embellishments but also to create continuity throughout the text on both imaginary and linguistic levels.[77] Associated words in a single passage draw attention to the bonds between related ideas to evoke certain overtones. Pivot words, or "poetic puns," are one of the most important poetic figures in Japan. They connect two phrases by overlapping one with the other; the last syllable(s) of a phrase also function(s) as the first syllable(s) of the next phrase. Pivot words enable sudden, sometimes stunning, logical leaps, while maintaining continuity on a phonetic level.

The following is the protagonist's entrance scene of *Izutsu*, another *mugen nō* by Zeami. In this scene, the ghost of a woman who was loved by the famous poet Ariwara no Narihira appears at a temple with water to offer the Buddha. The old temple is the place where she, as a small girl, used to play with Narihira, then the "boy next door." The scene, typical of a protagonist's entrance in Zeami's plays, exemplifies the rich use of the various rhetorical devices discussed above:

WOMAN (*shite*) [*shidai*]
Akatsuki goto no aka no mizu, akatsuki goto no aka no mizu, tsuki mo kokoro ya sumasu ran

---

77   Yokomichi 1987: 71–72.

[*sashi*]
    Sanaki dani mono no samishiki aki no yo no, hitome mare naru furutera no,
    niwa no matsukaze fukesugite, tsuki mo katabuku nokiba no kusa, wasurete
    sugishi inishie o, shinobu gao nite itsu made ka, matsu koto nakute nagaraen,
    geni nanigoto mo omoide no, hito ni ha nokoru yo no naka kana[78]

WOMAN (*shite*) [*shidai*]
    Water offered to the Buddha every dawn,
    water offered to the Buddha every dawn,
    is purified by the moon, and purified also will be my heart.
[*sashi*]
    In the autumn night desolate by nature,
    in this abandoned old temple rarely visited by anyone,
    the winds blow through the pine trees, the night wears on,
    and the moon sinks toward the eaves from which ferns grow.
    Missing the past long forgotten, burying myself in obscurity,
    how long shall I linger like this, waiting with no avail?
    Indeed, in this world, whatever remains to us are only memories.[79]

The scene opens with striking alliteration through words beginning with "*aka*," meaning "every dawn" (***akatsuki goto no***) and "water offered to the Buddha" (***aka no mizu***). As these two phrases are both repeated, the sound "*aka*" is heard four times in total. The following *sashi* section is densely packed with pivot words and associated words. The phrases "winds blow through pine trees" (*matsukaze **fuke***) and "the night wears on" (***fuke** sugite*) overlap through the pivot word "***fuke***." The terms meaning "forgotten" (*wasurete*), "missing" (*shinobu*), and "how long" (*itsu made*) are all words associated with "ferns (that) grow (on the eaves)" (*nokiba no kusa*), which is another name for "memory weeds" (*omoide gusa*). Additionally, "missing the past" (*inishie o **shinobu***) and "burying myself in obscurity" (***shinobu** gao nite*) are connected by the pivot word "***shinobu***."[80]

These phrases are connected not through grammar or logic but on the basis of sound and association. Therefore, any translations of nō texts—even translations in modern Japanese—always need to fill in logical gaps in the original

---

78   Itō, ed. 1983: 1:104. The use of commas follows this edition.
79   See Tyler, trans./ed. 1992: 125.
80   Itō, ed. 1983: 1:104.

text with conjunctions or other grammatical and expository additions.[81] The tentative translation above is no exception.

In the original text, however, the natural and emotional images of an autumn night, abandoned temple, winds, moon, grasses, a ghost's reflection of herself, and her everlasting longing for the past and her lover, are not presented in a logical order, but rather are "juxtaposed" and overlap with one another due to the strength of homonyms and poetic associations. Zeami excelled at this technique, often employing it to merge a protagonist's emotional state with the surrounding natural environment, as is clearly the case in the example above.[82]

Both associated words and pivot words are widely employed in Japanese poetry—namely, in *waka* and *renga*. What makes their use in nō plays different from that in poetry, however, is the fact that nō texts are much longer and continuously chanted, while in *waka* and *renga* each verse consists of only a few lines. As a result, in performances of nō plays, the juxtaposed and overlapping presentations of visual imagery and characters' emotions could go on for a significant length of time. This creates what could be called a linguistic montage.[83] Varied and fragmented imagery appears almost incessantly, connected but without logical coherence, thus making the audience perceive a fusion of scenery and emotions that transcends logical reasoning.

4.7.3 *Registers in Prose Sections*

Nō plays do not consist solely of language that heavily employs such rhetorical devices and citations of classic texts. The plays' highlights—when the protagonist expresses his or her inner thoughts, or the event of the main interest of the play is unrolled—are usually delivered through such highly poetic language. Yet, many nō plays also include sections in which the language is much less "poetic" and can even be called "prosaic," although it is still chanted with patterned intonations in a highly stylized way.

These prosaic sections can be roughly divided into two types, according to their registers: *nari-* and *sōrō-*style sections. The language of the former is that of oral storytelling and narratives, while the latter is closer to colloquial,

---

81   In his two cycles of translations of nō, *Pining Wind* and *Granny Mountains*, Royall Tyler made one of the most successful attempts to translate into English the multilayered meanings created by pivot words and associated words in nō (Tyler, trans. 1978a, 1978b). The facing-page translations by Chifumi Shimazaki also attempt to convey the word play both in the English versions and in commentary. For *Izutsu*, see Shimazaki 1977.
82   Miyake 2001: 38.
83   Yokoyama 2021; Yokoyama 2022. Paul Atkins discusses this technique employed in Zenchiku's plays, calling it a "kaleidoscopic" pattern of allusion. Atkins 2006: 61.

conversational language. Thus, nō texts consist of three different language styles: poetic, narrative, and colloquial. Three generic elements that make up nō theatre—poetry, narratives (orally performed or transmitted in written form), and drama—are reflected in these three language styles.[84]

4.8 Narration and Ambiguous Voice
Takeuchi Akiko

In theatre, enunciated words control audience perception of the physical onstage space.[85] The spectators of *Hamlet*, for example, *see* the onstage space as a castle in Denmark, no matter where the stage is *actually* located, simply because it is verbally described as such by the characters. In nō, with its bare stage, scarce usage of gestures, and static facial expressions, the audience is all the more encouraged to accept whatever the actors and chorus verbally describe about the scenes and actions onstage.

From the point of view of narratology, this powerful language in nō theatre has two distinct traits. First, both characters' speeches and narration are chanted onstage. In fact, nō shares this feature with other classical Japanese theatrical genres, such as *jōruri* puppetry and, to a lesser degree, kabuki. Second, nō texts often do not make clear who the speaker is, by which we mean not the identity of the speaker onstage but the speaker in the narratological sense. This creates problems for anyone attempting to translate nō plays into another language—including modern Japanese. This ambiguity is partly due to the grammatical characteristics of premodern Japanese, to the richly rhetorical language employed in nō texts, and to nō's theatrical conventions.

As a result of these two characteristics—the use of narration and the ambiguity of voice—many nō plays contain sections in which the narration and the speeches of the characters merge to become indistinguishable. The following discussion applies a narratological framework to examine the use of narration, the ambiguity of voice, and how the fusion of characters' speeches and narration impacts the stage-audience relationship in nō.[86]

4.8.1 Use of Narration
Before analyzing the use of narration in nō, it might be instructive to define what "narration" means in this context. What matters here is *not* "secondary

---

84 Yokomichi 1986: 30.
85 Issacharoff 1989: 157–60.
86 For more detailed discussion on this subject, see Takeuchi 2020.

narration," in which characters retrospectively describe an incident to another character, as in *Hamlet* when Queen Gertrude recounts to her husband and Laertes how Ophelia was drowned in a river. Such secondary narration is common in nō plays—especially in *mugen nō* with the central event retrospectively "told" to a living traveler by a ghost or other supernatural being—but it is also seen to varying degrees in other theatrical traditions. What is particular to nō is its employment of primary, or contemporaneous, narration, which depicts incidents as they occur in the dramatic present and is conveyed through either the present or past tense similarly to "narration" in novels and epics. This "primary narration" (hereafter, "narration") typically appears in nō at the conclusion of an act to describe a protagonist's disappearance or to provide final commentary on the whole incident, as demonstrated in the examples here:

– *Chikubushima*, the ending scene of the first act:

> CHORUS
> And the old man plunges (it seems)
> Into the deep, with this parting cry:
> I am this lake's own lord!
> Such are his words, before the waves
> Conceal him and he is gone.[87]

– *Shōkun*, the ending scene of the second act:

> CHORUS
> Like a flower she seems, seen dimly through
> The clouded skies of their sorrow.
> But it is her heart, clear as the crescent moon
> Shining in the distance,
> That is the mirror of her virtue.[88]

The chorus at the end of the first act of *Chikubushima* describes the action of the deity (*shite*) disguised as an old man, delivers his parting words, and then narrates his disappearance into the lake. The closing chorus of *Shōkun* relates the disappearance of the ghost of Shōkun (*shite*) and praises her high virtue.

Narration may also occur during an act. The ongoing activities of characters in the dramatic present are verbalized, sometimes by the chorus, sometimes by the actors who play those characters. In *Sumidagawa*, the *shite* actor in the

---

87   Tyler, trans./ed. 1992: 65; layout modified.
88   Keene, ed. 1970: 176; layout modified.

role of the mother narrates her own speechlessness when she finally finds the
tomb of her son after a long search for him:

MOTHER (*shite*)
  While the mother, overcome by sorrow,
  unable even to call the Name,
  lies there, prostrate, dissolved in weeping.[89]

The amount of narration varies from play to play, and in this respect, *mugen nō*
and *genzai nō* demonstrate opposing tendencies. On the one hand, in *genzai
nō* the main event unfolds in the dramatic present through the interactions of
characters, just as commonly seen in Western realistic theatre. There is a frequent
tendency to employ narration in its descriptions of events occurring in
the dramatic present. On the other, in *mugen nō* narration usually appears only
at the end of an act, and not all acts end with this narration.[90] From a narratological
viewpoint, Zeami's invention of the *mugen nō* style can be interpreted
as his attempt to minimize the use of (primary) narration by presenting the
main incident through a character's retelling to another character (secondary
narration), not as an event that happens in the dramatic present.

4.8.2   Fusion of Different Voices and Narration

Exemplary of the fusion of different voices and narration is the final scene
of *Takasago*, which is perhaps the most famous nō play. In this scene, the
Sumiyoshi deity (*shite*) manifests his true form before a traveling priest (*waki*)
and performs a dance to celebrate the peaceful reign and the country's people.
Linguistic ambiguity leads to numerous possible interpretations regarding the
identity of the "speaker" for the choral parts.
– *Takasago*, ending scene of the second act:

CHORUS
  Gracious manifestation of the god!
  Gracious manifestation of the god!
  To see the dance of the god under the bright moon—
  what a miraculous effect!
SUMIYOSHI DEITY (*shite*)
  Indeed, the clear voices of the various dancing shrine
  maidens are heard in Sumiyoshi,

---

89   Tyler, trans./ed. 1992: 262; layout modified.
90   Yokomichi 1986: 44–45.

> where the pine trees are reflected on the blue sea;
> it should be exactly like "Blue Sea Waves."[91]
>
> CHORUS
> The Way of Gods and the Way of the Emperor are both straight,
> leading to the spring of the capital—
>
> SUMIYOSHI DEITY
> Just like the dance of "Return to the Capital."
>
> CHORUS
> With a wish for an eternal life of the emperor,
>
> SUMIYOSHI DEITY
> Dressed in the ritual robe,
>
> CHORUS
> A dancing arm held out sweeps away the demon;
> an arm pulled in holds good fortune.
> The Dance of "Thousand Autumns" caresses the people;
> "Ten Thousand Years" extends their lives.
> The sound of the winds blowing through the paired pine trees
> is pleasing to the ear.
> The sound of the winds is pleasing to the ear![92]

The first choral part seems to be the priest's own exclamation at seeing the deity's manifestation; however, the subsequent alternate chanting between *shite* and chorus blurs the voice of the speaker. Spoken by an unidentified voice that could be the deity, priest, or narrator, the chorus describes every movement of the deity's dance as a bestowal of benediction upon the world.

Numerous commentaries and modern Japanese translations give diverse interpretations on the "voice" of these choral sections. Sanari Kentarō takes the first two choral parts as the priest's words and the third and fourth choral parts as the deity's words, except for the ending lines referring to "the sound of the winds," which he interprets as narration.[93] Koyama Hiroshi translates the first two choral parts as the priest's words, but he does not attribute the voice of the third and fourth choral parts to either a specific character or narration, thereby leaving the speaker undefined.[94] Amano Fumio translates the first, second, and third choral parts as the priest's words, and the whole fourth part

---

91   "Blue Sea Waves" (*Seigaiha*), "Return to the Capital" (*Genjōraku*), "Thousand Autumns" (*Senshūraku*), and "Ten Thousand Years" (*Manzairaku*) are the titles of famous *gagaku* dances.
92   Itō, ed. 1986: 2:291–92; see Tyler, trans./ed. 1992: 291–92.
93   Sanari 1954: 1872–73.
94   Koyama et al., eds. 1973: 64–65.

as the deity's words.⁹⁵ These different interpretations are all plausible, both in terms of grammar and of content.

4.8.3 The Effect of Narration and Ambiguity of Voice: Narratological Observations

What, then, is the effect of the ambiguity caused by the fusion of narration and different voices? Narratological studies may provide us with a clue in answering this question. They point out that narration possesses its own "credibility," or "absolute authority," which the reader (or listener) inevitably accepts. To borrow Seymour Chatman's words, we accept whatever the narration says, as if by "the contract that [we] willingly signed in picking up the book."⁹⁶ In other words, theatrical language, which is intrinsically able to control the audience's spatial perception of onstage space, becomes all the more persuasive when it employs narration.

This is especially true in nō, as we have already witnessed in examples above from *Chikubushima*, *Shōkun*, and *Sumidagawa*. At the end of *Chikubushima* the *shite* actor in the role of the deity remains onstage, and there are no stage props to suggest the lake. Nonetheless, the audience perceives the god's disappearance into the lake thanks to the narration chanted by the chorus. In *Shōkun*, the narration by the last chorus not only controls the spatial perception of the spectators—here again, the *shite* actor who plays the ghost remains onstage while the chant of the chorus describes her disappearance from view. The narration similarly controls their interpretation of the narrated scene through the addition of a comment. In *Sumidagawa*, the audience *sees* the mother weep, as verbally described by the actor's narration, even though the actor's masked face does not shed a tear.

Narratology also argues that this "authority" of narration is observed when the voices of the narrator and characters become inseparable, such as in free indirect discourse in Indo-European languages.⁹⁷ In the Japanese language, narration and the voices of the characters merge more readily, as clearly shown by the narratological studies of Heian-period literature.⁹⁸ In this language, the subject is generally omitted, verbs are not conjugated for the grammatical person, and the use of deixis and what is equivalent to personal pronouns is quite limited. Thus, it is often difficult to make a grammatical distinction between direct and indirect discourse. When a tag clause—the "(s)he said" phrase that

---

95   Amano et al., eds. 2013: 261.
96   Chatman 1978: 250–51.
97   Chatman 1978: 206.
98   Midorikawa 2003: 212.

accompanies character's discourse in prose narrative[99]—is omitted and the voice of discourse is not specified by the context, personal pronouns, deixis, or the use of honorifics, monologues tend to become indistinguishable from narration.[100]

In other theatrical genres, an actor's body may function as a "tag clause." Each actor plays a fixed character; he or she moves onstage as that character and speaks only that character's lines. This allows any words spoken onstage to be attributed to a specific character. This is not the case with nō, however. It is true that in nō theatre, there are also actors onstage, each of whom represents a specific character. Yet, the chorus recites both narration and the speech of various characters. The actors onstage chant not only their own characters' lines, they also provide narration, describing their own movements, as is shown in the example above from *Sumidagawa*. Sometimes, they even chant the words of different characters. In nō theatre, the "tag" is sometimes unreliable.

As a result, when there is no obvious onstage communication between characters, the discourse tends to become not only monologic but also narrative. Theatrically, words spoken by an actor (not the chorus) tend to be naturally taken as the words of the character he or she plays, rather than narration. When the chorus chants a lengthy passage without apparent inter-character communication, however, it can be taken either as narration or a character's words depending on the context.

A reexamination of the final scene of *Takasago* might be useful. The alternating chanting between the *shite* actor and chorus blurs the "voice" of the discourse, and even the distinction between narration and the characters' voices. This ambiguity continues until the end since the text gives no certain indication of who is the addresser or addressee of those words. While thus bearing the narrator's authority, the chorus directly addresses the spectators and reveals the transcendental meaning of each movement of the god's dance, which brings us peace and good fortune—that is, the god's benediction is delivered directly to the audience, endowed with the narrator's authority. In other deity plays by Zeami, a similar narration-infused ambiguous voice is often employed to deliver religious messages.

The clear-cut narration in nō, typically appearing at the end of an act, can be easily presented in another language. It has therefore appealed to modern Western dramatists through translations, who struggled to break away from the theatrical conventions in the West. Most notably, W. B. Yeats freely adapted the use of narration, especially its ability to create a poetic landscape

---

99   Prince 2003: 97.
100 Vincent 2015: 211.

unconstrained by realism, in his famous four plays modeled after nō (see ch. 8 *Reception*, 8.3). The ambiguity of voice and fusion of characters' voices and narration are usually lost in translation. Yet, they are essential elements for the textual richness of nō plays. Employing voice that is not restricted to a single character, and bears the authority of narration, nō plays continue to suggest new possibilities for theatrical texts.

4.9 Religious and Political Allegory in Nō
Susan Blakeley Klein

Nō theatre, like all literary and performative arts, was thoroughly embedded in its time. It is not surprising therefore that plays written to please powerful political and religious patrons might function as political and religious allegory. Nevertheless, for a variety of reasons, there is a tradition of treating nō plays as purely literary texts. These reasons include a paucity of performance records that could provide knowledge about the localized historical contexts in which plays were composed and performed, knowledge that would allow us to read the plays as political allegories. A second reason was the erasure of knowledge about medieval esoteric allegorical commentaries used to write plays (see sec. 4.10). As these secret medieval commentaries have been brought back into scholarly focus, nō's function as religious allegory has become clearer. Finally, in the twentieth century, the neutralization of allegorical political and religious content was exacerbated by modern critical methodologies, especially New Criticism, that treated nō as a purely aestheticized object of study, and its imagery as purely symbolic. As scholars have begun favoring a more historicizing approach, allegory, with its deep rhetorical connection to historical context, has become more critically appealing. In order to understand this last point, it is useful to begin by distinguishing the terms "symbol" and "allegory."

4.9.1 *A Definition of Allegory and Symbol*
Whether critics identify texts as allegorical or symbolic lies with three main features. First is the degree of the text's polysemic opacity—that is, the density of its rhetorical play. Metaphors that are easily naturalized are the most symbolic (e.g., "a life brief as cherry blossoms"); the more complex the trope—especially wordplay that allows for a secondary level of meaning—the more allegorical. Second is the degree of reliance on discourse extrinsic to the text. The more "universal" and easily understood the image (e.g., "the path of life"), the more symbolic the image is considered. The more the reader must rely on knowledge of discourses, usually political or religious, to make sense of the

text, the more allegorical the text is considered. Lastly, there is the degree of self-conscious reflexivity. Dense rhetorical play that relies on political or religious discourse external to the text tends to force the reader or viewer to attend to the process of interpretation more consciously. These characteristics, at least in terms of the historical use of the two terms "allegory" and "symbol," are what is required to call a text allegorical in any language or culture, regardless of the particular rhetorical techniques involved.

4.9.2 *Allegory in Nō: an Illustration*

Not all nō is allegorical, but the ideological goals of nō theatre—particularly as it developed under the patronage of the Ashikaga shōguns Yoshimitsu, Yoshimochi (1386–1428; r. 1394–1423), Yoshinori (1394–1441; r. 1429–1441), and Yoshimasa (1436–1490; r. 1449–1473)—and the rhetorical techniques employed made it conducive to allegory. To begin with, there is the language: *kakekotoba* (pivot words), *engo* (associated words), *uta makura* (poetic place names or toponyms), and *monotsukushi* (poetic lists or catalogues); every variety of polysemic play occurs in nō (see sec. 4.7). When this polysemic play takes as its theme the mirroring of political and religious cosmologies, nō tends toward allegory. For example, nō often plays on the figural meanings of *kage*, which contains the antithetical meanings of shade (陰) and reflected light (影), both figures for benevolence on the part of a superior who casts his shadow of protection and shelter, and in whose favor (reflected light) those who depend on him bask. This figural reading has been literalized within Japanese in the word *mikage*, a sovereign's benevolent protection of his subjects, a usage that also appears frequently in nō plays. Used in conjunction with other associated words such as *hikari* (light), *wakō* ([Buddha's] tranquil light), *ikō* (political light/power), and *eijiru* (to reflect), *kage* has not only political but also strongly religious connotations.

This kind of allegorical usage can be seen in the various plays on *kage* in the nō *Ukon*, in which one of the central thematic principles is that the enlightened power of the sun deity Amaterasu Ōmikami is reflected by or mirrored in the political power of an unnamed sovereign. For example, at the beginning of the second act of the play, we find the line *wakō no kage mo kumorinaki, kimi no ikō mo kage takaku* ("the reflection of [Buddha's] tranquil light is unclouded, the shelter/reflection of our sovereign's enlightened power/political glory is far-reaching/majestic").[101] The sovereign's political power, similar to Amaterasu's divine power as a reflection of Buddha's tranquil light, acts as a protective shelter for the imperial family, and by extension, the nation. When political

---

101   Itō, ed. 1983: 1:142–43. All translations are by the author, unless otherwise indicated.

and divine hierarchies mirror each other, their harmony brings peace to the nation as a whole. This identification of divine and political authority takes place through the figural compression of the word *kage*, as well as the use of the principle of analogical correspondences.

Nō can also function as religious allegory via its source-story texts. In the play *Kakitsubata*, attributed to Konparu Zenchiku, multiple levels of meaning are generated through allusions to the medieval commentaries that read Heian-period texts such as *The Tales of Ise* and the first imperial *waka* poetry collection *Kokin wakashū* as esoteric religious allegories. Commentaries such as *Waka chikenshū* (*A Collection of Revealed Knowledge of Waka*, ca. 1260s), *Reizei-ke ryū Ise monogatari shō* (*Selected Reizei School Comments on The Tales of Ise*, 14th c.), *Gyokuden jinpi no maki* (*Jeweled Transmission of Deep Secrets*, ca. 1273–78), and *Ise monogatari zuinō* (*Essence of The Tales of Ise*, ca. 14th c.) identified historical personages, such as the Heian-period courtier-poet Ariwara no Narihira, as incarnations of a variety of Buddhist and Shintō deities. *Kakitsubata*, which alludes to all the commentaries named above and more, represents Ariwara no Narihira as an avatar of the deity of yin and yang and the bodhisattva of song and dance who "left Buddha's Capital of Tranquil Light to bring salvation and blessings to all"[102] through his poems, all "miraculous sermons on the Buddha's Dharma."[103] In this world, poetry is not merely rhetoric, and dance is not simply movement. Both have the power to bring us to enlightenment if they are correctly interpreted (see sec. 4.3).

It is harder to find concrete examples of political allegory in nō because we have little knowledge about the contexts in which the plays were written. Very few records were kept of performances, and authorship lists were constructed long after most plays in the current repertory were composed. Amano Fumio has written extensively on hidden allusions to political contexts found in nō plays, especially plays involving deities that effectively align the power of Buddhist and Shintō deities in support of specific warrior patrons (e.g., *Naniwa, Oimatsu, Kinsatsu, Yumi Yawata, Takasago*).[104] He has also made a strong argument based on circumstantial evidence for *Haku Rakuten* being an overt, if light-hearted, allegory of a military crisis that sent the capital into turmoil in the summer of 1419.[105]

---

102   Itō, ed. 1983: 1:263.
103   Itō, ed. 1983: 1:262.
104   See Amano 2007.
105   Amano 2002; a slightly revised version appears in Amano 2007: 478–71; see also Klein 2021a.

4.9.3 A Case Study: Oshio

The likelihood that many other plays were originally written as political allegories is evinced in the example of *Oshio*, for which there is a rare record of its first performance as part of the *Kasuga Wakamiya onmatsuri* (Kasuga Wakamiya Grand Festival) in the ninth month of 1465. The centerpiece of the festival was a competition between the four major *sarugaku nō* troupes of Yamato Province (present-day Nara Prefecture)—today known as the Kanze, Konparu, Kongō, and Hōshō—before the reigning shōgun Ashikaga Yoshimasa and an entourage that included the crème de la crème of the warrior, courtier, and religious elite. It was a spectacular event, and because it featured so prominently in contemporary diaries we have considerable information about it: thirteen plays were performed during the course of a day, three in full armor with horses. Of those plays, the Konparu troupe's *Oharano hanami* (*Blossom Viewing at Oharano*, now known as *Oshio*) stands out because it was written specifically for this performance.[106] The troupe's lead actor, Konparu Zenchiku (then aged sixty), composed the play and performed in the main role. The spirit of the poet Ariwara no Narihira appears as a humble old woodcutter in the first act, and returns in the second act in his "true identity" as both the Oshio deity of the Ōharano Shrine and deity of yin and yang. Narihira as deity manifests at the height of the cherry-blossom season to mingle with the flowers and to reenact in song and dance a perfect moment from the long-lost past: the ninth-century pilgrimage by Fujiwara no Takaiko, Empress of the Second Ward, to her family's tutelary shrine at Ōharano. According to episode 76 in *The Tales of Ise*, Narihira accompanied the empress and wrote a famous poem commemorating the occasion, a poem that could also be interpreted as alluding to a love affair between the two long ago.

The choice of topic was strikingly apt. Although ostensibly about the distant past, the play's title simultaneously evoked a much more recent event: a flower-viewing procession led by Yoshimasa and his wife Hino Tomiko that had taken place only six months earlier. Over a three-day period in the third month, 1465, Yoshimasa and his entourage visited a series of temples in

---

106 The title given in the diary *Inryōken nichiroku* is 小原野花見 (*Oharano hanami*), although the shrine's actual name is 大原野 (Ōharano). *Inryōken nichiroku*, 1465.9.25, 1465.9.26, in Kikei 2007. For more detailed discussion on this play, see Klein 2021a. See Klein 2021b for English translation.

Higashiyama, indulging in *renga* sessions and extravagant banquets, before ending at Ōharano Shrine for blossom viewing. The procession was meant as a very public display of the power and splendor of Yoshimasa's shogunate. And to all those in attendance at the Konparu troupe's performance of *Oharano hanami*, it would have been abundantly clear that the play was meant as a political allegory commemorating that display, blessed by the Oshio deity at Ōharano as a recreation of an ancient and perfect harmony between ruler and ruled: "The hour, day, and verdant month this view conjoins in perfect harmony: at Ōhara's Mount Oshio, today truly the Age of the Gods has been realized."[107] The underlying ideological message of *Oharano hanami* is that such a splendid cultural, political, and religious event, in which a benevolent deity demonstrates its approval of those in power, is still possible, if only for a brief, shining moment.

And yet, within a relatively short space of time, the title of the play was changed to *Oshio* (the name of the mountain where Ōharano Shrine is located and of the deity enshrined there), and the political subtext erased. The proximate cause was undoubtedly the disastrous *Ōnin bunmei no ran* (Ōnin Disturbances, 1467–1477), which laid waste to the capital and put all public cultural activity on hold for a decade. In the aftermath, texts such as the *Ōnin ki* (*Chronicle of the Ōnin Era*, late 15th–the mid-16th c.) singled out both the flower-viewing procession and the nō competition at the *Kasuga Wakamiya onmatsuri* as two of the most egregious examples of Yoshimasa's wildly extravagant conspicuous consumption, extravagance seen as a major contributing factor leading to the civil war. So it may well have seemed prudent to the Konparu troupe, led by Zenchiku's grandson Zenpō (1454–?), to disassociate Zenchiku's play from Yoshimasa's flower-viewing event, and the first step would have been to change its name to *Oshio*. Performance records indicate that after the initial performance at the Nara temple Kōfukuji, the play was never again performed under the title *Oharano hanami*. And *Oshio* came to be seen as just another play celebrating the ineffable beauty of cherry blossoms and the beneficence of a deity blessing the land.

The political and religious allegorical meaning of nō plays may not always be easy for modern viewers to discern. Nevertheless, as this discussion on allegory in nō demonstrates, by re-embedding plays within the complex society in which they first emerged and by reestablishing their sources in religious commentaries, we can begin to recover the medieval reception of plays. This helps extend the range and depth of our understanding of nō in this period.

---

107   Itō 1983: 1:227.

4.10 Medieval Commentaries and Nō Theatre
Susan Blakeley Klein

It is clear to contemporary scholars that secret medieval literary commentaries on works such as *The Tales of Ise* and the first imperial *waka* poetry anthology *Kokin wakashū* had a powerful bearing on the composition of nō plays and treatises. This included some of the most famous and popular plays in the repertory today. But for most of the Edo and much of the modern period that influence was unrecognized for a number of reasons. By the late fifteenth century, the esoteric (and especially tantric) content of the commentaries began to be seen as highly problematic, even distasteful, by the foremost scholars of the age: Shōtetsu (1381–1459), Ichijō Kaneyoshi (1402–1481), and Sōgi (1421–1502). By the Edo period (1603–1868), the esoteric commentaries had largely faded from scholarly view, lying forgotten in family and temple archives, although as secret texts they still remained a source of prestige for the families and institutions that owned them. This process of suppression and erasure made it difficult for modern scholars to acknowledge the esoteric commentaries as a source for nō plays. Beginning in the 1960s and 1970s, however, Japanese scholars began focusing serious attention on the esoteric commentaries as exemplary of the religious mindset of the medieval period, and a rich body of work on the relationship between medieval commentaries and nō subsequently emerged.

4.10.1 *The Original Development of Esoteric Literary Commentaries*
In the late thirteenth century, the relatively obscure poet-monk Fujiwara no Tameaki (ca. 1230s–ca. 1290s), son of Fujiwara no Tameie (1198–1275) and grandson of the influential poet Fujiwara no Teika (1162–1241), introduced a *waka* initiation ceremony based on the esoteric Buddhist ordination and transmission system of initiation (*Shingon kanjō*). At these poetic initiations, a "*waka* mandala" was displayed along with portraits of the Sumiyoshi deity (the patron deity of *waka* poetry) and the poets Kakinomoto no Hitomaro (d. ca. 708–715) and Ariwara no Narihira (825–860), who were considered the founders of the Way of Poetry. Incense was burned, elaborate gifts of money and clothing were presented, and after appropriate poetic mantras were recited, commentaries containing esoteric poetic "secrets" were transmitted to the initiate along with genealogical documents purportedly authenticating an unbroken line of transmission. These secret commentaries transformed Heian-period canonical texts, such as *The Tales of Ise* and the *Kokin wakashū*, into complex religious allegories, and poets such as Narihira, who was understood as the central figure in *The Tales of Ise*, into tantric deities. The idea caught on quickly and soon every major

poetic house had its own esoteric *waka* initiation ceremony, and many of their associated commentaries contained material that Tameaki had originated.

4.10.2 *Medieval Commentaries and Nō*

In the Muromachi period (1336–1573), these supposedly top-secret commentaries began to seep into popular culture, where they had an inordinate influence. Already beginning in the late fourteenth century, material appears openly in nō and *otogizōshi* (short prose tales). Of the medieval commentaries on the *Kokin wakashū*, Tameaki's *Chikuenshō* (*Edited Selections from a Bamboo Grove*, ca. 1265–70), written for novice poets, provides an introduction to allegory as a rhetorical trope and had a significant impact for Zeami's treatise *Rikugi* (*Six Models*, 1428), which correlated the *rikugi* (the "Six Models" of how poetry expresses meaning) from the *Kokin wakashū* preface with Zeami's *kyūi*, or "nine levels," of nō performance. The most common plot source for plays related to the *Kokin wakashū* were Tameaki's middle-level commentary *Kokin wakashūjo kikigaki: sanryūshō* (*Lecture Notes on the Preface to the Kokin wakashū: Selected Comments from the Three Schools*, late 13th c.) and its descendant text, the *Nijōke-ryū Bishamondōbon Kokinshū chū* (*Nijō School Bishamon Hall Commentary on the Kokin wakashū*, first half 14th c.). Commentaries in the lineage of the *Kokin wakashūjo kikigaki* provided anecdotal backstories for phrases from the *Kokin wakashū* preface. These stories underlie nō plays as varied as *Takasago* ("growing old together with the twin pines of Takasago and Suminoe"), *Ominameshi* ("recalling the olden days of Man Mountain and mourning the brief blossoming of the damsel flower"), *Matsumushi* ("yearning for a friend at the sound of the pining cricket"), and *Fujisan* ("comparing one's smoldering passion to Mount Fuji's rising smoke"). Important allusions to commentary material also appear in the nō plays *Haku Rakuten*, *Kinsatsu*, *Naniwa*, *Ukai*, *Asagao*, and *Sotoba Komachi*, among others (see sec. 4.3).

Of the commentaries on *The Tales of Ise*, the two most critical for nō were *Waka chikenshū* (*A Collection of Revealed Knowledge of Waka*, ca. 1260s) and *Reizeike-ryū Ise monogatari shō* (*Selected Reizei School Comments on The Tales of Ise*, 14th c.). Material from these commentaries provided the plot, characters, and poetic imagery for the five plays related to *The Tales of Ise* that remain in the *nō* repertory (*Unrin'in*, *Izutsu*, *Ukon*, *Kakitsubata*, *Oshio*).

Tameaki was also associated with the production of commentaries for higher-level initiates that were heavily influenced by combinatory *kami* worship and esoteric Shingon Buddhism, including *Gyokuden jinpi no maki* (*Jeweled Transmission of Deep Secrets*, ca. 1273–78), *Waka Kokin kanjō no maki* (*Initiation on Waka of the Kokin wakashū*, ca. 1280s), and *Ise monogatari zuinō* (*Essence of the Ise monogatari*, ca. 14th c.). For the most part, content from these more esoteric commentaries appears only in Konparu Zenchiku's plays and treatises, especially the plays *Kakitsubata* and *Oshio*, and the treatise *Meishukushū* (*Collection Illuminating the Indwelling Deity*, ca. 1460s). Zenchiku's plays and treatises deploy esoteric commentary material to develop the Narihira character into a complex, multivalent persona, presenting Narihira as the deity of yin and yang and the bodhisattva of song and dance (see sec. 4.3; ch. 6 *Treatises*, 6.4).

There are Edo-period texts on nō such as *Utaishō* (*Selected Nō Texts*, early 17th c.) and *Yōkyoku shūyōshō* (*Gathered Leaves of Nō Texts*, 1772) that identify a number of allusions to the esoteric commentaries, but for the most part modern scholarship ignored their influence until Miwa Masatane and Katagiri Yōichi began the process of publishing commentaries in the 1960s and 1970s.[108] Itō Masayoshi (1930–2009) began publishing articles on the relationship of nō and medieval commentaries in the 1970s.[109] His three-volume edited collection of nō plays with annotations to the commentaries gave both Western and Japanese scholars a clearer understanding of their impact. Furthermore, it paved the way for other nō scholars to examine in detail the relationship between commentaries and individual nō plays.

4.11 *Bangai kyoku* and *Shinsaku nō*: Noncanonical Plays and Modern Nō Plays

Fukazawa Nozomi and Takeuchi Akiko (Translated in part by Steven Nelson and Michael Watson, with assistance from Diego Pellecchia)

During the Edo period, nō troupes were required to submit official repertories, with each troupe presenting a list of plays (*kakiage*) to the Tokugawa shogunate. Actors were expected to be ready to perform any play in their lists at a moment's notice (see ch. 1 *History*, 1.3). Today, the plays included in official repertories of the five troupes number around two hundred and forty, most of which were composed during the Muromachi period.[110] These represent less than 10 percent of surviving plays, however, and it is believed that between 2,500 and 3,000 nō plays have been written since that time. Of these, approximately 2,000 were created up to the middle of the Edo period, and some

---

108   Katagiri, ed. 1971–1987.
109   Itō, ed. 1983, 1986, 1988.
110   For a list of plays divided by school, see Yoshimura 2014. For an online resource, see Watson 2020.

1,000 date to the Muromachi.¹¹¹ The result is that there is far greater number of plays that are not part of the current repertory, and these are referred to as "noncanonical" or "extra canonical" plays (*bangai kyoku*).¹¹²

Some of these noncanonical plays were once performed but either failed to enter or have fallen out of the established repertories. Reasons for this vary from their fading popularity among the audience, difficulty of preparing the stage props, to decisions made by the head of a troupe.¹¹³ Many of the noncanonical plays were never staged, most notably those composed during the Edo period that were intended to be enjoyed only through chanting (*su-utai*), rather than through performance. This does not suggest that they are less worthy of close examination, and in fact, they have become the subject of increased scholarly interest, both in Japan and abroad.¹¹⁴ Recent scholarship has gone some way toward clarifying the creative motivation behind new works by known authors in the Edo period and the contexts in which they were used.¹¹⁵

This section will present a historical overview of *bangai kyoku* from the late sixteenth century (post-Muromachi period) until the present day. It will also review the modern plays of the Meiji period and after, now commonly referred to as *shinsaku nō* ("newly created nō"). The different motives behind their composition (political, recreational, religious, ethical) and the different social status of their authors (people in power, those who serve them, townsmen, dramatists, Japanese/non-Japanese scholars and nō practitioners) reflect the art's shifting social function over the last four hundred years.

4.11.1 *Plays Celebrating Toyotomi Hideyoshi*

In the last years of the sixteenth century, nō received the patronage of the powerful de facto ruler of Japan, Toyotomi Hideyoshi (1537–1598). Not only did Hideyoshi offer financial support to the various nō troupes by putting them under his protection, he was himself a practitioner of nō chant and dance. He even commissioned new nō plays to ensure his own legacy.

---

111 Tanaka 1980: 229–30.
112 For a list of plays dating from the Muromachi to the early Edo periods, see Nishino 1998: 699–729.
113 These plays are commonly referred to as *haikyoku*, or "discarded plays." In the early Meiji period, the head of the Hōshō troupe decided to discard thirty plays from the troupe's repertory for the reasons mentioned above.
114 For English translations of noncanonical plays, see Goff 1991 (five plays); Tyler, trans. 2024 (four plays); and Oyler and Watson, eds. 2013 (three plays). For noncanonical plays related to the Genpei War, see Watson 2007.
115 Examples are Ikai 2012; Miyamoto 2013.

The terms *hōkō nō* (Nō for Lord Toyo [Toyotomi Hideyoshi]), and *taikō nō* (Nō for the Regent [Toyotomi Hideyoshi]) refer to the plays commissioned by Hideyoshi. The texts of the plays were written by his official chronicler (*otogishū*) Ōmura Yūko (1535?–1596), with music by the head of the Konparu troupe, Yasuteru (1549–1621). Six of these plays survive: *Akechi uchi* (*The Conquest of Akechi*), *Hōjō*, *Kōya sankei* (*Pilgrimage to Mount Kōya*), *Shibata*, *Yoshino mōde* (*Pilgrimage to Yoshino*), and *Kono hana* (*This Flower*).[116] All of the six plays, apart from *Kono hana*, were performed by Hideyoshi in the third month of 1594 at Osaka Castle. Extant records show that *Kōya sankei* and *Yoshino mōde* had at least one further performance, both in collaboration with Hideyoshi.

These plays, written under Hideyoshi's orders, eulogize him and celebrate his achievement. *Yoshino mōde*, for example, was composed before his pilgrimage to Yoshino in 1594 and was staged as a dedicatory act (*hōnō*) during the pilgrimage, with Hideyoshi acting as himself in performance before the temple's main hall. In the play, Hideyoshi is on his way to view the cherry blossoms of Yoshino when two celestial beings appear—a heavenly maiden (*tennyo*) and the temple's tutelary deity Zaō Gongen. They bestow a blessing on the realm and promise to protect him on his return journey to the capital. These Hideyoshi-commissioned works were very unusual in their subject matter, and for that reason were not staged during the Edo period. They witnessed a degree of revival in the Meiji period, performed in the context of events commemorating Hideyoshi.[117]

Other noncanonical nō related to Hideyoshi include several created in his memory in 1604. After his death in 1598, Hideyoshi was deified at the Toyokuni Shrine built expressly for that purpose in the Higashiyama area of Kyoto. As part of sixth-year memorial services, new nō plays were performed by the Kanze, Hōshō, Konparu, and Kongō troupes: *Buō* (*King Wu*), *Taishi* (*Prince*), *Tachibana* (*Orange*), and *Son Shibaku* (*Sun Simiao*, the name of an ancient Chinese physician) (see ch. 1 *History*, 1.3).[118]

---

116 For texts, see Nonomura, ed. 1928; Tanaka 1963–1980 (1964). *Akechi uchi* has been translated into English; see Brown 2001.

117 *Shibata* was performed in 1898 as part of the tricentennial commemorations of Hideyoshi's death. *Akechi uchi* was staged in 1989 to celebrate the completion of the film *Rikyū*, which deals with Hideyoshi's tea master Sen no Rikyū (1522–1591). Open-air "firelight" or "torchlight" nō (*takigi nō*) performances have been given of *Hōjō* (1990), *Yoshino mōde* (2000), and *Kono hana* (2001), while *Kono hana* was also staged in 2002.

118 Tanaka, ed. 1963–1980 (1964): 192–94; Haga and Sasaki, eds. 1914: 382–86, 394–99, 492–97.

4.11.2 Plays by Daimyō and Those Who Serve Them

From Hideyoshi's time, nō troupes were patronized by political leaders, a practice that the Edo shogunate continued. The staging of nō plays as part of shogunal ceremonies became an important duty for nō actors, and performances on official occasions meant that the same canonical works were staged repeatedly. Ultimately, this contributed to the establishment of a fixed repertory. Nō actors also met the demand for teaching these plays to regional daimyō who wished to participate in performances, and not be just spectators.

The receipt of regular stipends meant that nō performers did not need to compete with other troupes in the creation of new works. Instead, new plays tended to be produced on demand for close patrons, and in feudal domains where nō was popular, plays were occasionally written by the daimyō themselves. Examples of such plays include *Iwatesan* (*Mount Iwate*) and *Kanameishi*. *Iwatesan* was written by the fifth daimyō of the Nanbu (Morioka) domain in the northern province of Mutsu [region that spans present-day Aomori, Iwate, and Akita Prefectures], Nanbu Yukinobu (1642–1702), and was performed at Morioka Castle in 1668. *Kanameishi* deals with the sacred stone of Kashima Shrine (in present-day Ibaraki Prefecture), and was the work of the ninth daimyō of the Mito domain, Tokugawa Nariaki (1800–1860). A chant book (*utaibon*) of the play survives with a colophon dated to 1844.

Many other plays that commemorate or celebrate local festivals and history were created by nō actors who served shogunal domains, such as *Kurokawa*, which was inspired by the regional performance practice of Kurokawa nō (see ch. 3 *Training*, 3.4). The play was composed by the nō performer Fujino Seizaburō (dates unknown), who was supported by the Tsuruoka domain (present-day Yamagata Prefecture).

Another daimyō play, *Suriage*, offers a fairly clear understanding of how the work was created. The plot deals with the 1589 Battle of Suriagehara (in present-day Fukushima Prefecture), when the forces of Date Masamune (1567–1636) of the Sendai domain vanquished the opposing forces. The play has a *mugen nō* structure, in which a traveling *renga* master encounters the spirit of Date Shigezane (1568–1646), a warrior and senior retainer of the Date clan known for his military prowess, who then reenacts the battle. The libretto was written by Hiraga Kurando Yoshimasa (1724–1802), a senior vassal in service to the seventh shōgun Date Shigemura (1742–1796) of the Sendai domain. The music and choreography were by Sakurai Kanomo (dates unknown), a nō actor patronized by the Sendai domain, on orders of the tenth daimyō Narimune (1786–1819). It was first performed at Sendai Castle in 1815 and thereafter the play was transmitted down through the Sakurai family as a play of great significance, even though the opportunities for its performance were extremely limited.[119]

There are numerous records of performances of plays that were created for the enjoyment of figures of power and authority. In some cases, surviving libretti are complemented by other records detailing stage performance, such as written instructions for choreography and costuming, and pictorial representations of props. It is clear that the plays were made for stage performance, but they did not enter the regular repertory of nō troupes.

4.11.3   Plays by Commoners in the Edo Period

In the Edo period, nō chanting (*su-utai*) became an extremely popular pastime among the commoner class. This was done without any staging or elements of stage performance, such as masks and costumes, and was therefore more easily accessible to the general populace. The amateur enthusiasts who became familiar with the basic structure of nō plays through *su-utai* practice began to compose new nō plays, not destined for stage performance but rather to be enjoyed through chanting. The composition of new nō plays was also taken up as a creative literary activity. The *Mikan yōkyokushū* (*Previously Unpublished Nō Playtexts*), a modern collection of over 2,400 nō plays that are not in the current repertory, provides evidence of this.[120] Among these plays are a considerable quantity of new nō plays by Edo-period amateurs. By the mid-Edo period, nō chanting also became established as an integral part of elementary education, and numerous collections of short nō chanting (*koutai*, or "short songs") were published to meet this demand.

These plays, created by amateur nō enthusiasts to be enjoyed through chanting only, tended to be somewhat makeshift in nature, often adaptations, reworkings, or imitations of earlier works, and sometimes nothing more than collages. The enormous quantity of new works from this period might entail a time-consuming search to unearth works worthy of study, but the largely unexplored nature of the field means that there are undoubtedly many more riches to be discovered (see ch. 1 *History*, 1.6; ch. 7 *Material Culture*, 7.7).

---

119   In 1989, the play was revived in Sendai; see Sendaishi-shi Hensan Iinkai, ed. 2008: 501–52 for *Suriage* and related materials. This includes a DVD recording of a reconstructed performance.

120   Tanaka, ed. 1963–1980; Tanaka, ed. 1987–1998; see also Tanaka, ed. 1950; Tanaka, ed. 1952.

4.11.4 *The Revival of Noncanonical Plays*

In the Edo period, there were sporadic movements to revive noncanonical plays. The fifth Tokugawa shōgun Tsunayoshi (1646–1709; r. 1680–1709), a fervent nō aficionado, and his successor the sixth shōgun Ienobu (1662–1712; r. 1709–1712), ordered nō troupes to perform a great many plays that had long not been included in the repertory. This led to the reintroduction of more than thirty plays into the repertory, including some that are highly appreciated today, such as *Kinuta*, *Semimaru*, and *Ohara gokō*. The 15th head of the Kanze troupe, Kanze Motoakira (1722–1774), drastically reformed the troupe's repertory, discarding seven plays and adding fifty-seven noncanonical plays. Although his reform was mostly abrogated soon after his death, some of the plays he revived remained in the repertory (e.g., *Minazuki-barae*) (see ch. 1 History, 1.7).[121]

There have been numerous attempts to resuscitate these forgotten plays since the Meiji period, particularly after World War II and particularly those plays that were once performed but then failed to enter the official repertory. The revival of the plays related to Toyotomi Hideyoshi, for example, was one result of this trend. Moreover, the increased interest in Zeami in the modern nō world also stimulated the renewal of plays composed by him and his contemporaries, including *Shigehira* (also known as *Kasa sotoba*), *Matsura Sayohime*, *Taisanpukun*,[122] *Tadatsu no Saemon*, *Hakozaki*, *Furu*, and *Akoya no matsu* (*The Akoya Pine*).[123]

The revival of noncanonical plays is generally based on what little information remains, sometimes only the lyrics with scant performance notes. Since much of nō theatre's knowledge of a play is acquired through direct experience of performing or watching, reviving plays is a difficult task. In order to do this, actors often reconstruct a play by comparing it with similar plays in the current repertory. Play structures, character types, and other elements of performance such as music sections, dances, or mask/costume combinations follow conventions, allowing for ample data necessary to reconstruct a "lost" play. It should be noted that in the majority of cases, reviving a play does not entail a historical reconstruction of its last performance. Current performance

---

121   For a scene-by-scene summary, see *Minazuki-barae*, or "Summer Purification Rite," in Emmert 2012–2017 (vol. 3, 2014): 100–2. The title has also been translated as *The Lustrations of Early Fall* in Hare 1986.

122   *Taisanpukun* was revived by the Kongō school in 1960. In 2000, the Kanze school revived the play under the title *Taisanmoku*.

123   Kanze Motoakira left performance notes (*kogaki*) on *Akoya no matsu*, suggesting that the play was probably performed on private occasions. The record of its performance was not found until its revival in the twentieth century.

conventions would be applied to the text, in keeping with how the rest of the repertory is staged today.

Many plays that have been revived since the Meiji period are performed in one-off events, but several plays have entered the official repertory, such as *Taisanpukun*, *Go*, *Matsura Sayohime*, and more recently, *Susuki*.[124] Several others, especially Zeami-related plays, including *Furu*, *Hakozaki*, and *Shigehira*, are not in the official repertory but are performed relatively often. In fact, they are performed more frequently than some of the plays in the official repertory that are rarely staged. This demonstrates the vague line between canonical and noncanonical plays.

4.11.5 Plays from the Meiji Period and After (shinsaku nō)

Since the Meiji period the composition (and performance) of new plays was also revived.[125] Modern nō plays from after the Edo period, or *shinsaku nō* ("newly created nō"), were written by poets, dramatists, professional nō performers, and nō scholars, who had a profound knowledge of nō theatre. These works frequently exhibit a departure from traditional nō in terms of the sources, themes, structures, stage conventions, and even language.

The renowned haiku poet Takahama Kyoshi (1874–1959), for example, wrote *Tetsumon* (*Iron Gate*, 1916), later renamed *Zenkōji mōde* (*Pilgrimage to Zenkōji*), an adaptation of Maurice Maeterlinck's *The Death of Tintagiles* (1894). After composing other new plays, in 1943, Takahama wrote *Oku no hosomichi* (*Narrow Road to the Deep North*) to commemorate the 250th anniversary of the death of the revered haiku poet Matsuo Bashō (1644–1694). This play draws upon an episode in Bashō's famous travelogue of the same title.[126]

The most prolific librettist of *shinsaku nō* in the prewar to postwar era was the poet, scholar, and journalist Toki Zenmaro (1885–1980). He composed fifteen new plays in collaboration with the 15th head of the Kita school, Kita Minoru (1900–1986). A number of them feature religious figures (including from Christianity) as the protagonists, as is seen in *Kennyo* (1942), *Shito Pauro* (*Paul the Apostle*, 1960), *Shinran* (1961), *Fukkatsu* (*The Resurrection*, 1963), and *Ganjin wajō* (*Monk Ganjin*, 1964).[127]

---

124 *Taisanpukun*, *Go*, and *Susuki* were admitted in the Kongō school's repertory, while *Matsura Sayohime* entered the Kanze school's repertory.
125 Hata 1987: 301–62.
126 Takahama 1944.
127 See Toki 1976 for texts of these plays together with six others: *Yumedono* (*Dream Pavilion*), *Shōe no nyonin* (*Woman in Blue*), *Sanetomo*, *Hidehira*, *Shimen soka* (*Amidst Enemies*), and *Tsuru* (*Crane*).

Works written during periods of war were deeply influenced by and mirrored current affairs. Many works of the Meiji period praised the war efforts of the First Sino-Japanese (1894–1895) and Russo-Japanese (1904–1905) wars, while others have strongly nationalistic themes.[128] This tendency became especially pronounced during World War II, when nō was used as a tool to raise military morale.[129] In 1941, the Association for Exalting the Merits of the War Dead (Dainihon Chūrei Kenshōkai) commissioned a work entitled *Chūrei* (*Loyal Spirits*) from the Kanze school, and in 1943 a Rear Admiral Sako wrote *Miikusabune* (*Sacred Warship*).[130] Collections of newly composed short nō chanting that promoted the war effort were also published.[131]

In the postwar period, a considerable number of plays were inspired by foreign literature. The nō scholar Yokomichi Mario (1916–2012) wrote two works based on Yeats's nō-inspired *At the Hawk's Well* (1916): *Taka no izumi* (*Hawk's Well*, 1949) and the more experimental *Takahime* (*The Hawk Princess*, 1967) (see ch. 8 Reception, 8.3).[132] The Japanese scholar of French literature Kimura Tarō (1899–1989) adapted Paul Claudel's *La Femme et son ombre* (1923) for his 1968 *Onna to kage* (*Woman and Shadow*). Claudel's play has recently been adapted to the nō stage by Kongō Hisanori, the head of the Kongō troupe, as *Omokage* (*Remnant Shadow*, 2017). The theatre scholar Mōri Mitsuya based his *Fukkatsu no hi* (*Day of Resurrection*, 2008) on Henrik Ibsen's *When We Dead Awaken* (1899).

A proportion of contemporary plays deal with pressing social issues and tragic historical events. The immunologist Tada Tomio (1934–2010) wrote on the theme of brain death in his 1991 *Mumyō no i* (*Well of Ignorance*), as well as on war-related themes in his *Genbakuki* (*Anniversary of the Bomb*, 2005), *Nagasaki no seibo* (*Holy Mother in Nagasaki*, 2005), and *Okinawa zangetsuki* (*Moon over Okinawa*, 2009).[133] *Shiranui* (*Unknown Fires*, 2002) by Ishimure Michiko (1927–2018) is a requiem for victims of Minamata disease.[134]

---

128 See Scholz-Cionca and Oshikiri 2004 for the discussions and partial translations in German of two such plays, *Washi* (*Eagle*) and *Ikusagami* (*War God*).
129 Smethurst and Smethurst 2008.
130 On *Miikusabune*, see Tanaka, ed. 1987–1998 (1994); Higashiya 2017.
131 These include *Shina jihen koutaishū* (*A Collection of Koutai on the China Incident*, 1937) and *Daitōa sensō koutaishū* (*A Collection of Koutai on the Greater East Asia War*, 1944; see fig. 1.28); see Ejima, ed. 1937; Ejima, ed. 1944.
132 For *Taka no izumi* and *Takahime*, see Masuda et al., eds. 1977: 222–24; 224–29.
133 See Tada 2012 for English translations of *Mumyō no I*, *Genbakuki*, and three other plays.
134 Ishimure 2003. Allen and Masami 2016 has an essay by Bruce Allen on *Shiranui* and Ishimure Michiko, and a translation of the play by Aihara Yūko and Bruce Allen. Christina Laffin translated Ishimure's play *Oki no miya*; see Scholz-Cionca and Oda 2006 for the German translations (and discussions) of Ishimure's *Shiranui*, Tada's *Bōkonka*

Shinsaku nō can be written in archaic or modern Japanese, or in other languages. The first major play in modern Japanese was *Chieko shō* (*Portrait of Chieko*, 1957), written and produced by theatre director and critic Takechi Tetsuji (1912–1988), with music by the celebrated nō actor Kanze Hisao (1925–1978), who performed the main role at the work's premiere. Umehara Takeshi (1925–2019), a prominent philosopher and dramatist, created three nō plays in contemporary Japanese, including *Sūpā nō Zeami* (*Super Nō Zeami*, 2013), which made use of nontraditional performance devices such as lights and properties and was premiered by the highly respected nō actor Umewaka Minoru IV. Many *shinsaku nō* plays have been produced and staged in English, most notably by Theatre Nohgaku, an international nō performance group founded in 2000 by Richard Emmert. Theatre Nohgaku's plays include *At Hawk's Well* (2002), *Crazy Jane* (2007), and more recently, *Blue Moon over Memphis* (2015), which has the character of Elvis Presley as the *shite* (fig. 4.6).

Contemporary authors creating *shinsaku nō* who are not themselves nō performers often need to collaborate with nō actors and musicians to shape a subject or text into the conventional form of a nō play. In the most cases, these nō performers are the ones who eventually stage the play. One of the greatest challenges faced is the adaptation of the text to the poetic meter of nō, which needs to match the patterns played by the instrumentalists. Noteworthy is the fact that, as any other activity within the conventional world of nō, actors are not free to perform a new nō play independently. Depending on the school, individuals wishing to perform a *shinsaku nō* play are required to submit a report to the troupe or to obtain the permission of the head of the troupe (*iemoto*).

There are also a number of nō-inspired contemporary theatre plays in Japan and abroad. The aforementioned *At the Hawk's Well* by Yeats is the earliest example (see ch. 8 Reception, 8.3). The degree to which they draw from traditional nō theatre varies. In some, this is primarily in the influence from the plots of existing nō plays (e.g., Mishima Yukio's *Five Modern Nō Plays* and Hosokawa Toshio's opera *Matsukaze*, choreographed by Sasha Walts). Others employ nō theatrical conventions, such as *mugen nō*, the chorus, and the bare square stage, or (adapted) physical techniques of nō chanting and dance, with or without the adaptation of the storylines of known nō plays (e.g., Yeats' *The Dreaming of the Bones*, Ku'nauka Theatre Company's *Othello*, and plays in the

(*Lament for Unrequited Grief*), and Dōmoto Masaki's *Sadako: Genbaku no ko* (*Sadako: Hiroshima's Child*).

FIGURE 4.6
Blue Moon Over Memphis. Shite (Elvis Presley), John Oglevee. 2017
IMAGE © DAVID SURTASKY. COURTESY OF THEATRE NOHGAKU

Contemporary Nō Performance series by Ren'niku Kōbō).[135] Some of these were created and performed in collaboration with professional nō actors.

This raises the question: "What are the boundaries of the nō genre?" To what extent can a recently composed nō play bend the rules of convention by, for example, introducing new costumes, masks, or music patterns? Where can we draw the line between newly created nō and nō-inspired experimental plays? There is no clear-cut, solid consensus in the nō world today about these questions. In general, however, if a new play does not follow the most basic theatrical conventions of nō, such as the art form's chanting and dancing styles as well as the building units (*shōdan*), it is categorized as a *nō-inspired* work and not a *shinsaku nō*.[136] In other words, adding textual, choreographic, or musical

---

[135] See Motohashi 2016 for the discussions on *Othello* by the Ku'nauka Theatre Company; on Ren'niku Kōbō, see Okamoto, ed. 2003.

[136] As Yamanaka Reiko noted, "to be called nō, a performance should consist of the traditional, well-known, existing units" (Yamanaka 2008a: 84).

elements that do not disrupt these basics would permit consideration of the work as "nō." They nonetheless always risk the criticism of not being "true nō" depending on the degree of their divergence from existing conventions. Since it requires years of training to master nō's chanting and dancing techniques, most *shinsaku nō* are performed by professional nō actors.

The creation and performance of a *shinsaku nō* is an extremely time-consuming enterprise that requires the collaboration of many professionals from different fields. Most of these works are never staged again after their premieres. Rare exceptions are Yokomichi Mario's *Takahime* and Tada Tomio's *Mumyō no i*, which have been performed several times in Japan and abroad. Although their "success" is relative and should be taken with reservations, it is still meaningful given the daring deviations from the norm. In *Takahime*, the chorus members play the role of "rocks," donning costumes, moving around onstage, and even chanting in a circular canon. *Mumyō no i* deals with the issue of heart transplants, one of the most controversial bioethical problems in Japan, posing the philosophical question on how one can define human death.

Shifts in the nō world may be too slow, or too fast, depending on one's standpoint. Nonetheless, the function of noncanonical plays, including *shinsaku nō*, within actual nō performance will continue to be the index of how nō adapts and survives in an ever-changing contemporary world.

4.12 Conclusion
Takeuchi Akiko

Most nō plays in the current repertory were profoundly influenced by diverse literary, religious, and social developments in the medieval period, when the great majority of nō's canonical plays were created. They were also governed by various theatrical conventions: patterns of topics, themes, protagonists, structures, and rhetorical devices. These "patterns" were not observed blindly as infallible rules, however. Even though Zeami formulated the basic conventions of nō, he often deviated from them in his playwriting. His *Kinuta*, for example, has quite an irregular structure, with the first act a *genzai nō* and the second act *mugen nō*. In another play by Zeami, *Yamanba*, the protagonist is an old woman demon. The play does not fall into any of the character types that Zeami lists in his treatises.

Likewise, while repeatedly advocating the importance of producing plays faithful to their original stories, Zeami's plays always alter certain aspects or nuances of the original episodes and add something new to their source materials. As noted above, the *mugen nō* structure that Zeami invented was itself a tactful device that permitted a well-known episode to be dramatized from a new perspective through the purely subjective recollections of a ghost. *Atsumori*, for example, draws its source material from *The Tale of the Heike* in depicting the flight of the Heike, Atsumori's death by the hand of Kumagai Naozane, and Naozane's subsequent taking of the tonsure. At the same time, the play adds a new episode that is not mentioned in the source material: the banquet of the Heike on the night before Atsumori's death. The recollection of this banquet occurs at the play's climax, accompanied by an elegant dance by the ghost of Atsumori. Moreover, the play's overall structure—the encounter between Atsumori's ghost and the monk Renshō (formerly Naozane) that leads to his pardon by Atsumori at the play's end—is entirely the invention of the playwright. It can be argued that the play offers redemption to Naozane, who in the original story has to kill young Atsumori against his own will.

Nō is made up of various conventions, but each play acquires its own individual allure through deviations from these conventions. Its most representative structure pattern is *mugen nō*, which is a tool to present a familiar story with novel twists. Moreover, the conventions, especially the elastic expression of time and the predominance of verbal description over the audience's spatial perception, also allow a creative handling of time-space onstage, free from the imperative of realism. Nō is thus equipped with a flexibility that enables it to adopt a wide range of themes and characters, as fully demonstrated in modern nō plays, topics of which span from organ transplantation to Elvis Presley. In nō theatre, conventions and flexibility can be likened to the two sides of the same coin. From Zeami's time onward, they developed nō into what it is, continuing to inspire new works.

4.13   Excursus: Dramaturgy in Nō and Greek Tragedy
Mae J. Smethurst

A great distance—spatial, temporal, and cultural—stretches between fifth-century BCE Greece and the fourteenth/fifteenth-century CE Japan, when the best-known writers of tragedy (Aeschylus, Sophocles, Euripides) and of nō (Kan'ami, Zeami, Zenchiku) created their classic dramas.[137] Since there is no evidence of any influence of one theatrical form upon the other until our times, a comparison of them is perforce ahistorical. The political and cultural milieus of the two forms of drama differed greatly. For example, Greek tragedy

---

137   This text is an abbreviated version of a longer essay in Smethurst 2013: 151–60, Japanese translation in Smethurst 2014; see also Smethurst 1989.

was a public affair, open to the citizens and thus democratic. In nō, for the most part of its history, the main target audience was the people in power and elite members of the society. The languages differ—the Greek verb is equipped with three persons and three numbers, the noun with five cases, and so forth. Therefore, it is never unclear, unless deliberately made so, who is talking at any given time in epic, lyric, or drama. In Japanese ambiguity in the identity of the speaker arises easily in a language that is not highly inflected (see sec. 4.8).

And yet, somehow and somewhere, the cultures shared elements in common, enough to nurture these two similar types of creative activity. It does not seem irrelevant that once the theatres were established, governmental authorities exiled Aeschylus and Zeami, while Euripides and Zenchiku went into self-imposed exile. If nothing else, this similarity in itself makes a cogent statement about the fragility of success in both cultures, not only in artistic endeavors but also in political endeavors, a fragility that is all too apparent in their drama.

There are significant parallels between the performances of nō and Greek tragedy that set them apart from other theatres. In each, three or more serious plays, often with a religious message, and the comic kyōgen and satyr plays were performed on religious or public occasions in outdoor theatres that contained few props or architectural structures compared with much of later Greek tragedy and other types of Japanese and Western drama. From the three sides of these outdoor auditoria, the audience's attention was directed toward the small all-male casts, in its primary roles limited to two or three actors, one of whom might be the playwright himself. These actors were supplemented in some cases by mute extras, but always by choruses and musical instrumentalists—a flutist and two or three drummers in nō, a player of a double-reed instrument (*auloi*) and perhaps a lyre player in Greek tragedy. In both forms, the dances, movements, and gestures enhanced the appearance of those members of the cast who were dressed in masks and costumes, and also complemented the words of the texts. Finally, in both, the texts were poetic, were delivered in a variety of ways: sung to the accompaniment of instruments, recited, narrated, and spoken.

At the very least, the similarities allow us to posit one conclusion about nō and Greek tragedy that sets them apart from many theatres. They prevent members of an audience from mistaking a performance not only for everyday reality, as is true of some theatres, but also for the degree of realism even, for example, of a Shakespearean or kabuki play. Various elements, such as the masks, the small number of male actors, and the presence "onstage" of the chorus and the instrumentalists throughout a performance, create a special aesthetic relationship between the plays and the audiences. The use of masks or, in some cases in nō, of expressionless faces, submerges the personalities of the actors. The words because they are for the most part poetic, the stage because it is devoid of sets and many props, and the movements because they are arranged by a choreographer (the playwright himself) do not reproduce their counterparts in the real world. The scarcity, but importance, of the visual features helps the playwright in turn to focus on what in his mind is essential for the audience to appreciate in any given play.

References

Allen, Bruce, and Yūki Masami 結城正美. 2016. *Ishimure Michiko's Writing in Ecocritical Perspective: Between Sea and Sky.* Lanham: Lexington Books.

Amano Fumio 天野文雄. 2002. "*Haku Rakuten* to Ōei no gaikō: Kume Kunitake to Takano Tatsuyuki no shosetsu o kenshō suru"《白楽天》と応永の外寇：久米邦武と高野辰之の所説を検証する. *Zeami* 世阿弥 1: 128–46.

Amano Fumio 天野文雄. 2007. *Zeami ga ita basho: nō taiseiki no nō to nōyakusha o meguru kankyō* 世阿弥がいた場所：能大成期の能と能役者をめぐる環境. Tokyo: Perikansha.

Amano Fumio 天野文雄, Tsuchiya Keiichirō 土屋恵一郎, Nakazawa Shin'ichi 中沢新一, and Matsuoka Shinpei 松岡心平, eds. 2013. *Zeami: Kami to shura to koi* 世阿弥：神と修羅と恋, supervised by Umehara Takeshi 梅原猛 and Kanze Kiyokazu 観世清和. *Nō o yomu* 能を読む 2. Tokyo: Kadokawa Gakugei Shuppan.

Atkins, Paul S. 2006. *Revealed Identity: The Noh Plays of Komparu Zenchiku.* Michigan Monograph Series in Japanese Studies 55. Ann Arbor: Center for Japanese Studies, University of Michigan.

Bethe, Monica, and Richard Emmert, trans./eds. 1992–1997. *Noh Performance Guides. Matsukaze* (1992); *Fujito* (1992); *Miidera* (1993); *Tenko* (1994); *Atsumori* (1995); *Ema* (1996); *Aoi no ue* (1997). Tokyo: National Noh Theatre.

* Bohner, Hermann. 1956. *Nô: die einzelnen Nô.* Tokyo: Deutsche Gesellschaft für Natur- und Völkerkunde Ostasiens.

* Bohner, Hermann. 1959. *Nô: Einfuhrung.* Tokyo: Deutsche Gesellschaft für Natur- und Völkerkunde Ostasiens.

Bowring, Richard. 1992. "The *Ise monogatari*: A Short Cultural History." *Harvard Journal of Asiatic Studies* 52, no. 2: 410–80.

* Brazell, Karen. 1997. "Subversive Transformations: Atsumori and Tadanori at Suma." In *Currents in Japanese Culture: Translations and Transformations,* edited by Amy Vladeck Heinrich, 35–52. New York: Columbia University Press.

Brazell, Karen, ed. 1997. *Traditional Japanese Theatre: An Anthology of Plays.* New York: Columbia University Press.

* Brazell, Karen, ed. 1988. *Twelve Plays of the Noh and Kyōgen Theaters*. Cornell East Asia Series 50. Ithaca: Cornell University East Asia Program.
Brown, Steven T. 2001. *Theatricalities of Power: The Cultural Politics of Noh*. Stanford: Stanford University Press.
Chatman, Seymour. 1978. *Story and Discourse: Narrative Structure in Fiction and Film*. Ithaca: Cornell University Press.
* de Poorter, Erika. (1986) 2002. *Zeami's Talks on Sarugaku. An Annotated Translation of the Sarugaku Dangi with an Introduction on Zeami Motokiyo*. Amsterdam: J. C. Gieben. Reprinted in the series Japonica Neerlandica 2. Leiden: Hotei Publishing, 2002.
Ejima Ihei 江島伊兵衛, ed. 1937. *Shina jihen koutaishū* 支那事変小謡集. Tokyo: Wan'ya Shoten.
Ejima Ihei 江島伊兵衛, ed. 1944. *Daitōa sensō koutaishū* 大東亜戦争小謡集. Tokyo: Wan'ya Shoten.
Emmert, Richard. 2012–2017. *The Guide to Noh of the National Noh Theatre: Play Summaries of the Traditional Repertory*. Tokyo: National Noh Theatre. Vol. 1 (A–G), 2012; vol. 2 (H–Ki), 2013; vol. 3 (Ko–M), 2014; vol. 4 (N–Sc), 2015; vol. 5 (Sh–Tok), 2016; vol. 6 (Tom–Z), 2017.
Goff, Janet Emily. 1991. *Noh Drama and The Tale of Genji: The Art of Allusion in Fifteen Classical Plays*. Princeton Library of Asian Translations. Princeton: Princeton University Press.
* Gundert, Wilhelm. 1925. *Der Schintoismus im japanischen Nô-Drama*. Band XIX. Tokyo: Verlag der Deutschen Gesellschaft für Natur- und Völkerkunde Ostasiens.
Haga Yaichi 芳賀矢一 and Sasaki Nobutsuna 佐々木信綱, eds. 1914–1915. *Kōchū yōkyoku sōsho* 校註謡曲叢書. 3 vols. Tokyo: Hakubunkan.
Hare, Thomas Blenman. 1986. *Zeami's Style: The Nō Plays of Zeami Motokiyo*. Stanford: Stanford University Press.
Hare, Thomas Blenman (Tom), trans. 2008. *Zeami: Performance Notes*. Translations from the Asian Classics. New York: Columbia University Press.
Hata Hisashi 羽田昶. 1987. "Kinsaku nō, kindai nō, gendai nō no sakusha to sakuhin" 近作能、近代能、現代能の作者と作品. In *Nō no sakusha to sakuhin* 能の作者と作品. *Iwanami kōza: nō kyōgen* 岩波講座―能・狂言 III, edited by Yokomichi Mario 横道萬里雄, Nishino Haruo 西野春雄, and Hata Hisashi 羽田昶, 301–62. Tokyo: Iwanami Shoten.
Higashiya Sakurako 東谷櫻子. 2017. "Shinsakunō *Miikusabune* no shomondai" 新作能「皇軍艦」の諸問題. *Shōwa Joshi Daigaku Nihon bungaku kiyō* 昭和女子大学日本文学紀要 29: 17–31.
Ikai Takamitsu 伊海孝充. 2012. "Yōkyoku *Shiroururi* no seiritsu to haikei: *Tsurezuregusa* no hiden, chūsei Shintō setsu, utai bunka ga kōsa suru tokoro" 謡曲「白うるり」の成立

と背景──『徒然草』の秘伝・中世神道説・謡文化が交叉するところ. *Nōgaku kenkyū* 能楽研究 36: 65–86.

Ishimure Michiko 石牟礼道子. 2003. *Shiranui* 不知火. Tokyo: Heibonsha.

Issacharoff, Michael. 1989. *Discourse as Performance*. Stanford: Stanford University Press.

Itō Masayoshi 伊藤正義, ed. 1983–1988. *Yōkyokushū* 謡曲集. 3 vols. Vol. 1 (*jō*): 1983; vol. 2 (*chū*): 1986; vol. 3 (*ge*): 1988. Shinchō Nihon koten shūsei 新潮日本古典集成 57, 73, 79. Tokyo: Shinchōsha.

Katagiri Yōichi 片桐洋一, ed. 1971–1987. *Chūsei kokinshū chūshakusho kaidai* 中世古今集注釈書解題. 6 vols. Kyoto: Akaoshō Bundō.

Keene, Donald, ed., with the assistance of Royall Tyler. 1970. *20 Plays of the Nō Theatre*. New York: Columbia University Press.

Kikei Shinzui 季瓊真蘂. 2007. *Inryōken nichiroku* 蔭涼軒日録. In *Dai Nihon bukkyō zensho* 第日本佛教全書 134, edited by Bussho Kankōkai 仏書刊行会. Tokyo: Daihōrinkaku.

Klein, Susan Blakeley. 2002. *Allegories of Desire: Esoteric Literary Commentaries of Medieval Japan*. Harvard-Yenching Institute Monograph Series 55. Cambridge: Harvard University Asia Center.

* Klein, Susan Blakeley. 2006. "Esotericism in Noh Commentaries and Plays: Komparu Zenchiku's *Meishukushū* and *Kakitsubata*." In *The Culture of Secrecy in Japanese Religion*, edited by Bernhard Scheid and Mark Teeuwen, 229–54. New York: Routledge.

Klein, Susan Blakeley. 2013. "Noh as Political Allegory: The Case of *Haku Rakuten*." In *Like Clouds or Mists: Studies and Translations of Nō Plays of the Genpei War*, edited by Elizabeth Oyler and Michael Watson, 399–462. Cornell East Asia Series 159. Ithaca: Cornell University East Asia Program.

Klein, Susan Blakeley. 2021a. *Dancing the Dharma: Religious and Political Allegory in Japanese Noh Theater*. Harvard East Asian Monographs 435. Cambridge: Harvard University Asia Center.

Klein, Susan Blakeley. 2021b. "Zenchiku's Noh Play *Oshio*: Introduction and Translation." In *An* Ise monogatari *Reader: Contexts and Receptions*, edited by Joshua S. Mostow, Yamamoto Tokurō 山本登朗, and Kurtis Hanlon, 113–48. Brill's Japanese Studies Library 69. Leiden: Brill.

* Kominz, Laurence R. 1995. *Avatars of Vengeance: Japanese Drama and the Soga Literary Tradition*. Michigan Monograph Series in Japanese Studies 13. Ann Arbor: Center for Japanese Studies, University of Michigan.

Koyama Hiroshi 小山弘志, Satō Kikuo 佐藤喜久雄, and Satō Ken'ichirō 佐藤健一郎, trans./eds. 1973. *Yōkyokushū* 1 謡曲集 1. Nihon koten bungaku zenshū 日本古典文学全集 33. Tokyo: Shōgakukan.

* Lim Beng Choo. 2005. "Performing *Furyū Nō*: The Theatre of Konparu Zenpō." *Asian Theater Journal* 22, no. 1: 33–51.

* Lim Beng Choo. 2012. *Another Stage: Kanze Nobumitsu & the Late Muromachi Noh Theater*. Cornell East Asia Series 163. Ithaca: Cornell University East Asia Program.

* Looser, Thomas D. 2008. *Visioning Eternity: Aesthetics, Politics, and History in the Early Modern Noh Theater*. Cornell East Asia Series 163. Ithaca: Cornell University East Asia Program.

Masuda Shōzō 増田正造, Kobayashi Seki 小林責, and Hata Hisashi 羽田昶, eds. 1977. *Nō: honzetsu to tenkai* 能—本説と展開. Tokyo: Ōfūsha.

* Matisoff, Susan. 1978. *The Legend of Semimaru, Blind Musician of Japan*. Studies in Oriental Culture 14. New York: Columbia University Press.

McCullough, Helen Craig, trans. 1966. *Yoshitsune: A Fifteenth-Century Chronicle*. Tokyo: University of Tokyo Press.

* Meyer, Harald, ed. 2008. *Wege der Japonologie: Festschrift für Eduard Klopfenstein*. Munster: LIT Verlag.

Midorikawa Machiko 緑川真知子. 2003. "Coming to Terms with the Alien: Translations of 'Genji Monogatari'." *Monumenta Nipponica* 58, no. 2: 193–222.

Mishima Yukio 三島由紀夫. 1975. "*Hanjo* haiken"「班女」拝見. Originally published in *Kanze* 観世 (July 1952). Reprinted in *Mishima Yukio zenshū* 三島由紀夫全集 25, 532–37. Tokyo: Shinchōsha.

Miyake Akiko 三宅晶子. 2001. "Zeami no sakushi hō" 世阿弥の作詞法. Originally published in *Kokugo kokubun* 国語国文 (April 1980), under the title of "Motomasa no sakushi hō: *Sumidagawa* to *Morihisa* ni mirareru shinjō hyōgen" 元雅の作詞法—「隅田川」と「盛久」にみられる心情表現. Reprinted in *Kabunō no kakuritu to tenkai* 歌舞能の確立と展開, 27–39. Tokyo: Perikansha.

Miyamoto Keizō 宮本圭造. 2013. "Utai kōshaku no sekai: kinsei yōkyoku kyōju no ichisokumen" 謡講釈の世界：近世謡曲享受の一側面. In *Shintō suru kyōyō: Edo no shuppan bunka to iu kairo* 浸透する教養：江戸の出版文化という回路, edited by Suzuki Ken'ichi 鈴木健一, 163–92. Tokyo: Bensei Shuppan.

Mostow, Joshua S., and Royall Tyler, trans. 2010. *The Ise Stories: Ise monogatari*. Honolulu: University of Hawai'i Press.

Motohashi, Ted. 2016. "Shakespeare's Asian Journey or 'White Mask, Black Handkerchief': A Case Study for Translation Theory in Miyagi Satoshi's 'Mugen-Noh' *Othello* and Omar Porras's 'Bilingal' *Romeo and Juliet*." In *Shakespeare's Asian Journey's Critical Encounters, Cultural Geographies, and the Politics of Travel*, edited by Bi-qi Beatrice Lei, Judy Celine Ick, and Poonam Trivedi, 67–86. New York: Routledge.

* Nishihara Daisuke 西原大輔. 2021. *Muromachi jidai no nichimin gaikō to nō kyōgen* 室町時代の日明外交と能狂言. Tokyo: Kasama Shoin.

Nishino Haruo 西野春雄. 1998. "Kokon kyokumei ichiran" 古今曲名一覧. In *Yōkyoku hyakuban* 謡曲百番, edited by Nishino Haruo, 699–729. *Shin Nihon koten bungaku taikei* 新日本古典文学大系 57. Tokyo: Iwanami Shoten.

Nonomura Kaizō 野々村戒三, ed. 1928. *Yōkyoku sanbyaku gojūban-shū* 謡曲三百五十番集. Tokyo: Nihon Meicho Zenshū Kankōkai.

Nonomura Kaizō 野々村戒三, ed. 1978. *Yōkyoku nihyaku gojūban-shū* 謡曲二百五十番集. 2 vols. Revised by Ōtani Tokuzō 大谷篤蔵. *Kaidai sakuin sōkan* 解題索引双刊 6. Kyoto: Akao Shōbundō.

* Ochiai Hiroshi 落合博志. 1995. "Nō kyōgen shutten ichiran" 能狂言出典一覧. In *Nō kyōgen hikkei* 能狂言必携, edited by Takemoto Mikio 竹本幹夫 and Hashimoto Asao 橋本朝生, 175–82. *Bessatsu kokubungaku* 別冊国文学 48. Tokyo: Gakutōsha.

Okamoto Akira 岡本章, ed. 2003. *Ren'niku kōbō: Hamuretto mashīn zenkiroku* 練肉工房・ハムレットマシーン全記録. Tokyo: Ronsōsha.

Oyler, Elizabeth, and Michael Watson, eds. 2013. *Like Clouds or Mists: Studies and Translations of Nō Plays of the Genpei War.* Cornell East Asia Series 159. Ithaca: Cornell University East Asia Program.

* Pellecchia, Diego. 2010–2013. Blog entries on "Shin-saku nō." *The Nō Diaries.* https://diegopellecchia.com.

Pellecchia, Diego. 2021. "Introducing Genzai Nō: Categorization and Conventions, with a Focus on Ataka and Mochizuki." *Mime Journal* 27: 1–16.

* Pinnington, Noel J. 2006. *Traces in the Way: Michi and the Writings of Komparu Zenchiku.* Cornell East Asia Series 132. Ithaca: Cornell University East Asia Program.

* Pinnington, Noel John. 2019. *A New History of Medieval Japanese Theatre: Nō and Kyōgen from 1300 to 1600.* Palgrave Studies in Theatre and Performance History. London: Palgrave Macmillan.

Prince, Gerald. 2003. *Dictionary of Narratology.* Revised Edition. Lincoln: University of Nebraska Press.

Quinn, Shelley Fenno. 2005. *Developing Zeami: The Noh Actor's Attunement in Practice.* Honolulu: University of Hawai'i Press.

Quinn, Shelley Fenno. 2013. "Morihisa." In *Like Clouds or Mists: Studies and Translations of Nō Plays of the Genpei War*, edited by Elizabeth Oyler and Michael Watson, 329–47 (essay), 349–78 (translation). Cornell East Asia Series 159. Ithaca: Cornell University East Asia Program.

* Renondeau, Gaston. 1954. *Nô.* 2 vols. Tokyo: Maison franco-japonais.

Rimer, Thomas. 1970. "*Taema*: A Nō Play Attributed to Zeami." *Monumenta Nipponica* 25, no. 3–4: 431–45.

Sanari Kentarō 佐成謙太郎. 1954. *Yōkyoku taikan* 謡曲大観. Vols. 3, 4. Tokyo: Meiji Shoin.

Sato, Hiroaki, and Burton Watson. 1981. *From the Country of Eight Islands.* Seattle: University of Washington Press.

* Scheid, Bernhard, and Mark Teeuwen, eds. 2006. *The Culture of Secrecy in Japanese Religion*. New York: Routledge.

Scholz-Cionca, Stanca. 1991. *Aspekte des mittelalterlichen Synkretismus im Bild des Tenman Tenjin im Nô*. Münchener Ostaisiatische Studien 59. Stuttgart: Franz Steiner Verlag.

Scholz-Cionca, Stanca, and Oshikiri Hōko. 2004. "Der Adler und die Chrysantheme: Nô-Spiele zum Russisch-Japanischen Krieg." NOAG 175–76: 23–59.

Scholz-Cionca, Stanca, and Oda Sachiko. 2006. "Drei zeitgenössische Nô-Dramen." NOAG 179–80: 209–53.

* Scholz-Cionca, Stanca, and Christopher Balme, eds. 2008. *Nō Theatre Transversal*. Munich: iudicium.

Sendaishi-shi Hensan Iinkai 仙台市史編纂委員会, ed. 2008. *Sendaishi-shi: shiryōhen* 仙台市史資料編 9. Sendai: Sendaishi.

Shimazaki, Chifumi 島崎千富美. 1977. *The Noh, Volume III: Woman Noh. Book 2*. Tokyo: Hinoki Shoten.

Shimazaki, Chifumi 島崎千富美. 1987. *The Nō, Volume II: Battle Nō in Parallel Translations with an Introduction and Running Commentaries*. Tokyo: Hinoki Shoten.

Shimazaki, Chifumi 島崎千富美. 1993. *Warrior Ghost Plays from the Japanese Nō Theater: Parallel Translations with Running Commentary*. Cornell East Asia Series 60. Ithaca: Cornell University East Asia Program.

Shimazaki, Chifumi 島崎千富美. 1998. *Troubled Souls from Japanese Nō Plays of the Fourth Group*. Cornell East Asia Series 95. Ithaca: Cornell University East Asia Program.

Shirane, Haruo, ed. 2007. *Traditional Japanese Literature: An Anthology, Beginnings to 1600*. New York: Columbia University Press.

* Shively, Donald H. 1957. "Buddhahood for the Nonsentient: A Theme in Nō Plays." *Harvard Journal of Asiatic Studies* 20, no. 1/2 (June): 135–61.

* Sieffert, René. 1960. *Zeami: la tradition secrète du nô, suivie de Une journée de nô*. Connaissance de l'Orient 3. Paris: Gallimard/Unesco.

Sieffert, René. 1979. *Nô et Kyôgen*. 2 vols. Paris: Publications orientalistes de France.

Smethurst, Mae J. 1989. *The Artistry of Aeschylus and Zeami: A Comparative Study of Greek Tragedy and Nō*. Princeton: Princeton University Press.

* Smethurst, Mae J. 1994. *Aisukyurosu to Zeami no doramaturugī: girishia higeki to nō no hikaku kenkyū* アイスキュロスと世阿弥のドラマトゥルギー：ギリシア悲劇と能の比較研究. Translated by Kiso Akiko 木曽明子. Suita: Ōsaka Daigaku Shuppankai.

Smethurst, Mae J., and Richard J. Smethurst. 2008. "Two New Nō Plays Written during World War II." In *Nō Theatre Transversal*, edited by Stanca Scholz-Cionca and Christopher Balme, 31–37. Munich: iudicium.

Smethurst, Mae J. 2013. *Dramatic Action in Noh and Greek Tragedy: Reading with and beyond Aristotle*. Lanham: Lexington Books.

Smethurst, Mae J. 2014. *Girisha higeki to nō niokeru gekitenkai: Arisutoterēsu o tebiki ni soshite kare o koete* ギリシャ悲劇と能における「劇展開」：アリストテレースを手引きに、そして彼を超えて. Translated by Watanabe Kōji 渡辺浩司 and Kiso Akiko 木曽明子, *Nōgaku kenkyū sōsho* 能楽研究叢書 2. Tokyo: Nogami Kinen Hōsei Daigaku Nōgaku Kenkyūjo.

Tada Tomio 多田富雄. 2012. *Tada Tomio Shinsakunō zenshū* 多田富雄新作能全集. Tokyo: Fujiwara Shoten.

Takahama Kyoshi 高浜虚子. 1944. '*Oku no hosomichi*' '*Saga nikki*' *nado: nō, shibai*「奥の細道」「嵯峨日記」など：能・芝居. Tokyo: Kōchō Shorin.

Takemoto Mikio 竹本幹夫. 2000. "Nō kyōgen to gunki oyobi ikusagatari" 能狂言と軍記および戦語り. In *Gunki gatari to geinō* 軍記語りと芸能, edited by Yamashita Hiroaki 山下宏明, 183–202. *Gunki bungaku kenkyū sōsho* 軍記文学研究叢書 12. Tokyo: Kyūko Shoin.

* Takeuchi Akiko 竹内晶子. 2004. "Dramatizing Figures: The Revitalization and Expansion of Metaphors in Nō." In "Hermeneutical Strategies: Methods of Interpretation in the Study of Japanese Literature," edited by Michael F. Marra. Special Issue, *Proceedings of the Association for Japanese Literary Studies* 5: 297–307.

Takeuchi Akiko 竹内晶子. 2020. "The Fusion of Narration and Character Voices in Noh Drama: A Narratological Approach to Zeami's God Plays and Warrior Plays." In "Narratological Perspectives on Premodern Japanese Literature," edited by Sebastian Balmes. Special Issue, *BmE* 7: 113–49.

Tanaka Makoto 田中允, ed. 1950. *Bangai yōkyoku: Tsunobuchi-bon* 番外謡曲：角淵本. *Koten bunko* 33. Tokyo: Koten Bunko.

Tanaka Makoto 田中允, ed. 1952. *Bangai yōkyoku zoku: Tsunobuchi-bon* 番外謡曲続：角淵本. *Koten bunko* 57. Tokyo: Koten Bunko.

Tanaka Makoto 田中允, ed. 1963–1980. *Mikan yōkyokushū* 未刊謡曲集. 31 vols. *Koten bunko* 194–407. Tokyo: Koten Bunko.

Tanaka Makoto 田中允. 1980. "Yōkyoku no genzon kyoku" 謡曲の現存曲. In *Sōgō shinteiban nōgaku zensho* 綜合新訂版能楽全書 3, edited by Nogami Toyoichirō 野上豊一郎 and Nishino Haruo 西野春雄, 227–34. Tokyo: Sōgensha.

Tanaka Makoto 田中允, ed. 1987–1998. *Mikan yōkyokushū zoku* 未完謡曲集続. 22 vols. *Koten bunko* 491–617. Tokyo: Koten Bunko. [*Chūrei*, vol. 9 (1992); *Miikusabune*, vol. 14 (1994)].

Toki Zenmaro 土岐善麿. 1976. *Shinsaku nō engi* 新作能縁起. Tokyo: Kōfūsha.

Tyler, Royall, trans. 1978a. *Pining Wind. A Cycle of Nō Plays*. Cornell East Asia Series 17. Ithaca: Cornell University East Asia Program.

Tyler, Royall, trans. 1978b. *Granny Mountains. A Second Cycle of Nō Plays*. Cornell East Asia Series 18. Ithaca: Cornell University East Asia Program.

* Tyler, Royall. 1987. "Buddhism in Noh." *Japanese Journal of Religious Studies* 14, no. 1: 19–52.

Tyler, Royall, trans./ed. 1992. *Japanese Nō Dramas*. Penguin Classics. London: Penguin Books.

* Tyler, Royall. 2014. *Zeami: Six Revived Bangai Plays*. Nōgaku kenkyū sōsho 能楽研究叢書 1. Tokyo: Nogami Kinen Hōsei Daigaku Nōgaku Kenkyūjo.

Tyler, Royall, trans. 2024. *Joy, Despair, Illusion, Dreams: Twenty Plays from the Nō Tradition*. New York: Columbia University Press.

Ueda, Makoto, trans. 1962. *The Old Pine Tree and Other Noh Plays*. Lincoln: University of Nebraska Press.

Vincent, J. Keith. 2015. "Sex on the Mind: Queer Theory Meets Cognitive Theory." In *The Oxford Handbook of Cognitive Literary Studies*, edited by Lisa Zunshine, 199–221. Oxford: Oxford University Press.

Wakabayashi, Haruko. 2012. *The Seven Tengu Scrolls: Evil and the Rhetoric of Legitimacy in Medieval Japanese Buddhism*. Honolulu: University of Hawai'i Press.

Waley, Arthur. 1921. *The Nō Plays of Japan*. London: G. Allen & Unwin, Ltd.

Watson, Michael. 2007. "Spirits of the Drowned: Sea Journeys in *Bangai* Noh from the Genpei War." In "Travel in Japanese Representational Culture: Its Past, Present, and Future," edited by Sekine Eiji. Special Issue, *Proceedings of the Association for Japanese Literary Studies* 8: 141–54.

* Watson, Michael. 2009. "Regenerating the Canon: One Hundred New Nō Plays." In *Ekkyō suru Nihon bungaku kanonkeisei jendā media* 越境する日本文学研究カノン形成・ジェンダー・メディア/*New Horizons in Japanese Literary Studies: Canon Formation, Gender, and Media*, edited by Haruo Shirane, 37–39. Tokyo: Benseisha.

* Watson, Michael. 2013. "Genpei Tales and the Nō." Premodern Japanese Studies Website. www.meijigakuin.ac.jp~pmjs/biblio/genpei-noh.html. Earlier version appeared as the appendix, "Nō Plays of the Genpei War, A Finding List." In *Like Clouds or Mists: Studies and Translations of Nō Plays of the Genpei War*, edited by Elizabeth Oyler and Michael Watson, 485–518. Cornell East Asia Series 159. Ithaca: Cornell University East Asia Program.

Watson, Michael. 2020. "Noh Translations: Noh Plays in Alphabetical Order of the Japanese Titles." Premodern Japanese Studies Website. www.meijigakuin.ac.jp/~pmjs/biblio/noh-trans.html.

Yamanaka Reiko 山中玲子. 1996. "Tengu no nō no sakufū: Ōnin no ran igo no nō" 天狗の能の作風―応仁の乱以後の能. *Chūsei bungaku* 中世文学 41: 13–21.

Yamanaka Reiko 山中玲子. 2008a. "What Features Distinguish Nō from Other Performing Arts?" In *Nō Theatre Transversal*, edited by Stanca Scholz-Cionca and Christopher Balme, 78–85. Munich: iudicium.

Yamanaka Reiko 山中玲子. 2008b. "*The Tale of Genji* and the Development of Female-Spirit Nō." In *Envisioning The Tale of Genji: Media, Gender, and Cultural Production*, edited by Haruo Shirane, 80–100. New York: Columbia University.

Yampolsky, Philip B. (1967) 1978. *The Platform Sutra of the Sixth Patriarch: The Text of the Tun-Huang Manuscript with Translation, Introduction, and Notes.* New York: Columbia University Press.

* Yasuda, Kenneth. 1989. *Masterworks of the Nō Theatre.* Bloomington: Indiana University Press.

Yip, Leo Shingchi. 2016. *China Reinterpreted: Staging the Other in Muromachi Noh Theater.* Lanham: Lexington Books.

Yokomichi Mario 横道萬里雄. 1986. *Nōgeki no kenkyū* 能劇の研究. Tokyo: Iwanami Shoten.

Yokomichi Mario 横道萬里雄. 1987. "Nōhon no gaikan" 能本の概観. In *Nō no sakusha to sakuhin* 能の作者と作品. *Iwanami kōza: nō kyogen* 岩波講座—能・狂言 III, edited by Yokomichi Mario 横道萬里雄, Nishino Haruo 西野春雄, and Hata Hisashi 羽田昶, 11–120. Tokyo: Iwanami Shoten.

Yokomichi Mario 横道萬里雄, and Omote Akira 表章, eds. 1960. *Yōkyokushū* 謡曲集 1. *Nihon koten bungaku taikei* 40. Tokyo: Iwanami Shoten.

* Yokota-Murakami, Gerry. 1997. *The Formation of the Canon of Nō: The Literary Tradition of Divine Authority.* Osaka: Osaka University Press.

Yokoyama Tarō 横山太郎. 2021. "Nō ni okeru kakekotoba to engo no shigaku: *Izutsu* o chūshin ni (1)" 能における掛詞と縁語の詩学:「井筒」を中心に（上）. *Kanze* 観世 88, no. 4: 46–53.

Yokoyama Tarō 横山太郎. 2022. "Nō ni okeru kakekotoba to engo no shigaku: *Izutsu* o chūshin ni (2)" 能における掛詞と縁語の詩学:「井筒」を中心に（下）. *Kanze* 観世 88, no. 6: 30–37.

Yoshimura Haruo 吉村春雄. 2014. *Bangumi sakusei sankō shiryō yōkyoku kōseihyō* 番組作成参考資料謡曲構成表. Tokyo: Hinoki Shoten.

5
Authors

Edited by Tom Hare and Yamanaka Reiko

5.1   **Introduction**
          Tom Hare and Yamanaka Reiko

Performing arts, unlike painting and sculpture, cannot be transmitted to subsequent generations as material objects. Once performances have ended, it is their fate to disappear. Even when a given performance has left a vivid impression on an audience, any memories of it will fade when the last member of the audience who witnessed it has died. All the same, the texts associated with such performances, and certain aspects of staging as well, may continue to be transmitted to later generations.

The repertory of nō today comprises some 240 pieces. The great majority of these were already composed by the sixteenth century. We know of many plays that were written and performed, but subsequently abandoned, because their playscripts have survived. It is important not to forget that among the most celebrated pieces in the modern repertory, there are a number of plays whose creators cannot be identified definitively.

Actors of nō performed successful plays time and time again, refining the performances as they did so, and from the seventeenth century onward, these plays were considered classical performing arts. There were many masters of legendary status in nō after that time, but with very few exceptions they did not produce new plays. They polished their technique as masters in the art and performed plays beautifully or exercised their ingenuity with new additions or amplifications to previously existing plays, thus concentrating their passion on the stage. Only rarely did the exercise of such ingenuity entail extensively rewriting existing plays (see ch. 2 *Performance*, 2.12). If, on the one hand, very significant changes have taken place with regard to performance techniques, masks and costumes, on the other, the playscripts of nō made between the late 1300s and the late 1400s remain authentically *the* dramatic literature of the Muromachi period (1336–1573). They have been transmitted continually since that time.

In circumstances such as these, who then can be said to have created nō? Here we can point to the celebrated early exponents of nō, father and son Kan'ami (1333–1384) and Zeami (1363 or 1364–1443?) (secs. 5.2, 5.3), along with

Zeami's oldest son Motomasa (?–1432), and his son-in-law Konparu Zenchiku (also Ujinobu, 1405–ca. 1470) (secs. 5.4, 5.5), the heir to Zeami's concept of *yūgen* and *mugen nō*. Mention can also be made of three performers who revitalized nō after the cataclysmic *Ōnin bunmei no ran* (Ōnin Disturbances) of 1467–1477—namely, the father and son pair, Kanze Kojirō Nobumitsu (1451 or 1452–1516) and Kanze Yajirō Nagatoshi (1488–ca. 1541), as well as Nobumitsu's artistic rival Konparu Zenpō (1454–?) (secs. 5.6, 5.7, 5.8). There is also the enigmatic figure of Miyamasu (5.9).

These individuals were also probably fine actors, although it is not possible to prove this definitively from our modern perspective. Our evaluations must be based on the characteristic plays bequeathed to us by these individuals. That said, however, they were first and foremost actors and musicians. The plays they produced were intended to be performed by themselves or by actors in their close entourage, and were not created for sale to others they did not know. The great majority of actors did not write plays—some, indeed, were not literate at all. Neither were there, apparently, "professional playwrights" who wrote playscripts exclusively, without performing themselves. As we shall see, there were rare exceptions to be found among samurai or, in one instance, a medical doctor who supposedly authored a play, but they were not professional playwrights.

In a small number of cases, nō plays written by these amateurs who had educated themselves in the classics such as *The Tale of Genji* (*Genji monogatari*) and the conventions of Japanese *waka* and *renga* (linked verse) poetry composition have remained in the modern repertory of nō. These individuals include samurai and court aristocrats and the aforementioned doctor Takeda Hōin Jōsei who happened to write a few nō plays. They have been called "amateurs" here, as they were neither actors nor professional nō playwrights (sec. 5.10).

When we speak of the "author" of a nō play, then, it is important to keep in mind that any such concept was very different when nō were first performed, as indeed is the case with Shakespeare. Zeami would change preexisting plays to some extent to suit the tastes of his audiences, and he recommended reworking earlier plays extensively to produce new nō plays (see ch. 6 *Treatises*).

In Zeami's artistic memoirs, *Zeshi rokujū igo sarugaku dangi* (*Talks on Sarugaku by Zeami after Sixty*, 1430; hereafter *Sarugaku dangi*), we find the following account: "*Ukai* and *Kashiwazaki* and the like were created by Enami no Saemon Gorō."[1] That said, however, Zeami took out the weak parts and inserted more attractive ones, such that those plays might be considered

---

1 Omote and Katō 1974: 291. English translation in de Poorter (1986) 2002: 114.

Zeami's own. He inserted the *kusemai* (see ch. 2 *Performance*, 2.7) from his play *Tsuchiguruma* into *Kashiwazaki* as known to us today.

In this specific example, therefore, the play *Ukai* is attributed to Zeami, rather than the original author, one Enami no Saemon Gorō, because of the revisions and improvements he effected on the play. *Kashiwazaki* is revised by the insertion of a song (and dance) originally composed for another of Zeami's plays. It is also important to point out that the term "author" in some instances may refer to what we would more likely call the "composer" of the music rather than to the "lyricist" or writer of the text.

A more complex instance concerns a play originally entitled *Shii no shōshō* (*Lesser Captain of the Fourth Rank*), known today as *Kayoi Komachi*. Immediately following a list of attributions Zeami makes in *Sarugaku dangi*, he outlines a complicated history of authorship, whereby an old play, created by a *shōdōshi* (a type of charismatic preacher), entered the repertory of Zenchiku's grandfather, the actor Konparu Gonnokami (dates unknown), and was later revised by Kan'ami. Another text, *Go-on* (*Five Sorts of Singing*, ca. 1429), informs us that Zeami further added one of his own songs to the first part of this play.[2]

5.2 Kan'ami
Tom Hare and Yamanaka Reiko

5.2.1 *Kan'ami's Life*

The first actor we know much about in the history of nō is Kan'ami (1333–1384). According to the account given in the 1430 memoir *Sarugaku dangi* by his son Zeami, his ancestors hailed from the western part of modern Mie Prefecture, around sixty kilometers east-southeast of Kyoto. Kan'ami himself appears to have been adopted into a troupe of *sarugaku* (as nō and kyōgen were called traditionally) in Yamato Province (present-day Nara Prefecture). His eldest brother was an early actor in the Hōshō troupe, showing the close connections that existed among the four Yamato troupes, direct ancestors of the five modern schools of nō. Kan'ami's personal name was Kiyotsugu, but he took the sobriquet Kan'ami, and was also sometimes known as "Kanze," a name that continues to be used today to refer to the Kanze school.

---

2 The scholar Yokomichi Mario, noting that such a complicated process of creation was particularly notable among old plays in the repertory, has characterized these as a "heritage compositions" (*keishōteki sakunō*). Yokomichi 1987: 103–6.

There are few resources to trace Kan'ami's early activity as an actor, but in the early 1370s he is known to have performed so successfully at the temple complex of Daigoji in southeastern Kyoto that he became something of a celebrity in the city. He thus gained the acquaintance of influential members of the shogunal administration and in 1374 or 1375 was commissioned to perform at the Imagumano Shrine in Kyoto before the shōgun Ashikaga Yoshimitsu (1358–1408; r. 1368–1394). This performance has been taken to represent the transition of *sarugaku* from a religious ritual into a dramatic entertainment. Yoshimitsu thereafter became an enthusiastic supporter of *sarugaku*, patronizing not only Kan'ami and his son Zeami but also rivals from Ōmi Province (present-day Shiga Prefecture), just east of Kyoto (see ch. 1 *History*, 1.2).

Kan'ami's reputation derives from his position as founder of the Kanze troupe, and additionally because he appropriated and adopted other performance styles into his own, most notably the *kusemai*, which exhibits a degree of rhythmic interest previously unknown in Yamato *sarugaku*. As an actor, Kan'ami is reported to have been remarkably skillful, able, despite his tall stature, to play the role of a young girl convincingly. His death in eastern Japan is said to have taken place after a particularly successful performance at the Asama Shrine nearly three hundred kilometers east of Kyoto. This suggests that his fame as an actor was not restricted to the area of Kyoto and Nara, but had a much wider reach.

5.2.2   *Kan'ami's Plays*

Kan'ami is credited with the creation of three important plays that remain in the modern repertory: *Jinen koji*, *Sotoba Komachi* (fig. 5.1), and *Kayoi Komachi*. All three were transmitted through Zeami's hands, and subject to his revisions, but they provide the best evidence for Kan'ami's style. The plays all display an interest in witty dialogue. *Kayoi Komachi* first enacts the encounter of a mysterious woman with a Buddhist priest. She brings him fruit and nuts and in giving them to him, delivers a song with numerous puns and plays on the names of the various items before disappearing, leaving him mystified. *Sotoba Komachi*, for its part, treats the poet in old age. Both plays focus, in their final scene, on short dances that reenact an attachment to her on the part of an ill-fated courtier. *Sotoba Komachi* is also famous for a "Zen dialogue" of sorts between the very elderly Komachi and some overconfident monks (see ch. 4 *Plays*, 4.4). *Jinen koji* treats the rescue of a young girl from slave traders, but is packed with interesting songs and dances. Kan'ami is also credited with the composition of songs that are still performed in two of the most celebrated plays in the nō repertory, *Eguchi* and *Matsukaze*, although the plays themselves were probably "authored" by Zeami.

FIGURE 5.1 *Sotoba Komachi*. From *An Illustrated Model of Nō* (*Nō on'ekagami*), vol. 2. By Kanō Shunko (d. 1726). Late 17th or early 18th century. Album (*orijō*), ink and color on paper. 42.2 × 48.5 cm. Noh Theatre Research Institute, Hōsei University, Tokyo

5.3 Zeami
Tom Hare and Yamanaka Reiko

5.3.1 *Zeami's Life*

Zeami is the central figure in the creation of nō. He inherited the responsibilities of troupe head when his father Kan'ami died in 1384, and he performed to great acclaim in the capital and secured patronage from the shōgun and other high officials during the most prosperous and stable period in Japan's "middle ages" (13th–16th c.). He authored many of the most celebrated plays in the nō repertory as well as remarkable texts on how to perform, how to train actors, how to ensure success for the troupe, and how to understand the aesthetics of this, at the time, relatively new dramatic form. His personal name as an adult was Motokiyo, but as a child he was known as Fujiwaka. He is known today as Zeami, which is a shortened form of the Buddhist name Zeamida-butsu. Certain historical documents reference him as Zea, but he sometimes signed his name as simply "Ze." A note in his 1430 memoir *Sarugaku dangi* claims that, as a mark of shogunal favor, he was directed by the third Ashikaga shōgun Yoshimitsu to pronounce the first syllable of this name as "Ze" rather than as the more common "Se."

Zeami was born in either 1363 or 1364 near the ancient capital Nara, but his early career is more closely connected with the then shogunal and imperial capital, modern-day Kyoto, where he saw his father's troupe rise to prominence in the mid-1370s. Even as Kan'ami excited the admiration of the military aristocracy and members of the court and religious elite with his performances, Zeami apparently attracted the attention of influential members of society, both onstage and off. He garnered the support of Yoshimitsu, who was about five years his senior, and may have shared a close relationship with him for a time. He is recorded as having been in Yoshimitsu's company once publicly on the occasion of the *Gion matsuri* (Gion Festival), exciting the derision of a jealous courtier, but other members of both the military and royal courts favored him, as did some important Buddhist clerics.

Although the circumstances of his education are not well understood, it is clear from his plays and from an exchange in the exacting form of *renga* with the court poet and statesman Nijō Yoshimoto (1320–1388) that he had a knowledge of poetics, of the *Ise monogatari* (*The Tales of Ise*) and, to a lesser extent, of *The Tale of Genji*. He was also well versed in the martial narratives of the *Heike monogatari* (*The Tale of the Heike*), along with certain Chinese classics and Buddhist scriptures.

Biographical detail regarding Zeami is limited to scattered references, mostly from early or late in his life, but it is clear that during his middle years he enjoyed great success as an actor, and brought his troupe fame and security in competition with several other *sarugaku* troupes. Zeami greatly respected a number of these actors and paid them compliments in the memoir recorded by his second son Motoyoshi (dates unknown), the *Sarugaku dangi*. Following the lead of his father, he adapted the virtues of some of these other troupes and mixed them with his own troupe's traditional strengths in the portrayal of other entertainers and demons (*oni*). In doing so, he was apparently answering to the tastes of the aristocratic audience who enjoyed singing and dance as much as or more than dramatic imitation. This led him to reject, for the most part, his tradition's reliance on the portrayal of demons, which in his view were too frightening to be interesting. And because demons were not real, they were unavailable for the kind of acute observation upon which he based his convictions regarding imitation (see ch. 6 *Treatises*, 6.2).

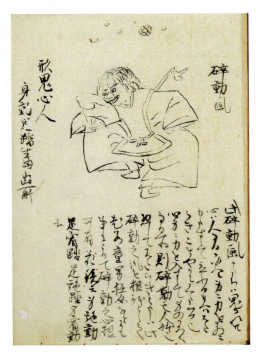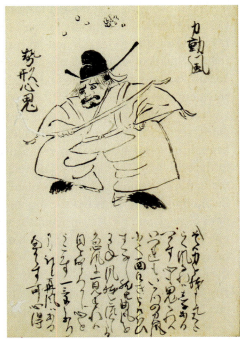

FIGURE 5.2 A human-hearted demon (left) and a demon-hearted demon (right). From *Figure Drawings of the Two Arts and the Three Modes* (*Nikyoku santai ningyō zu*). 1421. Hand-drawn/handwritten book, ink on paper. 26.7 × 20.7 cm. Noh Theatre Research Institute, Hōsei University, Tokyo

The singing and dance that he appropriated from rival troupes were tools in his performances for the creation of various aesthetic effects, the most famous of which is termed *yūgen*, a kind of mysterious elegance evoking the refinement and beauty of high-born court women of the Heian-period (794–1185). For Zeami, however, it was equally important to inject beauty into the portrayal of warriors, commoners, and a host of other stage characters. Even demons, he conceded, could be successfully imbued with enough beauty or pathos to satisfy aristocratic patrons, as long as they were "human-hearted" (fig. 5.2).

When Yoshimitsu, Zeami's most influential early patron died, his alienated son, Yoshimochi (1386–1428; r. 1394–1423), a painter and reputedly a man of refined taste, succeeded him on the shogunal throne. Among actors, Yoshimochi preferred Zōami (dates unknown) of the rival dramatic form, *dengaku*, to Zeami. Indeed, Zeami himself seems to have held Zōami in high esteem, speaking of his performances as "chillingly beautiful." Yet despite Yoshimochi's preference for Zōami, Zeami's troupe prospered in the early decades of the fifteenth century, until Yoshimochi died and was succeeded by his brother, Yoshinori (1394–1441; r. 1428–1441). Even though Yoshimochi did not patronize Zeami and his troupe, he did share with him a strong commitment to Zen Buddhism. Zeami had shown some familiarity with the religion as early as 1400, and he quotes a verse from the *Platform Sutra* in the "Daisan Mondō Jōjō" (Notes in Question-and-Answer Form) in *Fūshi kaden* (*Transmitting the Flower through Effects and Attitudes*, 1400–ca. 1418). It appears, however, that this quotation was a subsequent addition; in any case, Zeami's interest in Zen certainly increased late in his life and variously influenced his views on training and performance (see ch. 4 *Plays*, 4.4 for further details).

Yoshinori persecuted Zeami and his troupe, favoring instead a nephew Kanze Saburō Motoshige (also On'ami; 1398–1467), the son of Zeami's younger brother Shirō. It may be that Yoshinori felt On'ami to be the correct heir to Zeami's line, whereas Zeami clearly designated his son Motomasa for that role. Due to Yoshinori's machinations, Zeami's troupe was denied important performance commissions, which were instead transferred to On'ami, and in 1434, Zeami was exiled to Sado Island off the northwest coast of Japan (see ch. 1 *History*, 1.1). This represented the culmination of other tragic blows: in 1430 his son Motoyoshi abandoned the stage to take the tonsure; two years later his son and treasured heir, Motomasa, died in mysterious circumstances while on the road in Ano no tsu (or Anotsu) in Ise Province (present-day Mie Prefecture). Zeami may have returned from exile to the capital following Yoshinori's death, but the mainline lineage of the "Kanze" troupe was denied to his descendants in favor of On'ami's (see sec. 5.4). In his last decades, Zeami's artistic legacy seems to have been transmitted to his son-in-law, Konparu Zenchiku, the scion of another troupe that had its origins in the Nara area.

5.3.2 *Zeami's Plays*

It is difficult to speak of Zeami's plays without reference to those of his father, Kan'ami. Although Kan'ami's name is associated with a few plays in the modern repertory, every one of them passed through Zeami's hands before attaining the textual stability we observe today. Some of these plays have aesthetic aims that are very different from plays we link confidently with Zeami, but among plays that cannot be entirely attributed to either Kan'ami or Zeami, there are a few that testify to the common interest of father and son in the afterlives of ghosts. The play *Motomezuka*, for example, cannot be definitively attributed to either Kan'ami or Zeami, nonetheless it shows both structural and thematic features that Zeami would further refine to create the most characteristic plays in his oeuvre.

The central figure in act 1 of *Motomezuka* is a ghost in disguise. In an encounter with a monk, this figure arouses his suspicion; in response to the monk's questions, the ghost gives away some clues and recounts a narrative from the past. This mysterious figure then disappears, and only in the second act reappears in true form, asking for the monk's prayers. In Zeami's hands, the second act of a play like this generally contains a great deal of dance, accompanied by purely instrumental music and subsequently by instruments in combination with voice (see ch. 2 *Performance*, 2.3). In *Motomezuka*, there is, strictly speaking, no dance of this sort, rather an extended section of the performance is given over to the main character, when she enacts the story recounted in the text. It is not known how closely modern performances of the play resemble those of the fifteenth century. We can see in this structure, however, with its encounter of a monk and a ghost in disguise in act 1 and its revelation of the true identity of that ghost in act 2, the seeds of the full-fledged *mugen nō* ("dream" or "phantom" nō) that is emblematic of Zeami's plays and his legacy as a playwright (see ch. 4 *Plays*, 4.5).

By around 1423, Zeami had composed at least twenty-five plays, many of them among the most celebrated in the entire nō repertory. More than half are clearly *mugen nō* plays, and even when writing plays in the *genzai nō* category, in which the main character is alive in the dramatic present, Zeami sometimes adopted a structure closely resembling that of *mugen nō*. By the time of his death, Zeami had created about a dozen more plays of relatively reliable attribution. In addition, a number of plays in the nō repertory are based both formally and thematically on the patterns Zeami (and father Kan'ami) initiated. In general terms, this form has become the most typical in nō.

Plays about female subjects are perhaps the most prominent among Zeami's plays. Some of these, such as *Matsukaze*, *Izutsu*, and *Eguchi* (fig. 5.3) are among the most revered works in the repertory. In these plays, female characters query the pains and romantic pleasures of love from the perspective of death. In *Matsukaze*, two sisters poignantly recollect their all-too-short affair with a man temporarily exiled from the royal court while, as ghosts, they perform the arduous labor of extracting salt from seawater, one of the few commoners' occupations that Zeami allowed as appropriate material for aristocratic audiences. *Izutsu* takes a different tack in some regards, tracing the relationship between a boy and girl who were playmates as children; they grow up to be lovers and eventually marry. After a time, the husband began an affair with another woman, but his wife's patience and his perception of her suffering brought him back to her. All this is accomplished with repeated references to a couple of simple poems from *The Tales of Ise* that gain increasingly in meaning and complexity through the different contexts in which they occur in the performance. In this regard, the play is similar to *Matsukaze*, in which the two sisters recall with piercing sadness and beautiful song their time together with their joint lover. *Eguchi*, though formally quite similar to the other two plays,

FIGURE 5.3 *Eguchi*. From *An Illustrated Model of Nō* (*Nō on'ekagami*), vol. 1. By Kanō Shunko (d. 1726). Late 17th or early 18th century. Album (*orijō*), ink and color on paper. 42.2 × 48.5 cm. Noh Theatre Research Institute, Hōsei University, Tokyo

is thematically distinct from them in that it centers on the ghost of a beautiful courtesan who, in an exchange of poems with a monk, reveals herself actually to be the bodhisattva Fugen (Skt. Samantabhadra).

Many of Zeami's plays concentrate on women, yet he also bequeathed to the nō repertory numerous celebrated plays about the ghosts of warriors. In accordance with his insistence that these plays not only treat martial experience, but also bring out a connection with poetry and music, their main figures often claim particular talents in performing music or composing poetry, and several of the plays about them also contain instrumental dances and intricate songs. Most of the plays in this genre, which holds an important stake in the nō repertory, were composed by Zeami. Favorites include *Tadanori*, *Atsumori*, and *Sanemori*. All three characters are taken from famous episodes in *The Tale of the Heike*, but they show a refreshing range of treatment. While the first depicts the death of a brave warrior in detail, its focus is rather on his attachment to poetry, and to the question of whether, as a member of an outlawed clan, Tadanori can still claim the right to have his name attached to a poem included in a royally commissioned anthology of poems.

Atsumori uncovers the anguish of an older warrior who takes the tonsure after finding no way to avoid killing a sixteen-year-old boy, the eponymous hero. In the play, the older warrior encounters the ghost of the boy and reenacts the struggle in which he beheaded him. Atsumori, for his part, starts to attack his erstwhile enemy but is, at the last moment, reconciled with him on a higher plane of forgiveness. The boy Atsumori, praised for his valor and resolution, also does an elegant instrumental dance in the last act of the play, the music of which is otherwise only used in plays about women or female deities. *Sanemori*, by contrast, features an aged warrior who dyed his gray hair black so that he could take his place in battle as an equal to the younger members of his clan. After death, his ghost appears to a charismatic monk to seek release from the obsession of his anger and pride.

Zeami also composed some prominent plays about gods. These had an important ideological role in the development of nō, in that they were the most appropriate place to express an unalloyed celebration of life, political stability, and reverence for the traditional gods. Due to their ideological importance, Zeami argued that these plays should present their stories in a straightforward and formally orthodox manner. He singles out plays about gods as templates for nō in general, and *Takasago*, despite some small idiosyncrasies, sets the standard in terms for the repertory as a whole. That play commemorates marital fidelity, poetry, and the beauty of the pine, a tree that holds a special place in nō and in traditional poetry as a symbol of faithfulness because it does not drop its needles but remains ever green. It also praises political stability and does so without mentioning the theoretically contradictory roles of the "emperor" and the shōgun.

As stated earlier, the dramatic traditions of the *sarugaku* troupes that originated in the Nara basin valued the imitation of demons, and adapted the styles of other entertainers to their own ends. Zeami wrote or revised canonical plays along the lines of the latter, imbuing them with *yūgen* and allowing ample room in them for singing and dance. Although he warned against a reliance on demon plays, he nonetheless composed some of these as well. Among them, the play *Nue* exemplifies his interest in "demons with human hearts."[3] The central figure in this play is a hybrid monster with a monkey's head, a serpent's

---

3 *Saidōfūki*, explicated as "*katachi wa oni naredomo, kokoro wa hito nar[i]*." Omote and Katō 1974: 128; Hare, trans. 2008: 145. An English translation of *Nue* is in Yasuda 1989: 433–52.

tail, and tiger-striped legs and arms. (Its cry sounded like that of the nocturnal *nue* bird, thus the title.) In the play, the demise of the demon at the hands of a samurai is treated from two different perspectives, the one being that of the warrior himself, who is called upon by royal command to rid the palace of a dangerous pest, whereas the other shows much more sympathetically the point of view of the monster himself, "like a caged bird," floating disconsolately in the dugout where his corpse was abandoned, "groping in despair, like a blind tortoise who fumbles for a foothold on a piece of driftwood."

Nine playscripts in Zeami's own hand are still extant, along with one facsimile text, copied from an autograph manuscript that is no longer extant. They date from 1413 to 1429.[4]

5.3.3   *Zeami on Performance*

Among Zeami's most remarkable achievements is the creation of a large body of literature concerning performance. He treats performance from several viewpoints, articulating his first insights in texts from the early years of the fifteenth century. In his initial approaches, he discusses how to portray different kinds of roles and how to train young actors, as well as demonstrating his understanding of the aesthetic aims of performance. If these early texts, exemplified by *Fūshi kaden*, set the basic parameters for Zeami's interest in performance, then subsequent texts—there are at least twenty altogether—go into greater detail on many of the issues raised in *Fūshi kaden* (see ch. 6 *Treatises*, 6.1, 6.2, 6.3). Included among these are also brief letters and notes touching on the personal relationships he developed over the course of his career and the tragic events that marred the last decade of his life (see ch. 1 *History*, 1.2).

In addition to the texts that Zeami wrote—some still extant in his own hand—there is an important memoir of his experience as an actor, playwright, and critic of performance in the aforementioned memoir, *Sarugaku dangi*. This text was written down by his son Motoyoshi, nonetheless, it is understood to be a direct account of Zeami's own experience. It is not only filled with details about other actors and patrons, and anecdotes regarding specific occasions of performance and training, but also has an extensive discussion of the aesthetics of performance.

The texts Zeami wrote on performance comprise the first extended critical statements in Japanese history based on direct experience in performance. Although there are a number of earlier critical texts on the composition of

---

4   See Getsuyōkai, ed. 1997; Tyler 2013 contains English translations of Zeami's holograph playscripts *Akoya matsu, Furu, Matsuura Sayohime*, and *Tadatsu no Saemon* as well as *Hakozaki* and *Unoha*, the latter two *not* in Zeami's hand.

waka and *renga* poetry, they are prescriptive and often dauntingly abstract, whereas Zeami's remarks are practical and often acutely and poignantly rooted in his own experience onstage.

Among Zeami's achievements was a reconsideration of the narrative approaches of the incipient dramatic forms bequeathed to him by Kan'ami and other Nara troupes. He enlarged upon the attractions of dance and singing that his father had recognized among contemporary performers, including some important women. Among these, Kan'ami is said to have learned from, in particular, the style of one Otozuru (dates unknown). On this basis, Zeami fashioned something new. He did this initially by weaving the interiority of *waka* poetry and Buddhist devotionalism into myth, legend, and folklore. He found protean tools there for performances focused intently on the interior lives of their subjects, and with these he paired abstract formality in dance and singing. This constituted the ideal semiotic core from which, over the next two centuries, the stunningly beautiful material world of nō was created.

In taking such an approach, Zeami rejected some of the potential for a drama based on conflict or *agon* that one might have predicted from earlier *sarugaku* plays. But even when certain of his descendants came to give overt conflict a more prominent role in nō performance, Zeami's predispositions remained apparent. His son-in-law Zenchiku seems to have written plays with a darker outlook. All the same, he followed Zeami's formal conventions very faithfully and revered his aesthetic canons. Zeami's grandnephew, Nobumitsu, wrote exciting and melodramatic plays about malevolent specters and treacherous warriors. But even in these, there are abstract instrumental dances and centuries-old poetry—the legacy of Zeami. In the elegance and abstraction of the dramatic conventions of nō, Zeami's convictions about beauty, the integrity of the actor's vocation, and the fascination of paradox linger on.

5.4 Motomasa
Tom Hare and Yamanaka Reiko

5.4.1 *Motomasa's Life*
Zeami's son Kanze Jūrō Motomasa (?–1432) was an actor and playwright in his own right. Although he was designated as Zeami's successor as head of the Kanze troupe, he, as mentioned above, predeceased his father in mysterious circumstances. Zeami credits Motomasa with four plays, all of which remain in the modern repertory: *Sumidagawa*, *Yoroboshi*, *Morihisa*, and *Utaura*. While modern scholars consider Motomasa to be the "author" of these plays, strictly speaking, Zeami names him only as the "composer" of the music (see also sec.

5.1).⁵ Other plays have been ascribed to him as well, with varying degrees of credibility, as seen below. Motomasa also bore the given name Jūrō and may have been the otherwise mysterious "Mototsugu" referred to in the colophon in chapter 7 of the *Fūshi kaden* (this assumes that *Moto-* derives from Zeami's given name, *Moto*kiyo, and *-tsugu* from Kan'ami's given name, Kiyo*tsugu*). His posthumous Buddhist name is Zenshun. By Motomasa's time, his grandfather's artistic name, Kanze, had taken on the role of a surname. It is therefore historically correct to call him Kanze Motomasa.

Motomasa's birth order is not known definitely but he is generally believed to have been the eldest of at least three siblings. As noted above, a brother, Motoyoshi, was also an actor, but he took religious orders before Motomasa's death. A sister, whose personal name has not come down to us, was married to Konparu Zenchiku. After Motomasa's death, Zeami seems to have transmitted his writings on performance to Zenchiku rather than through Zeami's nephew On'ami and his progeny, the ancestors of the modern Kanze school. Indeed, even as early as 1428, one pivotal text, *Shūgyoku tokuka* (*Pick up a Jewel and Take the Flower in Hand*) was entrusted to Zenchiku, and Motomasa is stated to have shown a text "of great moment" (likely Zeami's *Kakyō*, or *A Mirror to the Flower*, ca. 1418–1424) to Zenchiku on his own initiative.⁶ This suggests a close professional connection between Zeami's artistic line and Zenchiku's even before Motomasa's death.

This connection holds more than merely genealogical interest because many of the misfortunes Motomasa and his immediate family suffered in the 1430s have by conjecture been posited as the result of a succession dispute in Zeami's line. According to one line of thought, Motoshige (later known as On'ami), the son of Zeami's younger brother Shirō, was formally adopted by Zeami and had some claim on the succession. When Motomasa, or some other son, was born to Zeami, On'ami was displaced.⁷ Decades later, the shōgun Ashikaga Yoshinori appears to have sided with and promoted On'ami, first sidelining and then persecuting Zeami and Motomasa (see ch. 1 *History*, 1.2). There is no clear evidence to entirely substantiate this theory, but neither are there other sound explanations for Yoshinori's treatment of Zeami and Motomasa. It therefore remains a distinct possibility.

---

5   In this context, Zeami's concern was with music rather than text, thus the designation "composer." Modern scholars believe, however, that unless stated otherwise, "composers" in a musical sense were also "authors" in a textual sense.
6   See Hare, trans. 2008: 203n1.
7   See Kōsai 1970: 82–97.

Some details from Motomasa's life are nonetheless known to us. In 1422, when Zeami took religious orders, Motomasa ostensibly became the head of the Kanze troupe. Then, in 1429, the shōgun Yoshinori chose On'ami to perform before the retired sovereign Gokomatsu (1377–1433; r. 1392–1412), thereby depriving Motomasa of this privilege. We do not know whether this was out of actual prejudice or malice or simply due to personal preference. Again in 1430, Yoshinori called upon On'ami to stage a festive torchlight performance, not Motomasa. The important role of the Director of Performances (*gakutōshiki*) for the Kiyotaki Shrine in the major Buddhist complex at Daigoji was also taken away from Zeami. In the same year, 1430, Motomasa's line was given over to On'ami.

Although few records remain of Motomasa's performances, there is one of particular interest: in 1427, he participated in a program with On'ami and another actor, Jūnijirō, at the temple Kōfukuji in Nara. Of the six plays Motomasa performed, at least two, *Morihisa* and *Utaura*, were his own compositions. Jūnijirō performed a few showy plays whereas those on On'ami's program demonstrate a commitment to plays associated with Kan'ami, with *Jinen koji* and the piece now known as *Kayoi Komachi* prominent among them. Motomasa and On'ami are recorded as having performed again on the same stage in 1429. On this occasion, however, the program describes them, among other troupes, as "the *two* Kanze troupes," an indication that a split had already occurred by this time.

In 1430, Motomasa dedicated a nō mask—today still extant—to the Tennokawa Shrine (today more commonly known as Tenkawa Shrine) in Yoshino south of the Nara basin. The dedication seems to have been offered in the hope of turning bad times to good, but if so, it was not successful. Motomasa died suddenly in the eighth month of that year in Ano no tsu (or Anotsu) in Ise Province.

5.4.2 *Motomasa's Plays*

Among the plays that can be securely attributed to Motomasa, both *Sumidagawa* (fig. 5.4) and *Yoroboshi* exhibit a different emotional orientation from the representative works of his father. Each work resides within the conventions of the lost-child play, but in *Sumidagawa*, the lost child has died, and the failure of an attempt to reunite with him is cast in truly tragic terms. In *Yoroboshi*, there is eventually a reunion with the parent, as in typical lost-child plays, but the son's fate is equally pitiful as he had been unjustly banished from the family home due to accusations of slander and during his subsequent exile went blind. This story is known elsewhere in Japanese literature, but in other

FIGURE 5.4 *Sumidagawa*. From *An Illustrated Model of Nō* (*Nō on'ekagami*), vol. 2. By Kanō Shunko (d. 1726). Late 17th or early 18th century. Album (*orijō*), ink and color on paper. 42.2 × 48.5 cm. Noh Theatre Research Institute, Hōsei University, Tokyo

versions the reunion is accompanied by the boy's miraculous regaining of sight. This is not the case in Motomasa's play.

Morihisa does close with a miracle: the eponymous warrior has been sentenced to death but must be taken east from the capital to Kamakura where the execution will take place. Much of the play is devoted to recounting the places Morihisa passes on his final journey. The conclusion, in which he is saved by the last-minute intervention of the bodhisattva Kannon, occupies only a fraction of stage time compared to his sad journey. If there is much prayer and devotion in the rest of the play, as Morihisa heads toward what he thinks will be his death, there is also much foreboding and bitter contrast between famous places in the landscape and the dread that occupies Morihisa's mind.

Although there is no documentary evidence on which to base an attribution, the literary excellence and dark emotional world of the plays *Tomonaga* and *Tomoakira* suggest a possible link to Motomasa. *Tomonaga* is about a teenager who, wounded in battle, takes his own life in an inn on the escape route. It is noteworthy that in this play the primary roles in acts 1 and 2 of the play are occupied by different characters, something not seen in Zeami's plays. *Tomoakira* is also about a teenage warrior's death in battle, but it is similarly unsettling because the boy dies before his father, having been separated from him during their attempts to escape.

While there is no evidence apart from the common thematic darkness and a focus on relationships between parents and children, these two plays deserve to be considered alongside possible works by Motomasa. We might, heuristically at least, regard these plays as "Motomasa-style" plays, and in doing so, mark the striking emotional and aesthetic differences they display when compared with plays by Zeami.

Hand in hand with the high esteem afforded *Sumidagawa* and *Yoroboshi*, the clear aesthetic difference that Motomasa asserts in these plays, when compared with his father's work, suggests that he was confident and creative, and no slave to tradition. An anecdote regarding the performance of *Sumidagawa* is particularly telling. The *Sarugaku dangi* records that since the lost child in the play is actually dead, Zeami opines that it would not be necessary for him to appear on the stage—in other words, that "it might be more interesting if he's not there." But Motomasa objects, asserting that "there's no way I could perform the play that way." Zeami ultimately yields to his son, noting that without giving it a try, one would never know.[8]

5.5 Zenchiku
Tom Hare and Takahashi Yūsuke

5.5.1 *Zenchiku's Life*
Konparu Zenchiku (1405–ca. 1470) is well known as the author of such nō plays as *Bashō* and *Teika*. His grandfather was Konparu Gonnokami, roughly a contemporary of Zeami. While still young, Zenchiku succeeded his father, Konparu Yasaburō, to the family headship and became the head of the Konparu troupe. At first he was known as Tsurauji, then in the early 1440s he changed his name to Ujinobu, and finally, on taking the tonsure, he took the religious appellation, Zenchiku.

---

8 In modern performances, the child almost always appears onstage. See de Poorter (1986) 2002: 91–92, section 43.

His first recorded appearance was around the tenth month of 1421, when he was around seventeen years old; he performed after the Vimalakirti Lectures at the temple Kōfukuji in Nara in appreciation of the efforts of the celebrant. In the third month of 1424, shortly after becoming head of the troupe, he held a subscription *sarugaku* performance in Kyoto at Hachijōbōmon in the third month of 1424, having by this time achieved some notoriety as an actor. It appears that he became Zeami's son-in-law around this time and as a result of that affiliation began to receive playscripts and textual transmissions about performance from Zeami. This is clearly attested to in a record, the *Nōhon sanjūgo-ban mokuroku* (*A List of Thirty-five Playscripts*) from the archives of the temple Hōzanji in the mountains west of Nara. In 1434, after Zeami was exiled to Sado Island, Zenchiku paid for his upkeep there and took care of his wife, Juchin. In a surviving letter to Zenchiku, in which Zeami thanked him for this support, the latter answers inquiries about the performance of the role of the demon in nō, which affords us solid proof of how Zenchiku had come to rely on Zeami as a mentor. After having studied Zeami's *Performance Notes*, Zenchiku wrote a number of texts on nō performance himself, among them, *Rokurin ichiro no ki* (*An Account of The Six Spheres and Single Dewdrop*), *Kabu zuinōki* (*The Essence of Singing and Dance*), *Go-on sangyokushū* (*Three Turns around Five Sorts of Singing*), and *Meishukushū* (*Collection Illuminating the Indwelling Deity*) (see ch. 6 *Treatises*, 6.4). Zenchiku's interactions with prominent intellectuals of the period are evident in the annotations to his *Rokurin ichiro no ki* by Shigyoku (1383–1463), a high-ranking cleric of the Kaidan-in at the Nara temple Tōdaiji, and the eminent statesman Ichijō Kaneyoshi. In addition to these, the Zen monk Nankō Sōgen (d. 1463) wrote an afterword to the text.

In his text *Kyakuraika* (*The Flower in ... Yet Doubling Back*, 1433), Zeami identified Zenchiku as a likely successor in the vocation of *sarugaku*, saying that he exhibited promise in becoming a distinguished performer, even if he was not yet a full-fledged master. Shigyoku praised him highly, calling him the "best actor in the realm."[9] In his *Hitorigoto* (*Solitary Ramblings*, 1468), the *renga* poet Shinkei (1406–1475) paired Zenchiku with On'ami as representing the two best actors in the land: it is apparent that after Zeami's death, Zenchiku and On'ami were the major exemplars in the world of nō at the time.

Zenchiku is thought to have relinquished his position as troupe head to his son Motouji around the age of sixty, but he remained active and in the ninth month of 1465 he performed before the eighth Ashikaga shōgun Yoshimasa

---

9   *Rokurin shaku*, written by the monk Shigyoku, is closely related to Zenchiku's *Rokurin ichiro no ki* and remains extant in manuscript form at Saikyōji in Shiga Prefecture.

(1436–1490; r. 1449–1473) at Ichijō-in at Kōfukuji on the occasion of a four-troupe competitive *sarugaku*. Zenchiku performed his own play *Ōhara no hanami* (now known as *Oshio*). In the second intercalary month of the following year, he appeared in a Konparu subscription nō (*kanjin nō*) in Sakamoto in Ōmi Province. At the same time, he expanded on his theories regarding performance in order to write the *Rokurin ichiro hichū* (*Notes on the Confidential Account of The Six Spheres and Single Dewdrop*, 1465) in the 1460s. In 1467, he went into retreat at the Monju Hall on Mount Inari where he celebrated the ritual for Kangiten (a Japanese Buddhist manifestation of Ganesha)—just one of the links he maintained with esoteric Buddhism.

5.5.2 Zenchiku's Plays

In their critical edition of Zenchiku's writings about nō, the *Konparu kodensho shūsei* (*A Collection of Old Treatises from the Konparu School*), Omote Akira and Itō Masayoshi attribute, with some confidence, the following plays to Zenchiku: *Ugetsu, Oshio, Kamo, Kogō, Shōki, Senju, Tatsuta, Tamakazura, Teika, Bashō,* and *Yōkihi*.[10] Internal evidence in these plays supports these attributions. Further analysis of individual plays has tentatively assigned the following to him as well: *Awadenomori*,[11] *Ōhara gokō, Kakitsubata, Kasuga ryūjin, Kamo monogurui, Kawazu* (*Frog*), *Saoyama, Tamura, Tōgan Botō* (two personal names), *Nureginu* (*Slander*), *Nonomiya, Matsumushi, Mekari,* and *Yuya*. As a result of these studies of potential attribution, numerous characteristics of his style have been identified, among them a stylistic preference for rhyme, especially head rhyme (*tōin*).

As a playwright, Zenchiku followed Zeami's lead in concentrating on singing and dancing, structurally patterning such plays as *Nonomiya*—if he is indeed its author—on Zeami's *Izutsu*. But Zenchiku also pioneered new approaches, introducing many innovations of his own. In addition, he created a number of *genzai nō*, still with a focus on singing and dancing. In composing the play *Kasuga ryūjin*, he formulated the genre of "dragon-god plays" (*ryūjin mono*), which served to expand the nō repertory. With his belief that Buddha nature resides in all phenomena, Zenchiku asserted that all things could be treated onstage in such a way as to engender the aesthetic value of *yūgen* (*yūgen sanrin*). This differed from Zeami's concept of *yūgen* in that Zenchiku held the view that the object of dramatic representation on the nō stage could not be restricted to superficial beauty.

---

10   Omote and Itō, eds. 1969: 62.
11   The title of the play is a (fictional) placename meaning something like "Erring Wood," for a play about a forest where a father fails to find his daughter alive.

Even while building upon works in the nō repertory established by his predecessors, Zenchiku added a further twist that influenced the development of nō in both its overall framework and in the fine details of expression. An example of the former is the play *Bashō*, in which a monk in the Chinese kingdom of Chu sets up his mountain hermitage in front of a plantain tree; the spirit of the tree appears to him and preaches the Buddhist doctrine about the salvation of non-sentient beings. In so doing, Zenchiku inverted the typical pattern of a *mugen nō* play in which it was the monk who enabled a spirit to attain enlightenment. Here, it is the spirit of the tree who enlightens the monk on the subtle points of Buddhist philosophy. The play reveals Zenchiku's familiarity with the medieval exegesis of the *Lotus Sutra*, even as it depicts a particular worldview in which a monk and a spirit engage each other at an ancient temple in the autumn.

The play *Yōkihi* depicts an encounter between the eponymous *shite* and a Daoist wizard, who has been dispatched by the Chinese Tang-dynasty emperor Xuanzong to search out the spirit of Yōkihi (C. Yang Guifei)—a beloved consort who was executed—in a palace on the Island of the Immortals (C. Penglai; J. Hōrai). The role of the wizard is played by the *waki*, and in a variation of the pattern typical of *mugen nō*, it is the *waki* who travels to the *shite*, where she recounts her memories of the emperor before her death.

Zenchiku regarded *waka* poetry as the lifeblood of nō and found his favorite poet in Fujiwara no Teika (1162–1241). The influence of Teika's poetry collection *Shūi gusō* (*Meager Gleanings*, 1216–1233) and other poetic treatises at one time attributed to Teika can be detected in Zenchiku's writings on nō. Moreover, Zenchiku's nō play *Teika* (fig. 5.5) envisions the poet's obsession with Princess Shokushi taking material form in a vine that tangles around the gravestone of the princess after her death. There is no historical plausibility to the idea of a love affair between Teika and Princess Shokushi, but the legend that Teika's spirit took the form of a strangling vine can be traced back to at least to an entry from Bun'ei 3 (1265).10.17 in the diary of the retired emperor Gofukakusa (1243–1304; r. 1246–1260). It also appears in medieval digests of *The Tale of Genji* such as *Genji taikō*, which was composed shortly after 1432.

Whereas Zeami sourced material for many of his plays from the Japanese classics in the centuries before him, Zenchiku was innovative in often taking the material for his plays from relatively recent times and from more vernacular sources. In *Teika*, for example, the intonation by the *waki* of the *Lotus Sutra* loosens the vine's strangling grasp on Princess Shokushi's grave and her spirit comes forth to express deep regret and humiliation, dancing a slow and elegant *jo no mai*. But then her spirit returns to the grave and the "*teika* vines" are seen once again to tighten their grasp over the gravestone. This represents a

FIGURE 5.5   *Teika*. From *An Illustrated Model of Nō* (*Nō on'ekagami*), vol. 1. By Kanō Shunko (d. 1726). Late 17th or early 18th century. Album (*orijō*), ink and color on paper. 42.2 × 48.5 cm. Noh Theatre Research Institute, Hōsei University, Tokyo

stark departure from the numerous nō plays in which the intonation of scripture frees a spirit from the limbo of its delusions and reveals a human world in which Buddhist devotion alone is inadequate to attain salvation.

The overall mood, the artistic effect, of Zenchiku's works has been described as "visual brilliance blanketed by deep sorrow" or "visual brilliance amidst deep sorrow." More recently, several of Zenchiku's plays have been identified as sharing an aesthetic atmosphere pervaded by rain, wind, and storms. *Teika*, for instance, begins with the *waki* taking shelter from an early winter drizzle in the Shigure Pavilion (*shigure* in fact means "drizzle"). *Senju* is the story of a consolatory encounter between Lady Senju and a condemned warrior, Taira no Shigehira, on a rainy night some time before his execution.

Ugetsu deals with a dispute between an elderly couple about whether they should thatch the eaves of their cottage: the one argues in favor of thatched eaves because of the lovely sound of rain hitting them, the other favors no thatch because the moonlight is easier to appreciate without it. In this way, just as the atmospheric mood of rain provides a thematic ground in Zenchiku's plays, one can also discern his conscious engagement on the theme in a treatise of his last years, *Shidō yōshō* (*An Abstract for Attaining the Way*, 1467), in which the image of an ancient cherry tree under the rain is a metaphor for what Zenchiku characterized as the highest aesthetic achievement in *kankyoku*.

Similarly, there are scenes near the conclusion of his plays *Bashō*, *Tatsuta*, *Tamakazura*, and *Oshio* in which the howling gale buffets, scattering blossoms and grasses. It is worth noting the connection between this and the form it takes in his theoretical writing through the concepts of *rangyoku*, by which he intends an aesthetically unrestricted form of expression matured through long experience, and *kankyoku*, indicating an elegance and grace in expression that has also been cultivated over time. (Zenchiku identified in total eight different kinds of music in his *Shidō yōshō*.) In considering the attractions of Zenchiku's works, one comes to understand the central importance of a beauty that is irreducible to any given plot per se.

5.6 Nobumitsu
Ikai Takamitsu and Lim Beng Choo

5.6.1 *Nobumitsu's Life*

Kanze Kojirō Nobumitsu (1451 or 1452–1516)[12] was the seventh child of Zeami's nephew, On'ami (Saburō Motoshige). A performer known particularly for his skill as an *ōtsuzumi* drummer, he was also a prolific playwright. About thirty nō plays are attributed to him, an output second only to that of his great uncle, Zeami.

Such an account of his role in nō might surprise scholars of the art outside Japan. The reference works read worldwide about him state that his birth year was 1435, and identify him as a versatile actor in *shite* and *waki* roles, as well as a *taiko* drummer. This was the long-held view of his career, but it changed dramatically with the publication of Omote Akira's *Kanze-ryū shi sankyū* (*A Study of the History of the Kanze School*) in 2008.

Basing his reconsideration on a study of historical documents such as the *Nobumitsu gazō san* (*The Inscription on Nobumitsu's Portrait*, 1503 or 1504), Omote proposed that Nobumitsu was born in 1450. Horikawa Takashi

---

12 Although some historians of nō still favor an earlier birth year of 1435, the current consensus is for 1451 or 1452.

subsequently made a yet closer examination of the textual history of *Nobumitsu gazō san*,[13] adjusting this date to 1451 or 1452, and such has become the widely accepted view ever since. While the portrait of Nobumitsu is sadly no longer extant, the inscription (*san*) on it has survived (fig. 5.6).

The revision in Nobumitsu's dates has significantly altered our understanding of Nobumitsu's career. It is, for example, no longer possible to consider him as the author of the plays *Kōso* (named after Gaozu, an emperor of the Chinese Han Dynasty) and *Ataka* (a place name). Omote's research has shown, moreover, that there are no records of Nobumitsu having acted in either *shite* or *waki* roles. This view, too, has become the standard view, and the one adopted in this discussion of Nobumitsu's plays. It should be remembered, however, that even though certain assumptions about Nobumitsu's career have changed in accordance with recent scholarship, his significance as an outstanding playwright and important performer remain constant.

Nobumitsu is believed to have had a wide social circle in which he interacted with both professional performers and amateur enthusiasts. The statesman, courtier, and prominent intellectual Sanjōnishi Sanetaka (1455–1537) is one of the best-known members of the cultural elite associated with him. As a nō enthusiast, Sanetaka wrote at least two nō plays that were revised and performed by Nobumitsu. Nobumitsu also had a close friendship with the Zen monks of Kyoto's *gozan* ("five mountains"), the five great Buddhist temples whose activities extended beyond the religious. Well versed in classical Chinese, these monks were often keenly interested in cultural activities such as linked verse (*renga*), tea (*chanoyu*), and nō. It was the *gozan* Zen monk, Keijo Shūrin (1440–1518), who wrote the inscription on the Nobumitsu portrait mentioned above. He describes Nobumitsu as a talented, much-liked figure. It would appear that the social spheres in which Nobumitsu circulated attracted patrons to the Kanze troupe, further establishing nō as a type of cultural asset. Despite his popularity and social connections, however, Nobumitsu did not become the formal head of the Kanze troupe. Following the death of his eldest brother Matasaburō (1429–1470), Nobumitsu supported another elder brother, Yukishige, who took over the position of head of the troupe. Nobumitsu had three children, all of whom became nō actors. The eldest son, Nagatoshi, likewise succeeded him as a playwright (see sec. 5.7).

---

13   In *Horikawa* 2019.

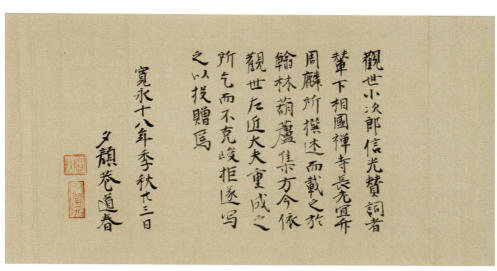

FIGURE 5.6   The inscription text from *The Inscription on Nobumitsu's Portrait* (*Kanze Nobumitsu gazō san*): (top) beginning of the scroll and (bottom) colophon. 1488. Copied by Hayashi Dōshun. Handscroll, ink on paper. 18.1 × 348.2 cm. Noh Theatre Research Institute, Hōsei University, Tokyo

5.6.2 Nobumitsu's Plays

Nobumitsu's numerous plays constitute an important part of the late Muromachi-period nō repertory. His plays illustrate the cultural landscape and the general characteristics of nō at this time. Nobumitsu composed a number of *mugen nō* of the sort that had become typical ever since Zeami's day (see ch. 4 *Plays*, 4.2), many of which have been characterized as *furyū* plays. While his *mugen nō* follow the general structure and style of earlier *mugen nō*, his *furyū*-style plays depart from that structure and thematic orientation. They often have a dramatic plot, a diverse range of sources, energetic music, numerous characters, as well as gorgeous costumes and an opulent design, and, overall, a strong emphasis on visual interest. Elaborate stage and hand props are regular elements, and it is on this basis that modern scholars have identified them by the term *furyū nō*.

Possibly the best known of Nobumitsu's *furyū*-style plays is *Funa Benkei* (fig. 5.7). The play starts with the arrival of the warrior monk Benkei and his lord Minamoto no Yoshitsune at Daimotsu Bay. Together with other retainers, they plan to cross the bay to escape pursuit by forces loyal to Yoshitsune's estranged brother, Yoritomo. Before that, however, Benkei insists that Yoshitsune must send away his beloved consort Shizuka. As a farewell act, she performs a dance expressing her intense grief at leaving Yoshitsune. In act 2, the group takes a boat out to sea, where they encounter the ghost of Taira no Tomomori, who rises from the waters to seek revenge. He is ultimately defeated by Benkei and Yoshitsune. The numerous characters in this play are allotted to various role types. Yoshitsune's part is taken by a child actor (*kokata*), those of retainers by *tsure*, and the boatman by a kyōgen actor. The *shite* plays Shizuka in the first act and Tomomori in the second, performing two different dances, one expressing sorrow, the other rage. The *waki*, Benkei, has a central dramatic role, planning the escape and defeating Tomomori's vengeful spirit.

Tomomori is not the only fearsome ghost that Nobumitsu created. In *Rashōmon*, the brave warrior Watanabe no Tsuna cuts off the arm of a demon hiding in the Rashōmon gate. In *Momijigari*, another warrior, Taira no Koremochi, fights the demon from Mount Togakushi (in present-day Nagano) with a sword he received in a dream, and in *Kōtei*, a spirit of illness almost kills the Chinese emperor's favorite consort.

In addition to featuring gallant warriors fighting powerful demons, the *furyū* plays are sometimes set in places far removed from the capital. In the late fifteenth century, nō troupes often ventured out to the provinces to expand their audience base. These new encounters may have inspired some of Nobumitsu's plays, such as *Momijigari*. Several other plays, mostly no longer performed or lost, or known to us only by a title, also showcase tales or characters from more distant regions.

FIGURE 5.7 *Funa Benkei*. From *An Illustrated Model of Nō (Nō on'ekagami)*, vol. 1. By Kanō Shunko (d. 1726). Late 17th or early 18th century. Album (*orijō*), ink and color on paper. 42.2 × 48.5 cm. Noh Theatre Research Institute, Hōsei University, Tokyo

Another important trait of Nobumitsu's plays is an apparent knowledge of Chinese literary sources. In *Kōtei*, a legendary Chinese exorcist battles a sickness demon, with extensive allusions to the Tang-dynasty poem *Song of Everlasting Sorrow* (C. *Changhenge*; J. *Chōgonka*) by Bai Juyi (772–846). Nobumitsu's skillful use of imagery and words from the Chinese poem transforms the play from a potentially tragic work into a lively play celebrating the defeat of a demon by the Daoist deity Zhong Kui (J. Shōki). Even in plays that do not have an explicit Chinese theme or protagonist, there are still frequent references to Chinese sources. One such play is *Kochō*, a *mugen nō*, in which a monk meets the spirit of a butterfly. This piece is imbued with beautiful imagery and poetry from both Japanese and Chinese classics, and includes an elegant butterfly dance (*chū no mai*; see ch. 2 *Performance*, 2.4) in act 2.

Yugyō Yanagi, also a *mugen nō*, is widely acknowledged as Nobumitsu's final play and was reportedly written a few months before his death. In this play, a monk wants to find the path that his predecessors followed to reach enlightenment. He arrives at a certain crossroads and cannot decide on the direction. At this point an old man appears, who insists that the monk proceed off the beaten path to seek an ancient willow tree. In act 2, the old man emerges as the spirit of the willow tree and performs an "old man dance" (here a *jo no mai*; see ch. 2 *Performance*, 2.4.). It is quite possible that Nobumitsu not only composed this play, but also performed in the ensemble to accompany the dance of the elegant old willow tree. Although there is no historical proof to substantiate this, it would have been a fitting performance to crown the final years of this remarkable performer.

5.7 Nagatoshi
Ikai Takamitsu and Lim Beng Choo

5.7.1 *Nagatoshi's Life*
Kanze Yājirō Nagatoshi (1488–ca. 1541) was one of the last composers of nō plays in the Muromachi period. He learned *waki* roles as a youth and as an adult, served as a right-hand man and chief administrator for the Kanze troupe leader (*tayū*). Nagatoshi was the eldest son of Kanze Kojirō Nobumitsu, and his plays and career trajectory demonstrate influences from his father. His significance as a nō performer, however, might be better understood by looking at the political and cultural context of his time.

Nagatoshi's greatest contribution to nō history might be the text *Nōhon sakusha chūmon* (*An Index to Nō Playwrights*), which was completed in 1524, and was the result of conversations with Yoshida Kanemasa (Kenshō, dates unknown), himself a nō enthusiast. This text contains lists of nō plays and their creators up to and including those of their own time, providing later generations with a critical source on Muromachi-period nō plays (see ch. 10 *Research Overview*, 10.2).

5.7.2 *Nagatoshi's Plays*
In *Nōhon sakusha chūmon*, Nagatoshi identified a total of twenty-five plays as his own, and these works span a wide range of themes, including tales of vengeance as well as praise for Buddhism and Shintō. Unfortunately, more than ten plays in this list have been lost and of those remaining, only a few—*Enoshima*, *Rinzō*, *Ōyashiro* (fig. 5.8), and *Shōzon*—are still performed today. With the

FIGURE 5.8 *Ōyashiro*. From *An Illustrated Model of Nō (Nō on'ekagami)*, vol. 1. By Kanō Shunko (d. 1726). Late 17th or early 18th century. Album (*orijō*), ink and color on paper. 42.2 × 48.5 cm. Noh Theatre Research Institute, Hōsei University, Tokyo

exception of *Enoshima*, *Rinzō*, *Ōyashiro*, most of Nagatoshi's better-known plays are *genzai nō* set in the dramatic present. Scholars generally acknowledge that the text of *Nōhon sakusha chūmon* must have been revised after its initial composition, as some of the plays Nagatoshi attributed to himself are likely to have been written only when he was older.

Enoshima tells how the eponymous island, the location of the Benzaiten Shrine, appeared mysteriously from out of the sea. In act 1 of the play, the Dragon King, disguised as an old man (*shite*), strikes up a conversation with the emperor's messenger. He appears in act 2 with the female deity Benzaiten and two young attendants. They then perform celebratory dances in praise of the island. In contemporary classification, *Enoshima* belongs to the first category deity plays and follows the structure of a two-part *mugen nō* (see ch. 2

Performance, 2.3). There are, however, other elements that are distinctively Nagatoshi's, and these differentiate this play from other deity plays. In act 2, the *nochi tsure*, a nameless companion to the main character, plays the deity Benzaiten. The actor in this role emerges from a veiled platform holding a prop torch and performs a dance (in modern performance, a *gaku*; see ch. 2 *Performance*, 2.4). Before the play ends, the Dragon King also performs a boisterous dance (a *mai-bataraki*; see ch. 2 *Performance*, 2.4), joined, once the chorus begins again to sing, by two *kokata*, in celebration of the shrine.

The dramatic plot, energetic music, numerous characters, and elaborate stage and hand props are some of the regular traits seen, not only in Nagatoshi's plays, but also in other late Muromachi-period nō plays. As noted above, modern scholars have labeled these "*furyū*," and in this regard the late Muromachi period is sometimes referred to as "the era of *furyū nō*." Among these late Muromachi plays, Nagatoshi's seem to have pushed the limits of *furyū* features the furthest. Other than the ending scene of *Enoshima* mentioned above, *Kasui*, which is set in China, is another play that illustrates the extent to which Nagatoshi used these *furyū* elements. In act 1, the imperial court grants the Dragon Princess a husband so that she will unleash the waters of a large river in an effort to end a drought. In act 2, the court is confronted with yet another disaster: the invasion from a neighboring state. The Dragon King then appears to assist in the battle, thereby defeating the enemy. The dramatic development of the play and the numerous characters involved are perhaps the two principal reasons why this play is not performed regularly.

There are probably a number of reasons to explain why Nagatoshi composed plays such as *Enoshima* and *Kasui*, one being the impact of his father Nobumitsu. Some of Nagatoshi's plays have plots and character types similar to those of Nobumitsu, such as the depiction of a pestilential demon in the Chinese court or deities leaping out of a prop. Nagatoshi was also liberal in assigning role types, another trait identifiable among late Muromachi nō plays, and most regularly seen in Nagatoshi's works. In plays such as *Rinzō*, the many characters occupy equal dramatic significance and perform various dances, a clear divergence from the *shite*-centered plays of Zeami. Clearly in Nagatoshi's time the composition of the audience and performance context differed from earlier periods.

The political situation In Japan remained unstable, to say the least, after the 1467–1477 Ōnin Disturbances. Troupes of nō actors traveled further from their home bases in order to expand performance opportunities and to create new plays inspired by their new encounters (see ch. 1 *History*, 1.1). In this way, audience members became more receptive to varied styles of presentation and content. At the same time, a broader cultural elite, including court officials and

Zen monks, actively engaged with nō by socializing with its performers, writing and performing nō, discussing the composition of nō plays, and appreciating nō masks. Nagatoshi's interactions with these members of the cultural elite would have had an impact on his nō plays.

Other than writing nō plays, historical records also reveal that Nagatoshi revised and edited the music in various nō plays, as his father had done, although the details are not clear. Like his father, Nagatoshi did not become the Kanze troupe leader, but he has been credited with overseeing the Kanze troupe when the designated troupe leader was young. After Nagatoshi died in his fifties, his son Motoyori (d. 1573?) continued to study *waki* roles.

5.8 Zenpō

Ikai Takamitsu and Lim Beng Choo

5.8.1 Zenpō's Life

Konparu Zenpō (1454–?), also known as Motoyasu, was a late Muromachi-period nō performer who wrote both nō plays and treatises. Zenpō is related to two of the best-known names in the early history of nō: he was the grandson of Konparu Zenchiku, who in turn was Zeami's son-in-law. Zenpō studied nō under both his father Konparu Sōin (dates unknown) and his grandfather Zenchiku; he succeeded as the Konparu troupe leader in his twenties when his father Sōin passed away.

As troupe leader Zenpō was regularly confronted with challenges, including when the Ashikaga shogunate forced two Konparu *waki* performers to join the Kanze troupe. Despite such hurdles, Zenpō, a talented nō performer and teacher, was able to sustain the livelihood of the troupe. He continued to perform in the Kyoto and Nara regions, and he also secured patronage from a military general from as far away as Kyushu, Japan's most southern large island.

Zenpō was a prolific writer and the author of several noteworthy treatises on diverse aspects of nō, including music, composition, and performance. Other than those he wrote, one of his disciples, Nakamura Tōemon (ca. 1457–ca. 1533), compiled a book called *Zenpō zōtan* (*Zenpō's Talks on Various Matters*) based on the teachings and conversational exchanges he had with Zenpō. *Zenpō zōtan* is representative of Zenpō's versatile talents: it not only discussed elements of nō but also other artistic endeavors and cultural practices of his time, such as kickball (*kemari*), tea (*chanoyu*), and linked verse (*renga*). Like other nō performers, he also contributed to the transmission of significant nō plays and writings by copying earlier Konparu family treatises and plays.

Zenpō's activity as a nō actor was not restricted to just performance onstage. Among his other activities, anecdotes tell of him teaching and interacting with students from Sakai and acquaintances from Kyoto. His relationship with other nō troupes seems to have been friendly. His daughter married the sixth Kanze troupe leader Motohiro (1472?–1523?), further strengthening the bond between the two families. The name by which we know him, "Zenpō," was adopted when he became a monk, first witnessed in extant texts in 1518. It is clear that by this time he had taken religious orders, otherwise very little is known about the final years of his life.

5.8.2 *Zenpō's Plays*

Five nō plays attributed to Zenpō are still performed today: *Arashiyama* (fig. 5.9), *Ikuta Atsumori*, *Hatsuyuki*, *Ikkaku Sennin*, and *Tōbōsaku*. Another play, *Kurokawa*, is believed to be an early work, but it is no longer performed (see ch. 4 *Plays*, 4.11). Despite their small number, they exhibit distinct characteristics that can be seen as hallmarks of a Zenpō style, especially in contrast to earlier plays.[14] Some scholars have argued that Zenpō's writings were a reaction to the Kanze troupe's plays, yet Zenpō's plays exhibit features seen in those by Nobumitsu and his son Nagatoshi, such as the bold dramatic presentation and a large cast. This similarity in style, however, should also be understood as an indication of the general trends in nō of the late Muromachi period. Nō performers, including Zenpō, received strong support from their patrons and audiences, and thus they looked further afield for possible sources in an effort to produce plays that met the demands of this expanded audience.

Hatsuyuki is probably the most interesting of Zenpō's plays in terms of structure and theme. The play begins with the daughter of a shrine priest being informed by her female attendant of the death of her pet chicken Hatsuyuki. The daughter, overcome by grief, decides to offer a seven-day prayer session for her beloved pet to help it achieve enlightenment. In act 2, the enlightened Hatsuyuki appears to perform a dance of thanksgiving (*chū no mai*; see ch. 2 *Performance*, 2.4). There is no *waki* in this play: *waki* do not wear masks and are therefore exclusively male characters, but here Zenpō has created a play with only female characters. Also noteworthy is the fact that in Zenpō's time, the enlightened pet in act 2 was performed by a child actor (*kokata*).

It would seem that Zenpō had a preference for roles with child actors. The orphan searching for his dead father in *Ikuta Atsumori*, as well as the deity's attendants in *Tōbōsaku*, were all performed by child actors. This is not to say, however, that this approach was monopolized by Zenpō. Such distribution of dramatic significance among different characters, rather than solely on the *shite* role, is a common trait of nō plays from the late Muromachi period, albeit

---

14   In *Zenpō zōtan*, for example, Nobumitsu's plays *Momijigari* and *Chōryō* are criticized for the excessive use of demons and dragons, and a lack of artistic sensibility.

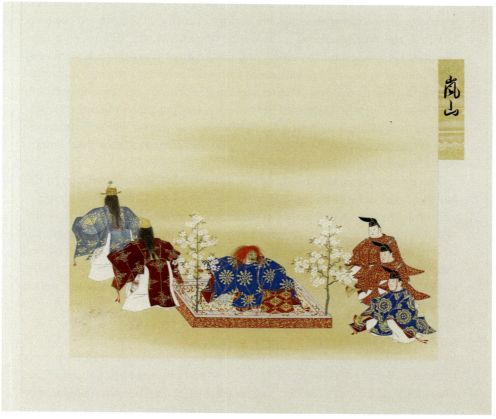

FIGURE 5.9 *Arashiyama*. From *An Illustrated Model of Nō* (*Nō on'ekagami*), vol. 1. By Kanō Shunko (d. 1726). Late 17th or early 18th century. Album (*orijō*), ink and color on paper. 42.2 × 48.5 cm. Noh Theatre Research Institute, Hōsei University, Tokyo

with variations. Moreover, Zenpō's plays have characters from distant lands with unusual appearances and powers, such as *Tōbōsaku*, the Chinese wizard in the play of the same name and the Queen Mother of the West in the eponymous *Seiōbō*. There are, of course, ferocious messengers from hell in *Ikuta Atsumori* and the enlightened pet chicken in *Hatsuyuki*.

5.9 Miyamasu

Ikai Takamitsu and Lim Beng Choo

5.9.1 *Miyamasu's Life*

Miyamasu is undoubtedly one of the most enigmatic nō performers of the Muromachi period. The name "Miyamasu," or sometimes "Miyamasu-dayū," appeared in historical records from as early as Zeami's time. Factors contributing to the mystery enshrouding this performer include the different contexts in which the name is listed in historical documents, the different Chinese characters employed for the name, and the different plays that are attributed to Miyamasu in two important late Muromachi-period nō records, the aforementioned *Nōhon sakusha chūmon* and the *Jika denshō* (*Transmissions Within the Konparu Line*). Nō historians have nonetheless pieced together the various sources to draw the conclusion that there were at least a few performers, as well as one musician, called Miyamasu, and that they were most likely members of a family with that surname.

The nō composer Miyamasu is said to have been active sometime in the late fifteenth century and was not directly affiliated with any of the four major nō troupes of the time. Researchers generally agree that this Miyamasu composed several nō plays and that he was a famous nō performer who specialized in *waki* roles.[15] Miyamasu-dayū, a talented *kotsuzumi* drummer named "Miyamasu," and a nō composer of the same name are now thought to be the same person.[16] It is now generally accepted that Miyamasu was not only a composer of nō plays but also a *waki* actor and drummer.

5.9.2 Miyamasu's Plays

In terms of nō plays, Miyamasu's name has been associated most frequently with works based on the vendetta of the Soga brothers, including *Genpuku Soga*, *Chōbuku Soga*, *Kosode Soga* (fig. 5.10), and *Youchi Soga*. These were inspired by the *Soga monogatari* (*The Tale of the Soga Brothers*, 14th c.). In this tale, Kawazu Saburō, the father of the Soga brothers Gorō and Jūrō, was murdered when the boys were very young. Their father's tragic death resulted in the remarriage of their mother, and they vowed to avenge their father's death. Seventeen years later, after much hardship and a few failed attempts, the brothers were able to carry out their vendetta. Episodes from the tale were incorporated into the nō dramatizations, which center on the poverty and humiliation endured by the brothers, their unsuccessful efforts to assassinate the enemy, the begging of forgiveness from their mother, and Jūrō's sad departure from his lover Tora Gozen (Ōiso no Tora).

Another group of nō plays known as the *Hōgan mono*, or plays about the Genji-clan general, Minamoto no Yoshitsune, such as *Eboshiori* and *Kurama tengu*, are also attributed to Miyamasu. These plays were based on the *Gikeiki* (*The Chronicle of Yoshitsune*, 14th–15th c.), and other popular legends regarding Yoshitsune that were circulating in the Muromachi period. The nō plays

---

15   Takemoto 1999: 606–25.
16   Yokomichi 1987: 244–45.

FIGURE 5.10   *Kosode Soga*. From *An Illustrated Model of Nō* (*Nō on'ekagami*), vol. 2. By Kanō Shunko (d. 1726). Late 17th or early 18th century. Album (*orijō*), ink and color on paper. 42.2 × 48.5 cm. Noh Theatre Research Institute, Hōsei University, Tokyo

attributed to Miyamasu center on specific events from these tales, even though they are all situated in the present (*genzai nō*). Other elements include a large cast and an emphasis on conversational exchanges and dramatic development.

In the second half of the fifteenth century, the canons and forms of nō were opened up to new authorial styles. While plays in the style originating with Zeami and Zenchiku retained their place onstage, these new types of plays were also successful. Thus, while Zeami and Zenchiku had created beautiful plays imbued with *yūgen*, subsequent nō performers and playwrights produced showier works adapted from popular narratives—the vendetta of the Soga brothers or the life of Yoshitsune—that focused on human relationships. Miyamasu is probably one of the best representatives of this latter group of nō performers and playwrights.

5.10 Amateurs
Ikai Takamitsu and Lim Beng Choo

Information on amateur nō performers and playwrights is understandably scant and fragmentary. Nō by the late Muromachi period had become an integral part of cultural life among the social elite, much like the linked verse (*renga*) or kickball (*kemari*) competitions. Amateurs are an integral part of nō history, not only because they were ardent and knowledgeable audience members but also because they participated as patrons, collaborators, and students. The written documents that they produced, including courtier diaries, temple records, and portrait inscriptions, have become invaluable historical sources for later generations. Some scholars argue that paradoxically these amateur performers tended to adhere closely to existing structures and conventions of nō composition so as not to be labeled "amateurs," and as a consequence, tend to be stereotypical.

The term "amateur" (*shirōto*) here refers to the group of nō enthusiasts, principally before the Edo period, who sometimes composed and performed nō or wrote nō treatises without being members of any particular nō troupe. The earliest mentions of amateur performers are in Zeami's *Go-on* and *Sarugaku dangi* with the names of three contemporaries: Nan'ami (d. 1381) and Rin'ami (dates unknown) appear in the former, while that of Yokoo Motohisa (dates unknown) as the attributed author of *Ukifune* in the latter. Various historical records described them as immensely talented in music and proficiency in literary classics. It is not until the second half of the Muromachi period that more information on amateur nō enthusiasts and their engagement with nō emerges. Most were members of the cultural elite: court officials, intelligentsia among the military class, professional poets, and religious practitioners.

Yokoo Motohisa was arguably one of the earliest members of the warrior class to participate in writing texts for nō, and not just a patron. He was a lower-ranking official of the Hosokawa clan and a *waka* poet. Although the play *Ukifune*, which is based on *The Tale of Genji*, is attributed to Motohisa, it was Zeami who would have composed the music and likely had a hand in revising the text. Following in Motohisa's footsteps were figures such as Ichijō Kaneyoshi (1402–1481), a high-ranking court official as well as a *renga* poet and historian. He was a close friend of the Konparu family, including Zenchiku and his son Sōin. It is said that he wrote the play *Sagoromo no nō* for Zenchiku, based on the courtly prose narrative *Sagoromo monogatari* (*The Tale of Sagoromo*, latter half 11th c.). Zenchiku supposedly revised the play but no text for it survives, nor are there any records of its having been performed.

FIGURE 5.11   *Zegai*. From *An Illustrated Model of Nō* (*Nō on'ekagami*), vol. 1. By Kanō Shunko (d. 1726). Late 17th or early 18th century. Album (*orijō*), ink and color on paper. 42.2 × 48.5 cm. Noh Theatre Research Institute, Hōsei University, Tokyo

Another noted amateur, Takeda Hōin Jōsei (1421–1508), was the official doctor to the shōgun Yoshimasa. *Nōhon sakusha chūmon* attributes the play *Zegai* (fig. 5.11) to him, but other records of his existence are extremely scarce. The play recounts the tale of the mythical *tengu* creature who visits Japan from China to obstruct the further transmission of Buddhism. He joins forces with a Japanese counterpart and battles Buddhist monks from Mount Hiei. This fifth category finale or *kiri nō* play is believed to be based on an eponymously named illustrated scroll dating to the first half of the fourteenth century.

A second play attributed to Takeda was recorded in the diary of Sanjōnishi Sanetaka, himself an amateur nō enthusiast. An entry in Sanetaka's extensive diary, the *Sanetaka kōki*, states that Takeda sought Sanetaka's assistance to revise the piece. The play is said to have been incorporated into one of Nobumitsu's lost works, although very little else is known about it. Sadly, it is no longer extant. Together these documents indicate that there was a close relationship among some nō enthusiasts and nō performers, and that their friendship facilitated the creation and production of nō plays. Moreover, the sharing of knowledge on or the joint creation of nō plays by professionals and amateurs was a recognized practice among the cultural elite.

As discussed in section 5.6, the middle-ranking courtier Sanjōnishi Sanetaka was friendly with Kanze Kojirō Nobumitsu, one of the best known Kanze nō performers of the era. Entries in Sanetaka's diary *Sanetaka kōki*—for which he is most celebrated—regularly mention nō-related activities including meetings with nō actors to discuss nō plays, to admire nō masks, or to attend nō performances. (There was at least one occasion when he remarked that his passion for nō caused a dispute with his wife!) Sanetaka also noted that he composed a nō play *Sagoromo* and that he had discussed with Kanze Nobumitsu. He records having seen the play performed. It should be noted that *Sagoromo* and the previously mentioned *Sagoromo no nō* are different plays.

Shimotsuma Nakataka (1551–1616; see ch. 1 *History*, 1.3), better known by his court rank as Shimotsuma Shōshin, was another significant amateur. His family served the Buddhist temple Honganji, and thanks to a good relationship with the cultural elite, he was quickly promoted to the court rank of *shōshin*. Commonly referred to by his rank, Shōshin studied with the Konparu troupe leader Yoshikatsu (Gyūren; 1510–1583) and is said to have been very proficient in nō. Shōshin wrote various texts on the details of performance (*katatsuke*), addressing a wide range of topics (see ch. 7 *Material Culture*, 7.6). He shared these writings with other amateur nō performers and with certain military figures. There are no examples of nō plays attributed to him, however, since by the latter half of the sixteenth century, there was a shift away from the creation of new plays to the refinement of existing works.

References

Atkins, Paul S. 2006. *Revealed Identity: The Noh Plays of Komparu Zenchiku*. Michigan Monograph Series in Japanese Studies 55. Ann Arbor: Center for Japanese Studies, University of Michigan.

Brown, Steven T. 2001. *Theatricalities of Power: The Cultural Politics of Noh*. Stanford: Stanford University Press.

de Poorter, Erika. (1986) 2002. *Zeami's Talks on Sarugaku: An Annotated Translation of the Sarugaku Dangi with an Introduction on Zeami Motokiyo*. Amsterdam: J. C. Gieben. Reprinted in the series Japonica Neerlandica 2. Leiden: Hotei Publishing.

Getsuyōkai 月曜会, ed. Supervised by Omote Akira. 1997. *Zeami jihitsu nōhonshū* 世阿弥自筆能本集. Tokyo: Iwanami Shoten.

Hare, Thomas Blenman. 1986. *Zeami's Style: The Noh Plays of Zeami Motokiyo*. Stanford: Stanford University Press.

Hare, Thomas Blenman (Tom), trans. 2008. *Zeami. Performance Notes*. New York: Columbia University Press.

Horikawa Takashi 堀川貴司. 2019. "Kanze Kojirō Gazō-san Saikō"「観世小次郎画像（賛）」再考. *Kokugo to kokubungaku* 国語と国文学 96.4: 3–17.

Kōsai Tsutomu 香西精. 1970. "Motomasa gyōnen kō: shin, Saburō Motoshige yōshishi setsu" 元雅行年考―新・三郎元重養嗣子説. In *Zoku Zeami shinkō* 世阿弥新考, edited by Kōsai Tsutomu, 82–97. Tokyo: Wan'ya Shoten.

Lim, Beng Choo. 2012. *Another Stage: Kanze Nobumitsu & the Late Muromachi Noh Theater*. Cornell East Asia Series 163. Ithaca: Cornell University East Asia Program.

Matisoff, Susan. 1979. "Images of Exile and Pilgrimage: Zeami's *Kintōsho*." *Monumenta Nipponica* 34, no. 4 (Winter): 449–65.

Nishino Haruo 西野春雄. 1987. "Miyamasu no nō" 宮増の能. In *Nō no sakusha to sakuhin* 能の作者と作品. *Iwanami kōza: nō kyōgen* 岩波講座―能・狂言 III, edited by Yokomichi Mario 横道萬里雄, Nishino Haruo 西野春雄, and Hata Hisashi 羽田昶, 243–55. Tokyo: Iwanami Shoten.

Omote Akira 表章. 2008. *Kanze-ryū shi sankyū* 観世流史参究. Tokyo: Hinoki Shoten.

Omote Akira 表章 and Itō Masayoshi 伊藤正義, eds. 1969. *Konparu kodensho shūsei* 金春古伝書集成. 1 vol. Tokyo: Wan'ya Shoten.

Omote Akira 表章 and Katō Shūichi 加藤周一. (1974) 1995. *Zeami Zenchiku* 世阿弥禅竹. *Nihon shisō taikei* 日本思想大系 24. Tokyo: Iwanami Shoten.

O'Neill, P. G. 1958. *Early Nō Drama: Its Background, Character and Development 1300–1450*. London: Lund Humphries.

Oyler, Elizabeth, and Michael Watson, eds. 2013. *Like Clouds or Mists: Studies and Translations of Nō Plays of the Genpei War*. Cornell East Asia Series 159. Ithaca: Cornell University East Asia Program.

Pinnington, Noel J. 2006. *Traces in the Way: Michi and the Writings of Komparu Zenchiku*. Cornell East Asia Series 132. Ithaca: Cornell University East Asia Program.

Quinn, Shelley Fenno. 2005. *Developing Zeami, the Noh Actor's Attunement in Practice*. Honolulu: University of Hawai'i Press.

Takemoto Mikio 竹本幹夫. 1999. *Kan'ami, Zeami jidai no nōgaku* 観阿弥・世阿弥時代の能楽. Tokyo: Meiji Shoin.

Thornhill, Arthur H. III. 1993. *Six Circles, One Dewdrop: The Religio-Aesthetic World of Komparu Zenchiku*. Princeton: Princeton University Press.

Tyler, Royall, trans./ed. 1992. *Japanese Nō Dramas*. Penguin Classics. London: Penguin Books.

Tyler, Royall, trans. 2014. *Zeami: Six Revived Bangai Plays*. Tokyo: The Nogami Memorial Noh Theatre Research Institute of Hōsei University.

Yasuda, Kenneth. 1989. *Masterworks of the Nō Theatre*. Bloomington: Indiana University Press.

Yokomichi Mario 横道萬里雄. 1987. "Nōhon no gaikan" 能本の概観. In *Nō no sakusha to sakuhin* 能の作者と作品. *Iwanami kōza: nō kyogen* 岩波講座—能・狂言 III, edited by Yokomichi Mario 横道萬里雄, Nishino Haruo 西野春雄, and Hata Hisashi 羽田昶, 11–120. Tokyo: Iwanami Shoten.

Printed in the United States
by Baker & Taylor Publisher Services